SHIPS
VISUAL ENCYCLOPEDIA

SHIPS
VISUAL ENCYCLOPEDIA

DAVID ROSS

amber
BOOKS

This edition printed in 2024

Copyright © 2022 by Amber Books Ltd

First published in 2010

All rights reserved. No part of this publication may be reproduced, stored in a retrieval system, or transmitted in any form or by any means, electronic, mechanical, photocopying, recording, or otherwise, without prior written permission of the copyright holder.

Published by
Amber Books Ltd
United House
North Road
London N7 9DP
United Kingdom
www.amberbooks.co.uk
Facebook: amberbooks
YouTube: amberbooksltd
Instagram: amberbooksltd
X(Twitter): @amberbooks

ISBN: 978-1-83886-499-6

Project Editor: Sarah Uttridge
Picture Research: Terry Forshaw
Design: Andrew Easton

Printed in China

CONTENTS

INTRODUCTION   6

SHIP TYPES TO 1899   8

SHIP TYPES 1900–1929   92

SHIP TYPES 1930–1949   214

SHIP TYPES 1950–1999   316

TWENTY-FIRST CENTURY SHIPS   428

Glossary   440

Index   442

INTRODUCTION

Three things were necessary for early humans to travel across large extents of water. One was a vessel to sit in or stand on, one was a means of driving it, and one was a way to steer it. It is likely that these were discovered or invented not once but many times, in different places, in the remote prehistory of humanity. The uses of the first boats can only be guessed at.

Depictions of ships are quite recent in history. The oldest we have were painted in Egyptian tombs about six thousand years ago. They show ships built from wooden planks and with sails. The earliest vessels most probably had practical and peaceful purposes – transport, fishing. From very early on, too, there may have been a spiritual aspect to our use of boats. The image of a boat carrying the spirits of the dead to the next world is a very ancient one. But, like every tool ever made, the ship also became a weapon of warfare. Ships could carry spearmen in a silent attack. The ship itself could be given a heavy pointed front to ram and disable others.

Fundamental Principles

Underlying all the huge range of adaptations, enlargements and additions that have been made to ships since those remote days, the basics still remain. Ships nowadays might seem impossibly large to our far-off ancestors; they can move far under the water or skim just above the surface, and they have equipment of immense power and sophistication. But these are elaborations on the three fundamentals.

Ship Development

If a graph of ship development were to be drawn against a timeline, its upward trend would be imperceptibly slight for most of its length, with rises to mark the introduction of the oar, the mast and square sail, the steering oar, then much later, the tiller and rudder, the compass, the lateen sail which was far more adjustable to the wind, and the steering wheel. From the 1790s the curve would become much steeper as a stream of innovations began: powered drive, iron and then steel construction, a dramatic increase in size. At exactly the same time, the destructive power of the warship showed a similar change, with the rifled gun, the high-explosive shell, the torpedo – leading towards the nuclear-tipped inter-continental ballistic missile. Innovations continue to be made, with new types of ship reflecting new needs. It is likely that coming years will see an array of remote-controlled vessels capable of operating on, and digging into, the ocean floors.

Complex Constructions

And yet the spectacle of a tall ship under full sail still bewitches us, drawing crowds that would not turn out to see the latest super-tanker. Ships have always had a combination of the practical and the miraculous, and have always been among the more complex of human constructions. Whether the most modern ships are as beautiful as some of their sail-driven predecessors is a matter of debate, but of one thing there is no dispute – ships retain their interest and fascination.

Above: USS *Ronald Reagan*, launched in 2001, belongs to the Nimitz-class supercarriers, the largest capital ships in the world.

SHIP TYPES TO 1899

It may be that the earliest true boats were made from bundled reeds, and not wood. If so, it is remarkable that on both the African and South American continents, similar techniques are still in use today.

The availability of materials, the early perfection of the construction method, and the unchanging purpose meant that further development was neither necessary nor possible. For similar reasons, rowing boats are still seen in every harbour. But this chapter shows how natural, and then mechanical, forces were exploited in ever-more effective ways by the ship-builders.

Left: Launched in 1869, *Cutty Sark* was one of the last racing clippers built for the China tea trade. At full speed it was faster than contemporary steamships.

SHIP TYPES TO 1899

Early Ships

Archaeology shows that boats made from bundled reeds were among the earliest craft, and the building technique developed both in Egypt and South America. But wooden vessels, first of hollowed-out logs, then of planking, are also of great antiquity. The origins of the sail and oars also date far back into prehistory.

Egyptian Reed Boat

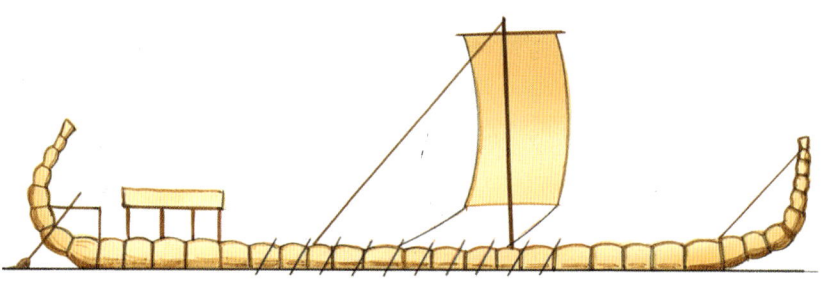

Trees were scarce in ancient Egypt, but tall papyrus trees were plentiful in the Nile delta, and this form of boat-construction goes back at least to 3200BCE. The steering oar is already in evidence. The life-span of a reed boat was a few months at most, but they were quick and cheap to construct.

SPECIFICATIONS
Type:	Egyptian papyrus boat
Dimensions:	16.5m x 2.7m x 1.5m (54ft x 9ft x 5ft)
Rigging:	Single mast, square sail
Cargo:	Fish, reeds, grain
Year:	3200BCE

Cheops Ship

Built of imported cedar, this is one of the oldest ships to be preserved. Its planking is held together by ropes, and there is no keel. Intended as a ceremonial vessel, it had two deck cabins. Oars, as well as a sail, helped it move against the wind as well as the Nile current.

SPECIFICATIONS
Type:	Egyptian cedarwood ship
Displacement:	95.5 tonnes (94 tons)
Dimensions:	43.6m x 5.7m x 1.45m (143ft x 18ft 7in x 4ft 9in)
Rigging:	Single mast, square sail
Complement:	12
Year:	2500BCE

TIMELINE

3200BCE  2500BCE   1550BCE

Nile Barge

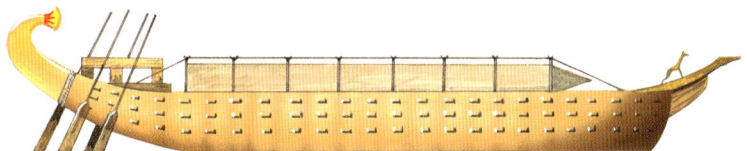

Substantial loads were carried in specialized craft, like this one designed to transport obelisks downriver from Aswan to Luxor. It could take two at a time. Unpowered, it was controlled by four steering oars and towed by 27 small oared vessels. Ropes were used to help support the huge structure.

SPECIFICATIONS	
Type:	Egyptian obelisk barge
Displacement:	1524 tonnes (1500 tons), loaded
Dimensions:	59.4m x 21.3m x 2.1m (195ft x 70ft x 7ft)
Rigging:	None
Complement:	900, including auxiliary crews
Year:	1550 BCE

Phoenician Cargo Ship

Egyptian tomb murals are the evidence for these trading vessels, wooden-built and intended to be rowed with the sail as a supplement. Notable features include the masthead rope-ladder, the large amphora for wine or water, and a wicker barrier probably intended to hold the deck cargo away from the oarsmen.

SPECIFICATIONS	
Type:	Phoenician oared cargo ship
Dimensions:	16.8m x 3.7m x 1.5m (55ft x 12ft x 5ft)
Rigging:	Single mast, square sail attached to upper and lower yards
Complement:	12
Cargo:	Timber, fish, grain, metals, wine
Year:	1500 BCE

Greek Cargo Ship

A tall mast and larger sail area suggest that this ship used oars only when necessary in harbour or calms. The hull is a lightweight construction of pine planking. The frontal ram indicates that the vessel could be pressed into action for naval warfare, as happened during the Persian War of 479 BCE.

SPECIFICATIONS	
Type:	Greek sailing cargo ship
Dimensions:	15.2m x 4.3m x 1.8m (50ft x 14ft x 6ft)
Rigging:	Single mast, reefable square sail
Complement:	8–10
Cargo:	Wine, timber, grain, wool, hides
Year:	500 BCE

SHIP TYPES TO 1899

War Galleys

Right up to the Middle Ages (and even later in the Mediterranean and Baltic Seas), the oared warship was the prime fighting vessel. Hull design went ahead faster than that of sails and steering gear, and the heavy galley, driven by up to 200 rowers, was employed for close-quarters fighting.

Egyptian Galley

Part of the fleet of Pharaoh Rameses III, this is a substantial craft, mounted on a keel and able to ram. Bulwarks shelter the oarsmen and there are fighting platforms fore and aft for close engagement with enemy craft. A look-out point is provided at the mast-head, and the sail-area can be reduced by brailing up.

SPECIFICATIONS
Type:	Egyptian war galley
Dimensions:	25.9m x 5.5m x 1.2m (75ft x 14ft x 5ft)
Rigging:	Single mast, square sail mounted on single two-piece yard
Cargo:	24 oarsmen plus officers and fighting men
Year:	1180BCE

Phoenician Bireme

For over 500 years, the Phoenicians were a major Mediterranean sea power. Some details of this bireme (double-banked galley) are conjectural, but it seems to have been built from a hollowed-out tree trunk. Construction is double-deck, with a full-length fighting platform above the oarsmen, and a ram prow.

SPECIFICATIONS
Type:	Phoenician war galley
Dimensions:	27.4m x 4.3m x 1.8m (90ft x 14ft x 6ft)
Rigging:	Single mast, square sail
Complement:	56 oarsmen plus officers and fighting men
Year:	c.700BCE

TIMELINE 1180BCE   700BCE   500BCE

WAR GALLEYS

Greek Trireme

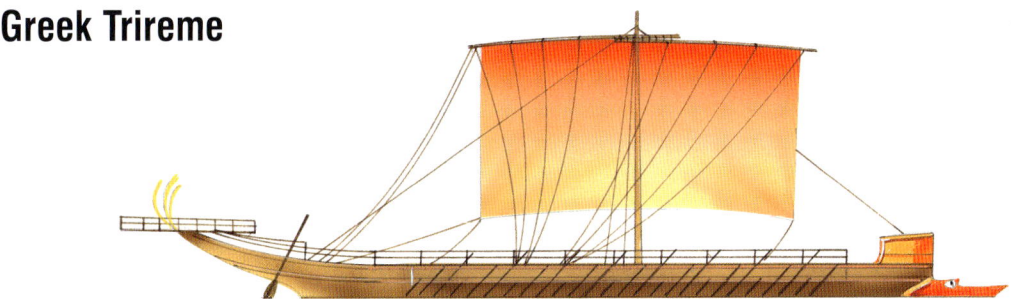

Triple banks of rowers propelled this ship at a ramming speed of 11.5 knots. Originating c.650BCE, probably in Corinth, the trireme was the most formidable warship of its time – large, fast and manoeuvrable. A platform deck ran full length and a short foremast could be fitted as well as the mainmast.

SPECIFICATIONS

Type:	Greek war galley
Displacement:	approx. 50 tonnes (49 tonnes)
Dimensions:	32.5m x 4.6m x 1.1m (106ft 7in x 15ft x 3ft 6in)
Rigging:	One or two masts, square sails on two-piece yards
Complement:	170 oarsmen plus officers and fighting men
Year:	500BCE

Roman Quinquereme

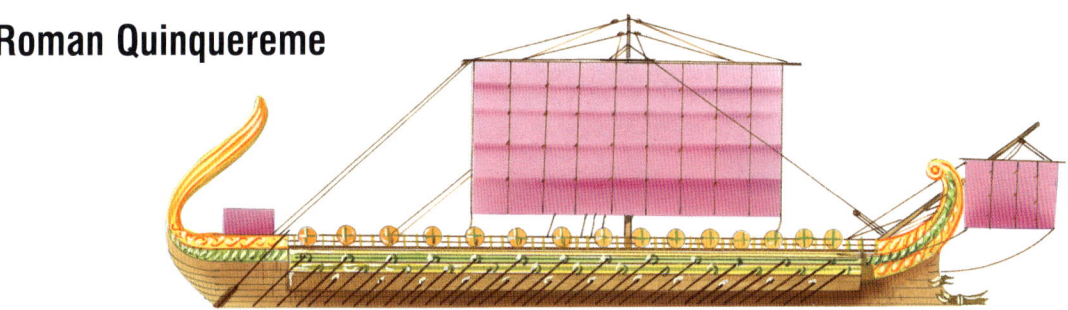

The name does not mean five banks of oars, but five rowers in each 3-level file: two to an oar on the upper levels, one on the lower level. Roman warships were generally more broad-beamed and heavier than Greek ones – giving them more power but less manouevrability in naval warfare.

SPECIFICATIONS

Type:	Roman war galley
Dimensions:	Beam 5m (16ft 4in)
Rigging:	Single dismountable mast, square sail
Armament:	Ballista (heavy catapult)
Complement:	300 oarsmen plus officers and 120 fighting men
Year:	350BCE

Roman Trireme

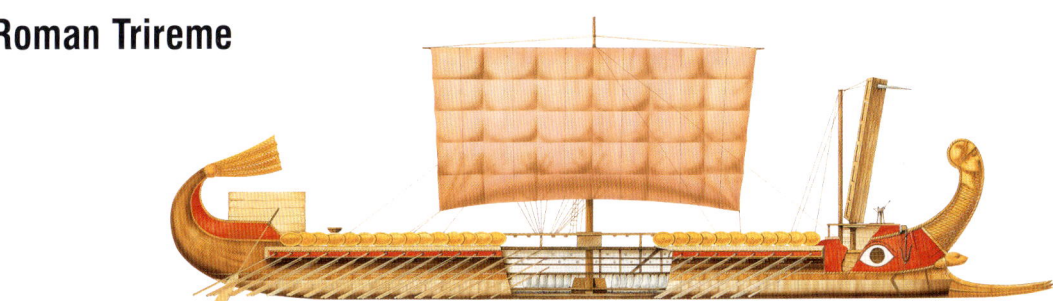

In the long war with Carthage, the Romans copied Carthaginian designs in these heavy triremes. In addition to the ram prow and the ballista's stone missiles, they could project fire-pots into enemy ships, and were also equipped with a heavy boarding platform, whose spike could be lodged in an enemy hull.

SPECIFICATIONS

Type:	Roman war galley
Dimensions:	35m x 4.6m x 1.5m (115ft x 15ft x 5ft)
Rigging:	Single mast, square sail
Complement:	190 oarsmen plus officers and fighting men
Year:	c.200BCE

350BCE

200BCE

SHIP TYPES TO 1899

Early Medieval Ships: Part 1

Growing populations, new technical ideas and developing international trade brought new developments in ship design. Sails became more important and mariners became more skilled in their use. The number of ships increased greatly. At this time, a merchant vessel could still be quickly converted for military purposes.

Mediterranean Cargo Ship

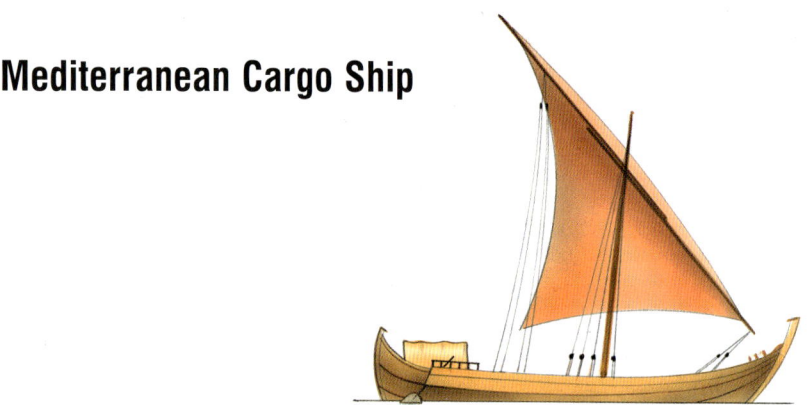

Many ships of this type sailed between Italy, Greece, North Africa and the Middle East. Masts now had lateral stays for better support. The lateen sail, which could be trimmed to keep the ship sailing close to the wind, was an innovation learned from the Arabs, whose ships were also prolific in the Mediterranean.

SPECIFICATIONS

Type:	Small sailing cargo ship
Dimensions:	24.4m x 7.6m x 2.7m (80ft x 25ft x 9ft)
Rigging:	Forward-tilted mast, lateen sail on double spar
Complement:	5–8
Cargo:	Wine, oil, grain, wood, hides
Year:	c.800CE

Scandinavian Longship

The Vikings were raiders or traders, and the longship was a fine vessel for either purpose. From its early development, it showed the northern practice of clinker-building (overlapping planks), with the mast set in a strong oak keel. It could carry men or animals, but the open hull was not well-suited for dry cargoes.

SPECIFICATIONS

Type:	Sailed galley
Dimensions:	36.6m x 6.1m x 1.1m (120ft x 20ft x 3ft 6in)
Rigging:	Single mast, square sail
Complement:	44–50 oarsmen
Year:	c.900CE

TIMELINE

800CE   900CE   1200

EARLY MEDIEVAL SHIPS: PART 1

Italian Cargo Ship

By 1200, this was becoming an old-world design, though some ships now had two masts (as illustrated) and so harnessed greater wind-power. Mediterranean ships were carvel-built (planks meeting edge to edge without overlap). The bow and stern platforms suggest that this vessel was built with fighting in mind.

SPECIFICATIONS	
Type:	Sailing cargo ship
Displacement:	approx. 76 tonnes (74.7 tons)
Dimensions:	21.3m x 7.6m x 2.7m (70ft x 25ft x 9ft)
Rigging:	Lateen rig with single or two masts and double spars
Complement:	6–10
Cargo:	Grain, wine, timber, oil, slaves
Year:	c.1200

Swedish Cargo Ship

Found in mud at Kalmar Bay in the 1930s, this is one of the oldest rudder-fitted ships known. The former steering oar is now a solid fixture. The ship is clinker-built and part-decked. The short bowsprit suggests a staysail was carried. The ship also has a windlass fitted, to pull in a net as well as to raise the anchor.

SPECIFICATIONS	
Type:	Sailing cargo ship
Displacement:	20 tonnes (19.7 tons)
Dimensions:	11.1m x 4.6m x 1.1m (36ft 6in x 15ft x 3ft 6in)
Rigging:	Single dismountable mast, square sail, foresail
Complement:	4
Cargo:	Dried fish, timber, ores, barrelled goods
Year:	c.1200

Hanseatic Cog

The Hanseatic League had many ships of this type, compact, seaworthy and efficient in their time, with a rounded hull to maximize carrying capacity. They might also carry a few passengers in a cabin below the stern platform. A typical cog was found in the Weser River, at Bremen, in 1962.

SPECIFICATIONS	
Type:	Sailing cargo ship
Displacement:	122 tonnes (120 tons)
Dimensions:	24m x 8m x 3m (78ft 9in x 26ft 3in x 10ft)
Rigging:	Single mast, square sail
Complement:	6–8
Cargo:	Coal, wood, wine, wool, hides, fish
Year:	1239

SHIP TYPES TO 1899

Henry Grace à Dieu

Built on the lines of a very large carrack, to carry and fire heavy guns, this was also Henry VIII's royal flagship. Known as *Great Harry,* it was refitted in 1536–39 with 21 heavy bronze cannon and 130 light iron guns. Renamed *Edward* after the accession of Edward VI, it was destroyed by fire in 1553.

Up to this time, English warships had been converted merchantmen, with all the difficulties involved in the hiring and refitting of them in time of war. *Henry Grace à Dieu*, a large carrack, was purpose-built as a warship, as were her sister-ships, the ill-fated *Mary Rose* and the *Great Galley*.

SPECIFICATIONS

Type:	English warship
Displacement:	approx. 1659 tonnes (1500 tons)
Dimensions:	57.9m x 15.2m (190ft x 50ft) approx
Rigging:	Four masts, square rigged on fore and main, lateen mizzens
Main armament:	43 heavy guns, 141 light guns
Launched:	1514

FIGHTING TOPS
The full rig of square sails made it difficult to incorporate effective fighting tops on the masts, unlike earlier ships.

STERNCASTLE
Great Harry had a long, two-decked sterncastle with suitable accommodation for the King and his accompanying party.

GUNPORTS
Unsecured or inadequate ports could lead to flooding, and rapid sinking, as happened with *Mary Rose* in 1545.

HENRY GRACE À DIEU

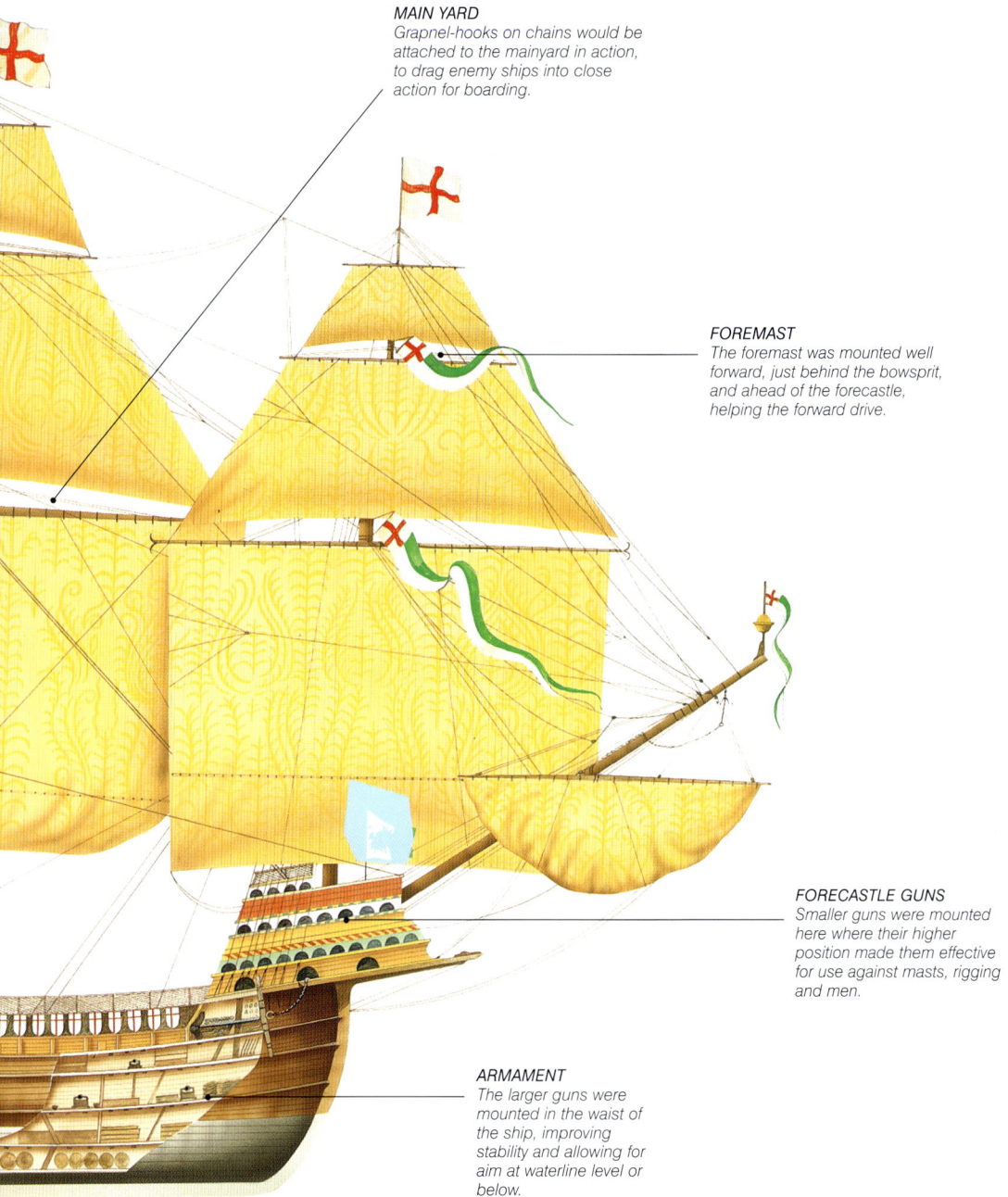

MAIN YARD
Grapnel-hooks on chains would be attached to the mainyard in action, to drag enemy ships into close action for boarding.

FOREMAST
The foremast was mounted well forward, just behind the bowsprit, and ahead of the forecastle, helping the forward drive.

FORECASTLE GUNS
Smaller guns were mounted here where their higher position made them effective for use against masts, rigging and men.

ARMAMENT
The larger guns were mounted in the waist of the ship, improving stability and allowing for aim at waterline level or below.

Early Medieval Ships: Part 2

Improvements in navigation, ship construction and ship handling made long-range warfare more effective as well as assisting trade and civilian travel. In many places, older-style ships with steering oars were still being built, and the single mast was still the general rule.

Venetian Crusader Ship

Venice profited by conveying troops and supplies from the European kingdoms to and from Palestine. By the late thirteenth century, two lateen-rigged masts were fitted to galley-type vessels like this, for speed of transit. Double-decked, it had steering oars, and the ram indicates it could also be used in battle.

SPECIFICATIONS	
Type:	Transport galley
Displacement:	approx. 122 tonnes (120 tons)
Dimensions:	25.8m x 6.4m x 3.4m (84ft 6in x 21ft x 11ft)
Rigging:	Two lateen-rigged masts, triple-piece yards
Complement:	Not known
Cargo:	Troops, horses, fodder, siege equipment, stores
Year:	1268

Christopher of the Tower

This was one of the earliest vessels to carry guns. Its three iron guns were intended to kill men on decks and in fighting castles. Its designation, *of the Tower*, indicates that it was fitted out by the Royal Armoury. Captured by the French in 1339, it was retaken by the English at the Battle of Sluys in 1340.

SPECIFICATIONS	
Type:	Sailing warship
Displacement:	305 tonnes (300 tons)
Dimensions:	Not known
Rigging:	Single mast with fighting top, square sail
Armament:	Three iron guns
Year:	c.1338

TIMELINE 1268 1338 1370

EARLY MEDIEVAL SHIPS: PART 2

English Warship

Up to 200 fighting ships of this size and general type could be assembled by England in the late fourteenth century. The hull, with a substantial aftercastle, owes much to the design of the cog. Despite its length, the bowsprit does not appear to have carried a sail.

SPECIFICATIONS	
Type:	Sailing warship
Displacement:	approx. 122 tonnes (120 tons)
Dimensions:	22.9m x 6.7m x 2m (75ft x 22ft x 6ft 6in)
Rigging:	Single mast, square sail, stays attached to bowsprit
Complement:	Around 10 seamen plus officers and fighting men
Year:	c.1370

Danish Warship

This is a merchant ship design adapted for warfare. Essentially the same design as the previous vessel, it has a different hull shape and the castle structures at bow and stern look like afterthoughts. Side spikes helped in grappling an enemy vessel. This ship is depicted on ceiling paintings in a church at Skamstrup.

SPECIFICATIONS	
Type:	Adapted sailing warship
Dimensions:	30.5m x 6.1m x 1.5m (100ft x 20ft x 5ft)
Rigging:	Single mast, square sail
Complement:	6–8 seamen plus officers and fighting men
Year:	1390

Spanish Warship (Não)

Não simply means ship, or large vessel, and Spain was a leader in design advances. A second mast, lateen-rigged, is placed on the long poop-deck, and the steeply raked bowsprit is well on the way to becoming a foremast. Of clinker construction, the hull comes to a point at the stern where the big rudder is fitted.

Type:	Sailing warship
Displacement:	152.5 tonnes (150 tons)
Dimensions:	19.8m x 6.7m x 2m (65ft x 22ft x 6ft 6in)
Rigging:	Mainmast with square sail; mizzen with lateen sail
Complement:	15–20 seamen plus officers and fighting men
Year:	1450

1390

1450

SHIP TYPES TO 1899

San Martin

Built for Portugal (which was annexed to Spain in 1580), this was Spain's flagship in the victory of Terceiro over the French in 1582, and again in the Armada expedition against England in 1588. Heavily engaged with English ships, it was hit by cannon-balls over 200 times. It survived defeat and storm to return to Spain.

San Martin

At the time of forming the Spanish Armada, the *San Martin* was found to be the best of the fleet and was chose as the flagship of the Armada commander-in-chief, the Duke of Medina Sidonia. She suffered heavy damage at the Battle of Gravelines in 1588 but she escaped the attack and led the Armada back to Spain through a fierce storm.

SPECIFICATIONS	
Type:	Spanish galleon
Displacement:	approx. 1016 tonnes (1000 tons)
Dimensions:	Beam 9.3m (30ft 9in)
Rigging:	Four masts, square rigged on fore and main, lateen mizzens
Main armament:	48 heavy guns
Complement:	350 seamen and gunners, 302 arquebusiers and musketeers
Launched:	c.1579

FIGHTING MEN
Musketeers and arquebusiers were placed on the lofty fore- and stern-castles, from where they could fire down into enemy vessels.

HULL
Iberian galleons were built high-sided to allow for effective grappling and boarding in close-quarters fighting.

SAN MARTIN

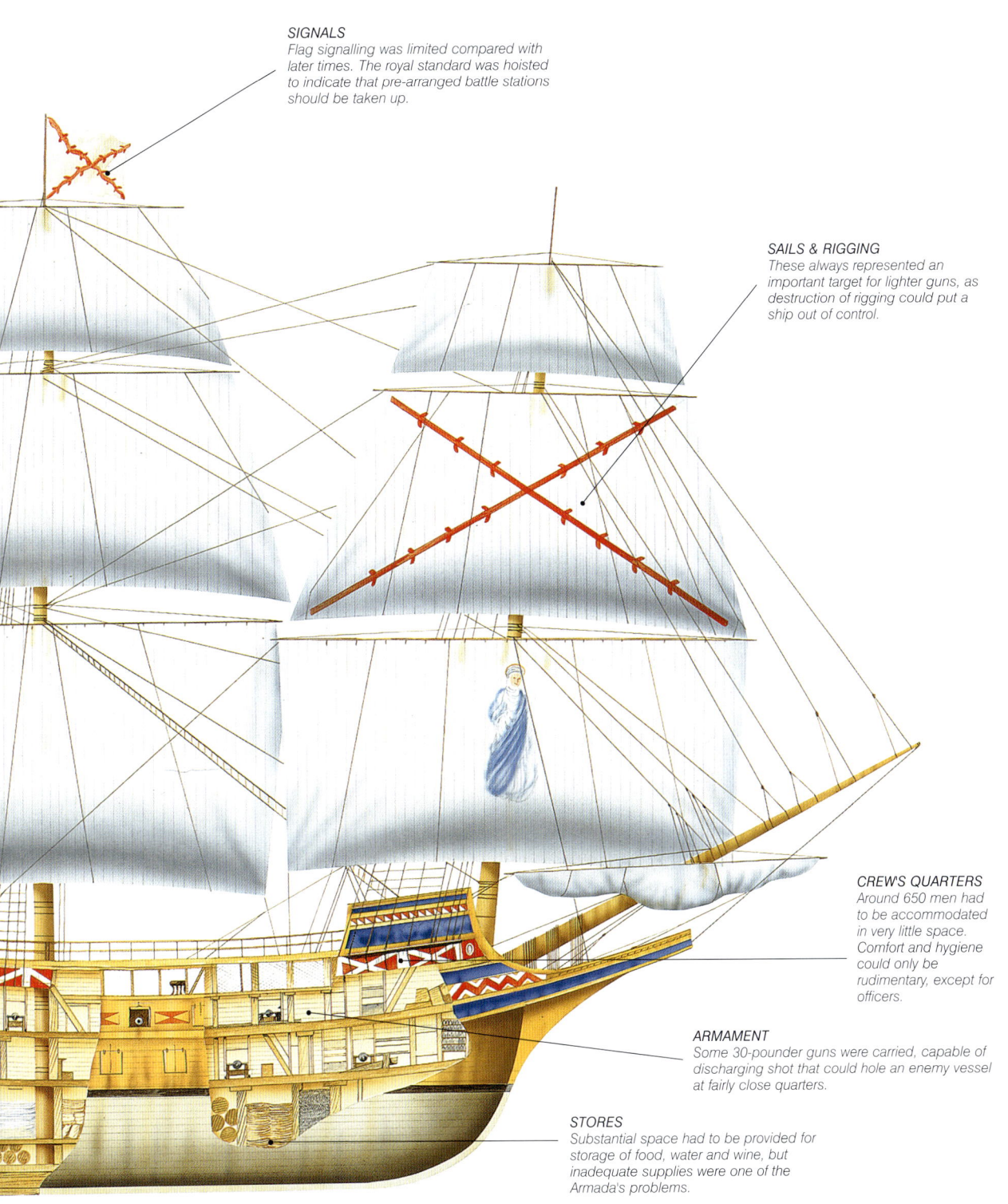

SIGNALS
Flag signalling was limited compared with later times. The royal standard was hoisted to indicate that pre-arranged battle stations should be taken up.

SAILS & RIGGING
These always represented an important target for lighter guns, as destruction of rigging could put a ship out of control.

CREW'S QUARTERS
Around 650 men had to be accommodated in very little space. Comfort and hygiene could only be rudimentary, except for officers.

ARMAMENT
Some 30-pounder guns were carried, capable of discharging shot that could hole an enemy vessel at fairly close quarters.

STORES
Substantial space had to be provided for storage of food, water and wine, but inadequate supplies were one of the Armada's problems.

SHIP TYPES TO 1899

The Age of Exploration

From the 1450s on, geographers and explorers were steadily extending the frontiers of knowledge. The process was led by Portugal and Spain, the great sea powers of the time, and ships were built and provisioned for far longer voyages than had been dared before. Precious cargoes were anticipated: gold, silver and spices.

Niña

Built as a lateen-rigged caravel (low-decked ship), *Niña* was re-rigged as a *caravela redonda,* with a third mast stepped in the bows, making her swift and seaworthy. In 1492, she was the flagship of Christopher Columbus in his first transatlantic voyage, and crossed the ocean at least another four times.

SPECIFICATIONS
Type:	Spanish sailing ship
Displacement:	approx. 76 tonnes (74.8 tons)
Dimensions:	18.3m x 5.5m x 2.1m (60ft x 18ft x 7ft)
Rigging:	Square rig on fore and main masts; lateen sail on mizzen
Complement:	24
Year:	c.1491

São Gabriel

Built to explore the sea route to India, this was the flagship of Vasco da Gama's squadron, which rounded the African continent between 1497 and 1499. A high-decked *não,* it shows many novel features, including the upper course of sails and the foresail on the bowsprit. These rapidly became standard on larger ships.

SPECIFICATIONS
Type:	Portuguese sailing ship
Displacement:	approx. 101.5 tonnes (100 tons)
Dimensions:	21.3 x 7 x 2.7m (70 x 23 x 9ft)
Rigging:	Square rig with upper course on fore and main masts; lateen rig on mizzen
Armament:	20 guns
Complement:	60
Year:	c.1497

TIMELINE

 1491   1497   1519

THE AGE OF EXPLORATION

La Dauphine

SPECIFICATIONS	
Type:	French caravel
Displacement:	101.5 tonnes (100 tons)
Dimensions:	24.5m x 5.8m x 4.6m (80ft x 19ft x 15ft)
Rigging:	Square rig with upper course on fore and main masts; lateen rig on mizzen
Complement:	50
Year:	1519

Of caravel design, this three-master crossed the Atlantic in 1523, commanded by Giovanni da Verrazzano, who hoped to find a sea-route to China. Instead, it sailed up the coast of North America, making some of the first maps and charts of the New England coast. The ship returned to Dieppe in July 1524.

Golden Hind

SPECIFICATIONS	
Type:	English galleon
Displacement:	approx. 152.5 tonnes (150 tons)
Dimensions:	21.3m x 5.8m x 2.7m (70ft x 19ft x 9ft)
Rigging:	Square rig with main and upper courses and topsails on fore and mainmasts; lateen rig on mizzen
Armament:	18 guns
Complement:	80–85
Year:	1576

Initially named *Pelican,* this was Francis Drake's flagship when circumnavigating the globe in 1577–80. Compact and well-armed, half-exploration craft and half-pirate ship, she had a double hull with tarred horsehair between the planks, to stave off marine worms. Preserved in London, the hull had rotted away by 1660.

Triumph

SPECIFICATIONS	
Type:	English war galleon
Displacement:	1117.6 tonnes (1100 tons)
Dimensions:	64m x 15.5m x 6.4m (210ft x 51ft x 21ft)
Rigging:	Four masts; square rig on fore and main masts; lateen mizzens
Armament:	60 guns
Complement:	300 seamen, 40 gunners, 180 fighting men
Year:	c.1580

The contest for supremacy between England and Spain led to the 'English galleon' – longer and narrower than the Spanish galleon, it had a square stern, and was faster and more manoeuvrable. *Triumph* was the largest of the type, and played an important part in the fight against the Spanish Armada in 1588.

1576   1580

23

SHIP TYPES TO 1899

Sovereign of the Seas

Opulently decorated to reflect the prestige of King Charles I, this was a real fighting ship, a giant of its time. It may have been the first to carry royals above the topgallants, but its bulk made it a sluggish sailer. Having seen action in three Anglo-Dutch wars, it was destroyed by accidental fire in 1703.

Sovereign of the Seas

The masterwork of the shipwright Phineas Pett, *Sovereign of the Seas* was intended to display the naval might of England and the prestige of the English-Scottish King. It had three complete gun decks and was the first man-of-war to carry 100 heavy guns.

SPECIFICATIONS	
Type:	English man of war
Displacement:	1159 tonnes (1141 tons)
Dimensions:	70.7m x 14.2m x 7.1m (232ft x 46ft 6in x 23ft)
Rigging:	Three masts, square rigged on fore and main, lateen mizzen with topsail
Main armament:	102 guns
Complement:	250 seamen, plus gunners and soldiers
Launched:	1637

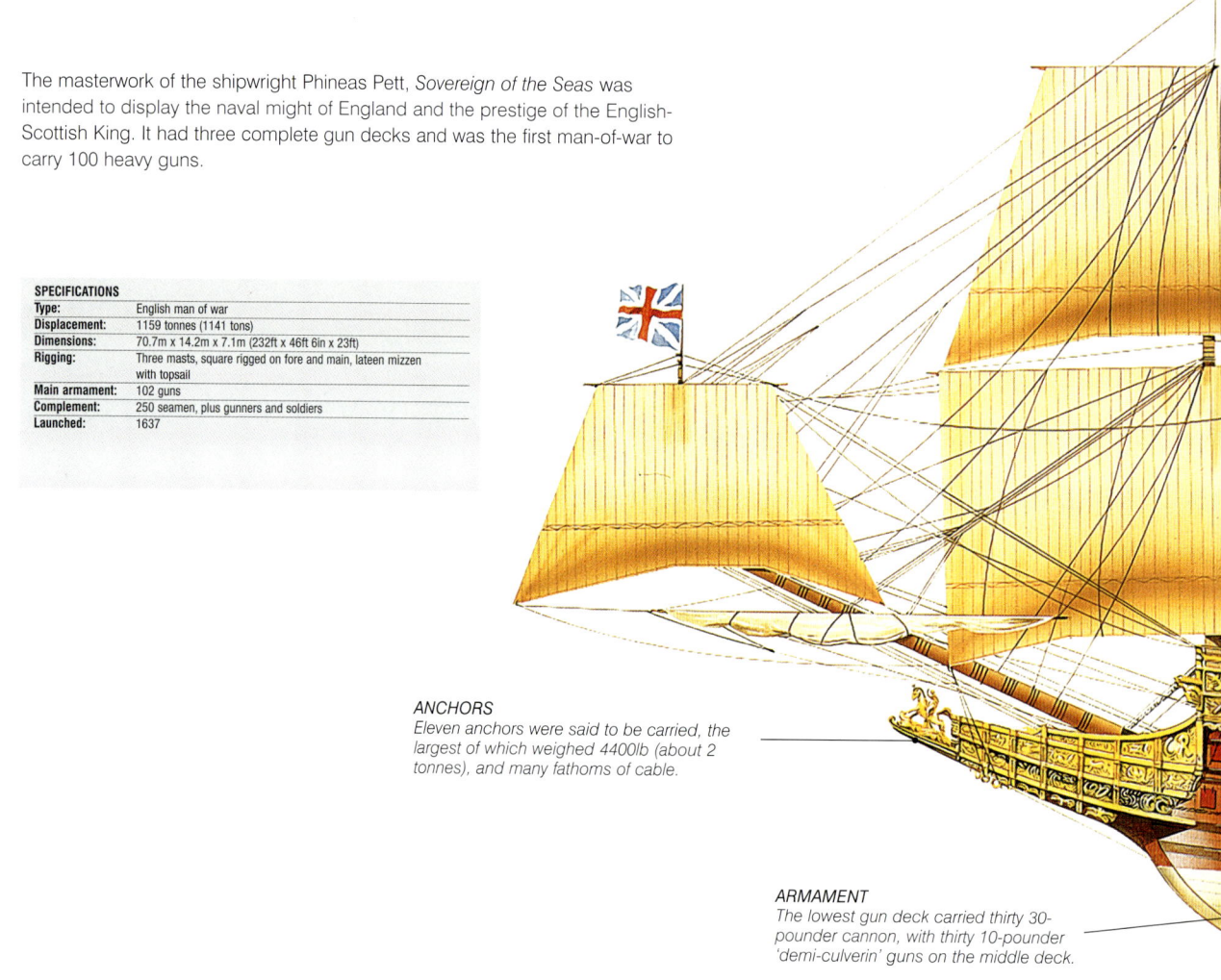

ANCHORS
Eleven anchors were said to be carried, the largest of which weighed 4400lb (about 2 tonnes), and many fathoms of cable.

ARMAMENT
The lowest gun deck carried thirty 30-pounder cannon, with thirty 10-pounder 'demi-culverin' guns on the middle deck.

SOVEREIGN OF THE SEAS

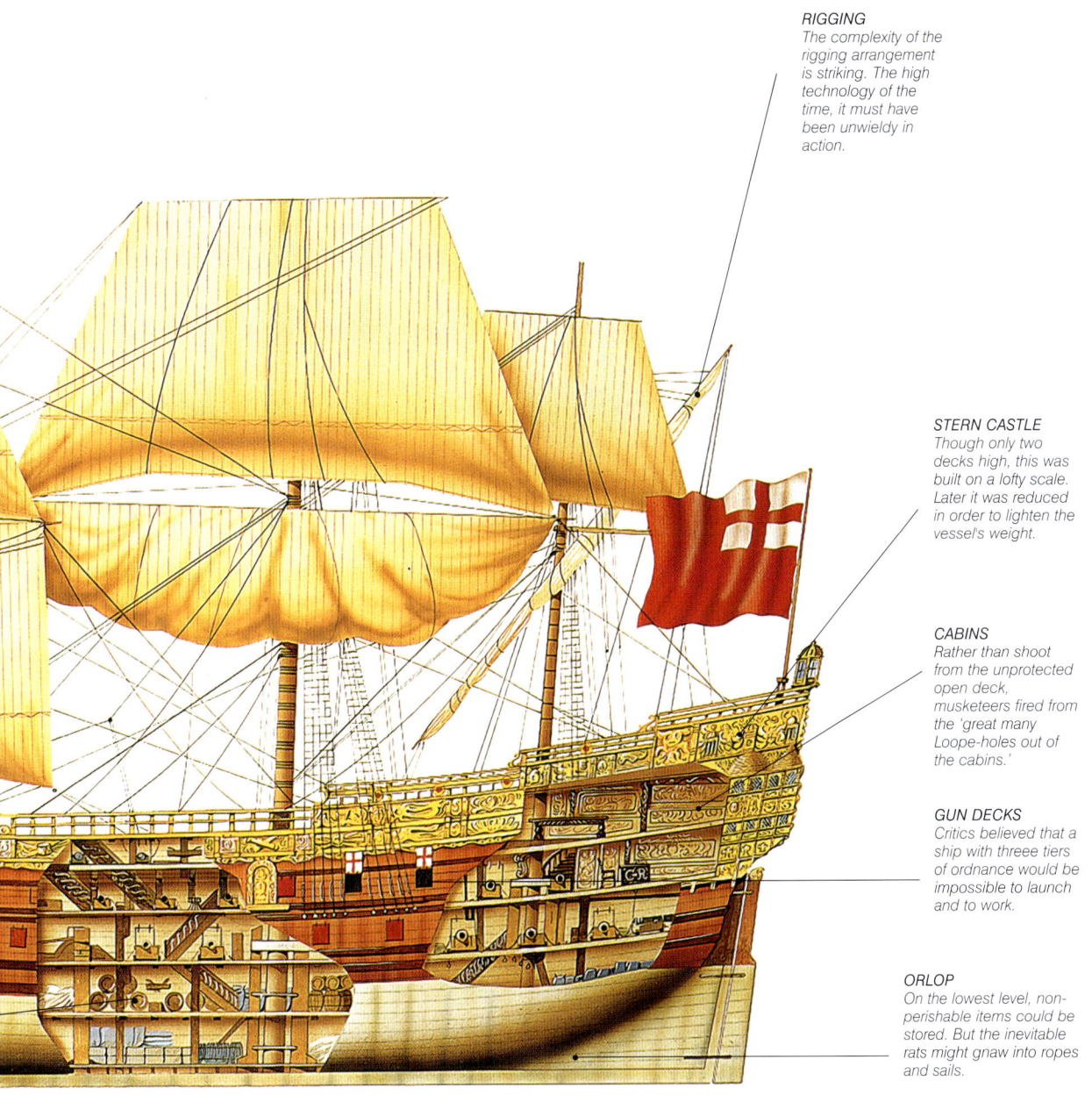

RIGGING
The complexity of the rigging arrangement is striking. The high technology of the time, it must have been unwieldy in action.

STERN CASTLE
Though only two decks high, this was built on a lofty scale. Later it was reduced in order to lighten the vessel's weight.

CABINS
Rather than shoot from the unprotected open deck, musketeers fired from the 'great many Loope-holes out of the cabins.'

GUN DECKS
Critics believed that a ship with threee tiers of ordnance would be impossible to launch and to work.

ORLOP
On the lowest level, non-perishable items could be stored. But the inevitable rats might gnaw into ropes and sails.

European Warships of the Seventeenth Century

Holland was now a major power, and naval rivalries, as well as mercantile opportunities, continued the drive towards bigger ships. Ship types became more varied, including coastal and short-sea craft as well as ocean-going vessels. But the largest ships, built for prestige, were rarely the most useful or successful.

Galleass

A combination of oared ship and galleon, the galleass was used by navies from the Mediterranean to the North Sea, from the 1580s until around 1700, though latterly in the Mediterranean only. This example is typical of the Venetian and Turkish galleasses of the 1650s, with its galleon-style poop and galley-type ram.

SPECIFICATIONS

Type:	Galleass
Dimensions:	48.7m x 9.1m x 3.6m (160ft x 30ft x 12ft)
Rigging:	Three masts all with lateen rig
Armament:	20 cannon plus 20–30 light swivel guns
Complement:	350 oarsmen, 30 seamen, 40 gunners
Year:	1650s

Dauphin Royal

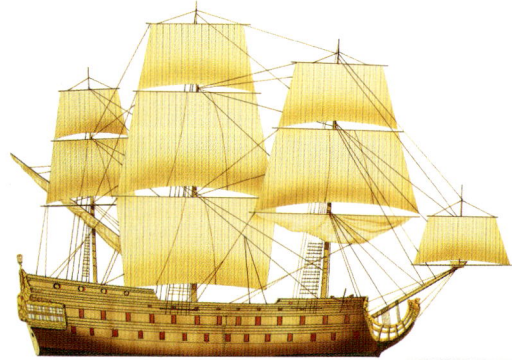

This was probably one of the first ships to have staysails (not shown here), and also studding sails on the mainmast. The two covered gun decks and high-sided hull were state of the art in the mid-century. *Dauphin Royal* took part in the unsuccessful action against the English and Dutch off Beachy Head in 1666.

SPECIFICATIONS

Type:	Sailing warship (vaisseau)
Displacement:	1077 tonnes (1060 tons)
Dimensions:	44m x 12.2m (144ft x 40ft) – depth unknown
Rigging:	Three masts, square rigged with topsails over lateen mizzen; sprit sail and bowsprit topsail
Armament:	104 guns
Complement:	760
Year:	1658

TIMELINE

 1650   1658    1665

EUROPEAN WARSHIPS OF THE SEVENTEENTH CENTURY

De Zeven Provinzien

SPECIFICATIONS	
Type:	Sailing warship
Dimensions:	44.7m x 11.8m x 4.4m (146ft 9in x 38ft 9in x 14ft 5in)
Rigging:	Three masts, square rigged with topsails over lateen mizzen; sprit sail and bowsprit topsail
Armament:	80 guns
Complement:	450
Year:	1665

Dismasted in the Battle of the Downs in 1665, this was the flagship of Admiral de Ruyter in the Dutch fleet that startled England by storming the Medway in 1666. This sturdy two-decker saw other action at Sole Bay, the Texel, and Cape La Hogue, in a career that lasted until it was broken up in 1694.

Chebeck

SPECIFICATIONS	
Type:	Oar-assisted sailing warship
Displacement:	193.5 tonnes (190 tons)
Dimensions:	31 x 6.7 x 2.5m (103ft 9in x 22 x 8ft 2in)
Rigging:	Three masts, originally all lateen-rigged; later square-rigged on mainsail and mizzen
Armament:	12–15 guns
Complement:	24 seamen plus fighting men
Year:	c.1670

The *chebeck* or *xebec* was a commerce raider, associated with North Africa's Barbary pirates. Its striking rig and fine underwater lines made it fast and manoeuvrable, easily able to run down a merchant ship, making a rapid exit from and return to shallow harbours and bays. Nine pairs of oars were carried.

Berlin

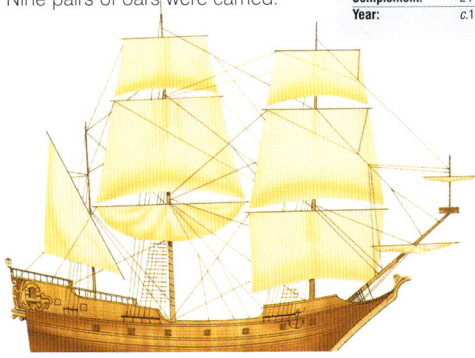

SPECIFICATIONS	
Type:	Light frigate
Dimensions:	22.7m x 6.3m, depth unknown (74ft 6in x 20ft 7in)
Rigging:	Three masts, square rigged with topsails over lateen mizzen; sprit sail and bowsprit topsail
Armament:	Twenty 24-pdr guns
Complement:	72
Cargo:	Timber, fish, grain, metals, wine
Year:	1674

The frigate – as a raider, escort craft and scout ship – was becoming important now. *Berlin*, built in Holland, was a small version of the type, built to operate along the Baltic coast of Brandenburg (later Prussia). Later it was sent on a long-distance cruise to the East Indies and was last heard of in January 1688.

1670    1674

27

SHIP TYPES TO 1899

Victory

Not put into commission until 1778, *Victory* was always an admiral's flagship, for Jervis at Cape St Vincent in 1797, and most memorably for Nelson at Trafalgar on 21 October 1805. *Victory* took heavy punishment but survived to bear Nelson's body back to England. Refitted, it served as flagship in the Baltic until 1812. It is the oldest warship still in commission.

Victory

Laid down in 1759 at Chatham Dockyard and launched in 1765, *Victory*, a First Rate of 100 guns, was not put into commission until 1778, when France allied herself with the American colonists. Nelson was shot on the deck during the decisive victory at Trafalgar; it went on to serve as flagship for Admiral Saumarez in the Baltic.

SPECIFICATIONS	
Type:	British ship of the line (First Rate)
Displacement:	2196.6 tonnes (2162 tons)
Dimensions:	56.7m x 15.8m x 6.5m (186ft x 51ft 10in x 21ft 6in)
Rigging:	Three masts, square rig
Main armament:	100 guns
Complement:	850
Launched:	1765

SECONDARY ARMAMENT
Twenty-eight 24-pounders, the same number of 12-pounders, and 16 6-pounder guns completed the triple-tiered array.

GREAT CABIN
This was divided into three units: Admiral's day cabin, dining-room, and sleeping cabin. Cannons could be installed for battle.

PRIMARY ARMAMENT
A pair of massive 68-pounder and 28 42-pounder guns were carried, to provide the basis of Victory's fire-power.

COPPER PLATING
The Royal Navy began copper-sheathing below the water-line in 1761. It made a major difference to ship-performance and life-span.

VICTORY

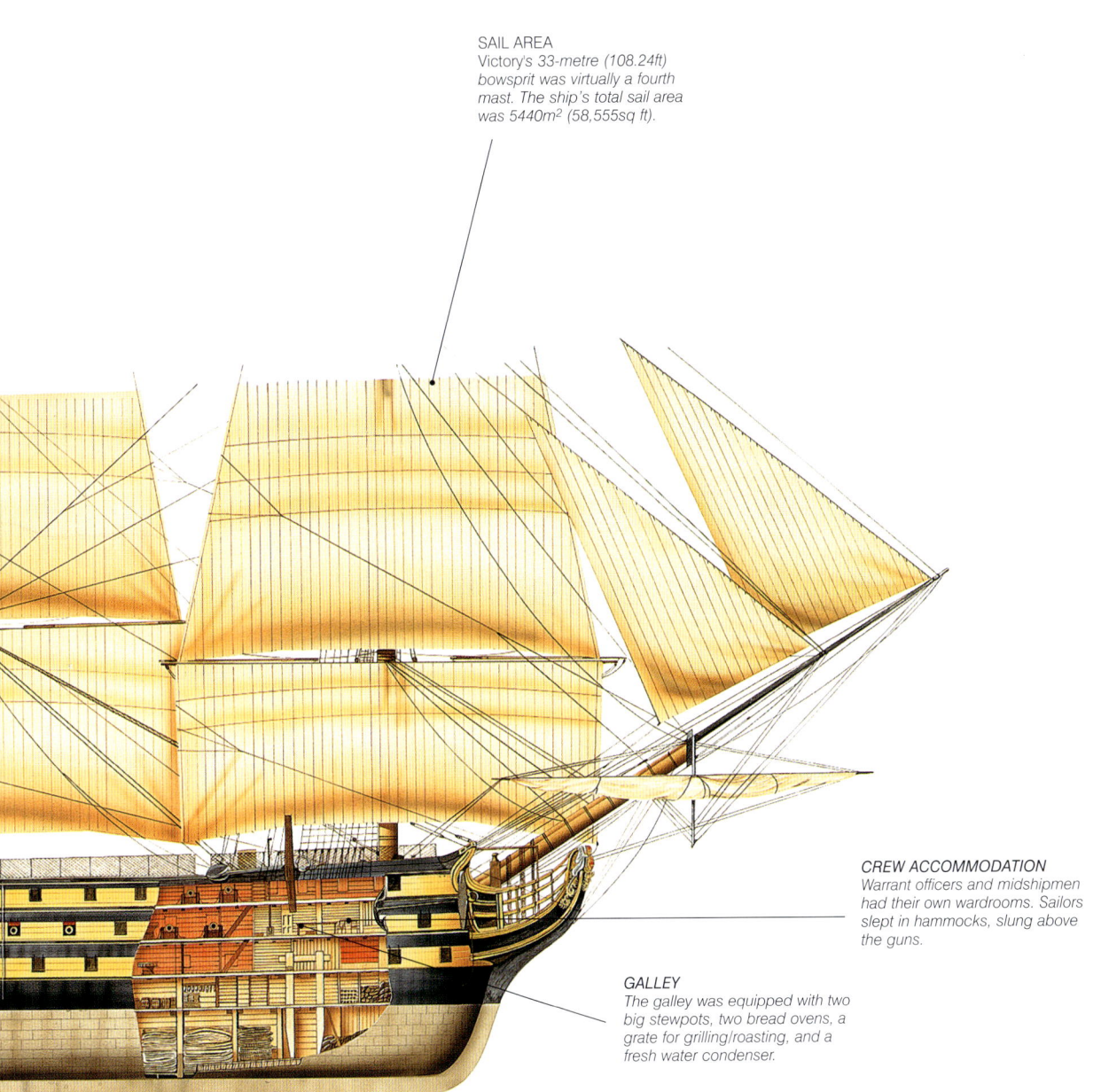

SAIL AREA
Victory's 33-metre (108.24ft) bowsprit was virtually a fourth mast. The ship's total sail area was 5440m^2 (58,555sq ft).

CREW ACCOMMODATION
Warrant officers and midshipmen had their own wardrooms. Sailors slept in hammocks, slung above the guns.

GALLEY
The galley was equipped with two big stewpots, two bread ovens, a grate for grilling/roasting, and a fresh water condenser.

SHIP TYPES TO 1899

Eighteenth-Century Warships

Warships were now more specialized. Line-of-battle ships – from First to Fourth Rate, dependent on number of guns – mounted both attack and defence. Frigates were 'the eyes of the fleet'. The cruiser, a cross between a frigate and a battleship, was developing. Smaller craft included sloops, corvettes and shell-firing bomb ships.

Ville de Paris

Major warships carried three decks of guns. Part of the French navy's expansion between 1763 and 1771, this was a First Rate, used as an admiral's flagship. In the Battle of the Saintes, April 1782, *Ville de Paris* surrendered to the British after running out of ammunition. It sank in a storm while being taken back to England.

SPECIFICATIONS
Type:	First-Rate sailing warship
Displacement:	2412 tonnes (2347 tons)
Dimensions:	56.5m x 16.3m x 6.7m (185ft 7in x 53ft 8in x 22ft 6in)
Rigging:	Three masts, square rig
Armament:	100 guns
Complement:	850
Launched:	1764

USS Hancock

Frigates were the prime weapons of the new American fleet. In the War of Independence, *Hancock* was captured by the British and renamed *Iris*. As a royal ship, it captured USS *Trumbull* in 1781. It was then captured by the French and sailed as *Iris* under French colours. It was blown up at Toulon in 1793.

SPECIFICATIONS
Type:	Sailing frigate
Displacement:	762 tonnes (750 tons)
Dimensions:	41.6m x 10.8m x 3.5m (136ft 6in x 35ft 6in x 11ft 6in)
Rigging:	Three masts, square rig
Armament:	Twenty-four 10-pdr guns, ten 6-pdr guns
Complement:	290
Launched:	1776

TIMELINE

 1764   1776

EIGHTEENTH-CENTURY WARSHIPS

Charles

Reminiscent of the galleass, this 'oared frigate' was used in the Mediterranean, built to match the *chebecks* of the Barbary corsairs in speed and exceed them in range and weight of artillery. The lower deck had positions for 15 oarsmen on each side. Its depth prevented it from close pursuit in shallow waters.

SPECIFICATIONS	
Type:	French oared frigate
Displacement:	1016 tonnes (1000 tons)
Dimensions:	45m x 11m x 4m (135ft x 38ft x 14ft)
Rigging:	Three masts, square rig
Armament:	40 guns
Complement:	330
Launched:	1776

Bomb Vessel

Bomb ships were usually solid little ketches, but this was a lightweight craft for the purpose. Discharge of its heavy mortar must have shaken its frame, even if reinforced. The mortar could be raked upwards but not turned; the whole boat had to be manoeuvred to point in the right direction.

SPECIFICATIONS	
Type:	Light mortar vessel
Displacement:	approx. 56 tonnes (55 tons)
Dimensions:	10.7m x 3.7m x 1.5m (35ft x 12ft x 5ft)
Rigging:	Single mast with spritsail and foresail
Armament:	One 330–381mm (13–15in) mortar; two light cannon
Complement:	18
Year:	c.1780

USS Constitution

As flagship of the Mediterranean Squadron, this frigate destroyed the Barbary pirates. Destroying HMS *Guerriere* in 1812 earned it the name of *Old Ironsides*, and other victories followed. A national campaign saved it from the breaker's yard in 1830, and *Constitution* still remains an American heirloom.

SPECIFICATIONS	
Type:	Sailing frigate
Displacement:	2235 tonnes (2200 tons)
Dimensions:	53.3m x 13.3m x 6.9m (175ft x 43ft 6in x 22ft 6in)
Rigging:	Three masts with square rig to upper topgallants
Armament:	Twenty 32-pdr guns, thirty-four 24-pdr guns
Complement:	450
Launched:	1797

1780

1797

SHIP TYPES TO 1899

Santissima Trinidad

Largest warship of the eighteenth century, this was a formidable vessel, able to deliver a broadside from four decks of guns. As Spanish flagship of the Combined Fleet, it was in the thick of the Battle of Trafalgar and even when dismasted and out of control, fought on, surrendering only after the battle to *HMS Prince*.

Santissima Trinidad

Built in Havana, Cuba in 1769, *Santissima Trinidad* was the most famous Spanish warship of her day. It was the only four-decker to see extensive service. It is likely that its performance, and ultimate loss at the Battle of Trafalgar was due to it being overloaded with ordnance.

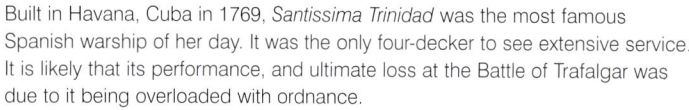

SPECIFICATIONS	
Type:	Spanish ship of the line (First Rate)
Displacement:	4851 tonnes (4572 tons)
Dimensions:	60.1m x 19.2m (200ft x 62ft 9in)
Rigging:	Three masts, square rig
Main armament:	130 guns
Complement:	950
Launched:	1769

VULNERABILITY
The large-windowed stern structure, though cannons could be mounted in it, allowed close-range fire to create destruction throughout the ship.

HELM
The rudder is quite substantial but the vessel was said to be unresponsive, especially in light winds, as at Trafalgar.

HULL
Eye-witness accounts recall that the hull was painted in broad red and white stripes in 1805, presumably the captain's choice.

SANTISSIMA TRINIDAD

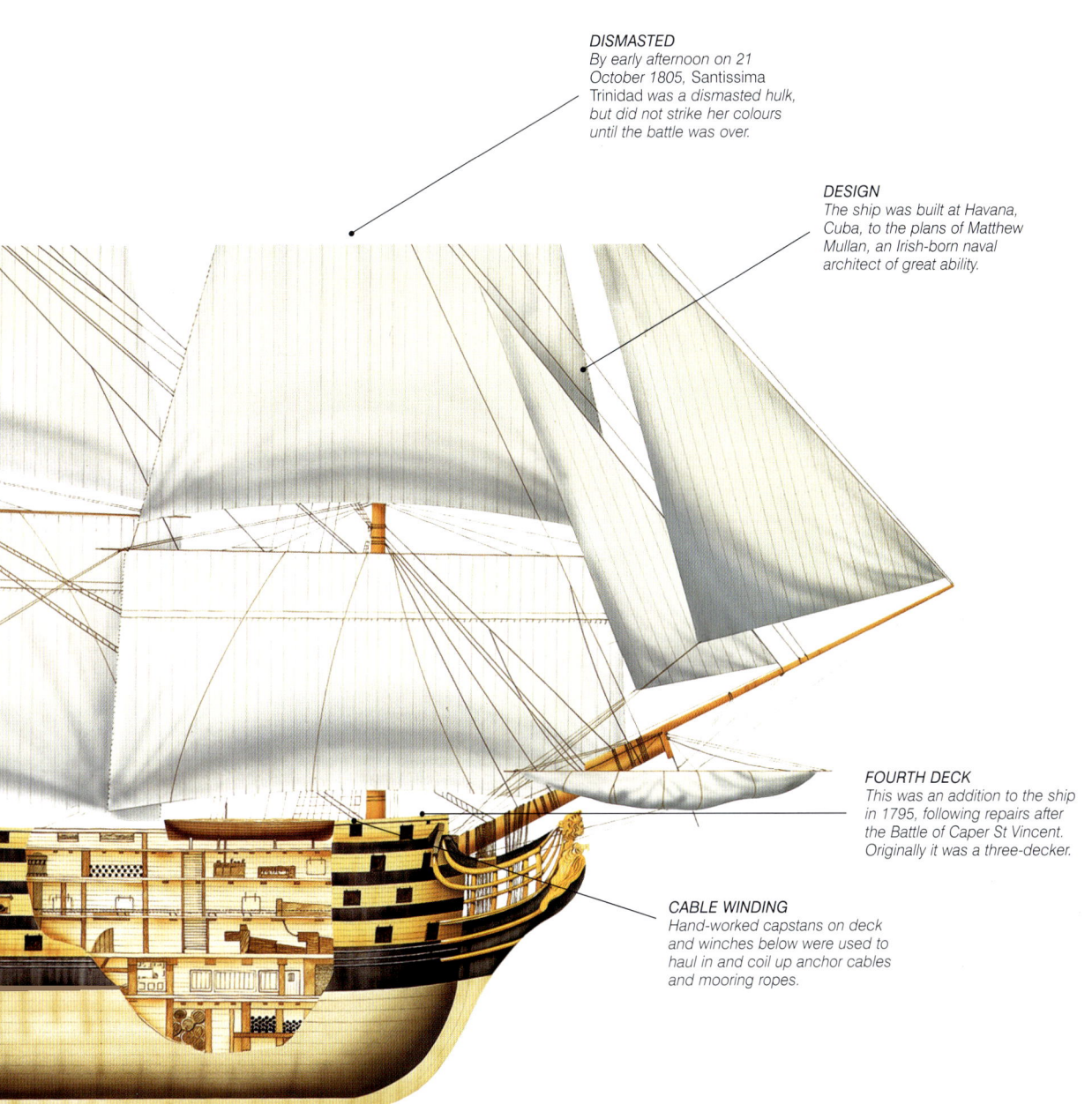

DISMASTED
By early afternoon on 21 October 1805, Santissima Trinidad was a dismasted hulk, but did not strike her colours until the battle was over.

DESIGN
The ship was built at Havana, Cuba, to the plans of Matthew Mullan, an Irish-born naval architect of great ability.

FOURTH DECK
This was an addition to the ship in 1795, following repairs after the Battle of Caper St Vincent. Originally it was a three-decker.

CABLE WINDING
Hand-worked capstans on deck and winches below were used to haul in and coil up anchor cables and mooring ropes.

SHIP TYPES TO 1899

Early Steam-Powered Craft

Developed in France and England, the steam engine had been used on land for decades before a version of suitable size and weight could be developed for marine use. Inventors on both sides of the Atlantic worked on the problem in the last decades of the eighteenth century, but saw little reward for their ingenuity.

John Fitch

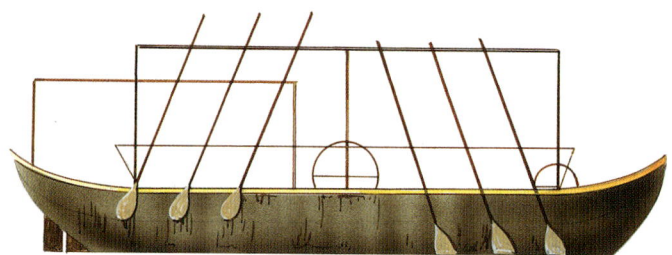

The American engineer John Fitch tried replicating manual oars with mechanical ones on this craft, which was trialled on the Delaware River. Crank rods linked the driving shafts to the cylinders. The ship was under-powered and failed. Fitch built other steam-powered craft in 1788 and 1790 but got no financial backing.

SPECIFICATIONS	
Type:	Experimental steamboat
Dimensions:	18.3m x 3.7m x 0.9m (60ft x 12ft x 3ft)
Machinery:	Steam boiler with pistons driving gantry-mounted oars
Complement:	2
Launched:	1787

Charlotte Dundas

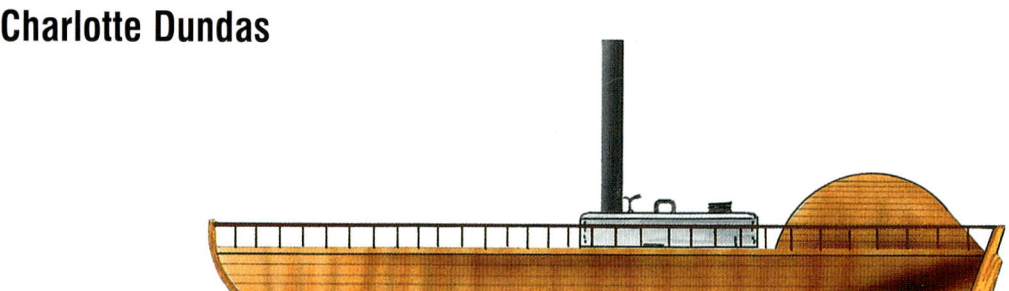

Built to tow canal barges, this was the first really effective steamship, with boiler and cylinders side by side to maintain balance. Unfortunately its stern-wheel drive created a wash that threatened to undermine the canal banks, and it was never used in regular service. It was finally scrapped in 1861.

SPECIFICATIONS	
Type:	Stern-wheeled steamboat
Dimensions:	17.1m x 5.5m x 2.4m (56ft x 18ft x 8ft)
Machinery:	Steam boiler with piston driving a stern wheel
Complement:	4
Launched:	1801

TIMELINE

1787　　　　1801　　　　1803

EARLY STEAM-POWERED CRAFT

Fulton

Robert Fulton, an American engineer living in Paris, pioneered the sidewheel steamship. This was his second attempt. Trialled in August 1803, it successfully pulled two laden barges against the current of the Seine. Fulton returned home and built the US Navy's first steam frigate, *Demologos*, launched in 1814.

SPECIFICATIONS	
Type:	Sidewheel steamboat
Displacement:	25.5 tonnes (25 tons)
Dimensions:	27.4m x 4.9m x 1.5m (90ft x 16ft x 5ft)
Machinery:	Single cylinder beam engine with pistons and cranks driving sidewheels
Speed:	4.5 knots
Complement:	2
Launched:	1803

Clermont

Designed by Fulton, and first known simply as *Steam Boat*, then *North River Steamboat*, *Clermont* was the first steamship in regular service. It carried up to 140 passengers between New York and Albany until 1814. Mocked by the river sloop men as 'Fulton's Folly', it foreshadowed the end of their business.

SPECIFICATIONS	
Type:	Sidewheel steamboat
Displacement:	101.6 tonnes (100 tons)
Dimensions:	40.5m x 4m x 2.1m (133ft x 13ft x 7ft)
Machinery:	Boulton & Watt steam engine with cog drive to paddle wheels
Rigging:	Two masts, square sail on foremast, gaff mizzen
Route:	Hudson River
Launched:	1807

Comet

By 1812, the high-pressure steam boiler was a reality, imparting a more powerful drive. Built by Henry Bell, *Comet* was the first steamship in commercial service in Europe, but technical improvements soon overtook it. It was wrecked on the Scottish coast on 13 December 1820, though the engine was salvaged.

SPECIFICATIONS	
Type:	Passenger steamship
Displacement:	23.4 tonnes (23 tons)
Dimensions:	13.3m x 3.4m x 1.7m (43ft 5in x 11ft 3in x 5ft 6in)
Machinery:	4hp steam engine driving double sidewheels
Complement:	6
Launched:	1811

1807

1811

SHIP TYPES TO 1899

Pioneering Steamships of the Nineteenth Century

Sceptics claimed that a steam-powered ship would need so much coal to cross the Atlantic there would be no room for cargo. New theoretical knowledge dispelled this myth, and improvements to the steam engine made ocean-going steamers a reality.

James Watt

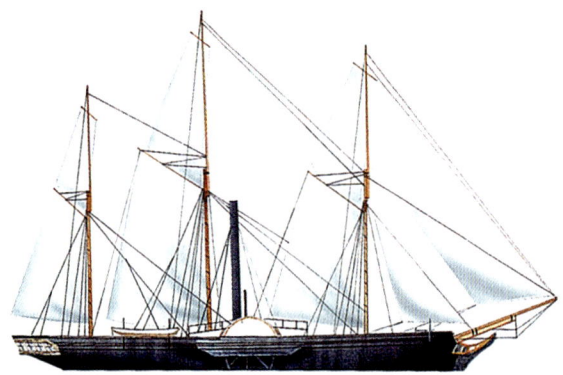

Until the advent of a railway network, coastal steamers like this pioneering ship were the prime means of long-distance transport up and down the British coast, and ran to a generally reliable timetable. The tall funnel provided draught for the fire as well as raising smoke clear of the deck and lower rigging.

SPECIFICATIONS	
Type:	British paddle steamer
Dimensions:	43m x 14.3m (141ft 8in x 47ft) beam across paddleboxes
Machinery:	100hp steam engine with two 508mm (20in) cylinders
Rigging:	Three masts, schooner rig
Top speed:	9 knots
Route:	Edinburgh to London
Launched:	1820

Curaçao

Launched at Dover, England, as *Calpe,* and sold to the Dutch and renamed, this was a lightly-armed colonial supply and defence ship. The first steamship in the Dutch navy, it made many runs between Rotterdam and Surinam, sometimes stationed in the Caribbean, sometimes in home waters. It was scrapped in 1850.

SPECIFICATIONS	
Type:	Dutch paddle steamer
Displacement:	445 tonnes (438 tons)
Dimensions:	39.8m x 8.2m x 4.1m (130ft 6in x 26ft 9in x 13ft 6in)
Rigging:	Three masts, barque rig
Machinery:	Side-lever steam engine, 100hp
Armament:	Two 12-pdr guns
Complement:	42
Route:	Netherlands–Caribbean
Launched:	1826

TIMELINE 1820 1826 1831

Royal William

SPECIFICATIONS	
Type:	British passenger–cargo steamship
Displacement:	573 tonnes (564 tons)
Dimensions:	53.3m x 8.2m x 5.3m (175ft x 27ft x 17ft 6in)
Rigging:	Three masts, barquentine rig
Machinery:	Steam engine, 200hp
Complement:	40
Cargo:	General goods, furs
Launched:	1831

Wooden-hulled, like most early steam vessels, this was one of the first ships fitted with watertight bulkheads (of iron) – a feature that proved its worth in a collision in 1839, when the ship stayed afloat. The ship ran for years on the Liverpool–Halifax route. Eventually moored at Dublin, it was broken up in 1888.

Beaver

SPECIFICATIONS	
Type:	Canadian paddle steamer
Displacement:	190 tonnes (187 tons)
Dimensions:	30.75m x 6.1m x 2.6m (100ft 10in x 20ft x 8ft 6in)
Rigging:	Two masts, brigantine rig
Machinery:	Side lever steam engine driving side paddle wheels
Armament:	4 brass cannon
Complement:	31
Cargo:	Furs, coal, general supplies
Launched:	1836

Built in London and initially operated by the Hudson's Bay Company, *Beaver* had an engine fitted at Fort Vancouver, becoming the first steamer in the North Pacific. A trading and survey ship, it operated along the north-west coast between Oregon and Alaska until wrecked in Burrard Inlet, Vancouver, in 1888.

Sirius

SPECIFICATIONS	
Type:	British paddle steamer
Displacement:	714 tonnes (703 tons)
Dimensions:	54m x 7.6m (178ft x 25ft)
Machinery:	Twin side-lever engines, paddle wheels
Top speed:	8 knots
Route:	North Atlantic
Launched:	1837

The first steamer to start a regular service across the Atlantic, *Sirius* left London on 28 March 1838 with forty passengers, and arrived in New York on 22 April. Its success was partly due to the newly-introduced surface condensers, which enabled fresh distilled water to be fed to the boilers. *Sirius* was wrecked in 1847.

1836  1837

SHIP TYPES TO 1899

The Iron Steamship

With the 'industrial revolution' in full swing – by mid-century iron-making techniques and production capacity were capable of being applied to large ships, with resultant benefits in construction time, strength and carrying capacity. Wrought-iron plates were riveted on an iron frame. Tall masts and sails were still retained, but as time passed these were used less frequently.

Great Britain

Brunel's *Great Britain* was the first iron-hulled, screw-propelled steamship, and the largest steamer of its day. It ran aground near Belfast in 1846, and a year later was refloated and rebuilt. After decades as a hulk in the Falkland Islands, it was towed to Bristol for restoration as a museum ship in 1970.

SPECIFICATIONS	
Type:	British liner
Displacement:	3322 tonnes (3270 tons)
Dimensions:	88m x 15m (289ft x 50ft)
Machinery:	Single screw, compound engine
Top speed:	9 knots
Launched:	July 1843
Date of profile:	1844

John Bowes

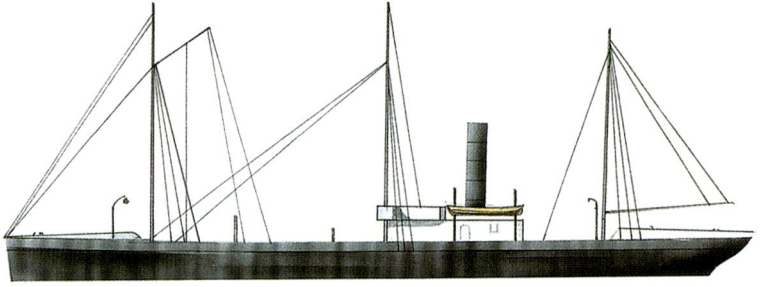

The launch of the *John Bowes* at Jarrow made the English fleet of collier brigs instantly obsolete. In five days it could transport 650 tons of coal to London and be back in Newcastle to reload. With a 20m (60ft) hatch, it could load quickly, and its water ballast could be pumped out. It cost £10,000 to build.

SPECIFICATIONS	
Type:	British bulk coal carrier
Displacement:	444 tonnes (437 tons)
Dimensions:	30m x 5.5m x 3m (98ft x 18ft x 9ft 6in)
Machinery:	Single screw, compound engine
Rigging:	Three masts, staysails
Top speed:	9 knots
Cargo:	Coal
Route:	Newcastle–London
Launched:	1852

TIMELINE

1844  1852  1853

Himalaya

While still under construction, *Himalaya* was converted from paddle to screw propulsion. Proving expensive to operate, it was sold to the British government as a troop ship. After service during the Crimean War, it became a depot ship until 1919. In 1920, it was sold as a coal hulk. It was sunk at Portland in 1940.

SPECIFICATIONS	
Type:	British liner
Displacement:	4765 tonnes (4690 tons)
Dimensions:	103.7m x 14m x 6.5m (340ft 5in x 46ft 2in x 21ft 5in)
Machinery:	Single screw, horizontal direct-acting trunk engines
Rigging:	Three masts, square rig
Top speed:	14 knots
Launched:	May 1853

Bremen

In June 1858, *Bremen* opened the North Atlantic route for the North German Lloyd Line. With 115 passengers, and 152 tonnes of cargo, it reached New York in just over 12 days. In 1874, *Bremen* was sold to a British company, the engines were removed and it served as a sailing ship until wrecked in 1882.

SPECIFICATIONS	
Type:	German liner
Displacement:	2717 tonnes (2674 tons)
Dimensions:	97m x 12m (318ft x 41ft)
Machinery:	Single screw, compound engine
Rigging:	Three masts, barque rig
Top speed:	10 knots
Route:	Hamburg/Bremen–New York
Launched:	1858

America

Built as a fast liner, *America* had capacity for 300 first class and 700 steerage class passengers. It was a heavy coal user and proved uneconomic to run, so the National Line sold it to the Italian government in 1887. Refitted and renamed *Trinacria*, it became the royal yacht. It was scrapped in 1925.

SPECIFICATIONS	
Type:	British liner, Italian royal yacht
Displacement:	5729 tonnes (5639 tons)
Dimensions:	135m x 15.5m (442ft 11in x 50ft 10in)
Machinery:	Single screw, compound engine
Rigging:	Two masts, square rig
Launched:	1884

1858

1884

SHIP TYPES TO 1899

The Last Great Sailing Ships

The sailing ship had the great advantage of free energy, and its builders took account of technical advances in hull design, rigging and sail-making. Every conceivable square inch of canvas was deployed and in favourable conditions the fastest sailing ships swept past slower steamers. New sailing ships were being built right up to the end of the century.

Flying Cloud

This celebrated wooden-hulled clipper, designed and built in Boston by Donald McKay, was perhaps the fastest of all in a full wind. From 1862, it ran on the Australian wool route for almost ten years. In 1874, it ran aground on the New Brunswick coast, and though salvaged, was stripped and burned in 1875.

SPECIFICATIONS
Type:	American full-rigged sailing ship
Displacement:	1812 tonnes (1783 tons)
Dimensions:	71.6m x 12.4m (235ft x 40ft 8in)
Rigging:	Three masts, full square rig
Top speed:	14+ knots
Cargo:	Tea, cotton, wool, nitrates
Launched:	1851

Formby

The first large steel-hulled ship, built for £24,000, *Formby* redeemed its price by its ability to carry 15 per cent more freight than an iron ship of equivalent tonnage. Its builders, Quiggin & Jones, also built the Confederate blockade-runner *Banshee*, the first steel-hulled steamship to cross the Atlantic (in 1862).

SPECIFICATIONS
Type:	British full-rigged sailing ship
Displacement:	1291 tonnes (1271 tons)
Dimensions:	63.85m x 10.95m x 7.15m (209ft 5in x 36ft x 23ft 6in)
Rigging:	Three masts, square rig
Cargo:	Mixed cargo
Launched:	1863

TIMELINE

1851    1863   1865

THE LAST GREAT SAILING SHIPS

Ariel

Ariel was a handsome, well-proportioned ship, able to make up to 16 knots for long periods. The length of the lower masts was longer than usual and with the deep sail set, *Ariel* made good speed in light winds. It left London in January 1872 bound for Sydney, Australia, but disappeared without trace.

SPECIFICATIONS	
Type:	British full-rigged sailing ship
Displacement:	1067 tonnes (1050 tons) full load
Dimensions:	59.4m x 10.3m (195ft x 33ft 9in)
Rigging:	Three masts, full square rig
Cargo:	Tea, general cargo
Routes:	Britain–China, Britain–Australia
Launched:	1865

Lawhill

Steel-hulled and one of the last big sailing vessels, *Lawhill* later transported various bulk items – kerosene barrels, grain and nitrates – on long-haul voyages. Under Finnish ownership, it was seized by the British in South Africa in 1941. That effectively marked the end of *Lawhill*'s career, though it survived until 1958.

SPECIFICATIONS	
Type:	British full-rigged sailing ship
Displacement:	2861 tonnes (2816 tons)
Dimensions:	96.7m x 13.7m x 7.6m (317ft 4in x 45ft x 25ft 2in)
Rigging:	Four masts, barque rig
Cargo:	Varied
Routes:	Worldwide
Launched:	1892

Dunkerque

Built at Rouen, and named for its home port, a steel-hulled bulk carrier intended specifically for the Chilean nitrate (fertilizer) trade, it followed the stormy Cape Horn route between the Chilean desert and European ports for almost 30 years. The traffic was one-way: the return leg to Chile was made in ballast.

SPECIFICATIONS	
Type:	French full-rigged sailing cargo ship
Displacement:	3392 tonnes (3334 tons)
Dimensions:	99.85m x 13.85m x 7.75m (327ft 8in x 45ft 6in x 25ft 6in)
Rigging:	Four masts, barque rig
Cargo:	Nitrates
Routes:	Northern Europe to Chile
Launched:	1896

1892   1896

SHIP TYPES TO 1899

Cutty Sark

Cutty Sark made only eight voyages to China before the tea trade was lost to steamships. From 1877 to 1883, it worked as a tramp, then transferred to the Australian wool route until 1895, after which it served as a Portuguese vessel for 27 years. *Cutty Sark* survived a fire in 2007 and is still preserved in London.

Cutty Sark

The *Cutty Sark* was designed by Hercules Linton and built in 1869 at Dumbarton, Scotland, by Scott & Linton, for Captain John Willis. The *Cutty Sark* is the only surviving tea clipper and is now preseved, in a dry dock at Greenwich in London. It was badly damaged by a fire in 2007 but is expected to be fully restored by 2011.

SPECIFICATIONS	
Type:	British full rigged ship (tea clipper)
Displacement:	978 tonnes (963 tons)
Dimensions:	65m x 11m x 6.4m (212ft 5in x 36ft x 21ft)
Rigging:	Three masts, full square rig
Top speed:	21 knots
Cargo:	Tea, wool, later general cargo
Routes:	Britain–China, Britain–Australia
Launched:	1869

DECKHOUSE
Known by its style as a 'Liverpool house', the deckhouse provided accommodation for the captain, officers and a few passengers.

BOATS
Two lifeboats, a cutter and a captain's gig were carried. The gig was fitted with a stepped mast and sails.

FRAME
The hull was of wood, built on a strong iron frame, with cross-braces, angle-irons, and a watertight bulkhead at each end.

CUTTY SARK

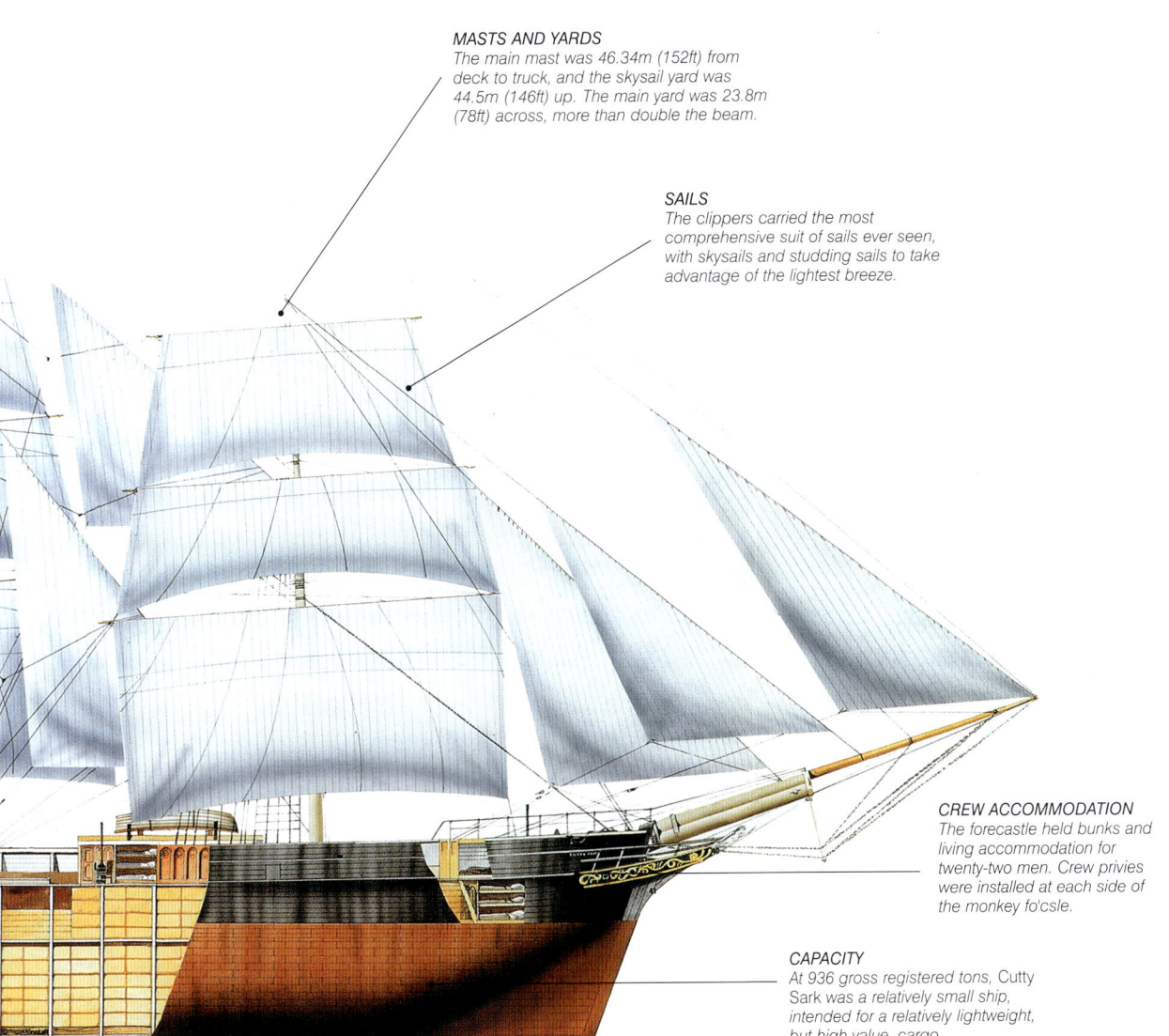

MASTS AND YARDS
The main mast was 46.34m (152ft) from deck to truck, and the skysail yard was 44.5m (146ft) up. The main yard was 23.8m (78ft) across, more than double the beam.

SAILS
The clippers carried the most comprehensive suit of sails ever seen, with skysails and studding sails to take advantage of the lightest breeze.

CREW ACCOMMODATION
The forecastle held bunks and living accommodation for twenty-two men. Crew privies were installed at each side of the monkey fo'csle.

CAPACITY
At 936 gross registered tons, Cutty Sark was a relatively small ship, intended for a relatively lightweight, but high value, cargo.

SHIP TYPES TO 1899

American Civil War Ironclads

Naval warfare was possible on the great rivers, especially the Mississippi, and in shore creeks as well as on the Atlantic coast. New-style gunboats were built or adapted for river warfare, capable of rapid movement, downstream at least. Between 1861 and 1865, many were used by the Confederate and Union navies.

Choctaw

Choctaw's independent wheels provided good steering and control. The forward casemate housed three 228mm (9in) guns plus one 100-pounder rifle. The second casemate contained two howitzers. In the stern were two 30-pounder rifles. Choctaw saw action around Vicksburg in the Civil War. It was sold in 1866.

SPECIFICATIONS
Type:	Union ironclad
Displacement:	1020 tonnes (1004 tons)
Dimensions:	79m x 13.7m x 2.4m (260ft x 45ft x 8ft)
Machinery:	Paddle wheels driven by compound engines
Top speed:	6 knots
Main armament:	Three 228mm (9in) guns
Launched:	1855

Atlanta

In November 1861, the blockade runner Fingal arrived at Savannah with a large cargo of war material. Unable to escape, she was bought by the Confederate Navy in January 1862, converted into an ironclad and renamed Atlanta. In June 1863, after a brief battle, Atlanta ran aground and surrendered to the Union.

SPECIFICATIONS
Type:	Confederate ironclad
Displacement:	1022 tonnes (1006 tons)
Dimensions:	62m x 12.5m x 4.7m (204ft x 41ft x 15ft 9in)
Machinery:	Single screw
Top speed:	7 knots
Main armament:	Two 178mm (7in) guns, two 165mm (6.4in) guns, one spar torpedo
Complement:	145
Launched:	c.1858

TIMELINE

1855　　1858　　1860

AMERICAN CIVIL WAR IRONCLADS

Baltic

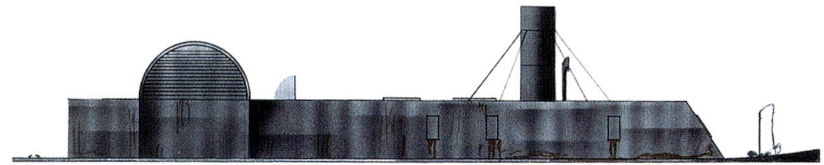

A wooden-hulled sidewheel river steamer, *Baltic* was built as a tow boat and adopted by the State of Alabama for conversion into an ironclad during the American Civil War. It laid mines in Mobile Bay, one of which sank the Union monitor *Tecumseh*. Its armour was later applied to CSS *Nashville*.

SPECIFICATIONS	
Type:	Confederate ironclad
Displacement:	652 tonnes (642 tons)
Dimensions:	56.5m x 11.5m x 2m (185ft 4in x 37ft 9in x 6ft 6in)
Machinery:	Inclined engines driving 8m (26ft 3in) diameter paddle wheels
Top speed:	6 knots
Main armament:	One 42-pdr gun, two 32-pdr gun
Complement:	86
Launched:	1860

Benton

Benton was originally a catamaran-hulled salvage vessel, *Submarine No. 7*. It was converted by planking-over the space between the hulls, adding a new bow and building a two-tier casemate over most of the hull. The armour was removed in 1865 and it was sold at auction for a fraction of the original cost.

SPECIFICATIONS	
Type:	Union ironclad
Displacement:	643 tonnes (633 tons)
Dimensions:	61.5m x 22m (202ft x 72ft 9in)
Machinery:	Inclined engines driving a single stern wheel
Top speed:	5.5 knots
Main armament:	Two 279mm (11in) guns
Complement:	176
Converted:	1861

Cairo

Cairo was a purpose-built gunboat designed by James Eades for the Mississippi squadron, with a low wooden hull surmounted by a large armoured casemate with inwards-sloping sides. Armour was mounted round the engines. *Cairo* was sunk by a mine on 2 December 1862, but raised, and it remains a museum ship.

SPECIFICATIONS	
Type:	US gunboat
Displacement:	902 tonnes (887 tons)
Dimensions:	53m x 16m x 2m (173ft 9in x 4ft 9in x 6ft 6in)
Machinery:	Single stern wheel driven by two non-condensing reciprocating engines
Top speed:	8 knots
Main armament:	Three 203mm (8in) guns, three 178mm (7in) guns
Armour:	68mm (2.5in) on casemate
Complement:	251
Launched:	December 1861

SHIP TYPES TO 1899

US Monitors

One of the side-effects of the Civil War was a powerful impetus to warship technology. These iron ships were generally known as monitors, a name coined by the inventor John Ericsson. The effectiveness of iron armour was shown in the inconclusive 4-hour battle between CSS *Merrimac* and USS *Monitor* on 9 May 1862.

Monitor

Ericsson's design for *Monitor* was quickly put in hand. It was a well-armoured vessel, and the low freeboard presented a poor target for gunfire. After the famous inconclusive battle with *Merrimac* at Hampton Roads in 1862, it served on the James River until it sank in a storm on 31 December 1862.

SPECIFICATIONS
Type:	US monitor
Displacement:	1000 tonnes (987 tons)
Dimensions:	52m x 12.6m x 2.5m (172ft x 41ft 6in x 8ft 4in)
Machinery:	Single screw, double trunk engines
Top speed:	6 knots
Main armament:	Two 280mm (11in) guns
Armour:	203mm (8in) on turrets, 127mm (5in) on hull
Complement:	49
Launched:	January 1862

Passaic

Passaic was lead ship in a class of 10 single-turret monitors that formed the backbone of the Union Navy during the Civil War. These were a development of the original *Monitor*, with increased displacement. Two were lost in the war. *Passaic* also served in the Spanish-American War of 1898. It was sold in 1899.

SPECIFICATIONS
Type:	US monitor
Displacement:	1905 tonnes (1875 tons)
Dimensions:	61m x 14m x 3.2m (200ft x 46ft x10ft 6in)
Machinery:	Single screw, trunk engines
Top speed:	7 knots
Main armament:	One 280mm (11in) gun, one 381mm (15in) gun
Armour:	280mm (11in) on turret, 127mm (5in) on hull
Complement:	75
Launched:	August 1862

TIMELINE

1862   1863

US MONITORS

Winnebago

For river operations, *Winnebago*'s was a good design. Four were built, with twin gun turrets: one of Ericsson type and and one produced by James Eades, who built *Winnebago*. Only the turrets, the funnel and a single ventilator showed above the turtleback deck. Side armour was solid plate. *Winnebago* was sold in 1874.

SPECIFICATIONS	
Type:	US monitor
Displacement:	1320 tonnes (1300 tons)
Dimensions:	70m x 17m x 1.8m (229ft x 56ft x 6ft)
Machinery:	Quadruple screws, horizontal compound engines
Top speed:	9 knots
Main armament:	Four 279mm (11in) guns
Armour:	203mm (8in) on turrets, 76mm (3in) on sides
Complement:	120
Launched:	1863

Monadnock

A double-turreted monitor, *Monadnock* was too late to serve in the American Civil War, and served on the Pacific coast. It was a good seaboat and steady gun platform even when the sea was washing across the deck, but the wooden planking quickly deteriorated and it was scrapped in 1875.

SPECIFICATIONS	
Type:	US monitor
Displacement:	3454 tonnes (3400 tons)
Dimensions:	78.8m x 16m x 3.9m (258ft 6in x 52ft 8in x 12ft 8in)
Machinery:	Twin screws, vibrating lever engines
Top speed:	9 knots
Main armament:	Four 380mm (15in) guns
Armour:	254mm (10in) on turrets, 127mm (5in) on hull, 51mm (2in) deck
Complement:	150
Launched:	1864

Monterey

This was the last twin-turret monitor built for the US Navy. In action, the low freeboard could be further reduced by flooding the ballast tanks. Completed in 1893 for service as a coast defence ship on the Pacific coastline, it served in the Philippines from 1898 to 1917, then at Pearl Harbor until it was sold in 1921.

SPECIFICATIONS	
Type:	US monitor
Displacement:	4000 tonnes (4084 tons)
Dimensions:	78m x 18m x 4.2m (256ft x 59ft x 14ft 10in)
Machinery:	Twin screws, vertical triple expansion engines
Main armament:	Two 254mm (10in) guns, two 305mm (12in) guns
Armour:	190–203mm (7.5–8in) on turrets, 127–330mm (5–13in) on belt
Launched:	April 1891

SHIP TYPES TO 1899

Civil War Ships

The American Civil War extended into the Atlantic Ocean, as the Union fleet sought to blockade Confederate ports, and the South built fast ships to outrun the patrols. There was sympathy for the Confederate states in the United Kingdom, and British shipbuilders profited from the struggle in building both civilian and naval ships.

Housatonic

Housatonic was laid down in 1861 as part of the Union Navy's expansion programme, and in 1862 briefly engaged the Confederate ironclad *Chicora* off Charleston. In 1864 it was attacked by the Confederate submarine *H. L. Hunley*, which succeeded in exploding a spar torpedo under her hull. Both vessels sank.

SPECIFICATIONS	
Type:	US cruiser
Displacement:	1964 tonnes (1934 tons)
Dimensions:	62m x 11.5m x 5m (205ft x 38ft x 16ft 6in)
Machinery:	Single screw, horizontal direct-acting engines
Rigging:	Three masts, barque rig
Top speed:	10 knots
Main armament:	One 280mm (11in), one 100-pdr, three 30-pdr guns
Complement:	214
Launch date:	1861

Iosco

The hazards of turning vessels in rivers called for speedy craft with a shallow draught able to travel in both directions. Consequently, *Iosco* and her class were given a rudder at each end, becoming known as 'double enders'. Machinery and boilers were positioned amidships, and both bow and stern were pointed.

SPECIFICATIONS	
Type:	US paddle gunboat
Displacement:	1191 tonnes (1173 tons)
Dimensions:	62m x 10.6m x 2.9m (205ft x 35ft x 9ft 6in)
Machinery:	Paddle wheels, direct acting inclined engines
Rigging:	Two masts, staysails
Top speed:	13 knots
Main armament:	Four 228mm (9in) guns, two 24-pdr guns, two 100-pdr guns
Complement:	145
Launched:	1863

TIMELINE

1861   1863  1864

CIVIL WAR SHIPS

Danmark

SPECIFICATIONS
Type:	Confederate steam warship
Displacement:	4823 tonnes (4747 tons)
Dimensions:	82.3m x 15.2m x 6m (270ft x 50ft x 19ft 6in)
Machinery:	Single screw, single expansion engine
Rigging:	Three masts, square rig
Armament:	Twelve 203mm (8in) guns, twelve 26-pdr guns
Armour:	115mm (4.5in) over teak frame
Complement:	530
Launched:	1864

Ordered and built in Glasgow for the Confederate navy, this ironclad would have been by far its most powerful vessel. Its broadside would have matched that of any Union ship. But by the time it was completed, the Civil War had ended, and the ship was sold to the Danish navy and named accordingly.

Florida

SPECIFICATIONS
Type:	US cruiser
Displacement:	4282 tonnes (4215 tons)
Dimensions:	108m x 13.8m x 6m (335ft x 45ft 2in x 19ft 10in)
Machinery:	Single screw, horizontal back-acting engines
Rigging:	3 masts, barque rig
Top speed:	17.7 knots
Armament:	Ten 228mm (9in) guns, three 60-pdr guns
Complement:	330
Launched:	1864

Designed by Benjamin Delano, considered to be a very fast ship, the wooden-hulled *Florida* was built as *Wampanoag*, to be a commerce raider in the event of war with Britain. The huge engines took up much of the hull space and it was not considered practicable as a regular warship. It was sold in 1885.

Stonewall

SPECIFICATIONS
Type:	Confederate armoured ram ship
Displacement:	1585 tonnes (1560 tons)
Dimensions:	60m x 32m x 16m (194ft x 31ft 6in x 15ft 8in)
Machinery:	Twin screws, horizontal direct-acting engines
Main armament:	One 228mm (9in) gun, two 70-pdr guns
Rigging:	Two masts, square rig
Armour:	89–115mm (3.5–4.5in) belt, 140mm (5.5in) over bow gun
Complement:	135
Launched:	June 1864

Stonewall was the last ironclad to serve in the Confederate Navy. Its main gun was housed in the bows above the ram, and could fire ahead or through a port on either side. In 1865, it was sold to Japan and re-named *Adzuma*. In 1888, it was removed from the effective list, and used as an accommodation ship.

SHIP TYPES TO 1899

Alabama

In a short career, *Alabama* was the most successful of Confederate raiders, destroying or capturing 66 ships, at an estimated value of over $6 million, between August 1862 and April 1864. Among them was the Union gunboat *Hatteras.* On 19 June 1864, *Alabama* was sunk off Cherbourg, France, by the US sloop *Kearsarge.*

Alabama

Alabama was built in secrecy by John Laird and Sons in North West England. Initially known as hull number 290, the ship was launched without fanfare on 29 July 1862 as *Enrica*. *Alabama* was probably the most famous vessel of the American Civil War because her commerce-raiding activities almost destroyed the Union's mercantile marine.

SPECIFICATIONS

Type:	Confederate armed sloop
Displacement:	1066.8 tonnes (1050 tons)
Dimensions:	67m x 9.6m x 4.2m (220ft x 31ft 8in x 14ft)
Machinery:	Single screw, steam engine
Rigging:	Three masts, barque rig
Top speed:	13 knots
Main armament:	One 162mm (6.4in) gun, one 68-pdr gun, six 32-pdr guns
Complement:	145
Launched:	1862

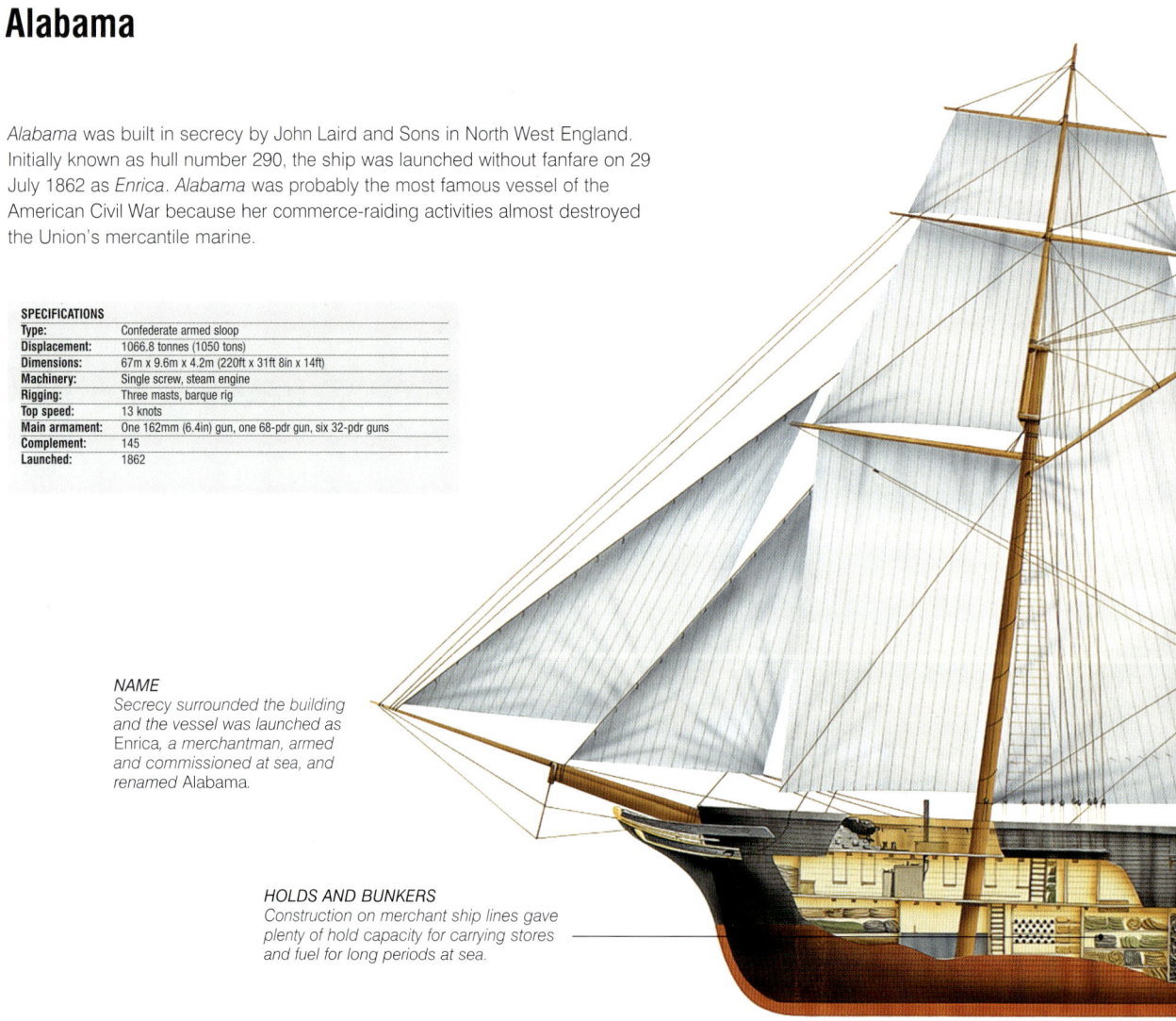

NAME
Secrecy surrounded the building and the vessel was launched as Enrica, *a merchantman, armed and commissioned at sea, and renamed* Alabama.

HOLDS AND BUNKERS
Construction on merchant ship lines gave plenty of hold capacity for carrying stores and fuel for long periods at sea.

ALABAMA

THE WRECK
Alabama's remains were found by French naval divers in 195ft (59m) of water, 6 miles (10km) off Cherbourg in November 1984.

MACHINERY
Coal-fired direct-acting 300ihp (252kW) steam engine. The engine added 3.25 knots to the ten achievable under sail.

IMPACT
Alabama's actions caused insurance rates for US-flag shipping to rise by 900%, and many ships were transferred to foreign ownership.

HULL
Alabama was wooden-hulled and unarmoured. Any contest with an iron or armoured ship was bound to be an unequal one.

SCREW PROPELLER
As often with ships where the engine was considered auxiliary to the sails, the screw was retractable, to reduce drag.

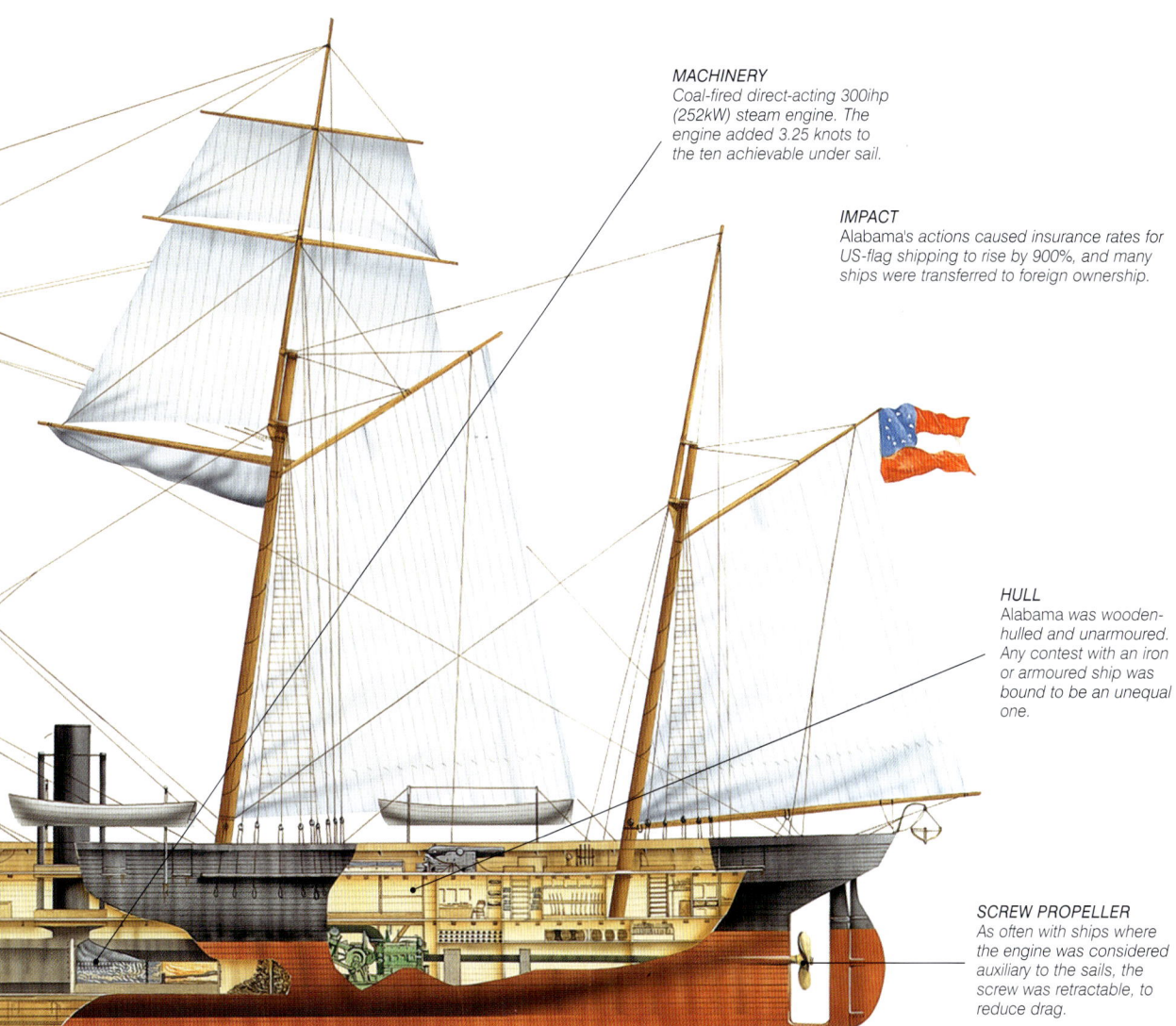

SHIP TYPES TO 1899

Paddle-driven Warships

Naval designers were never enthusiastic about paddle-driven ships, because of the vulnerability of the paddle wheels and the difficulty of protecting them. They much preferred the underwater screw propeller, and were relieved once its superiority was demonstrated. But numerous paddle warships were built, up to the 1860s.

Alecto

A wooden paddle-wheel frigate, *Alecto* was picked for trials in 1848 against the screw-driven gunboat *Rattler* to establish whether propeller propulsion was superior to that of paddles. The ships were of similar power and dimensions, but with *Alecto* making full steam ahead, *Rattler* pulled it backwards at 2.8 knots.

SPECIFICATIONS
Type:	British gunboat
Displacement:	816 tonnes (803 tons) full load
Machinery:	200hp engine driving two paddles
Launched:	1839

Gladiator

By the mid-1850s, the Royal Navy had 77 paddle-wheel warships, 41 on foreign stations. In 1860, *Gladiator* was part of a combined British and US squadron sent to capture William Walker, who had declared himself President of Nicaragua. 'Corvette' designated a smaller version of the frigate.

SPECIFICATIONS
Type:	British corvette
Displacement:	1229 tonnes (1210 tons)
Dimensions:	67m x 8.5m x 3m (220ft x 28ft x 10ft)
Machinery:	Paddle wheels, oscillating engines
Rigging:	Three masts, barque rig
Top speed:	9.5 knots
Main armament:	Six 24-pdr guns
Launched:	1844

TIMELINE

 1839    1844   1850

Paddle-Driven Warships

Hatteras

Formerly a New York harbour ferry craft, *Hatteras* was purchased by the US Navy in 1861. On blockade duty off Galveston, it pursued the Confederate raider *Alabama*. Heavily outgunned, *Hatteras* was sunk after a 13-minute battle – the only Union warship sunk by a Confederate cruiser during the Civil War.

SPECIFICATIONS
Type:	American gunboat
Displacement:	1144 tonnes (1126 tons)
Dimensions:	64m x 10.3m x 5.4m (210ft x 34ft x 18ft)
Machinery:	Sidewheels, side lever engine
Top speed:	8 knots
Main armament:	One 20-pdr gun, four 32-pdr guns
Complement:	120
Launched:	c.1850

Harriet Lane

A US Revenue cutter, *Harriet Lane* fired the first shot of the Civil War on 11 April 1861. Captured at Galveston, it served in the Texas Marine Department, and was converted as *Lavinia* into a blockade runner in 1864. In 1865, it sank at Havana but was raised. Re-named *Elliot Richie,* it was wrecked in 1884 off Brazil.

SPECIFICATIONS
Type:	American gunboat
Displacement:	610 tonnes (600 tons)
Machinery:	Paddle wheels
Rigging:	Two masts, barquentine rig
Top speed:	9 knots
Main armament:	Three 228mm (9in) guns
Launched:	November 1857

Fuad

Fuad and its three sisters were among the last paddle-driven warships to be built. Iron-hulled vessels with a light rig and two raked funnels, they served well as lightly-armed despatch boats and also performed escort duties. Their speed was not great, but they had a good cruising range. *Fuad* was discarded in 1898.

SPECIFICATIONS
Type:	Turkish despatch vessel
Displacement:	1075 tonnes (1058 tons)
Dimensions:	76.2m x 9.1m x 3.7m (250ft x 30ft x 12ft)
Machinery:	Paddle wheels
Rigging:	Two masts, light rig
Top speed:	12.5 knots
Main armament:	One 119mm (4.7in) gun plus three smaller guns
Launched:	1864

1857

1864

SHIP TYPES TO 1899

Gloire

Brain-child of the great ship designer Dupuy de Lôme, this armoured ironclad was the world's first 'modern' battleship. Plans proposed 68-pounder, smoothbore guns, but rifled versions of the same weapons were fitted, and it was later rearmed with modern guns. *Gloire* was deleted from the effective list in 1879.

Gloire

Gloire was constructed with a wooden hull and armour plating to the upper deck because French manufacturers were unable to provide sufficient plating and armour in time to construct an iron hull. The battleship's design was based on the steam frigate *Napoleon* in that it had a full-length battery along the hull.

SPECIFICATIONS	
Type:	French battleship
Displacement:	5720 tonnes (5630 tons)
Dimensions:	77.8m x 17m x 8.4m (255ft 6in x 55ft 9in x 27ft 10in)
Machinery:	Single screw, horizontal return engines
Top speed:	13 knots
Main armament:	Thirty-six 162.5mm (6.4in) guns
Armour:	Belt 119–110mm (4.7–4in)
Top speed:	12.5 knots
Complement:	570
Launched:	November 1859
Date of profile:	1860

ARMAMENT
A criticism of Gloire was that the guns were placed too close together, compared with the British iron warship Warrior *(1861).*

ARMOUR
The wooden hull was reinforced by 120mm (4.7in) iron plates, heavily secured with iron fastenings. The main deck was also of iron.

MACHINERY
Eight fire-tube boilers, two-cylinder horizontal return connecting rod engine developing 2100ihp (1864kW) formed the main drive, with sails as auxiliary.

54

Warrior

Warrior was the world's first iron-hulled capital ship. Designed by Isaac Watts, it was laid down in May 1859. High speed was achieved by the V-formation of the forward part of the hull. Restored during the 1980s, Warrior is preserved at Portsmouth Dockyard, England.

SPECIFICATIONS	
Type:	British battleship
Displacement:	9357 tonnes (9137 tons)
Dimensions:	115.8m x 17.8m x 8m (420ft x 58ft 4in x 26ft)
Machinery:	Single screw, single expansion trunk engine
Top speed:	14 knots
Main armament:	Twenty-six 68-pdr, four 70-pdr, ten 110-pdr guns
Armour:	114mm (4.5in) on belt and battery, 457mm wood (18in) backing
Launched:	December 1860

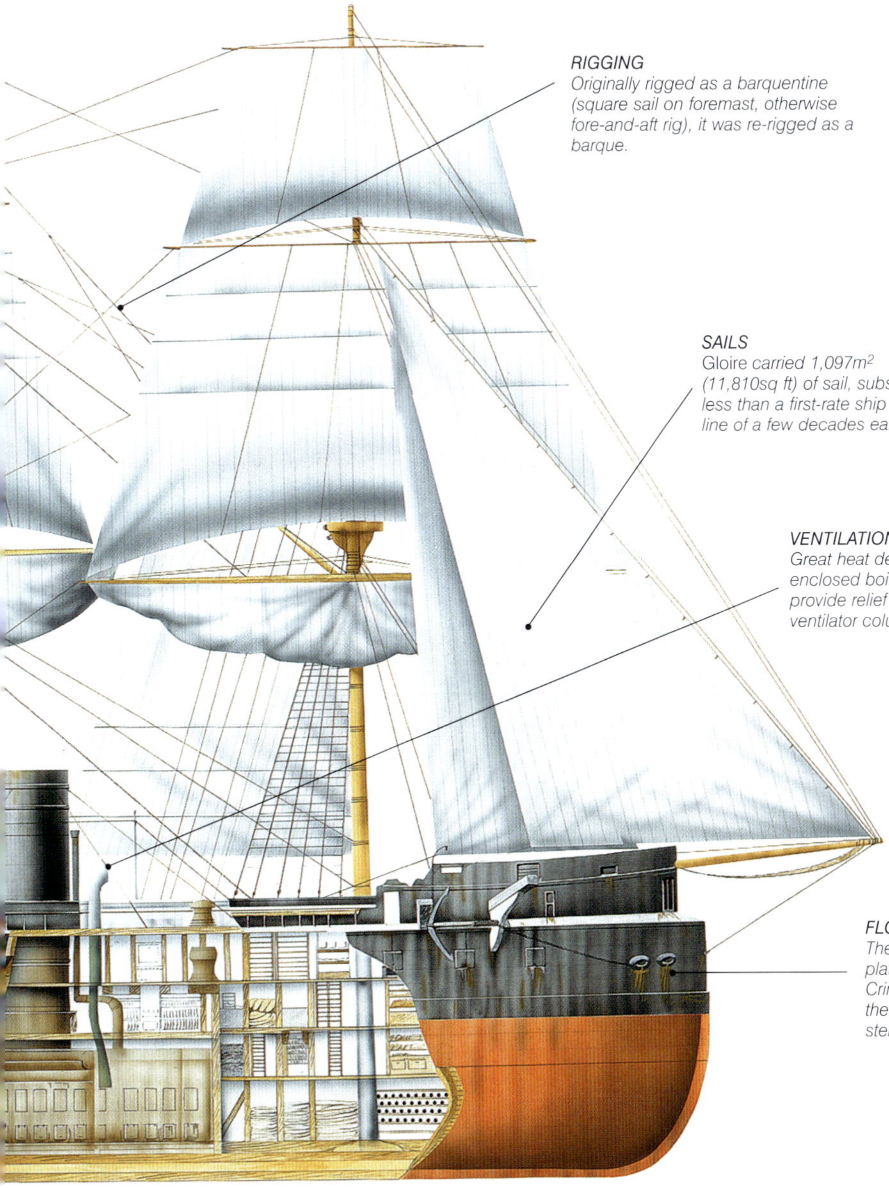

RIGGING
Originally rigged as a barquentine (square sail on foremast, otherwise fore-and-aft rig), it was re-rigged as a barque.

SAILS
Gloire carried 1,097m² (11,810sq ft) of sail, substantially less than a first-rate ship of the line of a few decades earlier.

VENTILATION
Great heat developed in the enclosed boiler rooms, and to provide relief for the stokers, cowled ventilator columns were fitted.

FLOATING BATTERY
The design of floating gun platforms used in the Crimean War influenced the blunt bow, convex stem and low freeboard.

SHIP TYPES TO 1899

Nineteenth-Century Screw-Propelled Warships: Part 1

In the first propeller-driven warships, the machinery was regarded as secondary, helpful mostly in calms and the confined spaces of anchorages. Sail power was still supreme. The screw was normally hinged or detachable and could be hoisted above the waterline to reduce drag. Getting under steam power was cumbersome.

Salamander

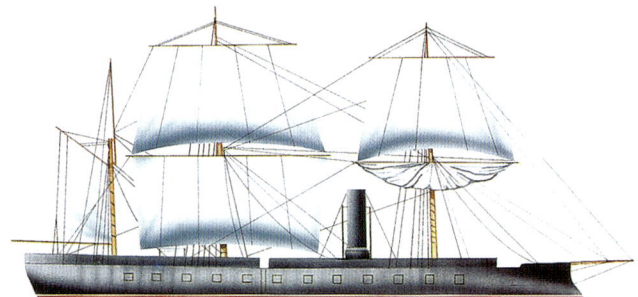

SPECIFICATIONS	
Type:	Austrian battleship
Displacement:	3075 tonnes (3027 tons)
Dimensions:	62.8m x 13.9m x 6.3m (206ft x 45ft 7in x 20ft 8in)
Machinery:	Single screw, horizontal low pressure engine
Rigging:	Three masts, barque rig
Top speed:	11 knots
Main armament:	Fourteen 150mm (5.9in) guns, fourteen 68-pdr guns
Complement:	346
Launched:	August 1861

Austria's first ironclad, *Salamander* had a full-length waterline protective belt, extended upwards to cover the battery each side of the foremast. In a refit in 1867–68, its sail area was increased to help compensate for a slow engine speed. Decommissioned in 1883, it remained in use as a mine store until 1896.

Agincourt

SPECIFICATIONS	
Type:	British battleship
Displacement:	10,812 tonnes (10,642 tons) (full load)
Dimensions:	124m x 18.2m x 8.5m (406ft 10in x 58ft 9in x 27ft 10in)
Rigging:	Five masts, square rig
Top speed:	15 knots
Main armament:	Four 229mm (9in) guns, twenty-four 178mm (7in) muzzle-loader rifled guns
Launched:	1862

With two sister-ships, this was the longest single-screw warship ever built. Though modern in many respects, it was among the last Royal Navy ships to be equipped with muzzle-loading guns. These were later replaced on *Agincourt* by breech-loading guns. The hull was not broken up until 1960.

TIMELINE

1861   1862  1865

Affondatore

SPECIFICATIONS	
Type:	Italian turret battleship
Displacement:	4393 tonnes (4324 tons)
Dimensions:	93.9m x 12m x 6.3m (308ft x 39ft 4in x 20ft 8in)
Machinery:	Single screw, single expansion engine, 8 boilers
Top speed:	12 knots
Main armament:	Two 229mm (9in) muzzle-loading rifled (MLR) guns
Rigging:	Two masts, staysails
Armour:	127mm (5in) belt and turrets
Complement:	309
Launched:	November 1865

Iron-hulled, originally schooner-rigged, *Affondatore* had a wrought-iron ram. It had two turrets, designed by the British Navy's Captain Cowper Coles. It was the flagship of Admiral Persano's fleet against the Austrians at the Battle of Lissa in July 1866. Rebuilt in 1885, it served with the Italian Navy for a further 20 years.

Armide

SPECIFICATIONS	
Type:	French battleship
Displacement:	3569 tonnes (3513 tons)
Dimensions:	70m x 14m x 7m (229ft 8in x 46ft x 23ft)
Machinery:	Single screw, horizontal compound engine
Rigging:	Three masts, barque rig
Top speed:	11.9 knots
Main armament:	Six 193mm (7.6in) guns
Armour:	152mm (6in) belt, 120mm (4.7in) on battery
Launched:	November 1867

Wooden-hulled with armour protection, this was one of six 'Alma' class vessels designed for long-range service, helping to maintain colonial rule. They were compact ships, with guns mounted in a central armoured battery. Fully rigged, it could make extensive use of the sails when cruising, to economize on coal.

Assari Tewfik

SPECIFICATIONS	
Type:	Turkish battleship
Displacement:	4762 tonnes (4687 tons)
Dimensions:	83m x 16m x 6.5m (272ft 4in x 52ft 6in x 21ft 4in)
Machinery:	Single screw, horizontal compound engine
Rigging:	Three masts, barque rig
Top speed:	13 knots
Main armament:	Eight 228mm (9in) guns
Armour:	152mm (6in) belt, 120mm (4.7in) on battery
Launched:	1868

The Ottoman Navy operated in the Mediterranean and Black Seas, and kept its ships for longer than West European navies. *Assari Tewfik*'s guns, mounted in battery formation amidships, were originally muzzle-loading. It served until 1913, when it struck a rock during the Balkan wars, and had to be abandoned.

1867  1868

SHIP TYPES TO 1899

Victoria

Few three-decker steam-powered warships were built. *Victoria,* built in response to the French three-decker *La Bretagne*, was unique in the placement of its machinery, with two funnels offset to port and starboard respectively. Within a decade, the design was obsolete and it was decommissioned, though not broken up until 1893.

Victoria

Victoria was the largest wooden battleship ever to enter service and was the world's largest warship until the completion of HMS *Warrior*, Britain's first ironclad battleship, in 1861. *Victoria* was also the first British battleship with two funnels.

SPECIFICATIONS

Type:	British battleship
Displacement:	7070 tonnes (6959 tons)
Dimensions:	79.2m x 18.3m x 7.8m (260ft x 60ft x 25ft 10in)
Machinery:	Single screw, horizontal compound engine
Rigging:	Three masts, square rig
Main armament:	Sixty-two 203mm (8in) guns, fifty-eight 32-pdr guns
Complement:	1000
Launched:	November 1859

HULL
Victoria was the largest wooden warship, and the last Royal Navy capital ship to be wooden-hulled, though diagonal iron braces were fitted.

MACHINERY
Eight boilers, Maudslay reciprocating steam engine developing 4403ihp (3283.3kW). Around 60 stokers and trimmers were needed.

VICTORIA

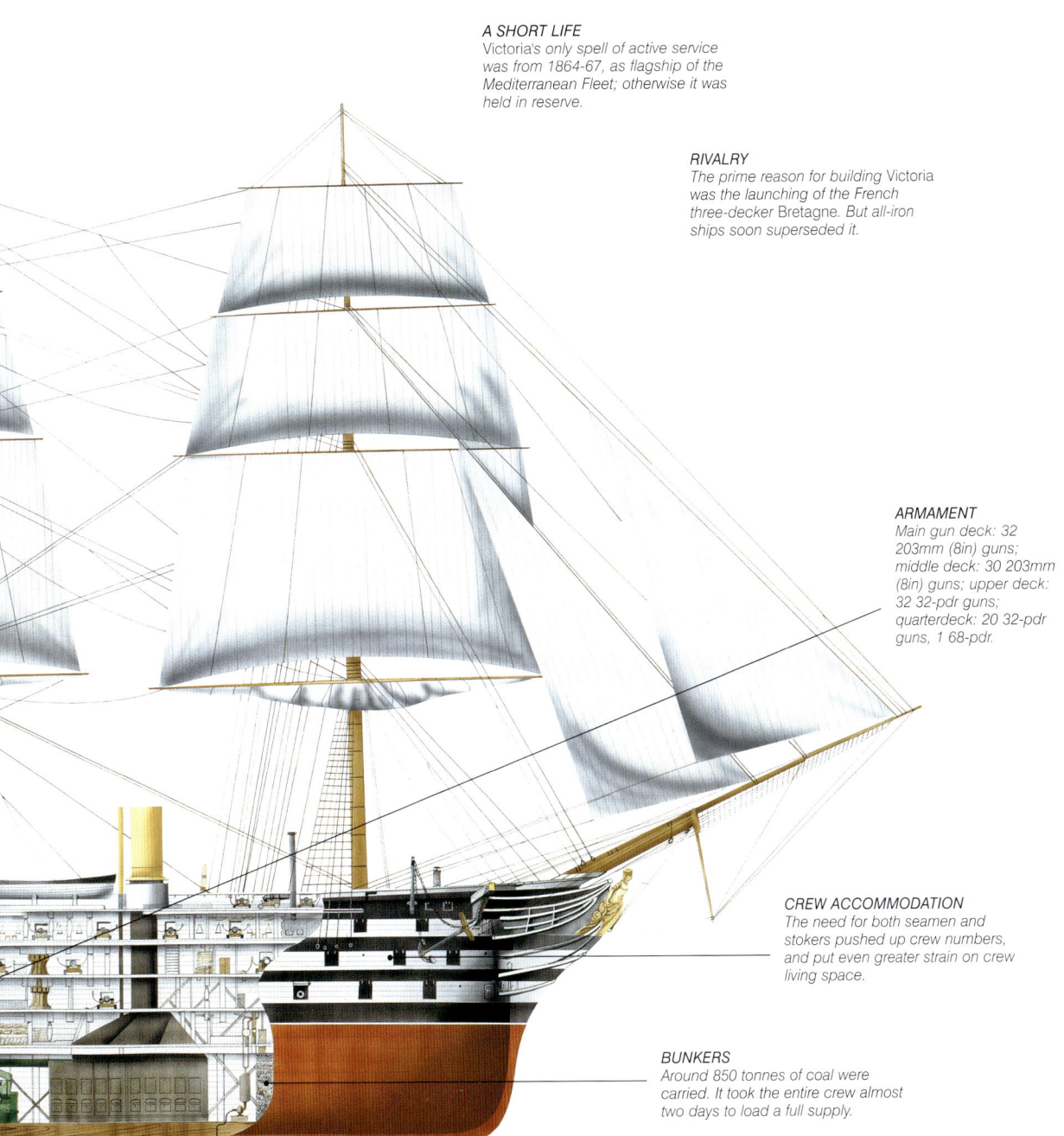

A SHORT LIFE
Victoria's only spell of active service was from 1864-67, as flagship of the Mediterranean Fleet; otherwise it was held in reserve.

RIVALRY
The prime reason for building Victoria was the launching of the French three-decker Bretagne. But all-iron ships soon superseded it.

ARMAMENT
Main gun deck: 32 203mm (8in) guns; middle deck: 30 203mm (8in) guns; upper deck: 32 32-pdr guns; quarterdeck: 20 32-pdr guns, 1 68-pdr.

CREW ACCOMMODATION
The need for both seamen and stokers pushed up crew numbers, and put even greater strain on crew living space.

BUNKERS
Around 850 tonnes of coal were carried. It took the entire crew almost two days to load a full supply.

Nineteenth-Century Screw-Propelled Warships: Part 2

By the 1870s, more powerful compound steam engines had become the chief means of propulsion, and the sails became the auxiliary, useful when there was a tail wind. To the end of the century, warships would make progressively less use of sails.

Vanguard

This central battery ship was built for overseas service, to encounter ironclads of other navies. Originally ship-rigged, it was barque-rigged from 1871, carrying 2202 square metres (23,700 sq ft) of canvas. In 1875, it sank after being accidentally rammed by *Iron Duke* in thick fog.

SPECIFICATIONS	
Type:	British battleship
Displacement:	6106 tonnes (6010 tons)
Dimensions:	85.3m x 16.4m x 6.8m (280ft x 54ft x 22ft 7in)
Machinery:	Twin screws, horizontal return connecting rod engines
Rigging:	Three masts, barque rig
Main armament:	Ten 228mm (9in) guns, four 152mm (6in) guns
Armour:	152–203mm (6–8in) belt, 203–254mm (8–10in) teak backing, 152mm (6in) on battery
Launched:	1870

Almirante Cochrane

Typically of the time, the guns were concentrated in a central battery, though its overhang permitted forward and rear fire as well as broadside. With its sister ship *Blanco Encalada*, it captured the Peruvian battleship *Huascar* in 1879. In 1891, it was sunk at anchor by two torpedo boats in the course of a revolution.

SPECIFICATIONS	
Type:	Chilean battleship
Displacement:	3631 tonnes (3574 tons)
Dimensions:	64m x 13.9m x 6.7m (210 x 45ft 7in x 22ft)
Machinery:	Twin screw horizontal compound engine
Rigging:	Three masts, barquentine rig
Top speed:	12.7 knots
Main armament:	Six 228mm (9in) guns
Armour:	115-152-229mm (4.5–6–9in) belt, 152–203mm (6–8in) on battery
Complement:	300
Launched:	1874

TIMELINE

 1870    1874    1879

Aragon

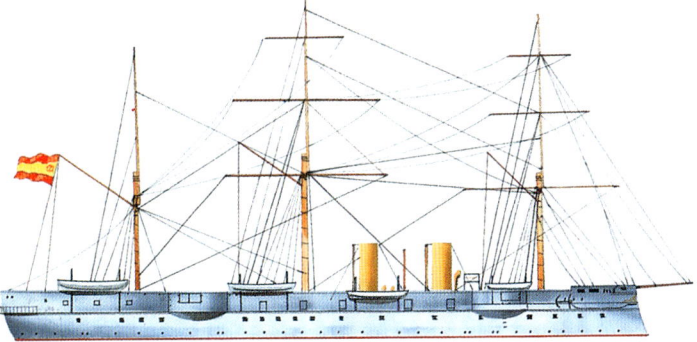

Aragon's wooden hull was intended to be protected by iron cladding, but this was never done. Sponson mounts at each end of the battery let it fire forwards and backwards. There were three cruisers in the class; one, *Castilla*, was sunk by US warships at Manila on 1 May 1898 during the Spanish–American War.

SPECIFICATIONS

Type:	Spanish cruiser
Displacement:	3342 tonnes (3289 tons)
Dimensions:	71.9m x 13.4m x 7.2m (236 x 44ft x 23ft 7in)
Machinery:	Single screw horizontal compound engine
Rigging:	Three masts, barquentine rig
Top speed:	14 knots
Main armament:	Six 163mm (6.4in) guns
Launched:	1879

Chen Yuan

Chen Yuan and her sister-ship *Ting Yuan* were Imperial China's only battleships, built to a turret design, with barbettes for the heavy guns, and an armoured central citadel protecting the engines and magazines. *Chen Yuan* took part in the 1894 Battle of the Yalu. Captured by the Japanese in 1895, it was scrapped in 1914.

SPECIFICATIONS

Type:	Chinese battleship
Displacement:	7792 tonnes (7670 tons)
Dimensions:	94m x 18m x 6m (307ft 9in x 59ft x 20ft)
Machinery:	Twin screw horizontal compound engines
Top speed:	15.7 knots
Main armament:	Four 304mm (12in) guns, two 152mm (6in) guns
Armour:	356mm (14in) belt, 356–305mm (14–12in) on barbettes
Complement:	350
Launched:	November 1882

Unebi

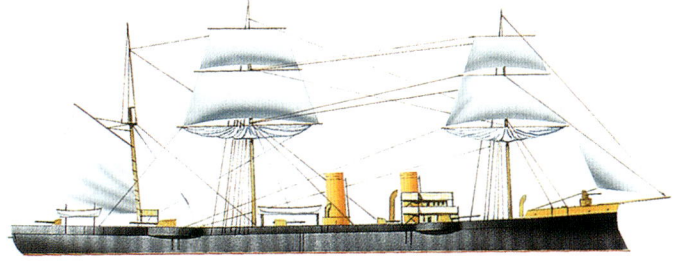

Built in France to French design, *Unebi* carried unusually heavy armament for a vessel of its displacement. The 238mm (9.4in) guns were placed on sponsons built out from the hull and the lighter guns were mounted on deck. *Unebi* never reached Japan, foundering in a typhoon on its outward voyage in October 1887.

SPECIFICATIONS

Type:	Japanese cruiser
Displacement:	36722 tonnes (3615 tons)
Dimensions:	98m x 13m x 5.7m (321ft 6in x 43ft x 18ft 9in)
Machinery:	Twin screw horizontal compound triple expansion engines
Rigging:	Three masts, barque rig
Main armament:	Four 238mm (9.4in) guns, seven 150mm (5.9in) guns
Armour:	67mm (2.5in) deck
Complement:	280
Launched:	April 1886

SHIP TYPES TO 1899

Coastal Defence Craft

The coastal defence craft was a product of the long-range heavy gun era. Relatively small but mounting one or two large guns, and able to operate in shallow waters, it was intended to intercept invasion attempts and also, while presenting a small target itself, to engage larger warships sent on coastal bombardment sorties.

Gorm

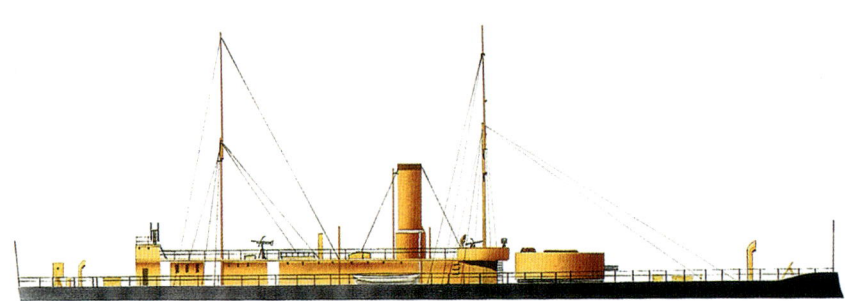

Powerfully armed, *Gorm* was designed for shallow-draught coast defence duty. A single turret forward housed 254mm (10in) Armstrong rifled muzzle-loaders, only 1.6m (5ft 5in) above water level. The original guns in the turret were replaced with 150mm (5.9in) weapons. *Gorm* was scrapped in 1912.

SPECIFICATIONS	
Type:	Danish coast defence ship
Displacement:	2381 tonnes (2344 tons)
Dimensions:	68.5m x 13.7m x 4.9m (225ft x 45ft x 16ft 4in)
Machinery:	Single screw, single expansion engines
Main armament:	Two 254mm (10in) guns
Armour:	178mm (7in) on hull, 203mm (8in) on turret
Launched:	1870

Gorgon

Several ships of this type were ordered in 1870–71, but as the threat of war with France receded, they became redundant. Poor sea-keeping qualities further limited their value. *Gorgon*, completed in 1874, spent most of its time in harbour at Devonport, used as a fleet tender, and was broken up in 1903.

SPECIFICATIONS	
Type:	British coast defence ship
Displacement:	3535 tonnes (3480 tons)
Dimensions:	70m x 15m x 4.3m (231ft x 49ft x14ft 3in)
Machinery:	Twin screw, horizontal direct acting engines
Main armament:	Four 254mm (10in) guns
Armour:	152–203mm (6–8in) on hull, 203–228mm (8–9in) on breastwork, 228–254mm (9–10in) on turrets
Launched:	1870

TIMELINE 1870   1871

COASTAL DEFENCE CRAFT

Haai

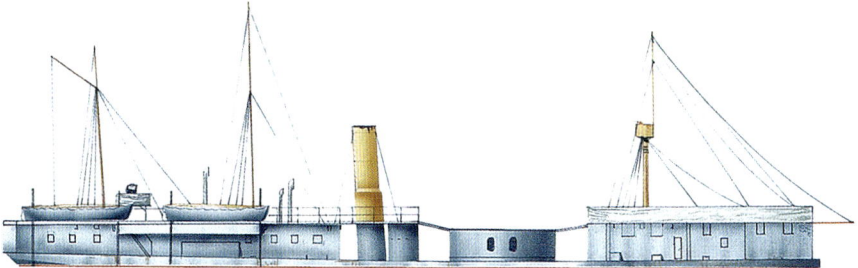

A monitor with its two big guns mounted in a single turret, *Haai* also had a ram bow. With four sister vessels, plus a dissimilar fifth, it formed the first large class of coast-defence ships built for the Dutch Navy. Later it was rearmed with one 279mm (11in) gun and additional lighter guns.

SPECIFICATIONS
Type:	Dutch coast defence ship
Displacement:	1580 tonnes (1555 tons)
Dimensions:	59.6m x 13.4m x 2.9m (195ft 5in x 44ft x 9ft 9in)
Machinery:	Twin screws, compound engines
Top speed:	8 knots
Main armament:	Two 228mm (9in) guns
Launched:	1871

Novgorod

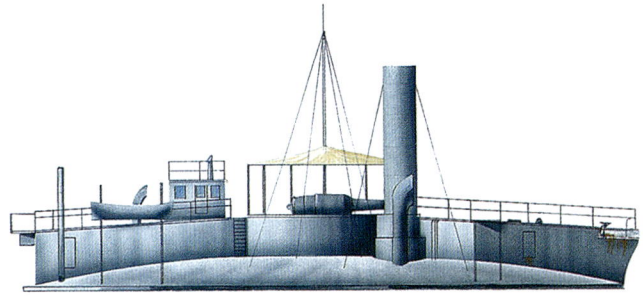

Designed by Admiral Popov, *Novgorod* was circular in form, with a longitudinal structure supporting a barbette that housed the two heavy guns. Two 'Popoffkas' of this type were built, in sections, the parts then being assembled. Two of the six propellers were later removed, and the vessel was scrapped around 1900.

SPECIFICATIONS
Type:	Russian coast defence ship
Displacement:	2500 tonnes (2491 tons)
Dimensions:	36.9m x 36.9m x 4.1m (121ft x 121ft x 13ft 6in)
Machinery:	Six screws, horizontal compound engines
Top speed:	6 knots
Main armament:	Two 280mm (11in) guns, two 86mm (3.4in) guns
Launched:	1876

Harald Haarfagre

Harald Haarfagre was a *panserskipet*, or armoured ship – Norway's first major warship. For patrolling inshore waters, it was compact and slow-moving. It was decommissioned in the 1930s, but taken over by German forces during World War II and converted into an anti-aircraft battery. It was scrapped in 1948.

SPECIFICATIONS
Type:	Norwegian coast defence ship
Displacement:	3919 tonnes (3858 tons)
Dimensions:	92.6m x 14.7m x 5.3m (304ft 6in x 48ft 6in x 17ft 8in)
Machinery:	Twin screws, triple expansion engines
Main armament:	Two 208mm (8.2in) guns, six 120mm (4.7in) guns
Armour:	102–178mm (4–7in) belt, 127–203mm (5–8in) on main turrets
Launched:	January 1897

1876  1897

SHIP TYPES TO 1899

Cruisers of the 1880s and 1890s: Part 1

In the late nineteenth century, a cruiser was often just a ship undertaking longer-range missions without escort. Some ships designated cruisers were smaller than the conventional cruiser of later years – ship types tend to get bigger with time.

Chao Yung

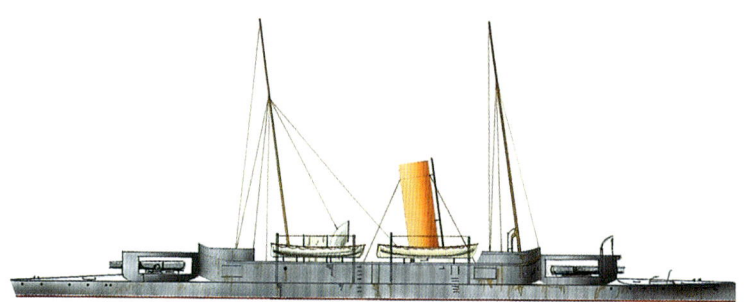

China's navy was organized in separate fleets with little central co-ordination. *Chao Yung* was ordered for the Peiyang fleet. Very fast for its day, it carried heavy guns on a small displacement. In 1894, in action against the Japanese at the Battle of the Yalu, it was set on fire and, listing badly, was later sunk.

SPECIFICATIONS	
Type:	Chinese cruiser
Displacement:	1566 tonnes (1542 tons)
Dimensions:	64m x 10m x 5m (210ft x 32ft x 15ft)
Machinery:	Twin screw, horizontal compound reciprocating engines
Main armament:	Two 254mm (10in) guns
Armour:	68mm (2.7in) deck, 25.5mm (1in) turrets
Complement:	177
Launched:	November 1880

Boston

The 1880s saw an increase in the size of the US Navy. *Boston* and its sister-ship *Atlanta* were powerful cruisers, with the 203mm (8in) guns mounted on barbettes fore and aft of the superstructure. The builders went bankrupt during construction and the ships were completed by the New York Naval Dockyard.

SPECIFICATIONS	
Type:	US cruiser
Displacement:	3240 tonnes (3189 tons)
Dimensions:	86.2m x 12.8m x 5.2m (283ft x 42ft x 17ft)
Machinery:	Single screw, horizontal compound engine
Rigging:	Two masts, square rig
Main armament:	Two 203mm (8in) guns, six 152mm (6in) guns
Armour:	50mm (2in) on barbettes, 37mm (1.5in) on deck
Complement:	317
Launched:	1884

TIMELINE

1880   1884

Calliope

Calliope had a steel hull, with a protective deck sloping downwards to its outer edges. Side-mounted sponsons carried the 152mm (6in) guns. By this time, some warships had their superstructure above the deck, but Calliope had none. Six locomotive-type boilers fed the two high- and two low-pressure cylinders.

SPECIFICATIONS	
Type:	British cruiser
Displacement:	2814 tonnes (2770 tons)
Dimensions:	71.6m x 13.6m x 6m (235ft x 44ft 6in x 19ft 11in)
Machinery:	Single screw, horizontal compound engines
Rigging:	Three masts, square rig
Top speed:	13.75 knots
Main armament:	Four 152mm (6in) guns, twelve 127mm (5in) guns
Armour:	37mm (1.5in) on deck
Complement:	317
Launched:	1884

Etna

Etna set the pattern for cruisers worldwide, combining good speed and heavy armament with protection and reasonable seakeeping qualities. In 1907, it was converted into a training ship and served until 1914, when it became a harbour defence ship, and later a depot ship at Taranto. It was discarded in 1921.

SPECIFICATIONS	
Type:	Italian cruiser
Displacement:	3881 tonnes (3820 tons)
Dimensions:	91.4m x 13.2m x 6.2m (300ft x 43ft 4in x 20ft 4in)
Machinery:	Twin screw double expansion engines
Top speed:	17.8 knots
Main armament:	Two 254mm (10in) guns, six 152mm (6in) guns
Launched:	September 1885

Forth

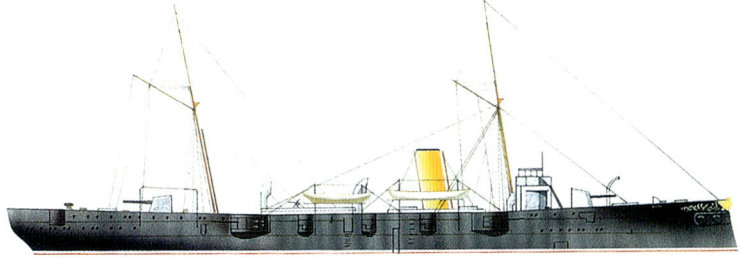

Forth and its sister-ships marked a complete break from previous Second Class cruisers and showed the way forward. Two pole masts with light rigging were fitted, but for the first time all sail power was done away with. Another first was the fitting of a full-length protective deck. Forth was sold in 1921.

SPECIFICATIONS	
Type:	British cruiser
Displacement:	4115 tonnes (4050 tons)
Dimensions:	96m x 14m x 5.9m (315ft x 46ft x 19ft 6in)
Machinery:	Twin screw, horizontal direct-acting compound engines
Main armament:	Two 203mm (8in) guns, ten 152mm (6in) guns
Armour:	76–50mm (3–2in) deck
Complement:	300
Launched:	October 1886

Cruisers of the 1880s and 1890s: Part 2

The cruiser, in its different forms, performed a variety of tasks. The availability of swift, effective warships for support and policing was a necessity for countries with colonial ambitions. The cruiser cost much less to build and run than a battleship.

Charleston

In 1887, plans for a new American cruiser type were purchased in Britain, based on designs already built for Japan and Chile. A 203mm (8in) gun was located at each end of the superstructure, and 152mm (6in) guns carried amidships. The first US cruiser without sail power, *Charleston* was wrecked in November 1899.

SPECIFICATIONS

Type:	US cruiser
Displacement:	4267 tonnes (4200 tons)
Dimensions:	97.4m x 14m x 6m (319ft 6in x 46ft x 18ft 4in)
Machinery:	Twin screw, horizontal compound engines
Top speed:	18.9 knots
Main armament:	Two 203mm (8in) guns, six 152mm (6in) guns
Complement:	300
Launched:	July 1888

Forbin

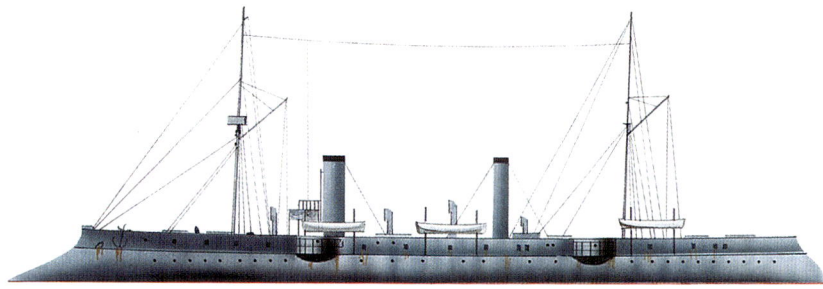

Forbin was one of three medium-sized cruisers with fine lines and a pronounced plough bow. The guns were mounted on sponsons with a good field of fire. The hull had a very marked tumblehome. A curved 41mm (1.6in) armoured deck ran the full length of the ship. Decommissioned, *Forbin* became a collier in 1913.

SPECIFICATIONS

Type:	French cruiser
Displacement:	1880 tonnes (1850 tons)
Dimensions:	95m x 9m x 5.2m (311ft 8in x 29ft 6in x 17ft 2in)
Machinery:	Twin screw, horizontal compound engines
Top speed:	19.5 knots
Main armament:	Four 140mm (5.5in) guns
Launched:	January 1888

TIMELINE

1888  1890

Chiyoda

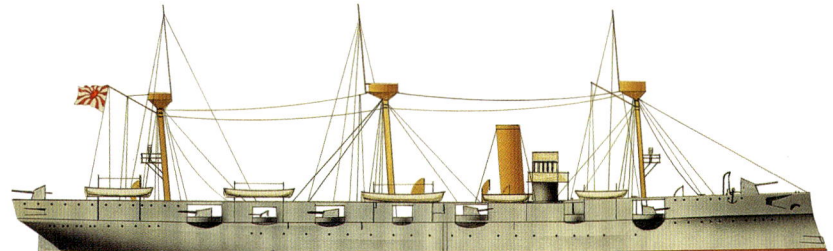

A replacement for the lost *Unebi*, this was Japan's first armoured cruiser, and very modern in its day, carrying the Elswick quick-firing gun, capable of a round every five seconds. Though three masts were fitted, the ship was not rigged for sails. Eight boilers provided 5600hp. The armoured belt was of chrome steel.

SPECIFICATIONS	
Type:	Japanese cruiser
Displacement:	2439 tonnes (2400 tons)
Dimensions:	94.5m x 13m x 4.3m (310ft x 42ft x 14ft)
Machinery:	Twin screws, vertical triple expansion engine
Top speed:	19 knots
Main armament:	Ten 119mm (4.7in) guns, three 356mm (14in) torpedo tubes
Armour:	Belt 115mm (4.5in), deck 38–25mm (1.5–1in)
Launched:	1890

Euridice

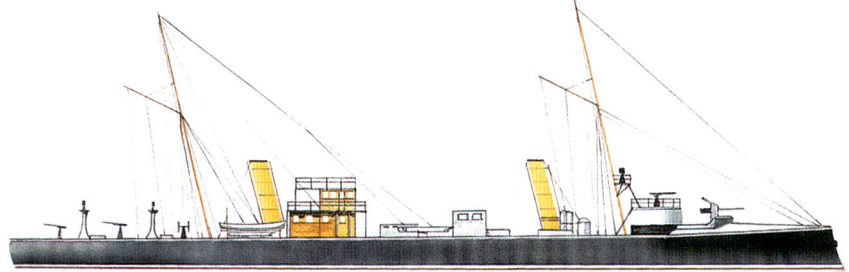

Euridice was one of eight ships classed as torpedo cruisers, improved versions of the *Tripoli* torpedo cruiser. They had steel hulls and originally carried a light fore and aft rig. They were intended to act as fast scouts on the fringes of the fleet, as well as acting independently. *Euridice* was discarded in 1907.

SPECIFICATIONS	
Type:	Italian cruiser
Displacement:	918 tonnes (904 tons)
Dimensions:	73.9m x 8.2m x 3.7m (242 ft 6in x 27ft x 12ft 2in)
Machinery:	Twin screw, triple expansion engines
Top speed:	20 knots
Main armament:	One 120mm (4.7in) gun, six 430mm (17in) torpedo tubes
Launched:	1890

Geiser

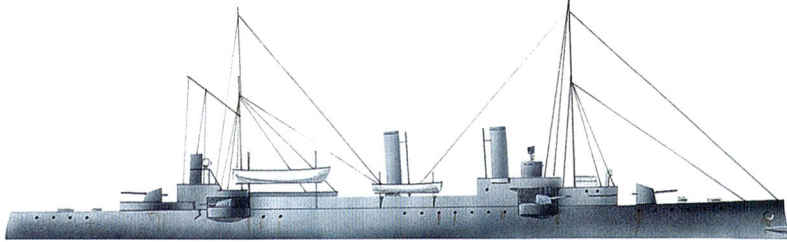

The Danish Navy patrolled the North Atlantic as far as Greenland and needed good sea ships. Though classed as a cruiser, *Geiser* was modestly armed for its time. Apart from some torpedo boats, it was the first warship fitted with the new Thornycroft water-tube boilers, giving greater efficiency and better performance.

SPECIFICATIONS	
Type:	Danish cruiser
Displacement:	1311 tonnes (1290 tons)
Dimensions:	78.5m x 8.4m x 4m (257ft 6in x 27ft 6in x13ft)
Machinery:	Twin screw vertical triple expansion engines
Main armament:	Two 119mm (4.7in) guns
Launched:	1892

Cruisers of the 1880s and 1890s: Part 3

By now the spars of a square rig were rarely seen on new warships. But tall masts were still needed for look-out posts and because ships still communicated by flag signals. Wooden hulls were obsolete and improved shells made armour vital.

Friant

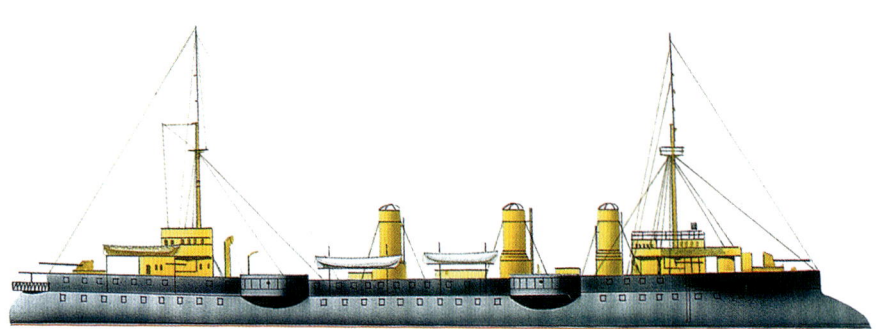

Its sides were unarmoured, but *Friant*'s deck had armour 30mm (1.2in) thick on the flat and 81mm (3.2in) thick on the slopes. A splinter deck was placed above the machinery spaces. An escort in the Mediterranean in World War I, it became a submarine tender in 1918, and was removed from the effective list in 1920.

SPECIFICATIONS	
Type:	French cruiser
Displacement:	3861 tonnes (3800 tons)
Dimensions:	95m x 13m x 6.4m (311ft 8in x 42ft 8in x 21ft)
Machinery:	Twin screw, triple expansion engines
Main armament:	Six 163mm (6.4in) guns, four 102mm (4in) guns
Launched:	April 1893

Gefion

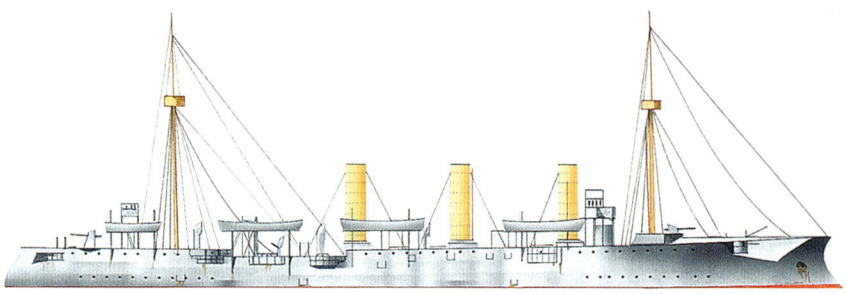

Gefion marked a change in German cruiser design. It was completed in June 1894 to carry 152mm (6in) guns, but the lighter 104mm (4.1in) weapon was chosen and this became the standard German cruiser weapon. Rebuilt as the merchant ship *Adolf Summerfield* after World War I, it was scrapped in 1923.

SPECIFICATIONS	
Type:	German cruiser
Displacement:	4275 tonnes (4208 tons)
Dimensions:	110.4m x 13.2m x 6.5m (362ft 2in x 43ft 4in x 21ft 3in)
Machinery:	Twin screw triple expansion engines
Top speed:	20.5 knots
Main armament:	Ten 104mm (4.1 in) guns
Launched:	May 1893

TIMELINE 1893 1895

General Garibaldi

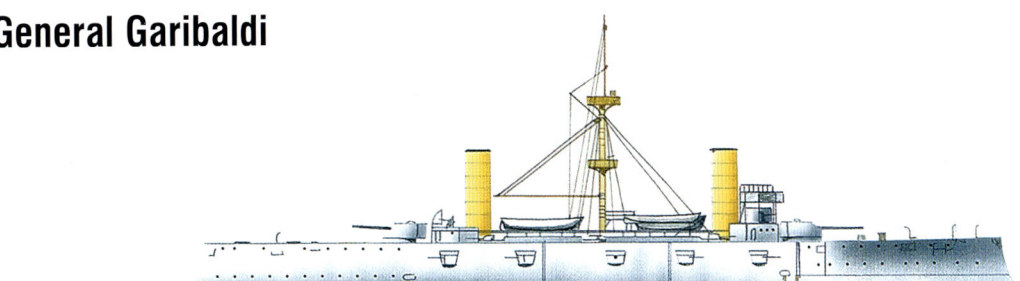

SPECIFICATIONS	
Type:	Argentinian cruiser
Displacement:	6949 tonnes (6840 tons)
Dimensions:	100m x 18.1m x 7.6m (328ft x 59ft 6in x 25ft)
Machinery:	Twin screw, triple expansion engines
Top speed:	19.9 knots
Main armament:	Two 254mm (10in) guns, ten 152mm (6in) guns, six 119mm (4.7in) guns
Launched:	May 1895

Laid down for the Italian Navy as the *Giuseppe Garibaldi*, this was purchased by Argentina with three sister-ships. The main guns were of unusually heavy calibre for ships of their size, and the cruisers made the Argentinian Navy the strongest on the eastern South American coast. *General Garibaldi* was discarded in 1935.

Gelderland

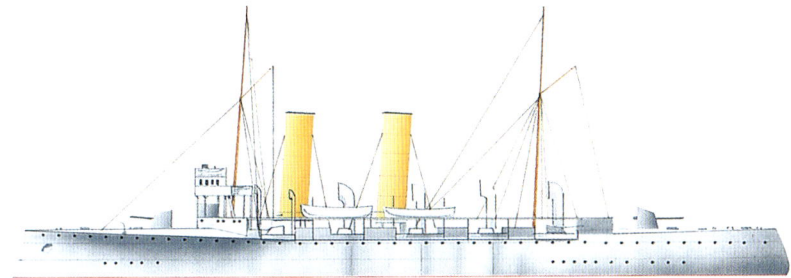

SPECIFICATIONS	
Type:	Dutch cruiser
Displacement:	4013 tonnes (3950 tons)
Dimensions:	95m x 14.7m x 5.4m (312ft x 48ft x 17ft 9in)
Machinery:	Twin screw, triple expansion engines
Top speed:	20.1 knots
Main armament:	Two 152mm (6in) guns, six 119mm (4.7in) guns
Launched:	1898

From 1920, this cruiser was used as a gunnery training ship, but on the fall of Holland in World War II it was converted by the Germans into a flak ship, *Niobe*, fitted with eight 104mm (4.1in) guns plus 20 smaller ones. It was bombed and torpedoed by Russian aircraft in July 1944.

Gromoboi

SPECIFICATIONS	
Type:	Russian cruiser
Displacement:	12,564 tonnes (12,367 tons)
Dimensions:	144m x 20.7m x 8.8m (472ft 6in x 68ft x 29ft)
Machinery:	Triple screws, triple expansion engines
Top speed:	20 knots
Main armament:	Sixteen 152mm (6in) guns, four 203mm (8in) guns, twenty 12-pdr guns
Armour:	152mm (6in) belt
Launched:	May 1899

An old-fashioned design, *Gromoboi* was well-protected and had substantial gun-power. It was attached to Russia's Pacific Fleet during the Russo–Japanese War in 1904. Menaced by a Japanese cruiser squadron, it outran them at a speed of 18 knots despite having been damaged by shell-fire. It was scrapped in 1922.

SHIP TYPES TO 1899

Natchez

Natchez had a reputation for speed, and in 1870 it forged upstream from New Orleans to St Louis at an average of 11.17 knots, sustained for 1672km (1039 miles). With three decks above the cargo space, there was ample room for passengers, who favoured the faster boats. Competition for trade was keen.

Natchez

Natchez was built to transport cotton, mail and passengers up and down the Mississippi River. *Natchez* sailed for nine and a half years and made 401 trips between New Orleans and the town of Natchez. She famously beat *Robert E Lee*, her rival, in a race between New Orleans and St Louis.

SPECIFICATIONS	
Type:	US sidewheel steamer
Displacement:	1578 tonnes (1547 tons)
Dimensions:	91.7m x 13m (301ft x 42ft 6in)
Machinery:	Side wheels driven by side lever engines
Service speed:	10 knots
Cargo:	Cotton bales, general cargo
Route:	Mississippi River
Launched:	1869

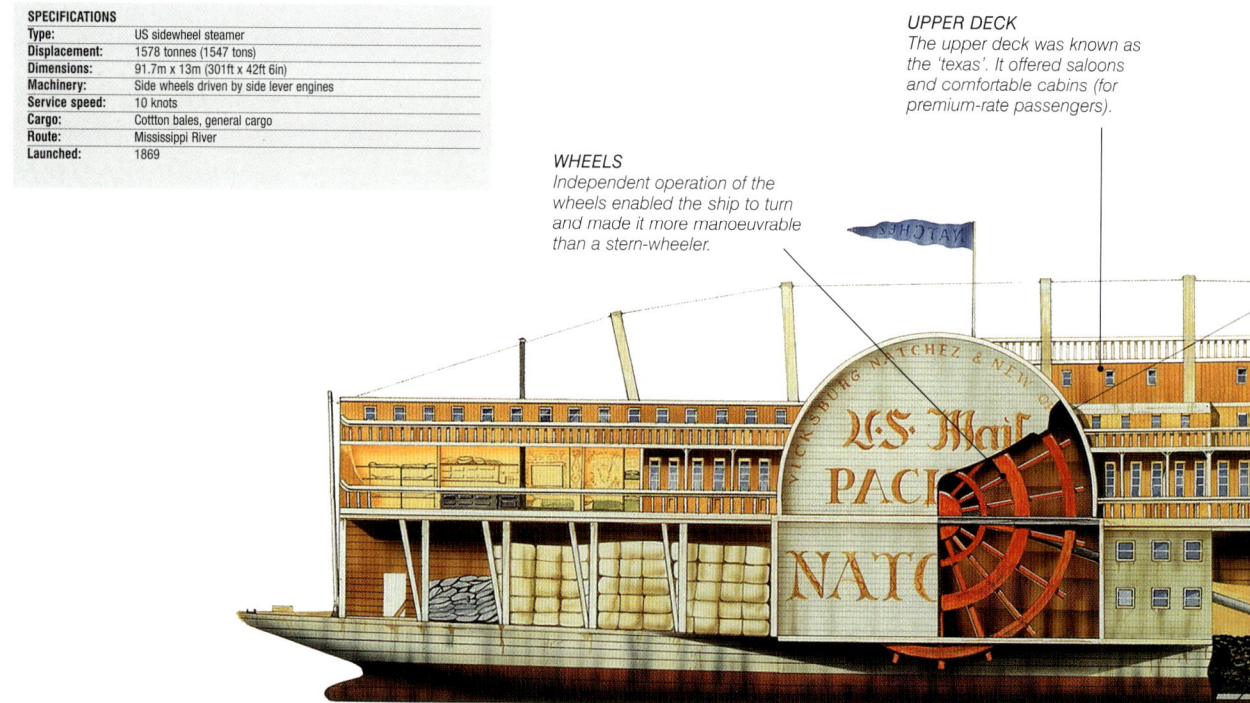

UPPER DECK
The upper deck was known as the 'texas'. It offered saloons and comfortable cabins (for premium-rate passengers).

WHEELS
Independent operation of the wheels enabled the ship to turn and made it more manoeuvrable than a stern-wheeler.

MACHINERY
Natchez normally burned coal. The engines in the ship's shallow-draught hull also stabilised the lofty but lightweight deckhouse.

NATCHEZ

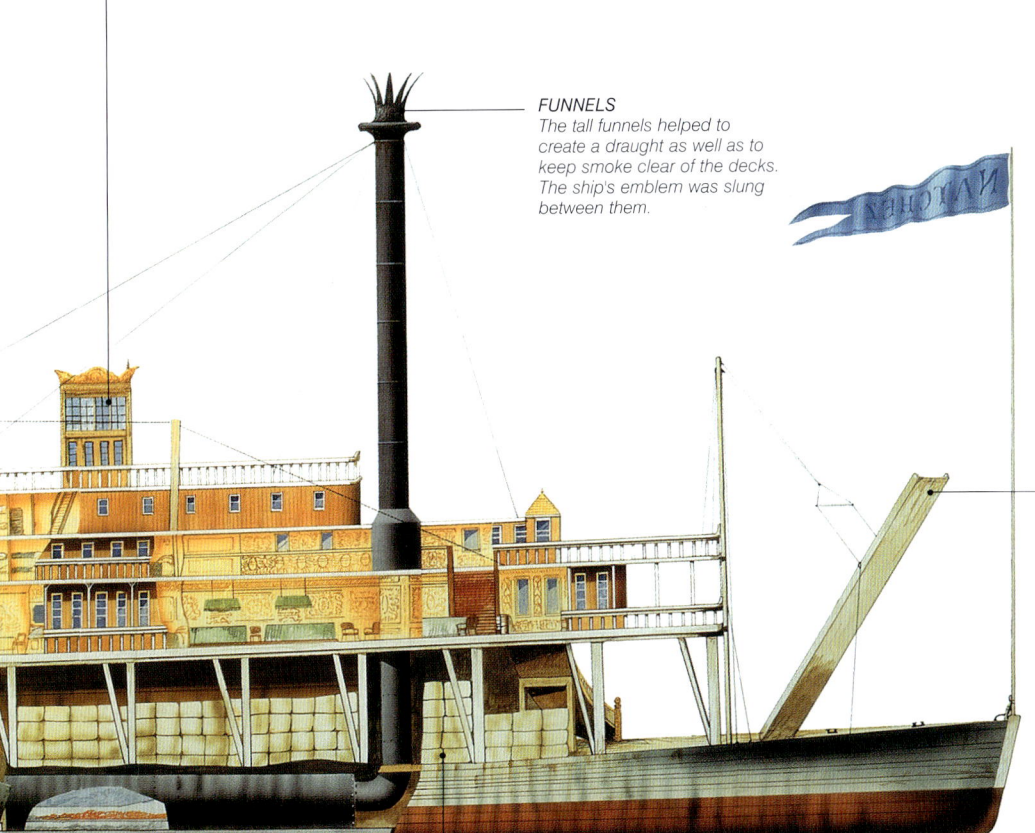

PILOT
A clear view ahead was essential in river navigation, to avoid shoals and mudbanks, rafts, and small boats.

FUNNELS
The tall funnels helped to create a draught as well as to keep smoke clear of the decks. The ship's emblem was slung between them.

GANGWAY
The long gang-plank was useful at places where the river was shallow or there was no proper jetty for berthing.

CARGO SPACE
Up to 5500 bales of cotton, or tobacco, stacked on the long main deck, helped to keep the vessel stable.

SHIP TYPES TO 1899

Paddle and Stern-Wheel Steamers: Part 1

By the late 1830s, the paddle steamer could cross oceans. Marine engineering became a specialized subject and engines were more reliable. But any long-distance steamer also carried sails, insurance against mechanical breakdown.

Britannia

Britannia, a wooden-hulled, three-masted barque with two decks, a single funnel and a clipper bow, started the first regular transatlantic mail service. Sold to the North German Confederation Navy in 1849, it was renamed *Barbarossa*. In 1852, it transferred to the Royal Prussian Navy and was sunk as a target ship in 1880.

SPECIFICATIONS	
Type:	British paddle steamer
Displacement:	2083 tonnes (2050 tons)
Dimensions:	70m x 17m (over paddle boxes) x 5m (228ft x 56ft x 16ft 10in)
Machinery:	Side wheels driven by side lever engines
Rigging:	Three masts, barque rig
Top speed:	8.5 knots
Launched:	February 1840

Washington

The first liner built for the Compagnie Générale Transatlantique, *Washington* carried 211 passengers, 128 in first class. In 1868, when many paddle ships were being scrapped, it was converted to a twin-screw vessel with single expansion engines, resulting in greater speed. It was scrapped only in 1900.

SPECIFICATIONS	
Type:	French liner
Displacement:	3462 tonnes (3408 tons)
Dimensions:	105m x 13m (345ft x 44ft)
Machinery:	Paddle wheels, side-lever engines
Rigging:	Three masts, square rigged on main and fore with mizzen spanker
Top speed:	9 knots
Route:	New York–Le Havre
Launched:	January 1847

TIMELINE

1840  1847  1848

California

SPECIFICATIONS	
Type:	US paddle steamer
Displacement:	1074 tonnes (1057 tons)
Dimensions:	10m (33ft) beam x 6.7m (22ft) depth
Machinery:	Paddle wheels, engine type not known
Rigging:	Two masts, barquentine rig
Complement:	75
Cargo:	General cargo, mails
Routes:	American west coast
Launched:	1848

Built in New York, *California* was the third steamship to pass Cape Horn, and the first to enter San Francisco Bay, in 1849. It worked on the US west coast for 28 years. In 1875, the engine was removed and it was rerigged as a barque. It was wrecked on the coast of Peru in 1895.

Arctic

SPECIFICATIONS	
Type:	US passenger liner
Displacement:	2896 tonnes (2850 tons)
Dimensions:	86m x 13.7m x 9.6m (282ft x 45ft x 31ft 6in)
Machinery:	Sidewheel
Top speed:	12.5 knots
Cargo:	Manufactured goods, mails
Route:	North Atlantic
Launched:	1849

A paddle steamer of the Collins Line, *Arctic* left the UK for New York with 246 passengers and 135 crew on 21 September 1854. On the 27th, in thick fog, it collided with the French steamer *Vesta*. Holed in three places, *Arctic* sank and 322 people drowned, including the wife and children of the line's owner.

Humboldt

SPECIFICATIONS	
Type:	US liner
Displacement:	2387 tonnes (2350 tons)
Dimensions:	85.9m x 12m (282ft x 40ft)
Machinery:	Paddle wheels, side-lever engines
Rigging:	Three masts, barque rig
Top speed:	10 knots
Cargo:	General cargo, mails
Routes:	North Atlantic
Launched:	1850

A pioneer steamship of the New York and Le Havre Steam Navigation Company, which took over the US mail contract from the Ocean Steam Navigation Company, *Humboldt* plied the route between New York, Southampton and Le Havre until it was wrecked on the Sister's Rock off Halifax, Nova Scotia, in 1853.

Paddle and Stern-Wheel Steamers: Part 2

Sailing craft were cheaper to operate, so the merchant steamship was confined to passenger (and mail) transport. Screw propulsion, though, offered higher speeds and paddles were relegated to shallow-draught ships only, especially river boats.

Powhatan

Powhatan's armament was concentrated on the upper deck, and was modified to one 280mm (11in) and ten 228mm (9in) guns in 1861. During the American Civil War, it also carried several 100-pounder rifled guns. It was kept in active service until the early 1880s, finally sold in 1886 and scrapped in 1887.

SPECIFICATIONS	
Type:	US cruiser
Displacement:	3825 tonnes (3765 tons)
Dimensions:	76.2m x 21.2m [over paddle boxes] x 6.3m (250ft x 69ft 6in x 20ft 9in)
Machinery:	Paddle wheels, inclined direct acting engines
Rigging:	Three masts, barque rig
Main armament:	Twelve 203mm (8in) guns
Launched:	February 1850

Arabia

The last wooden-hulled paddle-steamer to be built for the Cunard Line, *Arabia* was well equipped, with steam central heating and other passenger comforts. During the Crimean War of 1854, it was a troopship. In 1858, it suffered damage in a collision with *Europa*. Cunard sold it in 1864.

SPECIFICATIONS	
Type:	UK passenger liner
Displacement:	3962 tonnes (3900 tons)
Dimensions:	89.6m x 12.5m (284ft x 41ft)
Machinery:	Sidewheels, engine type not known
Rigging:	Two masts, square rig
Top speed:	15 knots
Cargo:	Light freight, mails
Route:	North Atlantic
Launched:	1851

TIMELINE			
	1850 	1851 	1854 

PADDLE AND STERN-WHEEL STEAMERS: PART 2

Quaker City

The merchant ship *Quaker City* was the only Union privateer during the American Civil War, fitted out by private subscription. Cruising in the Chesapeake Bay area, it captured four Confederate vessels. Later taken over by the Navy Department, it was decommissioned in 1865 and resumed commercial service.

SPECIFICATIONS	
Type:	US privateer
Displacement:	1625 tonnes (1600 tons)
Dimensions:	74.6m x 10.9m x 3.9m (244ft 8in x 36ft x 13ft)
Machinery:	Paddle wheels, side-lever engine
Rigging:	Two masts, schooner rig
Main armament:	Two 32-pdr guns, two 6-pdr guns
Launched:	1854

Adriatic

The largest and last of the Collins Line steamers, built at the Novelty Works, New York, *Adriatic* was sold to the Galway Line while still new. It survived a boiler explosion in 1864, being towed into Liverpool. Finally used as a stores ship at Bonny, West Africa, it was broken up in 1885.

SPECIFICATIONS	
Type:	US liner
Displacement:	5982 tonnes (5888 tons)
Dimensions:	105.1m x 15.2m (345ft x 50ft)
Machinery:	Paddle wheels, side-lever engines
Cargo:	General cargo, mails
Routes:	North Atlantic
Launched:	1856

Chaperon

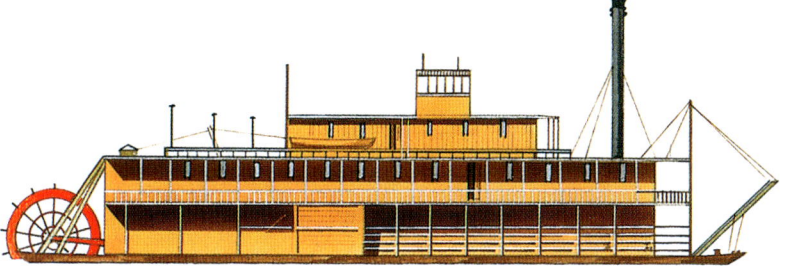

More than 5000 paddle-operated steamers served on the Mississippi during the nineteenth century. Built of wood, *Chaperon* had a typically long, low hull with minimum draught. It was strengthened fore and aft with strong supporting trusses stretched over spars above the upper deck – also typical.

SPECIFICATIONS	
Type:	US stern wheel steamer
Displacement:	812 tonnes (800 tons)
Dimensions:	37m x 6m x 2m (121ft x 21ft x 4ft)
Machinery:	Stern wheel, compound engine
Top speed:	8 knots
Launched:	1884

1856  1884

SHIP TYPES TO 1899

Passenger Liners of the Late Nineteenth Century

More passengers and larger ships promoted competition, especially on the route from north-west Europe to the eastern United States. Compound engines were overtaken by triple expansion. Sail power waned, and superstructures now rose above the hull: funnels rather than rigging dominated a ship's appearance.

City of Rome

Built for the Inman Line, *City of Rome* failed to reach the stipulated speed upon testing in 1881 and was sold on to the Anchor Line. It carried a mix of 520 first- and second-class passengers, and 810 third-class. Accommodation was luxurious and it was a popular ship. *City of Rome* was scrapped in 1902.

SPECIFICATIONS	
Type:	British liner
Displacement:	8550 tonnes (8415 tons)
Dimensions:	171m x 15.8m (560ft x 52ft)
Machinery:	Single screw, compound engines
Rigging:	Four masts, square rig with mizzen spanker
Top speed:	16 knots
Launched:	1881

Etruria

The Cunard liner *Etruria* and its sister-ship *Umbria* introduced the concept of the 'floating hotel', with luxurious accommodation for 550 saloon passengers, and magnificent décor and fittings. In May 1885, *Etruria* took the Blue Riband of the Atlantic for a record-breaking westbound passage. It was scrapped in 1909.

SPECIFICATIONS	
Type:	British liner
Displacement:	7841 tonnes (7718 tons)
Dimensions:	153m x 17m (502ft x 57ft)
Machinery:	Single screw, compound engines
Top speed:	19.9 knots
Launched:	1885

TIMELINE

1881    1885

PASSENGER LINERS OF THE LATE NINETEENTH CENTURY

La Champagne

SPECIFICATIONS	
Type:	French liner
Displacement:	6858 tonnes (6750 tons)
Dimensions:	154.8m x 15.7m x 7.3m (508ft x 51ft 8in x 24ft)
Machinery:	Single screw, triple expansion engines
Rigging:	Four masts, partial square rig
Top speed:	18.6 knots
Route:	North Atlantic
Launched:	April 1885

La Champagne and its sister-ship *Bretagne* were France's first luxury liners, built to compete with the American and British ships of the period. It carried 390 first-class, 65 second-class and 620 third-class passengers. At St-Nazaire on 28 May 1913, it dragged its anchors, ran aground, and became a total loss.

Augusta Victoria

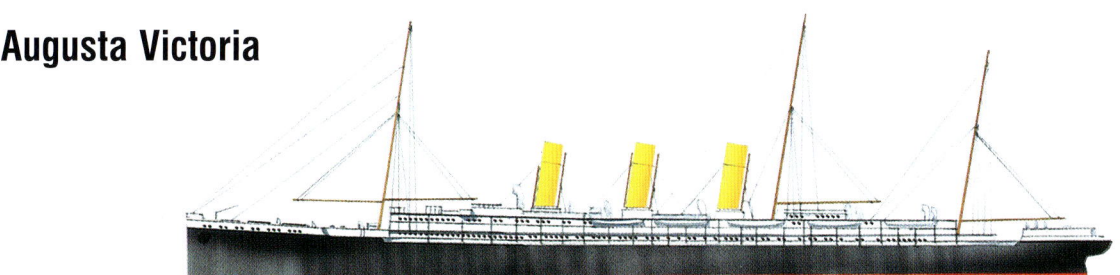

SPECIFICATIONS	
Type:	German liner
Displacement:	7783 tonnes (7661 tons)
Dimensions:	140m x 17m (459ft x 56ft)
Machinery:	Twin screws, vertical triple expansion engines
Rigging:	Three masts, staysails
Service speed:	18 knots
Route:	North Atlantic
Launched:	1889

Augusta Victoria's maiden transalantic voyage in 1889 was a record-breaker. In 1897 its displacement was increased to 8614 tonnes (8479 tons) and in 1904 it was sold to Russia as an auxiliary cruiser. Renamed *Kuban*, it acted as a decoy vessel for the fleet heading for the Straits of Tsushima. It was scrapped in 1907.

Gothland

SPECIFICATIONS	
Type:	Belgian liner
Displacement:	7880 tonnes (7755 tons)
Dimensions:	150m x 16m (491ft x 53ft)
Machinery:	Twin screws, triple expansion engines
Top speed:	14 knots
Cargo:	General cargo
Route:	North Atlantic
Launched:	1893

Built for the White Star Line as *Gothic*, *Gothland* was renamed when acquired by the Red Star Line in 1907. It had a long hull, straight stern and a single funnel topping a central superstructure that accommodated first-class passengers. In its last years, *Gothland* served as an emigrant ship. It was scrapped in 1926.

SHIP TYPES TO 1899

Early Submarines: Part 1

Submersible ships had been contemplated for years before the technology became sufficiently advanced for serious experiments to be made. As with many other forms of mechanical progress, the work of inventors was inspired by the demands of warfare. Here was the perfect 'stealth' ship, if only it could be made to work.

Turtle

Built by David Bushnell, *Turtle* was the first submarine to be used in action. It was also the first screw-propelled vessel, driven by a hand-crank, with a vertical screw for downward thrust. The external charge was attached to the target by an auger screwed into its hull. *Turtle* was destroyed to prevent capture by the British.

SPECIFICATIONS

Type:	American submersible
Displacement:	2 tonnes (2 tons)
Dimensions:	1.8m x 1.3m (6ft x 4.5ft)
Machinery:	Single screw, hand-cranked
Main armament:	One 68kg (150lb) detachable explosive charge
Launched:	1776

El Ictineo

Anticipating later submarines in shape, this craft also had a double hull. The engine was designed to operate when submerged, with a chemical conversion plant to supply oxygen. A compressed-air pump operated the ballast tanks. The technology was too far ahead of its time, and it proved unreliable in service.

SPECIFICATIONS

Type:	Spanish submersible
Displacement:	30.5 tonnes (30 tons)
Dimensions:	9m (30ft) length, 2m (7ft) depth
Machinery:	Single screw, steam engine
Complement:	3
Launched:	1858

TIMELINE

1776   1858   1862

EARLY SUBMARINES: PART 1

Intelligent Whale

SPECIFICATIONS	
Type:	US submarine
Displacement:	Unknown
Dimensions:	9.4m x 2.6m x 2.6m (31ft x 8ft 6in x 8ft 6in)
Machinery:	Single screw, hand-cranked
Top speed:	4 knots
Complement:	Six crankers, seven mine-planters
Launched:	1862

The Union Navy's first submarine was built to counter Confederate vessels of the same type. The cigar-shaped hull had a trap-door that let mine-planters exit to secure mines to the hulls of enemy vessels. The project was abandoned in 1872 and *Intelligent Whale* was put on display at the Washington Navy Yard.

H L Hunley

SPECIFICATIONS	
Type:	Confederate submarine
Displacement:	approx 2 tonnes (2 tons)
Dimensions:	12m x 1m x 1.2m (40ft x 3ft 6in x 4ft)
Machinery:	Single screw, hand-cranked
Main armament:	One spar torpedo
Launched:	1863

This was the first submarine to succeed against an enemy. The main part of the hull was shaped from a cylindrical steam boiler, with the tapered ends added. Eight crewmen turned the hand-cranked propeller; one steered. On 17 February 1864, it sank the Union ship *Housatonic*, but was dragged down with her.

Fenian Ram

SPECIFICATIONS	
Type:	Irish Republican submarine
Displacement:	19.3 tonnes (19 tons)
Dimensions:	9.4m x 1.8m x 2.2m (31ft x 6ft x 7ft 3in)
Machinery:	Single screw, petroleum engine
Main armament:	One 228mm (9in) gun
Launched:	May 1881

Built in New York for the Fenian Society, the vessel was towed to Newhaven in 1883. Never used as a war craft, it was exhibited at Madison Square Gardens in 1916 in order to raise funds for the Irish uprising that took place that year. It is housed in West Side Park, New York.

1863

1881

Early Submarines: Part 2

Key to submarine development was an effective underwater propulsion system. The electric motor, developed early in the nineteenth century, offered obvious potential. But the creation of electric power within a small hull remained a challenge. In 1860, the scientist Gaston Planté produced the first storage battery, showing the way.

Goubet I

By 1880, Planté's lead accumulator had been improved by coating the surface with red lead, providing a self-contained power source. Now a rechargeable underwater drive was feasible. Claude Goubet built one of the first successful electrically-driven submarines, quickly followed by his larger *Goubet II* in 1889.

SPECIFICATIONS	
Type:	French submarine
Displacement:	1.6 tonnes (1.6 tons) [surface], 1.8 tonnes (1.8 tons) [submerged]
Dimensions:	5m x 1.7m x 1m (16ft 5in x 5ft10in x 3ft 3in)
Machinery:	Single screw, electric motor
Top speed:	5 knots
Launched:	1887

Gymnôte

Dupuy de Lôme's designs for *Gymnôte* were revised by Gustave Zédé into a single-hull steel submarine with detachable lead keel. Electric power came from 204 cells spread along the lower part of the hull. *Gymnôte* made over 2000 dives in all. It sank at Toulon in 1907, was raised, and scrapped in 1908.

SPECIFICATIONS	
Type:	French submarine
Displacement:	30.5 tonnes (30 tons) [surface], 31.6 tonnes (31 tons) [submerged]
Dimensions:	7.3m x 1.8m x 1.6m (58ft 5in x 6ft x 5ft 6in)
Machinery:	Single screw, electric motor
Top speed:	7.3 knots [surface], 4.2 knots [submerged]
Main armament:	Two 355mm (14in) torpedo tubes
Launched:	September 1888

TIMELINE

1887　　　1888　　　1892

EARLY SUBMARINES: PART 2

Delfino

Italy was an early user of naval submarines. *Delfino* was built at La Spezia Naval Dockyard, and operated successfully for 10 years. It was rebuilt in 1902–04 with increased dimensions and displacement. A petrol motor was added and the conning tower enlarged. Serving throughout World War I, it was discarded in 1918.

SPECIFICATIONS	
Type:	Italian submarine
Displacement:	96 tonnes (95 tons) [surface], 108 tonnes (107 tons) [submerged]
Dimensions:	24m x 3m x 2.5m (78ft 9in x 9ft 5in x 8ft 4in)
Machinery:	Single screw [surface], electric motor [submerged]
Main armament:	Two 355mm (14in) torpedo tubes
Launched:	1892

Gustave Zédé

After initial problems of inadequate power and excessive weight of the 720-cell batteries, this was one of the first successful submarines, making over 2500 dives. It was the first to be fitted with a periscope, putting France at the forefront of submarine technology. *Gustave Zédé* was stricken from the Navy List in 1909.

SPECIFICATIONS	
Type:	French submarine
Displacement:	265 tonnes (261 tons) [surface], 274 tonnes (270 tons) [submerged]
Dimensions:	48.5m x 3.2m x 3.2m (159ft x 10ft 6in x 10ft 6in)
Machinery:	Single screw, electric motor
Top speed:	9.2 knots [surface], 6.5 knots [submerged]
Main armament:	One 450mm (17.7in) torpedo tube
Launched:	June 1893

Argonaut

Argonaut was built by Simon Lake for inshore salvage work. The engine could be connected to the front wheels for movement on the sea bed; the rear third wheel steered. An air chamber allowed divers to enter or leave. The vessel was rebuilt in 1899 and once made a trip of around 3200km (1684 miles).

SPECIFICATIONS	
Type:	US submarine
Displacement:	60 tonnes (59 tons) submerged
Dimensions:	11m x 2.7m (36ft x 9ft)
Machinery:	Single screw, 30hp gasoline engine
Complement:	5
Launched:	1897

1893

1897

Torpedo Boats: Part 1

Torpedoes had been pushed out on long spars, or towed, until Robert Whitehead developed the 'locomotive torpedo' in 1866. Its new potential as a weapon was clear. The Turkish ship *Intibah* was first to be sunk by a self-propelled torpedo, from a Russian craft, in 1878. By then, the first 'torpedo boat' was already in service.

Lightning

Lightning was the first boat built specially to fire Whitehead's locomotive torpedo. It was a slender launch-type vessel with a steel hull and reinforced steel conning-tower. Two reload torpedoes were mounted on rails behind the funnel. Other navies lined up to place orders for their own variants on the basic design.

SPECIFICATIONS	
Type:	British torpedo boat
Displacement:	27.4 tonnes (27 tons)
Dimensions:	26.5m x 3.3m x 1.6m (87ft x 10ft 9in x 5ft)
Machinery:	Single screw, compound engine
Top speed:	19 knots
Main armament:	One 356mm (14in) torpedo tube, three torpedoes
Complement:	15
Launched:	1877

Avvoltoio

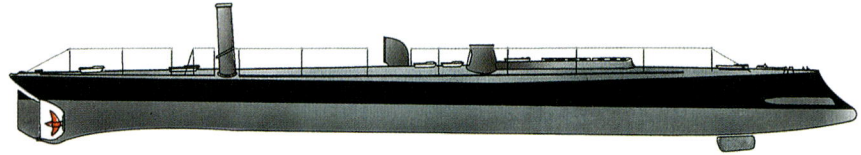

Avvoltoio was typical of the early torpedo boat, long with a low silhouette so that it could make a surprise appearance even in good visibility. Lightly built, it had scant protection apart from its speed, superior to that of large warships of the time. The second type adopted by the Italians, *Avvoltoio* was discarded in 1904.

SPECIFICATIONS	
Type:	Italian torpedo boat
Displacement:	25 tonnes (25 tons)
Dimensions:	26m x 3.3m x 1.3m (86ft x 11ft x 4ft 6in)
Machinery:	Single screw, vertical triple expansion engine. Steam supplied by a single locomotive boiler developing 420hp
Top speed:	21.3 knots
Main armament:	Two 356mm (14in) torpedo tubes, one 1-pdr revolving cannon
Launched:	1879

TIMELINE

1877   1879   1883

Euterpe

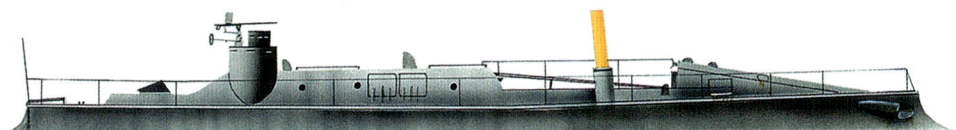

Euterpe was one of eight boats used for coast defence. Torpedo boats were now important, threatening battlefleets, especially in darkness. *Euterpe*'s conning tower was towards the stern, behind the torpedo storage space, with the launch tubes in front. *Euterpe* was discarded around 1897.

SPECIFICATIONS	
Type:	Italian torpedo boat
Displacement:	13.5 tonnes (13.3 tons)
Dimensions:	19.2m x 2.2m x 1.1m (63ft x 7ft 6in x 3ft 9in)
Machinery:	Single screw, vertical triple expansion engines
Main armament:	Two 355mm (14in) torpedo tubes, one 25mm (1in) machine gun
Launched:	1883

Fu Lung

Fu Lung was a steel-hulled ocean-going torpedo boat, with two torpedo tubes mounted side by side in the bows; two reloads were carried. It took part in the Battle of the Yalu in 1894, and was captured by the Japanese on 8 February 1895 at the fall of Wei-Hai-Wei. Renamed *Fukuryu*, it was broken up in 1908.

SPECIFICATIONS	
Type:	Chinese torpedo boat
Displacement:	130 tonnes (128 tons)
Dimensions:	44m x 5m x 2.3m (144ft 4in x 16ft 5in x 7ft 6in)
Machinery:	Single screw, triple expansion engine
Main armament:	Two 356mm (14in) torpedo tubes
Complement:	20
Launched:	1886

Balny

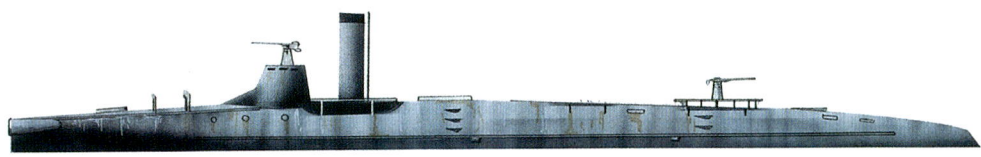

With *Balny*, the builders Normand attempted to produce a class of 10 sea-going torpedo boats, as a development of existing models. However, the vessels were not big enough for their task. They rolled badly, and deck access was very difficult. In 1890, all 10 were restricted to coastal defence.

SPECIFICATIONS	
Type:	French torpedo boat
Displacement:	66 tonnes (65 tons)
Dimensions:	40.8m x 3.4m x 1m (134ft x 11ft x 3ft 5in)
Machinery:	Single screw, compound engine
Top speed:	19 knots
Main armament:	Two 355mm (14in) torpedo tubes in the bow
Launched:	1886

Torpedo Boats: Part 2

The production of torpedo boats affected naval strategy and tactics. Small, fast and unobtrusive, they posed a deadly threat to capital ships that had seemed almost invulnerable. For a time, the balance of power among major navies seemed likely to collapse. Even countries unable to afford battleships could acquire torpedo boats.

Viborg

The largest torpedo boat of the time, Viborg was built at Thompson's Yard, Scotland, specialists in constructing this type. Two 37mm (1.5in) revolving Hotchkiss cannon were placed forward, abreast of the funnels. The turtle deck was thickly plated in front of the conning tower. Viborg was discarded in 1910.

SPECIFICATIONS	
Type:	Russian torpedo boat
Displacement:	169 tonnes (166 tons)
Dimensions:	43.4m x 5m x 2m (142ft 6in x 17ft x 7ft)
Machinery:	Twin screws, vertical compound engines
Rigging:	Three masts, gaff rig
Top speed:	20 knots
Main armament:	Three 381mm (15in) torpedo tubes
Launched:	1886

Habaña

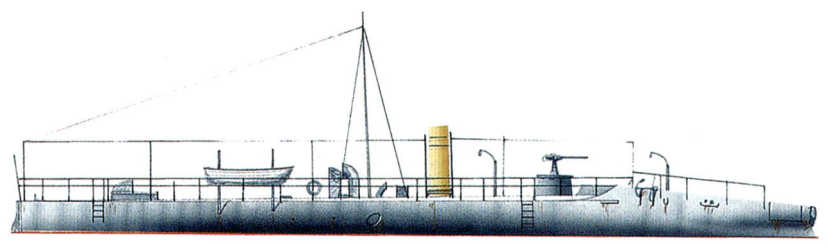

Habaña was built in England by Thornycroft, one of 13 steel-hulled boats constructed up to 1887 for the Spanish Navy, which was in the forefront of developments at the time, and saw their potential. The machine-gun was placed on the low conning tower; the two torpedo tubes were mounted in the bow.

SPECIFICATIONS	
Type:	Spanish torpedo boat
Displacement:	68 tonnes (67 tons)
Dimensions:	38.8m x 3.8m x 1.5m (127ft 7in x 12ft 7in x 5ft)
Machinery:	Single screw, triple expansion engines
Top speed:	24.5 knots
Main armament:	Two 355mm (14in) torpedo tubes, one machine-gun
Launched:	1887

TIMELINE

1886  1887  1890

Cushing

Cushing was the US Navy's first purpose-designed torpedo boat, with a conning tower at each end. In 1897 it was used as a despatch boat off Cuba, and in the 1898 war with Spain it captured four small Spanish transports. Based at Newport, it eventually became a target hulk, and was sunk in September 1920.

SPECIFICATIONS	
Type:	US torpedo boat
Displacement:	118 tonnes (116 tons)
Dimensions:	42m x 4.5m x 1.5m (140ft x 15ft 1in x 4ft 10in)
Machinery:	Twin screws, vertical quadruple expansion engines
Top speed:	23 knots
Main armament:	Three 457mm (18in) torpedo tubes, three 6-pounder guns
Launched:	January 1890

Havock

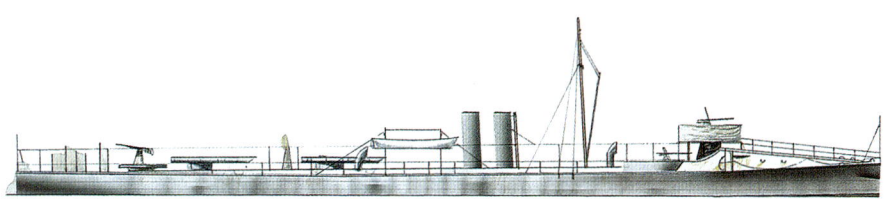

In 1892, Alfred Yarrow was asked to produce an answer to France's superb torpedo craft. *Havock* was completed in 1894. It could do everything a torpedo boat did, and its gun-power was sufficient to destroy torpedo boats as well. An excellent sea boat, soon nicknamed 'destroyer', *Havock* was scrapped in 1912.

SPECIFICATIONS	
Type:	British 'torpedo-boat destroyer'
Displacement:	243.8 tonnes (240 tons)
Dimensions:	54.8m x 5.6m x 3.3m (180ft x 18ft 6inx 11ft)
Machinery:	Twin screws, triple expansion engines
Top speed:	26 knots
Main armament:	One 12-pdr gun, three 6-pdr guns, three torpedo tubes
Launched:	August 1893

Forban

Forban was the first vessel to exceed 30 knots. It was also a superb sea boat. Designed and built by Normand, it followed on from the *Filibustier* class, which prompted the British to build the first destroyers in reply. In 1907, the torpedo tubes were replaced by 457mm (18in) ones. It was sold in 1920.

SPECIFICATIONS	
Type:	French torpedo boat
Displacement:	152 tonnes (150 tons)
Dimensions:	44m x 4.6m x 1.4m (144ft 4in x 15ft 3in x 4ft 5 in)
Machinery:	Twin screws, triple expansion engines
Top speed:	31 knots
Main armament:	Two 356mm (14in) torpedo tubes
Launched:	July 1895

SHIP TYPES TO 1899

Torpedo Gunboats

The threat of the torpedo boat was met in various ways, by increased battleship armour, and by the production of vessels that could intercept the torpedo boat, and sink it by gunfire. But this was not easy: the attacker could choose its moment, while the defender had to be permanently on the watch.

Bombe

Intended to counter the threat from torpedo boats, and endowed with sufficient speed to keep up with the battle fleet, the torpedo gunboat had its displacement held to the minimum, putting it at a disadvantage in rough weather. Navies had to rethink the concept of the escort. *Bombe* was broken up in 1921.

SPECIFICATIONS	
Type:	French torpedo gunboat
Displacement:	375 tonnes (369 tons)
Dimensions:	60m x 6m x 3m (194ft 3in x 19ft 7in x 10ft 5in)
Machinery:	Twin screws, vertical compound engines
Main armament:	Two 355mm (14in) torpedo tubes, two 3-pdr guns
Launched:	April 1885

Destructor

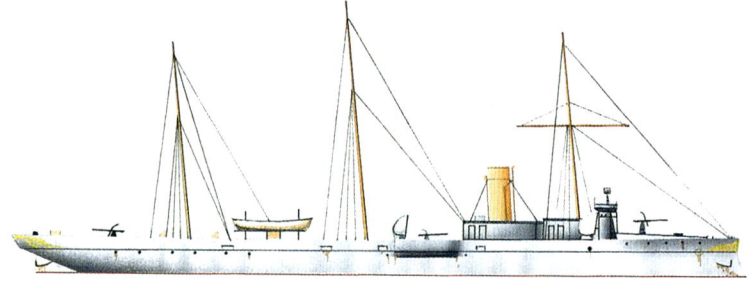

As typical in boats of this type, *Destructor* had a turtle-back fore section. One of the first vessels with triple expansion engines, it had side-by-side twin funnels and three hinged masts. Light protective plating was fitted on the conning tower and over the machinery room, and lighter weapons supplemented the main gun.

SPECIFICATIONS	
Type:	Spanish torpedo gunboat
Displacement:	465 tonnes (458 tons)
Dimensions:	58m x 7.6m x 2m (192ft 6in x 25ft x 7ft)
Machinery:	Twin screws, triple expansion engines
Main armament:	One 89mm (3.5in) gun, five 380mm (15in) torpedo tubes
Launched:	July 1886

TORPEDO GUNBOATS

Blitz

The torpedo gunboat was a short-lived design, its guns too ineffective and its seakeeping qualities insufficient to make it a serious threat to torpedo boats. The true answer was the destroyer, with its heavier armament. *Blitz* and its sister ship *Komet* were allocated to Italy in 1920 and were later broken up there.

SPECIFICATIONS	
Type:	Austrian torpedo gunboat
Displacement:	433 tonnes (426 tons)
Dimensions:	59m x 7m x 2m (193ft 6in x 22ft 5in x 6ft 10in)
Machinery:	Single screw, triple expansion engines
Main armament:	Nine 3-pdr guns, four 355mm (14in) torpedo tubes
Launched:	1888

Espora

Built by Lairds of Birkenhead, *Espora* was a steel-hulled boat with two sets of twin torpedo tubes carried in the lower midships section, and the fifth tube in the bows. It proved successful in action during the Chilean and Brazilian civil wars. The boilers and armament were changed in 1905. It was discarded in 1920.

SPECIFICATIONS	
Type:	Argentinian torpedo gunboat
Displacement:	528 tonnes (520 tons)
Dimensions:	60.9m x 7.6m x 2.5m (200ft x 25ft x 8ft 3in)
Machinery:	Twin screws, triple expansion engines
Top speed:	19.5 knots
Main armament:	Two 14-pdr guns, five 457mm (18in) torpedo tubes
Launched:	1890

Gustavo Sampaio

Built speculatively by Armstrongs of Newcastle, England, the steel-hulled *Aurora* was bought by Brazil in October 1893 and renamed *Gustavo Sampaio*. On 16 April 1894, it attacked the rebel ship *Aquidaban* and sank it with a torpedo. Despite sustaining 38 hits, *Gustavo Sampaio* survived. It was discarded in 1920.

SPECIFICATIONS	
Type:	Brazilian torpedo gunboat
Displacement:	487 tonnes (480 tons)
Dimensions:	59.9m x 6.1m x 2.5m (196ft 9in x 20ft x 8ft 6in)
Machinery:	Twin screws, triple expansion engines
Speed:	18 knots
Main armament:	Two 89mm (3.5in) guns, three 406mm (16in) torpedo tubes
Launched:	1893

SHIP TYPES TO 1899

Early Destroyers

The qualities required of the destroyer were adequate armament to quickly destroy a torpedo boat, good seakeeping qualities to maintain a constant patrol, and capacity to hold sufficient fuel, amunition and stores to accompany a battle fleet or large squadron. Inevitably, the size increased from early versions.

Furor

Built at Clydebank, Scotland, *Furor* was the Spanish Navy's first destroyer. Its speed and layout distinguished it from the torpedo gunboat. Attached to Admiral Ceveras's squadron during the Spanish–American War in 1898, it followed the cruisers out of Santiago on 3 July and was sunk by US ships lying in wait.

SPECIFICATIONS

Type:	Spanish destroyer
Displacement:	376 tonnes (370 tons)
Dimensions:	67m x 6.7m x 1.7m (219ft 10in x 22ft x 5ft 7in)
Machinery:	Twin screws, triple expansion engines
Top speed:	28 knots
Main armament:	Two 14-pdr guns, two 356mm (14in) torpedo tubes
Launched:	1896

Corrientes

Corrientes was modelled on the British ship *Havock*. Argentina, quick to appreciate its qualities, ordered four from the same builder, Yarrow. They had slightly greater length and displacement, with three funnels and a less steeply raked turtle foredeck. *Corrientes* was taken off the effective list in 1925.

SPECIFICATIONS

Type:	Argentinian destroyer
Displacement:	284 tonnes (280 tons)
Dimensions:	58m x 6m x 2m (190ft x 19ft 6in x 7ft 4in)
Machinery:	Twin screws, triple expansion engines
Main armament:	One 14-pdr gun, three 6-pdr guns, three 457mm (18in) torpedo tubes
Launched:	1896

TIMELINE

1896 1898

EARLY DESTROYERS

Bullfinch

The British commissioned a further group of destroyers in 1894, increasing the top speed to 30 knots. Following a basic design, the builders were allowed some latitude, so some ships featured two, three, or even four funnels. All had the same armament. *Bullfinch* was completed in June 1901 and scrapped in 1919.

SPECIFICATIONS
Type:	British destroyer
Displacement:	396 tonnes (390 tons)
Dimensions:	65m x 6m x 2.5m (214ft 6in x 20ft 6in x 7ft 10in)
Machinery:	Twin screws, triple expansion engines
Top speed:	30 knots
Main armament:	One 12-pdr gun, five 6-pdr guns, two 457mm (18in) torpedo tubes
Complement:	63
Launched:	February 1898

Farragut

Classified as a torpedo boat, this was in effect the US Navy's first destroyer. The engines developed 5878hp, with steam supplied by three Thornycroft boilers. Coal supply was 96 tonnes (95 tons). Her crew numbered 66. In August 1918, *Farragut* was renamed *Coast Torpedo Boat N° 5*. It was sold in 1919.

SPECIFICATIONS
Type:	US destroyer
Displacement:	283 tonnes (279 tons)
Dimensions:	65m x 6.3m x 1.8m (214ft x 20ft 8in x 6ft)
Machinery:	Twin screws, vertical triple expansion engines
Top speed:	33.7 knots
Main armament:	Six 6-pdr guns, two 457mm (18in) torpedo tubes
Launched:	July 1898

Framée

A prototype destroyer, with weapons and equipment in a narrow hull, *Framée* was top-heavy and rolled excessively. The class was not repeated, although the lessons learnt were incorporated in later designs. *Framée* was accidentally rammed and sunk on 11 August 1900 by the battleship *Brennus*.

SPECIFICATIONS
Type:	French destroyer
Displacement:	354 tonnes (348 tons)
Dimensions:	58.1m x 6.3m x 3m (190ft 7in x 20ft 8in x 9ft 10in)
Machinery:	Twin screws, triple expansion engines
Top speed:	26 knots
Main armament:	One 65mm (2.56in) gun
Launched:	October 1899

1899

SHIP TYPES TO 1899

Battleships of the 1880s & 1890s

Battleship design had to take account of the torpedo threat. It was appreciated that capital ships would have to be better armoured and faster than before, and so larger and more costly to build, operate and maintain. And the traditional concept of the 'broadside' had already given way to to a smaller number of heavy-calibre guns.

Italia

Italian naval strategy in the 1880s was to build a few ships so powerful that they could outfight any other. *Italia* had the largest guns of the time, on a huge barbette. By the time it entered service, the quick-firing gun and improved high-explosive shell had made these weapons obsolete. *Italia* was scrapped in 1921.

SPECIFICATIONS	
Type:	Italian battleship
Displacement:	15,904 tonnes (15,654 tons)
Dimensions:	124.7m x 22.5m x 8.7m (409ft 2in x 73ft 10in x 28ft 6in)
Machinery:	Four screws, vertical compound engines
Top speed:	17.8 knots
Main armament:	Four 431mm (17in) guns
Armour:	102mm (4in) deck, 482mm (19in) on barbette
Complement:	669
Launched:	September 1880

Courbet

Courbet and its sister-ship *Dévastation* were the largest central battery ships ever built. The hull sides were high, with a ram bow. Twin funnels set side-by-side rose through the main battery. By the 1890s, the rig had been modified, with each mast carrying two fighting tops. It was decommissioned in 1910.

SPECIFICATIONS	
Type:	French battleship
Displacement:	9855 tonnes (9700 tons)
Dimensions:	95m x 20m x 7.6m (312ft x 67ft x 25ft)
Machinery:	Twin screws, vertical compound engines
Top speed:	15 knots
Main armament:	Four 340mm (13.4in) guns, four 266mm (10.5in) guns
Armour:	381–178mm (15–7in) belt, 244mm (9.5in) on battery
Complement:	689
Launched:	April 1882

TIMELINE

1880  1882  1886

BATTLESHIPS OF THE 1880s & 1890s

Ekaterina II

Built for the Black Sea Fleet, this was one of the first major warships to have triple expansion engines. The six heavy guns were mounted on a pear-shaped redoubt amidships. Re-classified as a second-class battleship in 1906, *Ekaterina* became a target ship a year later, and as such was sunk off Tendra in 1907.

SPECIFICATIONS	
Type:	Russian battleship
Displacement:	11,224 tonnes (11,048 tons)
Dimensions:	100.9m x 21m x 8.5m (331ft x 68ft 11in x 27ft 11in)
Machinery:	Twin screws, vertical triple expansion engines
Top speed:	16 knots
Main armament:	Six 304mm (12in) guns
Armour:	203–406mm (8–16in) belt, 305mm (12in) redoubt
Launched:	May 1886

Kaiser Friedrich III

The most notable feature of the *Kaiser* class was its relatively light main and very extensive secondary armament. This arrangement did not survive the advent of the 'Dreadnought'. Of modest displacement for a battleship, *Kaiser Friedrich III* had armour weighing 3860 tonnes (3800 tons). It was scrapped in 1920.

SPECIFICATIONS	
Type:	German battleship
Displacement:	11,784 tonnes (11,599 tons)
Dimensions:	125.3m x 20.4m x 8.2m (411ft x 67ft x 27ft)
Machinery:	Triple screws, triple expansion engines
Top speed:	18 knots
Main armament:	Four 238mm (9.4in) guns, eighteen 152mm (6in) guns, twelve 86.3mm (3.4in) guns
Armour:	152–305mm (6–12in) belt, 254mm (10in) on main turrets, 152mm (6in) on secondary turrets and casemates
Complement:	651
Launched:	July 1896

Canopus

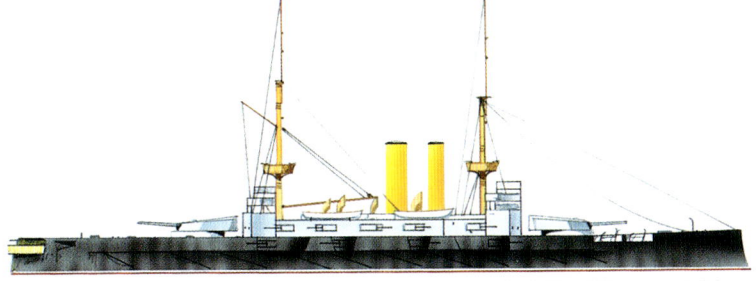

The *Canopus* class were Britain's first battleships to have water-tube boilers, for higher power and greater economy. At full speed, *Canopus* used 10 tonnes of coal per hour. Stationed at the Falkland Islands during World War I, it saw action against von Spee's squadron in December 1914. *Canopus* was sold in 1920.

SPECIFICATIONS	
Type:	British battleship
Displacement:	13,360 tonnes (13,150 tons)
Dimensions:	128m x 23m x 8m (421ft 6in x 74ft x 26ft)
Machinery:	Twin screws, triple expansion engines
Top speed:	18.3 knots
Main armament:	Four 305mm (12in) guns, twelve 152mm (6in) guns
Armour:	152mm (6in) belt, 305mm (12in) barbettes, 51mm (2in) deck
Complement:	682
Launched:	October 1897

1896  1897

SHIP TYPES 1900–1929

Until the twentieth century ships had been surface vessels and the reach of a warship had been restricted by the projective power of its guns.

In the decades from 1900 to 1929, new dimensions transformed the nature of naval warfare. One was the development of the submarine, linked with the invention of the self-propelled torpedo. The other was the development of powered flight. At an early stage, aircraft were taken to sea. In merchant fleets, liners reached new extremes of size, luxury and passenger capacity.

Left: In the 1900s, multiple funnels were an indication of power and speed. *Titanic's* fourth funnel was a dummy, intended to emphasise its supremacy in these respects.

SHIP TYPES 1900–1929

Aircraft Carriers to 1929: Part 1

The first aircraft used at sea were seaplanes or floatplanes, carried on warships or converted merchant ships, used primarily for reconnaissance. As the effectiveness and military value of aircraft increased, ships were designed with flying-off ramps. The advent of World War I speeded up development and led to larger-hulled ships.

Dédalo

The first specialized aircraft-launching ship, *Dédalo* could also fly an airship from the forward deck, supplied with gas from a hydrogen-producing plant. The seaplane deck, with crane, was aft of the deckhouse. Sunk in 1935 by Nationalist aircraft, the wreck was raised and broken up in 1940.

SPECIFICATIONS	
Type:	Spanish seaplane carrier
Displacement:	10,972 tonnes (10,800 tons)
Dimensions:	182m x 16.7m x 6m (597ft x 55ft x 20ft 6in)
Machinery:	Single screw, triple expansion engine
Main armament:	Two 102mm (4in) guns
Aircraft:	24
Launched:	1901

Ben-My-Chree

Ben-My-Chree, a passenger vessel on the Isle of Man route, was converted into an aircraft carrier in 1915. Fitted with a hangar aft, and a flying-off ramp on the fore-deck, it served in the Dardanelles campaign, its aircraft sinking two Turkish vessels. Anchored at Kastelorgio in 1917, it was sunk by Turkish shore batteries.

SPECIFICATIONS	
Type:	British aircraft carrier
Displacement:	3942 tonnes (3880 tons)
Dimensions:	114m x 14m x 5.3m (375ft x 46ft x 17ft 6in)
Machinery:	Twin screws, turbines
Aircraft:	4–6
Top speed:	24.5 knots
Launched:	March 1908

TIMELINE

1901   1908   1911

Engadine

SPECIFICATIONS	
Type:	British seaplane carrier
Displacement:	1702 tonnes (1676 tons)
Dimensions:	96.3m x 12.5m (316ft x 41ft)
Machinery:	Triple screws, turbines
Aircraft:	4–6
Top speed:	21 knots
Launched:	September 1911

In World War I, the British Admiralty requisitioned the cross-Channel steamers *Engadine* and *Riviera* for conversion into seaplane carriers. They were in action by December 1914. Further modified in 1915, *Engadine* served in the North Sea and the Mediterranean. It was re-converted as a ferry ship in 1919.

Courageous

SPECIFICATIONS	
Type:	British aircraft carrier
Displacement:	26,517 tonnes (26,100 tons)
Dimensions:	240m x 27m x 8m (786ft 5in x 90ft 6in x 27ft 3in)
Machinery:	Quadruple screws, turbines
Top speed:	31.5 knots
Main armament:	Sixteen 120mm (4.7in) guns
Armour:	76–50mm (3–2in) belt, 38–20mm (1.5–0.75in) decks
Aircraft:	48
Complement:	842
Launched:	February 1916

The cruiser *Courageous* was converted to a carrier in 1925–28. Forward of the hangar was an open flight deck. Above this was a full flight deck. With *Furious* and *Glorious*, it formed the backbone of Britain's carrier force in 1939. In the opening days of the war, *Courageous* was torpedoed and sunk by *U-29*.

Furious

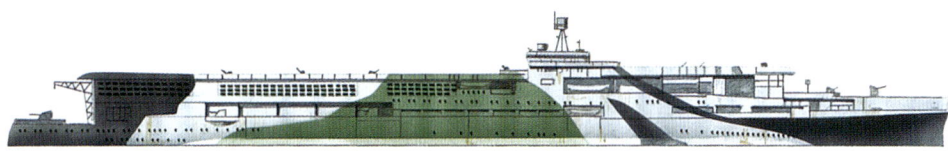

SPECIFICATIONS	
Type:	British aircraft carrier
Displacement:	22,758 tonnes (22,400 tons)
Dimensions:	239.6m x 27.4m x 7.3m (786ft 4in x 90ft x 24ft)
Machinery:	Quadruple screws, turbines
Top speed:	31.5 knots
Main armament:	Six 102mm (4in) guns
Aircraft:	36
Complement:	880
Launched:	August 1916

Furious, launched as as a heavy cruiser, was partially converted to a carrier in 1917–18, and given a complete flight deck in 1921–25. Refits followed in the 1930s. Active in World War II, it served in the Mediterranean, ferrying planes to Malta. In 1944, its aircraft attacked the *Tirpitz*. It was scrapped in 1948.

Aircraft Carriers to 1929: Part 2

By 1918, the concept of the aircraft carrier as an integral and important element in any major fleet was fully accepted, and the 'air arm' became part of the naval establishment. The first purpose-built carrier was laid down in 1917, its revolutionary design requiring careful balance of weights in order to achieve a level flight deck.

Europa

Originally a British merchant vessel, *Manila*, this was converted by the Italian Navy in 1915, acquiring two aircraft hangars. *Europa* carried eight seaplanes (six fighters, two reconnaissance), lifted and lowered by a crane. Based at Brindisi until January 1916, it transferred to Velona until 1918. It was scrapped in 1920.

SPECIFICATIONS	
Type:	Italian seaplane carrier
Displacement:	8945 tonnes (8805 tons)
Dimensions:	123m x 14m x 7.6m (403ft 10in x 46ft x 25ft)
Machinery:	Single screw, vertical triple expansion engines
Aircraft:	8
Top speed:	12 knots
Main armament:	Two 30mm (1.2in) anti-aircraft guns
Launched:	August 1895 (converted 1915)

Eagle

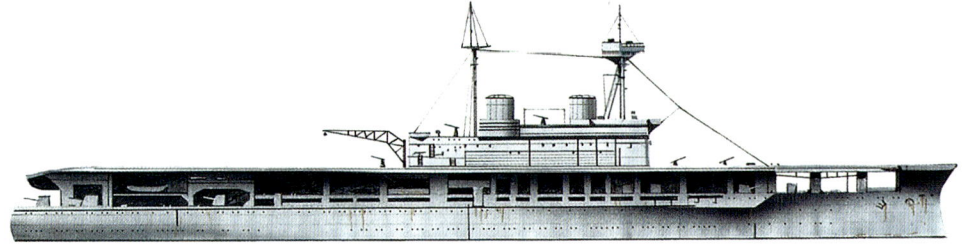

This was laid down as a super-dreadnought for the Chilean Navy, *Almirante Cochrane*, but work began at the outbreak of World War I to turn it into an aircraft carrier for the Royal Navy. Entering service in 1924, *Eagle* was sunk in the Mediterranean by *U-73*, in August 1942, attempting to carry aircraft to Malta.

SPECIFICATIONS	
Type:	British aircraft carrier
Displacement:	27,664 tonnes (27,229 tons)
Dimensions:	203.4m x 32m x 8m (667ft 6in x 105ft x 26ft 3in)
Machinery:	Quadruple screw, turbines
Main armament:	Nine 152mm (6in) guns, five 102mm (4in)
Armour:	114mm (4.5in) belt, 38mm (1.5in) deck
Aircraft:	24
Complement:	748
Launched:	June 1918

TIMELINE 1915 1918 1919

Hermes

SPECIFICATIONS	
Type:	British aircraft carrier
Displacement:	13,208 tonnes (13,000 tons)
Dimensions:	182.9m x 21.4m x 6.5m (600ft x 70ft 2in x 21ft 6in)
Machinery:	Twin screws, turbines
Top speed:	25 knots
Main armament:	Three 102mm (4in), six 140mm (5.5in) guns
Aircraft:	20
Launched:	1919

The first purpose-designed aircraft carrier, this provided the standard pattern. Built up on a cruiser-form hull, with the main deck providing the strength, were a hangar deck, then the flight deck. Deck structures and funnel were set to starboard. *Hermes* was sunk by Japanese aircraft off Ceylon on 9 April 1942.

Béarn

SPECIFICATIONS	
Type:	French aircraft carrier
Displacement:	28,854 tonnes (28,400 tons)
Dimensions:	182.5m x 27m x 9m (599ft x 88ft 11in x 30ft 6in)
Machinery:	Four screws, geared turbines, triple expansion engines
Aircraft:	35–40
Top speed:	21.5 knots
Main armament:	Eight 152mm (6in) guns
Launched:	April 1920

During World War II, *Béarn* was not employed as a front-line carrier because of its low speed, but gave valuable service as an aircraft ferry. After the fall of France in 1940, it was held at Martinique to prevent a return to France. After the war, it served off Indo-China (Vietnam). It was scrapped in 1949.

Hosho

SPECIFICATIONS	
Type:	Japanese aircraft carrier
Displacement:	10,160 tonnes (10,000 tons)
Dimensions:	168m x 21.3m x 6m (551ft 6in x 70ft x 20ft 3in)
Machinery:	Twin screws, turbines
Top speed:	25 knots
Main armament:	Four 140mm (5.5in) guns
Aircraft:	26
Complement:	550
Launched:	1921

This was the world's first commissioned aircraft carrier, entering service seven months before the British purpose-built *Hermes*. *Hosho* had a full-length flight deck, and the hangar was positioned amidships. It gave good service, but was relegated to secondary duties by the 1930s and scrapped in 1947.

SHIP TYPES 1900–1929

Aircraft Carriers to 1929: Part 3

The introduction of the carrier required new tactics. Large, but lightly armed and with varying degrees of armour protection, they were fast ships, intended to operate independently of the main battle fleet. The role of light cruisers and large destroyers was extended to provide carrier escorts, particularly as anti-submarine defence.

Kaga

Laid down as a battleship, *Kaga* was not completed until 1928 and was reconstructed with a full flight deck and island in 1934–35. Assigned to the 1st Carrier Division, and having participated in the Pearl Harbor attack, it was one of the Japanese carriers sunk by American aircraft in the Battle of Midway in 1942.

SPECIFICATIONS	
Type:	Japanese aircraft carrier
Displacement:	34,232 tonnes (33,693 tons)
Dimensions:	240.5m x 32.9m x 9.44m (798ft x 108ft x 31ft)
Machinery:	Quadruple screws, geared turbines
Aircraft:	90
Top speed:	27.5 knots
Main Armament:	Twenty-five 20mm (.75in) guns, thirty light AA guns
Armour:	279mm (11in) belt, 58.4mm (2.3in) deck
Complement:	1340
Launched:	1921

Giuseppe Miraglia

In 1923, the ex-liner *Citta di Messina* was re-named *Giuseppe Miraglia* and transformed into a seaplane carrier. It was used for catapult launching experiments, and during World War II served as an aircraft transport and carried out training duties. In 1943, it was surrendered to the British at Malta.

SPECIFICATIONS	
Type:	Italian seaplane carrier
Displacement:	5486 tonnes (5400 tons)
Dimensions:	115m x 15m x 5.2m (377ft 4in x 49ft 3in x 17ft)
Machinery:	Twin screws, turbines
Top speed:	21.5 knots
Main armament:	Four 102mm (4in) guns
Aircraft:	20
Launched:	December 1923

TIMELINE

1921　　1923　　1925

Lexington

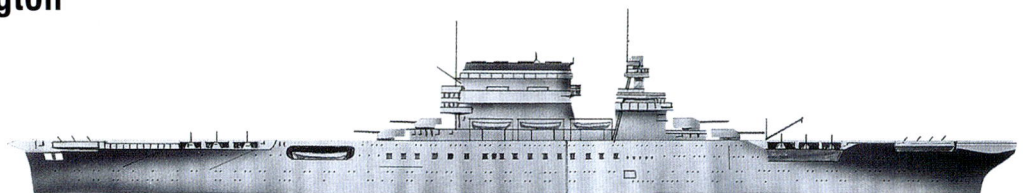

Laid down in 1921 as a battlecruiser, the design of Lexington was changed to that of an aircraft carrier. With a 137m x 21m (450ft x 70ft) hangar, it remained for many years the world's largest aircraft carrier. In 1942 it was set on fire during action with Japanese forces, and was scuttled by the US destroyer Phelps.

SPECIFICATIONS	
Type:	US aircraft carrier
Displacement:	48,463 tonnes (47,700 tons)
Dimensions:	270.6m x 32.2m x 9.9m (88ft x 105ft 8in x 32ft 6in)
Machinery:	Quadruple screws, turbo electric drive
Top speed:	33.2 knots
Main armament:	Eight 203mm (8in) guns, twelve 127mm (5in)
Armour:	178–127mm (7–5in) belt, 50mm (2in) deck
Aircraft:	90
Complement:	2327
Launched:	October 1925

Akagi

Akagi was intended as a 41,820 tonne (41,161 ton) battlecruiser. Built to dispatch up to 60 aircraft, it was later modified to carry heavier planes. Akagi led the Japanese carrier assault on Pearl Harbor on 7 December 1941. Seven months later, it was destroyed by US dive-bombers at the Battle of Midway.

SPECIFICATIONS	
Type:	Japanese aircraft carrier
Displacement:	29,580 tonnes (29,114 tons)
Dimensions:	249m x 30.5m x 8.1m (816ft 11in x 100ft x 26ft 7in)
Machinery:	Quadruple screws, turbines
Top speed:	32.5 knots
Main armament:	Ten 203mm (8in) guns, twelve 119mm (4.7in) guns
Armour:	152mm (6in) belt
Aircraft:	66 + 25 reserve
Launched:	1925

Aquila

The cruise ship Roma was requisitioned by the Italian Navy in 1941 and converted into the first Italian aircraft carrier. Powerful engines were installed and a second underwater keel, into which cement was poured to increase stability. Aquila never saw service, was scuttled, refloated in 1946 and scrapped in 1951.

SPECIFICATIONS	
Type:	Italian aircraft carrier
Displacement:	28,810 tonnes (28,356 tons)
Dimensions:	231.5m x 29.4m x 7.3m (759ft 6in x 96ft 5in x 24ft)
Machinery:	Quadruple screws, geared turbines
Top speed:	32 knots
Main armament:	Eight 135mm (5.3in) guns
Armour:	600mm (23.5in) reinforced concrete on bulge, 76mm (3in) steel plate on fuel tanks and magazines
Aircraft:	36
Complement:	1165 plus 243 aviation personnel
Launched:	1926

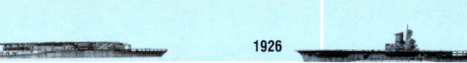

SHIP TYPES 1900–1929

Dreadnought

With the appearance of *Dreadnought,* a more advanced era of warship construction began, as well as a British–German arms race. The first 'all big gun' capital ship, it made previous battleships obsolete. Every navy now had to have 'dreadnoughts'. *Dreadnought* was scrapped in 1923, by which time it was itself obsolete.

Dreadnought

Dreadnought was the first battleship of her era to have a uniform main battery, rather than having a few large guns complemented by a heavy secondary battery of somewhat smaller guns. *Dreadnought* was the fastest battleship in the world at the time of its completion.

SPECIFICATIONS	
Type:	British battleship
Displacement:	22,194 tonnes (21,845 tons)
Dimensions:	160.4m x 25m x 8m (526ft 3in x 82ft x 26ft 3in)
Machinery:	Quadruple screws, turbines
Top speed:	21.6 knots
Main armament:	Ten 304mm (12in) guns
Armour:	203–280mm (8–11in) belt, 280mm (11in) on turrets
Launched:	February 1906

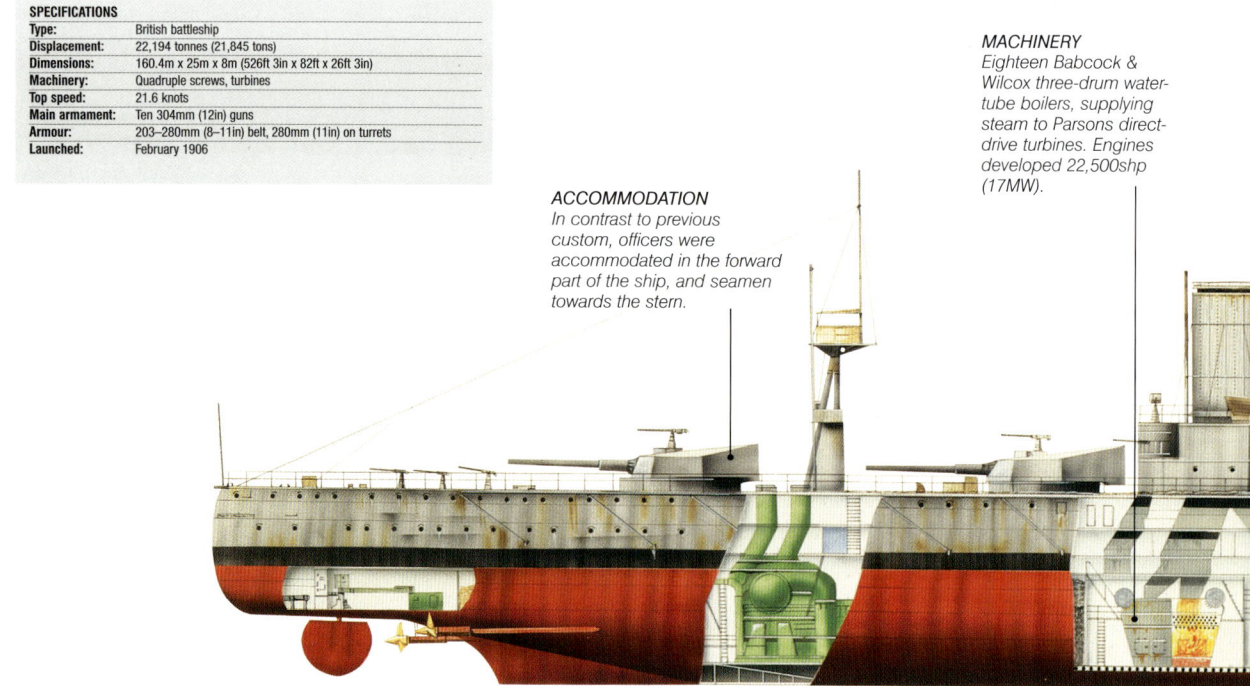

ACCOMMODATION
In contrast to previous custom, officers were accommodated in the forward part of the ship, and seamen towards the stern.

MACHINERY
Eighteen Babcock & Wilcox three-drum water-tube boilers, supplying steam to Parsons direct-drive turbines. Engines developed 22,500shp (17MW).

DREADNOUGHT

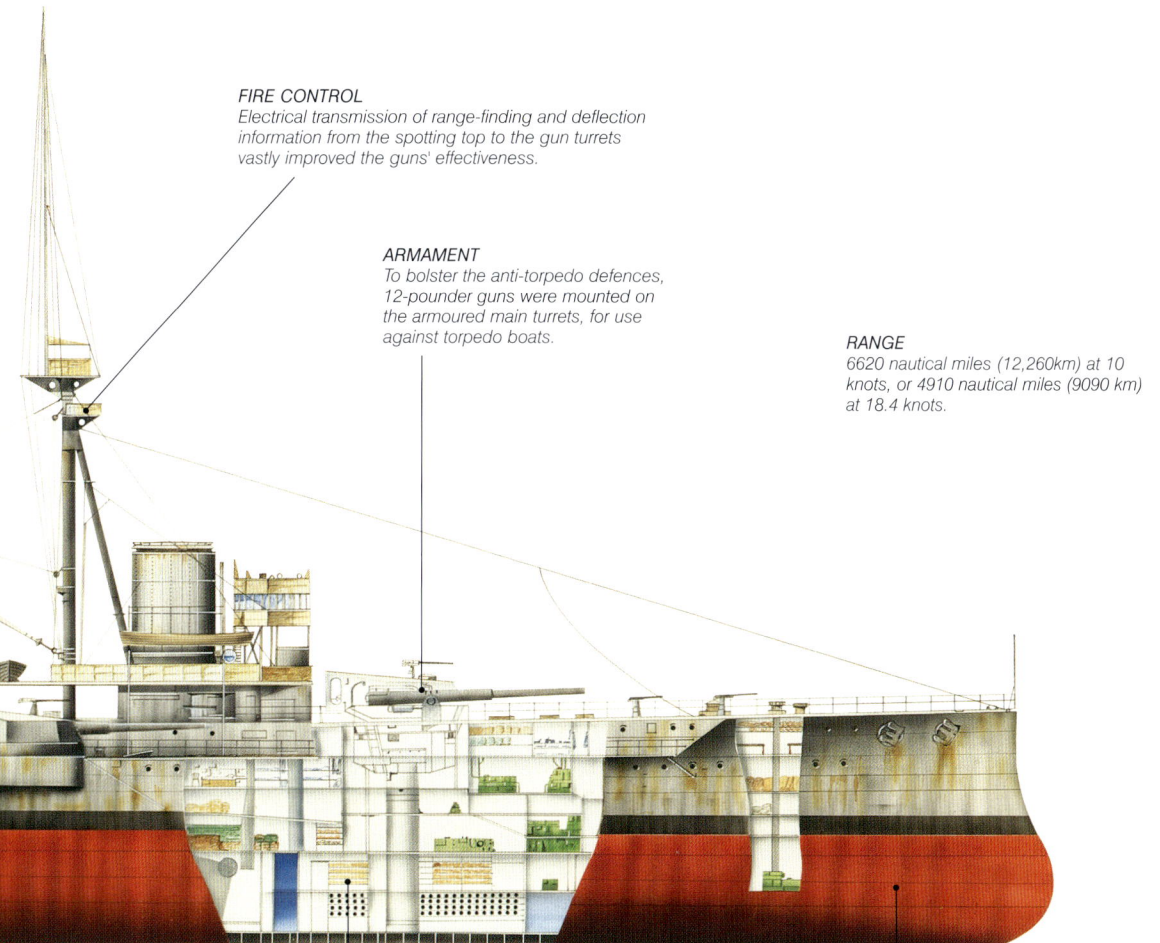

FIRE CONTROL
Electrical transmission of range-finding and deflection information from the spotting top to the gun turrets vastly improved the guns' effectiveness.

ARMAMENT
To bolster the anti-torpedo defences, 12-pounder guns were mounted on the armoured main turrets, for use against torpedo boats.

RANGE
6620 nautical miles (12,260km) at 10 knots, or 4910 nautical miles (9090 km) at 18.4 knots.

MAGAZINES
Shells were stored inside heavy armour plating and raised by hoist to the gun-turrets. Eight could be fired in a simultaneous broadside.

HULL
Its 'ram' was a modest one, but Dreadnought rammed and sank the German U-29 in the North Sea in March 1915.

Advent of the Dreadnought

New thinking in battleship design was going on in several countries around 1900. The appearance of HMS *Dreadnought* in 1906 confirmed and accelerated the trend towards an 'all big gun' ship that had weapons of uniform calibre, and which was driven by steam turbines and had heavy armour, including watertight bulkheads.

Conqueror

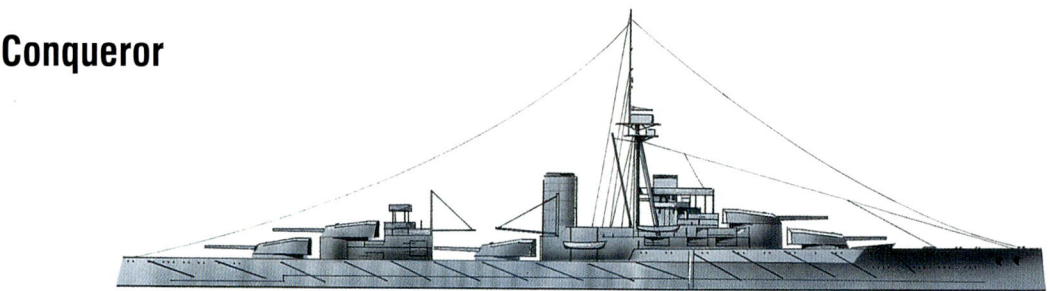

New 342mm (13.5in) guns firing 634kg (1400lb) shells to a range of 21,936m (24,000yds) made *Conqueror* one of the first 'super dreadnoughts', forming the Grand Fleet's 2nd Battle Squadron. Heavy guns were mounted on the centre-line, and it carried three 533mm (21in) torpedo tubes. It was broken up in 1922.

SPECIFICATIONS	
Type:	British battleship
Displacement:	26,284 tonnes (25,870 tons)
Dimensions:	177m x 27m x 9m (581ft x 88ft 7in x 28ft)
Machinery:	Quadruple screws, turbines
Top speed:	21 knots
Main armament:	Ten 342mm (13.5 in) guns, sixteen 102mm (4in) guns
Armour:	203–305mm (8–12in) belt, 279mm (11in) on turrets
Complement:	752
Launched:	May 1911

Monarch

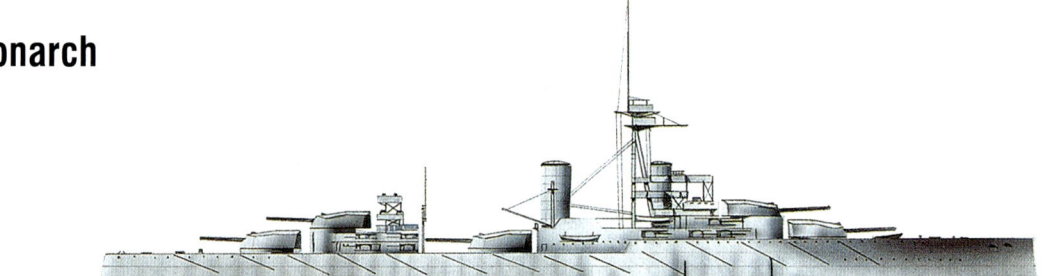

With an increase of 2540 tonnes (2500 tons) displacement over contemporary dreadnoughts, *Monarch* and its sisters were 'super dreadnoughts', the first capital ships to carry all the main guns on the centreline. Side armour rose to upper deck level 5m (17ft) above the waterline. *Monarch* was sunk as a target in 1925.

SPECIFICATIONS	
Type:	British battleship
Displacement:	26,284 tonnes (25,870 tons)
Dimensions:	177m x 26.9m x 8.7m (580ft x 88ft 6in x 28ft 9in)
Machinery:	Quadruple screws, turbines
Top speed:	20.8 knots
Main armament:	Ten 343mm (13.5in) guns, sixteen 102mm (4in)
Armour:	203–305mm (8–12in) belt, 280mm (11 in) on turrets
Launched:	March 1911

TIMELINE

1911   1913

Queen Elizabeth

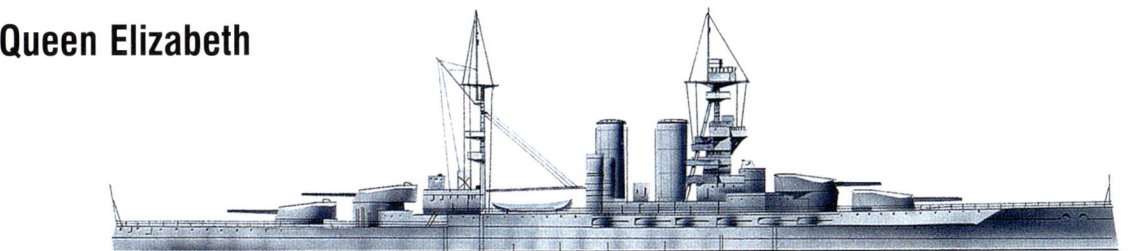

Marking a major advance in battleship development, this was the first capital ship to be built with oil-burning boilers, but her reliance upon oil fuel prompted forecasts of disaster if oil supplies should be interrupted. The following *Revenge* class carried both coal and oil fuel. *Queen Elizabeth* was scrapped in 1948/49.

SPECIFICATIONS	
Type:	British battleship
Displacement:	33,548 tonnes (33,020 tons)
Dimensions:	196.8m x 27.6m x 10m (646ft x 90ft 6in x 30ft)
Machinery:	Quadruple screws, turbines
Top speed:	23 knots
Main armament:	Eight 380mm (15in) guns, sixteen 152mm (6in) guns
Armour:	330–152mm (13–6in) belt, 330–279mm (13–11.5in) turrets, 76–25mm (3–1in) decks
Complement:	1297
Launched:	October 1913

Erin

Built for the Imperial Ottoman Navy, *Erin* was seized by the Royal Navy prior to completion, and served with the Grand Fleet in World War I, including participation in the Battle of Jutland. Beamier than most British battleships, refitted in 1917, it was placed in reserve in 1919 and broken up in 1922.

SPECIFICATIONS	
Type:	British battleship
Displacement:	25,654 tonnes (25,250 tons)
Dimensions:	170.5m x 27.9m x 8.6m (559ft 5in x 91ft 6in x 28ft 5in)
Machinery:	Quadruple screws, turbines
Main armament:	Ten 343mm (13.5in) guns
Armour:	300–100mm (12–4in) belt, 76–38mm (3–1.5in) deck, 280mm (11in) turret facings
Complement:	1070
Launched:	September 1913

Warspite

Warspite belonged to the *Queen Elizabeth* class, but displacement was increased by 2540 tonnes (2500 tons), and 6m (20ft) were added to the length. The 381mm (15in) guns fired an 871kg (1916lb) shell to a range of 32,000m (35,000yd). Active in both world wars, *Warspite* was scrapped in 1948.

SPECIFICATIONS	
Type:	British battleship
Displacement:	33,548 tonnes (33,020 tons)
Dimensions:	197m x 28m x 9m (646ft 9in x 90ft 6in x 29ft 10in)
Machinery:	Quadruple screws, turbines
Main armament:	Eight 381mm (15in) guns, sixteen 152mm (6in) guns
Armour:	102–330mm (4–13in) belt, 127–330mm (5–13in) on turrets, 102–254mm (4–10in) on barbettes
Launched:	November 1913

SHIP TYPES 1900–1929

Dreadnoughts of Other Navies: Part 1

Between 1906 and 1914, many new battleships on the Dreadnought model were built. Most notable was the rivalry between Great Britain and Germany, but other countries were equipping themselves with big-gun ships for long-range action.

Michigan

SPECIFICATIONS	
Type:	US battleship
Displacement:	18,186 tonnes (17,900 tons)
Dimensions:	138.2m x 24.5m x 7.5m (453ft 5in x 80ft 4in x 24ft 7in)
Machinery:	Twin screws, vertical triple expansion engines
Service speed:	18.5 knots
Main armament:	Eight 305mm (12in) guns, twenty-two 76mm (3in) guns
Armour:	228–305mm (9–12in) belt, 203–305mm (8–12in) on turrets
Complement:	869
Launched:	December 1906

Michigan was designed before, but built after, Britain's epoch-making *Dreadnought*. Most of the 76mm (3in) guns were concentrated in a box battery amidships, with the rest on the upper deck. Cage masts greatly reduced the target area offered to enemy gunners. *Michigan* was stricken in 1923.

Nassau

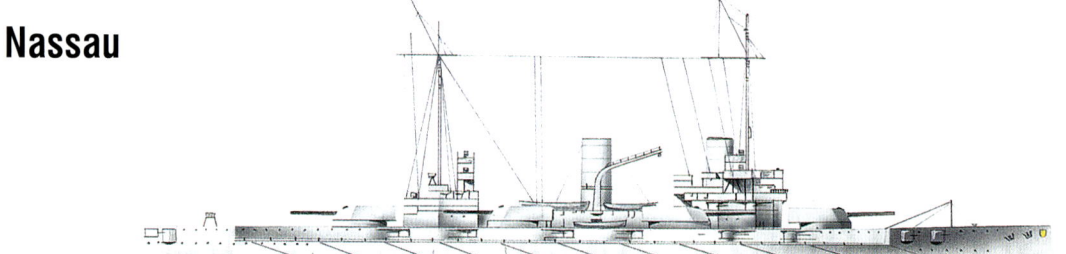

SPECIFICATIONS	
Type:	German battleship
Displacement:	20,533 tonnes (20,210 tons)
Dimensions:	146m x 27m x 8.5m (479ft 4in x 88ft 3in x 27ft 10in)
Machinery:	Triple screws, vertical triple expansion engines
Top speed:	20 knots
Main armament:	Twelve 280mm (11in) guns, twelve 150mm (5.9in) guns
Armour:	100–80mm (11–8in) belt, 280–220mm (11–8.6in) on turrets, 80mm (3.2in) deck
Complement:	1008
Launched:	March 1908

Nassau and three sisters were Germany's first dreadnought-type battleships, laid down in 1906. Shorter and wider than the British dreadnought, they had strong armour protection but carried less heavy guns. They also had a substantial secondary armament. *Nassau* was scrapped in 1921.

TIMELINE 1906   1908   1910

Dante Alighieri

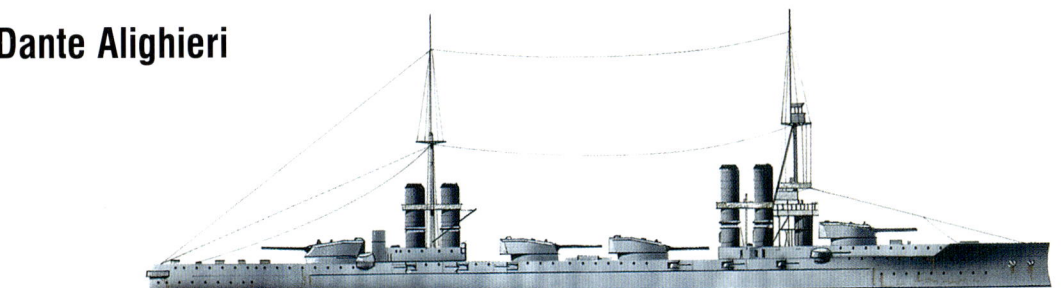

Italy's first dreadnought, designed by Engineering Admiral Masdea, was the first battleship to mount its big guns in triple turrets on the centreline, for maximum broadside fire. During World War I it was the flagship of the Southern Adriatic Fleet. Reconstructed in 1923 with a single tripod mast, it was scrapped in 1928.

SPECIFICATIONS	
Type:	Italian battleship
Displacement:	22,149 tonnes (21,800 tons)
Dimensions:	168m x 26.5m x 10m (551ft 2in x 87ft 3in x 31ft 10in)
Machinery:	Quadruple screws, turbines
Top speed:	22 knots
Armour:	152–249mm (6–9.8in) belt, 280mm (11in) on turrets
Complement:	987
Launched:	August 1910

Conte di Cavour

Conte di Cavour was completed in 1914, but a rebuild in the 1930s made it a virtually new ship. Sunk at Taranto by torpedoes dropped from British aircraft, it was refloated and towed to Trieste. Rebuilt, it was seized in September 1943 by the Germans, and sunk by bombs in 1945. The remains were broken up after 1945.

SPECIFICATIONS	
Type:	Italian battleship
Displacement:	29,496 tonnes (29,032 tons)
Dimensions:	186m x 28m x 9m (611ft 6in x 91ft 10in x 30ft)
Machinery:	Twin screws, turbines
Top speed:	21.5 knots
Main armament:	Ten 320mm (12.6in) guns, twelve 120mm (4.7in) guns
Armour:	250–127mm (10–5in) belt, 280mm (11in) on turrets, 170mm (6.6in) deck
Complement:	1136
Launched:	October 1911

Bretagne

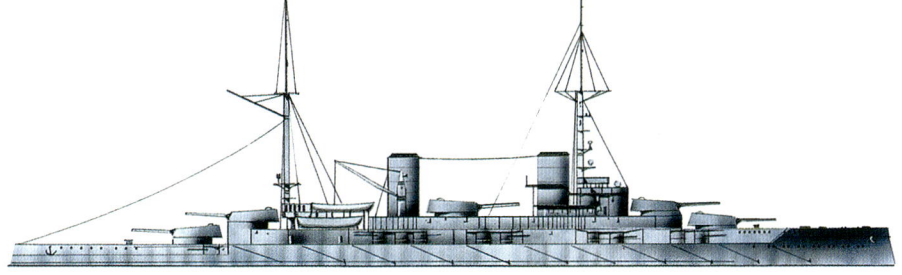

Based on the design of the *Courbet* class, *Bretagne* served in the Mediterranean from 1916 to 1918. It was modernized between the wars. On the surrender of France in 1940, and the French refusal to allow their fleet to leave port, *Bretagne* was destroyed with other ships by British guns and planes on 3 July 1940.

SPECIFICATIONS	
Type:	French battleship
Displacement:	29,420 tonnes (28,956 tons)
Dimensions:	166m x 27m x 10m (544ft 8in x 88ft 3in x 32ft 2in)
Machinery:	Quadruple screws, geared turbines
Top speed:	20 knots
Main armament:	Ten 340mm (13.4in) guns
Armour:	270–180mm (10.6–7in) belt, 430–250mm (16.8–9.8in) on turrets, 50mm (2in) deck
Complement:	1113
Launched:	April 1913

1911

1913

Dreadnoughts of Other Navies: Part 2

This was the high period of the battleship, when it was still the prime weapon of war, a symbol of national prestige as well as a defence of national security. Attack from the air was scarcely considered. An earlier generation of capital ships used net defences against torpedoes; the dreadnought relied on armour and speed.

Gangut

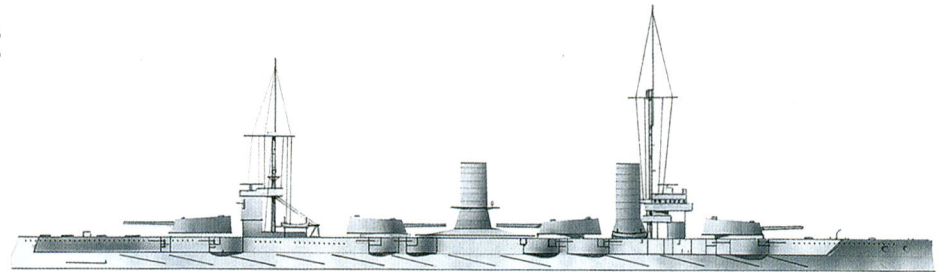

SPECIFICATIONS	
Type:	Russian battleship
Displacement:	26,264 tonnes (25,850 tons)
Dimensions:	182.9m x 26.5m x 8.3m (600ft x 87ft x 27ft 3in)
Machinery:	Quadruple screws, turbines
Main armament:	Twelve 305mm (12in) guns, sixteen 119mm (4.7in) guns
Armour:	102–226mm (4–8.9in) belt, 127–203mm (5–8in) on turrets, 203mm (8in) on barbettes
Complement:	1125
Launched:	October 1911

Gangut and its three sisters were Russia's first dreadnoughts. Russian industry could not produce enough high tensile steel, so an ingenious construction method was used. Building time was lengthy, and *Gangut* was not ready until 1914. Renamed *Oktyabrskaya Revolutsia* in 1919, it was scrapped in 1956–59.

España

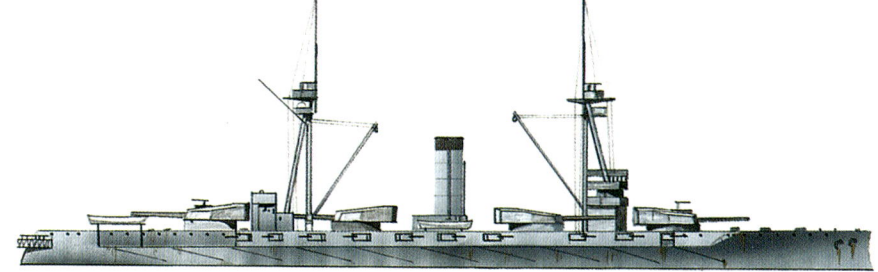

SPECIFICATIONS	
Type:	Spanish battleship
Displacement:	15,991 tonnes (15,740 tons)
Dimensions:	140m x 24m x 7.8m (459ft x 78ft 9in x 25ft 7in)
Machinery:	Quadruple screws, turbines
Top speed:	19.5 knots
Main armament:	Eight 304mm (12in) guns, twenty 102mm (4in) guns
Armour:	76–203mm (3–8in) belt, plus 76mm (3in) on battery, 203mm (8in) on turrets
Complement:	854
Launched:	February 1912

Of modest size for a dreadnought, *España* and its two sister ships were built to fit into unmodernized naval dockyards. On 26 August 1923, *España* hit an uncharted reef off Morocco and could not be salvaged. *Alfonso XIII*, one of the others, acquired the name in 1931, but was sunk by a mine in 1937.

Grosser Kurfürst

SPECIFICATIONS	
Type:	German battleship
Displacement:	28,598 tonnes (28,148 tons)
Dimensions:	175.7m x 29.5m x 8.3m (576ft 5in x 96ft 9in x 27ft 3in)
Machinery:	Triple screws, turbines
Service speed:	21 knots
Main armament:	Ten 305mm (12in) guns, fourteen 150mm (5.9in) guns, eight 86mm (3.4in) guns
Armour:	350–120mm (13.8–4.7in) belt, 300mm (11.8in) on turrets, 100mm (3.9in) deck
Complement:	1150
Launched:	May 1913

Grosser Kurfürst was a greatly improved version of the *Helgoland* type, with turbine engines and superfiring guns aft, allowing the broadside to be increased from six to ten 305mm (12in) guns. It fought at Jutland but at the end of World War I it was scuttled at Scapa Flow in 1919. It was raised for scrapping in 1936.

Nevada

SPECIFICATIONS	
Type:	US battleship
Displacement:	29,362 tonnes (28,900 tons)
Dimensions:	177.7m x 29m x 9.5m (583ft 3in x 95ft 3in x 31ft)
Machinery:	Twin screws, turbines
Top speed:	20.5 knots
Main armament:	Ten 355mm (14in) guns, twenty-one 127mm (5in) guns
Armour:	203–343mm (8–13.5in) belt, 228–406mm (9–18in) on turrets
Complement:	1049
Launched:	July 1914

With *Nevada,* its first battleship with triple turrets, the US Navy adopted the 'all-or-nothing' protection principle, applying the thickest possible armour to vital areas, and leaving the rest virtually unprotected. Reconstructed in 1927–30, *Nevada* supported the Normandy landings. It was sunk off Hawaii as a target in 1948.

Gustaf V

SPECIFICATIONS	
Type:	Swedish battleship
Displacement:	7757 tonnes (7635 tons)
Dimensions:	121.6m x 18.6m x 6.7m (399ft x 61ft x 22ft)
Machinery:	Twin screw, geared turbines
Top speed:	22.5 knots
Main Armament:	Four 283mm (11.1in) guns, eight 152mm (6in) guns, six 75mm (3in) guns
Armour:	200–60mm (7.8–2.4in) belt, 200–100mm (7.8–3.9in) on turrets
Complement:	443
Launched:	1918

This ship, one of Sweden's three 'pocket battleships', received many modifications in its life, including a tripod mast, the trunking of its two funnels into one, and partial conversion to oil burning. Anti-aircraft guns replaced some of the earlier armament. Serving until 1957, it was broken up in 1970.

SHIP TYPES 1900–1929

British & Australian Battlecruisers

The concept of the battlecruiser grew out of the armoured cruiser. It combined armament almost equal to that of a battleship with the speed of a cruiser. Inevitably this meant less armour protection, leaving it vulnerable in fleet actions.

Inflexible

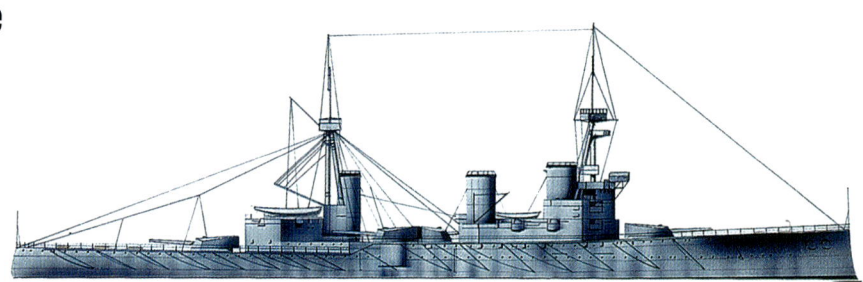

In 1904, the Japanese *Tsukuba* and *Ibuki* cruisers prompted the British Admiralty to develop the battlecruiser, starting with *Inflexible* and its sisters. *Inflexible* and *Invincible* sank *Scharnhorst* and *Gneisenau* in December 1914. *Invincible* was destroyed at Jutland in 1916. *Inflexible* and *Indomitable* were scrapped in 1922.

SPECIFICATIONS	
Type:	British battlecruiser
Displacement:	20,320 tonnes (20,000 tons)
Dimensions:	172.8m x 23.9m x 8m (567ft x 78ft 5in x 26ft 8in)
Machinery:	Quadruple screws, turbines
Service speed:	25 knots
Main armament:	Eight 305mm (12in) guns, sixteen 102mm (4in) guns
Armour:	102–152mm (4–6in) belt, 178mm (7in) on turrets
Launched:	June 1907

Lion

Lion was bigger than most battleships. Its biggest guns were mounted in twin turrets, two forward with one superfiring, one aft and one amidships between the second and third funnels. It was Beatty's flagship at Jutland in 1916, where speed instead of armour proved a failure in battle. *Lion* was scrapped in 1922.

SPECIFICATIONS	
Type:	British battlecruiser
Displacement:	30,154 tonnes (29,680 tons)
Dimensions:	213.3m x 27m x 8.7m (700ft x 88ft 6in x 28ft 10in)
Machinery:	Quadruple screws, turbines
Service speed:	26 knots
Main armament:	Eight 343mm (13.5in) guns, sixteen 102mm (4.2in) guns
Armour:	127–228mm (5–9in) main belt, 102–152mm (4–6in) upper belt, 102–228mm (4–9in) on turrets
Complement:	997
Launched:	August 1910

TIMELINE

1907   1910   1911

BRITISH & AUSTRALIAN BATTLECRUISERS

Australia

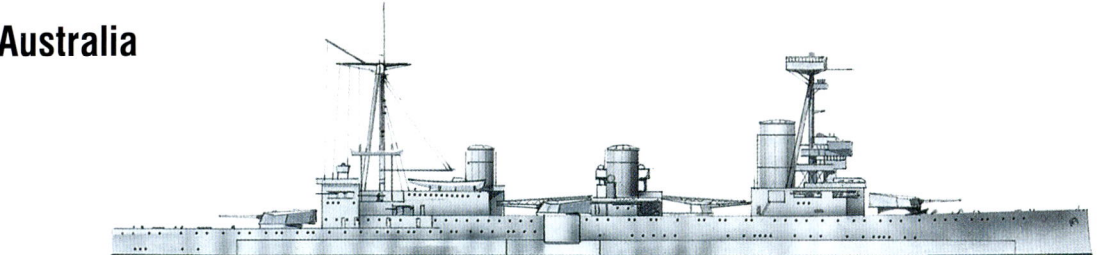

SPECIFICATIONS	
Type:	Australian battlecruiser
Displacement:	21,640 tonnes (21,300 tons)
Dimensions:	180m x 24.3m x 9m (590ft x 80ft x 30ft)
Machinery:	Four screws, geared turbines
Top speed:	26.9 knots
Main armament:	Eight 305mm (12in) guns
Armour:	152mm (6in) belt
Launched:	October 1911

The flagship of the new Commonwealth's navy, *Australia* served with the British Grand Fleet in 1915–18, and was twice damaged in collisions. Though fast, reduced armour protection of this class was responsible for the loss of its sister ship *Indefatigable* at Jutland. It was sunk in target practice off Sydney in 1924.

Tiger

SPECIFICATIONS	
Type:	British battlecruiser
Displacement:	35,723 tonnes (35,160 tons)
Dimensions:	214.6m x 27.6m x 8.6m (704ft x 90ft 6in x 28ft 5in)
Machinery:	Quadruple screws, turbines
Service speed:	30 knots
Main armament:	Eight 343mm (13.5in) guns, twelve 152mm (6in) guns
Armour:	229–76mm (9–3in) belt, 229mm (9in) on turrets, 76–25mm (3–1in) decks
Complement:	1121
Launched:	December 1913

Tiger was the fastest, as well as the largest, capital ship of its day. It was also the last coal-burning capital ship in the Royal Navy, and the only British battlecruiser to carry 152mm (6in) guns. *Tiger* was damaged in the Dogger Bank and Jutland battles. A refit was completed in 1924 and it was scrapped in 1932.

Hood

SPECIFICATIONS	
Type:	British battlecruiser
Displacement:	45,923 tonnes (45,200 tons)
Dimensions:	262m x 31.7m x 8.7m (860ft x104ft x 28ft 6in)
Machinery:	Quadruple screws, turbines
Top speed:	32 knots
Main armament:	Eight 381mm (15in) guns, twelve 140mm (5.5 in) guns
Armour:	305–127mm (12–5in) belt and barbettes, 381–279mm (15–11in) on turrets, 76–26mm (3–1in) deck
Complement:	1147
Launched:	August 1918

Hood was to have been the first of four battlecruisers, but was the only one completed. Its engines developed 144,000hp, and its range was 7600km (4000 miles) at 10 knots. Considered the most powerful warship afloat, it was sunk on 21 May 1941 by the German battleship *Bismarck* and the cruiser *Prinz Eugen*.

SHIP TYPES 1900–1929

Derfflinger

With a well-judged balance between armour and armament, *Derfflinger* and its sister ships *Hindenburg* and *Lützow* are considered the finest capital ships of their period. In 1916 *Derfflinger* severely damaged HMS *Queen Mary* and survived hits from 10 380mm (15in) and 10 304mm (12in) shells. It was scuttled at Scapa Flow in 1919.

Derfflinger

Derfflinger was part of a force of German warships that bombarded Scarborough and Whitby, on the northeast coast of England; shortly afterwards, in January 1915, it was seriously damaged in the Battle of Dogger Bank. In the following year it was involved in the Battle of Jutland where despite being badly damanged *Derfflinger* survived.

SPECIFICATIONS	
Type:	German battlecruiser
Displacement:	30,706 tonnes (30,223 tons)
Dimensions:	210m x 29m x 8m (689ft x 95ft 2in x 27ft 3in)
Machinery:	Quadruple screws, turbines
Top speed:	28 knots
Main armament:	Eight 304mm (12in) guns
Armour:	300mm (11.8 in) waterline belt
Launched:	July 1913

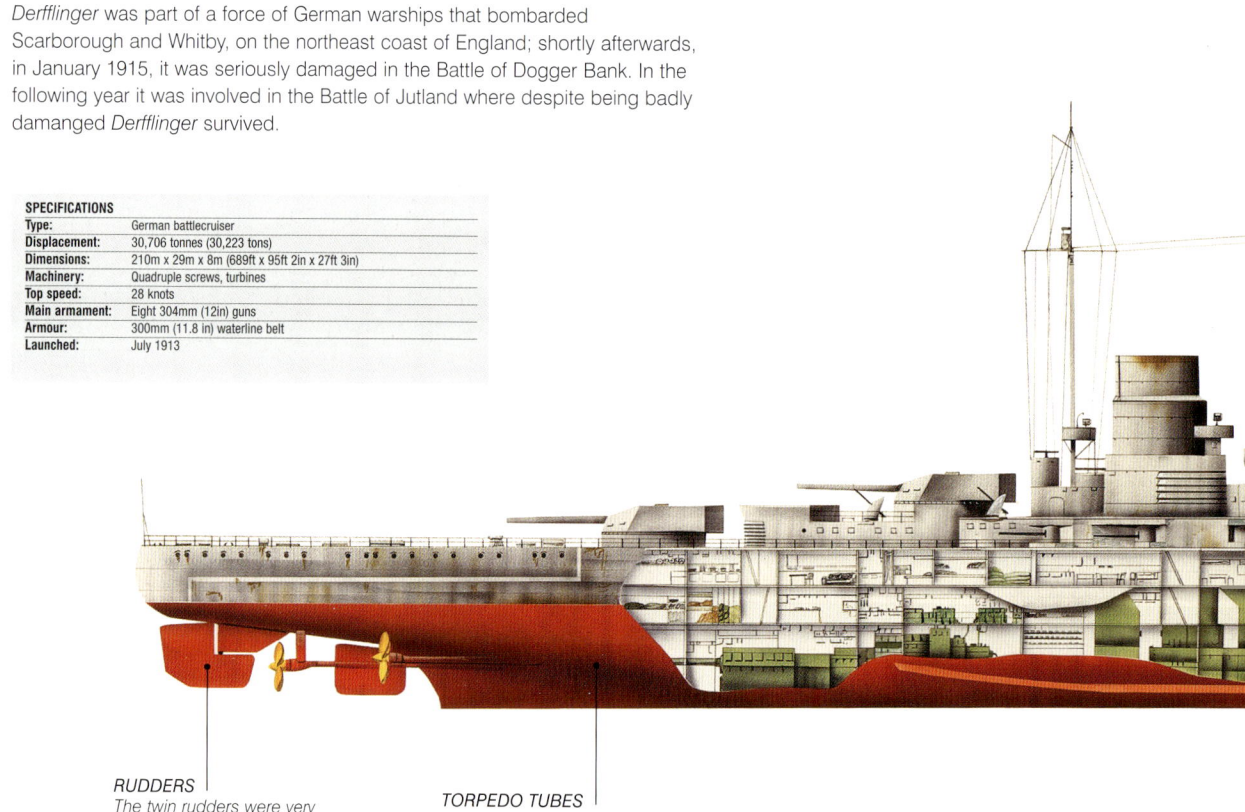

RUDDERS
The twin rudders were very effective. The ship might heel by 11° on a tight turn, and anti-roll tanks were fitted.

TORPEDO TUBES
Another unusual feature was four underwater torpedo tubes, two centrally placed, one at the bow and one at the stern.

DERFFLINGER

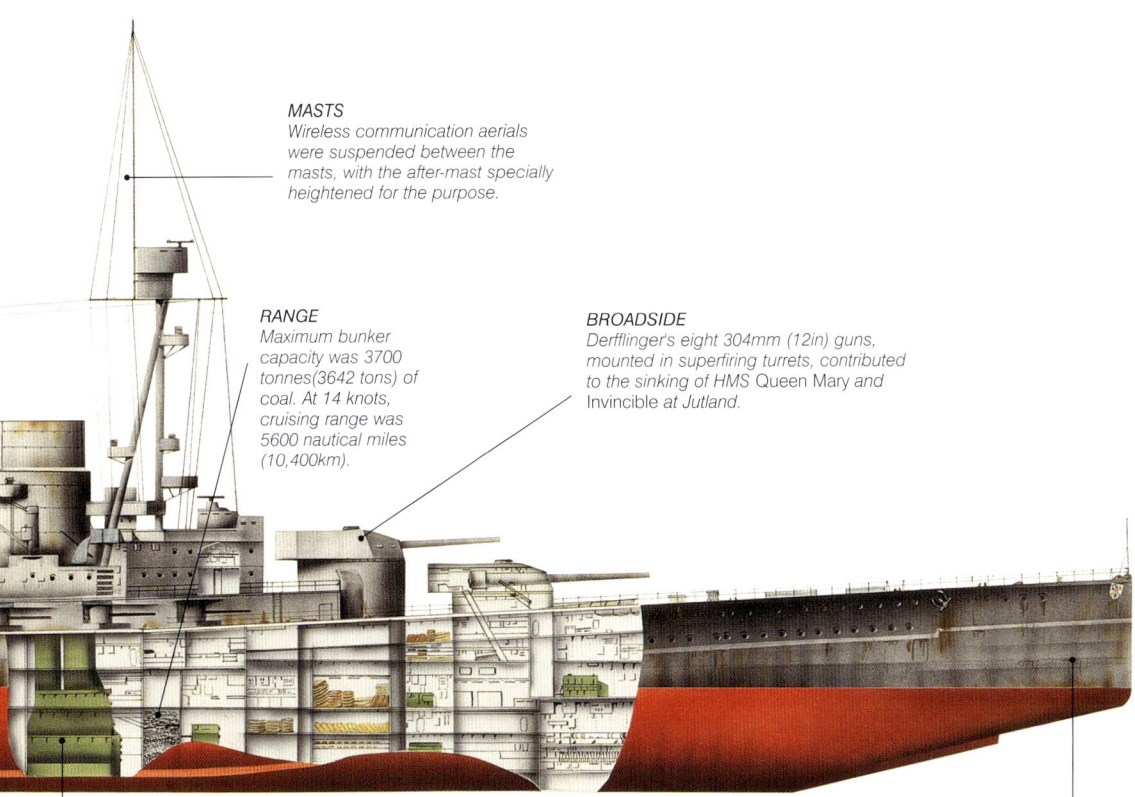

MASTS
Wireless communication aerials were suspended between the masts, with the after-mast specially heightened for the purpose.

RANGE
Maximum bunker capacity was 3700 tonnes (3642 tons) of coal. At 14 knots, cruising range was 5600 nautical miles (10,400km).

BROADSIDE
Derfflinger's eight 304mm (12in) guns, mounted in superfiring turrets, contributed to the sinking of HMS Queen Mary and Invincible at Jutland.

HULL
The faired bow design, reminiscent of an ice-breaker, was unique to the Derfflinger class among major warships.

MACHINERY
Fourteen coal-fired, and eight oil-fired boilers, drove two sets of high and low pressure turbines, with a shaft horse-power of 76,634 (57,000kW).

SHIP TYPES 1900–1929

German & Japanese Battlecruisers

Both Germany and Japan were expanding their naval power in the years before 1914, and both embraced the battlecruiser. German battlecruisers were less heavily armed than British ones, but more heavily armoured – an advantage in action.

Tsukuba

SPECIFICATIONS	
Type:	Japanese battlecruiser
Displacement:	15,646 tonnes (15,400 tons)
Dimensions:	137m x 23m x 8m (449ft 10in x 75ft 6in x 26ft 3in)
Machinery:	Twin screws, vertical triple expansion engines
Top speed:	20.5 knots
Main armament:	Four 305mm (12in) guns, twelve 152mm (6in) guns
Armour:	102–178mm (4–7in) belt, 178mm (7in) on turrets and barbettes, 76mm (3in) deck
Launched:	December 1905

Built at Kure Naval Dockyard, *Tsukuba* was first classified as an armoured cruiser. When commissioned in 1907, it was already a lightweight among battlecruisers. In January 1917, the magazine caught fire and it blew up in Yokosuka Bay. It was later raised and broken up.

Von der Tann

SPECIFICATIONS	
Type:	German battlecruiser
Displacement:	22,150 tonnes (21,802 tons)
Dimensions:	172m x 26.6m x 8m (563ft 4in x 87ft 3in x 26ft 7in)
Machinery:	Quadruple screws, turbines
Top speed:	27.7 knots
Main armament:	Eight 280mm (11in) guns, ten 150mm (5.9in) guns
Armour:	100–248mm (3.9–9.8in) belt, 228mm (9in) on barbettes and turrets, 50–76mm (2–3in) deck
Complement:	910
Launched:	March 1909

Germany's first battlecruiser, *Von der Tann* was the first German capital ship with turbines. Though hit by four shells at the Battle of Jutland, which caused fires and put the main guns out of action, it reached home. Scuttled at Scapa Flow in 1919, it was raised in December 1930, and broken up between 1931 and 1934.

TIMELINE 1905   1909   1911

GERMAN AND JAPANESE BATTLECRUISERS

Goeben

SPECIFICATIONS	
Type:	German battlecruiser
Displacement:	25,704 tonnes (25,300 tons)
Dimensions:	186.5m x 29.5m x 9.2m (611ft 10in x 96ft 9in x 30ft 2in)
Machinery:	Quadruple screws, turbines
Top speed:	28 knots
Main armament:	Ten 280mm (11in) guns, twelve 150mm (5.9in) guns
Armour:	266–95mm (10.5–3.7in) belt, 50mm (2in) deck
Complement:	1107
Launched:	March 1911

Excellent design and safety features, and heavy armament, made *Goeben* a formidable warship. Stationed in the eastern Mediterranean, it was transferred to the Turkish Navy, sinking two British ships in 1918. Renamed *Yavuz Sultan Selim*, it was modernized between 1926 and 1930, and served into the 1960s.

Haruna

SPECIFICATIONS	
Type:	Japanese battlecruiser
Displacement:	32,715 tonnes (32,200 tons)
Dimensions:	214.5m x 28m x 8.4m (703ft 9in x 91ft 10in x 27ft 6in)
Machinery:	Quadruple screws, turbines
Top speed:	27.5 knots
Main armament:	Eight 355mm (14in) guns, sixteeen 152mm (6in) guns
Armour:	76–203mm (3–8in) belt, 228mm (9in) on turrets
Launched:	November 1912

Haruna was one of the first dreadnought-type warships to be built in a Japanese yard. In 1927–28, after a major refit, it was reclassified as a battleship. The three funnels were reduced to two. New boilers were installed, and the armour increased. Sunk by US aircraft in July 1945, it was broken up in 1946.

Graf Spee

SPECIFICATIONS	
Type:	German battlecruiser
Displacement:	36,576 tonnes (36,000 tons)
Dimensions:	223m x 30.4m x 8.4m (731ft 8in x 99ft 9in x 27ft 7in)
Machinery:	Quadruple screws, turbines
Top speed:	28 knots
Main armament:	Eight 350mm (13.8in) guns, twelve 150mm (5.9in) guns
Armour:	305–120mm (12–4.7in) belt and turrets, 30mm (1.7in) deck
Complement:	1186
Launched:	September 1917

Graf Spee was an improved version of the *Hindenburg*. The main armament was updated, the guns positioned in four twin turrets, two superfiring fore and aft. Secondary armament was concentrated in a long upper deck battery. Launched in 1917, it was not completed by the end of the war, and scrapped in 1921–23.

SHIP TYPES 1900–1929

North Sea Adversaries

In a 10-year arms race, Britain and Germany both spent huge sums in constructing large warships. The Grand Fleet and the High Seas Fleet faced each other across the narrow North Sea. There was only one major confrontation, off Jutland, on 31 May 1916. The Germans came off better, but the British kept control of the seas.

Helgoland

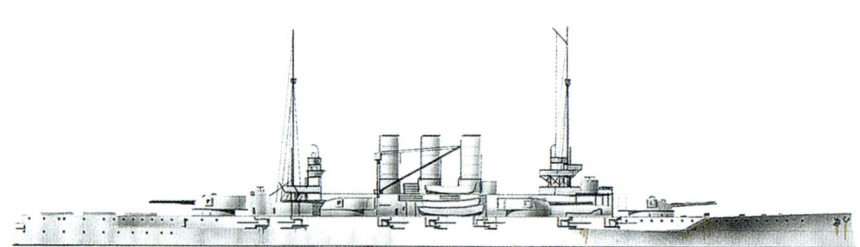

Helgoland was the last three-funnelled German battleship, and the first to be equipped with the 304mm (12in) gun as a main armament. All ships in her class served in World War I, two being damaged at the Battle of Jutland in 1916. *Helgoland* was broken up in 1924.

SPECIFICATIONS	
Type:	German battleship
Displacement:	24,700 tonnes (24,312 tons)
Dimensions:	166.4m x 28.5m x 8.3m (546ft x 93ft 6in x 27ft 6in)
Machinery:	Triple screws, triple expansion engines
Service speed:	20.3 knots
Main armament:	Twelve 304mm (12in) guns, fourteen 150mm (5.9in) guns
Armour:	102–300mm (4–11.8in) belt, 280mm (11in) on turrets, 76–170mm (3-6.7in) on casemates
Complement:	1100
Launched:	1909

Iron Duke

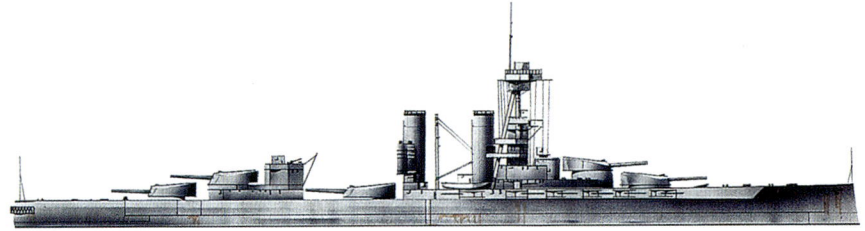

The British flagship at the Battle of Jutland, the super-dreadnought *Iron Duke* remained with the Grand Fleet until 1919, then was deployed to the Black Sea and later the Mediterranean. From 1931 it became a training ship, and was a depot ship at Scapa Flow during World War II. It was broken up in 1946.

SPECIFICATIONS	
Type:	British battleship
Displacement:	30,866 tonnes (30,380 tons)
Dimensions:	189.8m x 27.4m x 9m (622ft 9in x 90ft x 29ft 6in)
Machinery:	Quadruple screws, turbines
Top speed:	21.6 knots
Main armament:	Ten 342mm (13.5in) guns, twelve 152mm (6in) guns
Armour:	102–305mm belt (4–12in), 228mm (9in) middle belt, 51–152mm (2–6in) on battery
Complement:	1193
Launched:	October 1912

TIMELINE 1909 1912 1914

NORTH SEA ADVERSARIES

Royal Oak

Completed in 1916, *Royal Oak* was in action at Jutland. Refitted in the 1920s, it served in the Mediterranean, and after further refitting was attached to the Home Fleet in 1935. In 1939 it was assigned patrol duty in northern waters. On 13/14 October 1939, it was sunk in Scapa Flow by torpedoes fired from *U-47*.

SPECIFICATIONS	
Type:	British battleship
Displacement:	31,699 tonnes (31,200 tons)
Dimensions:	190.3m x 27m x 8.7m (624ft 3in x 88ft 6in x 28ft 7in)
Machinery:	Quadruple screws, turbines
Top speed:	23 knots
Main Armament:	Eight 381mm (15in) guns, fourteen 152mm (6in) guns
Armour:	102–25mm (4–1in) deck
Complement:	936
Launched:	1914

Barham

Barham carried newly designed 381mm (15in) guns, more accurate than the previous 343mm (13.5in) guns, and carried a bigger bursting charge. In the Battle of Jutland (1916), it was damaged, but repaired, and modernized in the 1930s. *Barham* was sunk in the Mediterranean by *U-331* on 25 November 1941.

SPECIFICATIONS	
Type:	British battleship
Displacement:	32,004 tonnes (31,500 tons)
Dimensions:	196m x 27.6m x 8.8m (643ft x 90ft 6in x 29ft)
Machinery:	Quadruple screws, turbines
Top speed:	24 knots
Main armament:	Eight 381mm (15in) guns, fourteen 152mm (6in) guns
Launched:	October 1914

Bayern

With *Bayern*, German designers matched the gunpower of the British 380mm (15in) gun battleships. *Bayern* was a stable vessel in short seas, and a good gun platform. Internal subdivision was effective and some design features were later incorporated into *Bismarck*. *Bayern* was scuttled at Scapa Flow in 1919.

SPECIFICATIONS	
Type:	German battleship
Displacement:	32,412 tonnes (32,000 tons)
Dimensions:	182.4m x 30m x 8m (598ft 5in x 99ft x 27ft 10in)
Machinery:	Triple screws, geared turbines
Top speed:	22 knots
Main armament:	Eight 380mm (15in) guns, sixteen 150mm (5.9in) guns
Armour:	350mm (13.8in) lower waterline belt, 170–249mm (6.7–9.8in) upper belt, 350mm (13.8in) on turrets
Launched:	1915

1915

SHIP TYPES 1900–1929

Imperial Japan 1900–1920

In the throes of a belated industrial revolution, with the national economy and ambition both expanding dynamically, Japan developed its navy into one of the world's most modern fleets, transforming the balance of power in the Pacific Ocean. In 1905, it inflicted a devastating defeat on the Russians at the Battle of Tsushima.

Kasuga

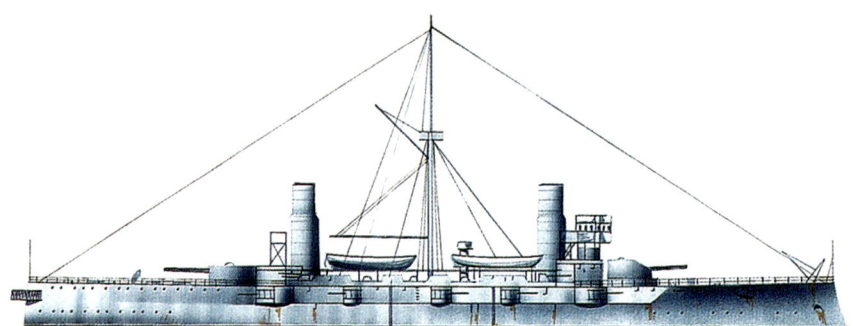

Kasuga was built for Argentina at Ansaldo, Genoa, but was purchased by Japan in 1903 just prior to completion. It was almost a duplicate of the Italian *Garibaldi* cruiser, with good protection, powerful armament and fair speed. Partially disarmed in the 1920s, it became a training ship, and was scrapped in 1948.

SPECIFICATIONS	
Type:	Japanese cruiser
Displacement:	7750 tonnes (7628 tons)
Dimensions:	111.7m x 18.9m x 7.3m (366ft 7in x 62ft x 24ft)
Machinery:	Twin screws, vertical triple expansion engines
Top speed:	20 knots
Main armament:	One 254mm (10in) gun, two 203mm (8in) guns, fourteen 152mm (6in) guns
Armour:	70–150mm (2.8–5.9in) belt, 25–38mm (.98–1.5in) deck, 100–150mm (3.9–5.9 in) on barbettes
Launched:	October 1902

Ibuki

Ibuki was the first Japanese warship to be fitted with turbine engines, developing 24,000hp. Coal supply was 2032 tonnes (2000 tons), plus 221 tonnes (218 tons) of oil fuel. *Ibuki* served as an escort for Australian troops on their way to the Dardanelles during the early part of World War I. It was scrapped in 1924.

SPECIFICATIONS	
Type:	Japanese battlecruiser
Displacement:	15,844 tonnes (15,595 tons)
Dimensions:	148m x 23m x 8m (465ft x 75ft 4in x 26ft 1in)
Machinery:	Twin screws, turbines
Top speed:	21 knots
Main armament:	Four 304mm (12in) guns, eight 203mm (8in) guns, fourteen 120mm (4.7in) guns
Armour:	102–178mm (4–7in) belt, 127–178mm (5–7in) on turrets
Complement:	820
Launched:	November 1907

TIMELINE

1902 1907 1914

IMPERIAL JAPAN 1900–1920

Fuso

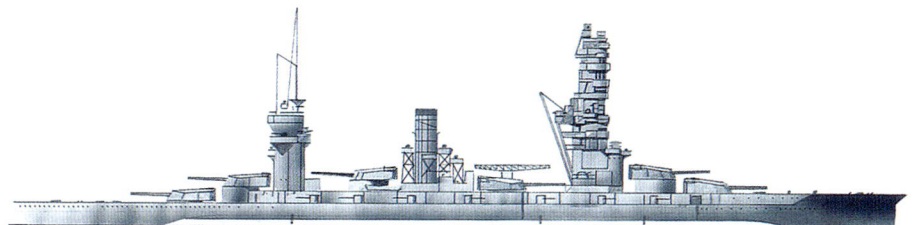

Fuso was Japan's first home-built battleship. It originally had two funnels, the first between the bridge and third turret, but this was replaced by a massive bridge structure in the 1930s. Underwater protection was improved and new machinery fitted. Fuso was sunk by gunfire and torpedoes from US ships in October 1944.

SPECIFICATIONS	
Type:	Japanese battleship
Displacement:	36,474 tonnes (35,900 tons)
Dimensions:	205m x 28.7m x 8.6m (672ft 6in x 94ft x 28ft)
Machinery:	Quadruple screws, turbines
Top speed:	23 knots
Main armament:	Twelve 357mm (14in) guns, sixteen 152mm (6in) guns
Armour:	102–306mm (4–12in) belt, 119–306mm (4.5–12in) on turrets, 204mm (8in) on barbettes
Complement:	1193
Launched:	March 1914

Ise

An improvement of the Fuso class, Ise carried twin superfiring guns amidships. It was modernized after World War I, and by 1937 had been lengthened aft by 7.6m (25ft). After Midway in June 1942, it was converted to a hybrid battleship-carrier. Sunk at Kure in early 1945, it was raised and scrapped in 1946.

SPECIFICATIONS	
Type:	Japanese battleship
Displacement:	32,576 tonnes (32,063 tons)
Dimensions:	208.2m x 28.6m x 8.8m (683ft x 94ft x 29ft)
Machinery:	Quadruple screws, turbines
Top speed:	23 knots
Main armament:	Twelve 355mm (14in) guns, twenty 140mm (5.5in) guns
Armour:	305–102mm (12–4in) belt, 305mm (12in) on turrets, 55–25mm (2.16–1in) deck
Complement:	1360
Launched:	November 1916

Nagato

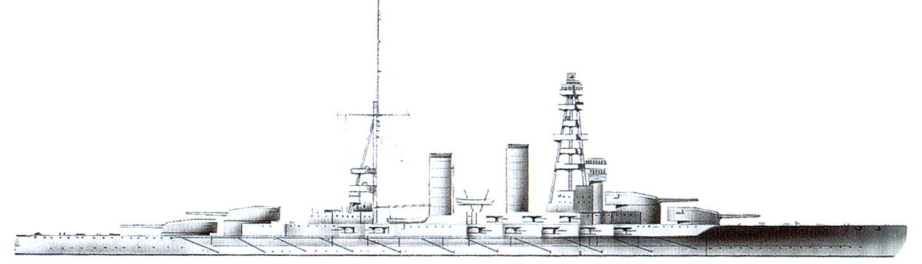

Nagato and Mutsu were first with the 406mm (16in) gun, which had a range of 40,233m (44,000yd). A tripod rose above the bridge, and in the mid-1920s the first funnel was angled back. Machinery requiring only one funnel was installed in 1934–36. Nagato was destroyed in the Bikini atomic bomb tests of July 1946.

SPECIFICATIONS	
Type:	Japanese battleship
Displacement:	39,116 tonnes (38,500 tons)
Dimensions:	215.8m x 29m x 9m (708ft x 95ft 1in x 29ft 10in)
Machinery:	Quadruple screws, turbines
Top speed:	23 knots
Main armament:	Eight 406mm (16in) guns, twenty 140mm (5.5in) guns
Launched:	November 1919

SHIP TYPES 1900–1929

Imperial Russia 1900–1917

The Russian Empire had to maintain first-rate fleets in the Baltic and Black Seas and the Pacific Ocean, a heavy demand even on so vast a country. Naval design was treated scientifically and methodically, but in the Russo–Japanese War of 1905, the Russian fleet was defeated by the Japanese at the Battle of Tsushima in May 1905.

Aurora

The armoured cruiser *Aurora* took part in the Battle of Tsushima in 1905, when it was badly damaged and interned. Anchored in the Neva river when the 1917 Russian Revolution broke out, it is credited with firing the first shots of the conflict. It remains anchored there, as a monument to the revolution.

SPECIFICATIONS	
Type:	Russian cruiser
Displacement:	6939 tonnes (6830 tons)
Dimensions:	125m x 16.7m x 6.5m (410ft x 55ft x 21ft 6in)
Machinery:	Triple screws, vertical triple expansion engines
Top speed:	19 knots
Main armament:	Eight 152mm (6in) guns
Launched:	1900

Retvisan

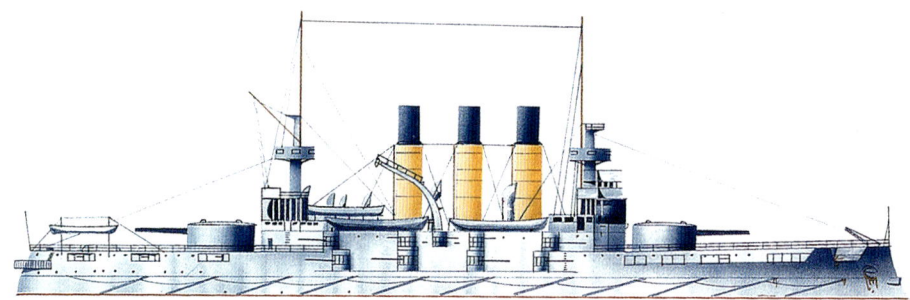

Retvisan was the only capital ship to be built for the Russians by a US yard, to standard American type, flush-decked with a central superstructure. In 1904, it was torpedoed off Port Arthur. When Port Arthur fell in 1905, it was surrendered to the Japanese. Re-named *Hizen,* it was sunk as a target in 1924.

SPECIFICATIONS	
Type:	Russian battleship
Displacement:	13,106 tonnes (12,900 tons)
Dimensions:	117.8m x 22m x 7.9m (386ft 8in x 72ft 2in x 26ft)
Machinery:	Twin screws, vertical triple expansion engines
Top speed:	18.8 knots
Main armament:	Four 305mm (12in) guns, twelve 152mm (6in) guns, twenty 11-pdr guns
Launched:	October 1900

TIMELINE

1900   1901

IMPERIAL RUSSIA 1900–1917

Tsessarevitch

SPECIFICATIONS	
Type:	Russian battleship
Displacement:	13,122 tonnes (12,915 tons)
Dimensions:	118.5m x 23.2m x 7.9m (388ft 9in x 76ft x 26ft)
Machinery:	Twin screws, vertical triple expansion engines
Top speed:	18.5 knots
Main armament:	Four 305mm (12in) guns, twelve 152mm (6in) guns, twenty 3-pdr guns
Armour:	178–254mm (7–10in) belt, 254mm (10in) on main turrets, 152mm (6in) on secondary turrets
Launched:	1901

Built in 1903, to plans based on French practice, with a high forecastle and pronounced tumblehome, *Tsessarevitch* was the flagship of the First Pacific Squadron at Port Arthur, and damaged during the Yellow Sea battle in 1904. In the Baltic in World War I, it was renamed *Grashdanin*, and scrapped in 1922.

Kniaz Souvarov

SPECIFICATIONS	
Type:	Russian battleship
Displacement:	13,732 tonnes (13,516 tons)
Dimensions:	121m x 23.2m x 8.1m (397ft x 76ft x 27ft)
Machinery:	Twin screws, vertical triple expansion engines
Top speed:	18.2 knots
Main armament:	Four 305mm (12in) guns, twelve 152mm (6in) guns
Armour:	190–152mm (7.5–6in) belt, 254–102mm (10–4in) on turrets, 76mm (3in) magazines, 55mm (2in) deck
Complement:	835
Launched:	September 1902

Rozhestvensky's flagship at Tsushima (May 1905) was a relatively short, broad-beamed vessel, *Kniaz Souvarov,* so loaded down with coal and ammunition that its main armour belt protection was below the waterline. It was sunk by Japanese torpedoes, and two other battleships of its class were also lost.

Admiral Nakhimov

SPECIFICATIONS	
Type:	Russian cruiser
Displacement:	8128 tonnes (8000 tons)
Dimensions:	154.5m x 15.4m x 5.6m (506ft 11in x 50ft 5in x 18ft)
Machinery:	Twin screws, geared turbines
Top speed:	29.5 knots
Main armament:	Fifteen 130mm (5.1in) guns
Armour:	76mm (3in) belt, 38mm (1.5in) deck
Complement:	630
Launched:	1915

This ship was launched in 1915, but the revolution delayed its completion until 1927, and it was commissioned into the Soviet fleet as *Chervona Ukrainia*. It carried six 533mm (21in) torpedo tubes. On 13 November 1941 it was sunk by German bombs while in support of action against German forces at Sevastopol.

1902

1915

SHIP TYPES 1900–1929

South American Neighbours & Rivals

National rivalries prompted the countries of South America to maintain battleworthy fleets; the arrival of a new warship in one country would lead to orders elsewhere. In general, South American capital ships had greater longevity than those of Europe.

Coronel Bolognesi

Coronel Bolognesi was a 'scout cruiser', but during its delivery voyage the boilers were allowed to run dry, causing extensive damage. It underwent a major refit in 1923–25 and was re-boilered in 1934–35, and 76mm (3in) AA guns were fitted in 1936. It was decommissioned in 1958 after exceptionally long service.

SPECIFICATIONS
Type:	Peruvian cruiser
Displacement:	3251 tonnes (3200 tons)
Dimensions:	116m x 12m x 4m (380ft x 40ft 4in x 14ft)
Machinery:	Twin screws, triple expansion engines
Top speed:	24.6 knots
Main armament:	Two 152mm (6in) guns
Launched:	November 1906

Minas Gerais

Originally designed as a pre-dreadnought battleship to answer the powerful vessels then building for Chile, the plans were modified to make it the first dreadnought built for a minor navy. It was extensively modernized in the United States in 1923, and again in Brazil from 1934 to 1937. It survived until 1954.

SPECIFICATIONS
Type:	Brazilian battleship
Displacement:	21,540 tonnes (21,200 tons)
Dimensions:	165.8m x 25.3m x 8.5m (544ft x 83ft x 27ft 10in)
Machinery:	Twin screws, vertical triple expansion engines
Top speed:	21 knots
Main armament:	Twelve 305mm (12in) guns, twenty-two 120mm (4.7in) guns
Armour:	230–102mm (9–4in) belt, 230–203mm (9–8in) on turrets
Complement:	850
Launched:	September 1908

TIMELINE

1906 1908 1909

Bahia

Bahia and her sister-ship *Rio Grande Do Sul* served in World War I, operating off north-west Africa. In 1925–26, both were re-boilered and re-engineered, giving a speed of nearly 29 knots. They served with the Allies in World War II, but in July 1945 *Bahia* was torpedoed by a U-boat, exploded, and sank within minutes.

SPECIFICATIONS	
Type:	Brazilian cruiser
Displacement:	3200 tonnes (3150 tons)
Dimensions:	122.5m x 11.9m x 4.2m (401ft 6in x 39ft x 14ft)
Machinery:	Triple screws, turbines
Main armament:	Ten 114mm (4.7in) guns
Armour:	19mm (.75in) deck, 76mm (3in) conning tower
Launched:	April 1909

Moreno

Argentina ordered two dreadnoughts in 1910. *Moreno* and its sister *Rivadavia* were modernized in 1924–25. They were converted to oil, the lattice mast forward was shortened and the pole mast aft was replaced by a tripod. Displacement increased by 1016 tonnes (1000 tons). *Moreno* was sold in 1956.

SPECIFICATIONS	
Type:	Argentinian battleship
Displacement:	30,500 tonnes (30,000 tons)
Dimensions:	173.8m x 29.4m x 8.5m (270ft 3in x 96ft 9in x 27ft 10in)
Machinery:	Triple screws, turbines
Top speed:	22.5 knots
Main armament:	Twelve 305mm (12in) guns, twelve 152mm (6in) guns
Armour:	279–203mm (11–8in) belt, 76mm (3in) deck
Complement:	1080
Launched:	September 1911

Almirante Latorre

In 1914, *Almirante Latorre*, under construction in Britain, was bought by the Royal Navy and re-named *Canada*. Completed in 1915, it was one of the most effective battleships in the fleet and saw action at the Battle of Jutland in 1916. It was returned to Chile in 1920, served until 1958 and was scrapped in 1959.

SPECIFICATIONS	
Type:	British, later Chilean battleship
Displacement:	32,634 tonnes (32,120 tons)
Dimensions:	202m x 28m x 9m (660ft 9in x 92ft x 29ft)
Machinery:	Quadruple screws, geared turbines
Main armament:	Ten 355mm (14in) guns
Armour:	230mm (9in) belt, 38mm (1.5in) deck, 250mm (10in) turret
Launched:	November 1913

1911

1913

Cruisers of the 1900s – British

Cruisers came in a variety of sizes, dependent on purpose, from small scouting vessels to large armoured ships. The only common features were the intended ability to operate as an independent unit, and a speed greater than that of capital ships. Great Britain, with its worldwide colonial empire, had the largest cruiser fleet.

Hampshire

An improved version of the *Monmouth* class, *Hampshire* had engines that developed 21,508hp, offering a good speed, one reason for its choice to carry Lord Kitchener on a mission to Russia. On 5 June 1915, with Kitchener on board, *Hampshire* struck a German mine laid by *U-75* off Cape Wrath, and sank.

SPECIFICATIONS	
Type:	British cruiser
Displacement:	11,023 tonnes (10,850 tons)
Dimensions:	144.3m x 20.8m x 7.3m (473ft 6in x 68ft 6in x 24ft)
Machinery:	Twin screws, triple expansion engines
Top speed:	22 knots
Main armament:	Four 190mm (7.5in) guns, six 152 mm (6in) guns
Armour:	51–152mm (2–6in) belt, 127mm (5in) on turrets, 152mm (6in) on casemates, 51mm (2in) main deck
Launched:	September 1903

Foresight

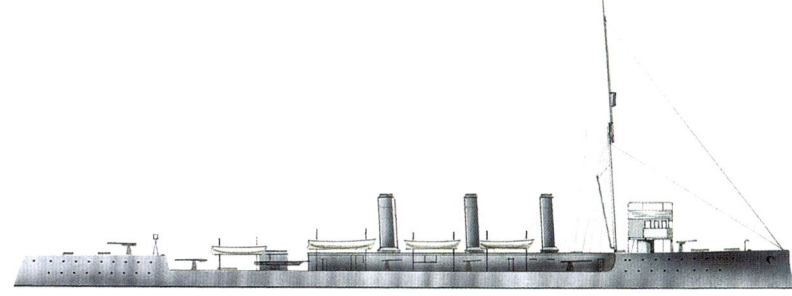

Foresight was one of eight broadly similar scout cruisers ordered by the Admiralty as destroyer group leaders, with a shallow draft for inshore operations. *Foresight* followed the traditional design of forecastle and poop-deck; six of the class had the modern feature of a clear run aft. *Foresight* was sold in 1921.

SPECIFICATIONS	
Type:	British cruiser
Displacement:	2896 tonnes (2850 tons)
Dimensions:	109.7m x 11.9m x 4.3m (360ft x 39ft x 14ft)
Machinery:	Twin screws, triple expansion engines
Top speed:	25.3 knots
Main armament:	Ten 12-pounder guns
Armour:	38mm (1.5in) deck
Launched:	October 1904

TIMELINE 1903 1904

Black Prince

SPECIFICATIONS	
Type:	British cruiser
Displacement:	13,716 tonnes (13,500 tons)
Dimensions:	154m x 23m x 8m (505ft 6in x 73ft 6in x 26ft)
Machinery:	Twin screws, triple expansion engines
Top speed:	23 knots
Main armament:	Six 228mm (9.2in) guns, ten 152mm (6in) guns
Armour:	76–152mm (3–6in) belt
Launched:	November 1904

Black Prince was not a successful design. The midships guns were mounted too low down, and consequently almost unworkable at sea. Also, in an attempt to reduce the usual high upper decks by eliminating bulwarks, the vessel proved very wet amidships. *Black Prince* was sunk at Jutland in May 1916.

Devonshire

SPECIFICATIONS	
Type:	British cruiser
Displacement:	11,023 tonnes (10,850 tons)
Dimensions:	144m x 21m x 7.3m (473ft 6in x 68ft 6in x 24ft)
Machinery:	Twin screws, triple expansion engines
Top speed:	22 knots
Main armament:	Four 190mm (7.5in) guns, six 152mm (6in) guns
Armour:	51–152mm (2–6in) belt, 127mm (5in) on turrets, 152mm (6in) on casemates, 51mm (2in) on deck
Launched:	April 1904

At the time of *Devonshire*'s construction, improvements in the quality of armour plate now made it possible to protect the vital parts of cruisers against 152mm (6in) shell fire using relatively thin and lightweight armour. This saved weight, which could be applied elsewhere. *Devonshire* was sold for scrapping in 1921.

Defence

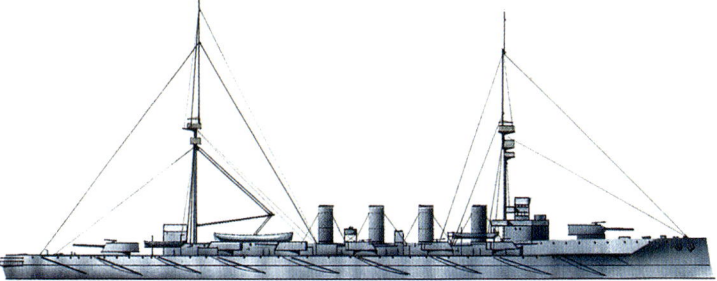

SPECIFICATIONS	
Type:	British cruiser
Displacement:	14,833 tonnes (14,600 tons)
Dimensions:	158m x 22m x 8m (519ft x 74ft 6in x 26ft)
Machinery:	Twin screws, triple expansion engines
Top speed:	22.9 knots
Main armament:	Four 228mm (9.2in) guns, ten 190mm (7.5in) guns
Armour:	152–76mm (6–3in) belt, 50–25mm (2–1in) deck
Launched:	May 1907

Though *Defence* was an enlarged cruiser design, to enable heavier armament to be carried, armour protection was slightly reduced. At the start of World War I, the *Defence* class formed part of a squadron looking for the German battleship *Goeben*. *Defence* was sunk at Jutland in 1916, and 893 lives were lost.

SHIP TYPES 1900–1929

Cruisers of the 1900s – Other Navies: Part 1

The wooden warship required only seamen, gunners and marines. The cruiser needed more: engineers, artificers, stokers, electricians and gunnery specialists, as well as materials that included coal fuel, lubricating oil and mechanical spare parts.

Gloire

Gloire was built midway through the development of the French armoured cruiser. Electric power was generated and used on board; the guns were electrically operated, and the hoist machinery was armoured. A high control station overlooked a short forecastle. Gloire was removed from service in 1922.

SPECIFICATIONS

Type:	French cruiser
Displacement:	10,375 tonnes (10,212 tons)
Dimensions:	139.7m x 20m x 7.6m (458ft 4in x 66ft 3in x 25ft 2in)
Machinery:	Triple screws, vertical triple expansion engines
Top speed:	21 knots
Main armament:	Two 193mm (7.6in) guns, eight 162mm (6.4in) guns, six 100mm (3.9in) guns
Armour:	102–170mm (4–7in) belt, 203mm (8in) on main turrets
Launched:	June 1900

Condé

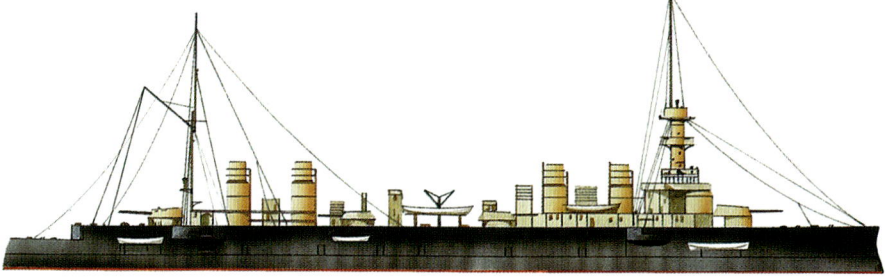

Condé was based on a concept of Admiral Fournier, who advocated the use of large, well-protected vessels as commerce raiders. There was extensive waterline protection, with two armoured decks bonding the upper and lower edges of the belt, forming a protective box. Condé was broken up in 1933.

SPECIFICATIONS

Type:	French cruiser
Displacement:	10,396 tonnes (10,233 tons)
Dimensions:	140m x 20m x 8m (458ft 8in x 66ft 3in x 25ft 2in)
Machinery:	Triple screws, vertical triple expansion engines
Top speed:	21.5 knots
Main armament:	Two 193mm (7.6in) guns, eight 162mm (6.4in) guns
Armour:	58–152mm (2.3–6in) waterline belt
Launched:	March 1902

TIMELINE

1900  1902

Francesco Ferruccio

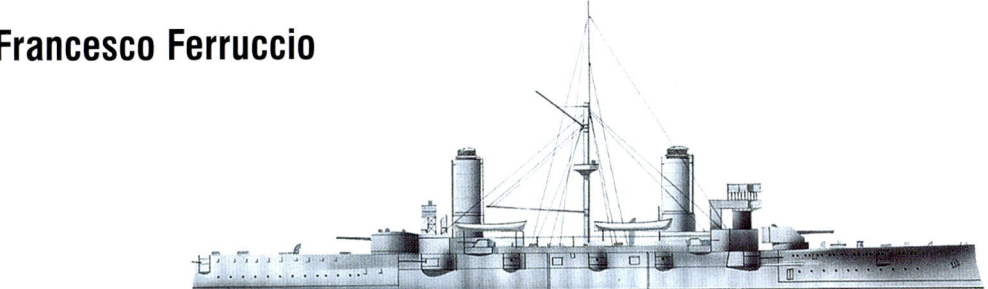

Francesco Ferruccio was one of a successful type designed during the early to mid-1890s and supplied to the navies of Argentina, Spain and Japan as well as Italy. Heavily armed, with good speed, this was a well-balanced design, able to withstand the fire of contemporary battleships and defeat any standard cruiser.

SPECIFICATIONS	
Type:	Italian cruiser
Displacement:	8230 tonnes (8100 tons)
Dimensions:	111.8m x 18.2m x 7.3m (366ft 10in x 59ft 9in x 24ft)
Machinery:	Twin screws, vertical triple expansion engines
Top speed:	20 knots
Main armament:	One 254mm (10in) gun, two 203mm (8in) guns, fourteen 152mm (6in) guns
Armour:	102–152mm (4–6in) belt and turrets
Launched:	1902

Berlin

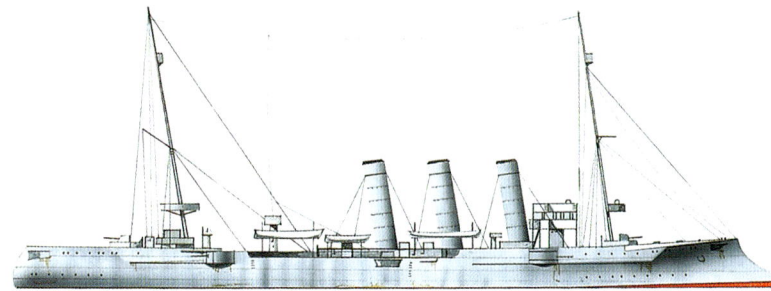

Berlin was one of a class of seven ships, intended for scouting purposes, with more powerful engines than previous German light cruisers. The 102mm (4in) guns were intended for rapid fire, but their lightweight shells were to prove inadequate in action. Berlin survived World War I and was stripped in 1935.

SPECIFICATIONS	
Type:	German cruiser
Displacement:	3816 tonnes (3756 tons)
Dimensions:	111m x 13m x 5.6m (364ft 9in x 43ft 8in x 18ft 5in)
Machinery:	Twin screws, triple expansion engines
Main armament:	Ten 102mm (4.1in) guns
Launched:	1903

Gneisenau

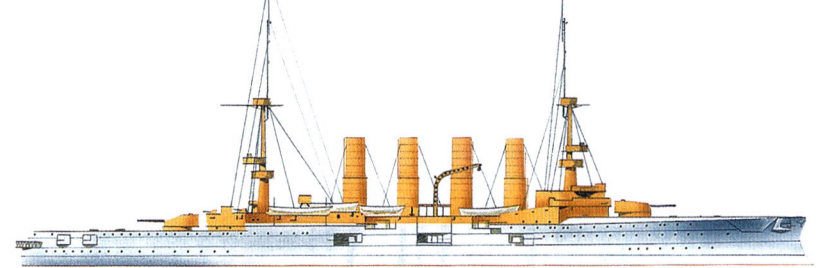

The armoured cruiser Gneisenau and its sister Scharnhorst were stationed in China when World War I broke out. On their way back to Germany, they met and defeated a British squadron off Coronel, but both vessels were sunk by the British off the Falkland Islands in December 1914.

SPECIFICATIONS	
Type:	German cruiser
Displacement:	12,985 tonnes (12,781 tons)
Dimensions:	144.6m x 21.6m x 8.3m (474ft 5in x 70ft 10in x 27ft 6in)
Machinery:	Triple screws, triple expansion engines
Top speed:	22.5 knots
Main armament:	Eight 208mm (8.2in) guns, six 152mm (6in) guns
Armour:	102–152mm (4–6in) belt, 152mm (6in) over battery, 170mm (6.75in) on turrets
Complement:	764
Launched:	June 1906

1903

1906

Cruisers of the 1900s – Other Navies: Part 2

Sails were now obsolete on large warships, but a new use was found for tall masts: supporting radio aerials. Wireless transmission of messages, initially by Morse code, was of obvious value. By 1910, the wireless operator had become indispensable.

Bayan

Bayan's effectiveness as a fast cruiser was affected by problems of internal design, which slowed down coal transfer from bunkers to furnaces. Stationed on the Pacific coast, it was a scout and patrol ship during the Russo–Japanese War, until captured by the Japanese in January 1905. It was sunk as a target in 1932.

SPECIFICATIONS	
Type:	Russian cruiser
Displacement:	7,924 tonnes (7,800 tons)
Dimensions:	135m x 17m x 6.7m (443ft x 55ft 9in x 22ft)
Machinery:	Twin screws, vertical triple expansion engines
Top speed:	21 knots
Main armament:	Two 203mm (8in) guns, eight 152mm (6in) guns
Armour:	203mm-76mm (8in-3in) belt, 178mm (7in) on turrets
Launched:	June 1900

Denver

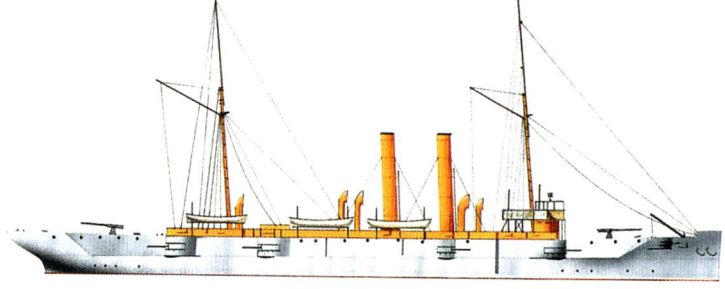

Built at Philadelphia, Denver, though slow for a light cruiser, served usefully in both the Atlantic and Pacific fleets. In World War I it was a convoy escort, and after 1918 operated on coastal patrols and goodwill missions in the Caribbean and along the South American coasts. Decommissioned in 1931, it was scrapped in 1933.

SPECIFICATIONS	
Type:	US cruiser
Displacement:	3570 tonnes (3514 tons)
Dimensions:	94m x 13m x 4.8m (308ft 10in x 44ft x 15ft 9in)
Machinery:	Twin screws, vertical triple expansion engines
Top speed:	16.7 knots
Main armament:	Ten 127mm (5in) guns
Complement:	339
Launched:	1902

TIMELINE

1900   1902

CRUISERS OF THE 1900S – OTHER NAVIES: PART 2

Izumrud

SPECIFICATIONS	
Type:	Russian cruiser
Displacement:	3098 tonnes (3050 tons)
Dimensions:	110.9m x 12.2m x 5m (345ft x 49ft x 16ft)
Machinery:	Twin screws, triple expansion engines
Top speed:	25 knots
Main armament:	Six 120mm (4.7in) guns
Armour:	51mm (2in) deck
Launched:	1903

Izumrud was one of Russia's first wireless-equipped warships. Its engines developed over 24,000hp, and consumed more than 25 tonnes (25 tons) of coal per hour. One of the few Russian warships to survive the Battle of Tsushima in May 1905, it ran aground in thick fog near Vladivostok due to compass failure.

Fylgia

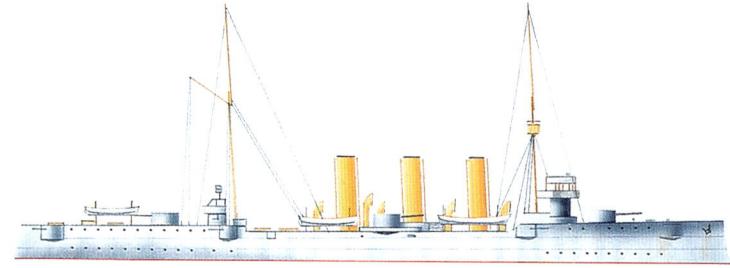

SPECIFICATIONS	
Type:	Swedish cruiser
Displacement:	4810 tonnes (3670 tons)
Dimensions:	115.1m x 14.8m x 6.3m (377ft 6in x 48ft 6in x 20ft 7in)
Machinery:	Twin screws, triple expansion engines
Top speed:	22.8 knots
Main armament:	Eight 152mm (6in) guns
Launched:	December 1905

Fylgia was the world's smallest armoured cruiser. The armoured belt, located amidships, ran from the fore to the aft turret, ending in a curved bulkhead that protected the vessel from end-on fire. The armoured deck was 51mm (2in) thick on the slopes, curving down at each end of the hull beyond the belt.

Edgar Quinet

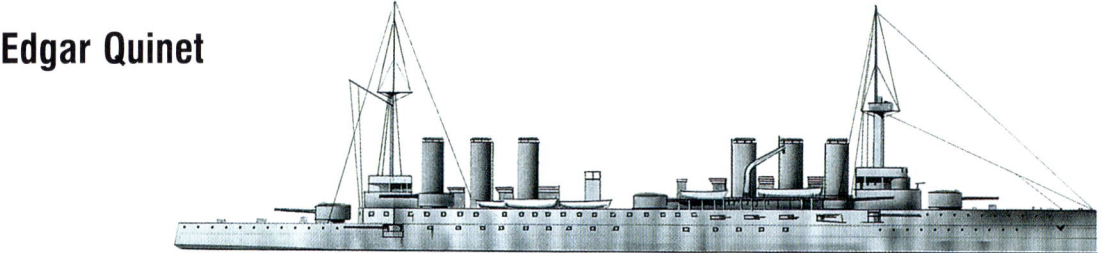

SPECIFICATIONS	
Type:	French cruiser
Displacement:	14,068 tonnes (13,847 tons)
Dimensions:	159m x 21.5m x 8.4m (521ft 4in x 70ft 6in x 27ft 7in)
Machinery:	Triple screws, vertical triple expansion engines
Top speed:	23.9 knots
Main armament:	Fourteen 193mm (7.6in) guns
Armour:	152–38mm (6–1.5in) belt, on turrets 203mm (8in)
Complement:	859
Launched:	September 1907

With light-calibre guns in relation to their size, the six-funnelled *Edgar Quinet* and *Waldeck-Rousseau* were the last armoured cruisers to enter the French Navy. Ten guns were mounted in double or single turrets, and four in casemates. *Edgar Quinet* became a training ship in 1928, and was wrecked off Algeria in 1930.

SHIP TYPES 1900–1929

British Cruisers, 1910–1929

The versatility of the cruiser was extended with the ability to launch aircraft at sea, beginning with the British *Arethusa* class. With the outbreak of World War I, cruisers stationed at colonial bases came under heavy pressure, notably Britain's South Atlantic Squadron, destroyed by Von Spee at Coronel in October 1914.

Calliope

Calliope and *Champion* were the first of the 22-strong C-class of light cruiser laid down between 1914 and 1917, intended for scouting despite not carrying a seaplane. These were the first two-funnelled British cruisers, made possible by a new arrangement of the boiler spaces. *Calliope* was broken up in 1931.

SPECIFICATIONS

Type:	British cruiser
Displacement:	4770 tonnes (4695 tons)
Dimensions:	136m x 12.6m x 5m (446ft 6in x 41ft 6in x 14ft 9in)
Machinery:	Quadruple screw geared turbines
Top speed:	28.5 knots
Main armament:	Two 152mm (6in) guns
Launched:	December 1914

Galatea

Gunfire from *Galatea* and HMS *Phaeton* shot down Zeppelin *L7* in May 1916. *Galatea*'s armour was worked into the structure to form part of the hull strength, enabling a weight reduction. Some of its class were the first warships to launch aircraft at sea, from a platform over the bows. *Galatea* was scrapped in 1921.

SPECIFICATIONS

Type:	British cruiser
Displacement:	4470 tonnes (4400 tons)
Dimensions:	132.9m x 11.9m x 4.1m (436ft x 39ft x 13ft 5in)
Machinery:	Quadruple screws, turbines
Top speeds:	28.5 knots
Main armament:	Two 152mm (6in) guns, six 102mm (4in) guns
Armour:	76–25mm (3–1in) belt, 25mm (1in) deck
Complement:	276
Launched:	1914

TIMELINE 1914   1921

BRITISH CRUISERS, 1910–1929

Effingham

SPECIFICATIONS	
Type:	British cruiser
Displacement:	9906 tonnes (9750 tons)
Dimensions:	184m x 20m x 6.2m (605ft x 65ft x 20ft 6in)
Machinery:	Quadruple screws, turbines
Top speed:	30.5 knots
Armament:	Seven 190mm (7.5in) guns
Armour:	38–76mm (1.5–3in) belt
Launched:	June 1921

The success of German commerce raiders in sinking British ships on the open seas led to the design in 1915 of a new class of fast cruisers for intercepting them. *Effingham* was wrecked on an uncharted rock off Norway on 18 May 1940 while escorting invasion ships for the abortive Norwegian campaign.

Cornwall

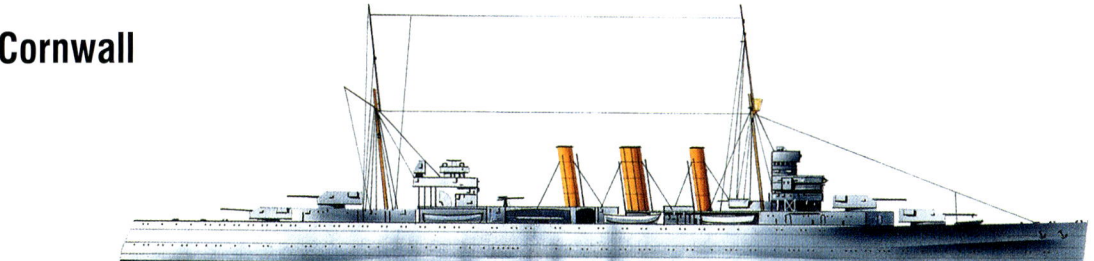

SPECIFICATIONS	
Type:	British cruiser
Displacement:	8382 tonnes (8250 tons)
Dimensions:	175m x 17.3m x 6m (574ft x 56ft 9in x 19ft 8in)
Machinery:	Quadruple screws, turbines
Top speeds:	32.3 knots
Main armament:	Six 203mm (8in) guns, four 102mm (4in) guns
Armour:	76mm (3in) belt, 100–25mm (4–1in) magazines
Complement:	623
Launched:	July 1928

Cornwall's working life was spent mainly in the Pacific and Indian Oceans. Early in 1941, it sank the German commerce raider *Pinguin*. Like most older ships, with modest anti-aircraft armament, it was vulnerable to air attack. On 5 April 1942, it and *Dorsetshire* were sunk off Ceylon by Japanese dive-bombers.

York

SPECIFICATIONS	
Type:	British cruiser
Displacement:	8,382 tonnes (8,250 tons)
Dimensions:	175m x 17.3m x 6m (574ft x 56ft 9in x 19ft 8in)
Machinery:	Quadruple screws, turbines
Main armament:	Six 203mm (8in) guns, four 102mm (4in) guns
Armour:	76mm (3in) belt, 100mm-25mm (4in-1in) magazines
Launched:	July 1928

York was the first attempt at building a powerful cruiser within the Washington Treaty limits. In order to give similar speed and protection to the *Kent* class, two 203mm (8in) guns were sacrificed. In 1941, *York* was beached at Suda Bay after being hit by an explosive motor boat. The wreck was broken up in 1952.

SHIP TYPES 1900–1929

Exeter

In December 1939, *Exeter* was in action in the South Atlantic against the German battleship *Admiral Graf Spee.* Sustaining severe damage from seven 280mm (11in) shells, the ship was effectively rebuilt in 1940–41. Deployed to Far Eastern waters, it was sunk in action at the Battle of the Java Sea in March 1942.

Exeter

Exeter featured modern innovations such as shipborne aircraft, but her own guns could not be elevated beyond 50 degrees, which limited their effectiveness against enemy aircraft. She remained unchanged throughout the 1930s until the outbreak of World War II when she was badly damaged. The basic armament was overhauled during repairs, the main gun turrets given a 70-degree elevation.

AIRCRAFT
Two planes and catapults were first carried; by 1939 one Supermarine Walrus floatplane was carried, with a single catapult.

SPECIFICATIONS	
Type:	British cruiser
Displacement:	10,657 tonnes (10,490 tons)
Dimensions:	175m x 17.6m x 6m (575ft x 58ft x 20ft 3in)
Machinery:	Quadruple screws, turbines
Top speed:	32 knots
Main armament:	Six 203mm (8in) guns, four 102mm (4in) guns
Armour:	76mm (3in) side armour, plus 25.4mm (1in) deck
Complement:	630
Launched:	July 1929

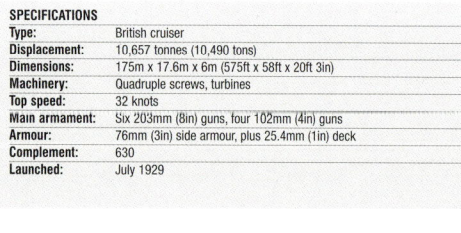

MACHINERY
Six of the eight boilers were put out of action in the Battle of the Java Sea, drastically reducing power and speed.

EXETER

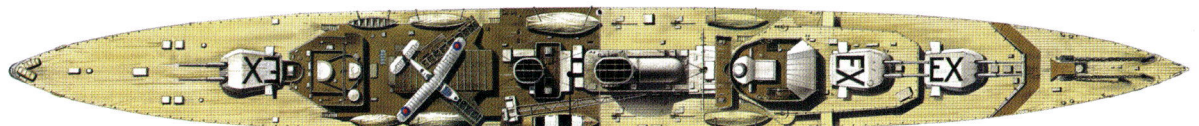

CENTRELINE
The deckplan reveals the typical centreline construction. Letters on the turret tops are to identify the ship to aircraft.

MASTS
The single-pole steel masts were reconstructed in 1941 as tripods to carry heavier look-out posts and Type 286M radar equipment.

RANGE
At a cruising speed of 12 knots, range was 9,635km (5200 nautical miles). Bunker capacity was 1930 tonnes (1900 tons) of fuel oil.

GUNS
'B' turret was rebuilt after being destroyed by an 280.5mm (11in) shell from Graf Spee; 'A' and 'Y' turrets were also put out of action.

CRANE
The crane was used to hoist up the floatplane and could also lower the ship's main launch and handle other bulky items.

SHIP TYPES 1900–1929

French, Italian & Greek Cruisers, 1910–1929

France and Italy had extensive colonial possessions and protectorates, and both countries had to protect and police their empires. Both maintained a substantial cruiser force. Greece's navy was much smaller, but long-running hostilities with the Ottoman Empire meant that it had to be effective in the Aegean and Ionian Seas.

Georgios Averroff

For many years the Greek flagship, *Georgios Averroff* was built in Italy as an armoured cruiser, and served in the Balkan wars prior to World War I and at the Dardanelles in 1916. A complete refit was made in the 1920s. In 1941, it escaped German capture. Stricken in 1946, *Averoff* is kept as a museum ship.

SPECIFICATIONS	
Type:	Greek cruiser
Displacement:	10,119 tonnes (9960 tons)
Dimensions:	140m x 21m x 7.5m (459ft x 69ft x 25ft 6in)
Machinery:	Twin screws, triple expansion engines
Top speed:	23 knots
Main armament:	Four 228mm (9.2in) guns, eight 189mm (7.5in) guns
Armour:	203–76mm (8–3in) belt, 165mm (6.5in) on turrets
Launched:	March 1910

Marsala

Two of *Marsala*'s 120mm (4.7in) guns were side-by-side on the forecastle, two were aft on the centreline, and two in echelon amidships. An armoured deck protected the machinery spaces, extending along the vessel's midships section before reducing at the bow and stern. *Marsala* was discarded in 1927.

SPECIFICATIONS	
Type:	Italian cruiser
Displacement:	4207 tonnes (4141 tons)
Dimensions:	140.3m x 13m x 4.1m (460ft 4in x 42ft 8in x 13ft 5in)
Machinery:	Triple screws, turbines
Top speed:	27.6 knots
Main armament:	Six 120mm (4.7in) guns, six 76mm (3in) guns
Launched:	March 1912

TIMELINE

1910   1912   1923

FRENCH, ITALIAN & GREEK CRUISERS, 1910–1929

Duguay-Trouin

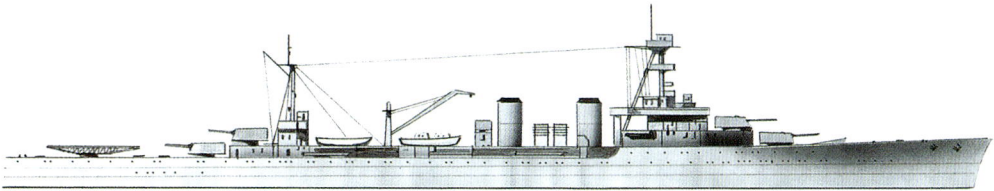

SPECIFICATIONS
Type:	French cruiser
Displacement:	9500 tonnes (9350 tons)
Dimensions:	184m x 17m x 6m (604ft 3in x 56ft 3in x 17ft 3in)
Machinery:	Quadruple screws, geared turbines
Top speed:	34.5 knots
Main armament:	Eight 152mm (6in) guns
Armour:	25mm (1in) on turrets, 19mm (.75in) deck
Complement:	578
Launched:	August 1923

Duguay-Trouin was the first major French warship built after World War I. The 152mm (6in) guns were of a new pattern also used by the French Army. Though lightly armoured, it was a successful design. Disarmed at Alexandria in 1940, the ship was then deployed with Free French forces. It was scrapped in 1952.

Trieste

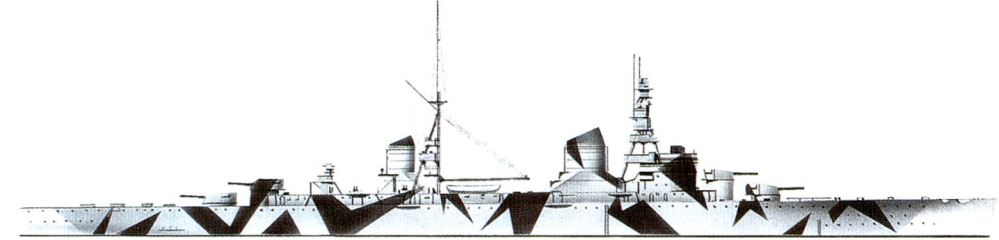

SPECIFICATIONS
Type:	Italian cruiser
Displacement:	13,540 tonnes (13,326 tons)
Dimensions:	196.9m x 20.6m x 6.8m (646ft 2in x 67ft 7in x 22ft 4in)
Machinery:	Quadruple screws, turbines
Top speed:	35.6 knots
Main armament:	Sixteen 100mm (3.9in), eight 203mm (8in) guns
Armour:	70mm (2.75in) belt, 100mm (3.9in) turrets, 78mm (2in) deck
Complement:	781
Launched:	1926

Trieste was one of two cruisers (see *Trento*) laid down to the Washington Naval Treaty limitation of 10,160 tonnes (10,000 tons). Even so, its displacement was over the limit. It was torpedoed and damaged by the British submarine *Utmost* in 1942, and badly damaged. It was sunk during an air raid on Sardinia in 1943.

Trento

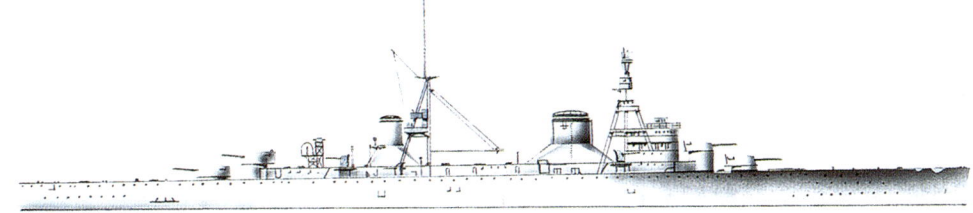

SPECIFICATIONS
Type:	Italian cruiser
Displacement:	13,547 tonnes (13,334 tons)
Dimensions:	196.9m x 20.6m x 6.8m (646ft 2in x 67ft 7in x 22ft 4in)
Machinery:	Quadruple screws, turbines
Top speed:	36 knots
Main armament:	Eight 203mm (8in) guns, sixteen 100mm (3.9in) guns
Armour:	70mm (2.75in) belt, 100mm (3.9in) on turrets, 78mm (2in) deck
Complement:	781
Launched:	October 1927

Trento produced similar difficulties to *Trieste*. It was a very fast cruiser, with engines developing 146,975hp, but the hull had to be strengthened to reduce heavy vibration at speed. Armour plating on the citadel superstructure protected the crew. It was sunk off Malta by the British submarine *Umbra* on 15 June 1942.

SHIP TYPES 1900–1929

Cruisers of Other Navies, 1920–29

In the post-1918 period, many warships were discarded, and international treaties limited the size of new ships. Steam turbines now drove large warships, increasing speeds: many cruisers could outrun all but the fastest of destroyers.

Java

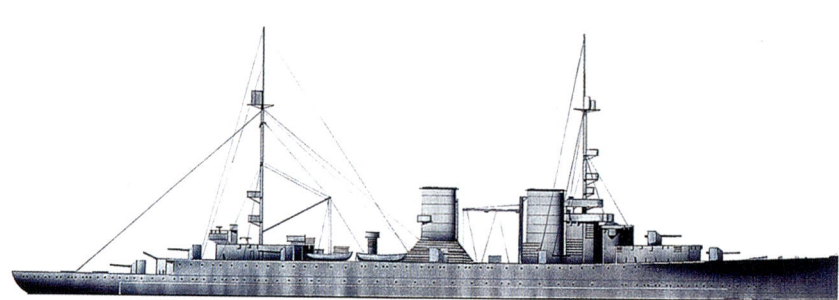

Designed and built in Germany, *Java* was laid down in 1916, but its completion was delayed until 1925. In 1935 it underwent a major refit and was given a new tubular foremast and a short pole mainmast near the second funnel. *Java* was sunk in action, off Java, on 27 February 1942 by superior Japanese forces.

SPECIFICATIONS	
Type:	Dutch cruiser
Displacement:	6776 tonnes (6670 tons)
Dimensions:	155m x 16m x 5.4m (509ft 6in x 52ft 6in x 18ft)
Machinery:	Triple screws, turbines
Top speed:	31 knots
Main armament:	Ten 150mm (5.9in) guns
Armour:	76–50mm (3–2in) belt, 50–38mm (2–1.5in) deck
Complement:	480
Launched:	August 1921

Memphis

The original plan was for ten 152mm (6in) guns on these 'scout cruisers', but this was increased during construction to 12 guns. *Memphis* and others in the class were fast but lacked armour protection, other than a strip 76mm (3in) wide covering the waterline near the machinery spaces. It was discarded in 1946.

SPECIFICATIONS	
Type:	US cruiser
Displacement:	9660 tonnes (9508 tons)
Dimensions:	169.5m x 16.9m x 4m (555ft 9in x 55ft 6in x 13ft 6in)
Machinery:	Quadruple screws, turbines
Top speed:	34.4 knots
Main armament:	Twelve 152mm (6in) guns
Armour:	76mm (3in) belt, 38mm (1.5in) deck
Complement:	458
Launched:	April 1924

TIMELINE 1921 1924 1925

Furutaka

The first large Japanese cruiser to be launched after the signing of the 1922 Washington Treaty, *Furutaka* was intended to compensate for the cancellation of larger ships. At first its 203mm (8in) guns were in single turrets, but these were later rearranged in three twins. *Furutaka* was sunk in October 1942.

SPECIFICATIONS	
Type:	Japanese cruiser
Displacement:	10,506 tonnes (10,341 tons)
Dimensions:	185.2m x 15.8m x 5.6m (607ft 6in x 51ft 9in x 18ft 3in)
Machinery:	Four screws, turbines
Top speed:	34.5 knots
Main armament:	Six 203mm (8in) guns
Armour:	76mm (3in) belt, 38mm (1.5in) deck
Complement:	625
Launched:	February 1925

Emden

The first post-1919 cruiser built for the *Kriegsmarine*, *Emden* was intended for overseas service, with a cruising range of 10,460 kilometres (6,500 miles). It took part in the invasion on Norway in World War II. After suffering bomb damage at Kiel, it was scuttled in May 1945. The wreck was broken up in 1948.

SPECIFICATIONS	
Type:	German cruiser
Displacement:	7102 tonnes (6990 tons)
Dimensions:	155m x 14m x 6.6m (509ft x 47ft x 21ft 8in)
Machinery:	Twin screws, turbines
Top speed:	29.4 knots
Main armament:	Eight 152mm (6in) guns
Armour:	38mm (1.5in) belt, 50mm (2in) on gunshields
Complement:	650
Launched:	January 1925

Aoba

Aoba and *Kinugasa* were improvements of the *Furutaka* class, and were the first Japanese cruisers fitted with catapults to launch aircraft. Modernization brought 203mm (8in) and heavier AA guns and increased displacement to 10,820 tonnes (10,650 tons). *Aoba* was sunk at Kure in July 1945 by US aircraft.

SPECIFICATIONS	
Type:	Japanese cruiser
Displacement:	8900 tonnes (8760 tons)
Dimensions:	185m x 15.8m x 5.7m (607ft 10in x 51ft 10in x 18ft 8in)
Machinery:	Four screws, geared turbines
Top speed:	33.5 knots
Main armament:	Six 203mm (8in) guns, four 120mm (4.7in) guns
Armour:	127mm (5in) on turrets, 50mm (2in) deck
Complement:	625
Launched:	September 1926

1926

Heavy Cruisers, 1900–1929

The term 'armoured cruiser' was fading, since all cruisers were to some extent armoured. The heavy cruiser designated a ship displacing at least 12,000 tonnes, normally armed with guns of at least 203mm (8in), and with a substantial secondary armament. Design and specifications changed considerably during this period.

Aboukir

The first British cruiser since 1886 to be built with a belt of armour for improved protection, *Aboukir* was sunk by the German submarine *U-9* on patrol in the North Sea on 22 September 1914, with her sister-ships *Cressy* and *Hogue,* leaving the British (and Germans) in no doubt about the U-boats' destructive power.

SPECIFICATIONS	
Type:	British armoured cruiser
Displacement:	12,240 tonnes (12,047 tons)
Dimensions:	144m x 21.2m x 7.6m (472ft 5in x 69ft 7in x 24ft 11in)
Machinery:	Twin screws, triple expansion engines
Top speed:	22.5 knots
Main armament:	Two 234mm (9.2in) guns, twelve 150mm (6in) guns
Armour:	150mm (6in) on sides and guns, 75mm (3in) on deck
Complement:	760
Launched:	May 1900

Montana

Montana served with the Atlantic Fleet until 1917, though sometimes deployed to the Mediterranean. During World War I, it escorted Atlantic convoys and after the war made one voyage as a troop transport for returning soldiers. It was renamed *Missoula* in 1920, but decommissioned in 1921 and sold for breaking in 1930.

SPECIFICATIONS	
Type:	US armoured cruiser
Displacement:	15,966 tonnes (15,715 tons) full load
Dimensions:	153.76m x 22.2m x 7.6m (504ft 6in x 72ft 11in x 25ft)
Machinery:	Twin screws, vertical triple expansion engines
Top speed:	22 knots
Main Armament:	Four 254mm (10in) guns, sixteen 152mm (6in) guns
Armour:	127mm (5in) belt, 229–127mm (9–5in) on turrets
Complement:	858
Launched:	1906

TIMELINE

 1900  1906

Rurik

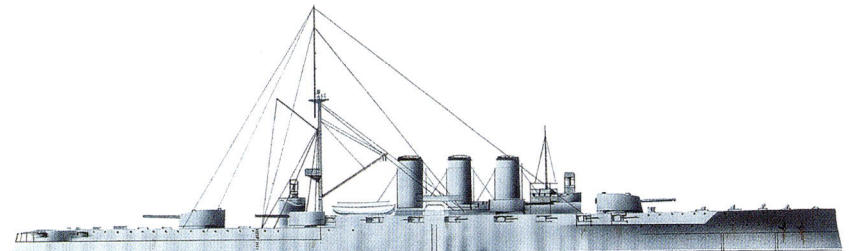

The last major Russian warship built abroad, *Rurik* was built by Vickers, to a design similar to the Italian *Pisa* class. It was one of several ships ordered after the losses incurred during the war with Japan, and its magazines were fitted with rapid flooding equipment, unique to the Russian Navy. It was broken up in 1923.

SPECIFICATIONS	
Type:	Russian cruiser
Displacement:	15,433 tonnes (15,190 tons)
Dimensions:	161.2m x 22.8m x 7.9m (529ft x 75ft x 26ft)
Machinery:	Twin screws, vertical triple expansion engines
Top speed:	21 knots
Main armament:	Four 254mm (10in) guns, eight 203mm (8in) guns, twenty 120mm (4.7in) guns
Armour:	102–152mm (4–6in) belt, 178–203mm (7–8in) on main turrets, 152–178mm (6–7in) on secondary turrets, 76mm (3in) on battery
Complement:	899
Launched:	1906

Pisa

Pisa was completed in September 1909. The 254mm (10in) guns were mounted in twin turrets. A single mast aft had searchlight platforms and two spotting tops. Later a foremast was added. In 1921, *Pisa* was reclassified as a coast defence vessel and served from 1925 to 1930 as a training ship. It was stricken in 1937.

SPECIFICATIONS	
Type:	Italian cruiser
Displacement:	10,770 tonnes (10,600 tons)
Dimensions:	140.5m x 21m x 7.1m (461ft 10in x 68ft 10in x 23ft 4in)
Machinery:	Twin screws, vertical triple expansion engines
Top speed:	23.4 knots
Main armament:	Sixteen 76mm (3in), eight 190mm (7.5in), four 254mm (10in) guns
Launched:	September 1907

San Giorgio

San Giorgio was laid down in 1905, and was an improved version of *Pisa*, then building. It was rebuilt as a training ship in 1937/38, and used as a floating battery in World War II. Scuttled in 1941 to prevent capture, it was refloated in 1952, but sank in heavy seas while under tow off Tobruk.

SPECIFICATIONS	
Type:	Italian cruiser
Displacement:	11,480 tonnes (11,300 tons)
Dimensions:	140.8m x 21m x 7.3m (462ft 10in x 68ft 10in x 24ft)
Machinery:	Twin screws, vertical triple expansion engines
Top speed:	23.7 knots
Main armament:	Four 254mm (10in) guns, eight 190mm (7.5in) guns, eighteen 76mm (3in) guns
Armour:	200mm (8in) belt and main turrets, 50mm (2in) deck
Complement:	700
Launched:	July 1908

SHIP TYPES 1900–1929

British Light Cruisers, 1900–1929

Gun calibre in light cruisers was typically 152mm (6in), outgunning destroyers and escort ships. A slender, lengthy profile with three or four funnels was typical of these ships, built for speed, and usually with good seakeeping qualities for rough weather.

Attentive

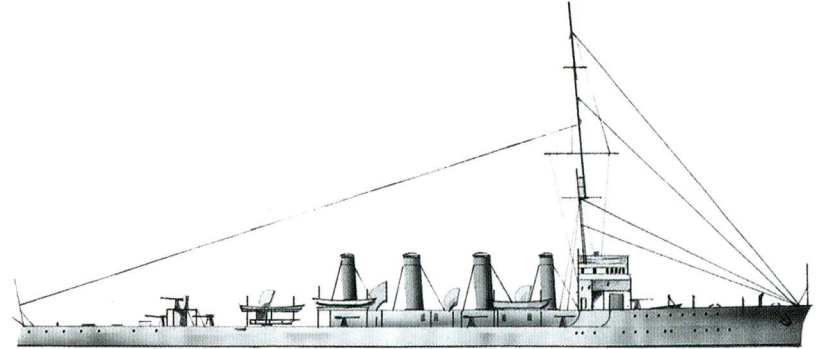

SPECIFICATIONS
Type:	British cruiser
Displacement:	2712 tonnes (2670 tons)
Dimensions:	114m x 11.6m x 4.2m (374ft x 38ft 3in x 13ft 6in)
Machinery:	Twin screws, triple expansion engines
Top speed:	25.6 knots
Main armament:	Ten 76mm (3in) guns
Launched:	1904

Attentive was one of eight small scout cruisers also intended as destroyer leaders, but their armament proved insufficient to be effective in the latter role. In 1911–12, all were rearmed with nine 102mm (4in) guns. All saw intensive action during World War I, with two being sunk. *Attentive* was sold for breaking in 1920.

Glasgow

SPECIFICATIONS
Type:	British cruiser
Displacement:	4876 tonnes (4800 tons)
Dimensions:	131m x 14m x 5.4m (430ft x 47ft x 17ft 9in)
Machinery:	Quadruple screws, turbines
Top speed:	25.8 knots
Main armament:	Two 152mm (6in) guns, ten 102mm (4in) guns
Armour:	50–20mm (2–1in) deck
Complement:	480
Launched:	September 1909

On the outbreak of World War I, *Glasgow* was part of Craddock's squadron sent to search for von Spee's cruiser force in the South Atlantic, and was the only British vessel to escape. In the Battle of the Falkland Islands in December 1914, it helped sink the cruiser *Leipzig*. It was broken up in 1927.

TIMELINE

1904    1909    1913

BRITISH LIGHT CRUISERS, 1900–1929

Birmingham

SPECIFICATIONS	
Type:	British cruiser
Displacement:	6136 tonnes (6040 tons)
Dimensions:	140m x 15.2m x 4.8m (457ft x 50ft x 16ft)
Machinery:	Quadruple screws, geared turbines
Top speed:	25.5 knots
Main armament:	Nine 152mm (6in) guns
Launched:	1913

Birmingham, of the First Light Cruiser Squadron, was one of the first British warships to claim victims in World War I, sinking two German merchant vessels in early August 1914. It sank *U-15*, the first U-boat to be destroyed by a British warship, on 9 August. *Birmingham* was scrapped in 1931.

Caroline

SPECIFICATIONS	
Type:	British cruiser
Displacement:	5017 tonnes (4733 tons)
Dimensions:	136m x 13m x 160m (446ft x 41ft 6in x 16ft)
Machinery:	Quadruple screws, geared turbines
Main armament:	Two 152mm (6in) guns, eight 102mm (4in) guns
Armour:	25–76mm (1–3in) belt
Launched:	September 1914

As the light cruiser developed the armament was increased, but *Caroline* was lightly gunned. In 1917–18 it had an extended fighter plane flying-off platform fitted so that it could engage Zeppelin airships. *Caroline* remains in commission at Belfast harbour, serving as a Royal Navy Volunteer Reserve (RNVR) drill ship.

Emerald

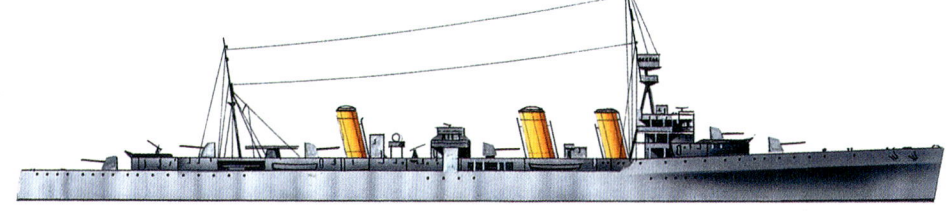

SPECIFICATIONS	
Type:	British cruiser
Displacement:	9601 tonnes (9450 tons)
Dimensions:	173.7m x 16.6m x 5.6m (570ft x 54ft 6in x 18ft 4in)
Machinery:	Quadruple screws, turbines
Top speed:	33 knots
Main armament:	Seven 152mm (6in) guns
Armour:	76–38mm (3–1.75in) belt, 25–15mm (1–0.5in) deck
Complement:	450
Launched:	May 1920

A fast cruiser designed to search out and destroy light cruisers and commerce raiders. A high length-to-beam ratio was used to achieve high speed, and a 9m (30ft) freeboard forward helped maintain speed in bad weather. *Emerald* was refitted in 1931, saw service in World War II, and was sold for scrap in 1948.

139

SHIP TYPES 1900–1929

German Light Cruisers, 1900–1929

Germany's light cruisers were similar to their British counterparts, though their guns were lighter, and their purpose more specific, as raiders or fleet scouts. Propulsion moved from vertical triple expansion engines to the turbine, improving speed.

Königsberg

German light cruisers were raiders or scout craft, and this was one of the former. Its 104mm (4.1in) guns were lighter than those of British counterparts but had the advantage of rapid fire, discharging up to 20 rounds per minute. Stationed in German East Africa, *Königsberg* was sunk in the Rufiji River in 1915.

SPECIFICATIONS

Type:	German light cruiser
Displacement:	3875 tonnes (3814 tons)
Dimensions:	114.8m x 13.2m x 5.2m (376ft 8in x 43ft 4in x 17ft)
Machinery:	Twin screws, vertical triple expansion engines
Top speed:	24 knots
Main Armament:	Ten 104mm (4.1in) guns
Complement:	352
Launched:	1905

Emden

Emden served in Asiatic waters until the outbreak of World War I. A short but intensive raiding career in the Indian Ocean, sinking 16 British vessels, was terminated on 9 November 1914 by the Australian cruiser *Sydney*. On fire, *Emden* was grounded by its crew. The wreck was partially dismantled in 1950.

SPECIFICATIONS

Type:	German cruiser
Displacement:	4336 tonnes (4628 tons)
Dimensions:	118m x 13m x 4.8m (389ft x 44ft x 16ft)
Machinery:	Twin screws, vertical triple expansion engines
Top speed:	25 knots
Main armament:	Ten 102mm (4in) guns
Armour:	30–20mm (1.75–0.75in) belt
Complement:	361
Launched:	May 1908

TIMELINE

1905  1908  1911

Breslau

For the first time on a light cruiser, a belt of nickel steel ran along most of *Breslau*'s length. Forming part of the structure, it saved weight yet strengthened the hull. In World War I, *Breslau* served in the Mediterranean with its crew under the Turkish flag as *Midilli*. It sank after striking mines in 1918.

SPECIFICATIONS	
Type:	German cruiser
Displacement:	5676 tonnes (5587 tons)
Dimensions:	138m x 14m x 5m (455ft x 44ft x 16ft 10in)
Machinery:	Quadruple screws, turbines
Main armament:	Twelve 102mm (4in) guns
Armour:	70mm (2.75in) belt, 57–38mm (2.25–1.5in) deck
Complement:	354
Launched:	May 1911

Karlsruhe

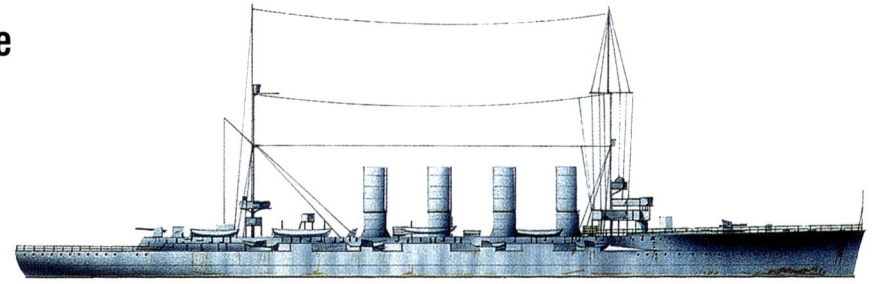

In a short career, *Karlsruhe* inflicted heavy damage on the British merchant marine. In 1914 it was stationed in the Caribbean, and sank 17 merchant vessels – more than 77,834 tonnes (76,609 tons). On 4 November 1914, *Karlsruhe* was destroyed by a magazine explosion.

SPECIFICATIONS	
Type:	German cruiser
Displacement:	6290 tonnes (6191 tons)
Dimensions:	142.2m x 13.7m x 5.5m (466ft 6in x 45ft x 18ft)
Machinery:	Twin screws, turbines
Top speed:	28.5 knots
Main armament:	Twelve 105mm (4.1in) guns
Armour:	18–60mm (0.7–2.4in) belt, 40–60mm (1.6–2.4in) deck
Complement:	373
Launched:	November 1912

Graudenz

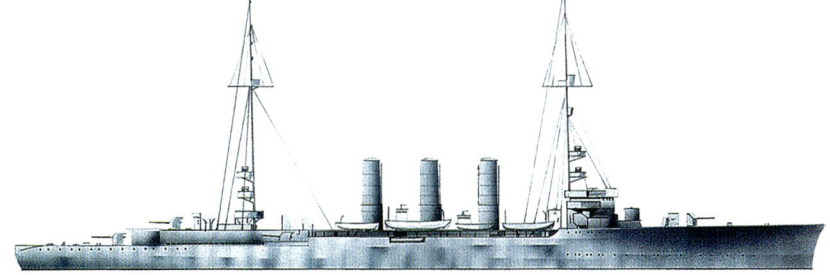

A light cruiser, but with three not four funnels, *Graudenz* had high-angle 104mm (4.1in) guns with good range. Later cruisers were given 150mm (5.9in) weapons – as, later, was *Graudenz*. It served with the main scouting group. Ceded to Italy in 1921, it became *Ancona*, and was scrapped in 1938.

SPECIFICATIONS	
Type:	German cruiser
Displacement:	6484 tonnes (6382 tons)
Dimensions:	142.7m x 13.8m x 5.7m (468ft 2in x 45ft 3in x 18ft 10in)
Machinery:	Twin screws, turbines
Top speed:	27.5 knots
Main armament:	Twelve 104mm (4.1in) guns
Armour:	60–18mm (2.25–0.75in) belt, 60–40mm (2.25–1.5in) deck
Complement:	442
Launched:	October 1913

SHIP TYPES 1900–1929

Köln

Electric welding was used to build *Köln*, which was fitted with 120 mines and new-type triple turrets, the two after turrets offset from the centreline. Its catapult and six of twelve 500mm (19.7in) torpedo tubes were removed early in World War II. Sunk by bombs while undergoing a refit, it was raised, and scrapped in 1946.

Köln

The Kreigsmarine's three *K-class* cruisers were the public face of the resurgent German navy during the 1930s. They were a bold new design that used modern techniques such as electric welding in their construction. For the first time a combinations of steam and diesel powerplants was fitted, though the two could only function separately.

GUNNERY CONTROL
Unusually, there were more heavy guns aft than forward. The rear turrets' off-centreline position was to give a better arc of fire.

SPECIFICATIONS	
Type:	German cruiser
Displacement:	8260 tonnes (8130 tons)
Dimensions:	174m x 15.3m x 6.3m (570ft 10in x 50ft 2in x 20ft 8in)
Machinery:	Twin screws, turbine and diesel engines
Top speed:	32 knots with turbines, 10 knots with diesels
Main armament:	Nine 150mm (5.9in) guns
Armour:	60–18mm (2.25–0.75in) belt, 60–38mm (2.25–1.5in) deck
Complement:	522
Launched:	May 1928

GUNS
In April 1945, following severe air raid damage, the ship's guns were removed for use in land defence at Wilhelmshaven.

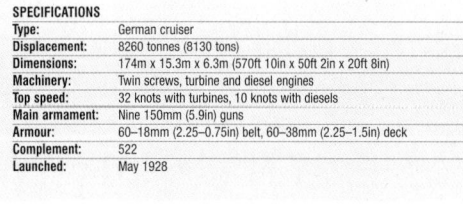

RANGE
Köln had a range of 13,140km (7300 nautical miles) at a speed of 17 knots. This was not considered sufficient for long-distance work and restricted its usefulness.

KÖLN

AIRCRAFT
At first two Heinkel He 60 aircraft were carried, with two catapults. From 1939 a single Flettner FL265 seaplane was carried, with a single catapult.

MACHINERY
Six boilers and two steam turbines were supplemented by two MAN 10-cylinder diesel engines. Total power was 52,050kW (69,800shp).

TORPEDO TUBES
Four sets of 503mm (19.7in) torpedo tubes were mounted. In addition Köln carried 120 mines.

HULL
The hull was 85 per cent welded and though this allowed for weight savings, it also led to structural weakness and vibration at speed.

SHIP TYPES 1900–1929

Light Cruisers of Other Navies, 1900–1929

World War I eclipsed earlier wars: between Spain and America in 1898, Russia and Japan in 1904–5, and Greece and Turkey in a long struggle in the Balkans. In all these, the light cruiser, as scout craft and fighting ship, played an important role.

Askold

Askold was laid down in the Krupp yard in 1898. It was fitted with nine of the new Schulz-Thornycroft boilers, exhausting through five funnels and taking up most of the long midships space. During the Russo–Japanese War, *Askold* was flagship to the cruiser squadron at Port Arthur. It was broken up in 1921.

SPECIFICATIONS

Type:	Russian cruiser
Displacement:	6198 tonnes (6100 tons)
Dimensions:	133.2m x 15m x 6.2m (437ft x 16ft 5in x 20ft 4in)
Machinery:	Triple screws, vertical triple expansion engines
Top speed:	23.8 knots
Main armament:	Twelve 152mm (6in) guns, twelve 76mm (3in) guns
Launched:	1900

Extremadura

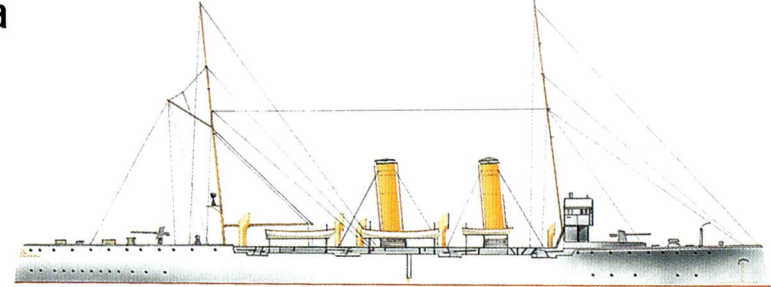

Extremadura was fitted with Armstrong quick-firing guns; the two 162mm (6.4in) main ones carried amidships on the broadside. A 13mm (0.5in) armoured deck ran the length of her hull, with a raised crown covering the engine room. Beneath were 11 separate watertight compartments. It was scrapped in 1930.

SPECIFICATIONS

Type:	Spanish cruiser
Displacement:	2168 tonnes (2134 tons)
Dimensions:	87m x 11m x 4.5m (288ft x 36ft x 14ft 6in)
Machinery:	Twin screws, triple expansion engines
Top speed:	20.5 knots
Main armament:	Four 162mm (6.4in) guns, four 120mm (4.7in) guns
Launched:	1900

TIMELINE

1900  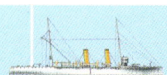 1907

Chester

SPECIFICATIONS	
Type:	US cruiser
Displacement:	4762 tonnes (4687 tons)
Dimensions:	129m x 14m x 5m (423ft x 47ft x 16ft 9in)
Machinery:	Quadruple screws, turbines
Top speed:	24 knots
Main armament:	Two 127mm (5in) guns, six 76mm (3in) guns
Armour:	50mm (2in) belt, 25mm (1in) deck
Complement:	359
Launched:	June 1907

Chester represented a new type of lightly-armed fast scout cruiser with high speed and good sea-keeping qualities to work directly with the battlefleet. With USS *Salem*, it was one of the first US warships with turbine engines, though these caused problems. Renamed *York* in 1928, it was scrapped in 1930.

Nagara

SPECIFICATIONS	
Type:	Japanese cruiser
Displacement:	5560 tonnes (5570 tons)
Dimensions:	163m x 14.2m x 4.6m (535ft x 46ft 9in x 15ft 10in)
Machinery:	Quadruple screws, turbines
Top speed:	36 knots
Main armament:	Seven 140mm (5.5in) guns
Armour:	63mm (2.5in) belt, 32mm (1.25in) deck
Launched:	April 1921

Nagara was the first Japanese ship to carry 610mm (24in) torpedo tubes, two in the break between the bridge and first funnel, two placed aft of the third funnel. Above the foredeck was a flying-off platform for a light floatplane, removed in 1931–32, when a tripod mainmast was fitted. It was sunk in August 1944.

Mendez Nuñez

SPECIFICATIONS	
Type:	Spanish cruiser
Displacement:	6140 tonnes (6043 tons)
Dimensions:	140.8m x 14m x 4.7m (462ft x 46ft x 15ft 5in)
Machinery:	Quadruple screws, turbines
Top speed:	29.2 knots
Main armament:	Six 152mm (6in) guns
Armour:	76mm (3in) midships belt, reducing to 31mm (1.25in) at either end; 25mm (1in) deck
Complement:	343
Launched:	March 1923

Mendez Nuñez was a light cruiser based on a British design, with three guns at each end of the vessel. Engines developed 43,776hp, and coal supply was 800 tonnes (787 tons), plus 500 tonnes (492 tons) of oil. Twelve 533mm (21in) torpedo tubes were carried. *Mendez Nuñez* was discarded in 1963.

SHIP TYPES 1900–1929

Development of the Destroyer to 1929: Part 1

In the early 1900s, the destroyer was a small vessel, not much bigger than the torpedo boats it hunted. Powered by triple expansion engines, it owed its speed to its lightness. But it lacked the fuel and ammunition capacity for sustained service.

Decatur

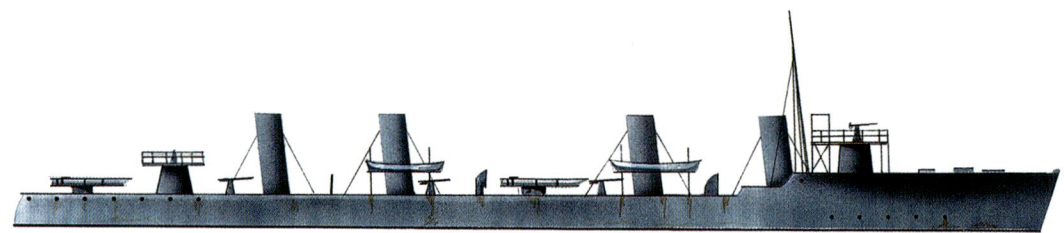

SPECIFICATIONS	
Type:	US destroyer
Displacement:	426 tonnes (420 tons)
Dimensions:	77m x 7m x 2m (252ft 7in x 23ft 6in x 6ft 6in)
Machinery:	Twin screws, vertical triple expansion engines
Top speed:	29 knots
Main armament:	Two 76mm (3in) guns, five 6-pdr guns, two 457mm (18in) torpedo tubes
Launched:	September 1900

Previous US destroyers had been 'one-off' vessels of between 238 and 283 tonnes (235–279 tons). *Decatur* was lead ship of a class of five, authorized in 1898. Deployed with the Pacific fleet, they served mainly in the Philippines. In 1917, *Chauncey* was sunk in a collision. The others were decommissioned in 1920.

Borea

SPECIFICATIONS	
Type:	Italian destroyer
Displacement:	386 tonnes (380 tons)
Dimensions:	64m x 6m x 2.3m (210ft x 19ft 6in x 7ft 6in)
Machinery:	Twin screws, triple expansion engines
Main armament:	Five 76mm (3in) guns, four 355mm (14in) torpedo tubes
Launched:	December 1902

Extended versions of the torpedo boat, *Borea* and five sister-ships were the first major class of small destroyers built for the Italians. They were later re-boilered, and the armament was modified. In 1915 minelaying equipment was added. *Borea* was sunk by Austrian destroyers *Csepel* and *Balaton* on 14 May 1917.

TIMELINE

1900   1902

Byedovi

SPECIFICATIONS	
Type:	Russian destroyer
Displacement:	355 tonnes (349 tons)
Dimensions:	56.6m x 6m x 3m (185ft 6in x 19ft 6in x 9ft 8in)
Machinery:	Twin screws, vertical triple expansion engines
Top speed:	26.5 knots
Main armament:	One 12-pdr gun, five 3-pdr guns, three 380mm (15in) torpedo tubes
Launched:	1902

Byedovi was one of 22 destroyers laid down in Russian yards between 1900 and 1903. Many served in the Russo–Japanese War of 1904–05. After the Battle of Tsushima in 1905, *Byedovi* was captured by the Japanese while trying to escape with the injured Admiral Rozhestvensky aboard. It was scrapped in 1922.

Gromki

SPECIFICATIONS	
Type:	Russian destroyer
Displacement:	355 tonnes (350 tons)
Dimensions:	64m x 6.4m x 2.5m (210ft x 21ft x 8ft 6in)
Machinery:	Twin screws, vertical triple expansion engines
Top speed:	26 knots
Main armament:	One 11-pdr gun, five 3-pdr guns guns, three 380mm (15in) torpedo tubes
Launched:	1904

This small destroyer formed part of the Second Pacific Squadron. During the Battle of Tsushima in 1905, it was attacked by a group of Japanese vessels. After a two-hour conflict, *Gromki* was crippled. Without surrendering, it sank at midday on 28 May 1905, two-thirds of the crew having been killed or wounded.

G132

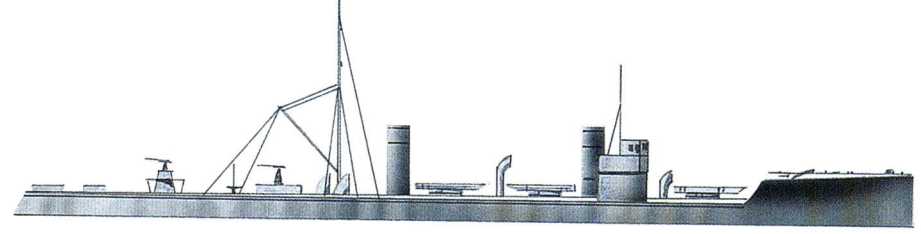

SPECIFICATIONS	
Type:	German destroyer
Displacement:	553 tonnes (544 tons)
Dimensions:	65.7m x 7m x 2.6m (215ft 6in x 2ft 8ft 6in)
Machinery:	Twin screws, triple expansion engines
Top speed:	28 knots
Main armament:	Four 51mm (2in) guns, three 450mm (17.7in) torpedo tubes
Launched:	May 1906

In the 1900s, Germany was building a force of destroyers to act with the battle fleet by breaking through the enemy battle line and attacking it with torpedoes. Attacks on enemy destroyers were a secondary function. When *G132* was built, design was still evolving and later G-ships showed numerous differences

SHIP TYPES 1900–1929

Development of the Destroyer to 1929: Part 2

With naval powers watching each other closely, developments were soon improved upon. Thus, from 1909, destroyers increased in size, and the growing number of submarines, and the demands of unrestricted ocean warfare, had a profound effect.

Grasshopper

In 1907 the British Admiralty obtained plans of German destroyers and planned to outdo them. *Grasshopper* and its 15 sisters burned coal. They carried a new torpedo, which was fitted with a heater to improve performance and had a range of 10,972m (12,000yds) at 30 knots. *Grasshopper* was sold in 1921.

SPECIFICATIONS	
Type:	British destroyer
Displacement:	937 tonnes (923 tons)
Dimensions:	82.6m x 27.5m x 9.7m (271ft x 27ft 10in x 9ft 6in)
Machinery:	Triple screws, turbines
Top speed:	27 knots
Main armament:	One 102mm (4in) gun, three 12-pdr guns
Launched:	November 1909

Garibaldino

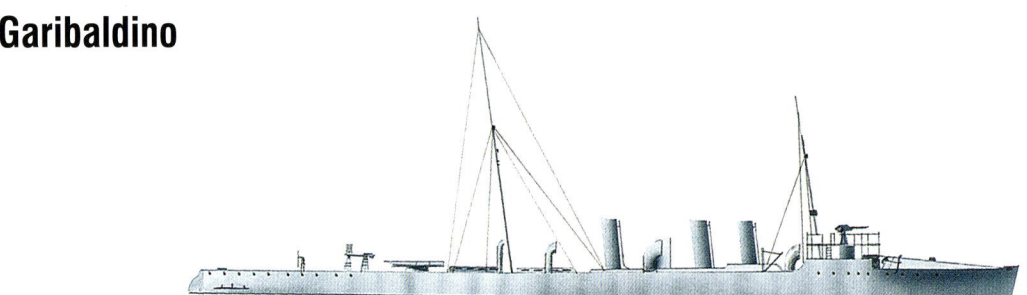

Garibaldino burned coal, though later members of the *Soldato* or *Alpino* class burned oil. The engines developed 6000hp, with a range of 2850km (1500 miles) at 12 knots or 760km (400 miles) at 23.5 knots. It was sunk on 16 July 1918, after colliding with the British destroyer *Cygnet* off Villefranche, southern France.

SPECIFICATIONS	
Type:	Italian destroyer
Displacement:	419 tonnes (412 tons)
Dimensions:	65m x 6.1m x 2.1m (213ft 3in x 20ft x 7ft)
Machinery:	Twin screws, triple expansion engines
Top speed:	28 knots
Main armament:	Three 76mm (3in) guns, three 450mm (17.7in) torpedo tubes
Launched:	1910

TIMELINE

1909 1910 1911

Ferret

Lead ship of a class of 20, designed by J.S. White, *Ferret* could maintain over 30 knots for eight hours. However, although the fore funnel was set well back, exhaust fumes still caused problems for those on the bridge. This was rectified later when the funnel was raised. *Ferret* was scrapped in 1921.

SPECIFICATIONS	
Type:	British destroyer
Displacement:	762 tonnes (750 tons)
Dimensions:	75m x 7.8m x 2.7m (246ft x 25ft 8in x 8ft 9in)
Machinery:	Twin screw turbines
Top speed:	33 knots
Main armament:	Two 102mm guns
Launched:	April 1911

Gromki

Gromki joined the Black Sea Fleet in 1913. Five twin torpedo tubes were carried on the centreline, with one 102mm (4in) gun forward and two aft. Engines developed 25,500hp, but not all the vessels in this class reached the designed All ships served in World War I. *Gromki* was scuttled at Sevastopol in June 1918.

SPECIFICATIONS	
Type:	Russian destroyer
Displacement:	1483 tonnes (1460 tons)
Dimensions:	98m x 9.3m x 3.2m (321ft 6in x 30ft 6in x 10ft 6in)
Machinery:	Twin screws, turbines
Main armament:	Three 102mm (4in) guns, ten 457mm (18in) torpedo tubes
Launched:	December 1913

Garland

Part of the British–German 'destroyer race' that paralleled the rival dreadnought construction, this 1911–12 class was to be armed with two 102mm (4in) guns plus four 12-pounders, but three 102mm (4in) guns were installed, making them among the most powerful destroyers of the era. *Garland* was broken up in 1921.

SPECIFICATIONS	
Type:	British destroyer
Displacement:	1005 tonnes (989 tons)
Dimensions:	81.5m x 8.2m x 2.8m (267ft 6in x 27ft x 9ft 3in)
Machinery:	Twin screws, semi-geared turbines
Main armament:	Three 102mm (4in) guns, two 533mm (21in) torpedo tubes
Launched:	April 1913

Development of the Destroyer to 1929: Part 3

By 1914, destroyers had turbine propulsion, increasing their speed to over 30 knots, enabling them to make a rapid charge when a torpedo boat or submarine periscope was sighted. Greater displacement gave more internal capacity and endurance.

Guadiana

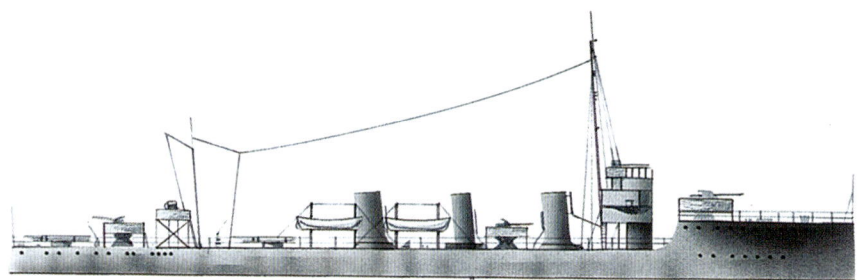

Guadiana was one of four British-type destroyers assembled in Portugal, at that time the largest single order placed by the Portuguese Navy for many years. The two twin torpedo mounts were on the centreline. Engines developed 11,000hp, and range at 15 knots was 3040km (1600 miles). It was discarded in 1934.

SPECIFICATIONS

Type:	Portuguese destroyer
Displacement:	670 tonnes (660 tons)
Dimensions:	73.2m x 7.2m x 2.3m (240ft 2in x 23ft 8in x 7ft 6in)
Machinery:	Twin screws, turbines
Main armament:	One 102mm (4in) gun, two 76mm (3in) guns, four 457mm (18in) torpedo tubes
Launched:	September 1914

G101

One of four ordered by the Argentinian Navy and laid down at Germaniawerft, Kiel, in 1914, but taken over on completion for the German Navy, G101 and its sisters were among the most powerful and fast destroyers afloat. Their turbines developed 29,500hp. All were interned at Scapa Flow and scuttled there in 1919.

SPECIFICATIONS

Type:	German destroyer
Displacement:	1873 tonnes (1843 tons)
Dimensions:	98m x 9.4m x 3.9m (321ft 6in x 30ft 9in x 12ft 9in)
Machinery:	Twin screws, turbines
Top speed:	36.5 knots
Main armament:	Four 85mm (3.3in) guns, six 508mm (20in) torpedo tubes
Launched:	1914

G40

Boats such as *G40* and its three sister-ships were regarded as too big to be safely used in close attack formation. But they were useful, seaworthy craft. A lateral torpedo tube was placed at each side of the bridge structure. The rest of the tubes were set in pairs on the centreline.

SPECIFICATIONS	
Type:	German destroyer
Displacement:	1068 tonnes (1051 tons)
Dimensions:	79.5m x 8.36m x 3.74m (261ft x 27ft 6in x 12ft 1in)
Machinery:	Twin screws, turbines
Top speed:	4.5 knots
Main armament:	Three 85mm (3.3in) guns, six 508mm (20in) torpedo tubes
Launched:	February 1915

Frunze

Originally named *Bistry*, *Frunze* was a very successful destroyer design. Two sets of triple 450mm (17.7in) torpedo tubes were carried on the centreline abaft the superstructure, with another triple set carried in front. Its armament was updated or altered several times. *Frunze* was sunk by German aircraft in 1941.

SPECIFICATIONS	
Type:	Russian destroyer
Displacement:	1321 tonnes (1300 tons)
Dimensions:	93m x 9.3m x 2.8m (305ft x 30ft 6in x 9ft 2in)
Machinery:	Twin screws, turbines
Top speed:	34 knots
Main armament:	Four 102mm (4in) guns, one 75mm (3in) gun
Launched:	1915

Walker

Many 'V and W' class destroyers of 1917–19 were adapted in World War II as short-range escorts or anti-aircraft battery ships. *Walker* was fitted with depth charge launchers, a Hedgehog AS mortar and 20mm guns. The forward boiler room was converted to fuel storage. It was scrapped in 1946.

SPECIFICATIONS	
Type:	British destroyer
Displacement:	1117.6 tonnes (1100 tons)
Dimensions:	95.1m x 9m x 3.2m (312ft x 29ft 6in x 10ft 6in)
Machinery:	Twin screws, geared turbines
Top speed:	34 knots
Main armament:	Four 102mm (4in) guns, six 533mm (21in) torpedo tubes
Complement:	127
Launched:	1917

1917

Development of the Destroyer to 1929: Part 4

In the 1920s, the steam torpedo boat was obsolete. Though destroyers' guns were improved, the standard Whitehead torpedo still had a range of 1000m (3280ft) and a warhead similar to that of 1906. Only Japan was undertaking development work.

Gwin

Gwin was an early 'flush-decker' destroyer with typical unprotected guns of the period. The foremast extended up from the superstructure, and two of its 102mm (4in) guns were mounted on a deck structure by the middle funnel. Many of this type served during World War II, but Gwin was sold in 1939.

SPECIFICATIONS

Type:	US destroyer
Displacement:	1205 tonnes (1187 tons)
Dimensions:	96.2m x 9.3m x 2.7m (315ft 7in x 30ft x 9ft)
Machinery:	Twin screws, turbines
Top speed:	32 knots
Main armament:	Four 102mm (4in) guns, twelve 533mm (21in) torpedo tubes
Launched:	December 1917

Gillis

The four-funnelled Gillis could be a fast ship, though its full cruising range of 4750km (2500 miles) needed a speed kept down to 20 knots or so. The turbines developed 27,000hp. Modified and adapted with more crew protection during World War II, the ship was broken up in 1946.

SPECIFICATIONS

Type:	US destroyer
Displacement:	1328 tonnes (1308 tons)
Dimensions:	95.8m x 9.4m x 3m (314ft 4in x 30ft 10in x 9ft 10in)
Machinery:	Twin screws, turbines
Top speed:	35 knots
Main armament:	Four 102mm (4in) guns, twelve 533mm (21in) torpedo tubes
Launched:	April 1919

TIMELINE

1917 1919 1923

Calatafimi

SPECIFICATIONS	
Type:	Italian destroyer
Displacement:	894 tonnes (880 tons)
Dimensions:	85m x 8m x 3m (278ft 9in x 26ft 3in x 9ft 9in)
Machinery:	Twin screws, turbines
Top speed:	34 knots
Main armament:	Four 102mm (4in) guns, six 444mm (17.5in) torpedo tubes
Launched:	March 1923

Ordered in 1915, *Calatafimi* was delayed by a materials shortage. By the 1930s, it was considered small for a destroyer and was reclassified as a torpedo boat in 1938. A single 102mm (4in) weapon replaced the twin mount aft. In 1943, the Germans captured *Calatafimi* and gave it the name *TA 19*. It was sunk in 1944.

Bourrasque

SPECIFICATIONS	
Type:	French destroyer
Displacement:	1930 tonnes (1900 tons)
Dimensions:	106m x 10m x 4.2m (347ft x 31ft 9in x 14ft)
Machinery:	Twin screws, geared turbines
Main armament:	Four 127mm (5in) guns
Launched:	1925

Bourrasque was well armed and compared favourably with its contemporaries. But the rate of fire of its guns was slow, only four to five rounds per minute. All ships in the class underwent armament modifications, and some were stripped of the aft gun to improve stability. *Bourrasque* was lost at Dunkirk in May 1940.

Ardent

SPECIFICATIONS	
Type:	British destroyer
Displacement:	2022 tonnes (1990 tons)
Dimensions:	95.1m x 9.8m x 3.7m (312ft 3in x 32ft 3in x 12ft 3in)
Machinery:	Twin screws, geared turbines
Top speed:	35 knots
Main armament:	Four 120mm (4.7in) guns, eight 533mm (21in) torpedo tubes
Launched:	1929

With *Ardent*'s 'W' class, the Royal Navy resumed destroyer construction, after a lapse of eight years from 1918. *Ardent* was sunk in June 1940 by *Scharnhorst* and *Gneisenau*, while escorting the aircraft carrier *Glorious*, which also fell prey to the German guns. Three other 'W' class ships were lost during the war.

SHIP TYPES 1900–1929

Flotilla Leaders, Italian & British

Some navies used light cruisers as destroyer leaders, controlling the movement of ships in squadron formation; others built ships for the task, essentially larger destroyers, with increased accommodation for command and communications.

Swift

The flotilla leader was a new concept, requiring a speed of 36 knots. Changes to the propeller and heightened funnels enabled *Swift* to make just over 35 knots, and it was commissioned in 1910, after two years of trials. The light construction made it vulnerable in North Sea storms. *Swift* was broken up in 1921.

SPECIFICATIONS	
Type:	British flotilla leader
Displacement:	2428 tonnes (2390 tons)
Dimensions:	107.8m x 10.4m x 3.2m (353ft 8in x 34ft 2in x 10ft 6in)
Machinery:	Quadruple screws, turbines
Top speed:	35 knots
Main armament:	Four 102mm (4in) guns, two 457mm (18in) torpedo tubes
Launched:	December 1907

Guglielmo Pepe

Guglielmo Pepe was one of three flotilla leaders laid down in Genoa in 1913. In 1916, it was given two 76mm (3in) anti-aircraft guns, but these were removed the next year. In 1921, the ship was reclassified as a destroyer and in June 1938 was transferred to Spain. Renamed *Teruel*, it served until scrapped in 1947.

SPECIFICATIONS	
Type:	Italian destroyer
Displacement:	1235 tonnes (1216 tons)
Dimensions:	85m x 8m x 2.8m (278ft 10in x 26ft 3in x 9ft 2in)
Machinery:	Twin screws, turbines
Top speed:	31.5 knots
Main armament:	Six 102mm (4in) guns, four 450mm (17.7in) torpedo tubes
Launched:	September 1914

TIMELINE

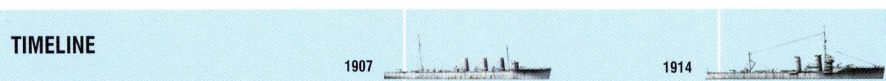

1907   1914

FLOTILLA LEADERS, ITALIAN & BRITISH

Faulknor

Designed by J. S. White in 1912 as *Almirante Simpson* for the Chilean Navy, the ship was taken over by the British in August 1914. *Faulknor* was more heavily armed than British destroyers, with four guns firing forward. After 1918, it was restored to Chile and served until stricken from the effective list in 1933.

SPECIFICATIONS	
Type:	British flotilla leader
Displacement:	2024 tonnes (1993 tons)
Dimensions:	100m x 10m x 6.4m (330ft 10in x 32ft 6in x 21ft 1in)
Machinery:	Triple screws, turbines
Top speed:	29 knots
Main armament:	Six 102mm (4in) guns, four 533mm (21in) torpedo tubes
Launched:	February 1914

Augusto Riboty

Augusto Riboty and two sister-ships were planned as lightly-armoured light cruisers but emerged as flotilla leaders, the flagships of destroyer groups, with heavier armament. *Carlo Alberto Racchia* and *Carlo Mirabello* were sunk by mines, but *Augusto Riboty* survived the World Wars, to be scrapped in the 1940s.

SPECIFICATIONS	
Type:	Italian flotilla leader
Displacement:	2003 tonnes (1972 tons)
Dimensions:	103.7m x 9.7m x 3.6m (340ft x 32ft x 12ft)
Machinery:	Twin screws, turbines
Main armament:	Eight 102mm (4in) guns
Launched:	1916

Falco

Laid down in 1913 for the Romanian fleet as *Viscol*, it was taken over by the Italian Navy in July 1916, renamed *Falco* and reclassified as a scout, but not completed until 1920. In 1937, it was transferred to Spanish service for the Nationalists and renamed *Ceuta*. It was discarded in 1948.

SPECIFICATIONS	
Type:	Italian flotilla leader
Displacement:	1788 tonnes (1760 tons)
Dimensions:	94.7m x 9.5m x 3.6m (310ft 8in x 31ft 2in x 11ft 10in)
Machinery:	Twin screws, turbines
Top speed:	35.2 knots
Main armament:	Three 152mm (6in) guns
Launched:	August 1919

  1916  1919

SHIP TYPES 1900–1929

Minelayers & Minesweepers

Nautical mines had a long history, but mass production in 1914–18 made them into a greater menace than ever before. Minelaying and minesweeping were among the more hazardous of routine tasks that naval ships had to undertake. Some sweepers were also fitted out to lay mines, but the two activities were very different.

Fugas

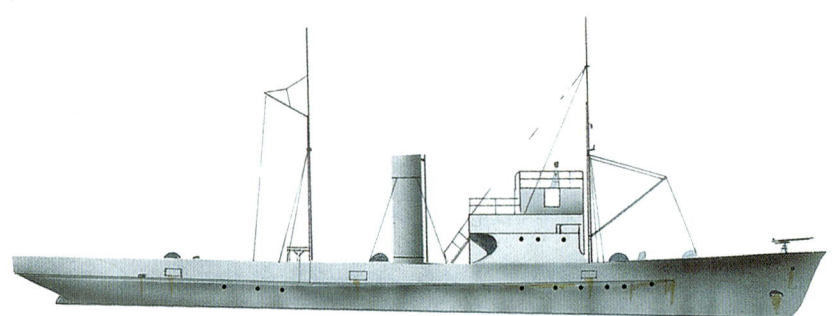

Mines were of concern to the Russian Navy after its defeat by the Japanese in 1904. Designated as a minesweeper, this light vessel could also lay mines. *Fugas* was mined off Saurop in November 1916; three of its four sisters were also mined during World War I, the fourth surviving to be scrapped in 1930.

SPECIFICATIONS	
Type:	Russian minesweeper
Displacement:	152 tonnes (150 tons)
Dimensions:	45.1m x 6.1m x 1.9m (148ft x 20ft x 6ft)
Machinery:	Twin screws, double expansion engines
Main armament:	One 63mm (2.5in) gun
Launched:	1910

Helle

Originally ordered as a light cruiser for the Chinese Navy, *Helle* was bought from its US builders by Greece. In 1928, it was rebuilt as a minelayer, with substantial changes to the superstructure and internal arrangements, as well as new engines and boilers. It was sunk in August 1940 by the Italian submarine *Delfino*.

SPECIFICATIONS	
Type:	Greek minelayer
Displacement:	2641.6 tonnes (2600 tons)
Dimensions:	98.1m x 9.75m x 4.3m (322ft x 39ft x 14ft)
Machinery:	Triple screws, turbines
Top speed:	18 knots
Main armament:	Two 152mm (6in) guns
Armour:	50–25mm (2–1in) deck
Complement:	232
Launched:	1912

TIMELINE — 1910 — 1912 — 1913

Chamäleon

Stealth and speed were essential for minelaying. *Chamäleon* was the most successful minelayer in the Austrian Navy. Rails were set into the main deck for handling the mines. Light armament for use against torpedo craft and aircraft was carried. In 1920, it was surrendered to the British, and scrapped in Italy.

SPECIFICATIONS	
Type:	Austrian minelayer
Displacement:	1184 tonnes (1165 tons)
Dimensions:	88m x 9m x 3m (288ft 8in x 30ft 2in x 8ft 10in)
Machinery:	Twin screws, vertical triple expansion engines
Main armament:	Four 90mm (3.5in) guns, 300 mines
Launched:	December 1913

Daffodil

Daffodil was one of 12 multi-purpose surface vessels capable of serving as minesweepers, escorts and training ships. Steadying sails helped to keep their heads to the wind when sweeping. Initially *Daffodil* was used as a minesweeper, but it was transferred to convoy escort duties in 1917. It was sold in 1935.

SPECIFICATIONS	
Type:	British minesweeper/sloop
Displacement:	1219 tonnes (1200 tons)
Dimensions:	80m x 10m x 3m (262ft 6in x 33ft x 11ft)
Machinery:	Single screw, triple expansion engines
Top speed:	16.5 knots
Main armament:	Two 76mm (3in) guns
Launched:	August 1915

Pluton

A minelaying cruiser, *Pluton* was used in peacetime as a gunnery training ship. In 1939 it was renamed *La Tour d'Auvergne*. Based with the Mediterranean Fleet, it became a training ship for midshipmen. An accidental mine detonation set off internal explosions and destroyed it at Casablanca on 18 September 1939.

SPECIFICATIONS	
Type:	French minelayer
Displacement:	6604 tonnes (6500 tons) full load
Dimensions:	152.5m x 15.6m x 5.18m (500ft 4in x 51ft 2in x 17ft)
Machinery:	Twin screws, geared turbines
Top speed:	30 knots
Main armament:	Four 140mm (5in) guns, four 76mm (3in) guns, 290 mines
Complement:	424
Launched:	1929

Monitors & Large Gun-Boats, 1900–1929

In World War I, the idea of the monitor was revived, for coastal defence and the bombardment of shore targets. It punched well above its weight and was relatively cheap to construct, certainly compared with the battleships whose guns it shared.

Humber

One of three shallow-draught monitors built for Brazil and taken over by the Royal Navy in 1914, *Humber* saw considerable war service. In 1920 it was sold to a Dutch salvage company and converted to a crane barge, and was still operating as such in 1939. It was broken up some time after 1945.

SPECIFICATIONS	
Type:	British monitor
Displacement:	1544 tonnes (1520 tons)
Dimensions:	81m x 14.9m x 1.7m (266ft 9in x 49ft x 5ft 8in)
Machinery:	Twin screws, triple expansion engines
Top speed:	9.6 knots
Main armament:	Two 152mm (6in) guns, two 120mm (4.7in) mortars
Armour:	76mm (3in) belt, 51mm (2in) deck over magazines
Complement:	140
Launched:	June 1913

Glatton

Glatton was one of a pair originally ordered by Norway in 1913 and laid down in Britain later that year. In November 1914, both were bought by the Royal Navy for service in World War I, and modified to take standard British shells. *Glatton* blew up at Dover in September 1918, shortly after completion.

SPECIFICATIONS	
Type:	British coast defence ship
Displacement:	5831 tonnes (5740 tons)
Dimensions:	94.5m x 22.4m x 5m (310ft x 73ft 6in x 16ft 5in)
Machinery:	Twin screws, triple expansion engines
Top speed:	12 knots
Rigging:	Three masts, square rig
Main armament:	Two 233mm (9.2in) guns, four 152mm (6in) guns
Armour:	76–178mm (3–7in) belt, 203mm (9in) on turrets, 152–203mm (6–9in) on barbettes
Launched:	August 1914

TIMELINE

1913  1914

Bosna

Bosna was a shallow-draught monitor built for service on the River Danube and its tributaries. It was renamed *Temes* soon after being laid down in 1914. The original *Temes* was sunk that year but later raised and returned to service, and *Bosna* reverted to its old name in 1917. In 1920 it became the Yugoslav *Vardar*.

SPECIFICATIONS	
Type:	Austrian river monitor
Displacement:	590 tonnes (580 tons)
Dimensions:	62m x 10m x 1m (203ft 5in x 33ft 9in x 4ft 3in)
Machinery:	Twin screws, triple expansion engines
Top speed:	13.5 knots
Main armament:	Two 120mm (4.7in) guns, two 120mm (4.7in) howitzers
Launched:	1914

Marshal Soult

Fitting heavy gun mountings on a draught of only 3m (10ft) was a challenge, and the barbette rose 5m (17ft) above the deck. Design speed was nine knots, but the engines were underpowered for such speed. The ship was also hard to steer. Adapted as a training ship in 1921, *Marshal Soult* was discarded in 1946.

SPECIFICATIONS	
Type:	British monitor
Displacement:	7010 tonnes (6900 tons)
Dimensions:	108.4m x 27m x 3m (355ft 8in x 90ft 3in x 10ft 6in)
Machinery:	Twin screws, diesel engines
Top speed:	6 knots
Main armament:	Two 380mm (15in) guns
Armour:	102mm (4in) deck, 330mm (13in) on turret
Complement:	228
Launched:	August 1915

Erebus

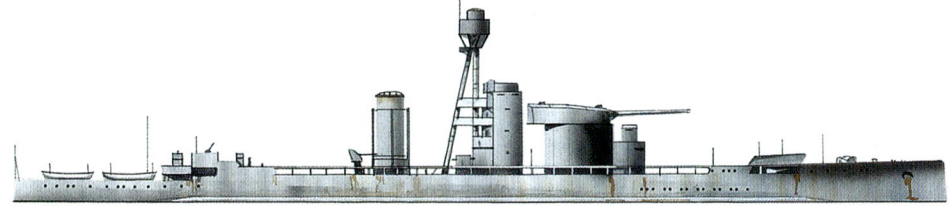

The two 380mm (15in) main guns were mounted in an armoured turret, placed on a tall barbette slightly forward of centre. Two 152mm (6in) guns were installed amidships. A low conning tower was placed forward of the main guns, and there was also a spotting station on the tripod mast. *Erebus* was broken up in 1946.

SPECIFICATIONS	
Type:	British monitor
Displacement:	8585 tonnes (8450 tons)
Dimensions:	123.4m x 26.9m x 3.6m (404ft 10in x 88ft 3in x 11ft 10in)
Machinery:	Twin screws, triple expansion engines
Top speed:	14 knots
Main armament:	Two 380mm (15in) guns, two 152mm (6in) guns
Armour:	102mm (4in) internal belt, 102mm (4in) over magazine, 330mm (13in) on turret face
Launched:	1916

SHIP TYPES 1900–1929

Fleet Auxiliaries 1900–29

A wide range of auxiliary ships existed to supply a fleet. Coal, oil, ammunition, water and food were the staples that had to be transported or ferried out to fleets or squadrons away from the permanent naval bases. Most of these were of merchant ship type, ranging from fishing boat size up to ships of several thousand tonnes.

Bengasi

As the Turkish transport *Derna*, *Bengasi* ran the Italian blockade of Tripoli. With the fall of Tripoli, it was sunk in harbour by the retreating Turks but raised in 1911 and taken into the Italian Navy, serving as a transport along the coast of the Mediterranean. It was sold into private ownership in November 1925.

SPECIFICATIONS
Type:	Italian naval transport
Displacement:	3617 tonnes (3560 tons)
Dimensions:	87.3m x 11.2m x 5.8m (286ft 8in x 37ft x 19ft)
Machinery:	Single screw, vertical triple expansion engines
Main armament:	Two 76mm (3in) guns
Launched:	1904

Bronte

A purpose-built fleet collier and oil carrier, with capacious holds and special equipment to carry out rapid refuelling of ships at sea, *Bronte* was captured by the British on 21 August 1941, renamed *Empire Peri* and used for the same purposes. It was returned to Italy in 1946 and discarded in the same year.

SPECIFICATIONS
Type:	Italian naval fuel carrier
Displacement:	9611 tonnes (9460 tons)
Dimensions:	119m x 14.3m x 7.5m (391ft x 47ft x 25ft)
Machinery:	Twin screws, vertical triple expansion engines
Top speed:	14.5 knots
Main armament:	Four 6-pounder guns
Launched:	1904

TIMELINE

1904   1916

Cyclop

Cyclop was twin hulled with massive gantries running their full length. Maximum lift was 1219 tonnes (1200 tons). Submarines were hoisted between the hulls and repaired *in situ*, or carried to a repair basin. *Cyclop* entered service in 1918. Handed over to Britain at the end of World War I, it was scrapped in 1923.

SPECIFICATIONS	
Type:	German submarine salvage vessel
Displacement:	4074 tonnes (4010 tons)
Dimensions:	94m x 19m x 6m (308ft 5in x 64ft 4in x 20ft 8in)
Machinery:	Twin screws, vertical triple expansion engines
Top speed:	9 knots
Launched:	1916

Blenheim

The Blue Funnel cargo liner *Achilles* was converted into a depot ship for destroyers early in World War II. Eight 20mm (0.8in) anti-aircraft guns were mounted. *Blenheim* was equipped with tools and spares for maintenance and light repair work, and to provide medical facilities. It was scrapped in 1948.

SPECIFICATIONS	
Type:	British depot ship
Displacement:	16,865 tonnes (16,600 tons)
Dimensions:	160m x 19m x 7.6m (528ft 6in x 63ft 3in x 25ft 3in)
Machinery:	Twin screws, geared turbines
Main armament:	Four 102mm (4in) guns
Launched:	1919

Dalmazia

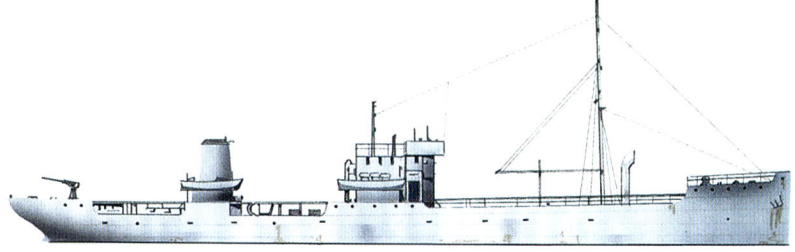

Originally a water carrier, *Dalmazia* served the Italian Navy for years, able to refuel vessels at sea as well as to supply naval oil depots. Its engines developed 1450hp at full speed. Cargo capacity was 1829 tonnes (1800 tons). It was armed with a 120mm (4.7in) gun and two 20mm (0.8in) anti-aircraft weapons.

SPECIFICATIONS	
Type:	Italian oiler
Displacement:	5080 tonnes (5000 tons)
Dimensions:	80m x 10m x 4.6m (260ft 6in x 32ft 6in x 15ft 3in)
Machinery:	Twin screws, triple expansion engines
Main Armament:	One 120mm (4.7in) gun
Launched:	1922

Submarines 1900–1909: Part 1

SHIP TYPES 1900–1929

From its uncertain beginnings in the previous century, the submarine had become a naval craft of increasing significance by the 1900s, though it was also plain that a great deal of development and crew training was necessary before its potential could be realized. Satisfactory surface propulsion was an unresolved problem.

Farfadet

A short-range electric-powered boat – 218.5km (115 miles) at 5.3 knots surfaced, and 53km (28 miles) at 4.3 knots submerged – *Farfadet* carried four torpedoes outside in cradles aft of the conning tower. It sank at Bizerta in 1905. Raised and recommissioned as *Follet* in 1909, it was removed from the effective list in 1913.

SPECIFICATIONS	
Type:	French submarine
Displacement:	188 tonnes (185 tons) [surface], 205 tonnes (202 tons) [submerged]
Dimensions:	41.3m x 2.9m x 2.6m (135ft 6in x 9ft 6in x 8ft 6in)
Machinery:	Single screw electric motors
Top speed:	6 knots [surface], 4.3 knots [submerged]
Main armament:	Four 450mm (17.7in) torpedo tubes
Launched:	May 1901

Espadon

By the 1880s, steam power was used to drive submarines on the surface, the machinery being shut down in order to switch to the newly introduced electric motors for underwater power. *Espadon* was one of this type of submarine. In service through World War I, it was removed from the effective list in 1919.

SPECIFICATIONS	
Type:	French submarine
Displacement:	159 tonnes (157 tons) [surface], 216 tonnes (213 tons) [submerged]
Dimensions:	32.5m x 3.9m x 2.5m (106ft 8in x 12ft 10in x 8ft 2in)
Machinery:	Single screw triple expansion steam engine [surface], electric motor [submerged]
Main armament:	Four 450mm (17.7in) torpedoes
Launched:	September 1901

TIMELINE

1901   1902

SUBMARINES 1900–1909: PART 1

A1

The 'A' class were the first British-designed submarines, and the first to have a proper conning tower to facilitate surface running. Originally one bow-mounted torpedo tube was fitted, but a second was installed from *A5* onwards. Between 1902 and 190, 13 were built. Some served during World War I, as training craft.

SPECIFICATIONS	
Type:	British submarine
Displacement:	194 tonnes (191 tons) [surface], 274.5 tonnes (270 tons) [submerged]
Dimensions:	30.5m x 3.4m (100ft x 11ft 2in)
Machinery:	160hp petrol motor [surface], 126hp electric motor [submerged]
Top speed:	9.5 knots [surface], 6 knots [submerged]
Main armament:	Two 460mm (18.1 in) torpedo tubes
Launched:	July 1902

B1

Even before the 'A' class submarines were completed, the 'B' class was underway, built by Vickers using their own engine design. The extended superstructure on the hull improved surface performance, while small hydroplanes on the conning tower assisted underwater handling. *B1* was scrapped in 1921.

SPECIFICATIONS	
Type:	British submarine
Displacement:	284 tonnes (280 tons) [surface], 319 tonnes (314 tons) [submerged]
Dimensions:	41m x 4.1m x 3m (135ft x 13ft 6in x 10ft)
Machinery:	Single screw petrol engine [surface], electric motor [submerged]
Main armament:	Two 457mm (18in) torpedo tubes
Launched:	October 1904

Hajen

Sweden's first naval submarine, *Hajen* was designed by engineer Carl Richson, who had studied submarine construction in America. Laid down at Stockholm in 1902, the boat underwent a major rebuild in 1916, and was lengthened by 1.8m (6ft). It was withdrawn from service in 1922 and remains a museum exhibit.

SPECIFICATIONS	
Type:	Swedish submarine
Displacement:	108 tonnes (107 tons) [surface], 130 tonnes (127 tons) [submerged]
Dimensions:	19.8m x 3.6m x 3m (65ft x 11ft 10in x 9ft 10in)
Machinery:	Single screw, paraffin engine [surface], electric motor [submerged]
Top speed:	9.5 knots [surface], 7 knots [submerged]
Main armament:	One 457mm (18in) torpedo tube
Launched:	July 1904

SHIP TYPES 1900–1929

U-9

Built at Danzig (Gdansk), *U-9* was a double-hulled boat, leader of a class of four. It was responsible for sinking four British cruisers in the North Sea during September–October 1914 (*Aboukir*, *Cressy*, *Hogue* and *Hawke*). In 1916 it was listed for training duties, and in 1918 it was handed over to Britain, and scrapped in 1919.

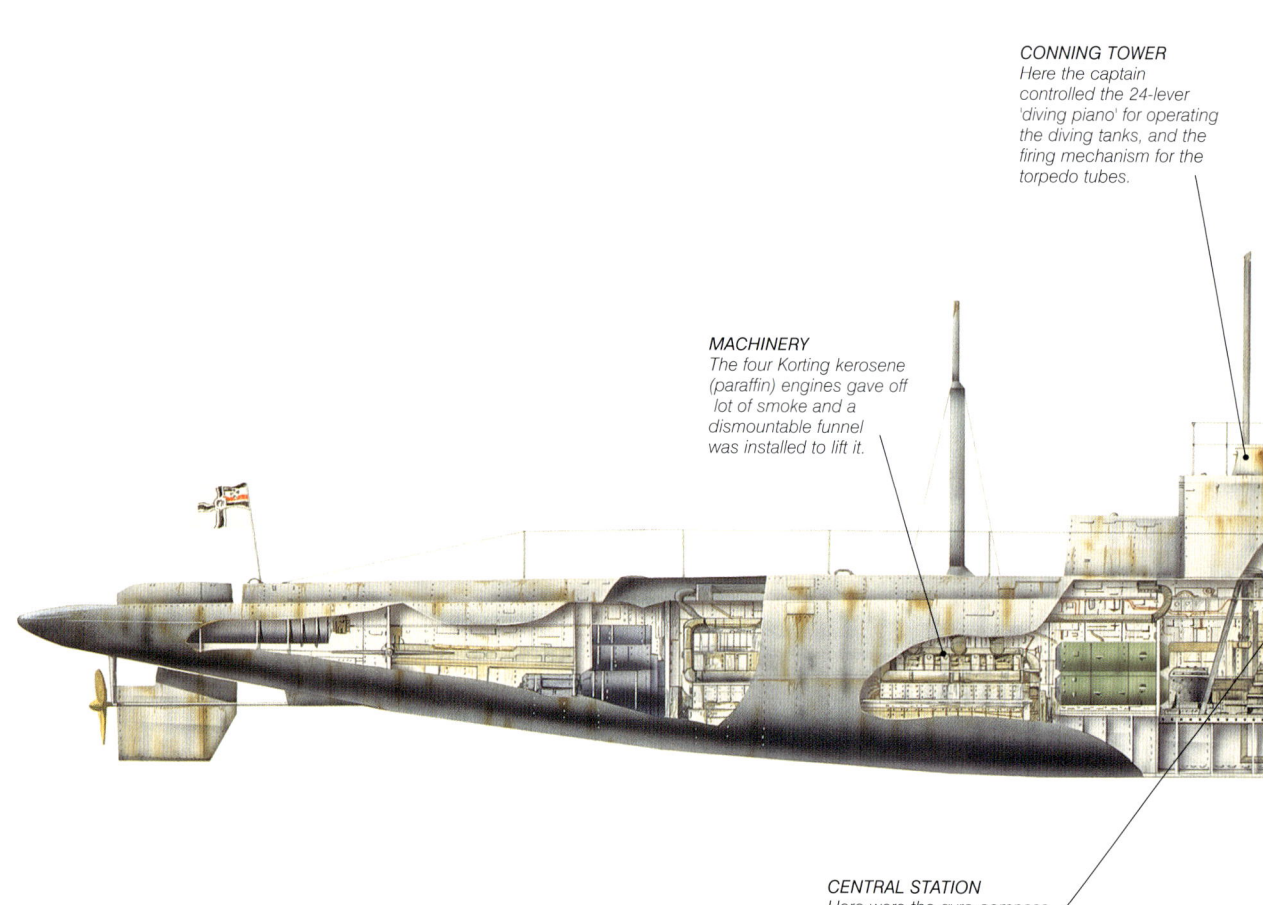

CONNING TOWER
Here the captain controlled the 24-lever 'diving piano' for operating the diving tanks, and the firing mechanism for the torpedo tubes.

MACHINERY
The four Korting kerosene (paraffin) engines gave off lot of smoke and a dismountable funnel was installed to lift it.

CENTRAL STATION
Here were the gyro-compass, hand-operating gear for the depth rudder, the bilge pumps and air compressors.

U-9

During World War I, the *U-9* sank three British cruisers – *Hogue*, *Cressy* and *Aboukir* – all in one hour. In total *U-9* sank 13 merchant ships and five warships during the war, creating a vast amount of wreckage.

SPECIFICATIONS	
Type:	German submarine
Displacement:	431.8 tonnes (425 tons) [surface], 610 tonnes (601 tons) [submerged]
Dimensions:	57.3m x 6m x 3.5m (188ft 7in x 19ft 7in x 11ft 6in)
Machinery:	Twin screws, kerosene engines [surface] electric motors [submerged]
Top speed:	14.2 knots [surface], 8 knots [submerged]
Main armament:	Four 450mm (17.7in) torpedo tubes, one 37mm (1.46in) gun
Launched:	1910

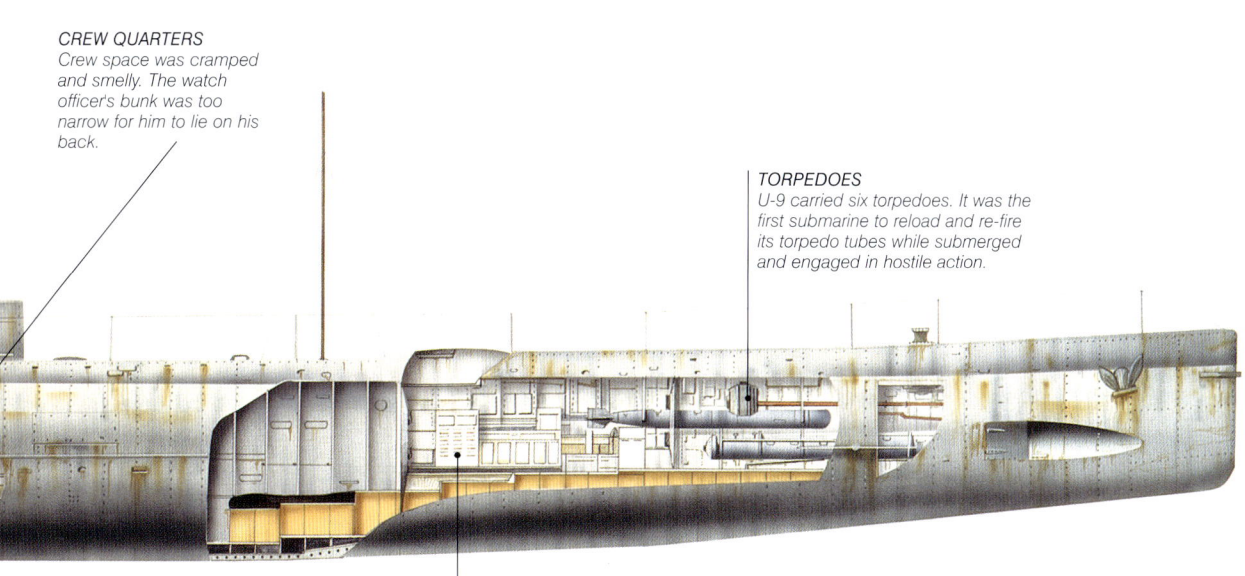

CREW QUARTERS
Crew space was cramped and smelly. The watch officer's bunk was too narrow for him to lie on his back.

TORPEDOES
U-9 carried six torpedoes. It was the first submarine to reload and re-fire its torpedo tubes while submerged and engaged in hostile action.

ELECTRICS
Electrical accumulators were placed throughout the forward section. Electrical equipment, especially the cooking stove, often short-circuited.

Submarines 1900–1909: Part 2

Work on submarine design and operation in several countries led to a succession of designs, each an improvement on the previous one. The diesel engine was introduced in France. Boats at this time were still relatively small and therefore had limited fuel capacity and torpedo storage, and extremely cramped crew quarters.

C Class

These were Britain's last petrol-engined submarines. All gave good service before and after World War I. Three were based at Hong Kong, and four were sent to the Baltic Sea, where they were deliberately sunk to prevent them falling into German hands. *C3* was used to blow up a viaduct at Zeebrugge in 1918.

SPECIFICATIONS	
Type:	British submarine
Displacement:	295 tonnes (290 tons) [surface], 325 tonnes (320 tons) [submerged]
Dimensions:	43m x 4m x 3.5m (141ft x 13ft 1in x 11ft 4in)
Machinery:	Single screw, petrol engine [surface], electric motor [submerged]
Top speed:	12 knots [surface], 7.5 knots [submerged]
Main armament:	Two 457mm (18in) torpedo tubes
Launched:	1906

U-1

Germany's first practical submarine was one of the most successful of the period. Surfaced range at 10 knots was 2850km (1500 miles). Submerged range at 5 knots was 80km (50 miles). *U-1* was a trial boat, and later a training vessel. Discarded in 1919, it was donated to the Deutsches Museum, München.

SPECIFICATIONS	
Type:	German submarine
Displacement:	241 tonnes (238 tons) [surface], 287 tonnes (283 tons) [submerged]
Dimensions:	42.4m x 3.8m x 3.2m (139ft x 12ft 6in x 10ft 6in)
Machinery:	Twin screws, kerosene engines [surface], electric motors [submerged]
Top speed:	10.8 knots [surface], 8.7 knots [submerged]
Main armament:	One 450mm (17.7in) torpedo tube
Launched:	August 1906

D1

As the first British submarines built for extended patrols away from coastal areas, the 'D' class marked a step forward in design. They had greater internal space and increased displacement, as well as diesel engines. They were also equipped for wireless communications. *D1* was sunk as a target in 1918.

SPECIFICATIONS	
Type:	British submarine
Displacement:	490 tonnes (483 tons) [surface], 604 tonnes (595 tons) [submerged]
Dimensions:	50m x 6m x 3m (163ft x 20ft 6in x 10ft 5in)
Machinery:	Twin screws, diesel engines [surface], electric motors [submerged]
Top speed:	14 knots [surface], 9 knots [submerged]
Main armament:	Three 457mm (18in) torpedo tubes, one 12-pdr gun
Launched:	August 1908

Grayling

Formerly numbered *D2*, *Grayling* later became *SS18*. It was one of the last submarines in the US Navy to have petrol engines, which were a source of constant anxiety to the 15-man crew. The engines developed 600hp, giving a surface range of 2356km (1240 miles) at 10 knots. It was discarded in 1922.

SPECIFICATIONS	
Type:	US submarine
Displacement:	292 tonnes (288 tons) [surface], 342 tonnes (337 tons) [submerged]
Dimensions:	41m x 4.2m x 3.6m (135ft x 13ft 9in x 12ft)
Machinery:	Twin screws, petrol engines [surface], electric motors [submerged]
Top speed:	12 knots [surface], 9.5 knots [submerged]
Main armament:	Four 457mm (18in) torpedo tubes
Launched:	June 1909

Dykkeren

Constructed by the Fiat-San Giorgio yards at La Spezia, Italy, *Dykkeren* was sold to the Danish Navy in October 1909, and used to patrol in the Kattegat and Skagerrak. In 1916 it collided with the Norwegian steamer *Vesta* and sank. Salvaged in 1917, it was sent for breaking up in the following year.

SPECIFICATIONS	
Type:	Danish submarine
Displacement:	107 tonnes (105 tons) [surface], 134 tonnes (132 tons) [submerged]
Dimensions:	34.7m x 3.3m x 2m (113ft 10in x 10ft 10in x 7ft 3in)
Machinery:	Twin screws, petrol engine [surface], electric motor [submerged]
Top speed:	12 knots [surface], 7.5 knots [submerged]
Main armament:	Two 457mm (18in) torpedo tubes
Launched:	June 1909

SHIP TYPES 1900–1929

World War I Submarines: Part 1

On one afternoon in September 1914, the German submarine *U-9* sank three British cruisers one after another in the North Sea, with the loss of over 1400 lives. That action brought home the fact that the submarine was now a lethal element in naval strategy. The U-boats almost succeeded in severing Britain's Atlantic supply lines.

Atropo

The *Medusa* class was German-designed. *Atropo* was commissioned in March 1912 and served through World War I, being stricken in 1919. It had two periscopes fitted, one in the conning tower and one in the central control room, both of which had tapered ends to reduce their visibility to the enemy.

SPECIFICATIONS	
Type:	Italian submarine
Displacement:	234.6 tonnes (231 tons) [surface], 325 tonnes (320 tons) [submerged]
Dimensions:	44.5m x 4.4m x 2.7m (146ft x 14ft 5in x 8ft 10in)
Machinery:	Twin screws, diesels [surface], electric motors [submerged]
Top speed:	15.2 knots [surface], 7.4 knots [submerged]
Main armament:	Two 450mm (17.7in) torpedo tubes
Launched:	1912

Euler

In 1914, France had the most effective submarine fleet, rapidly to be overtaken by Germany. *Euler* formed part of a large class of 16 boats. Range was 3230km (1700nm) at 10 knots on the surface, and 160km (84nm) at 5 knots submerged. *Euler* was removed from the effective list in the 1920s.

SPECIFICATIONS	
Type:	French submarine
Displacement:	403 tonnes (397 tons) [surface], 560 tonnes (551 tons) [submerged]
Dimensions:	52m x 5.4m x 3m (171ft x 17ft 9in x 10ft 3in)
Machinery:	Twin screws, diesel engines [surface], electric motors [submerged]
Top speed:	14 knots [surface], 7 knots [submerged]
Main armament:	One 450mm (17.7in) torpedo tube, four drop collars, plus two external cradles
Launched:	October 1912

TIMELINE

1912

WORLD WAR I SUBMARINES: PART 1

F4

F4 left Honolulu harbour on 25 March 1915 for a short trial run but never returned. It was located at a depth of 91m (300ft), well beyond the depth from which such a vessel had hitherto been raised. Five months later, however, it was successfully raised, thereby setting up a new world deep-sea diving record.

SPECIFICATIONS	
Type:	US submarine
Displacement:	335 tonnes (330 tons) [surface], 406 tonnes (400 tons) [submerged]
Dimensions:	43.5m x 4.7m x 3.7m (142ft 9in x 15ft 5in x 12ft 2in)
Machinery:	Twin screws, diesels [surface], electric motors [submerged]
Top speed:	11 knots [surface], 5 knots [submerged]
Main armament:	Four torpedo tubes
Launched:	January 1912

Gustave Zédé

Gustav Zédé's two reciprocating engines developed 3500hp, with electric motors developing 1640hp. Range was 2660km (1400 miles) at 10 knots surfaced, and 256km (135 miles) at 5 knots submerged. In 1921–22 it was fitted with diesel engines from U-165, and a new bridge. It was decommissioned in 1937.

SPECIFICATIONS	
Type:	French submarine
Displacement:	862 tonnes (849 tons) [surface], 1115 tonnes (1098 tons) [submerged]
Dimensions:	74m x 6m x 3.7m (242ft 9in x 19ft 8in x 12ft 2in)
Machinery:	Twin screws, reciprocating engines [surface], electric motors [submerged]
Top speed:	17.5 knots [surface], 11 knots [submerged]
Main armament:	Eight 450mm (17.7in) torpedo tubes
Launched:	May 1913

G1

The 'G' class, based on the 'E' class design, was ordered in 1914 after reports that Germany was planning a fleet of double-hulled, ocean-going submarines. Fifteen were built between 1915 and 1917, and used in the North Sea. G1 was scrapped in 1920; the last member of the class was broken up in 1928.

SPECIFICATIONS	
Type:	British submarine
Displacement:	704 tonnes (693 tons) [surface], 850 tonnes (836 tons) [submerged]
Dimensions:	57m x 6.9m x 4.1m (187ft x 22ft x 13ft 6in)
Machinery:	Twin screws, diesel engines [surface], electric motors [submerged]
Top speed:	14.25 knots [surface], 9 knots [submerged]
Main armament:	One 533mm (21in) and four 457mm (18in) torpedo tubes, one 76mm (3in) gun
Launched:	August 1915

SHIP TYPES 1900–1929

World War I Submarines: Part 2

Submarines got bigger during World War I, to undertake longer cruises and dive deeper. The preferred German tactic was for the submarine to approach submerged, then surface and despatch its target with gunfire, saving torpedoes. The British and French also fitted submarines with 76mm (3in) or even larger guns.

Dupuy de Lôme

A submarine gunship, *Dupuy de Lôme* served with the Morocco Flotilla from 1917 until the end of World War I, and was then reconstructed. The original steam engines were replaced by more powerful diesels taken from German submarines, which developed 2900hp. *Dupuy de Lôme* was discarded in 1935.

SPECIFICATIONS
Type:	French submarine
Displacement:	846 tonnes (833 tons) [surface], 1307 tonnes (1287 tons) [submerged]
Dimensions:	75m x 6.4m x 3.6m (246ft x 21ft x 11ft 6in)
Machinery:	Twin screws, three cylinder reciprocating steam engine [surface], electric motors [submerged]
Top speed:	15 knots [surface], 8.5 knots [submerged]
Main armament:	Eight 450mm (17.7in) torpedo tubes, two 76mm (3in) guns
Launched:	September 1915

J1

After some post-launch modification, this submarine could maintain 17 knots surfaced in heavy seas. Range at 12.5 knots surfaced was 9500km (5000 miles). Later a 102mm (4in) gun was installed at the front of the conning tower. *J1* was handed over to the Australian Navy in 1919. It was broken up in 1924.

SPECIFICATIONS
Type:	British submarine
Displacement:	1223 tonnes (1204 tons) [surface], 1849 tonnes (1820 tons) [submerged]
Dimensions:	84m x 7m x 4.3m (275ft 7in x 23ft x 14ft)
Machinery:	Triple screws, diesel engines [surface], electric motors [submerged]
Top speed:	17 knots [surface], 9.5 knots [submerged]
Main armament:	Six 457mm (18in) torpedo tubes, one 76mm (3in) gun
Launched:	November 1915

TIMELINE

1915

WORLD WAR I SUBMARINES: PART 2

E20

More than 50 strong, the 'E' class included the first submarines capable of extended overseas patrols, and were among the first to mount a deck gun. Deployed to the Eastern Mediterranean/Black Sea theatre, *E20* was sunk in 1915 by the German *UB-14*, becoming the first submarine to be sunk by another.

SPECIFICATIONS	
Type:	British submarine
Displacement:	677 tonnes (667 tons) [surface], 820 tonnes (807 tons) [submerged]
Dimensions:	55.6m x 4.6m x 3.8m (182ft 5in x 15ft x 12ft 6in)
Machinery:	Twin screws, diesel engine [surface], electric motors [submerged]
Main armament:	Five 457mm (18in) torpedo tubes, one 76mm (3in) gun
Top speed:	14 knots [surface], 9 knots [submerged]
Launched:	June 1915

Balilla

Originally ordered from Italian builders in 1913 by the German Navy as *U-42*, *Balilla* was taken over by the Italian Navy in 1915. It was deployed in the Adriatic Sea, but while on patrol on 14 July 1916 it was sunk by Austrian torpedo boats with the loss of all 38 crew members.

SPECIFICATIONS	
Type:	Italian submarine
Displacement:	740 tonnes (728 tons) [surface], 890 tonnes (876 tons) [submerged]
Dimensions:	65m x 6m x 4m (213ft 3in x 19ft 8in x 13ft)
Machinery:	Twin screws, diesel engines [surface], electric motor [submerged]
Top speed:	14 knots [surface], 9 knots [submerged]
Main armament:	Four 450mm (17.7in) torpedo tubes, two 76mm (3in) anti-aircraft guns
Complement:	38
Launched:	August 1915

L3

L3 was the first US submarine to mount a deck gun, which could be retracted vertically into a deckhouse, leaving only a small portion of the barrel exposed, reducing underwater drag. Range at 11 knots surfaced was 6270km (3300 miles) and at 5 knots submerged was 285km (150 miles). *L3* was broken up in 1932.

SPECIFICATIONS	
Type:	US submarine
Displacement:	457 tonnes (450 tons) [surface], 556 tonnes (548 tons) [submerged]
Dimensions:	51m x 5.3m x 4m (167ft 4in x 17ft 4in x 13ft 5in)
Machinery:	Twin screws, diesel engines [surface], electric motors [submerged]
Top speed:	15 knots [surface], 9 knots [submerged]
Main armament:	Four 457mm (18in) torpedo tubes, one 76mm (3in) gun
Launched:	February 1915

SHIP TYPES 1900–1929

World War I Submarines: Part 3

All the major powers built large submarine fleets. At the same time, intense effort was put into anti-submarine defence, with booms and nets across the entrances to naval anchorages. Belated employment by Britain of the convoy system made the U-boats' task more difficult, and many were sunk by escort warships.

N1

The seven 'N' class boats, slightly smaller than the previous 'L' class, had reduced engine power in order to achieve greater reliability. *N1* and her class were the first US submarines to have metal bridges, and the last until 1946 to be designed without deck guns. *N1*, re-numbered *SS53* in 1920, was broken up in 1931.

SPECIFICATIONS

Type:	US submarine
Displacement:	353 tonnes (348 tons) [surface], 420 tonnes (414 tons) [submerged]
Dimensions:	45m x 4.8m x 3.8m (147ft 4in x 15ft 9in x 12ft 6in)
Machinery:	Twin screws, diesel engines [surface], electric motors [submerged]
Top speed:	13 knots [surface], 11 knots [submerged]
Main armament:	Four 457mm (18in) torpedo tubes
Launched:	December 1916

Barbarigo

Barbarigo was one of a group of four medium-sized submarines. The batteries were placed in four watertight compartments under the horizontal deck that ran the length of the vessel. The *Barbarigo* class could dive to 50m (164ft) only, but underwater manoeuvrability was good. *Barbarigo* was sold in 1928.

SPECIFICATIONS

Type:	Italian submarine
Displacement:	774 tonnes (762 tons) [surface], 938 tonnes (923 tons) [submerged]
Dimensions:	67m x 6m x 3.8m (220ft x 19ft 8in x 12ft 6in)
Machinery:	Twin screws diesel [surface], electric motors [submerged]
Top speed:	16 knots [surface], 9.8 knots [submerged]
Main armament:	Six 450mm (17.7in) torpedo tubes, two 76mm (3in) guns
Launched:	November 1917

TIMELINE

1916   1917

WORLD WAR I SUBMARINES: PART 3

M1

M1's single 305mm (12in) gun was mounted in the front of the extended conning tower and, if already loaded, could be fired from periscope depth in 30 seconds, or 20 seconds if breaking the surface. *M1* served briefly in the war and was sunk in November 1925 after it was rammed by the merchant vessel *Vidar*.

SPECIFICATIONS
Type:	British submarine
Displacement:	1619 tonnes (1594 tons) [surface], 1977 tonnes (1946 tons) [submerged]
Dimensions:	90m x 7.5m x 4.9m (295ft 7in x 24ft 7in x 16ft)
Machinery:	Twin screws, diesel engines [surface], electric motors [submerged]
Top speed:	15 knots [surface], 9 knots [submerged]
Main armament:	One 305mm (12in) gun, four 533mm (21in) torpedo tubes
Launched:	July 1917

U-140

U-139 to *U-147* were the first German submersibles to be named (*U-140* was *Weddigen*). Fitted with six torpedo tubes but a limited torpedo supply, they also had two 150mm guns. The intention was for the submarine to surface and sink the target with gunfire when possible. *U-140* was sunk as a target in July 1921.

SPECIFICATIONS
Type:	German submarine
Displacement:	1960 tonnes (1930 tons) [surface], 2522 tonnes (2483 tons) [submerged]
Dimensions:	92m x 9m x 5.3m (301ft 10in x 29ft 10in x 17ft 4in)
Machinery:	Twin screws, diesel engines [surface], electric motors [submerged]
Top speed:	15.5 knots [surface], 7.5 knots [submerged]
Main armament:	Two 150mm (5.9in) guns, six 500mm (19.7in) torpedo tubes
Launched:	November 1917

H4

H4 was ordered from the Electric Boat Company for the Russian Tsarist navy, but after the Revolution was purchased for the US Navy in 1918. In 1920, the boat was renumbered *SS147*. The US 'H' class had a modest depth limit of 6m (20ft) but were considered very successful boats. *H4* was scrapped in 1931.

SPECIFICATIONS
Type:	US submarine
Displacement:	398 tonnes (392 tons) [surface], 529 tonnes (521 tons) [submerged]
Dimensions:	45.8m x 4.8m x 3.8m (150ft 3in x 15ft 9in x 12ft 6in)
Machinery:	Twin screws, diesel engines [surface], electric motors [submerged]
Top speed:	14 knots [surface], 10 knots [submerged]
Main armament:	Four 457mm (18in) torpedoes
Launched:	October 1918

1918

SHIP TYPES 1900–1929

Deutschland

Deutschland, of the *U-151* class, was a cargo-carrying submarine built to beat the British blockade of German ports. It made two trips to the United States for rubber, nickel and other high-value cargo before America entered World War I. *Deutschland* was then armed as *U-155.* Later ceded to Britain, it was scrapped in 1922.

Deutschland

Before America's entry into the war in 1917, the Germans were quick to recognize the potential of large, cargo-carrying submarines as a means of beating the blockade imposed on Germany's ports by the Royal Navy. The *U-151* was converted for mercantile use and named *Deutschland.*

SPECIFICATIONS	
Type:	German submarine
Displacement:	1536 tonnes (1512 tons) [surface], 1905 tonnes (1875 tons) [submerged]
Dimensions:	65m x 8.9m x 5.3m (213ft 3in x 29ft 2in x 17ft 5in)
Machinery:	Twin screws, diesel engines [surface], electric motors [submerged]
Top speed:	12.4 knots [surface], 5.2 knots [submerged]
Launched:	March 1916

EXPLOSION
During breaking-up at Birkenhead in 1921, the boat was ripped apart by an explosion which killed five young apprentices.

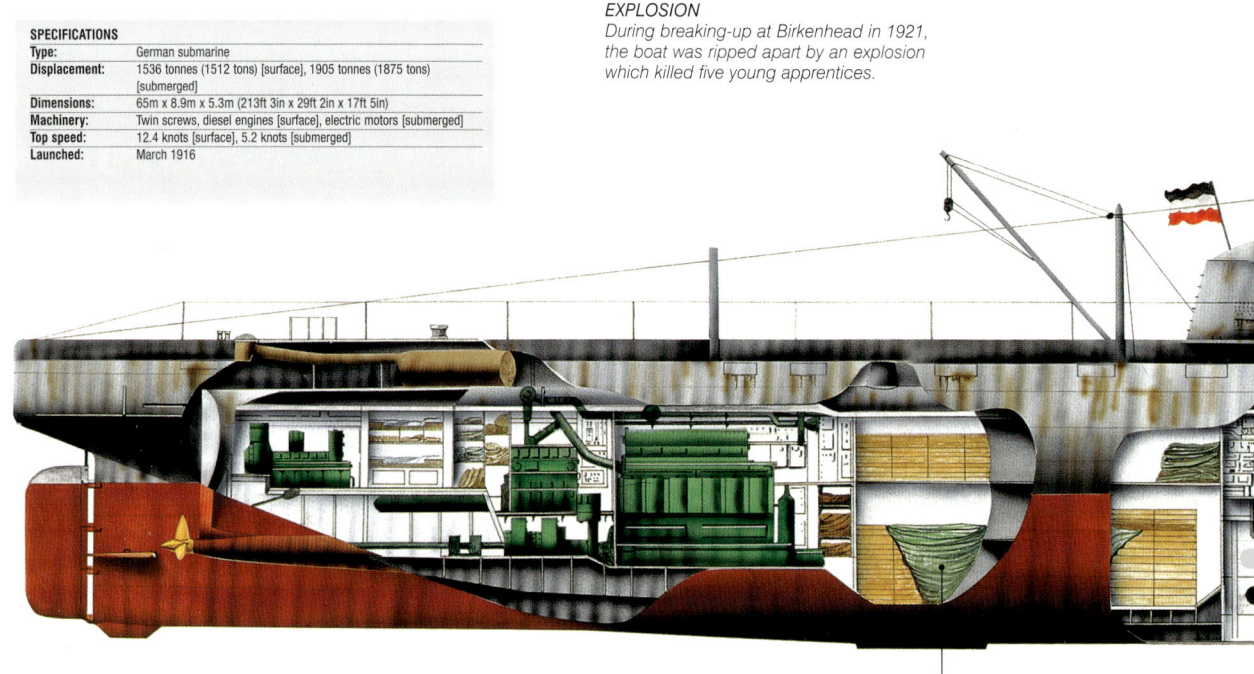

CARGO SPACE
Cargo capacity was 700 tonnes (690 tons). Items transported included chemical dyes, drugs, nickel, rubber, zinc, copper and silver.

DEUTSCHLAND

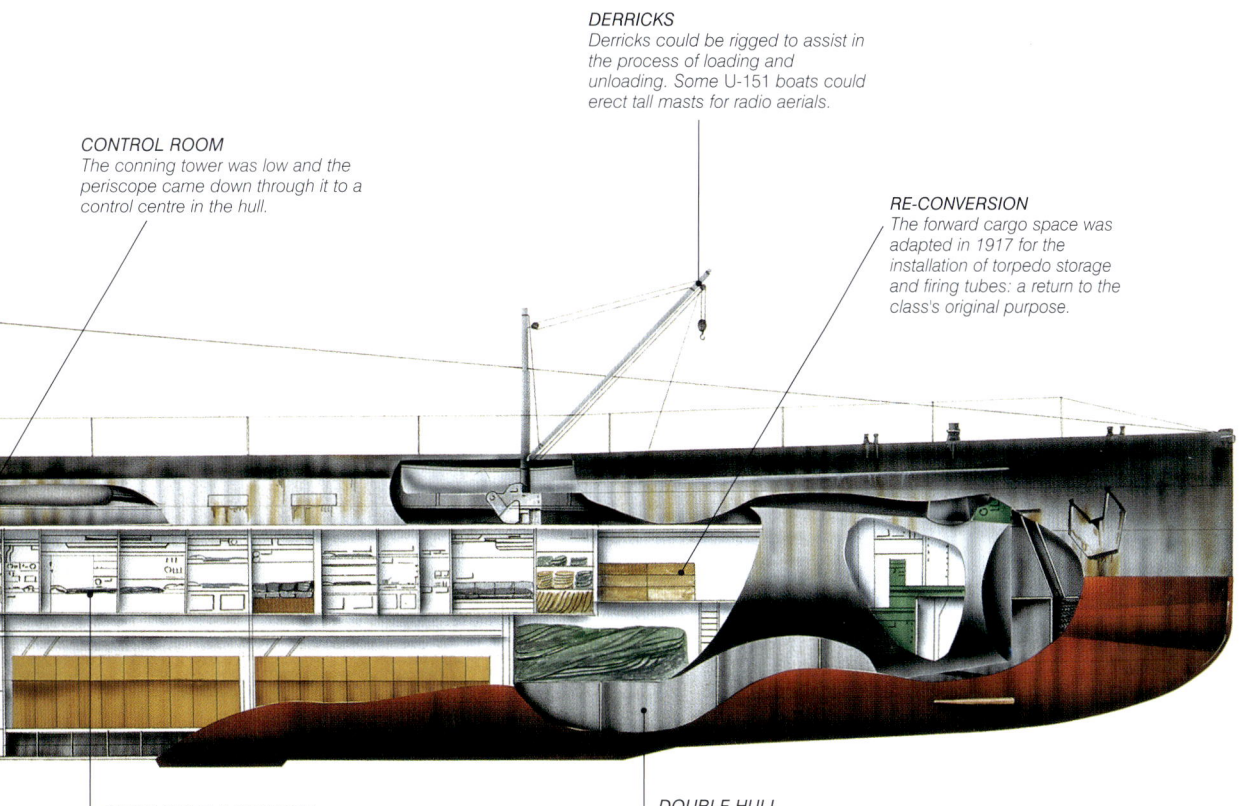

DERRICKS
Derricks could be rigged to assist in the process of loading and unloading. Some U-151 boats could erect tall masts for radio aerials.

CONTROL ROOM
The conning tower was low and the periscope came down through it to a control centre in the hull.

RE-CONVERSION
The forward cargo space was adapted in 1917 for the installation of torpedo storage and firing tubes: a return to the class's original purpose.

CREW ACCOMMODATION
Greater size meant slightly more generous crew space than on most U-boats, but conditions remained somewhat claustrophobic.

DOUBLE HULL
Part of the cargo of rubber was stored in the space between the outer hull and the inner pressure hull.

175

SHIP TYPES 1900–1929

Post-1919 Submarine Development: Part 1

The lesson of World War I, not fully digested by the world's admiralties at the time, was that aircraft carriers and submarines would be the key warships in future conflagrations. Development work continued on submarines, with attention given to improvements to the now almost-universal diesel-mechanical surface propulsion.

L23

L23 was one of the longest-surviving members of a large, successful class of single-hull submarines ordered and mostly built during World War I. By World War II, only *L23* and two others remained in service. *L23* survived the war and foundered on the way to the breakers in 1946.

SPECIFICATIONS	
Type:	British submarine
Displacement:	904 tonnes (890 tons) [surface], 1097 tonnes (1080 tons) [submerged]
Dimensions:	72.7m x 7.2m x 3.4m (238ft 6in x 23ft 8in x 11ft 2in)
Machinery:	Twin screws, diesel engines [surface], electric motors [submerged]
Top speed:	17.5 knots [surface], 10.5 knots [submerged]
Main armament:	Four 533mm (21in) torpedo tubes, one 102mm (4in) gun
Launched:	July 1919

I21

One of two vessels that were Japan's first ocean-going submarines, *I21* was built from Italian plans of the Fiat-Laurenti F1 type. It was built at Kawasaki's Kobe yard and completed in 1920. Its number was changed to *RO-2* in 1924, and it was stricken in 1930.

SPECIFICATIONS	
Type:	Japanese submarine
Displacement:	728 tonnes (717 tons) [surface], 1063 tonnes (1047 tons) [submerged]
Dimensions:	65.6m x 6m x 4.2m (215ft 3in x 19ft 8in x 13ft 9in)
Machinery:	Twin screws, diesel engines [surface], electric motors [submerged]
Top speed:	13 knots [surface], 8 knots [submerged]
Main armament:	Five 457mm (18in) torpedo tubes
Launched:	November 1919

TIMELINE

1919

K26

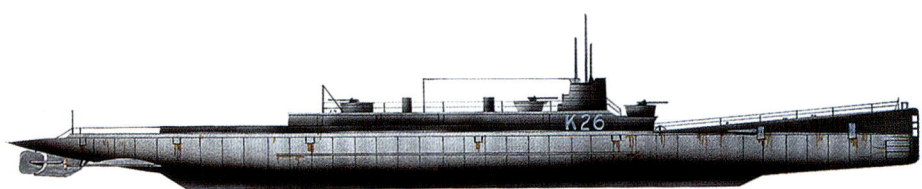

SPECIFICATIONS	
Type:	British submarine
Displacement:	2174 tonnes (2140 tons) [surface], 2814 tonnes (2770 tons) [submerged]
Dimensions:	107m x 8.5m x 5.2m (351ft 6in x 28ft x 17ft)
Machinery:	Twin screws, turbines [surface], electric motors [submerged]
Top speed:	24 knots [surface], 9 knots [submerged]
Main armament:	Ten 533mm (21in) torpedo tubes, three 102mm (4in) guns
Launched:	August 1919

In 1915, the British began a class of fast ocean-going submarines to keep up with the battlefleet. This required replacing diesel engines with steam turbines. Their machinery took up nearly 40 per cent of *K26*'s length. Giant lids covered the funnel uptakes. Completed in 1923, *K26* was scrapped in 1931.

Galathée

SPECIFICATIONS	
Type:	French submarine
Displacement:	619 tonnes (609 tons) [surface], 769 tonnes (757 tons) [submerged]
Dimensions:	64m x 5.2m x 4.3m (210ft x 17ft x 14ft)
Machinery:	Twin screws, diesel engines [surface], electric motors [submerged]
Top speed:	13.5 knots [surface], 7.5 knots [submerged]
Main armament:	Seven 551mm (21.7in) torpedo tubes, one 76mm (3in) gun
Launched:	December 1925

Galathée's group of medium-range submarines was the largest class of such vessels in the French Navy. Their long conning-towers gave them a distinctive profile. They operated until 1940 with great sucess despite a complex torpedo layout. *Galathée* was sunk in June 1944, while operated by the Free French.

X1

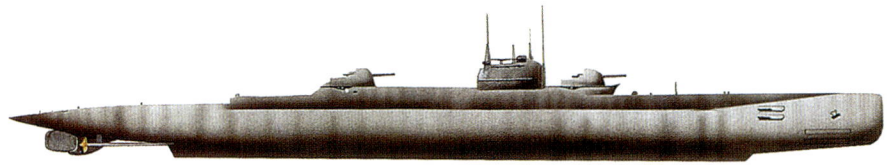

SPECIFICATIONS	
Type:	British submarine
Displacement:	3098 tonnes (3050 tons) [surface], 3657 tonnes (3600 tons) [submerged]
Dimensions:	110.8m x 9m x 4.8m (363ft 6in x 29ft 10in x 15ft 9in)
Machinery:	Twin screws, diesel engines [surface], electric motors [submerged]
Top speed:	20 knots [surface], 9 knots [submerged]
Main armament:	Four 132mm (5.2in) guns, six 533mm (21in) torpedo tubes
Launched:	1925

X1 was designed to test performance of a very large submarine. One of the first submarines fitted with Asdic, it proved to be an excellent sea boat, and a steady gun platform. Its 132mm (5.2in) guns were intended to defeat any destroyer or armed merchant cruiser in a surface action. It was scrapped in 1936.

Post-1919 Submarine Development: Part 2

Britain, France, Italy and the United States all studied German U-boats after World War I, incorporating many features in their own designs. Germany was prohibited from construction of submarines, but clandestine work began in the later 1920s.

Espadon

Espadon belonged to a group of minelaying submarines that were heavily armed, with four bow, two stern and two twin torpedo tubes mounted in containers in the upper hull. Eight of the group were lost during World War II, including *Espadon* which was scuttled in September 1943.

SPECIFICATIONS	
Type:	French submarine
Displacement:	1168 tonnes (1150 tons) [surface], 1464 tonnes (1441 tons) [submerged]
Dimensions:	78.2m x 6.8m x 5m (256ft 9in x 22ft 5in x 16ft 5in)
Machinery:	Twin screws, diesel engines [surface], electric motors [submerged]
Top speed:	15 knots [surface], 9 knots [submerged]
Main armament:	Ten 533mm (21in) torpedo tubes, one 100mm (3.9in) gun
Launched:	May 1926

Oberon

An ocean-going submarine developed from the 'L' type of World War I, originally *07*, *Oberon* was of advanced design for long-range operation, and was ideal for service in the Far East. Surfaced range at nine knots was 9500km (5000 miles), and submerged at four knots was 114km (60 miles). It was scrapped in 1945.

SPECIFICATIONS	
Type:	British submarine
Displacement:	1513 tonnes (1490 tons) [surface], 1922 tonnes (1892 tons) [submerged]
Dimensions:	83.4m x 8.3m x 4.6m (273ft 8in x 27ft 3in x 15ft)
Machinery:	Twin screws, diesel engines [surface], electric motors [submerged]
Top speed:	12 knots [surface], 17.5 knots [submerged]
Main armament:	Eight 533mm (21in) torpedo tubes
Launched:	September 1926

TIMELINE

1926   1927

Eurydice

A double-hulled, medium displacement submarine, intended for medium-range open sea work with an operational diving depth of 80m (262ft), *Eurydice* was one of a class of 26 boats built between 1925 and 1934. It was scuttled at Toulon in June 1944 and then raised, but was sunk in an Allied bombing raid.

SPECIFICATIONS	
Type:	French submarine
Displacement:	636 tonnes (626 tons) [surface], 800 (787 tons) tonnes [submerged]
Dimensions:	65.9m x 4.9m x 4m (216ft 2in x 16ft x 13ft 5in)
Machinery:	Twin screws, diesel [surface], electric motors [submerged]
Top speed:	14 knots [surface], 7.5 knots [submerged]
Main armament:	Seven 533mm (21in) torpedo tubes
Launched:	May 1927

Domenico Millelire

Domenico Millelire was one of four cruising boats that were the first large-displacement submarines built by the Italian Navy. Refitted in 1934, they were seconded to the Nationalist side in the Spanish Civil War in 1936–37. In 1941, *Domenico Millelire* was converted into the floating oil depot ship *GR248*.

SPECIFICATIONS	
Type:	Italian submarine
Displacement:	1473 tonnes (1450 tons) [surface], 1934 tonnes (1904 tons) [submerged]
Dimensions:	86m x 7.4m x 4.2m (282ft x 24ft 6in x 14ft)
Machinery:	Twin screws, diesel [surface], electric motors [submerged]
Top speed:	17.5 knots with diesel engines, 7 knots on ancillary motors [surface], 8.9 knots [submerged]
Main armament:	Six 533mm (21in) torpedo tubes, one 120mm (4.7in) gun
Launched:	September 1927

Argonaut

Argonaut was the only purpose-built minelaying submarine to serve in the US Navy. Operating depth was 91.5m (300ft) and maximum combat radius some 18,000 miles (28,800km). During World War II, it was used as a transport and special operations boat in the Pacific. *Argonaut* was lost off Lae in 1943.

SPECIFICATIONS	
Type:	US submarine/minelayer
Displacement:	2753 tonnes (2710 tons) [surface], 4145 tonnes (4080 tons) [submerged]
Dimensions:	116m x 10.4m x 4.6m (381ft x 34ft x 15ft 6in)
Machinery:	Twin screws, diesels [surface], electric
Top speed:	15 knots [surface], 8 knots [submerged]
Main armament:	Two 152mm (6in) guns, four 533mm (21in) torpedo tubes, 60 mines
Launched:	November 1927

Post-1919 Submarine Development: Part 3

In 1929, US engineers developed a diesel-electric submarine engine that generated power for an electric motor, and which could also recharge the boat's batteries. This was used in US 'S'-class boats and in the British 'U'-class.

Enrico Toti

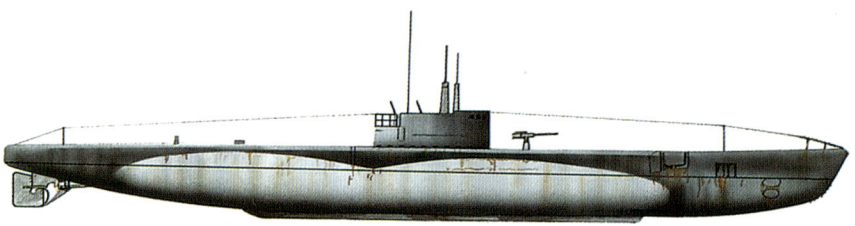

Enrico Toti was designed as a long-range vessel, with a diving depth of 90m (295ft). It was deployed by the Italian Navy to serve on the Nationalist side in the Spanish Civil War, 1936–38, but was too large to be effective in the Mediterranean, and was laid up in 1943.

SPECIFICATIONS
Type:	Italian submarine
Displacement:	1473 tonnes (1450 tons) [surface], 1934 tonnes (1904 tons) [submerged]
Dimensions:	87.7m x 7.8m x 4.7m (288ft x 25ft 7in x 15ft 5in)
Machinery:	Twin screws, diesel [surface], electric motors [submerged]
Top speed:	17.5 knots [surface], 8.9 knots [submerged]
Main armament:	Six 533mm (21in) torpedo tubes, one 120mm (4.7in) gun
Launched:	April 1928

Giovanni da Procida

Giovanni da Procida was one of a class of four. It served the Nationalist side in the Spanish Civil War. In 1942, higher-powered diesels were installed, increasing surface speed to 17 knots. From 1940 to 1943, it patrolled in the Mediterranean. In 1944 it became a training ship, and was scrapped in 1948.

SPECIFICATIONS
Type:	Italian submarine
Displacement:	843 tonnes (830 tons) [surface], 1026 tonnes (1010 tons) [submerged]
Dimensions:	64.6m x 6.5m x 4.3m (212ft x 21ft 4in x 14ft)
Machinery:	Twin screws, diesel engines [surface], electric motors [submerged]
Top speed:	17 knots [surface], 7 knots [submerged]
Main armament:	Six 533mm (21in) torpedo tubes, one 102mm (4in) gun
Launched:	April 1928

TIMELINE

1928   1929

Surcouf

A powerful surface gunship as well as a torpedo-launcher, *Surcouf* had a range of 19,000km (10,000 miles) at 10 knots. Diving depth was 80m (262ft 6in). The 203mm (8in) guns, in a watertight turret forward of the conning tower, could be fired 2.5 minutes after surfacing. *Surcouf* was lost in 1942.

SPECIFICATIONS	
Type:	French submarine
Displacement:	3302 tonnes (3250 tons) [surface], 4373 tonnes (4304 tons) [submerged]
Dimensions:	110m x 9.1m (360ft 10in x 29ft 9in)
Machinery:	Twin screws, diesel engines [surface], electric motors [submerged]
Top speed:	18 knots [surface], 8.5 knots [submerged]
Main armament:	Two 203mm (8in) guns, eight 551mm (21.7in), four 400mm (15.75m) torpedo tubes
Complement:	118
Launched:	1929

Henri Poincaré

Henri Poincaré was one of 29 double-hulled ocean-going submarines laid down between 1925 and 1931. The mixed armament of torpedo tubes was unusual. It was scuttled at Toulon in 1942, but was salvaged by the Italians. As *FR118*, it was sunk in September 1943 after being seized by German forces.

SPECIFICATIONS	
Type:	French submarine
Displacement:	1595 tonnes (1570 tons) [surface], 2117 tonnes (2054 tons) [submerged]
Dimensions:	92.3m x 8.2m x 4.7m (302ft 10in x 27ft x 15ft 5in)
Machinery:	Twin screws, diesel engines [surface], electric motors [submerged]
Top speed:	17–20 knots [surface], 10 knots [submerged]
Main armament:	Two 400mm (15.7in) and nine 550mm (21.7in) torpedo tubes, one 82mm (3.2in) gun
Launched:	April 1929

Ersh

Ersh belonged to a class of 88 boats, with a single hull and a maximum diving depth of 90m (295ft), designed for off-shore patrol. Thirty-two were lost during intensive operations in World War II, but the survivors remained in service with the Russian Navy until the late 1950s. *Ersh* was scrapped in 1958.

SPECIFICATIONS	
Type:	Russian submarine
Displacement:	595 tonnes (586 tons) [surface], 713 tonnes (702 tons) [submerged]
Dimensions:	58.5m x 6.2m x 4.2m (192ft x 20ft 4in x 13ft 9in)
Machinery:	Twin screws, diesel engines [surface], electric motors [submerged]
Top speed:	12.5 knots [surface], 8.5 knots [submerged]
Main armament:	Six 533mm (21in) torpedo tubes, two 45mm (1.8in) guns
Launched:	1931

1931

SHIP TYPES 1900–1929

Armed Merchant Ships, British & German

To import food and raw materials, Britain needed its merchant fleet. And Germany now deployed the commerce raider, which looked like an innocent merchant ship until within gunnery range. The British response was the 'armed merchant cruiser'.

Kronprinz Wilhelm

A fast ship, *Kronprinz Wilhelm* was armed at sea as a commerce raider in August 1914, capturing 15 Allied ships. In 1915, it was interned by the United States at Newport News, and on America's entry into the war in 1917 it was taken over as the troop transport *Von Steuben*. It was scrapped in 1940.

SPECIFICATIONS	
Type:	German liner
Displacement:	15,147 tonnes (14,908 tons)
Dimensions:	202m x 20.2m x 8.8m (663ft x 66ft 3in x 29ft)
Machinery:	Twin screws, quadruple expansion engines
Top speed:	23.3 knots
Launched:	March 1901

Carmania

Carmania was one of the first big merchant ships to be fitted with turbines, working the North Atlantic route. In 1914 it was taken over and refitted as an auxiliary cruiser and sank the German raider *Cap Trafalgar* in a fierce action, receiving over 300 hits in the fight. *Carmania* was sold for scrap in 1932.

SPECIFICATIONS	
Type:	British liner
Displacement:	19,836 tonnes (19,524 tons)
Dimensions:	205.7m x 22m (674ft 10in x 72ft 2in)
Machinery:	Triple screws, turbines
Top speed:	20 knots
Route:	North Atlantic
Launched:	February 1905

TIMELINE

1901   1905   1913

Cap Trafalgar

When World War I began, *Cap Trafalgar* was at Buenos Aires. It was immediately converted into an armed raider; the third funnel was removed, and it was armed with two 102mm (4in) guns, and lighter weapons. On 13 September, refuelling at Trinidada, it was sunk by the British armed merchant liner *Carmania*.

SPECIFICATIONS	
Type:	German liner
Displacement:	19,106 tonnes (18,805 tons)
Dimensions:	187m x 22m (613ft x 72ft 3in)
Machinery:	Triple screws turbines
Top speed:	17.8 knots
Launched:	July 1913

Bayano

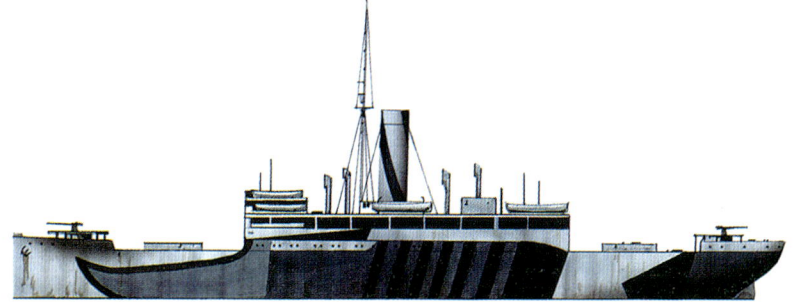

Bayano was one of 17 ships built for convoy protection work in the Atlantic, fitted with two anti-submarine howitzers. Medium-sized merchant ships of moderate speed, these were economic to run and more efficient to operate than armed merchant cruisers. *Bayano* was decommissioned in March 1919.

SPECIFICATIONS	
Type:	British escort vessel
Displacement:	6896 tonnes (6788 tons)
Main armament:	Four 152mm (6in) guns, two 102mm (4in) guns
Launched:	June 1917

Caledonia

A five-decked steamer, *Caledonia* was requisitioned by the British authorities in 1939. Converted to an auxiliary cruiser, it was given eight obsolete 152mm (6in) guns, plus two 76mm (3in) guns for anti-aircraft defence, and renamed *Scotstoun*. It was torpedoed and sunk on 13 June 1940 by the German submarine *U-25*.

SPECIFICATIONS	
Type:	British liner
Displacement:	17,319 tonnes (17,046 tons)
Dimensions:	168m x 22m x 9m (552ft x 72ft x 29ft)
Machinery:	Twin screws, geared turbines
Top speed:	17 knots
Route:	North Atlantic
Launched:	April 1925

SHIP TYPES 1900–1929

Herzogin Cecilie

Built as a training cargo ship, *Herzogin Cecilie* was lengthened in 1912 and was among the fastest bulk cargo sailers. After World War I, it was passed to France and eventually sold to Gustaf Erikson of Sweden. In April 1936, it grounded off England's Devon coast, was refloated, but grounded again and was wrecked.

Herzogin Cecilie

Herzogin Cecilie was one of the fastest merchant sailing ships of her time. The tall ships of the period remained only competitive against the steamers on the longer trade routes, such as the Australian *Weizenfahrt* wheat trade, carrying grain from Australia to Europe. This required rounding Cape Horn routinely, and were not well suited for steamers, as coal was in short supply there.

SPECIFICATIONS

Type:	German sail training ship
Displacement:	3294 tonnes (3242 tons)
Dimensions:	94.5m x 14m x 7.4m (310ft x 46ft x 24ft 7in)
Rigging:	Four masts, full square rig
Complement:	30 plus 70 cadets
Cargo:	Coal, grain, nitrates
Routes:	Europe–Australia, Cape Horn
Launched:	1902

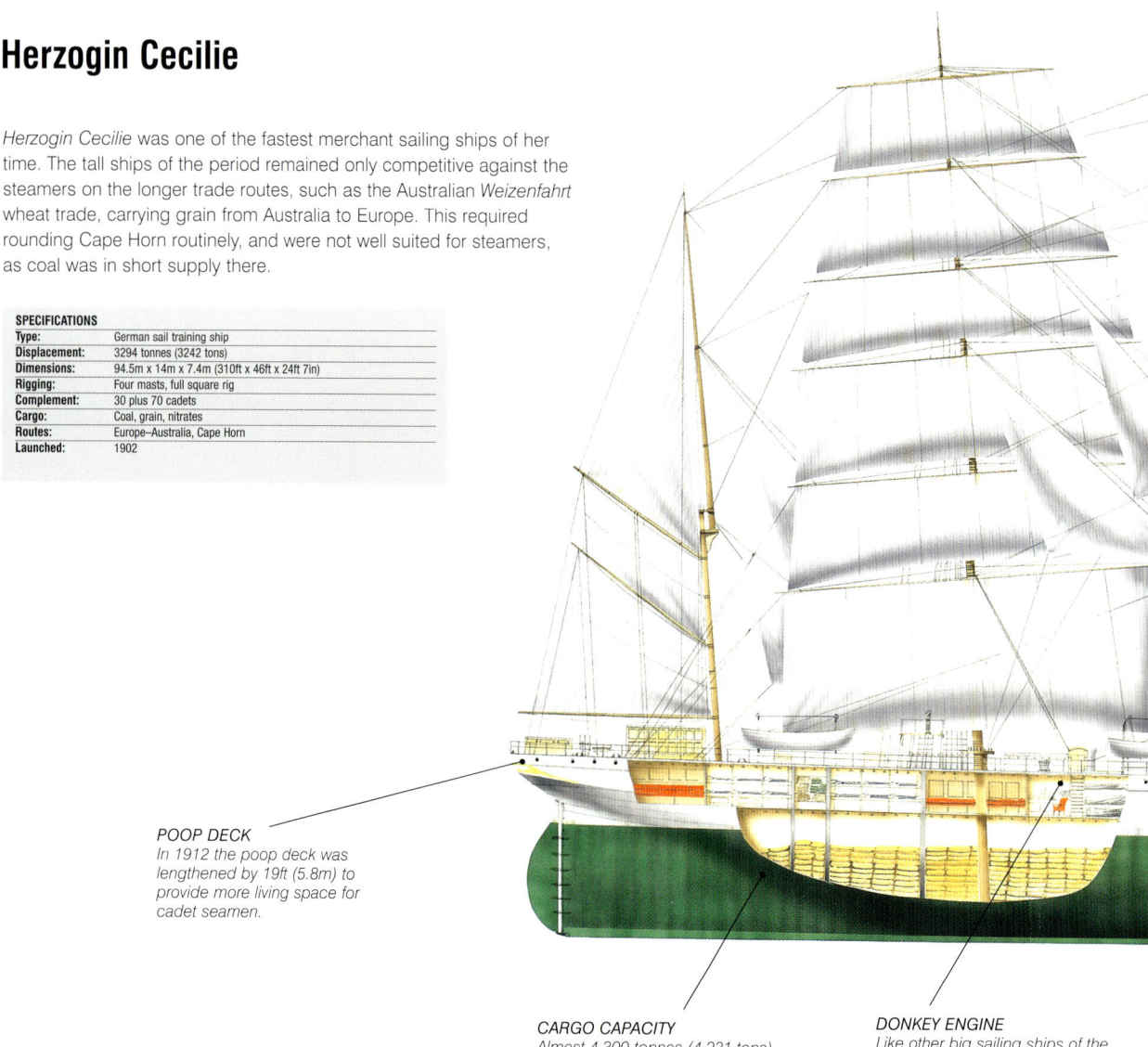

POOP DECK
In 1912 the poop deck was lengthened by 19ft (5.8m) to provide more living space for cadet seamen.

CARGO CAPACITY
Almost 4,300 tonnes (4,231 tons) of bulk cargo could be carried, more than doubling the gross registered tonnage.

DONKEY ENGINE
Like other big sailing ships of the time, a small steam engine was carried to provide power for the winches.

HERZOGIN CECILIE

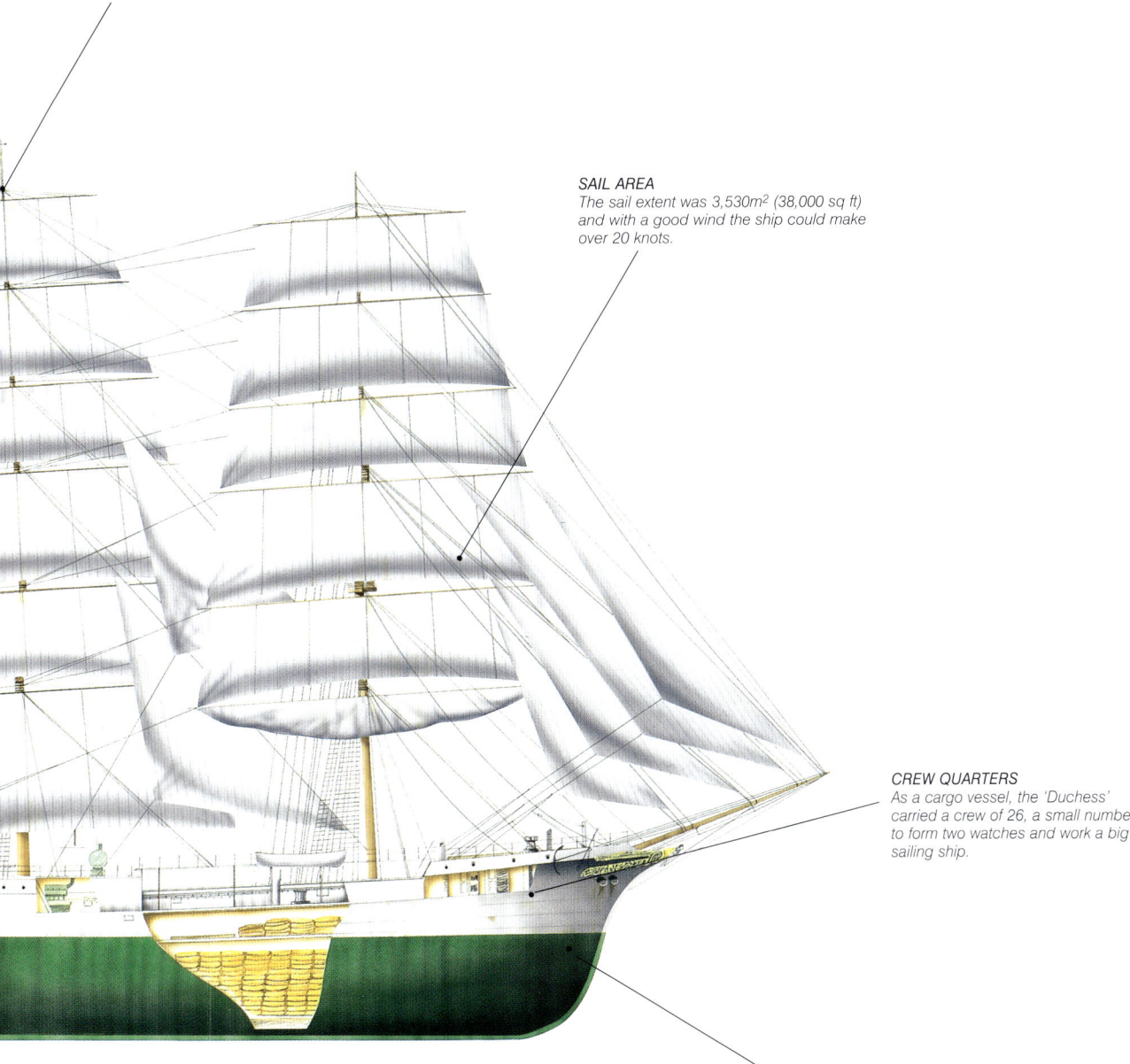

A TALL SHIP
The mainmast, tallest of the four, rose to 53.49m (175ft 6in) above the waterline. The main yards extended well beyond the ship's sides.

SAIL AREA
The sail extent was 3,530m² (38,000 sq ft) and with a good wind the ship could make over 20 knots.

CREW QUARTERS
As a cargo vessel, the 'Duchess' carried a crew of 26, a small number to form two watches and work a big sailing ship.

HULL
The hull, built of steel, had excellent lines, enabling the ship to slide through the water and helping it to eight victories in the Australian 'grain race'.

SHIP TYPES 1900–1929

Twentieth-Century Sailing Ships

Big merchant sailing ships continued to be built and used in the early decades of the twentieth century, but their numbers rapidly declined. Many were converted to steam propulsion, and by the 1930s only a handful were in regular operation. Those remaining afloat today are either training ships or preserved as museum pieces.

Thomas W. Lawson

Thomas W. Lawson, probably the largest schooner ever built and with a 4000m² (43,055 sq ft) spread of canvas, could carry 4064 tonnes (4000 tons) of coal. Later converted to an oil tanker, it was wrecked in 1907 off the Scilly Isles on its first transatlantic voyage with 2 million gallons of oil.

SPECIFICATIONS

Type:	US sailing ship
Displacement:	5301 tonnes (5218 tons)
Dimensions:	120.5m x 15m x 9.8m (395ft 4in x 49ft 3in x 32ft 2in)
Rigging:	7 masts, schooner rig
Complement:	35
Cargo:	Coal, oil
Routes:	US coastal, North Atlantic
Launched:	1902

Archibald Russell

A steel barque, *Archibald Russell* was one of the few sailing vessels with bilge keels, which enhanced steadiness in heavy seas. Many labour-saving devices were fitted. After World War I, it was sold to a Danish firm, became one of the last sailing ships used in the Australian grain trade, and was scrapped in 1949.

SPECIFICATIONS

Type:	British barque
Displacement:	2423 tonnes (2385 tons)
Dimensions:	88.7m x 13.1m x 7.3m (291ft x 43ft x 24ft)
Rigging:	Four masts, barque rig
Cargo:	Grain
Routes:	Europe–Australia
Launched:	1905

TIMELINE 1902 1905 1909

TWENTIETH-CENTURY SAILING SHIPS

Dar Pomorza

Built at Hamburg as *Prinzessin Eitel Friedrich*, fitted with auxiliary motors to aid passage in calms, this was a cargo carrier. Passed to France after World War I, it was acquired by the Polish Merchant Naval Academy in 1929 as a training ship and named *Dar Pomorza*. It is now a museum ship at Gdynia.

SPECIFICATIONS
Type:	Polish sailing ship
Displacement:	1646 tonnes (1620 tons)
Dimensions:	73m x 12m x 6.4m (239ft x 41ft x 21ft)
Machinery:	Auxiliary motors developing 360hp
Rigging:	Three masts, full square rig
Top speed:	6 knots
Launched:	1909

Commandant de Rose

During World War I, France ordered 40 wooden-hulled cargo-carrying schooners from a US shipbuilder. These were cheap to build, saved fuel and were not vulnerable to magnetic mines. But in the slump after the war, *Commandant de Rose* and its sisters were not a commercial success. It was broken up in 1923.

SPECIFICATIONS
Type:	French steam schooner
Displacement:	3556 tonnes (3500 tons)
Dimensions:	85m x 14m x 7m (280ft x 45ft 6in x 23ft)
Machinery:	Twin screws, triple expansion engines
Rigging:	Five masts, schooner rig
Cargo:	Barrelled oil and mixed freight
Launched:	July 1918

Kruzenstern

Built as the German barque *Padua* for the Laeisz sailing ship line, it was handed to Russia in 1946 as war reparations and renamed *Kruzenstern*. Based at Kaliningrad, it was used for hydrographic surveys. One of the largest surviving sailing ships and now a training ship, it circumnavigated the globe in 2005–6.

SPECIFICATIONS
Type:	Estonian full rigged cargo ship
Displacement:	3113 tonnes (3064 tons)
Dimensions:	114.5m x 14m x 6.85m (376ft x 46ft x 22ft 6in)
Machinery:	Twin screws, auxiliary diesels
Rigging:	Four masts, full square rig
Complement:	230 including cadets
Cargo:	Nitrates, wool, grain
Launched:	1926

 1918  1926

SHIP TYPES 1900–1929

Amerigo Vespucci

Based on an eighteenth-century 74-gun frigate, though rigged up to topgallants and with auxiliary power, *Amerigo Vespucci* was built as a sail training ship, even though such training was scarcely required by 1930. It remains part of Italy's merchant fleet. Its sister-ship *Cristoforo Colombo* was acquired by Russia in 1946.

Amerigo Vespucci

Amerigo Vespucci takes its name from the famous Italian sailor and cartographer who also lent his name to the New World. Except for the time during World War II, the *Amerigo Vespucci* has been continually active. Most of her training cruises are in European waters, but she has also sailed to North and South America, and navigated the Pacific. In 2002, *Amerigo Vespucc*i went around the world.

SPECIFICATIONS

Type:	Italian full rigged ship
Displacement:	4165.6 tonnes (4100 tons)
Dimensions:	82.1m x 15.5m x 6.7m (269ft 6in x 51ft x 22ft)
Machinery:	Single screw, auxiliary diesel-electric
Rigging:	Three masts, full square rig
Complement:	450 including cadets
Launched:	1930

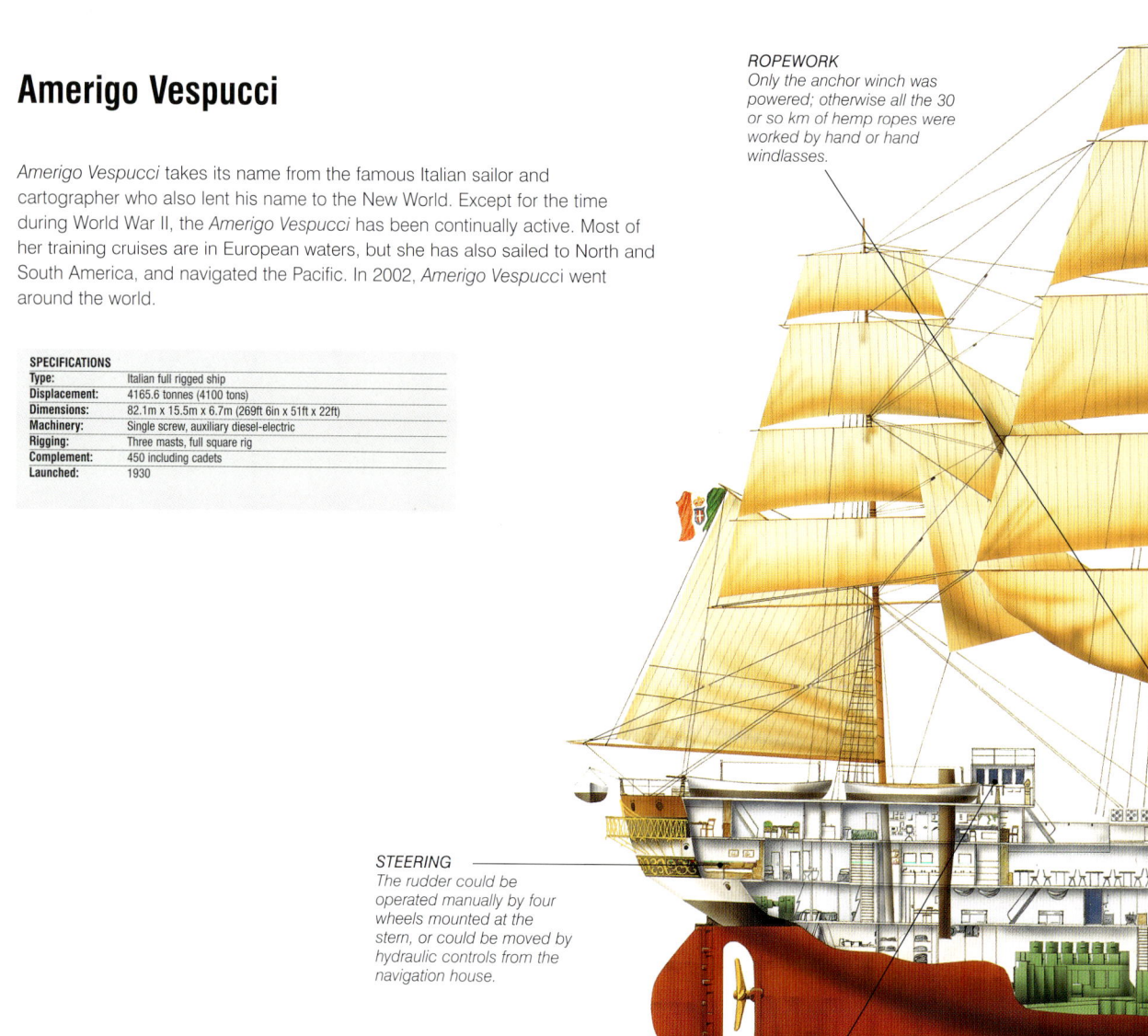

ROPEWORK
Only the anchor winch was powered; otherwise all the 30 or so km of hemp ropes were worked by hand or hand windlasses.

STEERING
The rudder could be operated manually by four wheels mounted at the stern, or could be moved by hydraulic controls from the navigation house.

WHEELHOUSE
An enclosed wheelhouse and navigation room at the break of the poop deck replaced the open 'cockpit' that an earlier ship would have had.

HULL
Designed specifically for the task by Francesco Rotundi, the steel hull was modelled on the lines of early nineteenth-century frigates.

AMERIGO VESPUCCI

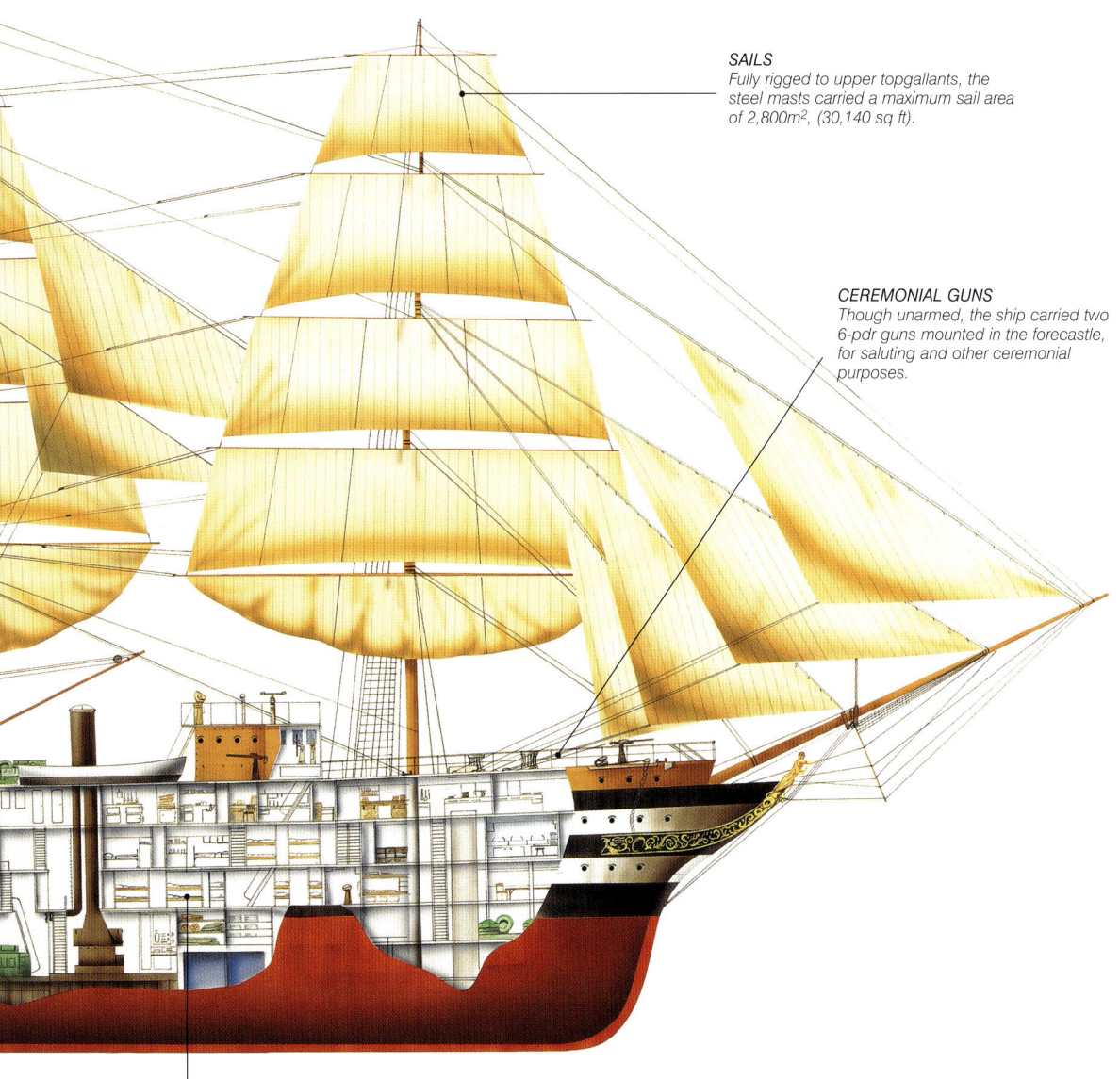

SAILS
Fully rigged to upper topgallants, the steel masts carried a maximum sail area of 2,800m², (30,140 sq ft).

CEREMONIAL GUNS
Though unarmed, the ship carried two 6-pdr guns mounted in the forecastle, for saluting and other ceremonial purposes.

CREW ACCOMMODATION
Space which would have been used for guns and ammunition was used to provide accommodation for cadets on three decks.

SHIP TYPES 1900–1929

Dry Cargo Ships 1900–1929: Pt 1

These three decades marked the heyday of the 'tramp steamer', a sturdy vessel that took contract cargoes anywhere in the world, then looked for another load, and might not return to its home port for a year or two. But many cargo ships also ran regular services on routes where there was a steady trade.

Cockerill

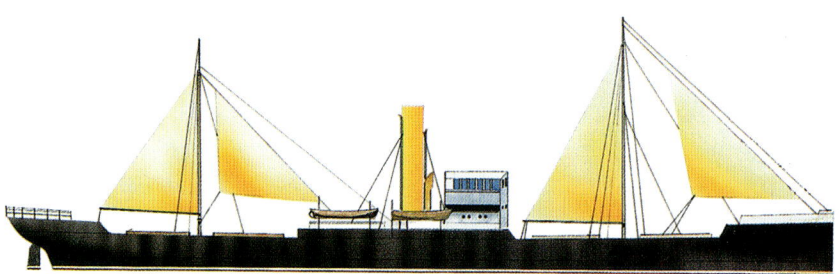

By 1900, the era of the sailing ship was nearing its end. *Cockerill* was an example of the new kind of general cargo vessel. Two main holds were separated by the boilers and engine room, with a deckhouse and bridge above. The light rig of steadying sails would soon be abandoned as unnecessary.

SPECIFICATIONS	
Type:	Belgian cargo steamer
Displacement:	2480 tonnes (2441 tons)
Dimensions:	88m x 14m (288ft 9in x 45ft)
Machinery:	Single screw, vertical compound engine
Top speed:	8 knots
Cargo:	Perishable goods
Route:	Antwerp–London
Launched:	1901

Atland

Doxford & Co. of Sunderland, England, built 178 ships of this type between 1890 and 1911. The 'turret' construction was of conventional shape beneath the waterline. It used less steel, was suitable for bulk cargoes and cost the owners less in harbour dues (based on deadweight). *Atland* sank after a collision in 1943.

SPECIFICATIONS	
Type:	Swedish turret-hull cargo ship
Displacement:	5109.4 tonnes (5029 tons)
Dimensions:	116m x 16m (388ft 9in x 52ft 4in)
Machinery:	Single screw, triple expansion engine
Top speed:	12.7 knots
Cargo:	Iron ore
Route:	Narvik–European ports
Launched:	1910

TIMELINE

1901   1910   1911

Karimoen

SPECIFICATIONS	
Type:	Dutch cargo ship
Displacement:	14,732 tonnes (14,500 tons)
Dimensions:	135m x 17m x 8.4m (445ft 6in x 55ft x 28ft 4in)
Machinery:	Single screw, triple expansion engine
Top speed:	16.5 knots
Cargo:	General merchandise, tropical products
Route:	Netherlands–East Indies
Launched:	1911

A cargo vessel, built to bring raw materials and agricultural products to Europe from the East Indies, *Karimoen* was well supplied with derricks to load and unload on to lighters in open roadsteads. It was also used on the Netherlands–Africa route and to transport Muslim pilgrims between Java and Jeddah.

Cabotia

SPECIFICATIONS	
Type:	British cargo ship
Displacement:	5243 tonnes (5160 tons)
Dimensions:	125.5m x 15.5m (411ft 7in x 50ft 8in)
Machinery:	Single screw, triple expansion engines
Top speed:	11 knots
Cargo:	General mixed cargo
Launched:	1917

Cabotia, originally *War Viper*, was a war-standard vessel built to replace merchant ships lost to German submarine attacks during World War I. *Cabotia* served on the North Atlantic route. In 1925 it acquired new owners who used it as a tramp steamer. It was sunk by a mine off the British coast in January 1940.

Canis

SPECIFICATIONS	
Type:	Norwegian coasting cargo steamer
Displacement:	949 tonnes (934 tons)
Dimensions:	56.4m x 11m x 5.2m (185ft 6in x 36ft x 17ft 5in)
Machinery:	Single screw, diesel
Top speed:	10 knots
Cargo:	General merchandise
Route:	Norwegian coast
Converted:	1918

This was built in 1888 as the sailing ship *Andrew Welch*. Then, like many others, the hull was fitted with an engine and new superstructure, to begin a new career. It was much cheaper than building a new ship. First renamed *Olga*, this vessel then became *Sophus Magdalen* and finally *Canis*, with Bergen as its home port.

Dry Cargo Ships 1900–1929: Part 2

While the majority of merchant steamers were fitted for 'general cargo', some were equipped for specific tasks, like the 'reefers' with refrigerated holds that carried meat, or the Scandinavian timber ships. Competition between carriers was often fierce, and many experiments were made in the hope of reducing operating costs.

Topaz

For four decades, ships of this type traded between harbours on the British coast. Coal was the most common cargo. Two holds occupied most of the hull, with a central deckhouse and bridge, and living accommodation and engines at the stern. Earlier examples often carried a mizzen mast with a steadying sail

SPECIFICATIONS	
Type:	British coastal steamer
Displacement:	586.2 tonnes (577 tons)
Dimensions:	50m x 8m x 4m (168ft x 27ft x 13ft)
Machinery:	Single screw, triple expansion engine
Top speed:	8 knots
Cargo:	Coal, cement, fertilizer, general merchandise
Route:	British coast
Launched:	1920

Carelia

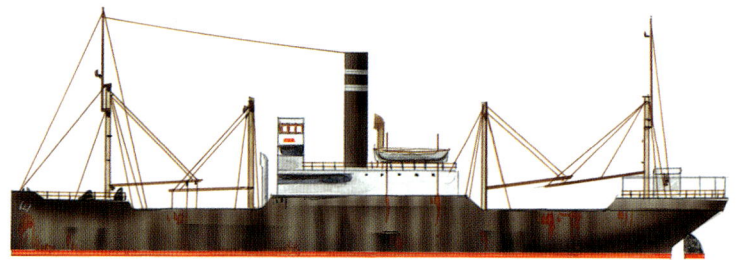

Softwood timber being lightweight in relation to its bulk, timber ships normally carried it stacked high on the well-decks as well as filling the holds. Many small steamships, able to use remote harbours and jetties, were built for this trade, mostly in Scandinavian yards. *Carelia* was scrapped in Holland in 1963.

SPECIFICATIONS	
Type:	Finnish timber carrier
Displacement:	1141 tonnes (1123 tons)
Dimensions:	66m x 10.4m x 4.6m (217ft x 34ft 5in x 15ft)
Machinery:	Single screw, triple expansion engine
Top speed:	8 knots
Cargo:	Lumber
Routes:	Finnish ports–European ports
Launched:	1921

TIMELINE

1920  1921  1926

Barbara

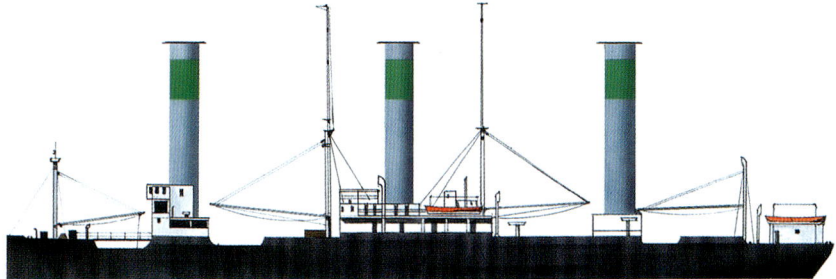

SPECIFICATIONS	
Type:	German merchant vessel
Displacement:	2110 tonnes (2077 tons)
Dimensions:	90m x 13m x 5.6m (295ft 3in x 42ft 8in x 18ft 4in)
Machinery:	Single screw, diesel engines
Rigging:	Three Flettner cylinders
Top speed:	13 knots
Cargo:	Mixed cargo
Launched:	1926

Flettner rotor towers use the 'Magnus Effect' of wind power to drive the ship along. This was to be first of 10 such vessels for the Hamburg–Amerika Line, but only one was fitted. *Barbara* could make six knots under rotor power. After a few voyages, the towers were removed. It served a Saudi firm until the 1970s.

Nerissa

SPECIFICATIONS	
Type:	British cargo/passenger liner
Displacement:	5672 tonnes (5583 tons)
Dimensions:	106m x 16.4m x 6.3m (349ft 6in x 54ft x 29ft 8in)
Machinery:	Single screw, triple expansion engines
Top speed:	16 knots
Routes:	UK–Canada; New York–West Indies
Launched:	March 1926

Nerissa was built in record time on the Clyde. The hull was strengthened, and the icebreaker-type stem sloped back to the keel from the waterline. There was accommodation for 229 passengers. In 1927, it was sold to Furness Withy Group for the West Indies–New York route. It was sunk by a U-boat in 1941.

Isar

SPECIFICATIONS	
Type:	German cargo ship
Displacement:	9170 tonnes (9026 tons)
Dimensions:	166m x 19.2m x 8m (564ft 6in x 63ft 6in x 28ft)
Machinery:	Single screw, triple expansion linked to geared turbine
Top speed:	14 knots
Cargo:	General merchandise
Route:	German ports–Far East
Launched:	1929

Isar was the first ship built with the Maierform hull to reduce drag, thus improving speed and fuel consumption. A turbine could be connected for further economy. In other respects, this was a standard-formation cargo liner of the time, with centrally-placed superstructure and engines, well equipped with derricks.

1929

SHIP TYPES 1900–1929

Cargo–Passenger Ships 1900–1929: Part 1

A surprising aspect of shipping history is the extent to which ships were bought and sold, acquiring new nationalities. The market was centred in London, but also in Hamburg, New York and Marseille, and some ships were sold several times.

Kiautschou

SPECIFICATIONS	
Type:	German liner
Displacement:	11,085 tonnes (10,911 tons)
Dimensions:	164.5m x 18m x 8.8m (540ft x 60ft x 29ft 11 in)
Machinery:	Twin screws, quadruple expansion engines
Top speed:	15 knots
Route:	Hamburg–Chinese ports
Launched:	1900

Kiautschou was built for the Hamburg Amerika Line's Far East service, to carry 240 first-class, 162 second-class and 1950 steerage-class passengers. In 1904, it changed ownership and was renamed *Princess Alice*. After World War I it was taken into the US merchant marine as *City of Honolulu*. Fire destroyed it in 1922.

Lake Champlain

SPECIFICATIONS	
Type:	British liner
Displacement:	7510 tonnes (7390 tons)
Dimensions:	140m x 15.8m (460ft x 52ft)
Machinery:	Twin screws, triple expansion nengines
Top speed:	13 knots
Route:	Britain–St Lawrence ports
Launched:	1900

Lake Champlain carried the first wireless fitted to a North Atlantic liner. In 1913 it transferred to Austria as *Tyrolia*. Back in Britain in 1914, it was briefly a decoy ship disguised as a dreadnought, then became the oiler *Ruthenia*. It was sent to Singapore in 1929, captured by the Japanese in 1942 and renamed *Choran*.

TIMELINE 1900 1902

CARGO–PASSENGER SHIPS 1900–1929: PART 1

Carpathia

Carpathia was built for Cunard's Atlantic route and was typical of the large mixed cargo/passenger vessels of the period, with no first-class accommodation. In April 1912, it picked up over 700 survivors from the sunken *Titanic*. In 1918, Carpathia was sunk by the German *U-55* while on the way to New York.

SPECIFICATIONS	
Type:	British cargo liner
Displacement:	13,781 tonnes (13,564 tons)
Dimensions:	170m x 20m (558ft x 64ft 4in)
Machinery:	Twin screws, quadruple engines
Cargo:	General cargo
Route:	North Atlantic
Launched:	August 1902

Hanoverian

This was launched as *Hanoverian*, but renamed *Mayflower* by new owners. It worked on the North Atlantic, carrying 1455 passengers in three classes. In 1904 it transferred to the Mediterranean as *Cretic*. From 1915 to 1919, it was a troop transport, before resuming its original role as *Devonian*. It was sold in 1929.

SPECIFICATIONS	
Type:	British liner
Displacement:	13,723 tonnes (13,507 tons)
Dimensions:	183.2m x 18.4m (601ft x 60ft 4in)
Machinery:	Twin screws, triple expansion engines
Top speed:	15 knots
Route:	North Atlantic
Launched:	February 1902

Corsican

Corsican had three-class accommodation for 1500 passengers. It collided with an iceberg in 1912, suffering slight damage. It operated as a troopship during World War I. In 1922, it was renamed *Marvale* and fitted out as a cabin-class vessel for Canadian Pacific. In 1923 it was stranded off Cape Race and lost.

SPECIFICATIONS	
Type:	British liner
Displacement:	11,619 tonnes (11,436 tons)
Dimensions:	157m x 19m (516ft x 61ft 4in)
Machinery:	Twin screws, triple expansion engines
Top speed:	16 knots
Route:	Glasgow–Montreal
Launched:	April 1907

 1907

Cargo–Passenger Ships 1900–1929: Part 2

World maps once showed shipping routes, with thicker or thinner lines indicating the density of traffic. Cargo–passenger ships usually followed the less 'thick' lines, routes needing regular service but not attracting many passengers or much freight.

George Washington

The largest German-built steamer of the pre-1914 years, accommodating 3017 passengers in three classes, the liner *George Washington* was taken over by the US government in 1917 and used as a troop transport. After 1919 it had various owners and was renamed *Catlin*. Laid up in 1947, it was burned out in 1951.

SPECIFICATIONS	
Type:	German liner
Displacement:	25,979 tonnes (25,570 tons)
Dimensions:	220.2m x 23.8m (722ft 5in x 78ft)
Machinery:	Twin screws, quadruple expansion engines
Top speed:	18 knots
Route:	Bremen–New York
Launched:	November 1908

Galway Castle

Galway Castle was a small Union Castle ship operating on the west coast route to South Africa until World War I broke out. It then served as a fast troopship. On 12 September 1918, it was torpedoed in the Atlantic. Superb seamanship kept it afloat in appalling weather long enough for the lifeboats to be launched.

SPECIFICATIONS	
Type:	British liner
Displacement:	8116 tonnes (7988 tons)
Dimensions:	143.3m x 17.1m x 8.2m (470ft x 56ft 3in x 27ft)
Machinery:	Twin screws, quadruple expansion engines
Top speed:	13.5 knots
Route:	Southampton–Cape Town
Launched:	1911

Cunene

SPECIFICATIONS	
Type:	Portuguese cargo vessel
Displacement:	8966 tonnes (8825 tons)
Dimensions:	137m x 17.6m x 7.7m (450ft x 58ft x 25ft 3in)
Machinery:	Single screw, triple expansion engine
Top speed:	12 knots
Cargo:	Grain, minerals, general cargo
Route:	Portugal–Angola
Launched:	1911

Formerly the German ship *Adelaide*, this was seized by the Allies in 1919 – as were all German merchant vessels over 1625 tonnes (1600 tons) – and given to Portugal. Renamed *Cunene*, it worked until 1925, then spent five years laid up. Brought back into service in 1930, it had a long career, scrapped only in 1955.

Czar

SPECIFICATIONS	
Type:	Russian liner
Displacement:	6607 tonnes (6503 tons)
Dimensions:	130m x 16m (426ft x 53ft)
Machinery:	Twin screws, quadruple expansion engines
Top speed:	15 knots
Route:	St Petersburg–New York, Britain–South America
Launched:	1912

The Russian Revolution in 1917 meant that *Czar* was transferred to the British registry, joining the Cunard fleet. It changed owners and names in 1921, 1930, 1935 and 1946, when it became the British Empire *Penryn*. For most of its life, it worked between British and South American ports, and was scrapped in 1949.

Suwa Maru

SPECIFICATIONS	
Type:	Japanese cargo ship
Displacement:	21,356 tonnes (21,020 tons)
Dimensions:	157.3m x 19m x 8.3m (516ft x 62ft 6in x 29ft)
Machinery:	Twin screws, triple expansion engines
Top speed:	15.5 knots
Cargo:	Manufactured products, general merchandise
Routes:	Japanese ports–Europe
Launched:	1914

Built in Japan, with its sister-ship *Fushimi Maru*, at launch *Suwa Maru* was Japan's largest merchant ship. Primarily a freighter, it also provided accommodation for 470 passengers (300 in the poop 'steerage' area). A long-haul ship, it carried 4000 tonnes of coal fuel. *Suwa Maru* was sunk by a US submarine in 1943.

Cargo–Passenger Ships 1900–1929: Part 3

For most cargo–passenger ships, cargo was the priority. Passengers were an extra, though often treated as well as on any luxury liner (at least in first or cabin class). But these ships were slower than liners, and likely to stop at intermediate ports.

Naldera

Naldera was ordered in 1914. In 1917 the Admiralty decided that it should be an armed merchant cruiser, then a fast cargo boat, a troopship, a hospital ship and an aircraft carrier. At the end of 1918, the unfinished hull was returned to P&O, who completed it as a liner in 1920. *Naldera* was scrapped in 1938.

SPECIFICATIONS

Type:	British liner
Displacement:	23,368 tonnes (23,000 tons)
Dimensions:	182.8m x 20.6m x 8.9m (600ft x 67ft 6in x 29ft 3in)
Machinery:	Twin screws, quadruple expansion engines
Top speed:	16 knots
Route:	London–Singapore and Australia
Launched:	1917

Lancashire

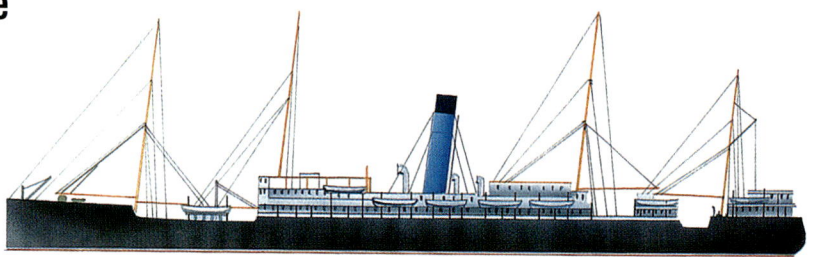

Lancashire was one of the last steam-powered ships to carry four masts. Entering service for the Bibby Line in July 1917, it became a troop transport running between Britain and India in 1930. It continued to serve as a troop transport during World War II, and was broken up in 1956.

SPECIFICATIONS

Type:	British liner
Displacement:	9704 tonnes (9552 tons)
Dimensions:	152m x 17.4m x 8.5m (500ft x 57ft 3in x 28ft 1in)
Machinery:	Twin screws, quadruple expansion engines
Top speed:	15 knots
Cargo:	General freight, cotton, rice
Route:	UK–Indian ports–Rangoon
Launched:	1917

TIMELINE

1917

Minnekahda

Ordered in 1913 as a luxury liner for the Atlantic Transport Line, *Minnekahda* served as a cargo carrier during World War I. In 1920 it entered the emigrant trade with accommodation for 2150 third-class passengers. In 1926 it was modified to carry 750 tourist-class passengers. It was scrapped in 1936.

SPECIFICATIONS	
Type:	US liner
Displacement:	17,500 tonnes (17,221 tons)
Dimensions:	196.9m x 20.3m (646ft x 66ft 3in)
Machinery:	Triple screws, triple expansion engines and low-pressure turbines
Top speed:	15 knots
Launched:	March 1917

Ballarat

Ballarat's design was based on the pre-World War I B-class vessels widely used in the P&O fleet. Employed on the UK–India–Australia route, her large passenger accommodation carried nearly 1200 third-class steerage pasengers. This type of vessel readily conveted to troop transport. *Ballarat* was broken up in 1935.

SPECIFICATIONS	
Type:	British cargo/passenger vessel
Displacement:	15,240 tonnes (15,000 tons)
Dimensions:	163.7m x 19.6m (537ft x 64ft 4in)
Machinery:	Twin screws, vertical triple expansion engines
Top speed:	13.5 knots
Route:	UK–Australia
Launched:	September 1920

Mount Clinton

Initially an emigrant ship from Europe to the United States, *Mount Clinton* was sold in 1925 to the Matson Line and worked in the Pacific Ocean, mostly between Hawaii and Californian ports. The cabin accommodation was designed for rapid conversion to storage space for light cargo in the absence of passengers.

SPECIFICATIONS	
Type:	US passenger/cargo liner
Displacement:	15,240 tonnes (15,000 tons)
Dimensions:	139m x 17.2m x 8.8m (457ft x 57ft x 28ft 9in)
Machinery:	Single screw, turbines
Top speed:	13 knots
Cargo:	Pineapples, sugar, general merchandise
Routes:	North Atlantic; USA–Hawaii
Launched:	1921

Cargo–Passenger Ships 1900–1929: Part 4

The development of the cargo–passenger ship was towards economy of operation, rather than speed. Turbine engines were fitted to only the largest ships, the owners being more interested in the improved marine diesel engines that operated at relatively low cost. The coal-fired triple expansion engine remained the most common.

Balmoral Castle

Balmoral Castle was the first Union Castle liner fitted with wireless. It carried 317 first-class, 220 second-class and 268 third-class passengers. In 1910 it served as a royal yacht during celebrations for the Union of South Africa, and during World War I was a troop transport. It was sold for scrap in 1939.

SPECIFICATIONS	
Type:	British liner
Displacement:	13,574 tonnes (13,360 tons)
Dimensions:	180m x 19.6m x 9.6m (590ft 6in x 64ft 4in x 31ft 6in)
Machinery:	Twin screws, quadruple expansion engines
Top speed:	17 knots
Route:	UK–South Africa
Launched:	November 1909

Conte Verde

Conte Verde was laid up at Shanghai in 1940–42, then journeyed between China and Japan. When Italy withdrew from the Axis in 1943, it was scuttled to prevent capture by the Japanese. They raised and refitted it as a troop transport. Sunk by US forces in 1944 and raised in 1949, it was scrapped in 1951.

SPECIFICATIONS	
Type:	Italian liner
Displacement:	19,065 tonnes (18,765 tons)
Dimensions:	170m x 23m (559ft 5in x 74ft 2in)
Machinery:	Twin screws, turbines
Top speed:	20 knots
Launched:	October 1922

Explorateur Grandidier

SPECIFICATIONS	
Type:	French liner
Displacement:	10,432 tonnes (10,268 tons)
Dimensions:	145m x 18.5m (475ft 9in x 60ft 8in)
Machinery:	Twin screws, triple expansion engines
Top speed:	14 knots
Cargo:	General goods, tropical products
Route:	Marseille–Madagascar
Launched:	1924

This was one of two ships built for the Far Eastern service, operating between France and Madagascar until laid up in Marseilles when France fell to the Germans in 1940. When the Germans evacuated Marseilles, *Explorateur Grandidier* was sunk to block the harbour entrance. It was broken up after 1945.

Highland Chieftain

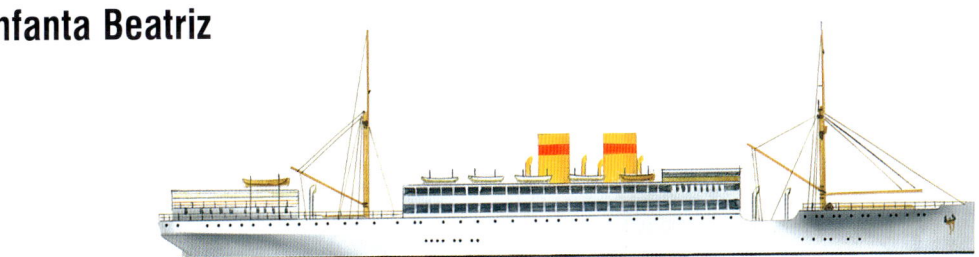

SPECIFICATIONS	
Type:	British liner
Displacement:	14,357 tonnes (14,13 tons)
Dimensions:	166m x 21m x 8.5m (544ft 6in x 69ft x 28ft 1in)
Machinery:	Twin screws, diesel engines
Top speed:	15 knots
Cargo:	General freight, grain, tinned beef
Route:	London–River Plate ports
Launched:	June 1928

Motor ships were economical, needing only 10,000hp to maintain 15 knots. *Highland Chieftain* provided three-class accommodation for 800 passengers. In 1955, it was sold to become the whaling ship *Calpean Star*. In 1960, under tow off Montevideo, it ran aground after an engine-room explosion, and it was lost.

Infanta Beatriz

SPECIFICATIONS	
Type:	Spanish passenger/cargo liner
Displacement:	6379.5 tonnes (6279 tons)
Dimensions:	125m x 16.8m x 6.4m (410ft x 52ft x 21ft 6in)
Machinery:	Twin screws, diesel motors
Top speed:	14 knots
Cargo:	Bananas
Route:	Germany–Canary Islands
Launched:	1928

Infanta Beatriz had well-appointed passenger accommodation, mostly first-class, for tourists, and capacious holds for the cool storage of bananas. During the Spanish Civil War it was renamed *Ciudad de Sevilla*, and was sunk at Barcelona by bombs from the Nationalist side. Later raised, it worked into the 1960s.

SHIP TYPES 1900–1929

Titanic

Built in Belfast for the White Star Line, *Titanic* had a fate that has preserved its fame. On the night of 14 April 1912, while on its maiden voyage from Southampton to New York, it struck an iceberg at full speed and flooded. Although more than two hours elapsed before it sank, 1503 passengers and crew (from a total of 2223) drowned.

Titanic

Titanic was intended to be one of the largest, most luxurious ships ever to operate. Sea trials took place just a few days before the maiden voyage and the ship was deemed seaworthy. A lack of planning and not enough lifeboats were the reason for so many deaths on that fateful night.

SPECIFICATIONS

Type:	British liner
Displacement:	47,069 tonnes (46,328 tons)
Dimensions:	259.85m x 28.2m x 10.35m (852ft 6in x 92ft 6in x 34ft)
Machinery:	Triple screws, triple expansion engines
Top speed:	22 knots
Route:	North Atlantic
Launched:	1911

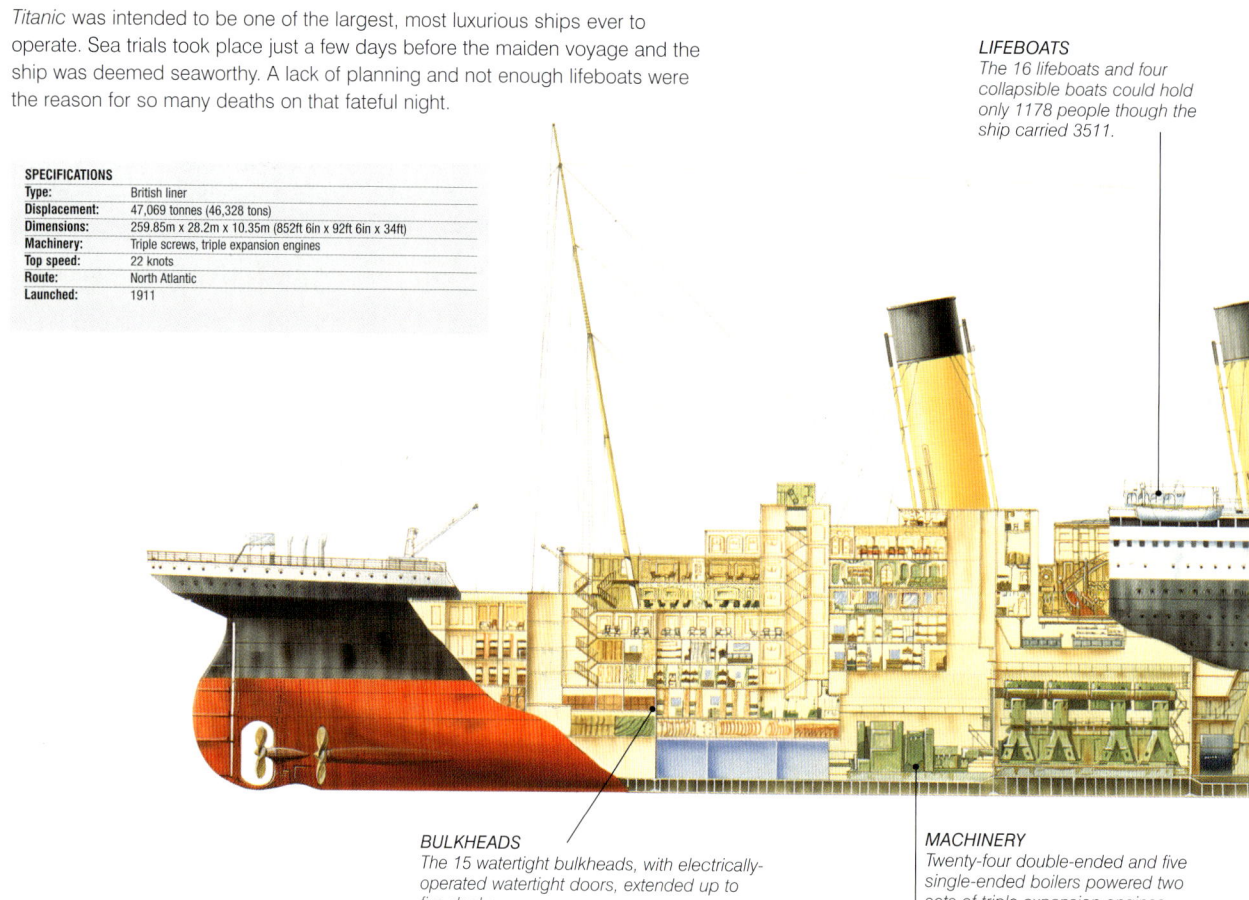

LIFEBOATS
The 16 lifeboats and four collapsible boats could hold only 1178 people though the ship carried 3511.

BULKHEADS
The 15 watertight bulkheads, with electrically-operated watertight doors, extended up to five decks.

MACHINERY
Twenty-four double-ended and five single-ended boilers powered two sets of triple expansion engines, and a low-pressure turbine which drove the centre screw.

TITANIC

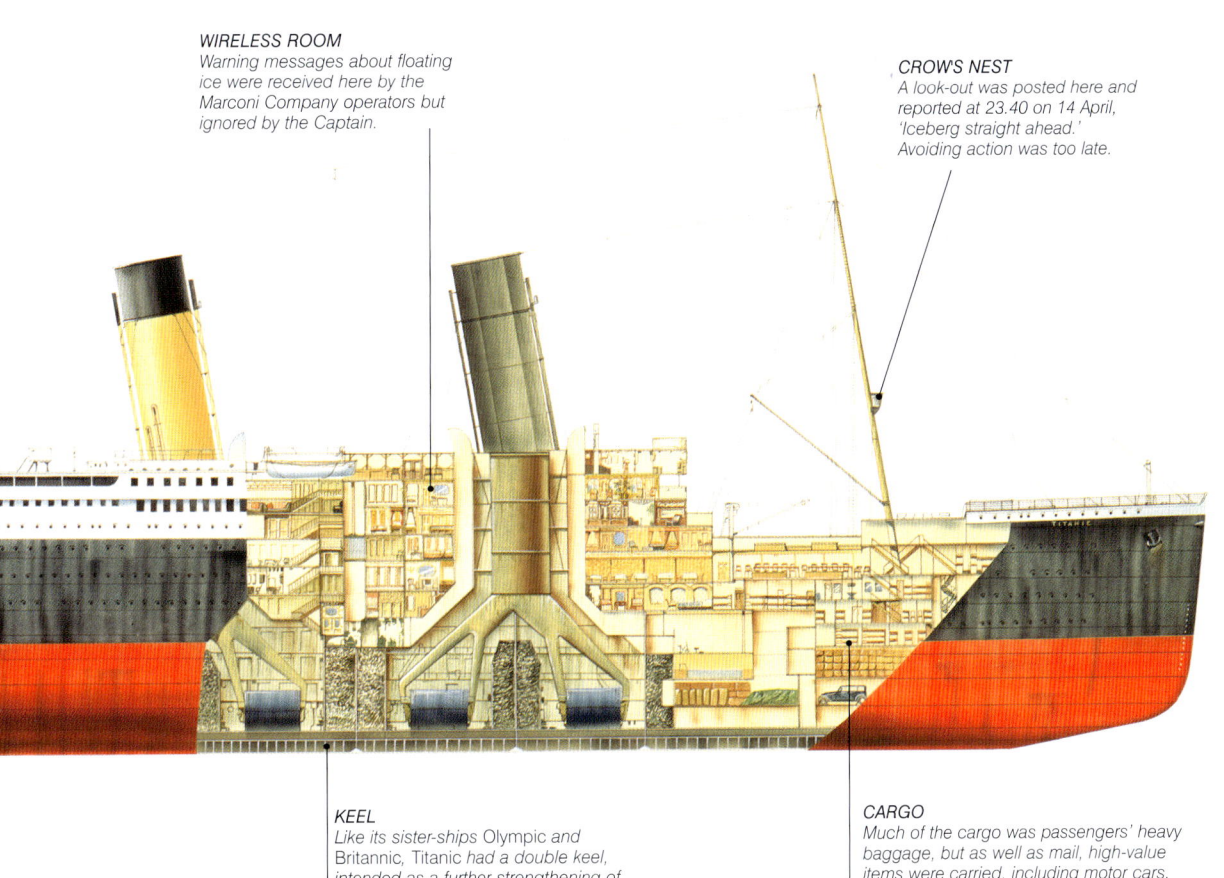

WIRELESS ROOM
Warning messages about floating ice were received here by the Marconi Company operators but ignored by the Captain.

CROW'S NEST
A look-out was posted here and reported at 23.40 on 14 April, 'Iceberg straight ahead.' Avoiding action was too late.

KEEL
Like its sister-ships Olympic *and* Britannic, Titanic *had a double keel, intended as a further strengthening of its 'unsinkable' steel hull.*

CARGO
Much of the cargo was passengers' heavy baggage, but as well as mail, high-value items were carried, including motor cars.

SHIP TYPES 1900–1929

Passenger Liners 1900–1929: Part 1

The routes from European ports to New York and Boston were heavily travelled, and competition was intense. Speed was key to success, and the Blue Riband, awarded to the ship making the fastest passage in each direction, was much coveted.

Deutschland

Built to be fastest across the Atlantic, *Deutschland* took the Blue Riband on its maiden voyage and held it for six years. In 1910 it was converted for cruising and renamed *Victoria Luise*. In 1914 it was fitted out as an auxiliary cruiser, though it never served in this role. It was broken up in 1925.

SPECIFICATIONS
Type:	German liner
Displacement:	16,766 tonnes (16,502 tons)
Dimensions:	208.5m x 20.4m (684ft x 67ft)
Machinery:	Twin screws, quadruple expansion engines
Top speed:	23.6 knots
Route:	Hamburg–New York
Launched:	January 1900

Blücher

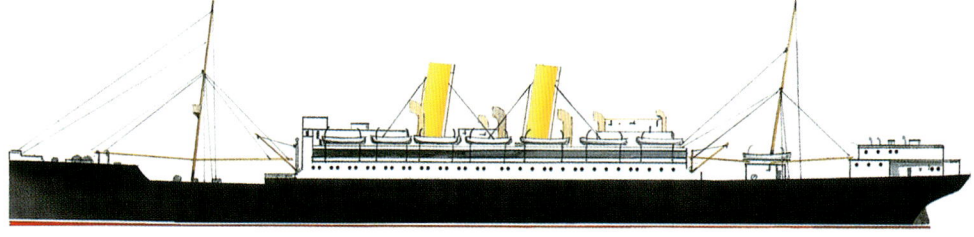

Blücher was built for the Hamburg–Amerika Line and on completion in 1902 was assigned to the Atlantic route. In 1917 it was taken over by the Allies, and in 1919 resumed the New York run under the French flag. Laid up from 1921–23, it was renamed *Suffren* on return to service. It was scrapped in 1929.

SPECIFICATIONS
Type:	German liner
Displacement:	12,531 tonnes (12,334 tons)
Dimensions:	168m x 19m (549ft 6in x 62ft)
Machinery:	Twin screws, quadruple expansion engines
Top speed:	15 knots
Route:	North Alantic
Launched:	1901

TIMELINE 1900   1901   1903

Baltic

SPECIFICATIONS	
Type:	British merchant vessel
Displacement:	24,258 tonnes (23,876 tons)
Dimensions:	221m x 23m (725ft x 75ft 6in)
Machinery:	Twin screws, triple expansion engines
Top speed:	17 knots
Cargo:	General cargo
Route:	North Atlantic
Launched:	November 1903

Baltic was built by Harland and Wolff of Belfast for the White Star Line. Capable of carrying nearly 900 passengers plus 2000 steerage, it was the world's largest ship when launched. Used as a troop transport during World War I, it was re-boilered in 1924 and laid up in 1932. It was broken up in 1933.

Empress of Britain

SPECIFICATIONS	
Type:	Canadian liner
Displacement:	14,416 tonnes (14,189 tons)
Dimensions:	167m x 20m (549ft x 66ft)
Machinery:	Twin screws, quadruple expansion engines
Top speed:	20 knots
Route:	Liverpool–Canada
Launched:	November 1905

Entering service for the Canadian Pacific Company in 1906, *Empress of Britain* carried 1460 passengers in three classes. On the outbreak of World War I, it was taken over as an auxiliary cruiser and later served as a troop transport. In 1924, it underwent a major refit, was renamed *Montroyal*, and was scrapped in 1930.

Lusitania

SPECIFICATIONS	
Type:	British liner
Displacement:	32,054 tonnes (31,550 tons)
Dimensions:	232m x 27m (761ft x 88ft)
Machinery:	Quadruple screws, turbines
Top speed:	24 knots
Route:	North Atlantic
Launched:	1906

At launch, *Lusitania*, built for Cunard's North Atlantic service, was the largest ship in the world, carrying 2165 passengers – and the Blue Riband holder in both directions in 1907. Returning from New York to Southampton in May 1915, it was sunk off Ireland by the German submarine *U-20* for the loss of 1198 lives.

Passenger Liners 1900–1929: Part 2

Despite an accent on luxury, all steam liner companies knew that most passengers travelled third class. They were segregated from first class but were still a cut above the bottom-rung 'steerage' passengers, mostly emigrants going one way only.

France

France was one of the smallest transatlantic liners, but also one of the fastest. In World War I, it was an auxiliary cruiser, troop transport and hospital ship. In 1919, it returned to the Atlantic route, so popular that passengers had to bid for their cabins. After a last crossing in 1932 it was broken up in 1934/35.

SPECIFICATIONS
Type:	French liner
Displacement:	27,188 tonnes (26,760 tons)
Dimensions:	217.2m x 23m (712ft 7in x 75ft 6in)
Machinery:	Four screws, turbines
Top speed:	25.9 knots
Route:	Le Havre–New York
Launched:	September 1910

Franconia

Similar in appearance to the other Cunard ships *Laconia* and *Caronia*, and used chiefly on the Liverpool–Boston service, *Franconia* also specialized in winter cruises. Passenger capacity was 300 first, 350 second and 2200 third class. A troopship during World War I, it was sunk by U-boat torpedoes in 1916.

SPECIFICATIONS
Type:	British passenger liner
Displacement:	18,441 tonnes (18,150 tons)
Dimensions:	182.95m x 21.75m (600ft 3in x 71ft 3in)
Machinery:	Twin screws, quadruple expansion engines
Top speed:	17 knots
Route:	North Atlantic, Mediterranean cruising
Launched:	1910

TIMELINE

1910   1911

Kaiser Franz Josef I

During World War I, *Kaiser Franz Josef I* was laid up at Trieste. In 1919 it was handed to Italy and renamed *Presidente Wilson*. From 1920 to 1922, it was Italy's largest liner. Transferred to the Lloyd Triestino and then Adriatica lines, it worked through the 1930s, and was scuttled at La Spezia in 1944.

SPECIFICATIONS	
Type:	Austrian liner
Displacement:	17,170 tonnes (16,900 tons)
Dimensions:	152.4m x 18.8m x 8.8m (500ft x 62ft x 29ft)
Machinery:	Twin screws, quadruple expansion engines
Top speed:	19 knots
Routes:	Trieste–New York, Trieste–Buenos Aires
Launched:	September 1911

Matsonia

Matsonia was built for Matson Lines, its machinery and funnel set unusually far back. Passenger accommodation in two classes was 329. During the 1932–37 slump, it was laid up. In both World Wars, it was used by the US government as an armed merchant cruiser. It was broken up in 1957.

SPECIFICATIONS	
Type:	US cargo/passenger liner
Displacement:	9886.5 tonnes (9728 tons)
Dimensions:	146m x 17.5m x 9m (480ft 6in x 58ft x 30ft 6in)
Machinery:	Single screw, triple expansion engine
Top speed:	15 knots
Cargo:	Tropical fruit, sugar, general merchandise
Route:	San Francisco–Hawaii
Launched:	1913

Britannic

Britannic was the largest of a trio of giant liners ordered by the White Star Line from Harland and Wolff, the others being *Olympic* and *Titanic*. In 1915, the Admiralty ordered its completion as a hospital ship. In 1916, it struck a German mine in the Aegean Sea, and an hour later it capsized and sank.

SPECIFICATIONS	
Type:	British hospital ship
Displacement:	48,928 tonnes (48,158 tons)
Dimensions:	275m x 27m (903ft x 94ft)
Machinery:	Triple screws, geared turbines
Top speed:	21 knots
Launched:	1914

SHIP TYPES 1900–1929

Passenger Liners 1900–1929: Part 3

Warfare emptied the passenger liners, though some companies leased their vessels as troopships or hospital ships. Many liners were laid up for the duration of World War I, and not recommissioned afterwards, being scrapped before their time.

Duilio

Italy's first home-built liner to exceed 20,320 tonnes (20,000 tons), *Duilio* was completed in 1923 for the North American route. In 1928 it switched to the South American route, and in 1933 began a South African service. It was chartered by the International Red Cross in 1942. Sunk in 1944, it was raised for scrap in 1948.

SPECIFICATIONS	
Type:	Italian liner
Displacement:	24,670 tonnes (24,281 tons)
Dimensions:	193.5m x 23.2m (634ft 10in x 76ft)
Machinery:	Quadruple screws, turbines
Routes:	Genoa–New York; Genoa–Buenos Aires
Launched:	1916

Columbus

Laid down in 1914 for Norddeutscher Lloyd, *Columbus*'s building was halted until 1920. Passenger capacity was 1837 in three classes and it was a popular ship. In 1929 new turbines were installed, increasing its speed. It was scuttled in the Atlantic in December 1939 to prevent capture by the British HMS *Hyperion*.

SPECIFICATIONS	
Type:	German liner
Displacement:	32,871 tonnes (32,354 tons)
Dimensions:	236m x 25m (775ft x 83ft)
Machinery:	Twin screws, triple expansion engine, replaced by turbines
Top speed:	19, later 23 knots
Route:	North Atlantic, Germany–United States
Launched:	August 1922

TIMELINE

1916    1922

Doric

The White Star Line's only turbine-driven liner, *Doric* was built for the Liverpool–Canada route, carrying 583 cabin class and 1688 third-class passengers. By 1930, it took 320 cabin class, 657 tourist class and 537 third-class passengers. Damaged in 1935 by a collision with the freighter *Formigny*, it was sold for scrap.

SPECIFICATIONS	
Type:	British liner
Displacement:	28,935 tonnes (28,480 tons)
Dimensions:	183m x 20.6m (600ft 6in x 67ft 6in)
Machinery:	Twin screws, turbines
Top speed:	16 knots
Route:	Liverpool–Halifax, Montreal
Launched:	1922

Eridan

The largest and most powerful motorship yet built in France, *Eridan* was built for the Australian service. During World War II, it was under Vichy control until captured in 1942. After a refit in 1947, *Eridan* served on the Indian route. In another refit in 1951, it acquired a large single funnel. It was broken up in 1956.

SPECIFICATIONS	
Type:	French liner
Displacement:	14,361 tonnes (14,135 tons)
Dimensions:	142.6m x 18.5m (468ft 7in x 61ft)
Machinery:	Twin screws, diesel engines
Top speed:	16 knots
Routes:	Marseille–New Caledonia; Marseille–India
Launched:	June 1928

Europa

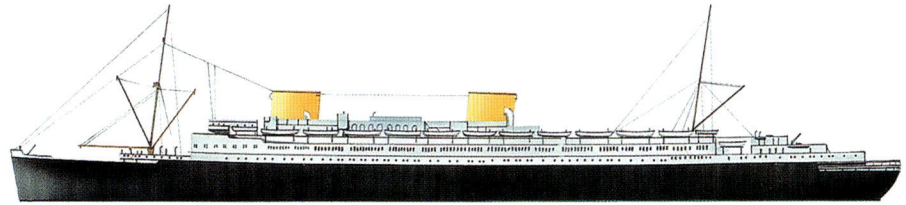

With an unusual raked bow and bulbous forefoot designed for easier passage through the water, *Europa* was completed in 1930. In 1946 it became the French *Liberté*, but while laid up, broke away and collided with the sunken wreck of the liner *Paris* and sank. Resuming service in 1950, it was broken up in 1962.

SPECIFICATIONS	
Type:	German liner
Displacement:	50,542 tonnes (49,746 tons)
Dimensions:	285m x 31m (930ft 9in x 102ft 1in)
Machinery:	Quadruple screws, turbines
Top speed:	27.9 knots
Route:	Bremen–Le Havre–New York
Launched:	July 1928

SHIP TYPES 1900–1929

Lake Steamers & River Vessels

Lake and river ships floated on fresh water, which is less buoyant than salt – something that designers had to bear in mind for bigger vessels. And some lake ships were large, particularly on the Great Lakes of North America. Most were modest-sized, like the steamers on Lake Titicaca and the East African Lakes.

Baikal

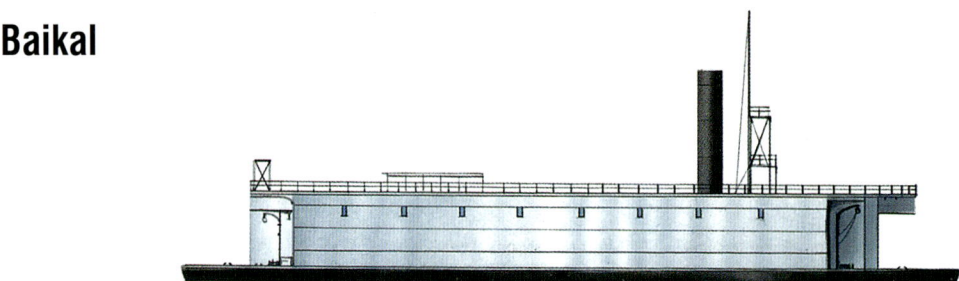

Baikal was built to connect the eastern and western sections of the Trans-Siberian railway across Lake Baikal, and was also used as an ice-breaker. Built on the Tyne in the 1890s, it was dismantled for transportation, and reassembled. It served on the lake until the railway was finally extended round the shore.

SPECIFICATIONS
Type:	Russian train ferry
Displacement:	2844 tonnes (2800 tons)
Dimensions:	76.2m x 19.2m (250ft x 63ft)
Machinery:	Twin screws, vertical triple expansion engines
Launched:	June 1900

Lady Hopetoun

Built in Sydney as an inspection boat for the officials of the Maritime Services Board, *Lady Hopetoun* worked in Sydney Harbour. It is a typical example of the steam pinnace, once a common sight. Most have vanished, but this one has been preserved and has been a museum craft in Sydney since 1991.

SPECIFICATIONS
Type:	Australian harbour inspection boat
Displacement:	38.6 tonnes (38 tons)
Dimensions:	23.45m x 4.2m x 2.05m (70ft x 13ft 9in x 6ft 9in)
Machinery:	Single screw, triple expansion engine
Launched:	1902

TIMELINE

1900　　　1902　　　1914

LAKE STEAMERS & RIVER VESSELS

Liemba

SPECIFICATIONS	
Type:	East African lake steamer
Displacement:	1600 tonnes (1575 tons)
Dimensions:	70.7m x 10.05m x 2.75m (232ft x 33ft x 9ft)
Machinery:	Twin screws, triple expansion engine
Top speed:	10 knots
Route:	Lake Tanganyika, Kigoma–Mpulungu
Launched:	1914

Built in sections in Germany and assembled at Kigoma (then a German colony), this ship was first named *Graf von Goetzen*. In 1916 it was scuttled to prevent the British taking it. Raised in 1924, it was refurbished, renamed *Liemba* and restored to service, carrying 384 passengers and light freight between railheads.

Oscar Huber

SPECIFICATIONS	
Type:	German river tug
Displacement:	203.2 tonnes (200 tons)
Dimensions:	75m x 20.7m x 1.55m (246ft x 67ft 10in x 5ft 1in)
Machinery:	Sidewheels, triple expansion engine
Route:	River Rhine
Launched:	1922

Steam tugs of this type towed long strings of barges on the Rhine and its linked waterways from central Germany to the coast. Sidewheels enabled them to have a shallow draught that could cope with reduced river flows. *Oscar Huber* is maintained as a museum craft at Duisburg, where it was built.

William G. Mather

SPECIFICATIONS	
Type:	US Great Lakes bulk carrier
Displacement:	8800 tonnes (8662 tons)
Dimensions:	183.2m x 18.9m x 5.5m (601ft x 62ft x 18ft)
Machinery:	Single screw, geared turbine engine
Top speed:	12 knots
Cargo:	Iron ore, wheat
Route:	Great Lakes
Launched:	1925

For navigating the Great Lakes and their linking canals, a unique ship design was produced, with command position and engines at opposite ends. The deck was free of equipment, since loading and unloading gear was available at both ends of the voyage. This example from the 1920s is retained as a museum ship.

SHIP TYPES 1900–1929

Specialized Vessels 1900–1929

Some ships were built for a specific purpose that required either a particular type of hull, perhaps ice-resistant or shallow-draught, or fitting with specialized equipment. Most common were tug-boats, from small harbour tugs to ocean-going salvage vessels, and the various kinds of dredger, but the range of requirements was wide.

Discovery

Built in Dundee, Scotland, and designed for Polar research work, *Discovery* had a wooden hull reinforced to withstand ice pressure. In 1901, it took Captain Scott to the Antarctic. Also used on numerous other research voyages, it was berthed on the Thames for many years and is now a museum ship in Dundee.

SPECIFICATIONS	
Type:	British exploration ship
Displacement:	1646 tonnes (1620 tons)
Dimensions:	52m x 10m x 4.8m (172ft x 34ft x 15ft 8in)
Machinery:	Single screw, triple expansion engine
Rigging:	Three masts, barque rig
Top speed:	8 knots
Launched:	March 1901

Industry

Industry's job was to keep the Murray's navigable channel free of obstructions such as floating logs and to act as a mobile workshop for maintenance work on locks and wharves. Its derrick could operate a bucket dredge to clear silt. In regular use until 1969, it is now a museum vessel at Renmark, South Australia.

SPECIFICATIONS	
Type:	Australian dredger and snag boat
Displacement:	92.4 tonnes (91 tons)
Dimensions:	34.15m x 5.65m x .94m (112ft x 18ft 6 in x 3ft 1in)
Machinery:	Sidewheels, 30hp steam engine
Route:	Murray River
Launched:	1911

TIMELINE

 1901  1911  1913

SPECIALIZED VESSELS 1900–1929

Acadia

Interest in Canada's northlands was strong around 1910 and *Acadia* was a specialized and well-equipped hydrographic research ship intended to provide valuable knowledge of the coastline and inshore waters, and to underline Canada's claim to the region. *Acadia* is preserved at Halifax, Nova Scotia.

SPECIFICATIONS	
Type:	Canadian hydrographic survey ship
Displacement:	859.5 tonnes (846 tons)
Dimensions:	51.8m x 10.25m x 3.65m (170ft x 33ft 6in x 12ft)
Machinery:	Single screw, vertical triple expansion engine
Top speed:	12.5 knots
Route:	Canadian east and north-east coasts
Launched:	1913

Inverlago

Serving the Venezuelan oilfield, ships like *Inverlago* were of restricted depth because of the shallow waters of the lake. Even so, it could carry 3200 tonnes (3156 tons) of crude oil from the well-heads to deep-water berths on the sea-coast. By 1953, the channels had been deepened and ships of such designs were not needed.

SPECIFICATIONS	
Type:	Dutch–Venezuelan oil tanker
Displacement:	2758.6 tonnes (2600 tons)
Dimensions:	92.5m x 11.6m x 4.05m (305ft x 38ft x 13ft 3in)
Machinery:	Single screw, triple expansion engine
Top speed:	10 knots
Cargo:	Crude oil
Route:	Lake Maracaibo
Launched:	1925

Artiglio II

Artiglio II was a small coaster adapted in 1929 to recover gold from the liner *Egypt*, which had sunk in 1922. The exercise marked a new era in underwater salvage, as the liner had gone down in a depth of 110m (360ft) – too deep for conventional diving gear. Most of the gold, valued at £1,054,000, was recovered.

SPECIFICATIONS	
Type:	Italian salvage vessel
Displacement:	305 tonnes (300 tons) (approx)
Dimensions:	42.6m x 7.6m x 2.1m (139ft 9in x 25ft x 7ft) (approx)
Top speed:	14 knots (approx)
Converted:	1929

SHIP TYPES 1930–1949

The economic depression of the 1930s slowed down the rate of construction of new ships, but technical development was intensified in the effort to get greater economy and efficiency.

Oil fuel replaced coal in all new vessels, and the diesel engine brought about the 'motor ship' to compete with the steamer. Attempts to agree on limits to warship sizes collapsed with the imminence of war in 1939. In World War II, more than twenty million tons of shipping were sunk, with huge loss of life, and yet most of it was speedily replaced.

Left: *Bismarck*, with *Tirpitz*, was the largest German warship ever built. Its one and only combat mission became a naval epic of World War II.

SHIP TYPES 1930–1949

Aircraft Carriers (Escort)

Large carriers took time to design and build, and from early in World War II, the hulls of existing ships were requisitioned and converted into small or medium-sized carriers in order to help provide air cover for battleships and convoys. Their facilities were usually limited, but they provided vital support at a crucial time.

Audacity

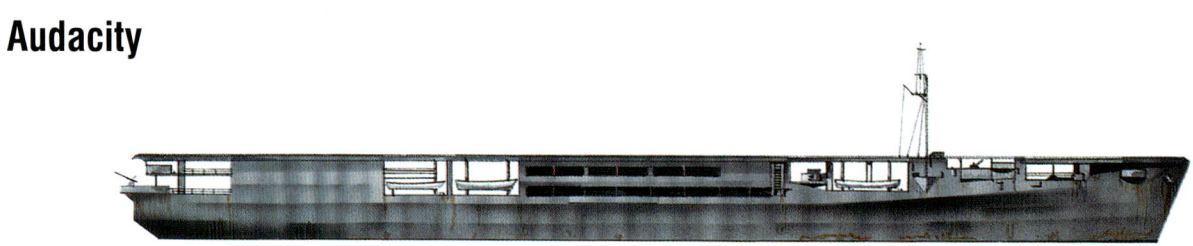

The captured German merchant ship *Hannover* was given a 140m x 18m (400ft x 60ft) flight deck above the hull. There was no hangar or elevator, so its aircraft had to remain on the deck, exposed to the weather. As *Audacity*, it served for only six months before it was torpedoed and sunk by *U-751* in December 1941.

SPECIFICATIONS

Type:	British escort carrier
Displacement:	11,176 tonnes (11,000 tons)
Dimensions:	142.4m x 17.4m x 7.5m (467ft 5in x 57ft x 24ft 6in)
Machinery:	Single screw, diesel engine
Top speed:	15 knots
Main armament:	One 102mm (4in) gun, eight AA guns
Aircraft:	Six Martlet fighters
Complement:	480
Launched:	1939 (converted 1941)

Sangamon

First a commercial tanker, then a fleet oiler, *Sangamon* was one of four similar ships converted to carriers. The aft-placed engines allowed for considerable hangar space. The wooden flight deck was fitted with two lifts and a catapult. The ships could carry 12,000 tonnes of oil, enabling them to act as refuellers.

SPECIFICATIONS

Type:	US escort carrier
Displacement:	24,257 tonnes (23,875 tons)
Dimensions:	168.55m x 32.05m x 9.3m (553ft 2in x 105ft 2in x 30ft 7in)
Machinery:	Twin screws, geared turbines
Top speed:	18 knots
Main armament:	Two 127mm (5in) guns
Aircraft:	30 (later 36)
Complement:	1080
Launched:	1939 (converted 1943)

TIMELINE

1939   1940

AIRCRAFT CARRIERS (ESCORT)

Dixmude

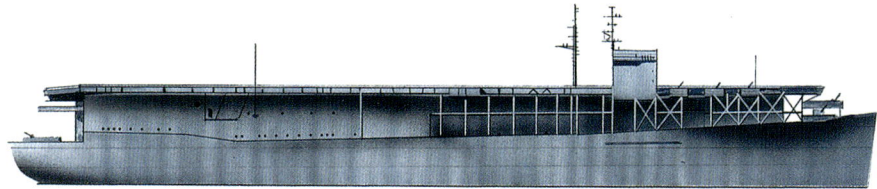

This ship was built in the United States as *Rio Parana* for lease to Britain. On arrival, the flight deck was increased to 134m (440ft) and the ship became HMS *Biter*. Passed to France in 1945, it was renamed *Dixmude*, serving as an aircraft transport. Disarmed as an accommodation ship, it was scrapped in 1966.

SPECIFICATIONS	
Type:	French aircraft carrier
Displacement:	11,989 tonnes (11,800 tons)
Dimensions:	150m x 23m x 7.6m (490ft 10in x 78ft x 25ft 2in)
Machinery:	Single screw, diesel engine
Top speed:	16.5 knots
Main armament:	Three 102mm (4in) guns
Aircraft:	15
Launched:	December 1940

Activity

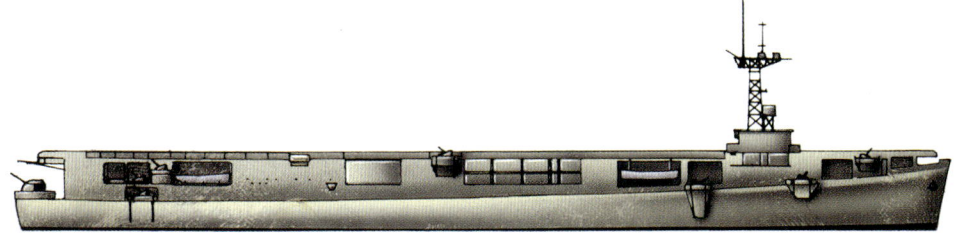

Built on the hull intended for a refrigerated cargo ship, *Activity* served as a carrier but was compromised by its restricted hangar space, only 31m (100ft long). But it was an effective escort to Arctic and Atlantic convoys and carried aircraft to the Far East. After 1945, it was reconstructed as the cargo ship *Breconshire*.

SPECIFICATIONS	
Type:	British escort carrier
Displacement:	14,529 tonnes (14,300 tons)
Dimensions:	156.3m x 20.3m x 7.95m (512ft 9in x 66ft 6in x 26ft)
Machinery:	Twin screws, diesels
Top speed:	18 knots
Main armament:	Two 102mm (4in) guns, twenty-four 20mm (0.78in) AA guns
Aircraft:	10
Complement:	700
Launched:	1942

Dédalo

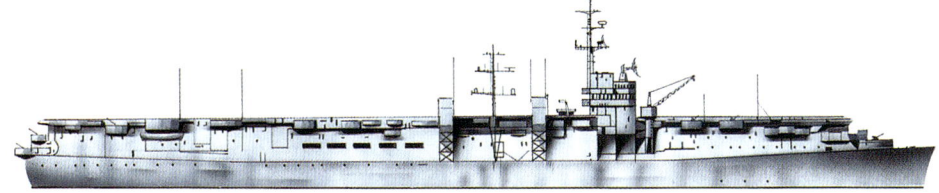

Dédalo began existence as the US carrier *Cabot*, completed in 1943. After service in World War II, it was decommissioned in 1947. Laid up for 20 years, it was lent to Spain in 1967, and purchased outright in 1972. It remained in service until the new carrier *Principe de Asturias* was commissioned in 1982.

SPECIFICATIONS	
Type:	Spanish aircraft carrier
Displacement:	16,678 tonnes (16,416 tons)
Dimensions:	190m x 22m x 8m (622ft 4in x 73ft x 26ft)
Machinery:	Quadruple screws, turbines
Top speed:	30 knots
Main armament:	Twenty-six 40mm (1.6in) guns
Aircraft:	20
Launched:	April 1943

SHIP TYPES 1930–1949

Enterprise

Commissioned in May 1938, *Enterprise* was engaged in almost every major carrier battle of World War II. At the Battle of Midway, its dive bombers helped sink four Japanese carriers. A refit was carried out in late 1943. In 1947, it was placed on the reserve list and it went for breaking in 1958.

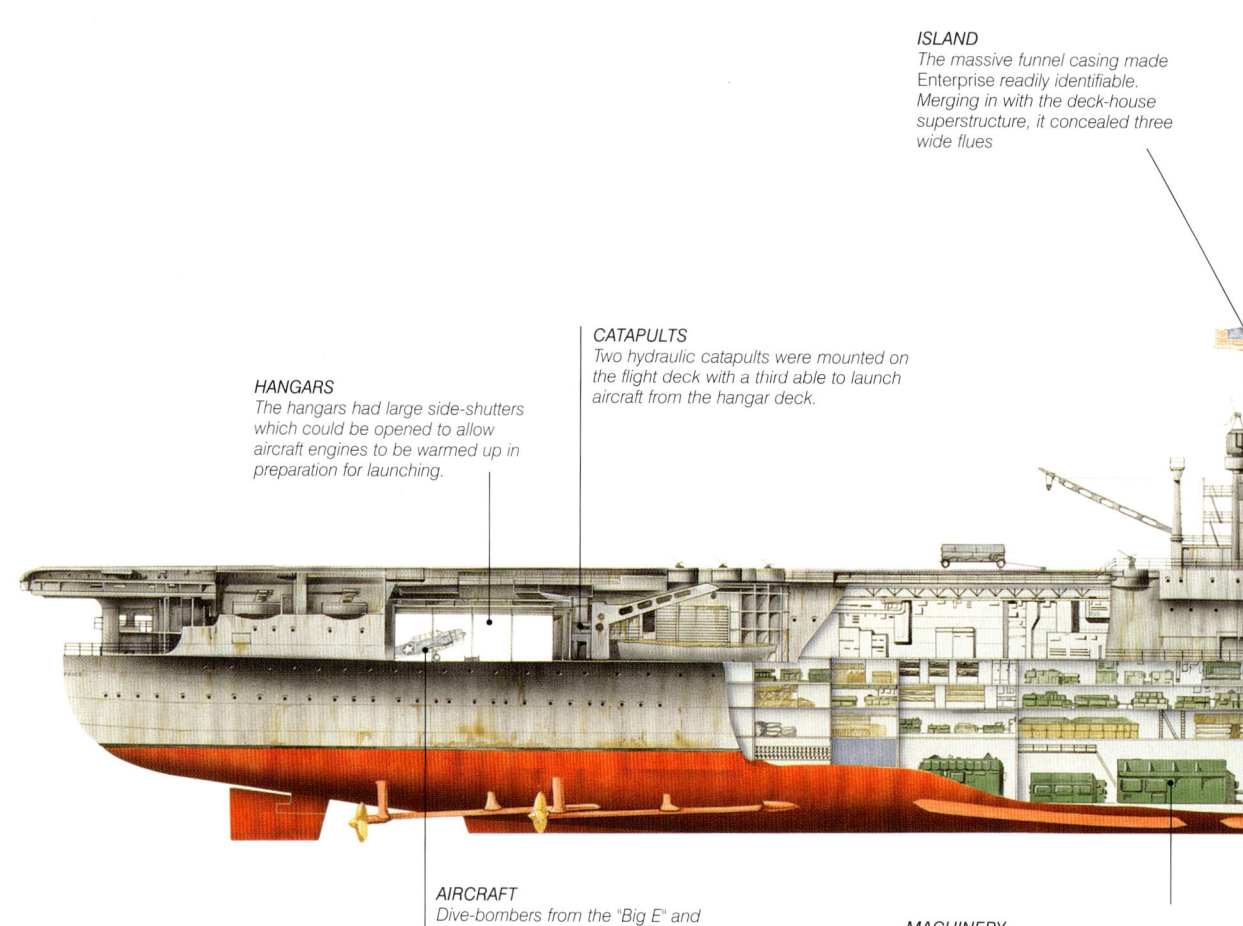

ISLAND
The massive funnel casing made *Enterprise* readily identifiable. Merging in with the deck-house superstructure, it concealed three wide flues

CATAPULTS
Two hydraulic catapults were mounted on the flight deck with a third able to launch aircraft from the hangar deck.

HANGARS
The hangars had large side-shutters which could be opened to allow aircraft engines to be warmed up in preparation for launching.

AIRCRAFT
Dive-bombers from the "Big E" and *Yorktown* sank four Japanese carriers and other ships at Midway in May 1942, a turning-point in the Pacific war.

MACHINERY
Nine oil-fired Babcock & Wilcox boilers supplied power to four Parsons geared turbines, generating 89,484kW (120,000 shp).

Enterprise

Enterprise was involved in Midway, Guadalcanal, the Eastern Solomons, the Gilbert Islands, Kwajalein, Eniwetok, the Truk raid, Hollandia, Saipan, the Battle of the Philippine Sea, Palau, Leyte, Luzon, Taiwan, the China coast, Iwo Jima and Okinawa. She received five bomb hits and survived two attacks by kamikazes off Okinawa.

SPECIFICATIONS	
Type:	US aircraft carrier
Displacement:	25,908 tonnes (25,500 tons)
Dimensions:	246.7m x 26.2m x 7.9m (809ft 6in x 86ft x 26ft)
Machinery:	Quadruple screws, turbines
Top speed:	37.5 knots
Main armament:	Eight 127mm (5in) guns
Aircraft:	96
Complement:	2175
Launched:	October 1936

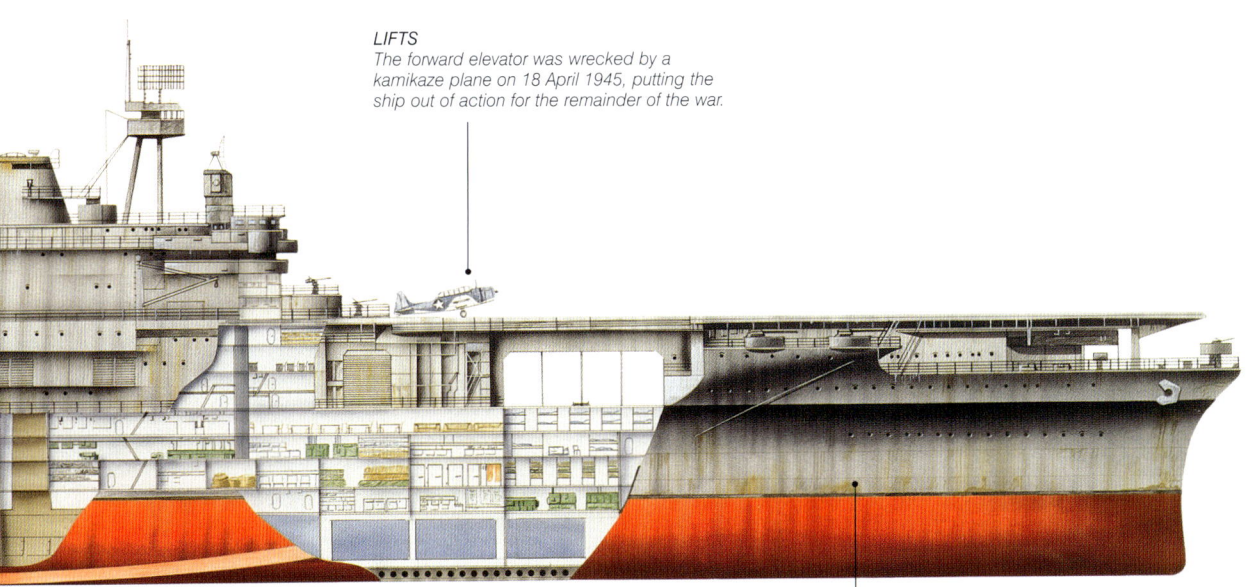

LIFTS
The forward elevator was wrecked by a kamikaze plane on 18 April 1945, putting the ship out of action for the remainder of the war.

HULL
Though purpose-built as a carrier, the hull design clearly shows how the form evolved from the cruiser hull.

SHIP TYPES 1930–1949

American Carriers

On entering World War II, the United States had few aircraft carriers, but began to construct them on an enormous scale, with many auxiliary and escort carriers built on merchant ship hulls. Carrier-borne aircraft played a vital role in the great battles of the Pacific Ocean, and became the prime destroyers of submarines.

Wasp

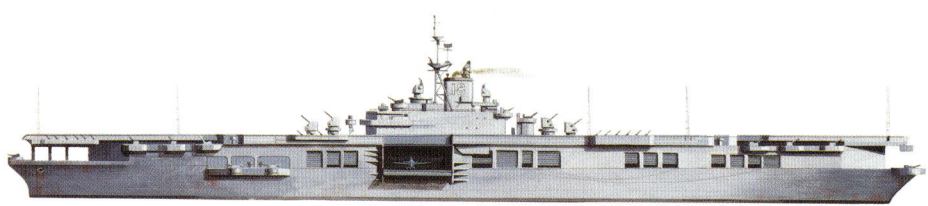

Notable among purpose-built US carriers for its lack of armour protection, *Wasp* was commissioned in April 1940. It helped in the defence of Malta by delivering 100 Spitfires. Transferred to the Pacific in June 1942, it was torpedoed by the Japanese submarine *I19* off Guadalcanal on 15 September, and abandoned.

SPECIFICATIONS	
Type:	US aircraft carrier
Displacement:	18,745.32 tonnes (18,450 tons)
Dimensions:	225.9m x 28.35m x 7.45m (741ft 3in x 93ft x 24ft 6in)
Machinery:	Twin screws, geared turbines
Top speed:	29.5 knots
Aircraft:	76
Main armament:	Eight 127mm (5in) guns
Armour:	37mm (1.5in) deck
Complement:	2167
Launched:	1939

Essex

The needs of the navy for air cover led to great increases in the size of aircraft carriers, with larger hulls to stow the fuel required for up to 91 aircraft. There were 24 vessels in the *Essex* class. *Essex* entered service in 1942, was removed from the effective list in 1969 and scrapped in 1973.

SPECIFICATIONS	
Type:	US aircraft carrier
Displacement:	35,438 tonnes (34,880 tons)
Dimensions:	265.7m x 29.2m x 8.3m (871ft 9in x 96ft x 27ft 6in)
Machinery:	Quadruple screws, turbines
Top speed:	32.7 knots
Aircraft:	90–100
Main armament:	Twelve 127mm (5in) guns
Launched:	July 1942

TIMELINE

1939 1942

AMERICAN CARRIERS

Independence

Borrowing the frame of a *Cleveland*-class light cruiser, *Independence* was part of an emergency carrier programme. Nine vessels entered service in 1943. *Independence* had room to ferry up to 100 aircraft. It was used as a target in the Bikini atomic bomb tests, and was sunk as a target in 1951.

SPECIFICATIONS	
Type:	US aircraft carrier
Displacement:	13,208 tonnes (13,000 tons)
Dimensions:	190m x 33m x 7.6m (623ft x 109ft 3in x 25ft 11in)
Machinery:	Quadruple screws, turbines
Top speed:	31 knots
Main armament:	Two 127mm (5in) guns
Armour:	140mm (5.5ins) belt, 51mm (2in) deck
Aircraft:	45
Launched:	August 1942

Gambier Bay

Gambier Bay was another of the 50-strong group of light escort carriers assembled on merchant ship hulls. All were built in under a year. In early 1944, *Gambier Bay* ferried aircraft to USS *Enterprise* and supported action off Saipan, in the Marianas and at Leyte. It was sunk by gunfire off Samar in October 1944.

SPECIFICATIONS	
Type:	US escort carrier
Displacement:	11,074 tonnes (10,900 tons)
Dimensions:	156.1m x 32.9m x 6.3m (512ft 3in x 108ft x 20ft 9in)
Machinery:	Twin screws, reciprocating engines
Top speed:	19 knots
Aircraft:	28
Launched:	November 1943

Attu

In 1942, shipbuilder Henry J. Kaiser was mass producing cargo vessels to replace those lost in war. With a severe shortage of aircraft carriers, the decision was taken to adapt 50 of the unfinished hulls as escort carriers. *Attu* was built in 75 days. It served in the Pacific until 1946, and was scrapped in 1949.

SPECIFICATIONS	
Type:	US escort carrier
Displacement:	11,076 tonnes (10,902 tons)
Dimensions:	156.1m x 32.9m x 6.3m (512ft 3in x 108ft x 20ft 9in)
Machinery:	Twin screws, reciprocating engines
Top speed:	19.3 knots
Main armament:	One 127mm (5in) gun
Launched:	1944

SHIP TYPES 1930–1949

British Carriers

In 1939, the British Navy had the advantage of twenty years' experience in carrier design and operation. But their number was not large. In 1938, a construction programme was got under way, and war demands and conditions prompted further designs in 1940. By then, the carriers were in the thick of naval warfare.

Ark Royal

Ark Royal was the Royal Navy's first large purpose-built aircraft carrier, with a long flight deck some 18m (60ft) above the deep water load line. Its full complement was 60 aircraft, although it never carried this many. Part of Force H in the Mediterranean, Ark Royal was sunk in November 1941 by submarine U-81.

SPECIFICATIONS	
Type:	British aircraft carrier
Displacement:	28,164 tonnes (27,720 tons)
Dimensions:	243.8m x 28.9m x 8.5m (800ft x 94ft 9in x 27ft 9in)
Machinery:	Triple screws, geared turbines
Top speed:	31 knots
Main armament:	Sixteen 114mm (4.5in) guns
Armour:	114mm (4.5in) belt, 7.6mm (3in) bulkheads
Aircraft:	50–60
Launched:	April 1937

Formidable

Formidable was modelled on Ark Royal but with one hangar deck. As the nature of the coming war was becoming clear, attention was given to its armour and defensive capacity; it withstood two kamikaze attacks in May 1945. The flight deck was widened to carry extra planes. Formidable was scrapped in 1953.

SPECIFICATIONS	
Type:	British aircraft carrier
Displacement:	28,661 tonnes (28,210 tons)
Dimensions:	226.7m x 29.1m x 8.5m (743ft 9in x 95ft 9in x 28ft)
Machinery:	Triple screws, turbines
Top speed:	30.5 knots
Main armament:	Sixteen 114mm (4.5in) guns
Armour:	115mm (4.5in) hangars, 76mm (3in) deck
Aircraft:	36, later 54
Complement:	1229, later 1997
Launched:	August 1939

TIMELINE

1937   1939   1940

BRITISH CARRIERS

Indomitable

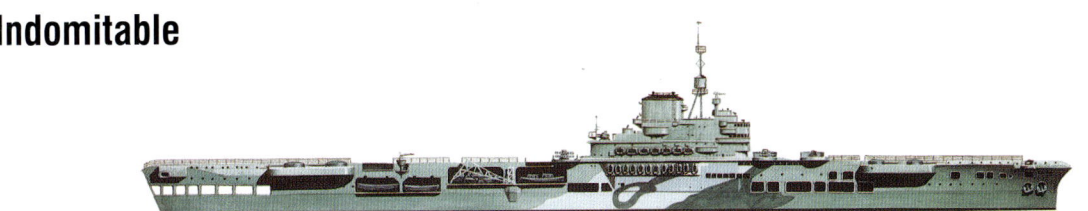

Indomitable was modified from the Illustrious class carriers, its armour weight sacrificed to provide more aircraft space, with an additional hangar deck. Indomitable was damaged by bombs in August 1942 and by an aerial torpedo in August 1943. Back in service from April 1944, it was broken up in 1955.

SPECIFICATIONS	
Type:	British aircraft carrier
Displacement:	30,205 tonnes (29,730 tons)
Dimensions:	229.8m x 29.2m x 8.85m (753ft 11in x 95ft 9in x 29ft)
Machinery:	Triple screws, geared turbines
Top speed:	30.5 knots
Main Armament:	16 114mm (4.5in) guns
Armour:	114mm (4.5in) belt, 37mm (1.5in) hangar sides, 76mm (3in) flight deck
Aircraft:	45 (later 56)
Complement:	1392 (later 2100)
Launched:	1940

Unicorn

Unicorn was meant to be a depot/maintenance support ship. It was modified during construction to operate its own aircraft, as well as repair those from other carriers. During World War II, it served in the Mediterranean, Atlantic and Pacific. It later became a depot ship in Hong Kong, and was scrapped in 1959/60.

SPECIFICATIONS	
Type:	British aircraft carrier
Displacement:	20,624 tonnes (20,300 tons)
Dimensions:	186m x 27.4m x 7.3m (610ft x 90ft x 24ft)
Machinery:	Twin screws, turbines
Top speed:	24 knots
Main armament:	Eight 102mm (4in) guns
Armour:	51mm (2in) flight deck, 76–51mm (3–2in) on magazines
Aircraft:	36
Complement:	1200
Launched:	November 1941

Eagle

During construction of the Illustrious class of 1938, designs were prepared in 1942 for their successors. These allowed for two complete hangars and ability to handle the heavier aircraft due to be introduced. Eagle entered service in 1951, was decommissioned in 1972 and was sent for breaking-up in 1978.

SPECIFICATIONS	
Type:	British aircraft carrier
Displacement:	47,200 tonnes (46,452 tons)
Dimensions:	245m x 34m x 11m (803ft 9in x 112ft 9in x 36ft)
Machinery:	Quadruple screws, turbines
Top speed:	31 knots
Main armament:	Sixteen 114mm (4.5in) guns; six GSW Seacat SAM (from 1962)
Aircraft:	80
Complement:	2750 including air group
Launched:	March 1946

1941    1946

SHIP TYPES 1930–1949

German & Japanese Aircraft Carriers

The Japanese Navy, an early user of carriers, built several in the 1930s and also ships easily convertible to carriers. Its carrier-borne aircraft attacked Pearl Harbor in December 1941. Germany, however, had been prevented from building carriers in the 1920s, and its designers and yards had no experience of this type of vessel.

Ryujo

Japan's first major purpose-built aircraft carrier was designed with a cruiser hull, restricting its width. A second hangar above the first gave excessive top weight, requiring post-launch modification. The hull was strengthened between 1934 and 1936, and the bulges widened. Aircraft from USS *Saratoga* sank it in 1942.

SPECIFICATIONS	
Type:	Japanese aircraft carrier
Displacement:	10,150 tonnes (9990 tons)
Dimensions:	175.3m x 23m x 5.5m (575ft 5in x 75ft 6in x 18ft 3in)
Machinery:	Twin screws, turbines
Top speed:	29 knots
Main armament:	Twelve 127mm (5in) guns
Aircraft:	48
Complement:	600
Launched:	April 1931

Zuiho

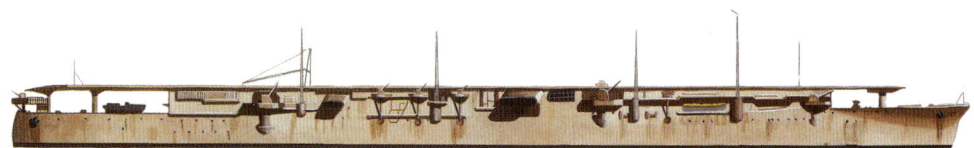

Many Japanese carriers had minimal deck superstructure. *Zuiho*, a submarine tender that was later converted, had none. Nor did it have armour protection. Damaged at Santa Cruz, it was repaired, and saw action at the Marianas and Guadalcanal. It was sunk at Cape Engano, in the Battle of Leyte Gulf.

SPECIFICATIONS	
Type:	Japanese aircraft carrier
Displacement:	14,528.8 tonnes (14,300 tons) full load
Dimensions:	204.8m x 18.2m x 6.65m (332ft x 59ft 89n x 21ft 9in)
Machinery:	Twin screws, geared turbines
Top speed:	28 knots
Main armament:	Eight 127mm (5in) guns
Aircraft:	30
Complement:	785
Launched:	1936

TIMELINE 1931 1936 1938

Graf Zeppelin

Construction of *Graf Zeppelin* to Wilhelm Hadeler's design began in 1935, but work was greatly delayed to make way for the U-boat programme. Never completed, the carrier was scuttled a few months before the end of World War II. It was raised by the Russians, but sank while under tow to Leningrad.

SPECIFICATIONS

Type:	German aircraft carrier
Displacement:	28,540 tonnes (28,109 tons)
Dimensions:	262.5m x 31.5m x 8.5m (861ft 3in x 103ft 4in x 27ft 10in)
Machinery:	Quadruple screws, turbines
Design speed:	35 knots
Main armament:	Twelve 104mm (4.1in) guns, sixteen 150mm (5.9in) guns
Armour:	88mm (3.5in) belt, 37mm (1.5in) hangar deck
Aircraft:	42
Launched:	December 1938

Zuikaku

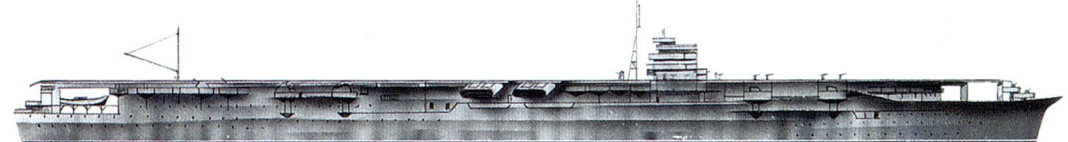

Zuikaku and its sister *Shokaku* were better armed and protected and carried more aircraft than Japan's previous purpose-built carriers. The flight deck, 240m (787ft) long and 29m (95ft) wide, was serviced by three lifts. *Zuikaku* helped sink USS *Lexington* but was sunk during the Battle of Leyte Gulf on 25 October 1944.

SPECIFICATIONS

Type:	Japanese aircraft carrier
Displacement:	32,618 tonnes (32,105 tons)
Dimensions:	257m x 29m x 8.8m (843ft 2in x 95ft x 29ft)
Machinery:	Quadruple screws, turbines
Top speed:	34 knots
Main armament:	Sixteen 127mm (5in) guns
Armour:	175–45mm (6.5–1.8in) belt, 155–100mm (5.9–3.9in) deck
Aircraft:	84
Complement:	1660
Launched:	November 1939

Junyo

Built on a hull laid down for a passenger liner, *Junyo* carried two hangar decks, though with limited headroom. It was in action at the Aleutian Islands, Santa Cruz and the Battle of the Philippine Sea. Badly damaged by torpedoes in December 1944, it was not repaired, and was broken up in 1947.

SPECIFICATIONS

Type:	Japanese aircraft carrier
Displacement:	24,181 tonnes (23,800 tons) full load
Dimensions:	166.55m x 21.9m x 8.05m (546ft 6in x 71ft 10in x 26ft 6in)
Machinery:	Twin screws, geared turbines
Top speed:	25 knots
Main armament:	Twelve 127mm (5in) guns
Armour:	25mm (1in) deck over machinery
Aircraft:	53
Complement:	1200
Launched:	1941

SHIP TYPES 1930–1949

Japanese Aircraft & Seaplane Carriers

Seaplanes were vital for Japanese strategy, to supply garrisoned islands with no airstrip. The Japanese fleet had nine seaplane carriers, but events later in the war forced a change of role, to conventional carriers or midget submarine mother ships.

Chitose

Chitose and sister-ship *Chiyoda* were seaplane carriers built for easy conversion into flush-decked aircraft carriers. In 1941 both were altered to enable the launch of midget submarines. They were refitted as conventional carriers between 1942 and 1944. *Chitose* was sunk in 1944 by aircraft from USS *Essex* and *Lexington*.

SPECIFICATIONS	
Type:	Japanese seaplane carrier
Displacement:	13,716 tonnes (13,500 tons)
Dimensions:	193m x 19m x 7m (631ft 7in x 61ft 8in x 23ft 8in)
Machinery:	Twin screws, turbines and diesel engines
Top speed:	29 knots
Main armament:	Four 127mm (5in) guns
Aircraft:	30
Launched:	November 1936

Mizuho

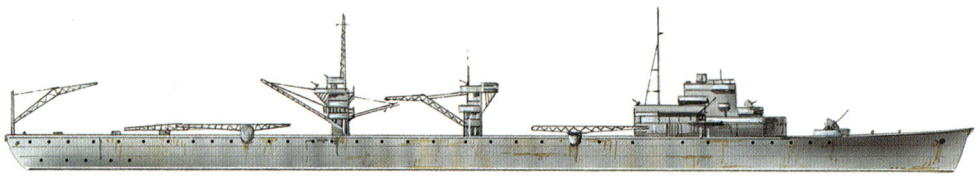

Mizuho was a sister-ship to *Chitose*, but slower, with diesel engines only. In 1941, the stern crane was removed and the ship was adapted to carry and service 12 midget submarines. There were plans for further conversion as a light aircraft carrier, but it was sunk by the US submarine *Drum* on 2 May 1942.

SPECIFICATIONS	
Type:	Seaplane (later submarine) support ship
Displacement:	11,110 tonnes (10,930 tons)
Dimensions:	192.m x 18.8m x 7.1m (631ft 6in x 61ft 8in x 23ft)
Machinery:	Twin screws, diesels
Top speed:	22 knots
Main armament:	Six 127mm (5in) guns
Aircraft:	24
Launched:	1938

TIMELINE   1936   1938   1943

JAPANESE AIRCRAFT & SEAPLANE CARRIERS

Taiho

Taiho was Japan's largest purpose-built aircraft carrier. The two-tier hangars were 150m (500ft) long, unarmoured at the sides. The flight deck could withstand a 455kg (1000lb) bomb hit. Armour protection came to 8940 tonnes (8800 tons) in total. Taiho was sunk by the US submarine Albacore in June 1944.

SPECIFICATIONS	
Type:	Japanese aircraft carrier
Displacement:	37,866 tonnes (37,270 tons)
Dimensions:	260.6m x 30m x 9.6m (855ft x 98ft 6in x 31ft 6in)
Machinery:	Quadruple screws, turbines
Top speed:	33.3 knots
Main armament:	Twelve 100mm (3.9in) guns, seventy-one 25mm (1in) guns
Armour:	76mm (3in) flight deck, 150mm (5.9in) machinery
Aircraft:	53
Complement:	1751
Launched:	April 1943

Unryu

A strike carrier, for use against convoys, Unryu was one of only three to be completed out of a planned class of 17. With the island sponsored out, it had a wide flight deck, served by two lifts. Unryu was sunk by the US submarine Redfish in December 1944, before it saw any action.

SPECIFICATIONS	
Type:	Japanese aircraft carrier
Displacement:	22,860 tonnes (22,500 tons) full load
Dimensions:	227.4m x 27m x 7.85m (746ft 1in x 88ft 6in x 25ft 9in)
Machinery:	Quadruple screws, geared turbines
Top speed:	34 knots
Main armament:	Twelve 127mm (5in) guns
Armour:	150–45mm (5.9–1.8in) belt, 50–25mm (2–1in) deck
Aircraft:	57 + 8
Complement:	1595
Launched:	1943

Shinano

On completion, Shinano was the world's largest aircraft carrier, a Yamato-class battleship hull converted into an auxiliary carrier with vast capacity for aircraft, fuel and spare parts. It never saw active service. On 29 November 1944, it was sunk by the US submarine Archerfish, on the way to Kure yard for final fitting-out.

SPECIFICATIONS	
Type:	Japanese aircraft carrier
Displacement:	74,208 tonnes (73,040 tons)
Dimensions:	266m x 40m x 10.3m (872ft 9in x 131ft 3in x 33ft 9in)
Machinery:	Quadruple screws, turbines
Top speed:	27 knots
Main armament:	145 25mm (1in) guns, 16 127mm (5in) guns, 336 rocket launchers
Armour:	205mm (8.1in) belt, 190mm (7.5in) hangar deck, 80mm (3.1in) flight deck
Aircraft:	70
Complement:	2400
Launched:	October 1944

SHIP TYPES 1930–1949

Attack Cargo Ships & Commerce Raiders

As in World War I, both Britain and Germany fitted out armed merchant ships, the Germans as commerce raiders, the British as defence vessels. These could mount enough gun-power to take on a cruiser. But the lack of armour was a disadvantage.

Jervis Bay

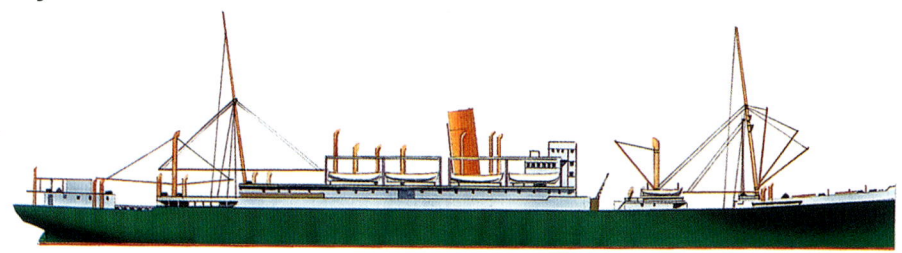

Built for the Australian emigrant trade in 1922, *Jervis Bay* was fitted out as an armed merchant cruiser with eight 152mm (6in) guns. In November 1939, its convoy was intercepted by the German battleship *Admiral Scheer*. *Jervis Bay* attacked and was sunk with heavy loss of life but the convoy was able to scatter.

SPECIFICATIONS	
Type:	British armed merchant cruiser
Displacement:	23,601 tonnes (23,230 tons)
Dimensions:	167m x 20m x 10m (549ft x 68ft x 33ft)
Machinery:	Twin screws, turbines
Top speed:	15 knots
Cargo:	Manufactured goods
Route:	London–Australian ports
Launched:	1922 (converted 1939)

Pinguin

Pinguin, originally the merchant ship *Kandelfels*, was Germany's most succesful commerce raider, sinking or capturing 32 Allied vessels, totalling (145,619 tons). Carrying 420 mines and two aircraft (later one), it travelled across the world. On 8 May 1941, it was sunk off the Seychelles by the British cruiser *Cornwall*.

SPECIFICATIONS	
Type:	German commerce raider
Displacement:	17,881.6 tonnes (17,600 tons)
Dimensions:	155m x 18.7m x 8.7m (508ft 6in x 61ft 4in x 28ft 6in)
Machinery:	Twin screws, double-acting diesels
Top speed:	16 knots
Main armament:	Six 150mm (5.9in) guns, one 76mm (3in) gun
Complement:	401
Launched:	1936 (converted 1940)

TIMELINE

1922   1936   1939

ATTACK CARGO SHIPS & COMMERCE RAIDERS

Komet

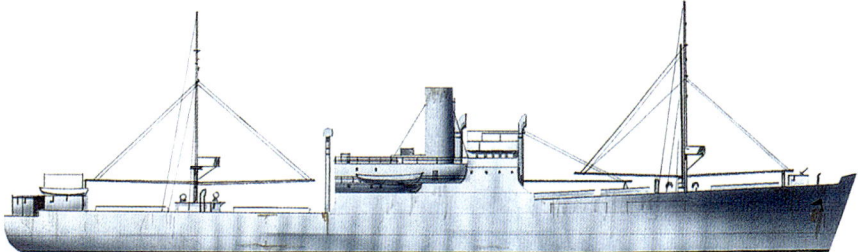

Komet was the best equipped of the German armed merchant cruisers. Armed with 150mm (5.9in) guns originally belonging to *Deutschland*-class battleships, it carried two scout planes and a motor torpedo boat (*LS2*). On its first outing, it sank 10 merchant ships, but it was sunk on a second sortie in 1942.

SPECIFICATIONS	
Type:	German commerce raider
Displacement:	7620 tonnes (7500 tons)
Dimensions:	115m x 15.3m x 6.5m (377ft 4in x 50ft 2in x 21ft 4in)
Machinery:	Single screw, diesel engines
Top speed:	14.5 knots
Main armament:	Six 150mm (5.9in) guns
Complement:	269
Launched:	1939

Kormoran

Kormoran, formerly the *Steiermark*, sank or captured 11 merchant ships totalling 69,366 tonnes (68,274 tons). Spotted by the Australian cruiser *Sydney* off Western Australia on 11 November 1941, it was taken to be a Dutch merchant vessel, until it opened fire. Both ships were destroyed in the battle.

SPECIFICATIONS	
Type:	German commerce raider
Displacement:	20,218 tonnes (19,900 tons)
Dimensions:	164m x 20m x 8.5m (538ft 3in x 66ft 3in x 27ft 10in)
Machinery:	Twin screws, diesel engines, electric motors
Service speed:	18 knots
Main armament:	Six 150mm (5.9in) guns
Complement:	400
Launched:	1939

Artemis

Class leader of 31 similar ships, *Artemis* was designed for invasion support, transporting 850 troops and their landing craft, which were swung down to the water, then loaded by using the ship's derricks. The hull was of wartime standard S4 pattern, able to be assembled cheaply and quickly in many yards.

SPECIFICATIONS	
Type:	US attack cargo ship
Displacement:	6848 tonnes (6740 tons) full load
Dimensions:	129.85m x 17.7m x 4.7m (426ft x 58ft x 15ft 6in)
Machinery:	Twin screws, geared turbines
Top speed:	18 knots
Main armament:	Twelve 20mm (0.78in) guns
Complement:	303
Launched:	1942

Battlecruisers & Heavy Cruisers

Only the British Navy used the term 'battlecruiser' as an official designation, but other navies had similar ships. However, new forms of combat, especially aerial attack, showed this type of ship to be ill-equipped for modern warfare.

Dunkerque

SPECIFICATIONS	
Type:	French battlecruiser
Displacement:	36,068 tonnes (35,500 tons)
Dimensions:	214.5m x 31m x 8.6m (703ft 9in x 102ft 3in x 28ft 6in)
Machinery:	Quadruple screws, turbines
Top speed:	29.5 knots
Main armament:	Eight 330mm (13in) guns, sixteen 127mm (5in) guns
Armour:	225–125mm (8.8–4.9in) on belt, turrets 345–330mm (13.5–13in), deck 140–130mm (5.5–5in)
Complement:	1431
Launched:	October 1935

Modelled on Britain's *Nelson* class to lead a fast battle-force, *Dunkerque* was a counterweight to the German *Deutschlands* of the 1930s. It carried four scout seaplanes. Damaged by British attacks at Mers-el-Kebir in July 1942, it was sailed to Toulon but scuttled in November when the Germans occupied the port.

Gneisenau

SPECIFICATIONS	
Type:	German battlecruiser
Displacement:	39,522 tonnes (38,900 tons)
Dimensions:	226m x 30m x 9m (741ft 6in x 98ft 5in x 30ft)
Machinery:	Triple screws, turbines
Service speed:	32 knots
Main armament:	Nine 280mm (11in) guns, twelve 150mm (5.9in) guns, fourteen 104mm (4.1in) guns
Armour:	350–170mm (13.75–6.75in) belt, 50mm (2in) deck, 355mm (14in) main turret faces
Complement:	1840
Launched:	December 1936

Gneisenau and its companion *Scharnhorst* had their bows lengthened in 1939, improving seaworthiness. In World War II, they attacked British commerce in the North Atlantic and sank the British aircraft carrier *Glorious*. Rendered unusable by RAF bombs in 1942, *Gneisenau* was broken up between 1947 and 1951.

TIMELINE   1935   1936   1938

BATTLECRUISERS & HEAVY CRUISERS

Prinz Eugen

Twelve 533mm (21in) torpedo tubes and 3 aircraft added to the capabilities of this *Hipper*-class ship, commissioned in 1940. It accompanied *Bismarck*, then *Scharnhorst* and *Gneisenau*, on their Atlantic sorties. Taken over by the US Navy after the war, it was used as a target in the 1946 Bikini Atoll atom bomb tests.

SPECIFICATIONS

Type:	German heavy cruiser
Displacement:	19,050 tonnes (18,750 tons) full load
Dimensions:	207.7m x 21.5m x 7.2m (679ft 1in x 70ft 6in x 23ft 7in)
Machinery:	Triple screws, geared turbines
Top speed:	32.5 knots
Main armament:	Eight 203mm (8in) guns, twenty-one 105mm (4.1in) guns
Armour:	80mm (3.3in) belt, 105mm (4.1in) turret faces, 50–30mm (2–1.2in) deck
Complement:	1600
Launched:	1938

Baltimore

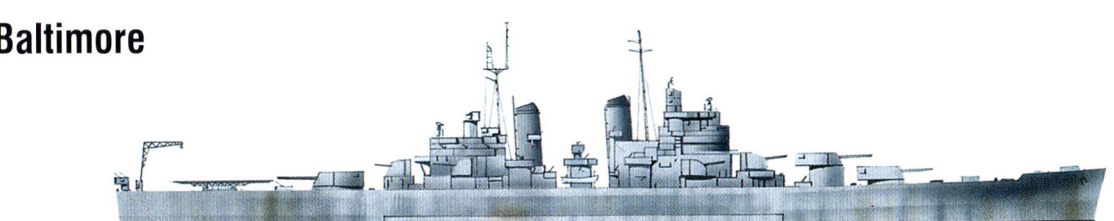

The *Baltimore* class were the first US cruisers built after the limits imposed by the Naval Treaties were lifted. Increased size improved sea-keeping qualities and protection. Two later became the first US guided-missile cruisers, others acted as fire support vessels in the Vietnam War. *Baltimore* was decommissioned in 1971.

SPECIFICATIONS

Type:	US heavy cruiser
Displacement:	17,303 tonnes (17,030 tons)
Dimensions:	205.7m x 21.5m x 7.3m (675ft 6in x 70ft 6in x 24ft)
Machinery:	Quadruple screws, geared turbines
Top speed:	33 knots
Main armament:	Nine 203mm (8in) guns
Armour:	152–102mm (6–4in) belt, 63mm (2.5in) deck
Complement:	2039
Launched:	July 1942

Guam

Larger versions of the cruiser *Baltimore*, with 305mm (12in) guns and upgraded armour, *Guam* and its sister *Alaska* were built to combat the (illusory) threat of Japanese fast raiders. *Guam* carried cranes and catapults for scout planes. Range at 15 knots was 22,800km (12,000 miles). *Guam* was scrapped in 1961.

SPECIFICATIONS

Type:	US battlecruiser
Displacement:	34,801 tonnes (34,253 tons)
Dimensions:	246m x 27.6m x 9.6m (807ft 5in x 90ft 9in x 31ft 9in)
Machinery:	Quadruple screws, geared turbines
Top speed:	33 knots
Main armament:	Nine 305mm (12in) guns, twelve 127mm (5in) guns, plus 90 40mm/20mm guns
Armour:	229–127mm (9–5in) belt, 102mm (4in) deck, 330mm (13in) barbettes and turret faces
Complement:	1517
Launched:	November 1943

1942  1943

SHIP TYPES 1930–1949

Scharnhorst

A fast commerce raider, *Scharnhorst* supported the invasion of Norway in April 1940, and sank the British carrier *Glorious* in May. In February 1942, it made a famous 'dash' through the English Channel from Brest to Germany. *Scharnhorst* was sunk in the North Atlantic in December 1943 by British ships led by HMS *Duke of York*.

Scharnhorst

Scharnhorst was attacked for the next two years after the invasion of Norway by surface ships and aircraft who considered it to be a deadly threat. She remained operational despite the attacks but came to an end when attacked by *Duke of York* and three cruisers when on the way to attack an Arctic convoy.

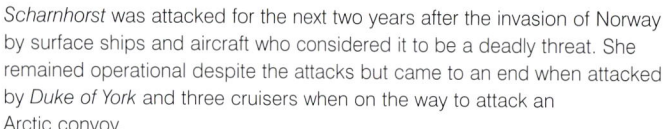

SPECIFICATIONS	
Type:	German battlecruiser
Displacement:	38,277 tonnes (38,900 tons)
Dimensions:	229.8m x 30m x 9.91m (753ft 11in x 98ft 5in x 32ft 6in)
Machinery:	Triple screws, geared turbines
Top speed:	32 knots
Main armament:	Nine 280mm (11in) guns, twelve 150mm (5.9in) guns
Armour:	350mm (13.8in) belt, 95mm (2.9in) deck
Crew:	1840
Launched:	30 June 1936

AIRCRAFT
Four Arado Ar 196A-3 folding-wing seaplanes were carried for reconnaissance and anti-submarine defence. From 1940 one of the two catapults was removed.

MACHINERY
Twelve Wagner 3-drum boilers raised steam for three Brown-Boveri geared turbines, with a maximum power output of 120.18MW (161,163 shp).

SCHARNHORST

CONTROL TOWER
From 1940 80cm wavelength radar was fitted. This was a relatively primitive system, and radar deficiency was always a handicap to German battleships.

GUNS
A proposal to replace the main guns with 380mm (15in) guns was made but never put into action. Such armament would have produced a formidable battleship.

ARMOUR
The 357mm (14in) waterline armour belt. Like Bismarck, Scharnhorst withstood intensive torpedo and shell-fire for many hours before finally succumbing.

RANGE
Bunker capacity was 6,200 tonnes (6,101 tons) of fuel oil, giving an operational range of 18,710km (10,100 nautical miles) at 19 knots.

HULL
The peaked 'Atlantic' bow was added in 1939, but Scharnhorst remained a 'wet' ship, and heavy seas could put its 'A' turret out of action.

SHIP TYPES 1930–1949

Battleships: Part 1

Battleships remained the prime heavy weapon of World War II fleets, with a psychological value as important as their strategic usefulness. The improvement of naval aircraft, particularly the dive bomber and the torpedo bomber, made capital ships vulnerable, and effective anti-aircraft armament became a necessity.

Admiral Graf Spee

In the 1930s, Germany built the three powerful *Deutschland* 'pocket battleships', as commerce-raiders. Savings were made by using electric welding and light alloys in the hulls. *Admiral Graf Spee* was scuttled off Montevideo, hemmed in by British ships, after the Battle of the River Plate in 1939.

SPECIFICATIONS

Type:	German pocket battleship
Displacement:	16,218 tonnes (15,963 tons)
Dimensions:	186m x 20.6m x 7.2m (610ft 3in x 67ft 7in x 23ft 7in)
Machinery:	Twin screws, diesels
Top speed:	28 knots
Main armament:	Six 280mm (11in) guns, eight 150mm (5.9in) guns
Armour:	76mm (3in) belt, 140-76mm (5.5-3in) turrets, 38mm (1.5in) deck
Complement:	926
Launched:	April 1933

Littorio

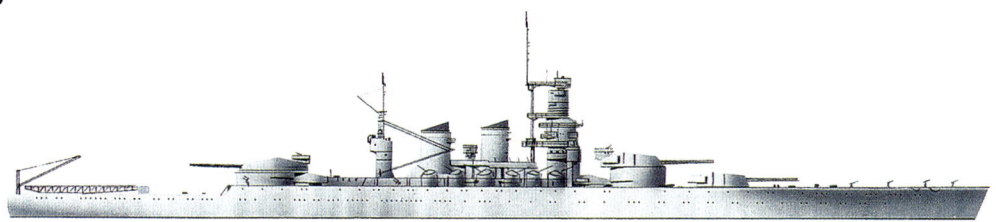

Littorio was one of the last battleships to be built for the Italian Navy. Its imposing profile was all the more striking due to the raised height of the aft turret, which was designed to avoid blast damage to the two fighter planes carried on the poop deck. *Littorio* was broken up between 1948 and 1950.

SPECIFICATIONS

Type:	Italian battleship
Displacement:	46,698 tonnes (45,963 tons)
Dimensions:	237.8m x 32.9m x 9.6m (780ft 2in x 108ft x 31ft 6in)
Machinery:	Quadruple screws, turbines
Top speed:	28 knots
Main armament:	Nine 380mm (15in) guns, twelve 152mm (6in) guns, four 120mm (4.7in) guns, twelve 89mm (3.5in) guns
Launched:	August 1937

TIMELINE

1933  1937

BATTLESHIPS: PART 1

Vittorio Veneto

SPECIFICATIONS	
Type:	Italian battleship
Displacement:	46,484 tonnes (45,752 tons)
Dimensions:	237.8m x 32.9m x 9.6m (780ft 2in x 108ft x 31ft 6in)
Machinery:	Quadruple screws, turbines
Top speed:	31.4 knots
Main armament:	Nine 381mm (15in) guns, twelve 152mm (6in) guns, four 120mm (4.7in) guns, twelve 89mm (3.5in) guns
Armour:	280mm (11in) belt, 162–45mm (6.4–1.8in) decks, 350–280mm (13.8–11in) barbettes, 350mm (13.8in) turret faces
Complement:	1830
Launched:	July 1937

Littorio, *Roma* and *Vittorio Veneto* made up a formidable trio of battleships. Torpedoed at the Battle of Matapan in March 1941 and again in December, *Vittorio Veneto* was damaged but repaired. Following the Italian surrender, it was laid up in the Suez Canal. It was broken up in Britain between 1948 and 1950.

North Carolina

SPECIFICATIONS	
Type:	US battleship
Displacement:	47,518 tonnes (46,770 tons)
Dimensions:	222m x 33m x 10m (728ft 9in x 108ft 3in x 32ft 10in)
Machinery:	Quadruple screws, geared turbines
Top speed:	28 knots
Main armament:	Nine 406mm (16in) guns, twenty 127mm (5in) guns
Armour:	305mm (12in) belt, 140mm (5.5in) deck, 406–373mm (16–14.7in) barbettes, 406mm (16in) turret faces
Complement:	1793
Launched:	June 1940

North Carolina's design specified 355mm (14in) guns, but as the Japanese refused to restrict their main armament, it was fitted with triple 406mm (16in) gun turrets. By 1945, these had been added to by 96 x 40mm (1.6in) and 36 x 20mm (0.8in) guns. Stricken in 1960, it is preserved at Wilmington, North Carolina.

Iowa

SPECIFICATIONS	
Type:	US battleship
Displacement:	56,601 tonnes (55,710 tons)
Dimensions:	270.4m x 33.5m x 11.6m (887ft 2in x 108ft 3in x 38ft)
Machinery:	Quadruple screws, turbines
Top speed:	32.5 knots
Main armament:	Nine 406mm (16in) guns, twenty 127mm (5in) guns
Armour:	310mm (12.2in) belt, 152mm (6in) deck, 440–287mm (17.3–11.3in) barbettes, 500mm (19.7in) turret faces
Complement:	1921
Launched:	August 1942

The Iowa class of fast battleships, America's last and largest, began in 1936 and had more power and heavier armour protection than the previous *South Dakota* class. A carrier escort in World War II, *Iowa* was reactivated in 1951–58 and in 1984–90 for bombardment of shore targets.

1940

1942

SHIP TYPES 1930–1949

Bismarck

Bismarck was in most respects a modern warship. But dated armour configuration meant that the steering gear and much of the communications and control systems were poorly protected. In May 1941, on a raiding mission into the Atlantic, it sank HMS *Hood*, before being sunk itself by a British force of battleships and cruisers.

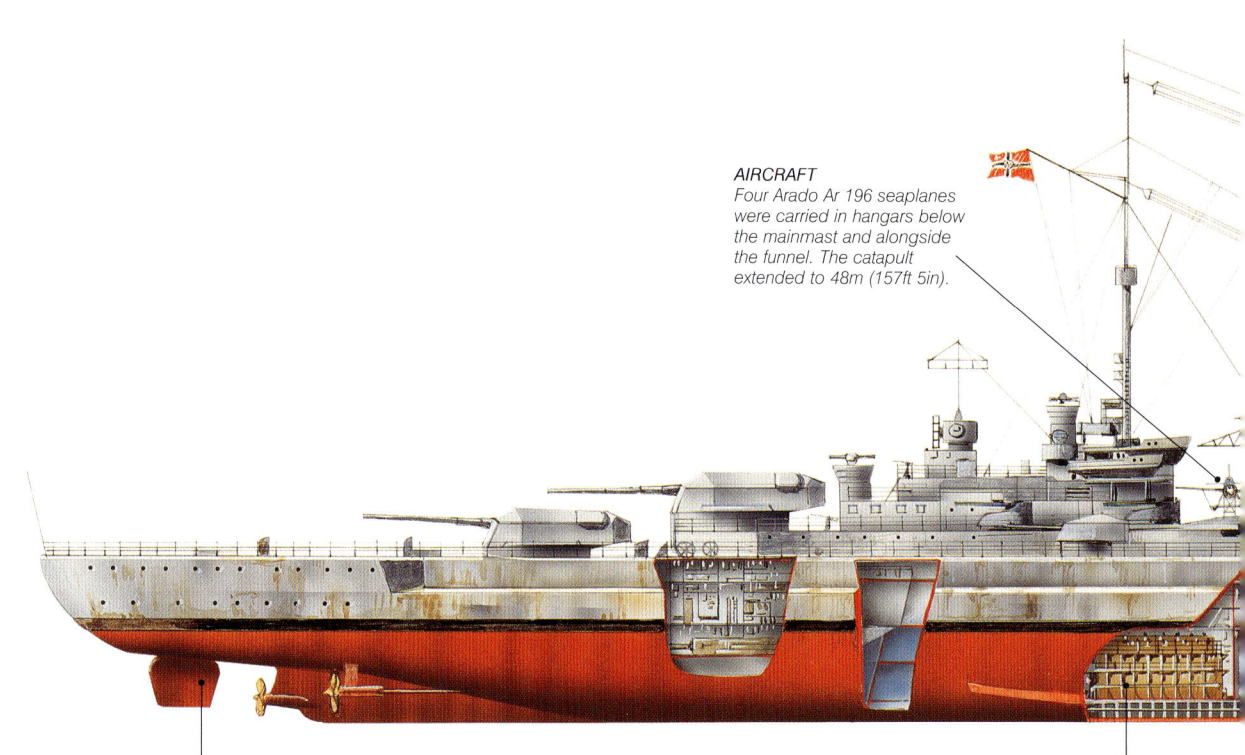

AIRCRAFT
Four Arado Ar 196 seaplanes were carried in hangars below the mainmast and alongside the funnel. The catapult extended to 48m (157ft 5in).

RUDDERS
The two parallel rudders made the ship highly manoeuvrable at speed. With an area of 24.2m² (260.5sq ft) each, they were at 80 divergence towards the centreline.

MACHINERY
Twelve Wagner Hochdruck (high pressure) oil-fired boilers powered three sets of Blohm & Voss turbines. Maximum power output was 111.92MW (150,170 shhp).

Bismarck

The 1919 Treaty of Versailles imposed tight restrictions on German naval developments. In spite of this, the Germans managed to carry out secret design studies, and when the Anglo-German Naval Treaty of 1935 came into force, were able to respond quickly. *Bismarck* and *Tirpitz* were constructed.

SPECIFICATIONS

Type:	German battleship
Displacement:	50,955 tonnes (50,153 tons)
Dimensions:	250m x 36m x 9m (823ft 6in x118ft x 29ft 6in)
Machinery:	Three screws, geared turbines
Top speed:	29 knots
Main armament:	Eight 380mm (15in) guns, twelve 150mm (5.9in) guns
Armour:	318–267mm (12.5–10.5in) belt, 362–178mm (14.25–7in) main turrets, 121mm (4.75in) deck
Complement:	2092
Launched:	February 1939

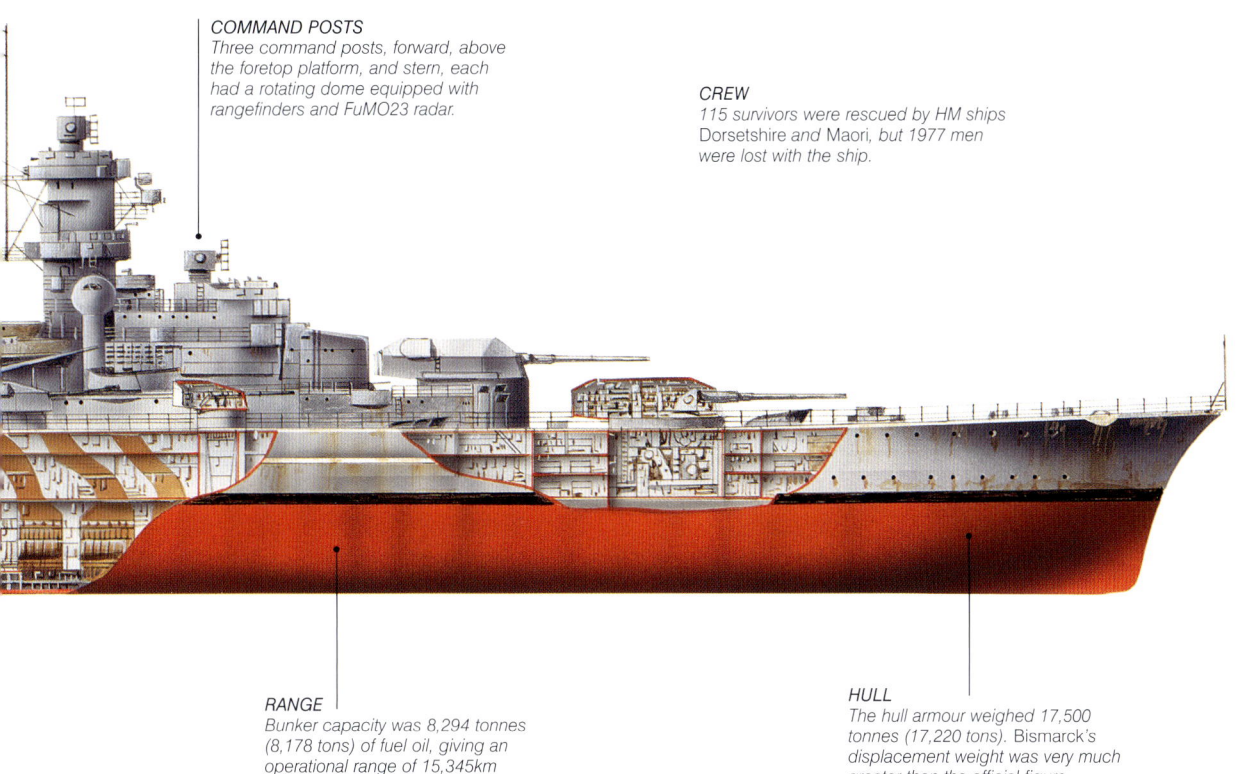

COMMAND POSTS
Three command posts, forward, above the foretop platform, and stern, each had a rotating dome equipped with rangefinders and FuMO23 radar.

CREW
115 survivors were rescued by HM ships Dorsetshire *and* Maori, *but 1977 men were lost with the ship.*

RANGE
Bunker capacity was 8,294 tonnes (8,178 tons) of fuel oil, giving an operational range of 15,345km (8,525 nautical miles) at 19 knots.

HULL
The hull armour weighed 17,500 tonnes (17,220 tons). Bismarck's displacement weight was very much greater than the official figure.

Battleships: Part 2

Although battleships took part in some of the Pacific battles, their primary role in the latter years of World War II, and in subsequent wars in Korea and Vietnam, was to bombard shore locations from long range with guns that could fire 1225kg (2700lb) high explosive shells at a range of 32km (20 miles) or more.

Washington

Washington's plans complied with the London Treaty, but when Japan refused to ratify the agreement, 406mm (16in) guns were installed, reducing top speed by 2 knots. With *South Dakota*, it sank the Japanese battlecruiser *Kirishima* at Guadalcanal in November 1942. *Washington* was scrapped in 1960/61.

SPECIFICATIONS

Type:	US battleship
Displacement:	47,518 tonnes (46,770 tons)
Dimensions:	222m x 33m x 10m (728ft 9in x 108ft 4in x 33ft)
Machinery:	Quadruple screws, turbines
Top speed:	28 knots
Main armament:	Nine 406mm (16in) guns, twenty 127mm (5in) guns
Armour:	168–305mm (6.6–12in) belt, 178–406mm (7–16in) main turrets
Launched:	June 1940

Howe

Much care was given to *Howe*'s torpedo protection. A sister-ship, *Prince of Wales,* was sunk by aerial torpedoes even before *Howe* was commissioned in 1942. It supported invasion forces in Sicily and Italy, and in 1945 was the British flagship in the Pacific. Placed in reserve in 1951, it was broken up in 1957.

SPECIFICATIONS

Type:	British battleship
Displacement:	42,784 tonnes (42,075 tons)
Dimensions:	227.05m x 31.4m x 9.5m (745ft x 103ft x 32ft 7in)
Machinery:	Quadruple screws, geared turbines
Top speed:	28 knots
Main armament:	Ten 356mm (14in) guns, sixteen 133mm (5.25in) guns
Armour:	380–356mm (15–13in) belt, 356mm (13in) barbettes and turret faces
Complement:	1422
Launched:	1940

TIMELINE

1940   1941

BATTLESHIPS: PART 2

Indiana

SPECIFICATIONS	
Type:	US battleship
Displacement:	45,231 tonnes (44,519 tons)
Dimensions:	207.2m x 32.9m x 10.6m (680ft x 108ft x 35ft)
Machinery:	Quadruple screws, geared turbines
Top speed:	28 knots
Main armament:	Nine 406mm (16in) guns, twenty 127mm (5in) guns
Armour:	309mm (12.2in) belt, 457mm (18in) turret facings
Complement:	1793
Launched:	November 1941

Indiana was the second of the four *South Dakota* class ships. Its 127mm (5in) guns were on two levels amidships, and the single funnel was faired into the rear of the bridge. In World War II, it was deployed mostly for carrier protection and shore bombardment. Decommissioned in 1947, it was scrapped in 1963.

Clemenceau

SPECIFICATIONS	
Type:	French battleship
Displacement:	48,260 tonnes (47,500 tons)
Dimensions:	247.9m x 33m x 9.6m (813ft 2in x 108ft 3in x 31ft 7in)
Machinery:	Four screws, geared turbines
Top speed:	25 knots
Main armament:	Eight 381mm (15in) guns
Launched:	1943

Clemenceau was only partially completed at Brest when the Germans arrived in 1940. After the D-Day invasion of 1944, they considered using it to block the harbour entrance. Before this could be done, it was sunk during a bombing raid in August. The illustration shows its appearance as indicated by the 1940 plans.

Vanguard

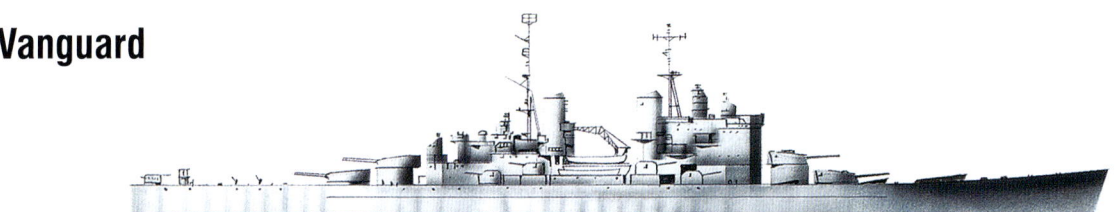

SPECIFICATIONS	
Type:	British battleship
Displacement:	52,243 tonnes (51,420 tons)
Dimensions:	248m x 32.9m x 10.9m (813ft 8in x 108ft x 36ft)
Machinery:	Quadruple screws, geared turbines
Top speed:	30 knots
Main armament:	Eight 380mm (15in) guns, sixteen 140mm (5.5in) guns
Armour:	114–355mm (4.5–14in) belt, 152–330mm (6–13in) on main turrets, 280–330mm (11–13in) on barbettes
Complement:	1893
Launched:	1944

The last, largest and fastest battleship built for the Royal Navy, *Vanguard* was ordered in 1941 but did not enter service until 1946. It had a long transom stern and considerable sheer forward. Though superior to its contemporaries, the concept of the big-gun battleship was now outmoded. It was scrapped in 1960.

SHIP TYPES 1930–1949

Yamato

Yamato and *Musashi* were the largest, most powerful battleships ever. Each main turret weighed 2818 tonnes (2774 tons), and the 460mm (18.1in) guns could fire two 1473kg (3240lb) shells per minute over a distance of 41,148m (45,000yd). Used just once, they sank an escort carrier and a destroyer in 1944. *Yamato* was sunk in 1945.

AA PROTECTION
By March 1944 24 127mm and 162 25mm anti-aircraft guns were fitted. But ten aerial torpedoes and 23 bombs destroyed Yamato on 7 April 1945.

NARROW ESCAPE
During the Battle of Leyte Gulf, a narrowly missed encounter with six American battleships would have severely tested Yamato's intended ability to deal with several opponents at once.

AIRCRAFT
Yamato could carry up to seven aircraft, launched from two catapults mounted at the stern, with a retrieval crane.

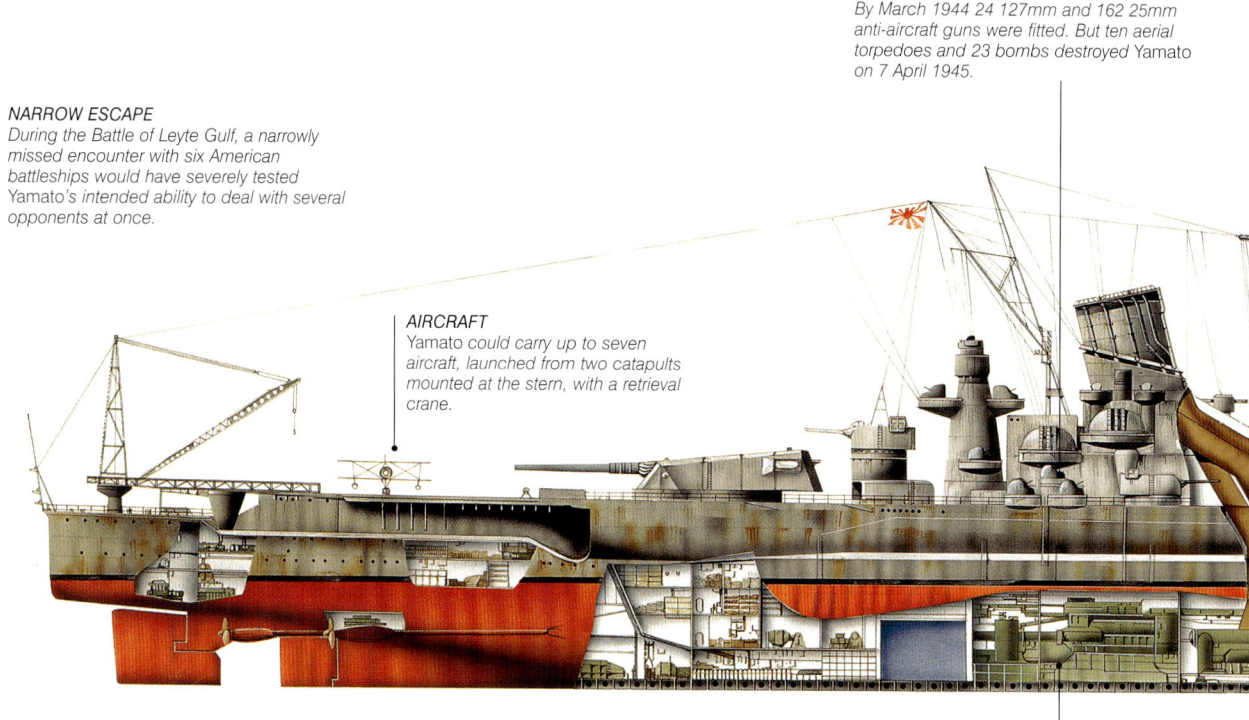

MACHINERY
At the design stage, it was planned to provide both steam turbine and diesel (or even diesel-only) power, but this was dropped.

Yamato

As flagship of the Combined Fleet *Yamato* saw action in the Battles of Midway, the Philippine Sea and Leyte Gulf. On 7th April 1945 it was sunk by US carrier aircraft 130 miles southwest of Kagoshima with the loss of 2498 lives.`

SPECIFICATIONS	
Type:	Japanese battleship
Displacement:	71,110 tonnes (71,659 tons)
Dimensions:	263m x 36.9m x 10.3m (862ft 10in x 121ft x 34ft)
Machinery:	Quadruple screws, turbines
Top speed:	27 knots
Main armament:	Nine 460mm (18.1in) guns, twelve 155mm (6.1 in) guns, twelve 127mm (5in) guns
Armour:	408mm (16.1in) belt, 546mm (21.5in) on barbettes, 193–650mm (7.6–25.6in) on main turrets, 200–231mm (7.9–9.1in) deck
Launched:	August 1940

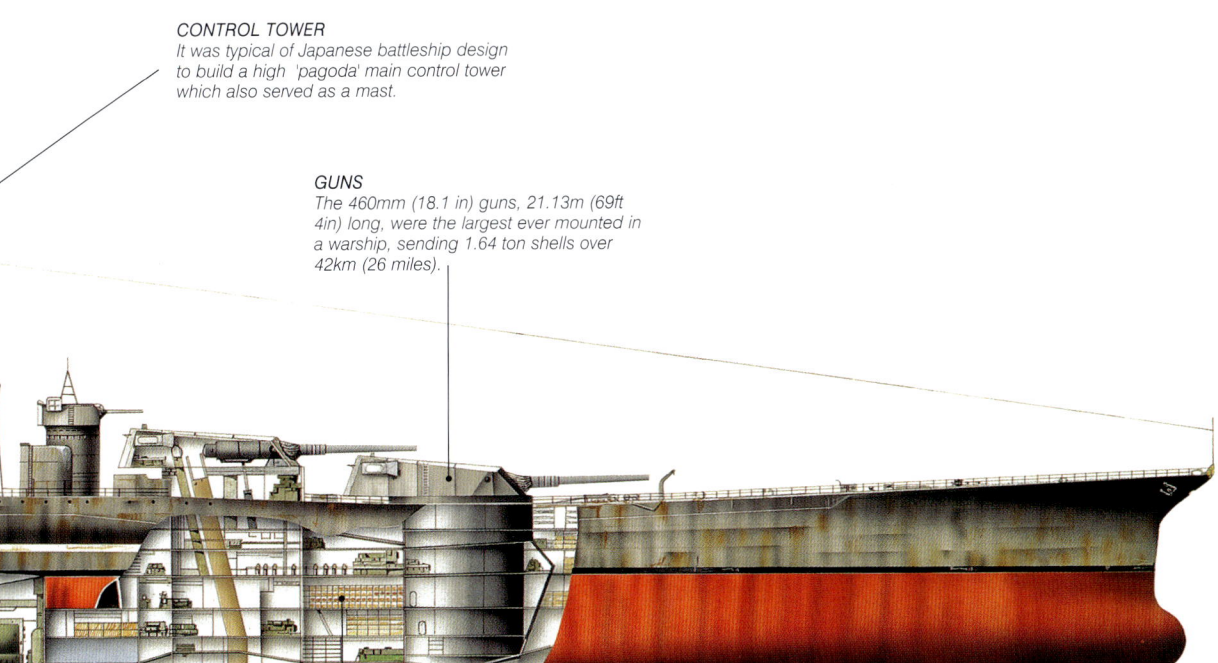

CONTROL TOWER
It was typical of Japanese battleship design to build a high 'pagoda' main control tower which also served as a mast.

GUNS
The 460mm (18.1 in) guns, 21.13m (69ft 4in) long, were the largest ever mounted in a warship, sending 1.64 ton shells over 42km (26 miles).

MAGAZINES
The ammunition magazines were normally floodable to prevent explosion, but only if the ship's pumps were working.

SHIP TYPES 1930–1949

Escorts & Patrol Ships: Part 1

Peacetime navies required few escort vessels, but in wartime these were needed in very large numbers for convoy protection, coastal patrols, anti-submarine and anti-aircraft work, and as support ships for the many amphibious operations carried out in the later years of World War II. Many were converted merchant ships.

Hashidate

SPECIFICATIONS	
Type:	Japanese gunboat
Displacement:	1168.4 tonnes (1150 tons) full load
Dimensions:	78.5m x 9.7m x 2.45m (257ft 7in x 31ft 10in x 8ft)
Machinery:	Twin screws, geared turbines
Top speed:	19.5 knots
Main armament:	Three 120mm (4in) guns
Complement:	170
Launched:	1936

Built to support the Japanese invasion of China, this shallow-draught ship operated in coastal waters and estuaries, its main purpose to bombard shore targets. Later, *Hashidate* was refitted as an escort ship, equipped with additional light guns and AS depth-charges. It was sunk by a US submarine in May 1944.

Tynwald

SPECIFICATIONS	
Type:	British anti-aircraft ship
Displacement:	2474 tonnes (2376 tons) as packet ship
Dimensions:	Length 96.26m (314ft 6in)
Machinery:	Twin screw, geared turbines
Top speed:	21 knots
Main armament:	Six 102mm (4in) guns, eight 2pdr pom-pom guns
Launched:	1936

Tynwald was converted in 1940 from an Isle of Man steamer to an auxiliary AA ship, part of the Royal Navy's effort to cope with the menace of attacks from the air. Sent to the Mediterranean to support the Operation Torch landings, it was lost in November 1942, victim of a submarine or floating mine.

TIMELINE

1936

ESCORTS & PATROL SHIPS: PART 1

Erie

SPECIFICATIONS	
Type:	US gunboat
Displacement:	2376 tonnes (2339 tons)
Dimensions:	100m x 12.5m x 3.4m (328ft 6in x 41ft 3in x 11ft 4in)
Machinery:	Twin screws, turbines
Top speed:	20.4 knots
Main armament:	Four 152mm (6in) guns
Complement:	236
Launched:	1936

Erie and its sister *Charleston* were the first US ships to carry the new 152mm (6in), 47-calibre gun, with its combined shell and powder. The unusual hull design enabled a relatively low 5941hp (4430kW) to maintain 20 knots. A scouting plane was carried, handled by crane. *Erie* was sunk by a U-boat off Curaçao in 1942.

Hachijo

SPECIFICATIONS	
Type:	Japanese escort
Displacement:	1020 tonnes (1004 tons)
Dimensions:	77.7m x 9m x 3m (255ft x 29ft 10in x 9ft Win)
Machinery:	Twin screws, diesel engines
Top speed:	19.7 knots
Main armament:	Three 120mm (4.7in) guns
Launched:	April 1940

Hachijo was a prototype for successive classes of Japanese escort. During World War II, its AA armament of four 25mm (1in) guns was increased to 15; and the depth-charge load of 12 increased to 25, then 60. It was broken up in 1948.

Bombarda

SPECIFICATIONS	
Type:	Italian escort vessel/corvette
Displacement:	740 tonnes (728 tons)
Dimensions:	64m x 9m x 2.5m (211ft x 28ft 7in x 8ft 4in)
Machinery:	Twin screw diesel engines
Top speed:	18 knots
Main armament:	One 102mm (4in) gun
Launched:	1942

Bombarda was one of a class of 59 escorts built to answer Italy's need for anti-submarine escort ships for supply convoys. When Italy surrendered, Germany seized *Bombarda,* among other vessels. Renamed *U-206*, it was scuttled in April 1945. Later salvaged and repaired, it remained in service until 1975.

1940

1942

Escorts and Patrol Ships: Part 2

Ships of this general type were variously classed, using traditional names that did not necessarily correspond with modern functions and weapons. 'Frigate' was applied to larger ships, and 'corvette' and 'sloop' to smaller escorts. Though smaller ships were quicker to build, anti-aircraft protection required a vessel of frigate size.

Danaide

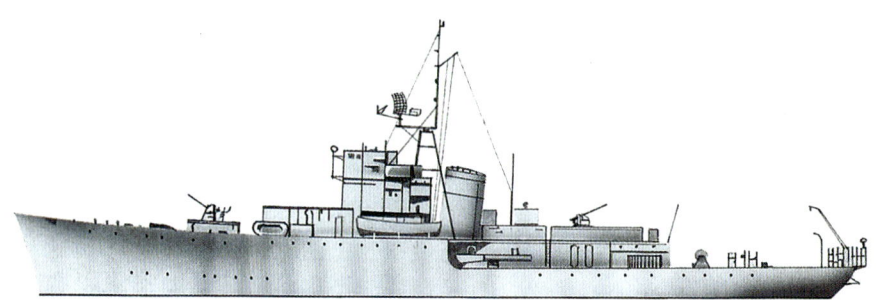

Completed only four months after launching and less than a year after being laid down, fitted for minesweeping, *Danaide* was converted to a corvette leader, with a small command deckhouse in front of the bridge replacing a depth-charge thrower. Many of its class survived the war, with 17 active in the mid-1960s.

SPECIFICATIONS	
Type:	Italian corvette
Displacement:	812 tonnes (800 tons)
Dimensions:	64m x 8.5m x 2.5m (211ft 3in x 28ft 3in x 8ft 6in)
Machinery:	Twin screws, diesel engines
Top speed:	18.5 knots
Main armament:	Four 40mm (1.6in) anti-aircraft guns
Launched:	October 1942

Avon

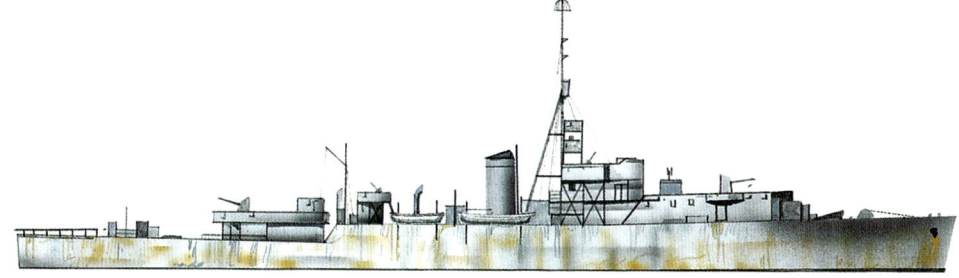

Avon was one of over 90 ocean-going, anti-submarine escorts of the 'River' class built between 1941 and 1944. Two sets of engines were installed. The original light armament was later increased. After World War II, many were passed to other navies, serving into the 1960s. *Avon* was sold to Portugal in 1949.

SPECIFICATIONS	
Type:	British frigate
Displacement:	2133 tonnes (2100 tons)
Dimensions:	91.8m x 11m x 3.8m (301ft 4in x 36ft 8in x 12ft 9in)
Machinery:	Twin screws, vertical triple expansion engines
Main armament:	Two 102mm (4in) guns
Launched:	1943

TIMELINE

1942  1943

Daga

Built to protect Mediterranean convoys, 16 of these escort craft were completed before Italy left the Axis alliance, and 15, including *Daga*, were seized by the Germans in 1943. Fast but lightly armed, they were vulnerable to larger destroyers. Thirteen were sunk, including *Daga* by mines in October 1944.

SPECIFICATIONS	
Type:	Italian escort ship
Displacement:	1138 tonnes (1120 tons)
Dimensions:	82m x 8.6m x 3m (270ft x 28ft 3in x 9ft 2in)
Machinery:	Twin screws, turbines
Top speed:	31.5 knots
Main armament:	Two 100mm (3.9in) guns, six 450mm (17.7in) torpedo tubes
Launched:	July 1943

Tintagel Castle

Intended for convoys, the 'Castle' corvettes were an enlargement of the 'Flower' class but with the same machinery. *Tintagel Castle* carried the triple-barrelled Squid mortar, which used position data derived from the ship's sonar system and fired 200kg (400lb) bombs to a range of 400m (430yds). It served until 1957.

SPECIFICATIONS	
Type:	British corvette
Displacement:	1615 tonnes (1590 tons) full load
Dimensions:	76.8m x 11.2m x 4.1m (252ft x 36ft 8in x 13ft 26n)
Machinery:	Single screw, vertical triple expansion reciprocating engine
Top speed:	16.5 knots
Main armament:	One 102mm (4in) gun, one 305mm (12in) AS mortar and depth charges
Complement:	120
Launched:	July 1943

Mikura

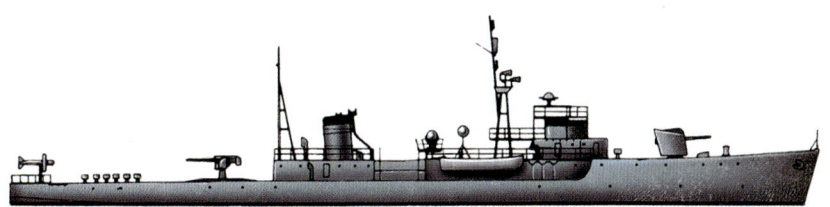

Normal construction standards were abandoned with this class of rapidly-built escort ships, whose later vessels used prefabricated parts and electric welding. But they gave good service, fitted with anti-submarine weaponry, including depth-charge racks. *Mikura*'s AA armament was much increased in 1945.

SPECIFICATIONS	
Type:	Japanese escort ship
Displacement:	1077 tonnes (1060 tons) full load
Dimensions:	78.8m x 9.1m x 3.05m (258ft 6in x 29ft 10ft)
Machinery:	Twin screws, turbines
Top speed:	19.5 knots
Main armament:	Three 120mm (4in) guns, 120 depth charges
Complement:	150
Launched:	1943

SHIP TYPES 1930–1949

Cruisers, Part 1: American

Cruiser construction in the 1930s was, in theory, governed by the terms of the London Naval Treaty of 1930, which specified maximum armaments. The United States, which had hosted the Washington Conference of 1921–22, abided fairly scrupulously by the limitations, but built many cruisers, especially in the later 1930s.

Indianapolis

Indianapolis was the last major US surface ship to be lost in World War II. Having delivered an atom bomb (one of the two to be dropped on Japan) to the forward air base at Tinian, it was returning from the task on 29 July 1945, when it was torpedoed and sunk by a Japanese submarine.

SPECIFICATIONS	
Type:	US cruiser
Displacement:	12,960 tonnes (12,755 tons)
Dimensions:	185.9m x 20m x 6.4m (610ft x 66ft x 21ft)
Machinery:	Quadruple screws, turbines
Top speed:	32.8 knots
Main armament:	Nine 203mm (8in) guns, eight 127mm (5in) guns
Armour:	57mm (2.25in) belt, 146–63mm (5.75–2.5in) deck
Complement:	917
Launched:	November 1931

Astoria

Astoria was one of seven heavy cruisers. It saw intensive war service in 1942, escorting carrier groups and taking part in the Coral Sea and Midway battles. Part of the Northern Covering Force supporting the Guadalcanal landings, it was damaged in action against Japanese cruisers, was abandoned, and sank.

SPECIFICATIONS	
Type:	US cruiser
Displacement:	12,662 tonnes (12,463 tons)
Dimensions:	179.2m x 18.8m x 6.9m (588ft 9in x 61ft 9in x 22ft 9in)
Machinery:	Quadruple screws, geared turbines
Top speed:	32.7 knots
Main armament:	Nine 203mm (8in) guns, eight 127mm (5in) guns
Armour:	127mm (5in) belt, 57mm (2.25in) deck
Complement:	868
Launched:	December 1933

TIMELINE

1931   1933   1936

Brooklyn

During the early 1930s, the US Navy upgraded the *Brooklyn* class cruiser design in response to the new Japanese *Mogami* class cruisers. Good protection was provided by weight saved in the hull. There were nine vessels in the new class, and all served during World War II. In 1951, *Brooklyn* was transferred to Chile.

SPECIFICATIONS	
Type:	US cruiser
Displacement:	12,395 tonnes (12,200 tons)
Dimensions:	185m x 19m x 7m (608ft 4in x 61ft 9in x 22ft 9in)
Machinery:	Quadruple screws, geared turbines
Main armament:	Fifteen 152mm (6in) guns
Launched:	November 1936

Wichita

Wichita was built on the same hull and with the same machinery as *Brooklyn* but heavier armour and guns, its 203mm (8in) guns mounted in three triple turrets. In 1945, its anti-aircraft armament was modernized. Conversion to a guided missile cruiser was considered but not effected. It was sold for breaking in 1959.

SPECIFICATIONS	
Type:	US cruiser
Displacement:	13,314 tonnes (13,015 tons)
Dimensions:	185.4m x 18.8m x 7.25m (608ft 4in x 61ft 9in x 23ft 9in)
Machinery:	Quadruple screws, geared turbines
Top speed:	33 knots
Main Armament:	Nine 203mm (8in) guns, eight 127mm (5in) guns
Armour:	152–102mm (6–4in) belt, 178mm (7in) barbettes, 203mm (8in) turret faces, 58mm (2.25in) deck
Complement:	929
Launched:	1937

Atlanta

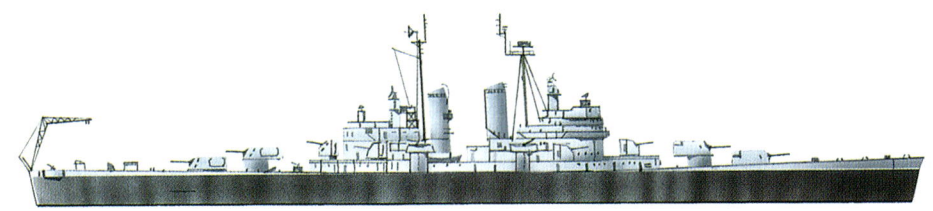

Atlanta was the lead ship in a class of 11, intended to patrol the exposed areas of the battle fleet as anti-aircraft vessels. Later members of the class carried better splinter protection, more guns and sonar capability. In 1942, *Atlanta* was torpedoed and disabled by the Japanese and finally sunk by US forces.

SPECIFICATIONS	
Type:	US cruiser
Displacement:	8473 tonnes (8340 tons)
Dimensions:	165m x 16.2m x 6.2m (541ft 6in x 53ft 2in x 20ft 6in)
Machinery:	Twin screws, turbines
Top speed:	32.5 knots
Main armament:	Sixteen 127mm (5in) guns
Launched:	1941

SHIP TYPES 1930–1949

Cruisers, Part 2: American & Japanese

Japan, though a signatory to the London Naval Treaty of 1930, walked out of the 1935 follow-up conference, and went on to develop the basis of a fleet that would be second to none as a naval power in the Pacific. Japanese cruisers were comprehensively armed, carrying torpedoes, mines and aircraft.

Maya

Maya had a modern look, with a high bridge. The 203mm (8in) guns had the high elevation of 70°. In 1943, Maya was badly damaged at Rabaul by US aircraft, and was completely rebuilt. In October 1944, it was sunk by four torpedoes fired from a US submarine shortly before the Battle of Leyte Gulf.

SPECIFICATIONS	
Type:	Japanese cruiser
Displacement:	12,985 tonnes (12,781 tons)
Dimensions:	202m x 18m x 6m (661ft 8in x 59ft x 20ft)
Machinery:	Quadruple screws, turbines
Top speed:	35.5 knots
Main armament:	Ten 203mm (8in) guns, four 120mm (4.7in) guns
Armour:	100mm (3.9in) belt, 125mm (4.9in) magazines, 38mm (1.5in) deck
Complement:	773
Launched:	November 1930

Mogami

Designated a light cruiser, Mogami was rather more. The 155mm (6.1in) guns were positioned in triple mounts along the centreline, and the dual-purpose 127mm (5in) guns in twin mounts amidships. An initially weak hull structure was reinforced. Mogami was sunk in 1944 by US torpedo bombers.

SPECIFICATIONS	
Type:	Japanese cruiser
Displacement:	11,169 tonnes (10,993 tons)
Dimensions:	201.5m x 18m x 5.5m (661ft x 59ft x 18ft)
Machinery:	Quadruple screws, turbines
Top speed:	37 knots
Main armament:	Fifteen 155mm (6.1in) guns, eight 127mm (5in) dual-purpose guns
Armour:	100mm (3.9in) belt, 125mm (4.9in) magazines, 61–31.4mm (2.4–1.4in) deck
Complement:	850
Launched:	March 1934

TIMELINE 1930  1934  1937

Tone

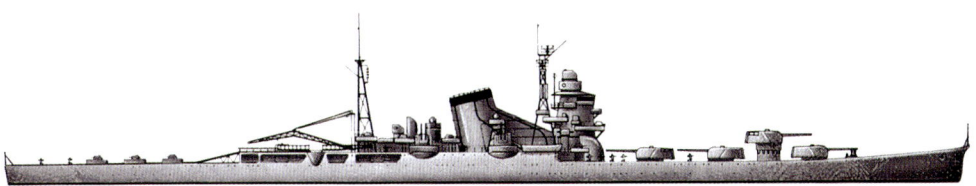

SPECIFICATIONS	
Type:	Japanese cruiser
Displacement:	15,443.2 tonnes (15,200 tons)
Dimensions:	201.5m x 18.5m x 6.5m (661ft 1in x 60ft 8in x 21ft 3in)
Machinery:	Quadruple screws, geared turbines
Top speed:	35 knots
Main armament:	Eight 203mm (8in) guns, eight 127mm (5in) guns, twelve 610mm (24in) torpedo tubes
Armour:	125–100mm (4.9–3.9in) belt, 25mm (1in) turrets, 65–30mm (2.5–1.2in) deck
Complement:	850
Launched:	1937

Tone and its sister vessel *Chikuma* shared an unusual layout, with all main guns mounted forward, leaving the after deck clear for operating six floatplane aircraft, launched by catapult and retrieved by crane. *Tone* was sunk in shallow water near Kure by US aircraft in July 1945, and was broken up in situ in 1948.

Agano

SPECIFICATIONS	
Type:	Japanese cruiser
Displacement:	8671.5 tonnes (8535 tons)
Dimensions:	174.1m x 15.2m x 5.63m (571ft 2in x 49ft 10in x 18ft 6in)
Machinery:	Quadruple screws, geared turbines
Top speed:	35 knots
Main armament:	Six 152mm (6in) guns, eight 610mm (24in) torpedo tubes
Armour:	56mm (2in) belt, 25mm (1in) turrets, 18mm (0.7in) deck
Complement:	730
Launched:	1941

Four ships formed the *Agano* class, intended as flotilla leaders for destroyer groups. Their Long Lance oxygen-powered torpedoes had three times the range of any Allied torpedo and a bigger warhead. Commissioned in October 1942, *Agano* was sunk by the US submarine *Skate* off Truk Island in 1944.

Des Moines

SPECIFICATIONS	
Type:	US cruiser
Displacement:	21,844 tonnes (21,500 tons) full load
Dimensions:	218m x 23m x 8m (717ft 6in x 75ft 6in x 26ft)
Machinery:	Quadruple screws, turbines
Top speed:	33 knots
Main armament:	Nine 203mm (8in) guns, twelve 127mm (5in) guns
Complement:	1799
Launched:	September 1946

The three ships of the *Des Moines* class were first to mount the complete automatic rapid-fire 203mm (8in) guns. Its two sisters were also the first warships to have air-conditioning. *Des Moines* remained active in the US fleet as an all-gun ship until 1961, when it was placed in reserve. It was stricken in 1991.

Cruisers, Part 3: British

British cruiser needs had not changed from previous years. A substantial number of middle-sized, up-to-date warships was needed to protect shipping lanes, for spells of duty at overseas stations like Simonstown (South Africa), Singapore and Hong Kong, and to maintain the balance of power against the main European navies.

Glasgow

Glasgow and four cruisers were built to match the Japanese *Mogami* class. Initial designs tried to reduce displacement to 8600 tonnes (8500 tons), but this was impracticable. A catapult was mounted between the funnels; a hangar for two aircraft formed an extension of the bridge. *Glasgow* was broken up in 1958.

SPECIFICATIONS	
Type:	British cruiser
Displacement:	11,652 tonnes (11,470 tons)
Dimensions:	187m x 19m x 5.5m (613ft 6in x 63ft x 18ft)
Machinery:	Quadruple screws, turbines
Top speed:	32 knots
Main armament:	Twelve 152mm (6in) guns
Armour:	114mm (4.5in) belt and magazines, 25mm (1in) turrets
Complement:	748
Launched:	June 1936

Belfast

Belfast was planned as a 10,160-tonne (10,000-ton) follow-on to the Southampton class, with triple-mounted 152mm (6in) guns that could elevate to 45°. It struck a mine four months after completion, but returned to service in October 1944, with added underwater protection. It is now a museum ship.

SPECIFICATIONS	
Type:	British cruiser
Displacement:	15,138 tonnes (14,900 tons)
Dimensions:	187m x 20m x 7m (613ft 6in x 66ft 4in x 23ft 2in)
Machinery:	Quadruple screws, geared turbines
Top speed:	32.5 knots
Main armament:	Twelve 152mm (6in) guns
Armour:	114mm (4.5in) belt, 102–51mm (3–2in) turrets, 76–51mm (3–2in) deck
Complement:	850
Launched:	1938

TIMELINE 1936  1938    1939

Dido

Designed for anti-aircraft defence, *Dido* carried three tiers of semi-automatic high-velocity 133mm (5.25in) guns on power-loaded mountings with a 70° elevation. A recovery crane was mounted between the funnels. Four of its class of 11 were lost during World War II, but *Dido* survived to be broken up in 1958.

SPECIFICATIONS	
Type:	British cruiser
Displacement:	6960 tonnes (6850 tons)
Dimensions:	156m x 15m x 5m (511ft 10in x 50ft 6in x 16ft 9in)
Machinery:	Quadruple screws, turbines
Top speed:	32.5 knots
Main armament:	Eight 133mm (5.25in) guns
Armour:	76mm (3in) sides, 51mm (2in) decks over magazines
Complement:	530
Launched:	July 1939

Gambia

More compact than earlier British cruisers, the '*Colony*' class formed the basis for later designs. Two were sunk in action in World War II, but most continued in the post-war Royal Navy, which still maintained numerous foreign stations. Two were sold to Peru in 1959, and one to India in 1957. *Gambia* was scrapped in 1968.

SPECIFICATIONS	
Type:	British cruiser
Displacement:	11,267 tonnes (11,090 tons)
Dimensions:	169.3m x 18.9m x 6.4m (555ft 6in x 62ft x 21ft)
Machinery:	Quadruple screws, turbines
Top speed:	33 knots
Main armament:	Twelve 152mm (6in) guns
Armour:	89mm (3.5in) midships belt, 51mm (2in) deck
Launched:	November 1940

Bellona

Bellona was one of five simplified *Dido* class cruisers, built as anti-aircraft ships, with new rapid-fire semi-automatic guns and lighter AA weapons. All saw active war service. After the war, *Bellona* and sister ship *Black Prince* were lent to the Royal New Zealand Navy. *Bellona* was returned in 1956 and scrapped in 1959.

SPECIFICATIONS	
Type:	British cruiser
Displacement:	7518 tonnes (7400 tons)
Dimensions:	156m x 15m x 5.4m (512ft x 50ft 6in x 18ft)
Machinery:	Quadruple screws, turbines
Top speed:	32 knots
Main armament:	Eight 133mm (5.25in) guns
Armour:	76mm (3in) side, 51–25mm (2–1in) deck
Complement:	530
Launched:	1942

SHIP TYPES 1930–1949

Cruisers, Part 4: Italian

Under Mussolini's Fascist regime, Italy was aggressive and expansionist, and a powerful fleet was deemed vital. Italian cruisers were well-balanced designs, notable for their high speed, but quite lightly armed compared to their British counterparts. Their specifications strained Naval Treaty obligations to the limit – and beyond.

Fiume

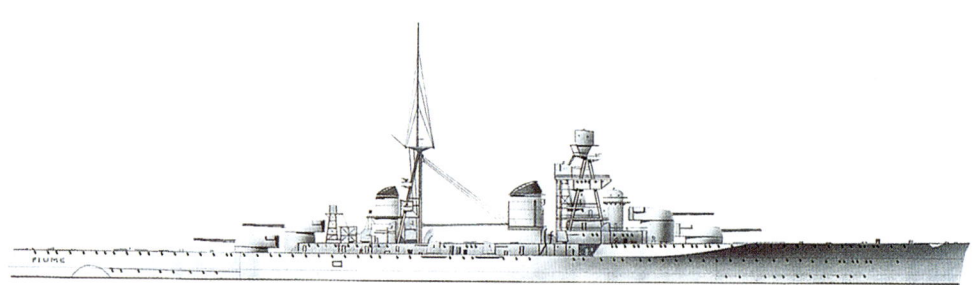

Fiume was originally designed to comply with the 10,160-tonne (10,000-ton) limit imposed by the Washington Treaty, but it was later modified. On trials the ship made 33 knots, generating 120,000hp. All four ships in the class were lost in World War II. *Fiume* was sunk in action with a British battleship in March 1941.

SPECIFICATIONS

Type:	Italian cruiser
Displacement:	14,394 tonnes (14,168 tons)
Dimensions:	182.8m x 20.6m x 7.2m (599ft 9in x 67ft 7in x 23ft 7in)
Machinery:	Twin screws, turbines
Top speed:	32 knots
Main armament:	Eight 203mm (8in) guns
Launched:	April 1930

Giovanni delle Bande Nere

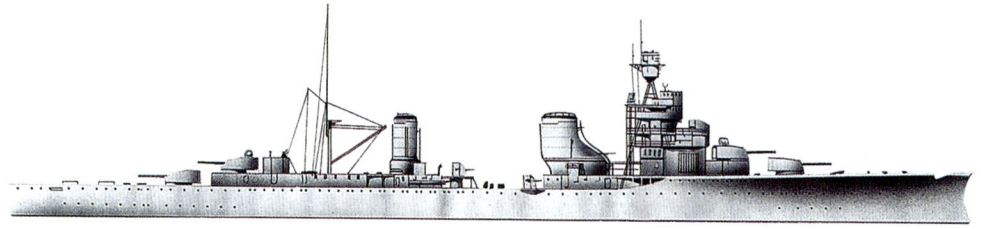

Italy built fast light cruisers to counter the large French *Jaguar*-class destroyers. Engines developed over 95,000hp, oil supply was 1250 tonnes (1230 tons) and range was 7220km (3800 miles) at 18 knots or 1843km (970 miles) at full speed. *Giovanni delle Bande Nere* was sunk by the British submarine *Urge* in April 1942.

SPECIFICATIONS

Type:	Italian cruiser
Displacement:	6676 tonnes (6571 tons)
Dimensions:	169.3m x 15.5m x 5.3m (555ft 6in x 50ft 10in x 17ft 5in)
Machinery:	Twin screws, turbines
Main armament:	Six 100mm (3.9in), eight 152mm (6in) guns
Launched:	April 1930

TIMELINE

1930　　　　　　　　　　　　　　　　　　1931

Pola

SPECIFICATIONS	
Type:	Italian cruiser
Displacement:	13,747 tonnes (13,531 tons)
Dimensions:	182.8m x 20.6m x 7.2m (599ft 9in x 67ft 7in x 23ft 8in)
Machinery:	Twin screws, turbines
Top speed:	34.2 knots
Main armament:	Eight 203mm (8in) guns, sixteen 100mm (3.9in) guns
Launched:	December 1931

To keep *Pola*'s displacement within reasonable limits, the superstructure was reduced and the flush deck of the *Trento* class (on which the design was based) was abandoned. Unlike its sister-ships, the bridge structure and fore-funnel were combined. Additional anti-aircraft guns were added later. *Pola* was sunk in 1941.

Luigi Cadorna

SPECIFICATIONS	
Type:	Italian cruiser
Displacement:	7113 tonnes (7001 tons)
Dimensions:	169.3m x 15.5m x 5.5m (555ft 6in x 50ft 10in x 18ft)
Machinery:	Twin screws, turbines
Main armament:	Eight 152mm (6in) guns, six 100mm (3.9in) guns
Launched:	1931

Italy's cruisers were faster than most of their contemporaries, speed achieved at the expense of protection. *Luigi Cadorna* was equipped with a new pattern of 152mm (6in) gun. It was also fitted as a minelayer, armed with 84–138 mines, according to type. *Luigi Cadorna* was removed from the effective list in 1951.

Giuseppe Garibaldi

SPECIFICATIONS	
Type:	Italian cruiser
Displacement:	11,485 tonnes (11,305 tons)
Dimensions:	187m x 18.9m x 6.7m (613ft 6in x 62ft x 22ft)
Machinery:	Twin screws, turbines
Top speed:	30 knots
Main armament:	Four 134mm (5.3in) guns, twin Terrier missile launcher, four Polaris missile launchers (later)
Launched:	April 1934

Giuseppe Garibaldi was one of the fifth group of cruisers of the 'Condottiere' type. Between 1957 and 1962, it was rebuilt and rearmed with a twin Terrier surface-to-air missile launcher and tubes for four Polaris missiles. Although the missiles were never carried, it was the only surface vessel to be so fitted.

SHIP TYPES 1930–1949

Cruisers, Part 5: Italian & Russian

Most cruisers built in the 1930s and '40s carried at least one aircraft, launched by crane or catapult, and retrieved by crane. Crane and catapult are both apparent on the Russian *Krasnyi Kavkaz.* The point was to extend the ship's observation range, though cruiser-borne aircraft could also carry heavy machine-guns and a torpedo.

Krasnyi Kavkaz

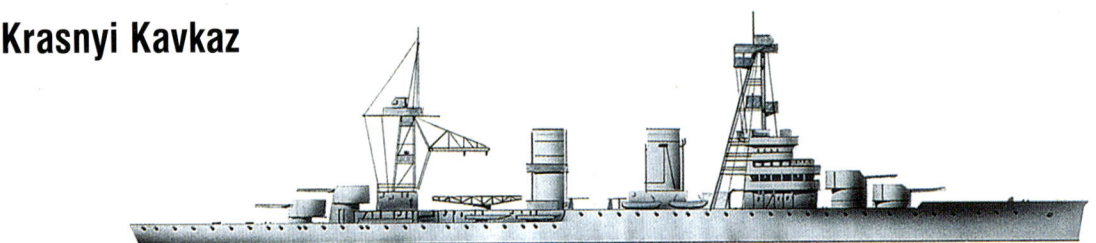

Laid down for the Russian Navy in 1913, *Krasnyi Kavkaz* was not completed until 1932, much modified from the original design. An aircraft crane formed an integral part of the mainmast. It served throughout World War II, suffering severe combat damage. It was finally sunk in 1956, as a target for the SSN-1 missile.

SPECIFICATIONS

Type:	Soviet cruiser
Displacement:	9174 tonnes (9030 tons)
Dimensions:	169.5m x 15.7m x 6.2m (556ft x 51ft 6in x 20ft 4in)
Machinery:	Twin screws, turbines
Top speed:	29 knots
Main armament:	Four 180mm (7.1in) guns, four 100mm (3.9in) guns
Completed:	1932

Emanuele Filiberto Duca D'Aosta

An enlargement of the *Montecuccoli* sub-class, it had the same armament but more powerful machinery and improved armour protection. *Emanuele Filiberto Duca D'Aosta* served extensively with Mediterranean convoys. Ceded to Russia in 1949, it was renamed *Stalingrad*, then *Kerch*, and discarded in the mid-1950s.

SPECIFICATIONS

Type:	Italian cruiser
Displacement:	10,540 tonnes (10,374 tons)
Dimensions:	187m x 17.5m x 6.5m (613ft 2in x 57ft 5in x 21ft 4in)
Machinery:	Twin screws, turbines
Top speed:	37.3 knots
Main armament:	Eight 152mm (6in) guns
Armour:	70mm (2.5in) belt, 90mm (3.5in) turrets
Complement:	694
Launched:	July 1935

TIMELINE

1932   1935

CRUISERS, PART 5: ITALIAN & RUSSIAN

Eugenio di Savoia

Eugenio di Savoia was one of two vessels provided for by the Italian naval programme of 1931–33. It was laid down at Ansaldo's yard in Genoa in July 1933 and completed in January 1936. In 1951, it was removed from the effective list, transferred to Greece, and renamed *Hella*. It remained in service until 1964.

SPECIFICATIONS	
Type:	Italian cruiser
Displacement:	10,842 tonnes (10,672 tons)
Dimensions:	186.9m x 17.5m x 6.5m (613ft 2in x 57ft 5in x 21ft 4in)
Machinery:	Twin screws, turbines
Top speed:	36.5 knots
Main armament:	Eight 152mm (6in) guns, six 100mm (3.9in) anti-aircraft guns, six 533mm (21in) torpedo tubes
Launched:	March 1935

Kirov

The Soviet Union's first home-built cruiser, *Kirov* was completed in 1938. The 180mm (7.1) guns were mounted in triple turrets, with the battery of 100mm (3.9in) guns in single mounts alongside the second funnel. A catapult was sited between the two funnels. *Kirov* was deleted from the list in the late 1970s.

SPECIFICATIONS	
Type:	Soviet cruiser
Displacement:	11,684 tonnes (11,500 tons)
Dimensions:	191m x 18m x 6m (626ft 8in x 59ft x 20ft)
Machinery:	Twin screws, turbines
Top speed:	35.9 knots
Main armament:	Nine 180mm (7.1in) guns, six 100mm (3.9in) guns
Armour:	50mm (2in) belt and deck, 75mm (3in) turrets
Complement:	734
Launched:	November 1936

Etna

Ordered for Siam in 1938, work on *Etna* ceased in December 1941, and in 1942 it was taken over by the Italian Navy. Major changes were introduced to turn it into an anti-aircraft cruiser. It was little over half complete when seized by German forces in 1943, but was finally scuttled that year, at Trieste.

SPECIFICATIONS	
Type:	Italian cruiser
Displacement:	5994 tonnes (5900 tons)
Dimensions:	153.8m x 14.4m x 5.9m (504ft 7in x 47ft 6in x 19ft 6in)
Machinery:	Twin screws, turbines
Top speed:	28 knots
Main armament:	Six 135mm (5.3in) guns
Launched:	May 1942

SHIP TYPES 1930–1949

Cruisers, Part 6: Other Navies

Cruisers in the 1930s and '40s were powered by turbine engines, in which steam from the boilers turns blades attached to a shaft. A cruiser's engines developed 60,246–67,770kW (80,000–90,000hp), a destroyer only 37,650kW (50,000hp). Gearing to the shafts made the ship economical at low speeds, extending its range.

Dupleix

Dupleix was the last of a group of four cruisers laid down each year from 1926 to 1929, modified versions of the *Tourville* class, and about two knots were sacrificed in favour of better protection. Scuttled at Toulon in 1942, *Dupleix* was raised in 1943, only to be sunk again by Allied bombing.

SPECIFICATIONS	
Type:	French cruiser
Displacement:	12,984 tonnes (12,780 tons)
Dimensions:	194m x 19.8m x 7m (636ft 6in x 65ft x 23ft 7in)
Machinery:	Triple screws, turbines
Top speed:	34 knots
Main armament:	Eight 203mm (8in) guns, eight 89mm (3.5in) guns
Armour:	51–57mm (2–2.25in) belt
Launched:	October 1930

Delhi

Delhi, then the British *Leander* class cruiser *Achilles*, helped to defeat the German battleship *Admiral Graf Spee* in December 1939. In 1948, it was sold to the Indian Navy, serving as the flagship until 1957. In 1959, when India began to modernize its fleet, *Delhi* was put into general service. It was scrapped in 1978.

SPECIFICATIONS	
Type:	Indian cruiser
Displacement:	9895 tonnes (9740 tons)
Dimensions:	166m x 16.7m x 6m (544ft 6in x 55ft 2in x 20ft)
Machinery:	Quadruple screws, turbines
Top speed:	32 knots
Main armament:	Six 152mm (6in) guns, four 102mm (4in) anti-aircraft guns
Launched:	September 1932

TIMELINE
1930  1932

Baleares

Designed by Sir Philip Watts, *Baleares* followed the British *Kent* class but with better speed and improved anti-aircraft armament. In the Spanish Civil War, it formed part of the Nationalist force and in 1938 encountered Government ships off Cape Palos, where it was torpedoed and sank with heavy loss of life.

SPECIFICATIONS	
Type:	Spanish cruiser
Displacement:	13,279 tonnes (13,070 tons)
Dimensions:	193.5m x 19.5m x 5.2m (635ft x 64ft x 17ft 4in)
Machinery:	Quadruple screws, geared turbines
Main armament:	Eight 203mm (8in) guns
Armour:	51mm (2in) belt, 114mm (4.5in) over magazines
Complement:	780
Launched:	1932

Gloire

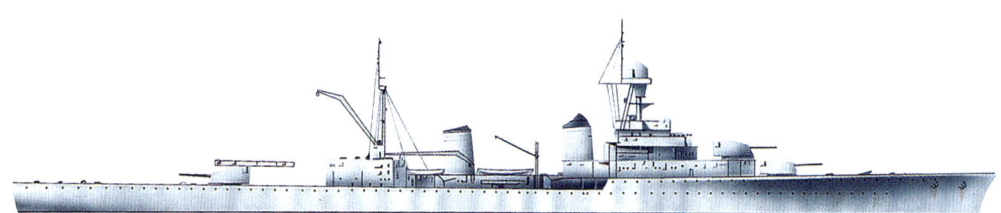

Gloire's 152mm (6in) guns were mounted in triple turrets, two superfiring forward and one aft. The aft superstructure comprised a large hangar with full repair facilities, and a long, open deck provided space to handle four aircraft. On top of the aft turret was a launching catapult. *Gloire* was scrapped in 1958.

SPECIFICATIONS	
Type:	French cruiser
Displacement:	9245 tonnes (9100 tons)
Dimensions:	179.5m x 17.4m x 5.3m (589ft x 57ft 4in x 17ft 7in)
Machinery:	Twin screws, turbines
Top speed:	36 knots
Main armament:	Nine 152mm (6in) guns, eight 88mm (3.5in) guns
Armour:	102mm (4in) belt
Launched:	1935

De Grasse

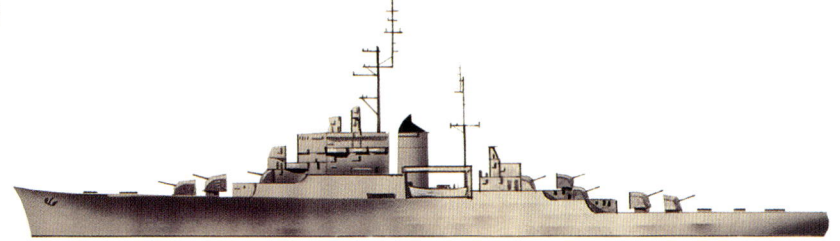

Its construction suspended during the German occupation of France. *De Grasse* was completed in 1956, as a fleet command ship for radar-controlled air strikes. In 1966, it was refitted to serve the Pacific Experimental Nuclear Centre. Several gun turrets were removed, and a lattice communications mast was fitted aft.

SPECIFICATIONS	
Type:	French cruiser
Displacement:	11,730 tonnes (11,545 tons)
Dimensions:	188m x 18.5m x 5.4m (617ft 2in x 61ft x 18ft 2in)
Machinery:	Twin screws, turbines
Top speed:	33.5 knots
Main armament:	Twelve 127mm (5in) dual-purpose guns
Launched:	1946

SHIP TYPES 1930–1949

De Ruyter

Enlarged during construction but still rather lightly armed, and stationed in the Dutch East Indies, this ship saw intensive action against Japanese forces. In February 1942 it was flagship of the Allied squadron opposing the Japanese invasion of Indonesia. It was sunk by torpedo in the Battle of the Java Sea, on 27 February 1942.

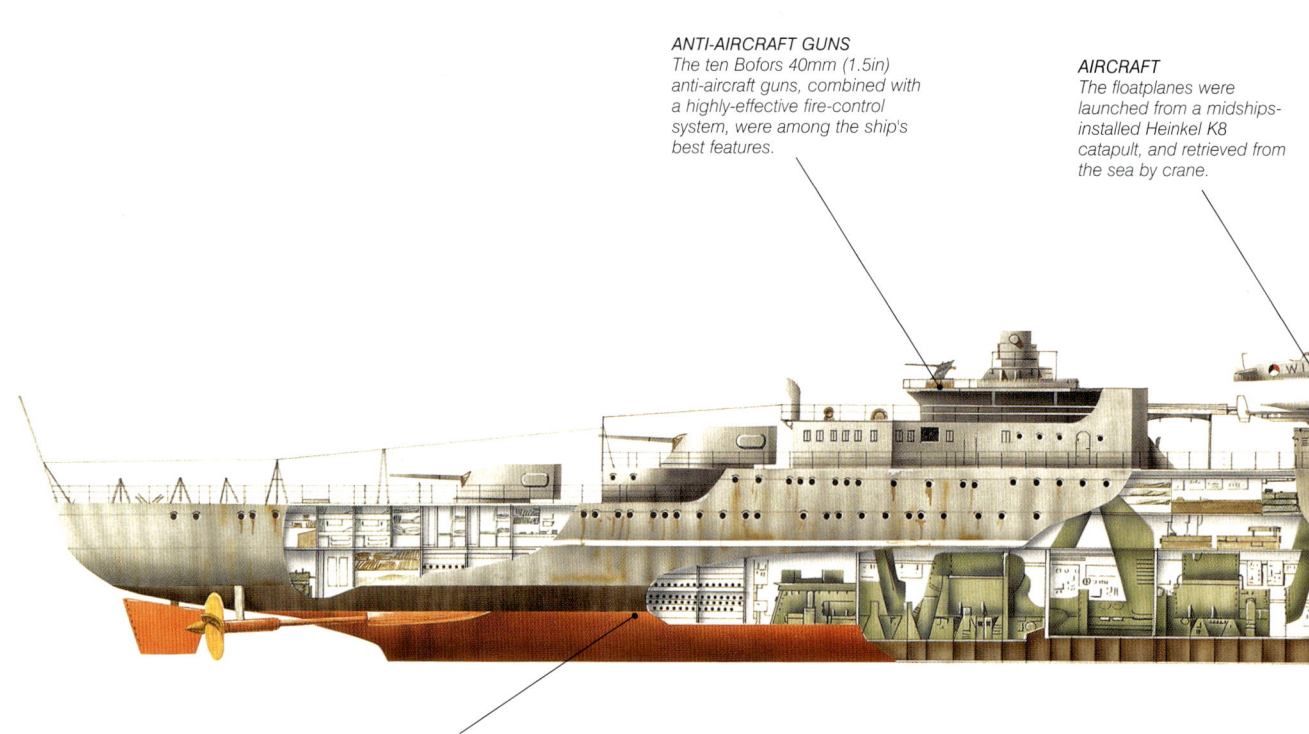

ANTI-AIRCRAFT GUNS
The ten Bofors 40mm (1.5in) anti-aircraft guns, combined with a highly-effective fire-control system, were among the ship's best features.

AIRCRAFT
The floatplanes were launched from a midships-installed Heinkel K8 catapult, and retrieved from the sea by crane.

OUTGUNNED
De Ruyter and its squadron were outgunned and outnumbered in the Battle of the Java Sea. A Japanese 'long lance' torpedo was responsible for sinking it.

De Ruyter

De Ruyter and De Zeven Provincien both took part in several NATO exercises and were often used as flagships for different naval task forces. De Zeven Provincien underwent a refit between 1962 and 1964 but a lack of funds meant De Ruyter did not undergo the same changes. De Ruyter was decommissioned in 1973.

SPECIFICATIONS	
Type:	Dutch cruiser
Displacement:	6,650 tonnes (6,545 tons)
Dimensions:	170.9m x 15.7m x 5.1m (561ft x52ft x 17ft)
Machinery:	Three screws, geared turbines
Top speed:	32 knots
Main armament:	Seven 150mm (6in) guns, ten 40mm (1.5in) guns
Armour:	50mm (2in) belt, 30mm (1.2in) deck and turrets
Aircraft:	Two Fokker C-11W floatplanes
Complement:	435
Launched:	1935

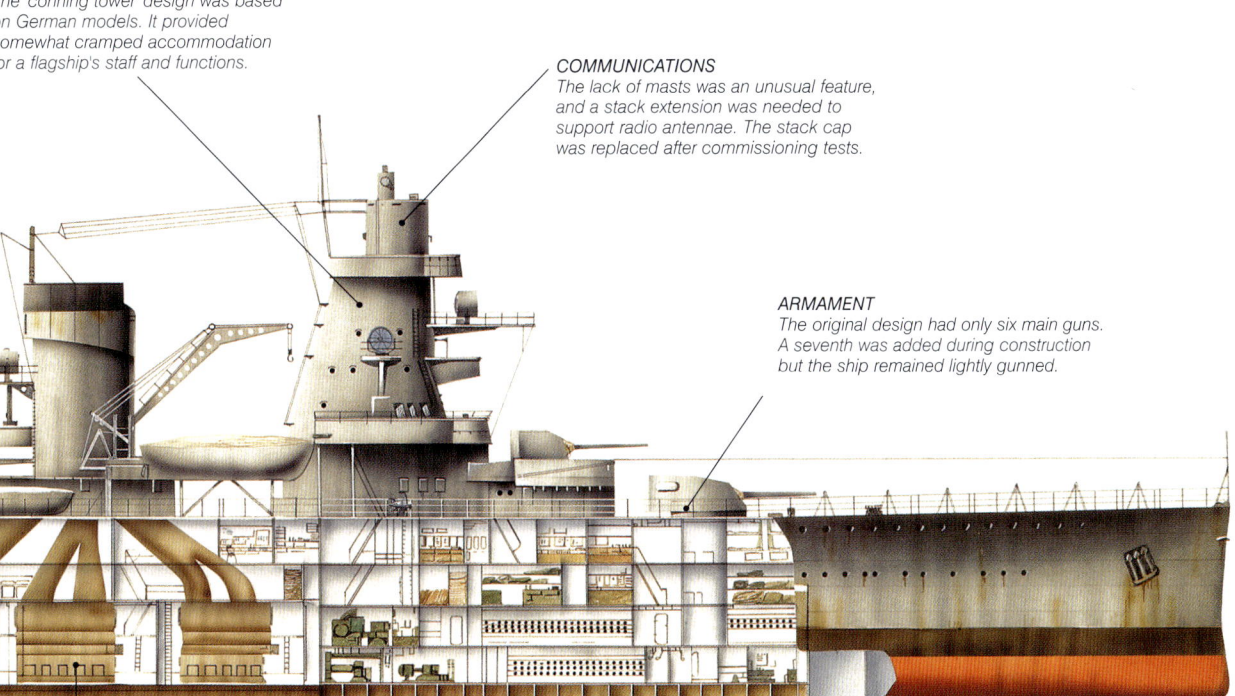

CONNING TOWER
The 'conning tower' design was based on German models. It provided somewhat cramped accommodation for a flagship's staff and functions.

COMMUNICATIONS
The lack of masts was an unusual feature, and a stack extension was needed to support radio antennae. The stack cap was replaced after commissioning tests.

ARMAMENT
The original design had only six main guns. A seventh was added during construction but the ship remained lightly gunned.

MACHINERY
Six boilers and three geared steam turbines generated 66,000shp (49,216 kW). 1,300 tonnes of oil gave a range of 6,800 nm (12,594km) at 12 knots.

Destroyers, Part 1: Russian

In the course of the 1930s, Soviet Russia set about expanding and modernizing its destroyer fleet, in successive five-year plans. Italian technical help was used and Soviet destroyers of the early 1930s closely resembled Italian types. Forty-eight fleet destroyers were built, most armed with mines as well as guns and torpedoes.

Minsk

Conceived as a type of super-destroyer for carrying out raiding missions in the Baltic, *Minsk* was built with technical aid from France and Italy. It was sunk in 1941, but refloated in 1942. In 1959, it became a training vessel.

SPECIFICATIONS
Type:	Soviet destroyer
Displacement:	2623 tonnes (2582 tons)
Dimensions:	127.5m x 11.7m x 4m (418ft 4in x 38ft 4in x 13ft 4in)
Machinery:	Triple screws, turbines
Top speed:	40 knots
Main armament:	Five 130mm (5.1in) guns, two 76mm (3in) guns
Launched:	November 1935

Bodryi

One of the first group of 28 ships, of the new Type 7, *Bodryi* was found insufficiently seaworthy for Arctic and Northern Pacific conditions. For this reason, a revised design was produced. By the start of World War II, 46 ships were complete, of which 20 were later lost. *Bodryi* was scrapped in 1958.

SPECIFICATIONS
Type:	Soviet destroyer
Displacement:	2072 tonnes (2039 tons)
Dimensions:	113m x 10m x 4m (370ft 3in x 33ft 6in x 12ft 6in)
Machinery:	Twin screws, geared
Main armament:	Four 127mm (5.1in) guns
Launched:	1936

TIMELINE
1935 1936

DESTROYERS, PART 1: RUSSIAN

Gromki

SPECIFICATIONS	
Type:	Soviet destroyer
Displacement:	2070 tonnes (2039 tons)
Dimensions:	112.8m x 10.2m x 3.8m (370ft 3in x 33ft 6in x 12ft 6in)
Machinery:	Twin screws, turbines
Main armament:	Four 130mm (5.1in) guns, two 76mm (3in) guns, six 533mm (21in) torpedo tubes
Launched:	1936

Gromki was a Type 7 destroyer, of Italian influence, completed in 1939. Its AA armament was uprated during the war. Engines developed 48,000hp, and oil fuel capacity was 548 tonnes (540 tons), enough for 1533km (807 miles) at full speed and 4955km (2608 miles) at 19 knots. *Gromki* was discarded in the 1950s.

Silnyi

SPECIFICATIONS	
Type:	Soviet destroyer
Displacement:	2443.5 tonnes (2405 tons)
Dimensions:	112.8m x 10.2m x 4.1m (370ft 7in x 22ft 6in x 13ft 5in)
Machinery:	Twin screws, geared turbines
Top speed:	36 knots
Main armament:	Four 130mm (5.1in) guns, six 533mm (21in) torpedo tubes
Complement:	207
Launched:	1938

Italian influence is evident in the design of the Type 7 destroyers. *Silnyi* was one of the second group, 7U, known as the *Storozhevoi* class, with strengthened hulls and more powerful engines. It carried 60 mines as well as the normal destroyer armament. Part of the Baltic fleet, it was withdrawn in the mid-1960s.

Ognevoi

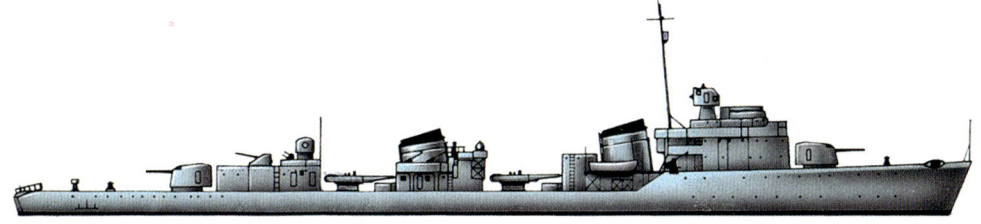

SPECIFICATIONS	
Type:	Soviet destroyer
Displacement:	2997.2 tonnes (2950 tons)
Dimensions:	117m x 11m x 4.2m (383ft 10in x 36ft 1in x 13ft 9in)
Machinery:	Twin screws, geared turbines
Top speed:	37 knots
Main armament:	Four 130mm (5.1in) guns, six 533mm (21in) torpedo tubes
Complement:	250
Launched:	1940

Only two ships of this two-funnelled class were completed before the end of World War II, but another 12 were built after 1945, known as the *Skoryi* class. Fast and well-armed, *Ognevoi* could carry 96 mines in addition to its secondary armament of two 76mm (3in) guns and four heavy 12.7mm (0.5in) machine guns.

SHIP TYPES 1930–1949

Destroyers, Part 2: British

The typical British destroyer of the 1930s displaced about 2000 tonnes and could reach about 35 knots top speed. Considerably larger than its predecessors, its function was considered to be the same, though gradually it took on a great variety of roles. As in other navies, it was later given much improved AA defences.

Ardent

SPECIFICATIONS	
Type:	British destroyer
Displacement:	2022 tonnes (1990 tons)
Dimensions:	95.1m x 9.8m x 3.7m (312ft x 32ft 3in x 12ft 3in)
Machinery:	Twin screws, geared turbines
Main armament:	Four 120mm (4.7in) guns, eight 533mm (21in) torpedo tubes
Top speed:	35 knots
Launched:	1929

With the 'W' class, the Royal Navy began a new era of destroyer construction, after a lapse of eight years. Completed in 1930, *Ardent* was sunk in June 1940 by *Scharnhorst* and *Gneisenau*, while escorting the aircraft carrier *Glorious*, which was also sunk. Three other 'W' class ships were lost during the war.

Crescent

SPECIFICATIONS	
Type:	British destroyer
Displacement:	1927 tonnes (1897 tons)
Dimensions:	97m x 10m x 3m (317ft 9in x 33ft x 8ft 6in)
Machinery:	Twin screws, turbines
Top speed:	36.4 knots
Main armament:	Four 120mm (4.7in) guns
Launched:	September 1931

A 'C' class destroyer, *Crescent* had increased fuel capacity compared to the 'B' class, and a 76mm (3in) anti-aircraft gun, as well as the 120mm (4.7in) guns and eight 533mm (21in) torpedo tubes. *Crescent* was transferred to the Royal Canadian Navy in 1937, and was sunk in a collision on 25 June 1940.

TIMELINE 1929 1931 1932

DESTROYERS, PART 2: BRITISH

Duncan

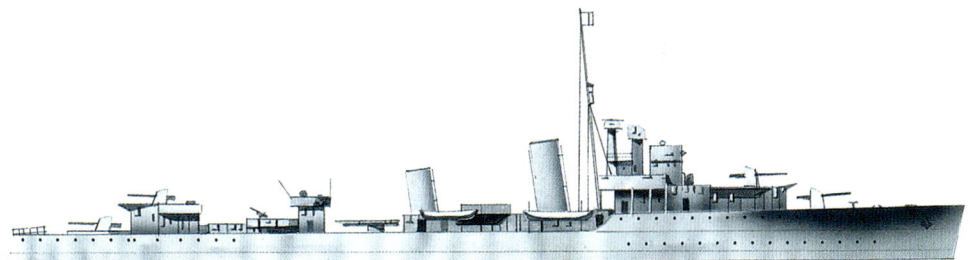

Fitted out originally as a destroyer leader, *Duncan* was a 'D' class vessel laid down in 1932, a slightly enlarged version of the 'B' class. During World War II, after the class had been greatly reduced by losses, the remaining vessels were converted into escort ships. *Duncan* was broken up in 1945.

SPECIFICATIONS	
Type:	British destroyer
Displacement:	1973 tonnes (1942 tons)
Dimensions:	100m x 10m x 4m (329ft x 32ft 10in x 12ft 10in)
Machinery:	Twin screws, turbines
Main armament:	Four 120mm (4.7in) guns
Launched:	July 1932

Exmouth

An enlarged version of the standard destroyer, with an additional 120mm (4.7in) gun and higher speed, *Exmouth* was an excellent sea boat. At 20 knots, just over 2 tonnes (2 tons) of oil fuel were consumed every hour. It was sunk with all hands in the Moray Firth in January 1940, probably by U-boat torpedo.

SPECIFICATIONS	
Type:	British destroyer leader
Displacement:	2041 tonnes (2009 tons)
Dimensions:	104.5m x 10.2m x 3.8m (342ft 10in x 33ft 9in x 12ft 6in)
Machinery:	Twin screws, turbines
Main armament:	Five 120mm (4.7in) guns
Launched:	February 1934

Cleveland

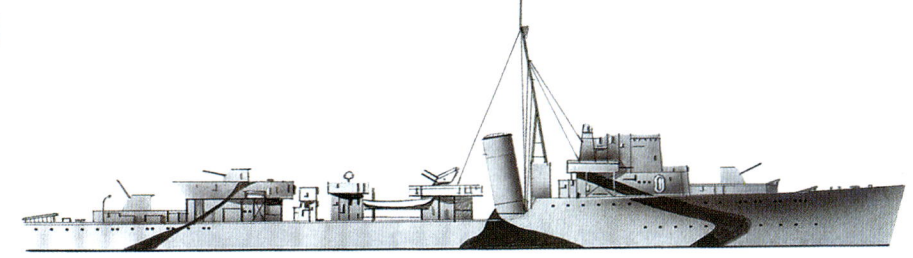

Cleveland was in the first group of the 'Hunt' class of destroyers, which eventually numbered 86. Designed to carry six 102mm (4in) guns, this armament proved too heavy, and the number was reduced to four. Though seaworthy, the ships tended to roll. *Cleveland* was wrecked en route to the breakers in June 1957.

SPECIFICATIONS	
Type:	British destroyer
Displacement:	1473 tonnes (1450 tons)
Dimensions:	85m x 9m x 4m (280ft x 29ft x 12ft 6in)
Machinery:	Twin screws, turbines
Top speed:	28 knots
Main armament:	Four 102mm (4in) guns
Launched:	April 1940

Cossack

A 'Tribal' class destroyer, *Cossack* made a dramatic rescue of British prisoners from the German vessel *Altmark*, in Norwegian waters, in February 1940, and was part of the force pursuing *Bismarck*, in May 1941. It also saw action with convoys to Malta, before being sunk in the North Atlantic by *U-563* on 26 October 1941.

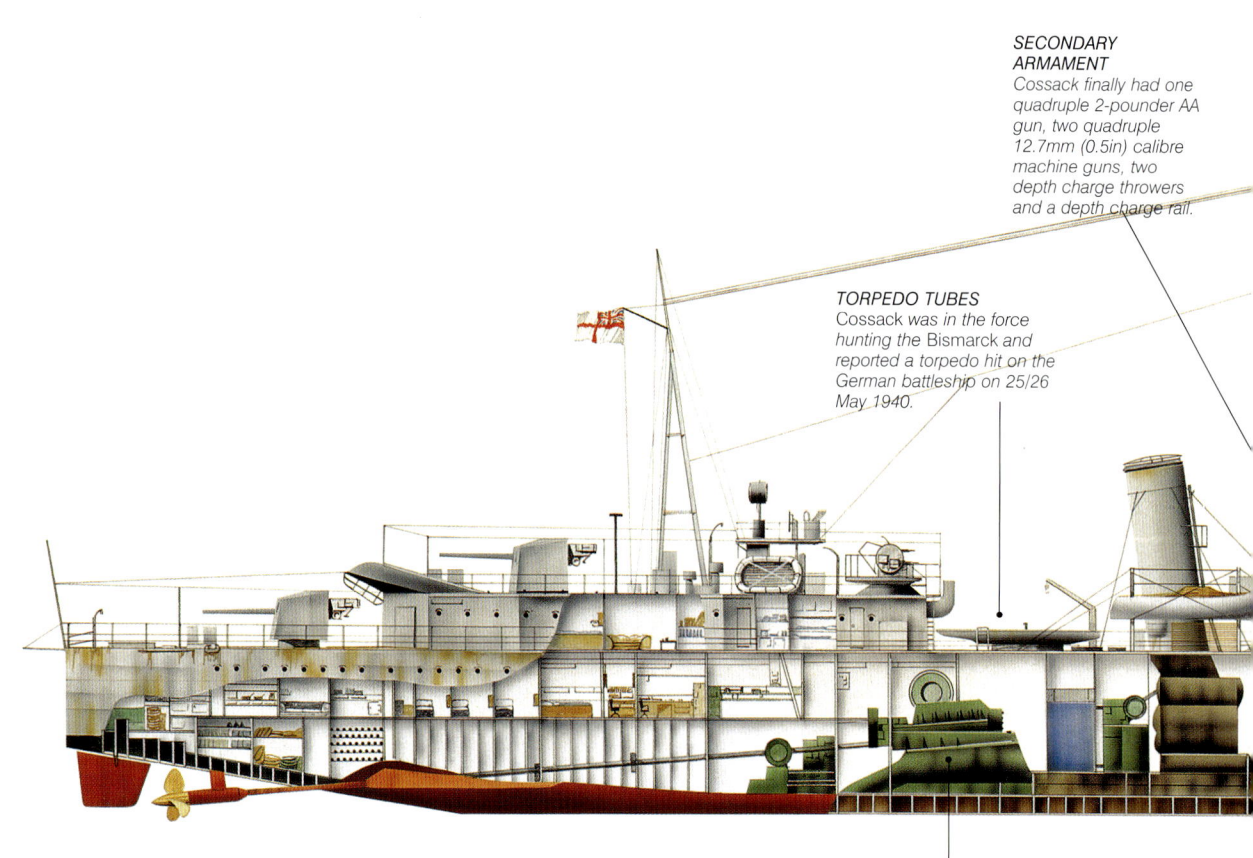

SECONDARY ARMAMENT
Cossack finally had one quadruple 2-pounder AA gun, two quadruple 12.7mm (0.5in) calibre machine guns, two depth charge throwers and a depth charge rail.

TORPEDO TUBES
Cossack was in the force hunting the *Bismarck* and reported a torpedo hit on the German battleship on 25/26 May 1940.

MACHINERY
Three Admiralty 3-drum boilers generated steam for two Parsons geared turbines, with a maximum power output of 33,131 kW (44,430 shp).

Cossack

In May 1941 Cossack participated in the pursuit and destruction of the *Bismarck*. While escorting Convoy WS-8B to the Middle East, Cossack and four other destroyers made several torpedo attacks in the evening and into the next morning. No hits were scored, but they made it easier for the battleships to attack her the next morning.

SPECIFICATIONS
Type:	British destroyer
Displacement:	1900 tonnes (1870 tons)
Dimensions:	111.5m x 11.13m x 4m (364ft 8in x 36ft 6in x 13ft)
Machinery:	Twin screws, geared turbines
Top speed:	36 knots
Main armament:	Eight 120mm (4.7in) guns, four 53mm (21in) torpedo tubes
Complement:	219
Launched:	June 1937

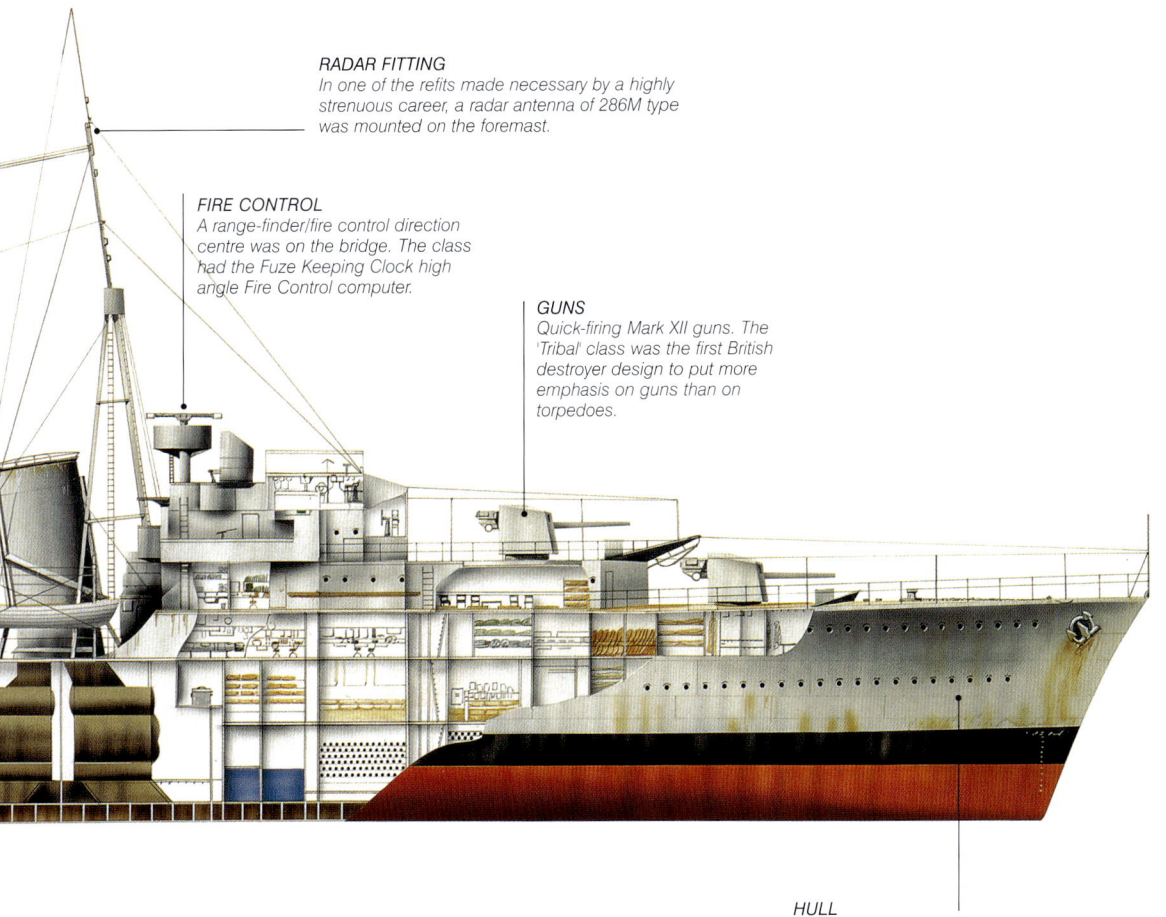

RADAR FITTING
In one of the refits made necessary by a highly strenuous career, a radar antenna of 286M type was mounted on the foremast.

FIRE CONTROL
A range-finder/fire control direction centre was on the bridge. The class had the Fuze Keeping Clock high angle Fire Control computer.

GUNS
Quick-firing Mark XII guns. The 'Tribal' class was the first British destroyer design to put more emphasis on guns than on torpedoes.

HULL
The 'Tribals' were fast and highly seaworthy ships, and looked it, with their clipper bows, and raked masts and funnels.

SHIP TYPES 1930–1949

Destroyers, Part 3: British & French

French destroyer design was influenced by Italian design, and vice versa, the competition producing classes that verged on the dimensions of the light cruiser. British destroyers were small and lightly gunned by comparison, but perhaps more suited to the rapid tactics and tight manoeuvring vital for a destroyer's true purpose.

Aigle

One of a class of six, the only four-funnelled destroyers of the 1930s, *Aigle* was fitted with new rapid-fire semi-automatic guns, capable of 12–15 rounds per minute. With two sister-ships, it was scuttled at Toulon in 1942 as German forces entered the port. Refloated, it was sunk again by air attack in 1943.

SPECIFICATIONS	
Type:	French destroyer
Displacement:	3190.3 tonnes (3140 tons)
Dimensions:	128.5m x 11.84m x 4.79m (421ft 7in x 38ft 10in x 16ft 4in)
Machinery:	Twin screws, geared turbines
Top speed:	36 knots
Main armament:	Five 140mm (5.5in) guns, six 550mm (21.7in) torpedo tubes
Complement:	230
Launched:	1931

L'Indomptable

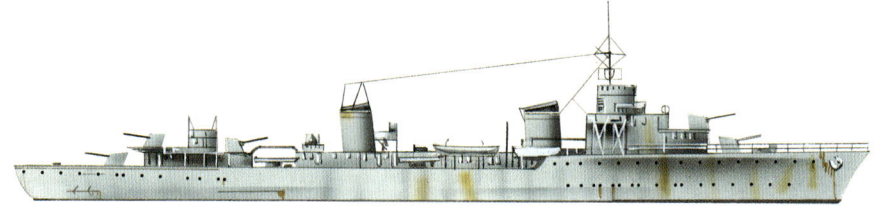

Each new Italian destroyer type prompted a bigger or better French one. The *Fantasque* class was fast, capable of over 40 knots. With *Le Triomphant* and *Le Malin*, *L'Indomptable* made a raid into the Skagerrak during the German invasion of Norway, engaging German patrol boats. It was scuttled at Toulon in 1942.

SPECIFICATIONS	
Type:	French destroyer
Displacement:	3352.8 tonnes (3300 tons)
Dimensions:	132.4m x 12.35m x 5m (434ft 4in x 40ft 6in x 16ft 4in)
Machinery:	Twin screws, geared turbines
Top speed:	40 knots
Main armament:	Five 138.6mm (5.46in) guns, three triple 533mm (21in) torpedo tubes
Complement:	210
Launched:	1933

TIMELINE

1931 1933 1941

Exmoor

Laid down as HMS *Burton*, this ship was renamed after the first *Exmoor*, also a 'Hunt' class destroyer, was sunk by a German E-boat in February 1941. *Exmoor*, of the second, slightly larger, group of 'Hunts', was transferred to the Danish Navy in 1953, as *Valdemar Sejr*. It was broken up in 1966.

SPECIFICATIONS	
Type:	British destroyer
Displacement:	1651 tonnes (1625 tons)
Dimensions:	85.3m x 9.6m x 3.7m (280ft x 31ft 6in x 12ft 5in)
Machinery:	Twin screws, turbines
Top speed:	26.7 knots
Main armament:	Six 102mm (4in) guns
Launched:	March 1941

Comet

Comet belonged to a 24-unit class of large destroyers, developed late in World War II. One, HMS *Contest*, was the first British destroyer with an all-welded hull. All vessels in the class survived the war. Four were passed to Norway in 1946, and four to Pakistan in the 1950s. *Comet* was broken up in 1962.

SPECIFICATIONS	
Type:	British destroyer
Displacement:	2575 tonnes (2535 tons)
Dimensions:	111m x 11m x 4m (362ft 9in x 35ft 8in x 14ft 5in)
Machinery:	Twin screws, turbines
Top speed:	36.7 knots
Main armament:	Four 114mm (4.5in) guns
Launched:	June 1944

Daring

Multi-purpose ships, *Daring* and seven others were the largest destroyers yet built for the Royal Navy and had an all-welded hull construction. The lattice foremast was built around the fore funnel. The 114mm (4.5in) guns were automatic and radar controlled. *Daring* was withdrawn and broken up in 1971.

SPECIFICATIONS	
Type:	British destroyer
Displacement:	3636 tonnes (3579 tons)
Dimensions:	114m x 13m x 4m (375ft x 43ft x 13ft)
Machinery:	Twin screws, turbines
Top speed:	31.5 knots
Main armament:	Six 114mm (4.5in) guns
Launched:	August 1949

SHIP TYPES 1930–1949

Destroyers, Part 4: USA

In December 1941, the United States had 68 destroyers in the Pacific and 51 in the Atlantic. In the course of 1942–45, another 302 were built, and the destroyer became the US Navy's all-purpose work-horse, as fleet and carrier escort, submarine hunter, anti-aircraft battery ship and landing support ship.

Sims

Fleet destroyers had to be fast and this required powerful engines. The *Sims* class destroyers were heavier than had been planned but were an effective class, capable of long range service, up to 12,000km (6500nm) at 12 knots. *Sims* was sunk by Japanese aircraft in the Battle of the Coral Sea, on 7 May 1942.

SPECIFICATIONS	
Type:	US destroyer
Displacement:	2388.6 tonnes (2315 tons)
Dimensions:	106.15m x 10.95m x 3.9m (348ft 4in x 36ft x 12ft 10in)
Machinery:	Twin screws, geared turbines
Top speed:	35 knots
Main armament:	Five 127mm (5in) guns, eight 533mm (21in) torpedo tubes
Complement:	192
Launched:	1938

Doyle

The large class to which *Doyle* belonged were the last destroyers designed for the United States before it entered World War II. Production was speeded up by simplified design, many being completed with straight-fronted bridge structures. Many were transferred to other navies after the war. *Doyle* was scrapped in 1970.

SPECIFICATIONS	
Type:	US destroyer
Displacement:	2621 tonnes (2580 tons)
Dimensions:	106m x 11m x 5.4m (348ft 6in x 36ft x 18ft)
Machinery:	Twin screws, turbines
Top speed:	37.4 knots
Main armament:	Four 127mm (5in) guns, five 533mm (21in) torpedo tubes
Launched:	March 1942

TIMELINE 1938  1942

Edsall

SPECIFICATIONS	
Type:	US destroyer escort
Displacement:	1625.6 tonnes (1600 tons) full load
Dimensions:	93.3m x 11.15m x 3.2m (306ft x 36ft 7in x 10ft 5in)
Machinery:	Twin screws, diesels
Top speed:	21 knots
Main armament:	Three 76mm (3in) guns, three 533mm (21in) torpedo tubes
Complement:	186
Launched:	1942

Speed was not vital for a merchant convoy escort ship, as the convoys were relatively slow; it had to be manoeuvrable and quick to respond to attack from surface craft and submarine alike. Hundreds of these ships were built in six very similar classes. *Edsall*'s diesel engines were driven through a reduction gearbox.

Gatling

SPECIFICATIONS	
Type:	US destroyer
Displacement:	2971 tonnes (2924 tons)
Dimensions:	114.7m x 12m x 4.2m (376ft 5in x 39ft 4in x 13ft 9in)
Machinery:	Twin screws, turbines
Top speed:	35 knots
Main armament:	Five 127mm (5in) guns
Launched:	June 1943

The *Gatling* class were the largest wartime destroyers built for the US Navy, with a displacement about 1000 tonnes greater than most predecessors, and firepower little less than that of some light cruisers. *Gatling* remained in service for over 30 years, being finally stricken from the Navy List in 1974.

Duncan

SPECIFICATIONS	
Type:	US destroyer
Displacement:	3606 tonnes (3549 tons)
Dimensions:	120m x 12.4m x 5.8m (390ft 6in x 41ft x 19ft)
Machinery:	Twin screws, geared turbines
Top speed:	33 knots
Main armament:	Six 127mm (5in) guns, ten 533mm (21in) torpedo tubes
Complement:	336
Launched:	October 1944

One of over 90 *Gearing* class ocean-going destroyers, provided with a powerful armament and sufficient fuel supplies for long-range action, *Duncan* was converted to a radar picket ship in 1945, losing its torpedo tubes. It was stricken from the Navy List in 1973, but several of the class served as late as 1980.

1943    1944

SHIP TYPES 1930–1949

Fletcher

Fletcher was lead ship of a class of 175, built to plans entirely different to its 1930s predecessors, flush-decked like earlier US destroyers, less top-heavy and so less inclined to roll. *Fletcher* gained 15 batttle stars in World War II and five more in the Korean War. Placed in reserve in 1962, it was stricken in 1967.

A THOUGHT-OUT DESIGN
The Fletchers were popular ships because they were fighting machines that took account of the needs of the human beings who worked them.

AMMUNITION HANDLING
Ammunition handling rooms are beneath each of the five turrets, with hoists to the magazines below the waterline.

CREW ACCOMMODATION
Galley and laundry are between the funnels. Most of the enlisted men's quarters are between the boiler room and the engine room.

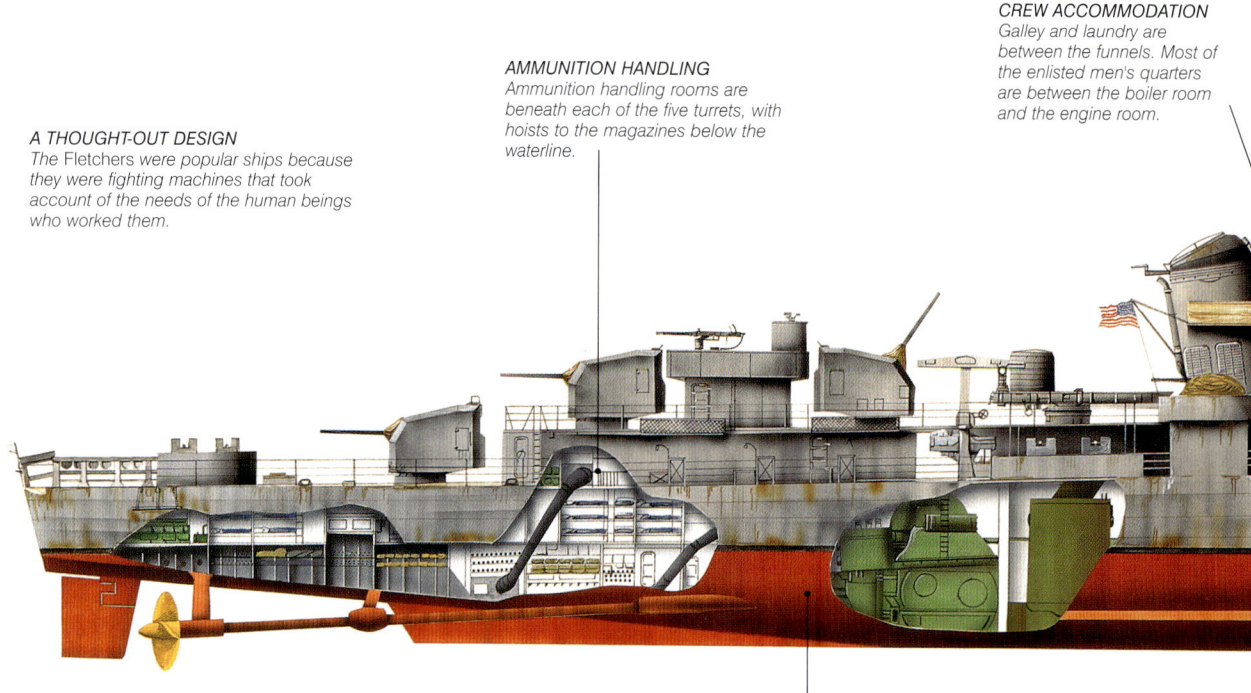

HULL
Displacement was 25 per cent up on the previous Gleaves class, allowing for heavier guns and slightly more crew space.

Fletcher

The *Fletcher* class was the largest class of destroyer ordered, and was also one of the most successful and popular with the destroyer crews themselves. Compared to earlier classes built for the Navy, they carried a significant increase in anti-aircraft (AA) weapons and other weaponry.

SPECIFICATIONS

Type:	US destroyer
Displacement:	2971 tonnes (2924 tons)
Dimensions:	114.7m x 12m x 4.2m (376ft 5in x 39ft 4in x 13ft 9in)
Machinery:	Twin screws, geared turbines
Top speed:	38 knots
Main armament:	Five 127mm (5in) guns, ten 533mm (21in) torpedo tubes
Complement:	273
Launched:	1942

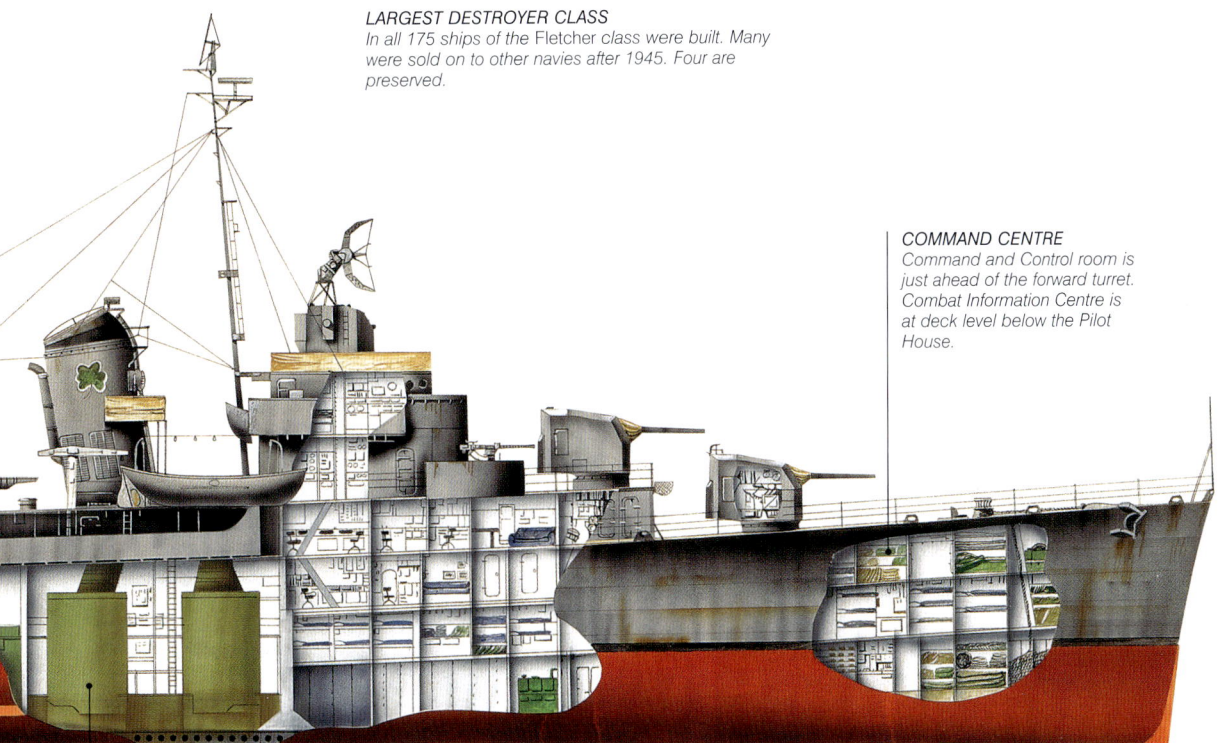

LARGEST DESTROYER CLASS
In all 175 ships of the Fletcher class were built. Many were sold on to other navies after 1945. Four are preserved.

COMMAND CENTRE
Command and Control room is just ahead of the forward turret. Combat Information Centre is at deck level below the Pilot House.

MACHINERY
Four Babcock & Wilcox boilers supplying steam to three General Electric geared turbines, with maximum power output of 45MW (60,000 shp).

SHIP TYPES 1930–1949

Destroyers, Part 5: Italian

Five destroyer classes were built by the Italians between 1930 and 1941, none of them numerous, amounting to 36 new ships. Large-sized, they were built very much with an eye on what the French were doing. They were fast, with 38 knots a common speed. The *Soldati* class carried a star-shell gun to help in night actions.

Alberto da Giussano

One of four ships built in response to the powerful French *Lion* class destroyers, *Alberto di Giussano* was a large and well-armed vessel, though lightly armoured. It was also very fast – one of the class achieved a speed of 42 knots during trials and maintained a steady 40 knots for eight hours.

SPECIFICATIONS	
Type:	Italian fast destroyer
Displacement:	5170 tonnes (5089 tons)
Dimensions:	169.4m x 15.2m x 4.3m (555ft 9in x 49ft 10in x 14ft 1in)
Machinery:	Twin screws, geared turbines
Top speed:	40 knots
Main armament:	Eight 152mm (6in) guns
Launched:	1930

Baleno

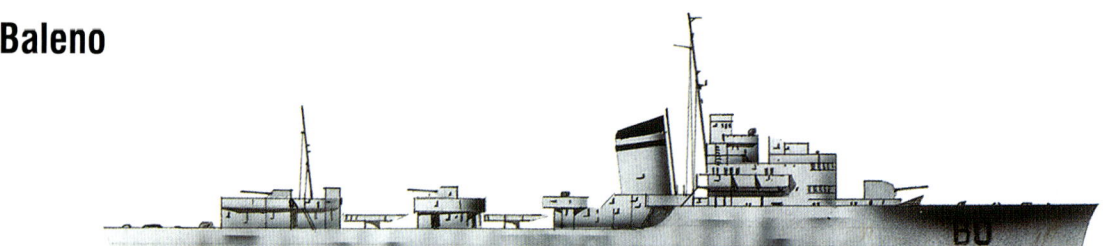

Single-funnelled, with a slimmer hull than its predecessors, *Balena* was sleek and fast. These ships saw hard service in the Mediterranean as convoy escorts, scouts and patrols. On 16 April 1941, it and another destroyer, *Luca Tango*, were in action with four British destroyers. *Baleno* capsized and sank the next day.

SPECIFICATIONS	
Type:	Italian destroyer
Displacement:	2123 tonnes (2090 tons)
Dimensions:	94.3m x 9.2m x 3.3m (309ft 6in x 30ft x 10ft 9in)
Machinery:	Twin screws, geared turbines
Top speed:	39 knots
Main armament:	Four 119mm (4.7in) guns, six 533mm (21in) torpedo tubes
Launched:	March 1931

TIMELINE
1930
1931

DESTROYERS, PART 5: ITALIAN

Fulmine

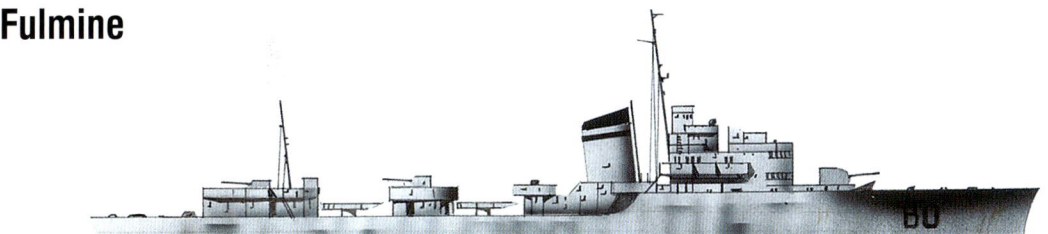

SPECIFICATIONS	
Type:	Italian destroyer
Displacement:	2124 tonnes (2090 tons)
Dimensions:	94.5m x 9.25m x 3.25m (309ft 6in x 30ft 6in x 11ft)
Machinery:	Twin screws, turbines
Top speed:	38 knots
Main armament:	Four 119mm (4.7in) guns
Launched:	August 1931

Destroyer design took a leap forward in 1929–30 with a new Italian class of eight single-funnelled ships with two banks of torpedo tubes placed on the centreline astern of the funnel. *Fulmine* was in the second group. Highly active in World War II, six were lost, including *Fulmine*, sunk in action against British forces.

Vincenzo Gioberti

SPECIFICATIONS	
Type:	Italian destroyer
Displacement:	2326 tonnes (2290 tons)
Dimensions:	106.7m x 10m x 3.4m (350ft x 33ft 4in x 11ft 3in)
Machinery:	Twin screws, turbines
Top speed:	39 knots
Main armament:	Four 120mm (4.7in) guns, six 533mm (21in) torpedo tubes
Launched:	September 1936

Vincenzo Gioberti was one in a class of four powerful destroyers. The torpedo tubes were mounted on triple carriages placed on the centreline. Later, 20mm (0.8in) anti-aircraft guns were fitted. It was built in 1936–37. On 9 August 1943, it was sunk by a torpedo from the British submarine *Simoom*.

Artigliere

SPECIFICATIONS	
Type:	Italian destroyer
Displacement:	2540 tonnes (2500 tons)
Dimensions:	106.7m x 10.2m x 3.5m (350ft x 33ft 4in x 11ft 6in)
Machinery:	Twin screws, geared turbines
Top speed:	38 knots
Main armament:	Four 120mm (4.7in) guns
Launched:	December 1937

Artigliere was in the *Soldati* class, the most numerous class of destroyer built for the Italian Navy. All 21 saw extensive war service as escorts able to give and take a deal of punishment. The anti-aircraft defence was inadequate and was soon improved. *Artigliere* was lost in action in October 1940.

SHIP TYPES 1930–1949

Destroyers, Part 6: Italian & Japanese

Japan entered World War II with a total of 110 destroyers, a number equivalent to the American total, deployed in six flotillas. But only 33 more were built. They were efficient craft, highly drilled for night actions when torpedoes were at their most effective, and sharing the Long Lance torpedo with the submarine fleet.

Asashio

The ten *Asashio* class of large destroyers marked Japan's abandonment of treaty limitations on warship construction. Their steam turbines proved unreliable at first, and defects in the steering gear was not corrected until December 1941. All ten ships were lost during World War II, *Asashio* was sunk by US carrier-borne aircraft.

SPECIFICATIONS

Type:	Japanese destroyer
Displacement:	2367 tonnes (2330 tons)
Dimensions:	118.2m x 10.4m x 3.7m (388ft x 34ft x 12ft)
Machinery:	Twin screws, geared turbines
Top speed:	35 knots
Main armament:	Six 127mm (5in) guns
Complement:	200
Launched:	December 1936

Hamakaze

The first Japanese destroyer with radar, *Hamakaze* and its 17 sisters were armed with six 127mm (5in) guns in twin turrets, but in 1943–44 the upper aft turret was replaced by anti-aircraft guns. The torpedo tubes were positioned amidships in enclosed quadruple mounts. *Hamakaze* was sunk by US aircraft on 7 April 1945.

SPECIFICATIONS

Type:	Japanese destroyer
Displacement:	2489 tonnes (2450 tons)
Dimensions:	118.5m x 10.8m x 3.7m (388ft 9in x 35ft 5in x 12ft 4in)
Machinery:	Twin screws, turbines
Top speed:	35 knots
Main armament:	Four 127mm (5in) guns, eight 610mm (24in) torpedo tubes
Launched:	November 1940

TIMELINE

1936   1940   1942

DESTROYERS, PART 6: ITALIAN & JAPANESE

Bombardiere

SPECIFICATIONS	
Type:	Italian destroyer
Displacement:	2540 tonnes (2500 tons)
Dimensions:	107m x 10m x 4m (350ft x 33ft 7in x 11ft 6in)
Machinery:	Twin screws, turbines
Top speed:	38 knots
Main armament:	Five 120mm (4.7in) guns
Launched:	March 1942

Bombardiere was one of the second group of *Soldati* destroyers, with minor modifications. Some were fitted with depth-charge throwers and all were given additional light AA guns. *Bombardiere* was one of 10 *Soldati* lost in World War II; it was sunk off Marettimo by the British submarine *United* on 17 January 1943.

Ariete

SPECIFICATIONS	
Type:	Italian destroyer
Displacement:	1127.8 tonnes (1110 tons)
Dimensions:	83.5m x 8.6m x 3.15m (274ft x 28ft 3in x 10ft 4in)
Machinery:	Twin screws, geared turbines
Top speed:	31.5 knots
Main armament:	Two 100mm (3.9in) guns, six 450mm (17.7in) torpedo tubes
Complement:	150
Launched:	1943

Built at Trieste, *Ariete* was the lead ship of Italy's final class of World War II destroyers, and the only one of the class to be commissioned before the surrender of Italy in 1943. After World War II, it was transferred to Yugoslavia as part of a war reparations package, and served as *Durmitor* until 1963.

Dragone

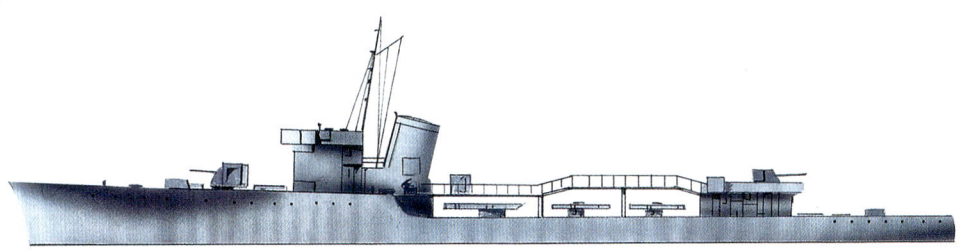

SPECIFICATIONS	
Type:	Italian destroyer/escort
Displacement:	1117 tonnes (1100 tons)
Dimensions:	83.5m x 8.6m x 3m (274ft x 28ft 3in x 10ft 4in)
Machinery:	Twin screws, turbines
Main armament:	Two 102mm (4in) guns, six 450mm (17.7in) torpedo tubes
Launched:	August 1943

Lightweight but slow destroyers, *Dragone* and its sisters were enlargements of the *Spica* class. Built economically, they were vulnerable to faster, more heavily gunned craft. Seized by the Germans after Italy's surrender and numbered TA30, *Dragone* was sunk in June 1944 by torpedoes fired from British MTBs.

1943

Destroyers, Part 7: Japanese & German

Germany's destroyers of the 1930s were advanced ships for their time, but their high-pressure boilers and turbines often failed. Compared to British destroyers they had limited range and magazine capacity. But, numbering only 40, they were a modest part of the *Reich* fleet compared to the hundreds of U-boats.

T1

Officially classed as torpedo boats, these were, in fact, small destroyers. There were 36 built for the *Kriegsmarine*, some larger than *T1*, though there was no special function for them. Too small for fleet work, too light for escort duty, their main virtue was speed, making them effective as North Sea raiding vessels.

SPECIFICATIONS	
Type:	German light destroyer
Displacement:	1107.4 tonnes (1090 tons)
Dimensions:	84.3m x 8.6m x 2.35m (276ft 7in x 28ft 3in x 7ft 8in)
Machinery:	Twin screws, geared turbines
Top speed:	35 knots
Main armament:	One 105mm (5in) gun, three 533mm (21in) torpedo tubes
Complement:	119
Launched:	1938

Z30

The 'Narvik' class, *Z23–30*, were officially class 36A. Their main guns were the heaviest mounted on destroyers but were not suitable for rapid fire, and their weight reduced the ships' seakeeping qualities. *Z30* was taken by the British at the end of World War II and destroyed in underwater explosive tests.

SPECIFICATIONS	
Type:	German destroyer
Displacement:	3750 tonnes (3691 tons) full load
Dimensions:	127m x 12m x 4.6m (416ft 8in x 39ft 4in x 15ft 2in)
Machinery:	Twin screws, geared turbines
Top speed:	38.5 knots
Main Armament:	Four 150mm (5.9in) guns, eight 533mm (21in) torpedo tubes
Complement:	321
Launched:	1940

TIMELINE — 1938 — 1940 — 1941

DESTROYERS, PART 7: JAPANESE & GERMAN

Akitsuki

SPECIFICATIONS	
Type:	Japanese destroyer
Displacement:	3759 tonnes (3700 tons) full load
Dimensions:	134.2m x 11.6m x 4.15m (440ft 3in x 38ft 1in x 13ft)
Machinery:	Twin screws, geared turbines
Top speed:	33 knots
Main armament:	Eight 100mm (3.9in) guns, four 610mm (24in) torpedo tubes
Complement:	300
Launched:	1941

Japan's final class of wartime destroyers carried a newly developed dual-purpose (anti-aircraft, anti-surface craft) gun and long-range torpedoes. *Akitsuki* was sunk by US aircraft at Leyte Gulf in October 1944. Six of its class of 12 survived the war, a high proportion in a fleet almost wholly destroyed.

Fuyutsuki

SPECIFICATIONS	
Type:	Japanese destroyer
Displacement:	3759 tonnes (3700 tons)
Dimensions:	134.2m x 11.6m x 4.2m (440ft 3in x 38ft 13ft 9in)
Machinery:	Twin screws, turbines
Top speed:	33 knots
Main armament:	Eight 96mm (3.8in) guns, four 607mm (23.9in) torpedo tubes in one quadruple mount
Launched:	January 1944

Fuyutsuki was one of a large class of big ocean-going destroyers, for which plans were drawn up in 1939. They were intended as fast anti-aircraft escort ships for the Japanese carrier task forces. By 1943, needs had changed and the design was modified to carry quadruple torpedo tubes for anti-ship attacks.

Fionda

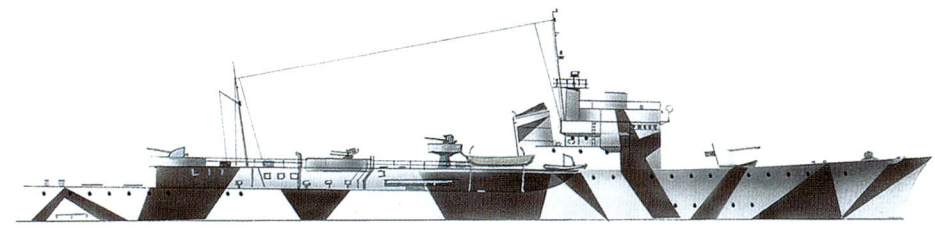

SPECIFICATIONS	
Type:	Italian destroyer
Displacement:	1138 tonnes (1120 tons) approx
Dimensions:	82.2m x 8.6m x 2.8m (270ft 3in x 9ft 2in)
Machinery:	Twin screws, turbines
Main armament:	Two 100mm (3.9in) guns
Launched:	Not completed

Italian war estimates provided for building 42 boats in *Fionda's* class. Only 16 were laid down, including *Fionda* in 1942. Captured by the Germans on the slips and designated *TA46*, it was damaged in an air raid in 1945. Construction began again, with the new name *Velebit*, but the ship was never completed.

Karl Galster

SHIP TYPES 1930–1949

Also known as *Z20, Karl Galster* was a considerable improvement on the earlier Type 36, with a new 'clipper' bow shape. Well-armed, with an array of AA guns and carrying 60 mines, it was the only ship of its class to survive World War II. Taken by the Soviets and renamed *Protshnyi*, it was decommissioned around 1960.

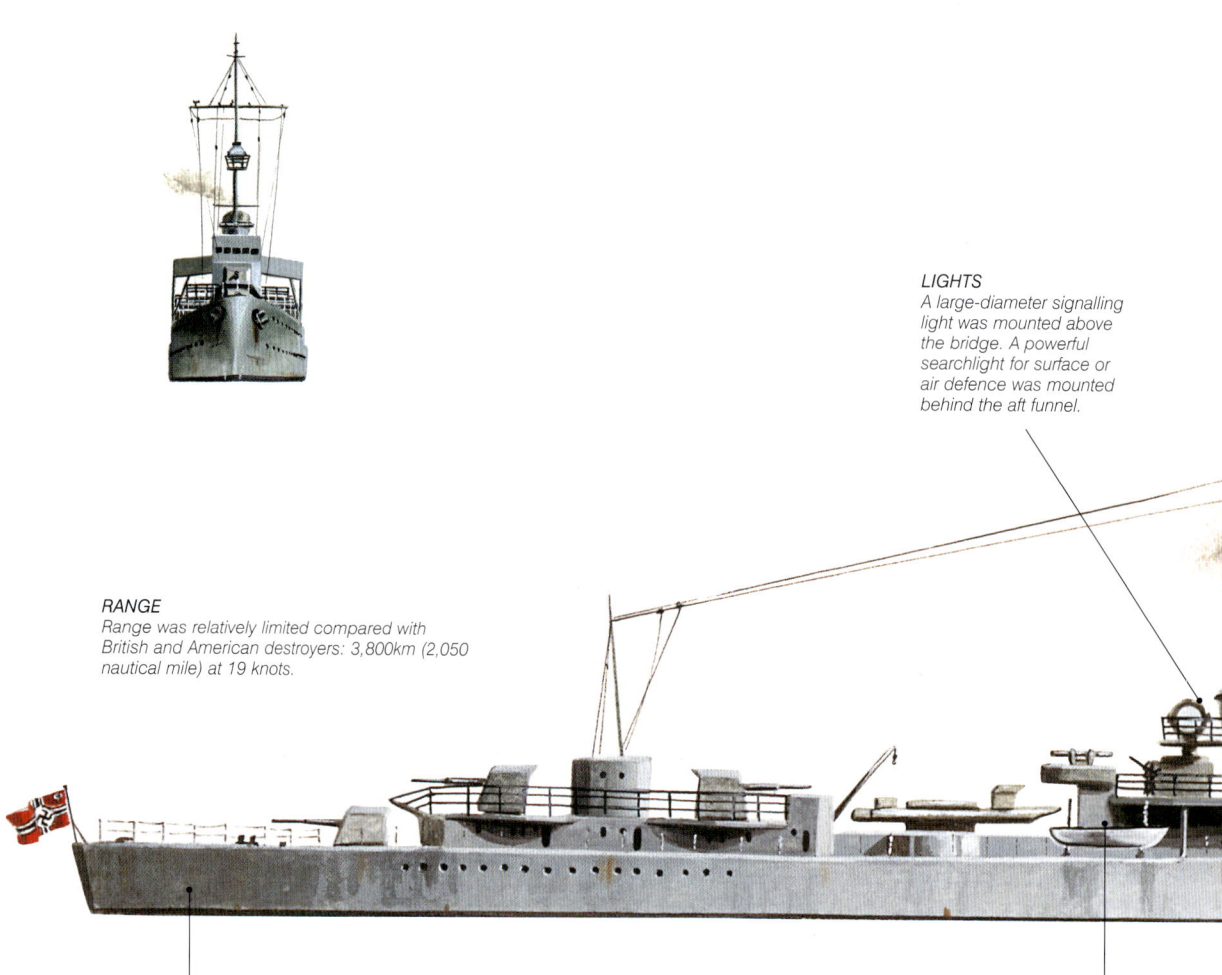

LIGHTS
A large-diameter signalling light was mounted above the bridge. A powerful searchlight for surface or air defence was mounted behind the aft funnel.

RANGE
Range was relatively limited compared with British and American destroyers: 3,800km (2,050 nautical mile) at 19 knots.

MINES
As often with German destroyers, most of the Z20 class were equipped for minelaying, with storage for 60 mines.

ANTI-AIRCRAFT AND SUBMARINE
Six 37mm (1.45in) AA guns were mounted, in pairs, and 12 20mm (0.79in) guns. Four anti-submarine depth-charge launchers were also carried.

Karl Galster

Karl Galster was the only one of its class to survive; the other five were sunk either at Narvik or in Rombaksfjord. In 1946 *Karl Galster* was handed over to the Soviet Navy as part of Germany's war reparations to the Soviet Union. She served in the Baltic fleet as the *Protshnyi* into the 1950s.

SPECIFICATIONS	
Type:	German destroyer
Displacement:	3469.7 tonnes (3415 tons) full load
Dimensions:	125m x 11.8m x 4m (410ft 1in x 38ft 8in x 13ft 1in)
Machinery:	Twin screws, geared turbines
Top speed:	36 knots
Main armament:	Five 127mm (5in) guns, eight 533mm (21in) torpedo tubes
Complement:	330
Launched:	1938

PROFILE
The class is distinguished from its 1934A predecessors by flatter funnel caps, marginally wider beam, and greater length (by 5m, or 15ft).

MACHINERY
The high pressure boilers and turbines, with a substantial power output of 55,554kW (74,500 shp), were more reliable than in previous classes.

BOATS
Four boats were normally carried: captain's gig, cutter, dinghy and Verkehrsboot or general purpose launch, for crew transport and intership trips.

Destroyers, Part 8: German & Other Navies

In the latter years of World War II and into the 1950s, the design and operation of destroyers were influenced by the experience of war. Armament, machinery and arrangement, tested in the ultimate conditions, were relatively unchanged. The main difference with pre-war destroyer types was more effective anti-aircraft defences.

Gravina

Gravina was one of 16 of the largest destroyers built for the Spanish Navy, virtual copies of the British *Scott* class flotilla leaders. All were launched between 1926 and 1933. The second octet, including *Gravina*, had large gun shields. Range at 14 knots was 8550km (4500 miles). The ship was stricken in the 1960s.

SPECIFICATIONS	
Type:	Spanish destroyer
Displacement:	2209 tonnes (2175 tons)
Dimensions:	101.5m x 9.6m x 3.2m (333ft x 31ft 9in x 10ft 6in)
Machinery:	Twin screws, turbines
Top speed:	36 knots
Main armament:	Five 120mm (4.7in) guns, six 533mm (21in) torpedo tubes
Launched:	December 1931

Goteborg

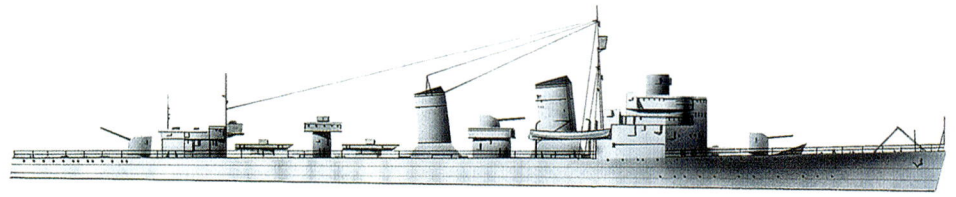

By 1934, Sweden began constructing new destroyers with a class of six to be completed by 1941. The 120mm (4.7in) guns were housed in single mounts, one forward, one aft and one amidships. Sunk by an internal explosion in 1941, then raised, it served until 1958, and was expended as a target in August 1962.

SPECIFICATIONS	
Type:	Swedish destroyer
Displacement:	1219 tonnes (1200 tons)
Dimensions:	94.6m x 9m x 3.8m (310ft 4in x 29ft 6in x 12ft 6in)
Machinery:	Twin screws, turbines
Top speed:	42 knots
Main armament:	Three 120mm (4.7in) guns, six 533mm (21in) torpedo tubes
Launched:	October 1935

TIMELINE 1931 1935 1938

DESTROYERS, PART 8: GERMAN & OTHER NAVIES

Vasilefs Georgios

Built for the Greek Navy in Glasgow to the British 'G'-class model, with modified armament, the ship was damaged at Salamis by German bombs. When Greece fell, it was made operational by the Germans as *ZG 3*, later named *Hermes*. Disabled by air attack in April 1943, it was scuttled in the harbour mouth at Tunis.

SPECIFICATIONS	
Type:	Greek destroyer
Displacement:	2123.4 tonnes (2090 tons) full load
Dimensions:	101.2m x 10.4m x 3m (332ft x 34ft 1in x 9ft 10in)
Machinery:	Twin screws, geared turbines
Top speed:	32 knots
Main armament:	Four 127mm (5in) guns, eight 533mm (21in) torpedo tubes
Complement:	215
Launched:	1938

Z51

This was intended as a prototype for fleet torpedo boats, more lightly armed than previous German destroyer types but more manoeuvrable, and with a greater array of anti-aircraft weapons. *Z51*, while under construction in Bremen, was sunk by RAF Mosquito bombers in March 1945. No others were built.

SPECIFICATIONS	
Type:	German destroyer
Displacement:	2674.1 tonnes (2632 tons)
Dimensions:	114.3m x 11m x 4m (375ft x 37ft 8in x 13ft 1in)
Machinery:	Triple screws, diesels
Top speed:	36.5 knots
Main armament:	Four 127mm (5in) guns, six 533mm (21in) torpedo tubes
Complement:	235
Launched:	1944

Araguaya

Araguaya and its five sisters were built to replace six Brazilian destroyers taken over by Britain's Royal Navy at the outbreak of World War II. They followed the same original design but used American equipment. All were built between 1943 and 1946 at the Ilha das Cobras Navy Yard. *Araguaya* was discarded in 1974.

SPECIFICATIONS	
Type:	Brazilian destroyer
Displacement:	1829 tonnes (1800 tons)
Dimensions:	98.5m x 10.7m x 2.6m (323ft x 35ft x 8ft 6in)
Machinery:	Twin screws, geared turbines
Top speed:	35.5 knots
Main armament:	Four 127mm (5in) guns, two 40mm (1.57in) guns
Launched:	1946

Gunboats & Motor Boats

Intended for close-quarters and inshore hostilities, the motor gun boat could also be used on short-range coastal raids. The torpedo boat was also motorized, and the Soviets in particular built many in the 1930s. Larger gunboats made longer-range patrols, or were designed for specific locations, including lakes and rivers.

Eritrea

Officially designated as a sloop, *Eritrea* could use its diesel and electric motors independently or together. Maximum range was 9500km (5000 miles) at 15.3 knots. Refitted as a minelayer in 1940–41, it was captured by the British in 1943. Handed to France in 1948, it was renamed *Francis Garnier*, serving until 1966.

SPECIFICATIONS	
Type:	Italian sloop
Displacement:	3117 tonnes (3068 tons)
Dimensions:	96.9m x 13.3m x 4.7m (318ft x 43ft 8in x 15ft 5in)
Machinery:	Twin screws, diesel engines plus electric drive
Top speed:	18 knots
Main armament:	Four 120mm (4.7in) guns
Launched:	September 1936

Dragonfly

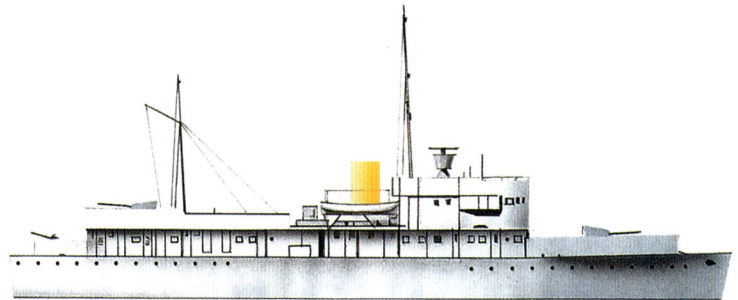

Dragonfly was one of a class of four river gunboats. These were compact with a shallow draught, able to navigate shallow rivers. Engines developed 3800hp and they carried 90 tonnes (90 tons) of fuel oil. *Dragonfly* was sunk by Japanese dive bombers while trying to escape from Singapore on 14 February 1942.

SPECIFICATIONS	
Type:	British gunboat
Displacement:	726 tonnes (715 tons)
Dimensions:	60m x 10m x 1.8m (196ft 6in x 33ft 8in x 6ft 2in)
Machinery:	Twin screws, turbines
Top speed:	17 knots
Main armament:	Two 102mm (4in) guns
Complement:	74
Launched:	1938

TIMELINE

1936  1938

GUNBOATS & MOTOR BOATS

G5

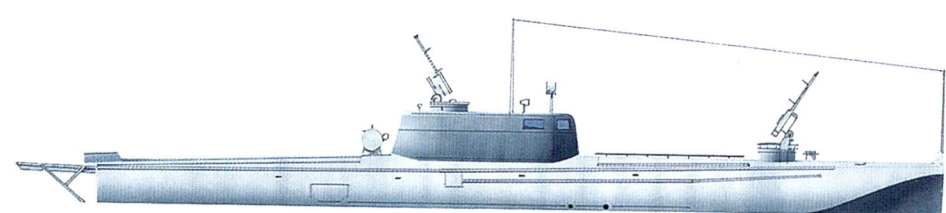

SPECIFICATIONS	
Type:	Soviet torpedo gunboat
Displacement:	14 tonnes (13.7 tons)
Dimensions:	19.1m x 3.4m x 0.75m (62ft 6in x 11ft x 2ft 6in)
Machinery:	Twin screws, petrol engines
Top speed:	45 knots
Main armament:	Two 12.7mm (.5in) guns, two 533mm (21in) torpedo tubes
Launched:	1938

G5 was one in a class of about 295 high-speed vessels, conceived in the early 1930s. Many had Isotta Fraschini engines, which were generally reliable, though Soviet-built versions had a poorer record. Torpedoes were launched from aft, and as they struck the water the vessel had to veer sideways out of their way.

D 3 Type MTB

SPECIFICATIONS	
Type:	Soviet motor torpedo boat
Displacement:	32.5 tonnes (32 tons)
Dimensions:	21.6m x 3.95m x 1.35m (71ft x 13ft x 4ft 6in)
Machinery:	Triple screws, GAM-34FN petrol engines
Top speed:	39 knots
Main armament:	Two 533mm (21in) torpedo cradles
Complement:	9–14
Launched:	1939–45

Around 130 craft of this type were built for the Soviet Navy, mainly for use in the Baltic Sea. The torpedoes were carried in and launched from cradles rather than tubes. Though small compared with their German counterparts, and basic in construction, they were effective boats, able to withstand severe sea conditions.

Fairmile Type C

SPECIFICATIONS	
Type:	British motor gunboat
Displacement:	70 tonnes (69 tons)
Dimensions:	33.55m x 6.5m x 1.75m (110ft x 17ft 5in x 5ft 8in)
Machinery:	Triple screws, petrol engines
Top speed:	27 knots
Main armament:	Two 2pdr pom-pom guns, eight machine-guns
Complement:	16
Launched:	Built from 1941

These wooden-hulled gunboats were enlargements of the RN's Type A motor launch, fitted with Hall-Scott petrol engines and four anti-submarine depth-charges. The type was a failure. The boats had wide turning circles and were exposed while exchanging fire, and noisy motors made clandestine use difficult.

1939

1941

SHIP TYPES 1930–1949

Light Cruisers: Part 1

The London Naval Treaty of 1930 made no distinction between light and heavy cruisers by displacement, but only by gun calibre. A light cruiser was permitted guns of 155mm (6.1in) or less, while a heavy cruiser could be armed with 205mm (8in) guns. The maximum displacement allowed was 10,000 tons (10,106 tonnes).

Arethusa

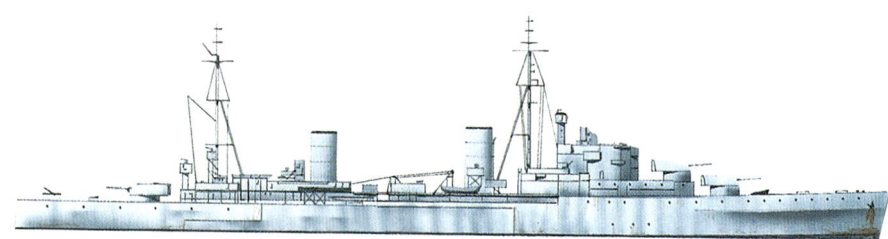

Arethusa and three companion ships were an attempt to create the smallest possible cruiser with reasonable armament and performance. They resembled the slightly longer *Perth* class of 1933. Two of the group were lost in World War II. *Arethusa* was broken up in 1950; one ship, *Aurora*, was sold to China in 1948.

SPECIFICATIONS
Type:	British cruiser
Displacement:	6822 tonnes (6715 tons)
Dimensions:	154m x 15.5m x 5m (506ft x 51ft x 16ft 6in)
Machinery:	Quadruple screws, geared turbines
Main armament:	Six 152mm (6in) guns, four 102mm (4in) guns
Armour:	51mm (2in) belt
Launched:	1932

Emile Bertin

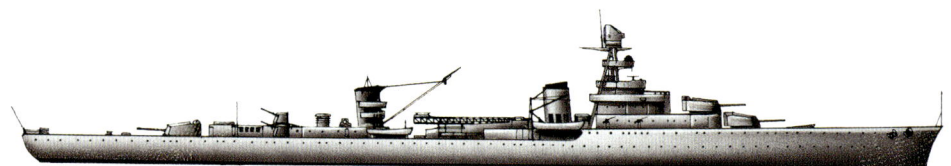

This light cruiser was built to hunt commerce raiders and submarines, with a seaplane. On the fall of France in 1940, it was at Martinique, where it was disarmed. In 1944–45, it was refitted in the United States, with new armament. The aircraft catapult was removed. *Emile Bertin* was scrapped in 1959.

SPECIFICATIONS
Type:	French cruiser
Displacement:	8615.7 tonnes (8480 tons)
Dimensions:	177m x 16m x 6.6m (580ft 8in x 52ft 6in x 21ft 8in)
Machinery:	Quadruple screws, geared turbines
Top speed:	34 knots
Main armament:	Nine 152mm (6in) guns, six 550mm (21.7in) torpedo tubes
Armour:	25mm (1in) magazines and deck
Complement:	711
Launched:	1933

TIMELINE

1932  1933

LIGHT CRUISERS: PART 1

Gotland

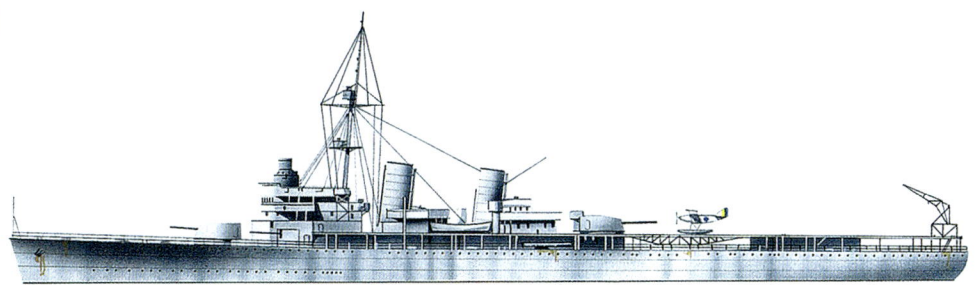

SPECIFICATIONS	
Type:	Swedish cruiser
Displacement:	5638 tonnes (5550 tons)
Dimensions:	134.8m x 15.4m x 5.5m (442ft 3in x 50ft 6in x 18ft)
Machinery:	Twin screws, turbines
Top speed:	28 knots
Main armament:	Six 152mm (6in) guns
Launched:	1933

Gotland was planned as a aircraft carrier with 12 float planes, but the design was revised and the designation changed to aircraft cruiser. It usually carried six planes aft, but had room for eight on deck and three below. In 1943–44, it was converted into an anti-aircraft cruiser. It was removed from the list in 1960.

Tromp

SPECIFICATIONS	
Type:	Dutch cruiser
Displacement:	4337.8 tonnes (4860 tons)
Dimensions:	132m x 12.4m x 4.2m (433ft x 40ft 8in x 13ft 9in)
Machinery:	Twin screws, geared turbines
Top speed:	33.5 knots
Main armament:	Six 150mm (5.9in) guns, six 533mm (21in) torpedo tubes
Armour:	15mm (.7in) belt, 30mm (1.2in) sides, 25mm (1in) deck
Complement:	309
Launched:	1937

A scout cruiser, *Tromp* escaped to Britain when the Germans occupied Holland and served as an Allied ship throughout World War II, mostly in the Far East. It carried one reconnaissance aircraft. After 1945, it remained in the Dutch Navy until 1958, when it was decommissioned but used as an accommodation ship.

Chapayev

SPECIFICATIONS	
Type:	Soviet cruiser
Displacement:	15,240 tonnes (15,000 tons) full load
Dimensions:	201m x 19.7m x 6.4m (659ft 5in x 64ft 8in x 21ft)
Machinery:	Twin screws, geared turbines, cruising diesels
Top speed:	34 knots
Main armament:	Twelve 152mm (6in) guns, eight 100mm (3.9in) guns
Complement:	840
Launched:	1940

Laid down at St Petersburg (then Leningrad), *Chapayev* was not completed until 1950. With a standard displacement of 11,480 tonnes (11,300 tons), it was a large ship to carry only 152mm (6in) guns. The design and armament were virtually obsolete and in 1960 it was disarmed and hulked. It was broken up in 1964.

Light Cruisers: Part 2

Great Britain had by far the largest number of light cruisers, with 81 in commission in 1939, some of them quite elderly. Twenty-three were lost in the course of World War II. The US Navy had 47, Italy had nine, France 12, and the Soviet Union four.

Jacob van Heemskerck

Jacob van Heemskerck was envisaged as a flotilla leader, but the plans were changed in 1938. Then, after the Nazi invasion of Holland in 1939, the ship was taken to Britain for completion and 102mm (4in) guns were mounted, as heavier armament was not available. *Jacob van Heemskerck* was scrapped in 1958.

SPECIFICATIONS

Type:	Dutch cruiser
Displacement:	4282 tonnes (4215 tons)
Dimensions:	131m x 12m x 4.5m (433ft x 40ft 9in x 15ft)
Machinery:	Twin screws, turbines
Top speed:	34.5 knots
Main armament:	Eight 102mm (4in) guns
Launched:	September 1939

Attilio Regolo

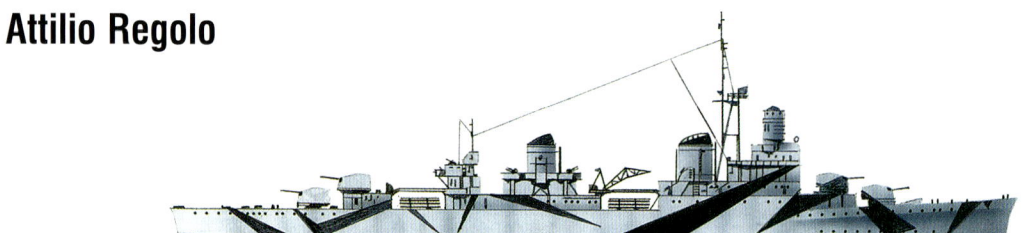

Attilio Regolo was one of 12 fast cruisers of the 'Capitani Romani' class laid down in 1939. Five of the class were not completed, and broken up on the stocks; three were lost in action; and one was scuttled to avoid capture. *Attilio Regolo* was transferred to France in 1948.

SPECIFICATIONS

Type:	Italian cruiser
Displacement:	5419 tonnes (5334 tons)
Dimensions:	142.9m x 14.4m x 4.9m (469ft x 47ft 3in x 16ft)
Machinery:	Twin screws, turbines
Top speed:	42 knots
Main armament:	Eight 135mm (5.4in) guns
Armour:	20mm (0.8in) over guns
Launched:	August 1940

TIMELINE

1939 1940 1941

LIGHT CRUISERS: PART 2

Caio Mario

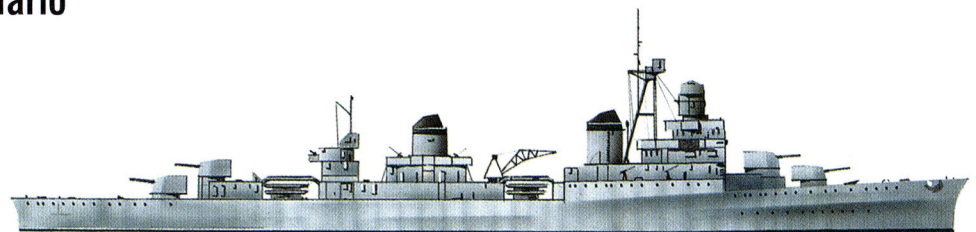

Caio Mario was one of a class of fast cruisers intended as anti-destroyer escorts as well as scouts. High speed was achieved at the expense of protection, and only a splinter-proof deck covered the machinery. It was not yet completed when it was scuttled at La Spezia in 1943 to prevent capture by the Germans.

SPECIFICATIONS	
Type:	Italian cruiser
Displacement:	5419 tonnes (5334 tons)
Dimensions:	143m x 14m x 4.8m (469ft 1in x 46ft x 15ft 7in)
Machinery:	Twin screws, turbines
Top speed:	40 knots
Main armament:	Eight 135mm (5.3in) guns
Launched:	August 1941

Ulpio Traiano

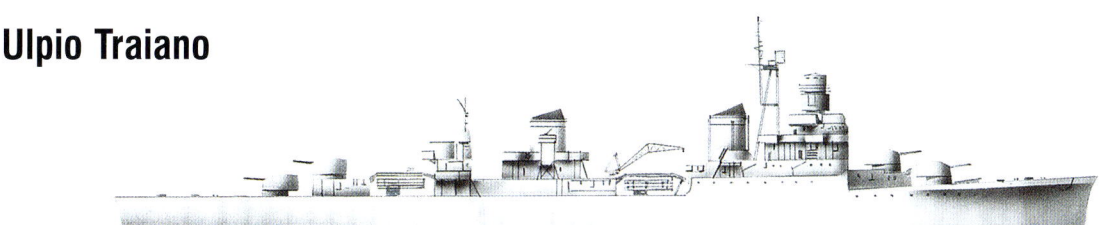

Ulpio Traiano was a sister ship of Attilio Regolo. To achieve a high operating speed, protective plating was only 15mm (0.6in) thick on the bridge, and 20mm (0.8in) on the four twin turrets. Ulpio Traiano was sunk by British 'human torpedo' commando units while still completing at Palermo harbour in 1943.

SPECIFICATIONS	
Type:	Italian cruiser
Displacement:	5420 tonnes (5334 tons)
Dimensions:	143m x 14.4m x 4.9m (468ft 10in x 47ft 3in x 16ft)
Machinery:	Twin screws, turbines
Top speed:	40 knots
Main armament:	Eight 135mm (5.3in) guns
Launched:	1942

Göta Lejon

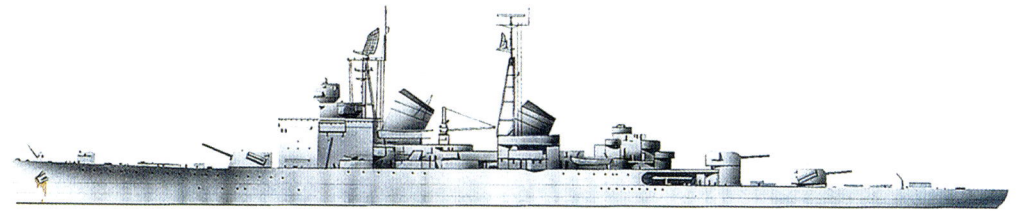

Sweden laid down two well-armed and strongly protected cruisers in 1943. Two raked funnels gave Göta Lejon and its sister Tre Kronor a distinctive appearance, enhanced on Göta Lejon by the tower bridge structure added during rebuilding in 1957–58. Göta Lejon was sold to Chile in 1971.

SPECIFICATIONS	
Type:	Swedish cruiser
Displacement:	9347 tonnes (9200 tons)
Dimensions:	182m x 6.7m x 6.5m (597ft x 22ft x 21ft 4in)
Machinery:	Twin screws, turbines
Top speed:	33 knots
Main armament:	Seven 152mm (6in) guns
Launched:	November 1945

SHIP TYPES 1930–1949

Landing Craft & Command Ships

Thousands of landing craft were built between 1942 and 1945 to carry and disembark combat-ready troops, tanks, trucks and support vehicles. Varying in size from 200 to several thousand tonnes, they were a new item in the naval armoury. Supported by escort craft, most also carried light weapons against air attack.

LCI (L)

The Landing Craft Infantry (Large) was designed in the UK as a vessel for raids, carrying up to 188 troops. Over 1000 were built in the United States and Britain. With a range of 15,750km (8,500nm), they could cross the Atlantic. Full load doubled their displacement and gave a stern depth of 1.5m (5ft).

SPECIFICATIONS	
Type:	US–British landing craft
Displacement:	197 tonnes (194 tons)
Dimensions:	48.3m x 7.2m x .8m (158ft 6in x 23ft 8in x 2ft 8in)
Machinery:	Twin screws, diesels
Top speed:	15.5 knots
Main armament:	Four 20mm (0.79in) guns
Complement:	24
Launched:	1942–44

Ashland

A self-propelling dry-dock, the LSD pumped its ballast tanks full or dry to lower or raise the stern section for the entrance and exit of landing craft (LCT). Three of these could be fitted, each holding five medium-size tanks. *Ashland* remained on the Navy list until 1970. The concept has been refined in later naval craft.

SPECIFICATIONS	
Type:	US landing ship (LSD)
Displacement:	8057 tonnes (7930 tons) full load
Dimensions:	139.5m x 22m x 4.8m (457ft 9in x 72ft 2in x 15ft)
Machinery:	Twin screws, triple expansion reciprocating engines
Top speed:	15.5 knots
Main armament:	One 127mm (5in) gun, twelve 40mm (1.57in) and sixteen 20mm (0.79in) guns
Complement:	254
Launched:	1942

TIMELINE

1942  1943

LANDING CRAFT & COMMAND SHIPS

Appalachian

SPECIFICATIONS	
Type:	US command ship
Displacement:	14,133 tonnes (13,910 tons)
Dimensions:	132.6m x 19.2m x 7.3m (435ft x 63ft x 24ft)
Machinery:	Single-screw, turbine
Speed:	17 knots
Main armament:	Two 127mm (5in) guns, eight 40mm (1.57in) guns
Launched:	1943

Appalachian acted as a headquarters vessel ensuring communication and coordination in the large-scale amphibious assaults on Japanese-held islands during World War II. It served briefly as Pacific Fleet flagship in 1947, before being removed from the active list that year. It was broken up in 1960.

LSM (R)

SPECIFICATIONS	
Type:	US landing craft/fire support ship
Displacement:	795.5 tonnes (783 tons)
Dimensions:	62m x 10.5m x 1.68m (203ft 6in x 34ft 6in x 5ft 6in)
Machinery:	Twin screws, diesels
Top speed:	13 knots
Main armament:	One 127mm (5in) gun, four 108mm (4.2in) mortars, rockets, light AA guns
Complement:	143
Launched:	Built 1944–45

The R variant of the Landing Ship Medium was a fire-support ship, bristling with guns, mortars and rocket launchers to give fire support during troop landings. Dimensions and specifications varied during construction. The earlier ships had a greater operating range, though all could make ocean passages.

T1

SPECIFICATIONS	
Type:	Japanese landing-ship
Displacement:	2235.2 tonnes (2200 tons) full load
Dimensions:	96m x 10.2m x 3.6m (315ft x 33ft 5in x 11ft 10in)
Machinery:	Single screw, geared turbines
Top speed:	22 knots
Main armament:	Two 127mm (5in) guns
Launched:	1944

Instead of the dock-type or crane-fitted landing ship, the Japanese produced this type, able to launch five fully-loaded landing craft from rails running off the specially shaped stern. Some of the 22 built were modified in 1945 to launch cradle-mounted midget submarines. Only a few *T1*s survived the war.

1944

SHIP TYPES 1930–1949

Minelayers

Estimates of the number of mines laid between 1939 and 1945 range from 600,000 to over a million. Aircraft dropped mines but the majority were laid from ships. The classic minelayer was a fast ship, purpose-built, but many ships were adapted for the purpose, and destroyers often carried a stock of mines.

Gouden Leeuw

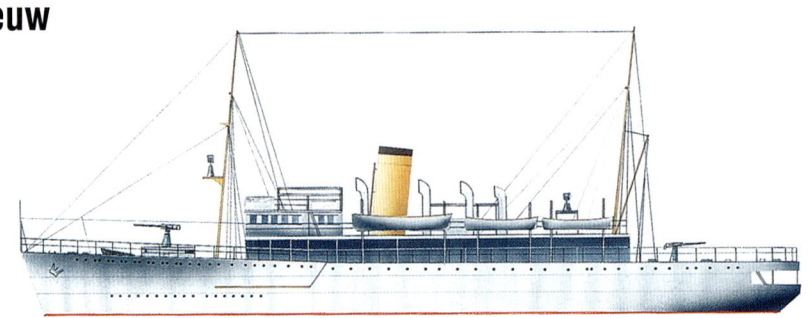

Built for service in the Far East, *Gouden Leeuw* could carry up to 250 mines, depending on size and type, held in a magazine aft, and laid from rails that led to the stern. It was caught and sunk by Japanese warships off Tarakan on 12 January 1942, less than a month after the start of the war in the Pacific.

SPECIFICATIONS	
Type:	Dutch minelayer
Displacement:	1311 tonnes (1291 tons)
Dimensions:	65.8m x 11m x 3.3m (216ft x 36ft x 11ft)
Machinery:	Twin screws, triple expansion engines
Top speed:	15 knots
Main armament:	Two 76mm (3in) anti-aircraft guns
Launched:	1931

Gryf

Gryf was primarily a minelayer carrying 600 mines, though it was also intended to function as a training vessel and as a state yacht. Built in France, delivered in 1938, it was deliberately sunk in a floating dry-dock at Hela, as a defensive battery, on 1 September 1939. On the 3rd it was destroyed by German aircraft.

SPECIFICATIONS	
Type:	Polish minelayer
Displacement:	2286 tonnes (2250 tons)
Dimensions:	103.2m x 13.1m x 3.6m (338ft 7in x 43ft x 11ft 10in)
Machinery:	Twin screws, diesels
Top speed:	20 knots
Main armament:	Six 120mm (4.7in) guns
Complement:	205
Launched:	1936

TIMELINE
1931 1936 1940

MINELAYERS

Tsugaru

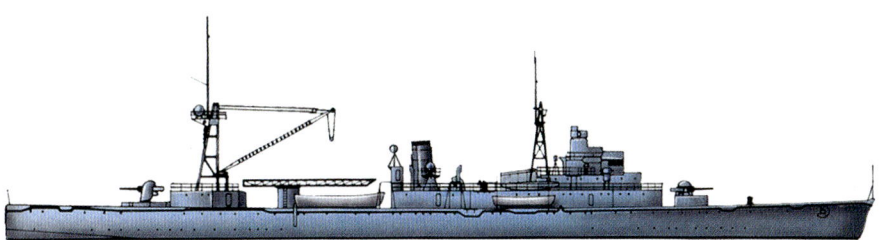

SPECIFICATIONS	
Type:	Japanese minelayer
Displacement:	6705.6 tonnes (6600 tons) full load
Dimensions:	124.5m x 15.6m x 4.9m (408ft 6in x 51ft 3in x 16ft 2in)
Machinery:	Twin screws, geared turbines
Top speed:	20 knots
Main armament:	Four 127mm (5in) guns
Launched:	1940

Comparable in size to the British *Abdiel* class (see *Ariadne*), this was one of only two larger Japanese minelayers. As with the British ships, the mines were held on a deck running almost full length, and dropped from the stern. *Tsugaru* also carried an aircraft. It was torpedoed by a US submarine in June 1944.

Artevelde

SPECIFICATIONS	
Type:	Belgian minelayer and royal yacht
Displacement:	2306 tonnes (2270 tons)
Dimensions:	98.5m x 10.5m x 3.3m (323ft 2in x 34ft 5in x 10ft 10in)
Machinery:	Twin screws, geared turbines
Top speed:	28.5 knots
Main armament:	Four 104mm (4.1in) guns, 120 mines
Launched:	1940

This multi-purpose vessel was also intended to operate as a fishery patrol ship. Captured while still building in May 1940, *Artevelde* was completed by the Germans and renamed *Lorelei*. At the end of World War II, it was returned to Belgium, where it served until the early 1950s. It was broken up in 1954–55.

Ariadne

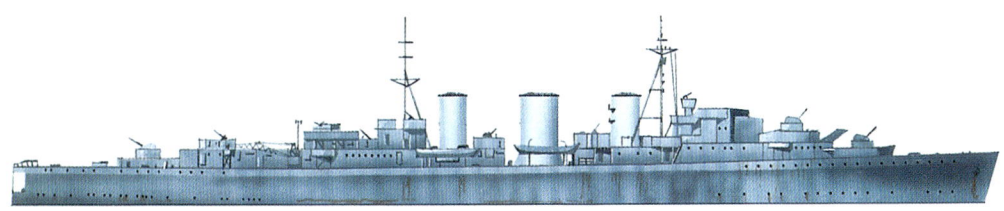

SPECIFICATIONS	
Type:	British cruiser/minelayer
Displacement:	4064 tonnes (4000 tons)
Dimensions:	127.4m x 12.2m x 4.5m (418ft x 40ft x 14ft 9in)
Machinery:	Twin screws, turbines
Top speed:	40 knots
Main armament:	Six 102mm (4in) guns, 100–156 mines
Launched:	1943

Ariadne was one of six fast minelaying cruisers. They had a small silhouette, and good armament against both air and surface attack. All saw extensive war service, including hazardous ammunition runs to Malta, using their high speed. Three were sunk through enemy action. *Ariadne* was broken up in 1965.

1943

SHIP TYPES 1930–1949

Minesweepers

Between 600,000 and a million mines were laid in World War II. Magnetic mines, invented in Germany, replaced contact mines that exploded on touch. The Allies had to find new ways to deal with them. Instead of cutting wires, minesweepers towed electrically-charged cables between two ships. Their task remained hazardous.

Espiègle

One of the *Algerine* class of minesweepers, *Espiègle* was among relatively few to have turbine engines. Early minesweepers had often been converted trawlers, but this was a more substantial and capable ship. With a range of 22,000km (12,000 miles) at 12 knots, it could go further and stay at sea much longer.

SPECIFICATIONS	
Type:	British minesweeper
Displacement:	995.7 tonnes (980 tons)
Dimensions:	65.6m x 10.8m x 3.2m (225ft x 35ft 6in x 10ft 6in)
Machinery:	Twin screws, turbines
Top speed:	16.5 knots
Main Armament:	One 102mm (4in) gun
Complement:	85
Launched:	1942

YMS 100

The Yard Mine Sweepers were wooden-hulled small warships intended for coastal service. Even so, many made trans-ocean voyages to act as advance way-clearers for invasion forces far from the United States. A submarine-chaser version was tried, but the diesel motors could not produce the necessary speed.

SPECIFICATIONS	
Type:	US minesweeper
Displacement:	365.7 tonnes (360 tons)
Dimensions:	41.45m x 7.45m x 2.35m (136ft x 24ft 6in x 7ft 9in)
Machinery:	Twin screws, diesels
Top speed:	15 knots
Main Armament:	One 76mm (3in) gun
Complement:	60
Launched:	Built 1942–44

TIMELINE 1942 1943

MINESWEEPERS

T 371

SPECIFICATIONS	
Type:	Soviet minesweeper
Displacement:	152.4 tonnes (150 tons)
Dimensions:	39m x 5m x 1.5m (127ft 11in x 18ft x 4ft 11in)
Machinery:	Twin screws, diesels
Top speed:	14 knots
Main Armament:	Two 45mm (1.8in) guns
Complement:	32
Launched:	1943

The 'T' class minesweepers, intended for inshore work, were war-production vessels, built quickly and economically from welded flat steel sections and driven by modified tank engines. Protection was minimal. About 145 had been launched by the end of World War II, and another 100 or so were built later.

Daino

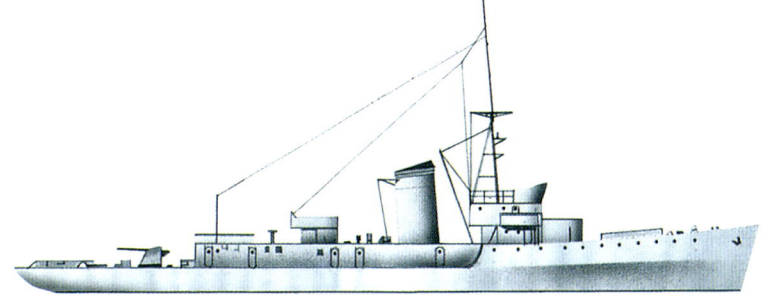

SPECIFICATIONS	
Type:	Italian minesweeper
Displacement:	850 tonnes (838 tons)
Dimensions:	68m x 9m x 2m (224ft 6in x 29ft 6in x 7ft 3in)
Machinery:	Twin screws, triple expansion engines
Top speed:	14 knots
Launched:	1945

Built of prefabricated sections as the German minesweeper *B2* (later *M802*), this served with the German Minesweeping Administration in the North and Baltic seas at the end of World War II. Transferred to Italy in 1949 as *Daino*, it was a minesweeper, then an escort ship. In 1960 it became an unarmed survey vessel.

Guadiaro

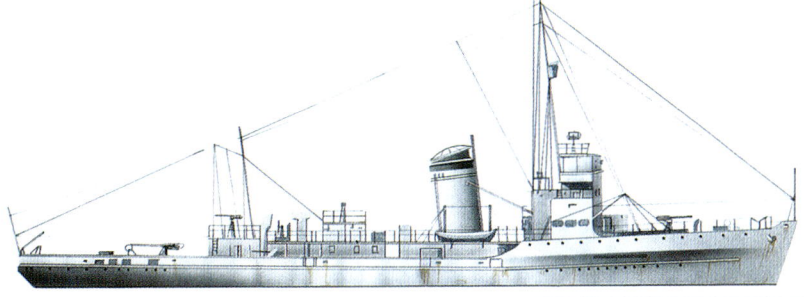

SPECIFICATIONS	
Type:	Spanish minesweeper
Displacement:	782 tonnes (770 tons)
Dimensions:	74.3m x 10.2m x 3.7m (243ft 9in x 33ft 6in x 12ft)
Machinery:	Twin screws, triple expansion engines plus exhaust turbines
Top speed:	16 knots
Main armament:	Two 20mm (0.79in) anti-aircraft guns
Launched:	June 1950

Guadiaro was in the first group of minesweepers built for the Spanish Navy after World War II. The design was modelled on the successful *Bidasoa*, launched in 1943 and built to the plan of the coal-fired German M1940 sweepers. *Guadiaro* was modernized between 1959 and 1960, and withdrawn from service by 1980.

1945    1950

SHIP TYPES 1930–1949

Repair, Supply & Support Ships

The increasing scale of fleets, especially in submarines and destroyers, required 'mother ships' to supply food, stores and fuel. The complexity of air-sea combined operations, and the advance of radar and other wireless technology, also brought about the command ship, a centre for co-ordination and communication.

Gustave Zédé

The German submarine depot ship *Saar* was acquired by France in 1947, and commissioned into the French Navy in 1949 as *Gustave Zédé*. During the 1960s, it was France's only ship to carry a fully comprehensive command system. By 1967, the vessel had become the flagship of the Fleet Training Centre.

SPECIFICATIONS

Type:	French command ship
Displacement:	3282 tonnes (3230 tons)
Dimensions:	93.8m x 13.5m x 4.2m (308ft x 44ft 3in x 14ft)
Machinery:	Twin screws, diesel engines
Top speed:	16 knots
Main armament:	Three 104mm (4.1in) guns
Launched:	April 1934

Togo

Togo was a merchant vessel, equipped as an armed raider, *Coronel*, but it failed to break out through the English Channel. With its original name, it was refitted to operate Freya and Würzburg radar, and radio communications systems. Stationed in the Baltic Sea, it was later used to carry troops, and then refugees.

SPECIFICATIONS

Type:	German fighter direction ship
Displacement:	12,903 tonnes (12,700 tons)
Dimensions:	134m x 17.9m x 7.9m (439ft 7in x 58ft 9in x 25ft)
Machinery:	Single screw, two-stroke double-acting diesel engine
Top speed:	16 knots
Main armament:	Three 105mm (4.1in) guns, two 40mm (1.57in) guns
Launched:	1940

TIMELINE

1934  1940

REPAIR, SUPPLY & SUPPORT SHIPS

Fulton

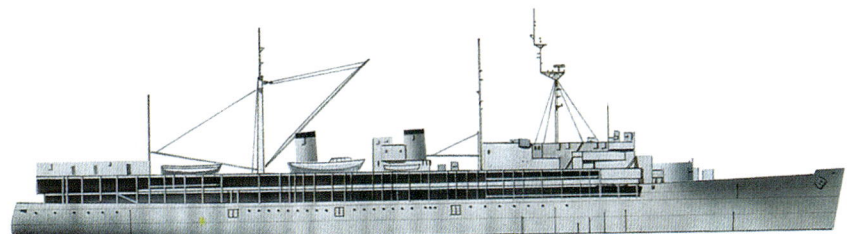

SPECIFICATIONS	
Type:	American submarine tender
Displacement:	18,288 tonnes (18,000 tons)
Dimensions:	161.5m x 22.4m x 7.8m (529ft 10in x 73ft 6in x 25ft 7in)
Machinery:	Twin screws, diesel electric engines
Top speed:	15 knots
Launched:	December 1940

One of a class of seven ships, *Fulton* established seaplane bases in the Panama Canal in December 1941, a prelude to the setting-up of a defence zone around the canal. It served as a submarine tender at Midway during 1942. In the 1950s, its facilities were updated to enable it to support nuclear attack submarines.

Jason

SPECIFICATIONS	
Type:	US repair ship
Displacement:	16,418 tonnes (16,160 tons)
Dimensions:	161.3m x 22.3m x 7m (529ft 2in x 73ft 2in x 23ft 4in)
Machinery:	Twin screws, turbines
Top speed:	19.2 knots
Main armament:	Four 127mm (5in) guns
Complement:	1336
Launched:	December 1940

In 1938, the US Navy authorized *Jason* as a purpose-built repair vessel, with three similar ships to follow. Capable of a multitude of repair and maintenance tasks, it could serve several major surface vessels at once. By the 1980s, the 127mm (5in) guns had been replaced with four 20mm (0.79in) guns.

Norton Sound

SPECIFICATIONS	
Type:	US seaplane tender
Displacement:	15,341.6 tonnes (15,100 tons)
Dimensions:	164.7m x 21.1m x 6.8m (540ft 5in x 69ft 3in x 22ft 3in)
Machinery:	Twin screws, geared turbines
Top speed:	19 knots
Main armament:	Four 127mm (5in) guns
Complement:	1247
Launched:	1943

One of four *Currituck*-class tenders, commissioned in 1944, *Norton Sound* was built to warship standards. Its after-deck mounted an H-5 hydraulic catapult. Most seaplane tenders, built on merchant ship hulls, were discarded after 1945, but this ship served into the 1980s, latterly as a guided-missile trials ship.

1943

SHIP TYPES 1930–1949

Submarines of the 1930s: Part 1

Big-gun submarines were banned by treaty in 1930, so designers focused their attention on the submarine as a torpedo vehicle. Engine improvements were also pursued, and in the United States lightweight, high-power diesel engines were developed, affording more space for fuel, spare torpedoes and the crew.

Nautilus

Nautilus was one of three V-class submarines. These were slow to dive due to their size and shape – a raised centre deck to improve the guns' field of fire. Re-numbered SS16 in 1931, Nautilus was refitted in 1940 to carry 5104 litres (19,320 gallons) of aviation fuel for seaplanes. It was scrapped in 1945.

SPECIFICATIONS	
Type:	US submarine
Displacement:	2773 tonnes (2730 tons) [surface], 3962 tonnes (3900 tons) [submerged]
Dimensions:	113m x 10m (370ft x 33ft 3in)
Machinery:	Twin screws, diesel engines [surface], electric motors [submerged]
Top speed:	17 knots [surface], 8 knots [submerged]
Main armament:	Two 152mm (6in) guns, six 533mm (21in) torpedo tubes
Launched:	March 1930

Delfino

Delfino was completed in 1931. A long-range boat, it was equipped with a gun of sufficient calibre to sink merchant ships when surfaced. A light anti-aircraft gun was mounted on the rear platform of the conning tower. From 1942, Delfino was used for training and transport duties. It was sunk in 1943.

SPECIFICATIONS	
Type:	Italian submarine
Displacement:	948 tonnes (933 tons) [surface], 1160 tonnes (1142 tons) [submerged]
Dimensions:	70m x 7m x 7m (229ft x 23ft 7in x 23ft 7in)
Machinery:	Twin screws, diesel engines [surface], electric motors [submerged]
Top speed:	15 knots [surface], 8 knots [submerged]
Main armament:	Eight 533mm (21in) torpedo tubes, one 102mm (4in) gun
Launched:	April 1930

TIMELINE 1930 1932

SUBMARINES OF THE 1930s: PART 1

Dolphin

SPECIFICATIONS	
Type:	US submarine
Displacement:	1585 tonnes (1560 tons) [surface], 2275 tonnes (2240 tons) [submerged]
Dimensions:	97m x 8.5m x 4m (319ft 3in x 27ft 9in x 13ft 3in)
Machinery:	Twin screws, diesel engines [surface], electric motors [submerged]
Top speed:	17 knots [surface], 18 knots [submerged]
Main armament:	Six 533mm (21in) torpedo tubes, one 102mm (4in) gun
Launched:	March 1932

Dolphin was an experimental boat, but the attempt to pack too many features from bigger craft into a relatively small hull was not a success, and the US Navy did not develop a class from it. During World War II, it was used for crew training duties. It was broken up in 1946.

U-2

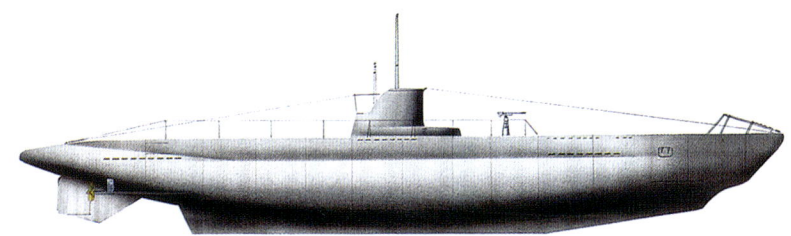

SPECIFICATIONS	
Type:	German submarine
Displacement:	254 tonnes (250 tons) [surface], 302 tonnes (298 tons) [submerged]
Dimensions:	40.9m x 4.1m x 3.8m (133ft 2in x 13ft 5in x 12ft 6in)
Machinery:	Twin screws, diesel engines [surface], electric motors [submerged]
Top speed:	13 knots [surface], 7 knots [submerged]
Main armament:	Three 533mm (21in) torpedo tubes, one 20mm (0.79in) gun
Launched:	July 1935

Forbidden to build or possess submarines after World War I, Germany set up clandestine design teams in Spain, Holland and the Soviet Union in the 1920s. A first boat built for Finland in 1927 was the basis for *U-2*, intended for coastal service. All early Type II boats were used for training. *U-2* was sunk in April 1944.

Enrico Tazzoli

SPECIFICATIONS	
Type:	Italian submarine
Displacement:	1574 tonnes (1550 tons) [surface], 2092 tonnes (2060 tons) [submerged]
Dimensions:	84.3m x 7.7m x 5.2m (276ft 6in x 25ft 3in x 17ft)
Machinery:	Twin screws, diesel engines [surface], electric motors [submerged]
Top speed:	17 knots [surface], 8 knots [submerged]
Main armament:	Eight 533mm (21mm) torpedo tubes, two 120mm (4.7in) guns
Launched:	October 1935

Enrico Tazzoli took part in the Spanish Civil War, and served in the Mediterranean for the early part of World War II. In 1940, it transferred to the Atlantic. In 1942, it was refitted to transport supplies to Japan, but on its first voyage in 1943 it disappeared without trace in the Bay of Biscay.

1935

Submarines of the 1930s: Part 2

Italy built over 100 submarines in the 1930s and many served, sometimes covertly, on behalf of Franco's Nationalist forces in the Spanish Civil War (1936–39). These were mainly short-range boats, as were most British submarines of the era. The Americans were more concerned with submarines capable of long-range cruising.

Aradam

SPECIFICATIONS	
Type:	Italian submarine
Displacement:	691 tonnes (680 tons) [surface], 880 tonnes (866 tons) [submerged]
Dimensions:	60.2m x 6.5m x 4.6m (197ft 6in x 21ft 4in x 15ft)
Machinery:	Twin screws, diesel engines [surface], electric [submerged]
Top speed:	14 knots [surface], 7 knots [submerged]
Main armament:	Six 530mm (21in) torpedo tubes, one 100mm (4in) gun
Launched:	1936

Aradam was one of a class of 17 sturdy short-range vessels. All operated in the Mediterranean Sea during World War II, except *Macalle*, which served in the Red Sea. *Aradam* was scuttled in September 1943 in Genoa harbour to avoid capture. Raised by the Germans, it was sunk by bombing the following year.

Diaspro

SPECIFICATIONS	
Type:	Italian submarine
Displacement:	711 tonnes (700 tons) [surface], 873 tonnes (860 tons) [submerged]
Dimensions:	60m x 6.4m x 4.6m (197ft 5in x 21ft 2in x 15ft)
Machinery:	Twin screws, diesel engines [surface], electric motors [submerged]
Top speed:	14 knots [surface], 8 knots [submerged]
Main armament:	Six 533mm (21in) torpedo tubes, one 100mm (3.9in) gun
Launched:	July 1936

Diaspro was one of 10 short-range boats of the *Perla* class, designed for use in Mediterranean waters, with a maximum operational depth of 70–80m (230–262ft). All were engaged in the Spanish Civil War, on Spain's east coast, and served in World War II. *Diaspro* was removed from the Navy List in 1948.

TIMELINE

1936

SUBMARINES OF THE 1930s: PART 2

Corallo

Corallo was a short-range submarine of the *Perla* class, all of which served in the Spanish Civil War, where two were ceded to the Nationalist forces. They also served in World War II, and one sank the British cruiser *Bonaventure*. Five were lost, including *Corallo*, sunk in December 1942 by the British sloop *Enchantress*.

SPECIFICATIONS	
Type:	Italian submarine
Displacement:	707 tonnes (696 tons) [surface], 865 tonnes (852 tons) [submerged]
Dimensions:	60m x 6.5m x 5m (197ft 5in x 21ft 2in x 15ft 5in)
Machinery:	Twin screws, diesel engines [surface], electric motors [submerged]
Top speed:	14 knots [surface], 8 knots [submerged]
Main armament:	Six 533mm (21in) torpedo tubes, one 100mm (3.9in) gun
Launched:	August 1936

Dagabur

Dagabur was one of a class of 17. While serving the Nationalists in the Spanish Civil War, two boats were modified to carry small assault craft. These were later used to inflict serious damage on the British vessels *Valiant* and *Queen Elizabeth* in 1941. *Dagabur* was sunk by the British destroyer *Wolverine* in 1942.

SPECIFICATIONS	
Type:	Italian submarine
Displacement:	690 tonnes (680 tons) [surface], 861 tonnes (848 tons) [submerged]
Dimensions:	60m x 6.5m x 4m (197ft 6in x 21ft x 13ft)
Machinery:	Twin screws, diesel engines [surface], electric motors [submerged]
Top speed:	14 knots [surface], 8 knots [submerged]
Main armament:	Six 533mm (21in) torpedo tubes, one 100mm (3.9in) gun
Launched:	November 1936

U-32

U-32 was one of the early Type VII ocean-going submarines, and the basis for all later construction. They were compact, relatively cheap and simple to build, easy to operate and reliable. Between 1941 and 1943, their success in sinking merchant shipping almost defeated Britain. *U-32* was sunk in October 1940.

SPECIFICATIONS	
Type:	German submarine
Displacement:	626 tonnes (616 tons) [surface], 745 tonnes (733 tons) [submerged]
Dimensions:	64.5m x 5.8m x 4.4m (211ft 8in x 19ft x 14ft 5in)
Machinery:	Twin screws, diesel engines [surface], electric motors [submerged]
Top speed:	16 knots [surface], 8 knots [submerged]
Main armament:	Five 533mm (21in) torpedo tubes, one 88mm (3.5in) gun
Launched:	April 1937

1937

Submarines of the 1930s: Part 3

In 1939, the US submarine *Squalus* and the British *Thetis* both accidentally flooded within days of each other, and many lives were lost. The two disasters led to greater attention to safety on board, with interlocks to prevent doors being inadvertently opened, and escape chambers to allow crew members to get out in an emergency.

Dandolo

SPECIFICATIONS	
Type:	Italian submarine
Displacement:	1080 tonnes (1063 tons) [surface], 1338 tonnes (1317 tons) [submerged]
Dimensions:	73m x 7.2m x 5m (239ft 6in x 23ft 8in x 16ft 5in)
Machinery:	Twin screws, diesel engines [surface], electric motors [submerged]
Top speed:	17.4 knots [surface], 8 knots [submerged]
Main armament:	Eight 533mm (21in) torpedo tubes, two 100mm (3.9in) guns
Launched:	November 1937

The *Dandolo*s, single-hull boats with internal ballast tanks, were among Italy's best submarines of World War II. Surface range at 17 knots was 4750km (2500 miles); submerged at 9 knots it was 14,250 kilometres (7500 miles). Maximum operational depth was 100m (328ft). All were lost in action except *Dandolo*.

Brin

SPECIFICATIONS	
Type:	Italian submarine
Displacement:	1032 tonnes (1016 tons) [surface], 1286 tonnes (1266 tons)
Dimensions:	70m x 7m x 4.2m (231ft 4in x 22ft 6in x 13ft 6in)
Machinery:	Twin screws, diesel engines [surface], two electric motors [submerged]
Top speed:	17 knots [surface], 8 knots [submerged]
Main armament:	Eight 533mm (21in) torpedo tubes
Launched:	1938

A long-range boat, *Brin* had a partial double hull developed from the *Archimede* class. Early in World War II, it served in the Mediterranean and Atlantic. In 1943 it was stationed in Ceylon, and after the Italian surrender, helped to train British anti-submarine units in the Indian Ocean.

TIMELINE

Durbo

All 17 vessels in the 600 Series *Adua* class, including *Durbo*, gave good service in World War II, but only one survived it. In 1940, *Durbo* was caught on a patrol close to Gibraltar by the British destroyers *Firedrake* and *Wrestler*. Forced to the surface by depth charges, it was scuttled by its crew.

SPECIFICATIONS	
Type:	Italian submarine
Displacement:	710 tonnes (698 tons) [surface], 880 tonnes (866 tons) [submerged]
Dimensions:	60m x 6.4m x 4m (197ft 6in x 21ft x 3ft)
Machinery:	Twin screws, diesel engines [surface], electric motors [submerged]
Top speed:	14 knots [surface], 7.5 [submerged]
Main armament:	Six 533mm (21in) torpedo tubes, one 100mm (3.9in) gun
Launched:	March 1938

Galvani

Galvani was one of a group of four long-range submarines, developed from the *Archimede* class. Attached to the Red Sea Flotilla, based at Massawa and other ports on the Ethiopian and Somali coast, it sank the British sloop *Pathan* on 23 June 1940, but was itself was sunk on the following day by HMS *Falmouth*.

SPECIFICATIONS	
Type:	Italian submarine
Displacement:	1032 tonnes (1016 tons) [surface], 1286 tonnes (1266 tons) [submerged]
Dimensions:	72.4m x 6.9m x 4.5m (237ft 6in x 22ft x 14ft 11in)
Machinery:	Twin screws, diesel engines [surface], electric motors [submerged]
Top speed:	17.3 knots [surface], 8 knots [submerged]
Main armament:	Eight 533mm (21in) torpedo tubes, one 99mm (3.9in) gun
Launched:	May 1938

Thistle

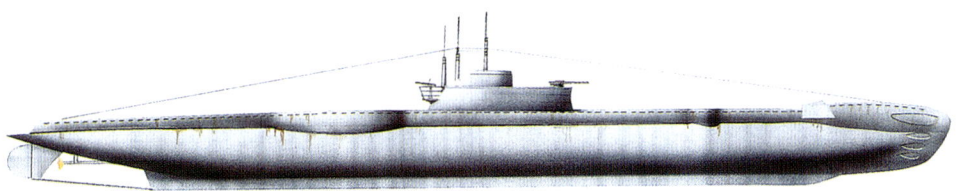

Thistle was one of the first of 21 British 'T'-class submarines, built to replace the previous 'O', 'P' and 'R' classes of ocean-going submarines, and designed to remain at sea for patrols of up to 42 days. *Thistle* was lost in the North Sea on 14 April 1940. Some of the 'T' class continued to serve until 1963.

SPECIFICATIONS	
Type:	British submarine
Displacement:	1347 tonnes (1326 tons) [surface], 1547 tonnes (1523 tons) [submerged]
Dimensions:	83.6m x 8m x 3.6m (274ft 3in x 26ft 6in x 12ft)
Machinery:	Twin screws, diesel engines [surface], electric motors [submerged]
Top speed:	15.25 knots [surface], 9 knots [submerged]
Main armament:	Ten 533mm (21in) torpedo tubes, one 102mm (4in) gun
Launched:	1939

SHIP TYPES 1930–1949

World War II Submarines: Part 1

In 1939, Germany had 57 submarines, of which 38 were considered serviceable. Britain had 58, Italy had 105, and the Soviet Union had 218. In the course of the war, the British total would reach 270, with 73 lost in action; the Soviets built another 54 and lost 109; Germany built over 800 and lost 812.

Barbarigo

Barbarigo's short range, 1425km (750 miles) on the surface, or 228km (120 miles) submerged at three knots, was adequate for Mediterranean operations. In 1943 it was converted into a submersible transport but was spotted on the surface in the Bay of Biscay by Allied aircraft, which sank her in June 1943.

SPECIFICATIONS	
Type:	Italian submarine
Displacement:	1059 tonnes (1043 tons) [surface], 1310 tonnes (1290 tons) [submerged]
Dimensions:	73m x 7m x 5m (239ft 6in x 23ft x 16ft 6in)
Machinery:	Twin screws, diesel engines [surface], electric motors [submerged]
Top speed:	17.4 knots [surface], 8 knots [submerged]
Main armament:	Eight 533mm (21in) torpedo tubes; two 100 mm (3.9 in)/47 guns four 13.2 mm (0.52 in) machine guns
Launched:	1938

Archimede

The 100mm (3.9in) conning tower gun was replaced by a 120mm (4.7in) weapon on the foredeck. At the outbreak of World War II, Archimede was operating in the Red Sea and the Indian Ocean, then in May 1941 transferred to the Atlantic. It was sunk by Allied aircraft off the Brazilian coast on 14 April 1943.

SPECIFICATIONS	
Type:	Italian submarine
Displacement:	1032 tonnes (1016 tons) [surface], 1286 tonnes (1266 tons) [submerged]
Dimensions:	72.4m x 6.7m x 4.5m (237ft 6in x 22ft x 5ft)
Machinery:	Twin screws, diesel engines [surface], electric motor [submerged]
Top speed:	17 knots [surface], 8 knots [submerged]
Main armament:	Eight 533mm (21in) torpedo tubes, one 100mm (3.9in) gun
Launched:	March 1939

Bronzo

SPECIFICATIONS	
Type:	Italian submarine
Displacement:	726 tonnes (715 tons) [surface], 884 tonnes (870 tons) [submerged]
Dimensions:	60m x 6.5m x 4.5m (197ft x 21ft 4in x 14ft 9in)
Machinery:	Twin screws, diesels on surface, electric motors submerged
Top speed:	15 knots [surface], 7.7 knots [submerged]
Main Armament:	Six 533mm (21in) torpedo tubes, one 99mm (9.4in) gun
Launched:	1941

Bronzo, a Series 600 boat of the *Acciaio* class, operating in the Mediterranean, was captured by four British minesweepers on 12 July 1943 after surfacing off Syracuse. After a spell as the British submarine *P714*, it was handed over to the Free French in January 1944, and renamed *Narval*. It was broken up in 1948.

Seraph

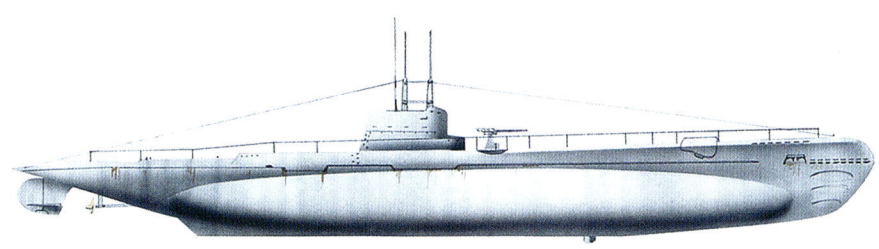

SPECIFICATIONS	
Type:	British submarine
Displacement:	886 tonnes (872 tons) (surface), 1,005 tonnes (990 tons) (submerged)
Dimensions:	66.1m x 7.2m x 3.4m (216ft 10in x 23ft 8in x 11ft 2in)
Machinery:	Twin screws, diesels (surface), electric motors (submerged)
Top speed:	14.7 knots [surface], 9 knots [submerged]
Main armament:	One 76mm (3in) gun, six 533mm (21in) torpedo tubes
Launched:	1941

Seraph was a medium-range boat with a diving depth of 95m (310ft). The diesel engines developed 1900hp, and surfaced range at 10 knots was 11,400km (6000 miles). The class, numbering 63 units, gave excellent service both during and after World War II. *Seraph* was broken up in 1965.

Drum

SPECIFICATIONS	
Type:	US submarine
Displacement:	1854 tonnes (1825 tons) [surface], 2448 tonnes (2410 tons) [submerged]
Dimensions:	95m x 8.3m x 4.6m (311ft 9in x 27ft 3in x 15ft 3in)
Machinery:	Twin screws, diesel [surface], electric motors [submerged]
Top speed:	20 knots [surface], 10 knots [submerged]
Main armament:	Ten 533mm (21in) torpedo tubes, one 76mm (3in) gun
Launched:	May 1941

Construction of the *Drum* class was the largest warship project undertaken by the United States: over 300 were built. Double hulled, ocean-going, they were excellent submarines with good seakeeping qualities and range. *Drum* was preserved on decommissioning, and has been a museum ship since 1968.

World War II Submarines: Part 2

A relatively small number of German U-boats operating in 'wolf packs' sank 712 ships between June 1942 and June 1943. But from the end of 1942, U-boats were being sunk at an increasing rate, with aircraft accounting for half of the losses. In May 1943, 41 U-boats were destroyed. They had lost the Battle of the Atlantic.

Grouper

In 1951, *Grouper* was converted into one of the first hunter/killer submarines. The concept required a boat to be quiet and carry long-range sonar with high bearing accuracy. It could lie off enemy bases, or in narrow straits, and intercept hostile submarines. In 1958, it became a test vessel, and was scrapped in 1970.

SPECIFICATIONS	
Type:	US submarine
Displacement:	1845 tonnes (1816 tons) [surface], 2463 tonnes (2425 tons) [submerged]
Dimensions:	94.8m x 8.2m x 4.5m (311ft 3in x 27ft 15ft)
Machinery:	Twin screws, diesel engines [surface], electric motors [submerged]
Top speed:	20.25 knots [surface], 10 knots [submerged]
Launched:	October 1941

Enrico Tazzoli

Enrico Tazzoli began as the US submarine *Barb,* completed in 1943 as part of the World War II *Gato* class. It was transferred to the Italian Navy in 1955 after it was fitted with the Guppy snorkel, including a modified structure and 'fairwater' for better underwater performance. Range was 19,311km (12,000 miles) at 10 knots.

SPECIFICATIONS	
Type:	Italian submarine
Displacement:	1845 tonnes (1816 tons) [surface], 2463 tonnes (2425 tons) [submerged]
Dimensions:	94m x 8.2m x 5m (311ft 3in x 27ft x 17ft)
Machinery:	Twin screws, diesel engines [surface], electric motors [submerged]
Top speed:	20 knots [surface], 10 knots [submerged]
Main armament:	Ten 533mm (21in) torpedo tubes
Launched:	April 1942

TIMELINE

C1

This large group of submarines was laid down from the early 1940s. Most were patrol boats; some became supply transports for beleaguered Japanese forces on the Pacific islands. Later, some were converted to carry four of the small *Kaiten*, or suicide boats, on the rear hull casing just aft of the conning tower.

SPECIFICATIONS	
Type:	Japanese submarine
Displacement:	2605 tonnes (2564 tons) [surface], 3702 (3761 tons) [submerged]
Dimensions:	108.6m x 9m x 5m (256ft 3in x 29ft 5in x 16ft 4in)
Machinery:	Twin screws, diesel engines [surface], electric motors [submerged]
Top speed:	17.7 knots [surface], 6 knots [submerged]
Main armament:	Six 533mm (21in) torpedo tubes, one 140mm (5.5in) gun
Launched:	1943

CB12

The CB programme of miniature submarines was begun in 1941. Its operating range was 2660km (1400 miles) at 5 knots on diesel engines, 95km (50 miles) at 3 knots submerged. Maximum diving depth was 55m (180ft). Complement was one officer and three crew. In all, 22 units were built, by Caproni Taliedo of Milan.

SPECIFICATIONS	
Type:	Italian midget submarine
Displacement:	25 tonnes (24.9 tons) [surface], 36 tonnes (35.9 tons) [submerged]
Dimensions:	15m x 3m x 2m (49ft 3in x 9ft 10in x 6ft 9in)
Machinery:	Single screw, diesel engine [surface], electric motor [submerged]
Top speed:	7.5 knots [surface], 6.6 knots [submerged]
Main armament:	Two 450mm (17.7in) torpedoes in exterior cages
Launched:	August 1943

Diablo

A double-hulled ocean-going submarine, *Diablo* was a development of the *Gato* class, more strongly built and with improvements to the internal layout, which increased the displacement by about 40.5 tonnes (40 tons). Transferred to Pakistan, it was renamed *Ghazi* in 1964. It was sunk in the 1971 war with India.

SPECIFICATIONS	
Type:	US submarine
Displacement:	1890 tonnes (1860 tons) [surface], 2467 tonnes (2420 tons) [submerged]
Dimensions:	95m x 8.3m x 4.6m (311ft 9in x 27ft 3in x 15ft 3in)
Machinery:	Twin screws, diesel engines [surface], electric motors [submerged]
Top speed:	20 knots [surface], 10 knots [submerged]
Main armament:	Ten 533mm (21in) torpedo tubes, two 150mm (5.9in) guns
Launched:	1944

1944

U-47

U-47 on 13–14 October 1939 penetrated Scapa Flow and sank the 27,940-tonne (27,500-ton) battleship *Royal Oak*. It had already sunk three small merchant ships, and accounted for 27 more before it disappeared in the North Atlantic on 7 March 1941, perhaps sunk by the corvettes HMS *Arbutus* and *Camellia*.

U-47

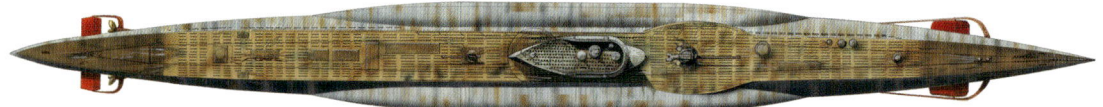

U-47 was an early Type VIIB submarine, which in 1939 sunk the battleship HMS *Royal Oak* inside Scapa Flow. It was one of the most daring submarine attacks of the war and a bitter blow to British prestige.

SPECIFICATIONS	
Type:	German submarine
Displacement:	765 tonnes (753 tons) [surface], 871 tonnes (857 tons) [submerged]
Dimensions:	66.5m x 6.2m x 4.7m (218ft x 20ft 3in x 15ft 6in)
Machinery:	Twin screws, diesel engines [surface], electric motors [submerged]
Top speed:	17.2 knots [surface], 8 knots [submerged]
Main armament:	Five 533mm (21in) torpedo tubes, one 88mm (3.5in) gun
Complement:	44
Launched:	1938

RANGE
A good range was important: U-47 could run for 15,660km (8700 nautical miles) at a surface speed of 10 knots.

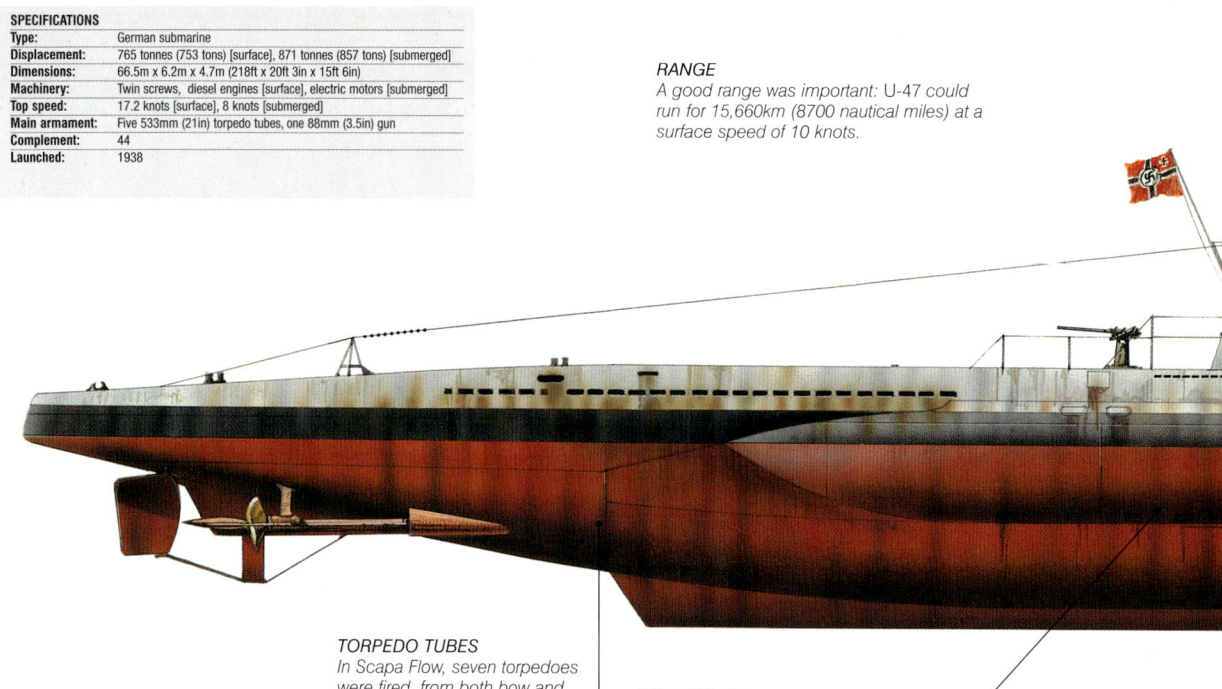

TORPEDO TUBES
In Scapa Flow, seven torpedoes were fired, from both bow and stern tubes; four struck, three in the captain's words 'went to blazes.'

MACHINERY
The two diesel engines developed 1MW (1400 shp) on the surface, and two electric motors generated 280kW (375 shp) underwater.

U-47

HULL
Compared with Type VIIA, the VIIB boats carried an extra 33 tonnes (32.5 tons) of oil in external saddle tanks, increasing their range.

TORPEDOES
Despite the successes, there were problems with German torpedoes, centred on faults in the magnetic pistol and a tendency to run too deep.

GUNS
The 88mm (3.5in) gun was removed from some boats in favour of an AA gun, as the air threat to submarines increased.

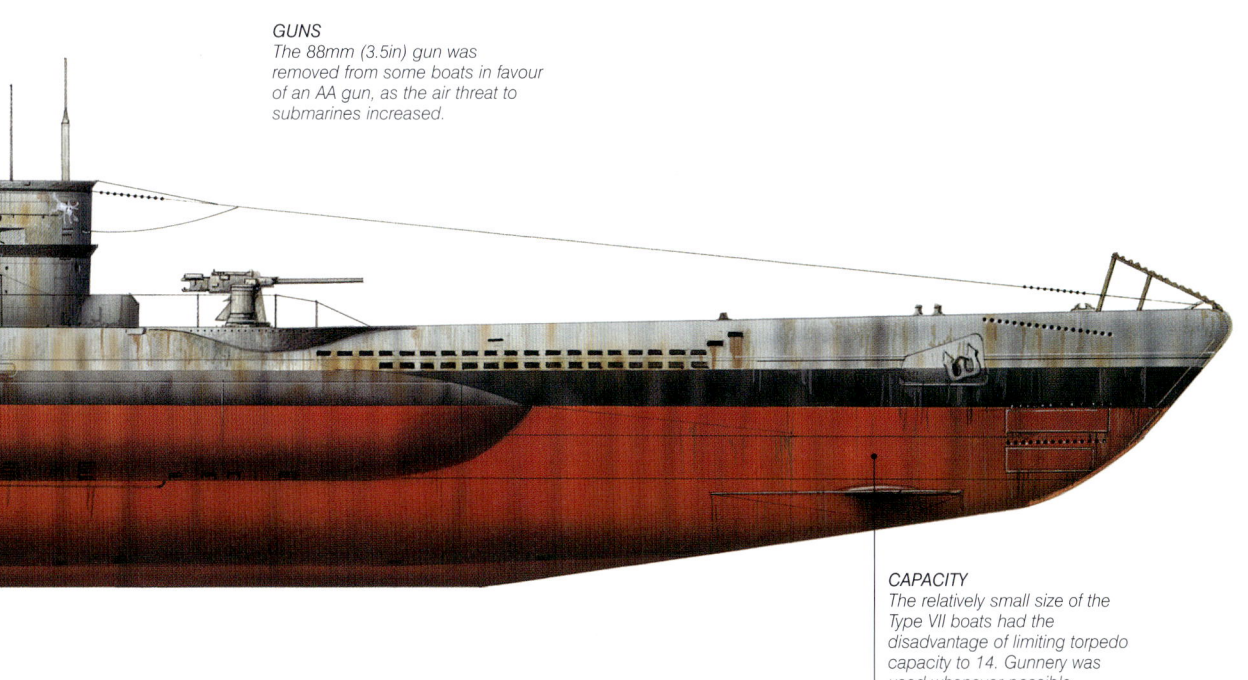

CAPACITY
The relatively small size of the Type VII boats had the disadvantage of limiting torpedo capacity to 14. Gunnery was used whenever possible.

SHIP TYPES 1930–1949

World War II Submarines: Part 3

Submarine warfare racked up daunting statistics. US submarines sank about 1300 Japanese ships (5.5 million tonnes), and U-boats sank 14.6 million tonnes of Allied shipping, mostly in the Atlantic. Casualty rates among submariners were the highest of all services: among US crews, it was 22 per cent, and among German crews, 63 per cent.

I201

I201, with a smooth all-welded hull, was twice as fast underwater as US contemporaries – but heavy electricity consumption was the price. Surface range was 15,200km (8000 miles) at 11 knots, but submerged it was only 256km (135 miles) at 3 knots. In August 1945, it surrendered to US forces.

SPECIFICATIONS

Type:	Japanese submarine
Displacement:	1311 tonnes (1291 tons) [surface], 1473 tonnes (1450 tons) [submerged]
Dimensions:	79m x 5.8m x 5.4m (259ft 2in x 19ft x 17ft 9in)
Machinery:	Twin screws, diesel engines [surface], electric motors [submerged]
Top speed:	15.7 knots [surface], 19 knots [submerged]
Main armament:	Four 533mm (21in) torpedo tubes
Complement:	31
Launched:	1944

I351

I351 was intended to provide support and supplies to seaplanes in forward areas where shore facilities and surface ships were not available. Up to 300 tonnes of aviation fuel could be carried. Two units were built. *I351* was sunk by the US submarine *Bluefish* on 14 July 1945, after only six months in service.

SPECIFICATIONS

Type:	Japanese submarine
Displacement:	3568 tonnes (3512 tons) [surface], 4358 tonnes (4290 tons) [submerged]
Dimensions:	110m x 10.2m x 6m (361ft x 33ft 6in x 20ft)
Machinery:	Twin screws, diesel engines [surface], electric motors [submerged]
Top speed:	15.7 knots [surface], 6.3 knots [submerged]
Main armament:	Four 533mm (21in) torpedo tubes
Complement:	90
Launched:	1944

TIMELINE

1944

WORLD WAR II SUBMARINES: PART 3

I400

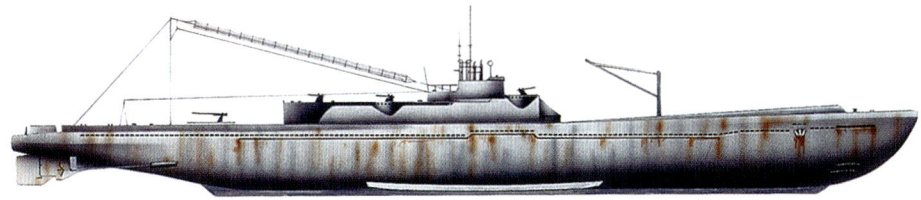

Three floatplanes were carried and could be launched from this class (of two), the largest ever diesel-electric submarines. *I400* would surface, the machines would be warmed up in the hangar, then rolled forward, their wings unfolded, and launched off a catapult rail. All aircraft could be airborne in 45 minutes.

SPECIFICATIONS
Type:	Japanese submarine
Displacement:	5316 tonnes (5233 tons) [surface], 6665 tonnes (6560 tons) [submerged]
Dimensions:	122m x 12m x 7m (400ft 3in x 39ft 4in x 23ft)
Machinery:	Twin screws, diesel engines [surface], electric motors [submerged]
Top speed:	18.7 knots [surface], 6.5 knots [submerged]
Main armament:	Eight 533mm (21in) torpedo tubes, one 140mm (5.5in) gun
Aircraft:	Three M6A1 Seiran floatplanes, plus components for a fourth
Launched:	1944

U-2501

The Type XXI was double-hulled, with a high submerged speed, and ran silently at 3.5 knots. The outer hull was of light plating. The inner hull was of 28–37mm (1–1.5in) carbon steel plating. Batteries let it run submerged for three days on a single charge. By 1945, 55 had entered service. *U-2501* was scuttled in 1945.

SPECIFICATIONS
Type:	German submarine
Displacement:	1647 tonnes (1621 tons) [surface], 2100 tonnes (2067 tons) [submerged]
Dimensions:	77m x 8m x 6.2m (251ft 8in x 26ft 3in x 20ft 4in)
Machinery:	Twin screws, diesel engines [surface], electric motors [submerged]
Top speed:	15.5 knots [surface], 10 knots [submerged]
Main armament:	Six 533mm (21in) torpedo tubes, four 30mm (1.18in) guns
Launched:	1944

Entemedor

The *Gato* class had been planned in December 1941, and 54 submarines were built in an accelerated programme. Fuel tanks, with up to 480 tonnes (472 tons), were sited in the central double hull section. Maximum diving depth was 95m (312ft). *Entemedor* was transferred to Turkey in 1973.

SPECIFICATIONS
Type:	US submarine
Displacement:	1854 tonnes (1825 tons) [surface], 2458 tonnes (2420 tons) [submerged]
Dimensions:	95m x 8.3m x 4.6m (311ft 9in x 27ft 3in x 15ft 3in)
Machinery:	Twin screws, diesel engines [surface], electric motors [submerged]
Top speed:	20.2 knots [surface], 8.7 knots [submerged]
Main armament:	Ten 533mm (21in) torpedo tubes
Launched:	December 1944

SHIP TYPES 1930–1949

Passenger Liners

Questions of national rivalry and prestige, as well as strict commerce, entered into the construction of large transatlantic liners. France's *Normandie*, Italy's *Rex* and *Conte di Savoia*, and Britain's *Queen Mary* all entered service in the 1930s, each claiming ways in which they were the best, or biggest, ships of the day.

Empress of Britain

The Canadian Pacific's largest passenger vessel, it could carry a total of 1195 passengers. In 1939, it was taken over as a troop transport. Attacked by a German bomber off the Irish coast in October 1940, it was taken in tow by the Polish destroyer *Burza*. However, on 28 October it was sunk by submarine *U-32*.

SPECIFICATIONS	
Type:	Canadian liner
Displacement:	43,025 tonnes (42,348 tons)
Dimensions:	231.8m x 29.7m (760ft 6in x 97ft 5in)
Machinery:	Quadruple screws, geared turbines
Top speed:	25.5 knots
Route:	Canada–Europe
Launched:	June 1930

Georges Philippar

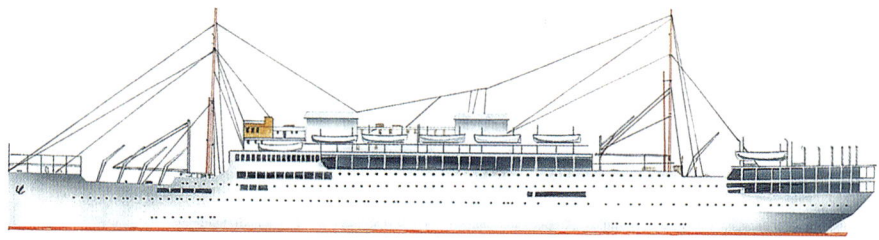

The motor ship *Georges Philippar* was short-lived. Built for Messageries Maritimes of Marseille, it made its maiden voyage to the Far East in February 1932. During the return trip, an electrical fire broke out, and the vessel sank 233km (145 miles) north-east of Cape Guardafui. Fifty-four passengers died.

SPECIFICATIONS	
Type:	French liner
Displacement:	17,819 tonnes (17,539 tons)
Dimensions:	172.7m x 20.8m (19ft 10in x 68ft 3in)
Machinery:	Twin screws, diesel engines
Top speed:	17 knots
Launched:	November 1930

TIMELINE   1930   1931

PASSENGER LINERS

Rex

Italy's largest passenger liner, *Rex* was an emblem of national prestige, intended to capture the Atlantic Blue Riband, which it did until the arrival of the French *Normandie* in 1935. Laid up from the spring of 1940, it was sunk by RAF planes at Trieste in September 1944 and was broken up in 1947.

SPECIFICATIONS	
Type:	Italian liner
Displacement:	49,278 tonnes (48,502 tons)
Dimensions:	248.3m x 30m (814ft 8in x 96ft 2in)
Machinery:	Quadruple screws, geared turbines
Top speed:	29.5 knots
Route:	Genoa–New York
Launched:	October 1931

Conte di Savoia

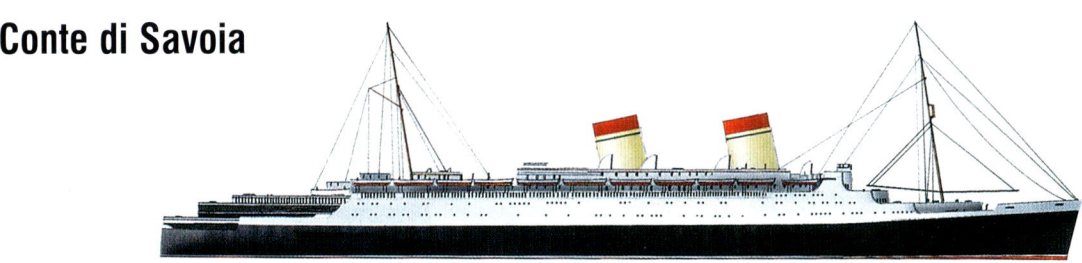

A stylish and elegantly fitted liner, built at Trieste, carrying up to 2060 passengers, *Conte di Savoia* was equipped with a gyro-driven stabilizer, the first to be used on so large a vessel. Laid up near Venice in 1939, it was sunk by Allied bombing in September 1943. Raised in 1946, it was scrapped in 1950.

SPECIFICATIONS	
Type:	Italian liner
Displacement:	51,879 tonnes (51,062 tons)
Dimensions:	268m x 29.25m x 8.55m (879ft x 96ft x 28ft)
Machinery:	Quadruple screws, geared turbines
Service speed:	27 knots
Route:	Genoa–New York
Complement:	750
Launched:	October 1931

Nieuw Amsterdam

Berthed at New York when World War II broke out, *Nieuw Amsterdam* served as a troopship when the United States entered the war, and covered over 800,000km (500,000 miles) in this role. Refitted after the war, it resumed regular transatlantic service. From 1971, it was a cruise liner, until scrapped in 1974.

SPECIFICATIONS	
Type:	Dutch liner
Displacement:	36,867.6 tonnes (36,287 tons)
Dimensions:	321.2 x 26.9m (758ft 6in x 88ft 4in)
Machinery:	Twin screws, geared turbines
Top speed:	20.5 knots
Route:	Rotterdam–New York
Launched:	1937

1937

SHIP TYPES 1930–1949

Queen Mary

Built to be the biggest and fastest, *Queen Mary* held the Blue Riband until 1952. It carried 2739 passengers, but as a wartime troopship some 15,000 servicemen could be accommodated. After 1001 Atlantic crossings in mercantile service, it was sold in 1967 to Long Beach, California, where it is moored as a museum-cum-hotel.

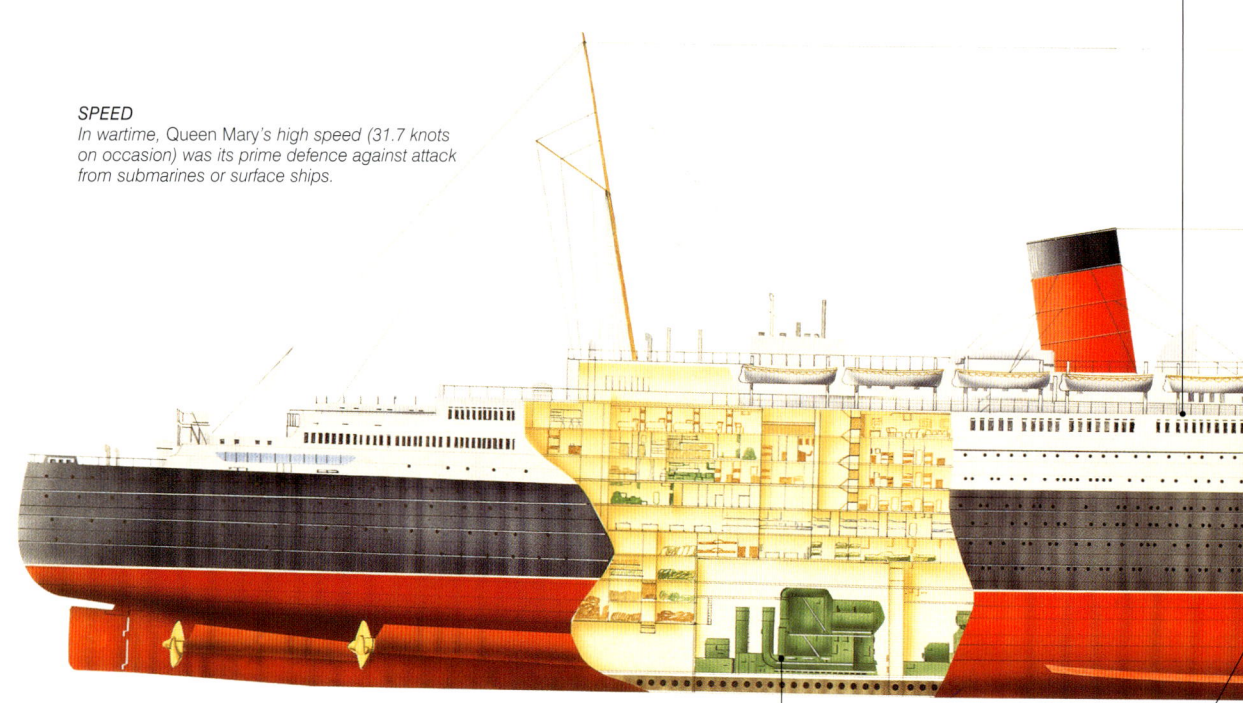

VENTILATION
Ventilation funnels and fans brought cooler air down to the boiler spaces. Ships of this period were not air-conditioned.

SPEED
In wartime, Queen Mary's high speed (31.7 knots on occasion) was its prime defence against attack from submarines or surface ships.

MACHINERY
24 Yarrow boilers served four sets of Parsons single-reduction geared steam turbines. Maximum power output was 119.3MW (160,000 shaft horse-power).

ACCOMMODATION
On one troopship voyage, 16,6— soldiers and crew were packed the maximum passenger numb— ever carried.

Queen Mary

The ship was named after Queen Mary, the consort of King George V. Until the launch the name it was to be given was kept a closely guarded secret. Legend has it that Cunard intended to name the ship 'Victoria', in keeping with company tradition of giving its ships names ending in 'ia'.

SPECIFICATIONS	
Type:	British liner
Displacement:	82,537 tonnes (81,237 tons)
Dimensions:	310.75 x 36.15m (1019ft 6in x 118ft 7in)
Machinery:	Quadruple screws, geared turbines
Top speed:	29 knots
Route:	Southampton–New York
Launched:	1934

FIRST-CLASS AREA
An indoor swimmming pool, cinema, cocktail lounge, library and drawing room, squash and deck tennis courts were among the amenities.

PASSENGERS
As in virtually all pre-war liners there were three classes; First: 776, Tourist: 784, Third: 579. The crew numbered 1071.

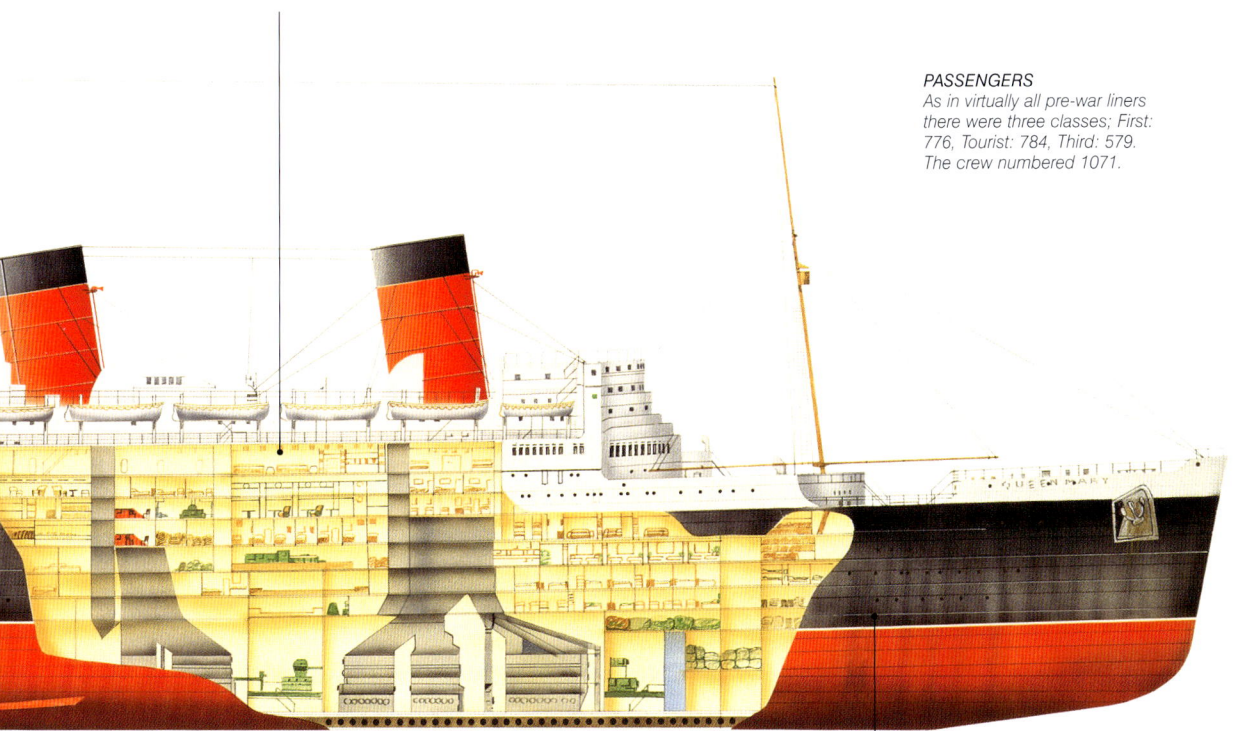

HULL
Queen Mary was the second 1000ft (300m)-plus liner, after the French Normandie (1935) which was ten feet (3m) longer.

SHIP TYPES 1930–1949

Passenger–Cargo Liners

The depression years of the 1930s saw a reduction in merchant shipbuilding generally. Construction of some ships was delayed, and many vessels were laid up for a few years. In new ships, the accent was on economy and efficiency. Oil fuel replaced coal and crew numbers were reduced.

Empire Windrush

Launched as the German liner *Monte Rosa*, this was a troopship in 1942, then a repair workshop for the battleship *Tirpitz*. Damaged in 1944 by mines, it became a hospital ship. After 1945, as the British liner *Empire Windrush*, it brought the first immigrants from the West Indies. In March 1954, the ship caught fire and sank.

SPECIFICATIONS	
Type:	British liner
Displacement:	14,104 tonnes (13,882 tons)
Dimensions:	160m x 20m (524ft x 66ft)
Machinery:	Twin screws, geared diesels
Top speed:	14.5 knots
Launched:	1930

Clan Macalister

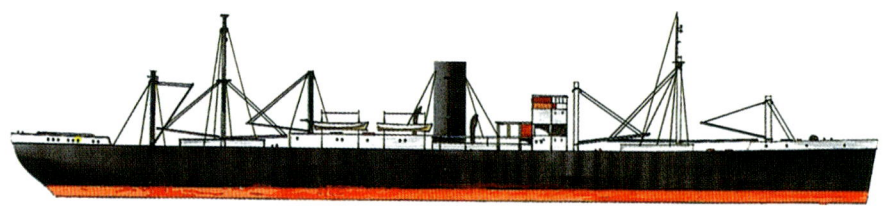

This general-purpose cargo liner was built for the Clan Line. In May 1940, it was commandeered to carry eight landing craft to Dunkirk to assist in the evacuation of British troops. Having unloaded the landing craft, it was attacked by German aircraft and caught fire. Efforts to control the blaze failed, and it was abandoned.

SPECIFICATIONS	
Type:	British cargo vessel
Displacement:	6896 tonnes (6787 tons)
Dimensions:	138m x 19m (453ft 8in x 62ft 3in)
Machinery:	Twin screws, triple expansion engines
Routes:	Britain–Africa and Far East
Launched:	1930

TIMELINE

1930   1931

PASSENGER–CARGO LINERS

Europa

SPECIFICATIONS	
Type:	Danish liner
Displacement:	10,387 tonnes (10,224 tons)
Dimensions:	147.6m x 19m (484ft 3in x 62ft 4in)
Machinery:	Single screw, diesel engines
Top speed:	17.2 knots
Cargo:	General plus 64 passengers
Routes:	North Atlantic
Launched:	1931

The motor ship was popular with smaller shipping companies, like Denmark's East Asiatic Co., being more economical to run, and needing fewer engine-room staff. When Denmark was occupied in 1940, *Europa* transferred to the British flag. In May 1941, it was burnt out at Liverpool docks after a German air raid.

Carthage

SPECIFICATIONS	
Type:	British liner
Displacement:	14,533 tonnes (14,304 tons)
Dimensions:	165m x 22m (540ft x 71ft)
Machinery:	Twin screws, geared turbines
Top speed:	19.5 knots
Route:	London–Far East ports
Cargo:	General cargo
Launched:	August 1931

As *Canton*, *Carthage* ran between London and Hong Kong from 1931, carrying passengers and mixed cargo. In 1940, it was refitted as an armed merchant cruiser with anti-aircraft weapons. In 1943, it was a troop transport. Renovated in 1947–48, it returned to commercial service. It was broken up in Japan in 1961.

Derbyshire

SPECIFICATIONS	
Type:	British liner
Displacement:	11,836 tonnes (11,650 tons)
Dimensions:	153m x 20m (502ft x 66ft 4in)
Machinery:	Twin screws, diesel engines
Top speed:	15 knots
Cargo:	General merchandise, rice, teak
Route:	London–Indian ports and Rangoon
Launched:	June 1935

Derbyshire was a one-class liner; its 291 passengers were mostly government employees travelling to and from British stations overseas. From 1939 to 1942, it served as an armed merchant cruiser, and then became a troopship. Refitted in 1946, it was a passenger/cargo liner 1948 to 1963, and was then sold for scrap.

1935

SHIP TYPES 1950–1999

A significant development of this era was the digital computer and subsequent advances in electronic technology, which were seized on in ship design, construction and operation.

Huge merchant ships with automated navigational, mechanical and cargo-handling systems could be operated by a handful of crewmen. Satellite tracking and GPS locating were incorporated into navigation. In other developments, the passenger liner, made redundant by wide-bodied jet aircraft, evolved into the cruise ship. In naval operations, the nuclear reactor and the ballistic missile prompted a fundamental change of strategy, based on the nuclear submarine.

Left: *Nautilus* was the world's first nuclear-powered submarine. Early trials saw records broken including the first submerged transit across the North Pole.

SHIP TYPES 1950–1999

Aircraft Carriers – USA

Among surface warships, the aircraft carrier took on the role of biggest and most dominant. The US Navy had many more and much larger carriers than any other fleet. Its *Kitty Hawk* and *Nimitz* classes, developed over decades, were vast ships with crew numbers running into thousands, and possessed of devastating firepower.

Forrestal

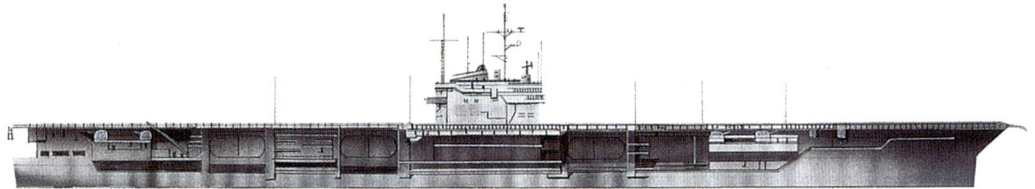

SPECIFICATIONS	
Type:	US aircraft carrier
Displacement:	80,516 tonnes (79,248 tons)
Dimensions:	309.4m x 73.2m x 11.3m (1015ft x 240ft x 37ft)
Machinery:	Quadruple screws, turbines
Top speed:	33 knots
Main armament:	Eight 127mm (5in) guns
Aircraft:	90
Complement:	2764 plus 1912 air wing
Launched:	December 1954

Forrestal and its three sisters were authorized in 1951. Large size was needed for combat jets, which needed more fuel than their piston-engined predecessors. *Forrestal* had space for 3.4 million litres (750,000 gallons) of aviation fuel. Decommissioned since 1993, it is to be sunk as a fishing reef.

Enterprise

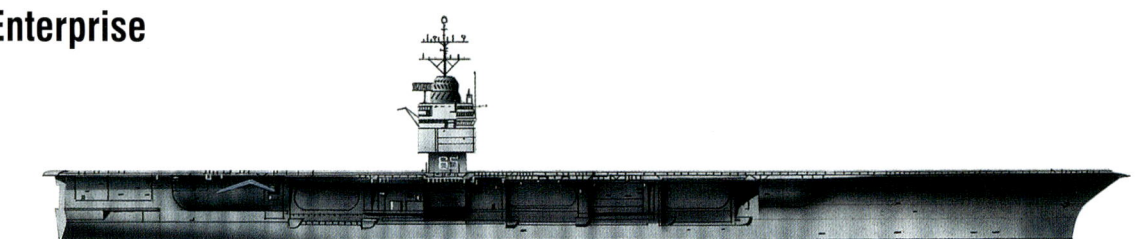

SPECIFICATIONS	
Type:	US aircraft carrier
Displacement:	91,033 tonnes (89,600 tons) full load
Dimensions:	335.2m x 76.8m x 10.9m (1100ft x 252ft x 36ft)
Machinery:	Quadruple screws, turbines, steam supplied by eight nuclear reactors
Top speed:	35 knots
Aircraft:	99
Complement:	5500 including air wing
Launched:	September 1960

When completed in 1961, *Enterprise* was the largest ship in the world, and only the second nuclear-powered warship. Eight reactors gave it a range of 643,720km (400,000 miles) at 20 knots. It was re-fitted between 1979 and 1982, with a new island structure, and reconstructed in 1990–94 to serve until 2012–14.

TIMELINE

1954   1960   1964

AIRCRAFT CARRIERS – USA

America

SPECIFICATIONS	
Type:	US aircraft carrier
Displacement:	81,090 tonnes (79,813 tons)
Dimensions:	324m x 77m x 10.7m (1063ft x 252ft 7in x 35ft)
Machinery:	Quadruple screws, geared turbines
Top speed:	33 knots
Main armament:	Three Mark 29 launchers for Sea Sparrow SAMs, three 20mm (0.79in) Phalanx CIWS
Aircraft:	82
Complement:	3306 excluding air wing
Launched:	1964

The *Kitty Hawk* class were the first carriers not to carry conventional guns. *America* was the first carrier equipped with an integrated Combat Information Centre (CIC). It took part in US engagements from Vietnam to Desert Storm (1991). Decommissioned in 1996, it was scuttled in 2005 after use as a target.

John F. Kennedy

SPECIFICATIONS	
Type:	US carrier
Displacement:	82,240 tonnes (80,945 tons)
Dimensions:	320m x 76.7m x 11.4m (1052ft x 251ft 8in x 36ft)
Machinery:	Quadruple screws, geared turbines
Top speed:	33.6 knots
Main armament:	Three Sea Sparrow octuple launchers, three Mk15 Phalanx 20mm (0.79in) CIWS
Complement:	3306 plus 1379 air wing
Launched:	1967

Kennedy was the first to have an underwater protection system. Completed in May 1968, it was based in the North Atlantic and Mediterranean. In the 1980s, it was deployed off Lebanon and Libya, and off Iraq in 1991. It flew bombing missions against Al Qaeda targets in 2002. From 2007, it has been in the Reserve Fleet.

George Washington

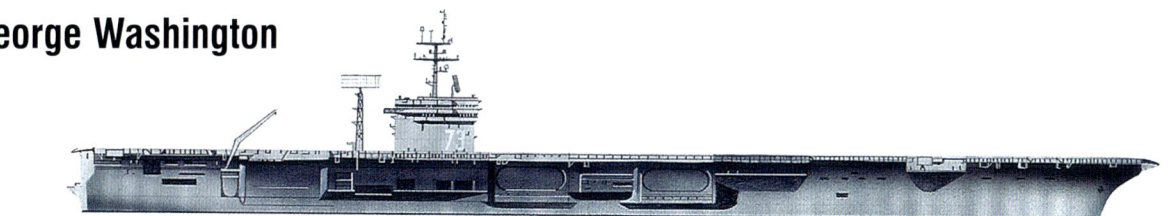

SPECIFICATIONS	
Type:	US aircraft carrier
Displacement:	92,950 tonnes (91,487 tons)
Dimensions:	332.9m x 40.8m x 11.3m (1092ft 2in x 133ft 10in x 37ft)
Machinery:	Quadruple screws, two water-cooled nuclear reactors, turbines
Top speed:	30 knots+
Main armament:	Four Vulcan 20mm (0.79in) guns plus missiles
Aircraft:	70+
Launched:	September 1989

A *Nimitz*-class supercarrier, *George Washington* carries damage-control systems, including armour 63mm (2.5in) thick over parts of the hull, plus box protection over the magazines and machinery spaces. Aviation equipment includes four lifts and four steam catapults. In 2010, it was operating from Yokosuka, Japan.

SHIP TYPES 1950–1999

Invincible

Commissioned in 1980, *Invincible*'s 7° (later 12°) 'ski-jump' let its Sea Harriers take off at low, fuel-saving speed. It was deployed with the Falkland Islands Task Force in April–June 1982; in the Adriatic Sea during the Yugoslav wars in 1993–95; and off Iraq in 1988–99. *Invincible* was decommissioned in August 2005.

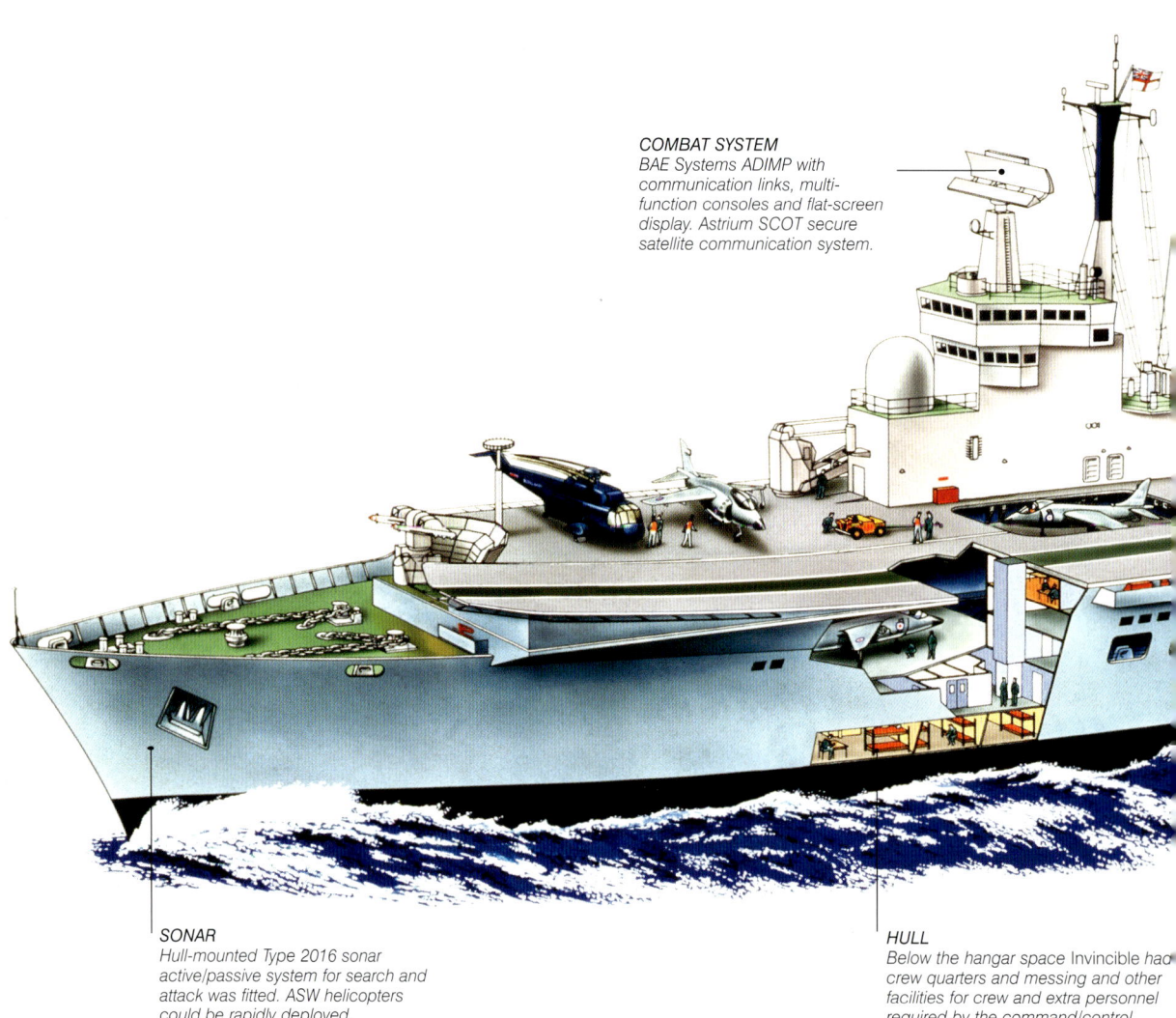

COMBAT SYSTEM
BAE Systems ADIMP with communication links, multi-function consoles and flat-screen display. Astrium SCOT secure satellite communication system.

SONAR
Hull-mounted Type 2016 sonar active/passive system for search and attack was fitted. ASW helicopters could be rapidly deployed.

HULL
Below the hangar space Invincible had crew quarters and messing and other facilities for crew and extra personnel required by the command/control function.

HMS INVINCIBLE 1977

Invincible

The Royal Navy maintains that *Invincible* could be deployed should the need arise and that navy policy assumes that it is still an active aircraft carrier. But *Invincible* was stripped of some parts for sister ships, so bringing the ship to a state of operational readiness would require 18 months.

SPECIFICATIONS	
Type:	British aircraft carrier
Displacement:	21,031 tonnes (20,700 tons)
Dimensions:	210m x 36m x 8.8m (689ft x 118ft 1in x 28ft 10in)
Machinery:	Twin screws, gas turbines
Top speed:	28 knots
Main armament:	Sea Dart anti-air and anti-missile missiles (removed c.1995), Goalkeeper CIWS
Aircraft:	Eight Harrier GR7/GR9, 11 Sea King helicopters
Complement:	726 plus 384 air wing
Launched:	1977

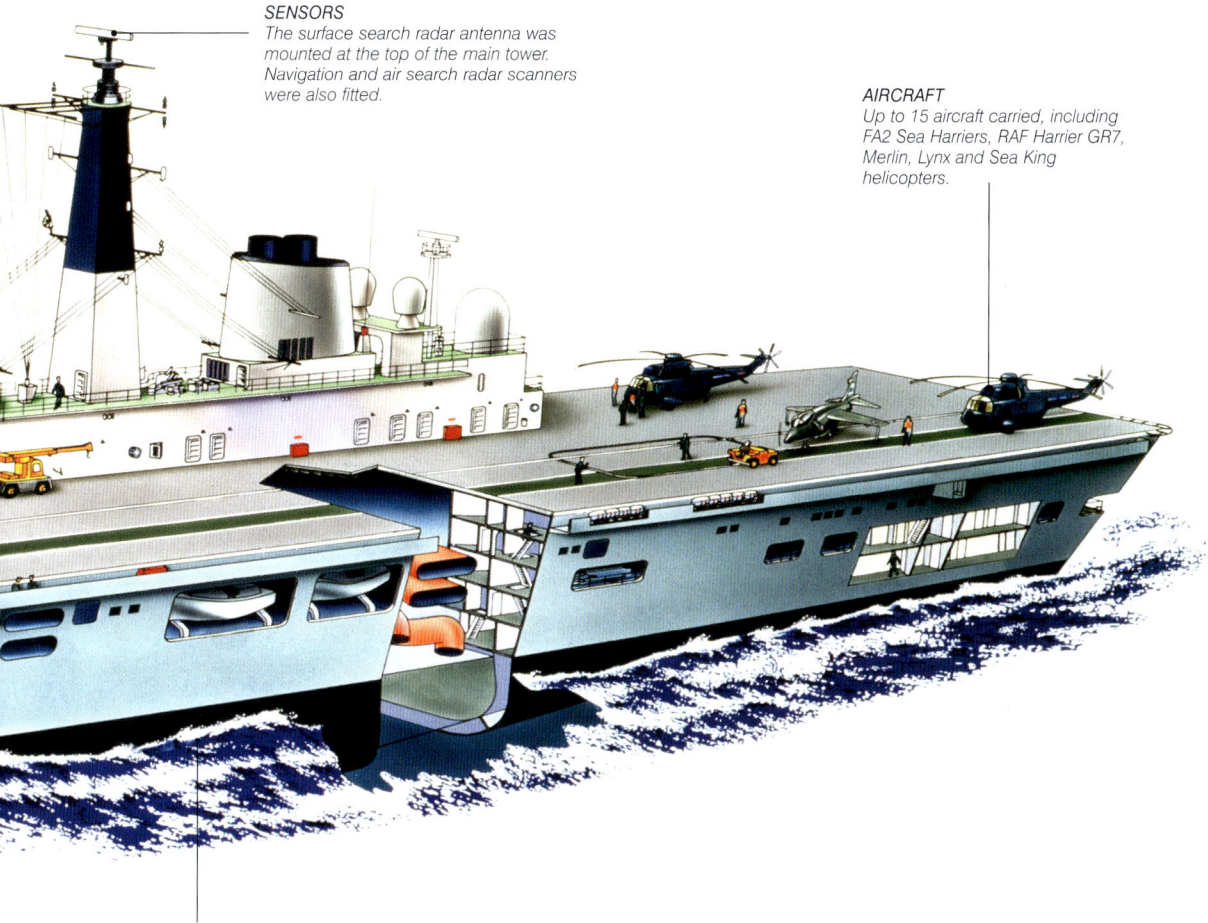

SENSORS
The surface search radar antenna was mounted at the top of the main tower. Navigation and air search radar scanners were also fitted.

AIRCRAFT
Up to 15 aircraft carried, including FA2 Sea Harriers, RAF Harrier GR7, Merlin, Lynx and Sea King helicopters.

MACHINERY
COCAG drive with four Rolls-Royce Olympus TM 3B marine gas turbines and eight Paxman Valenta diesel motors, producing 75MW (97,000hp).

SHIP TYPES 1950–1999

Aircraft Carriers – Other Navies

Several carriers of World War II had unexpectedly long lives. Knowing the tactical importance of fixed-wing aircraft and helicopters, numerous countries sought to retain carriers or to acquire them second-hand. The introduction of angled flight decks and 'ski-jump' ramps enabled older ships to deploy modern aircraft.

Hermes

Plans for *Hermes* went back to 1943. After many design changes, the ship was finally completed in 1959. By 1979, it was handling the new Harrier vertical take-off jets. In 1982 it served as flagship in the Falklands War. In 1989, it was sold to India as *Viraat*, and was still operational in 2010.

SPECIFICATIONS

Type:	British aircraft carrier
Displacement:	25,290 tonnes (24,892 tons)
Dimensions:	224.6m x 30.4m x 8.2m (737ft x 100ft x 27ft)
Machinery:	Twin screws, turbines
Top speed:	29.5 knots
Main armament:	Thirty-two 40mm (1.6in) guns
Aircraft:	42
Launched:	February 1953

Clemenceau

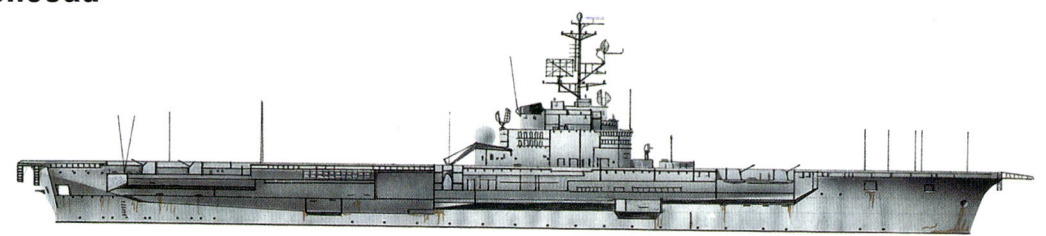

Clemenceau underwent modification during design and construction. It served in the Pacific, off Lebanon and in the 1991 Gulf War. Aircraft comprised 16 Super Etendards, three Etendard IVP, 10 F-8 Crusaders, seven Alize, plus helicopters. It was decommissioned in 2005 and sent for breaking in 2009.

SPECIFICATIONS

Type:	French aircraft carrier
Displacement:	33,304 tonnes (32,780 tons)
Dimensions:	257m x 46m x 9m (843ft 2in x 150ft x 28ft 3in)
Machinery:	Twin screws, geared turbines
Main armament:	Eight 100mm (3.9in) guns
Aircraft:	40
Launched:	December 1957

TIMELINE

1953   1957   1961

AIRCRAFT CARRIERS – OTHER NAVIES

Vikrant

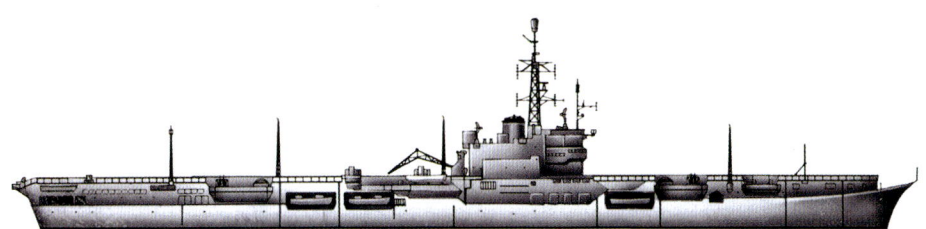

Formerly the British light carrier *Hercules*, *Vikrant* was refitted in 1961 to carry Sea Hawk fighter-bombers. After the Indo-Pakistan war of 1971, it was refitted, including the provision of a ski-jump, in 1987–89, to carry Sea Harriers. It was withdrawn in 1996. India's new home-built carrier *Vikrant* is due for launch in 2010.

SPECIFICATIONS	
Type:	Indian aircraft carrier
Displacement:	19,812 tonnes (19,500 tons)
Dimensions:	213.4m x 39m x 7.3m (700ft x 128ftx 24ft)
Machinery:	Twin screws, geared turbines
Top speed:	23 knots
Main armament:	Fifteen 40mm (1.57in) cannon
Aircraft:	16
Complement:	1250
Launched:	1945 (modernized 1961)

Veinticinco de Mayo

First HMS *Venerable*, then the Dutch *Karel Doorman*, *Veinticinco de Mayo* was bought by Argentina in 1968. The flight deck was extended in 1979, and flew A-4Q Skyhawks, Super Etendards, S-2A Trackers and Sea King helicopters. It was engaged in the Falklands War of 1982. In 1997, it was broken up.

SPECIFICATIONS	
Type:	Argentinian aircraft carrier
Displacement:	20,214 tonnes (19,896 tons) full load
Dimensions:	211.3 x 36.9 x 7.6m (693ft 2in x 121ft x 25ft)
Machinery:	Twin screws, turbines
Top speed:	23 knots
Main armament:	Twelve 40mm (1.57in) cannon
Aircraft:	22
Complement:	1250
Launched:	1943 (modernized 1968)

Kiev

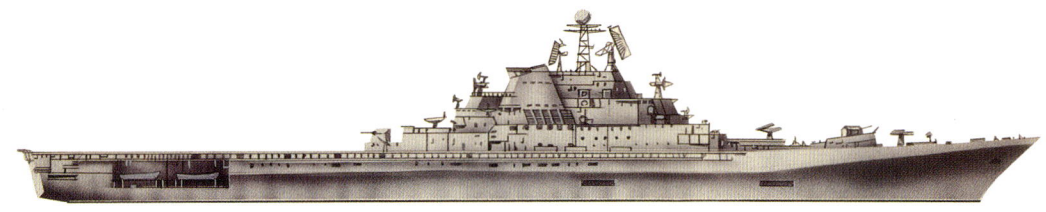

Completed in May 1975, *Kiev* was the first Russian aircraft carrier to be built with a full-length flight deck and a purpose-built hull. Apart from aircraft, it was armed with an array of missiles including the SS-N-12 Shaddock. Withdrawn in 1993, it has been an exhibit in a Chinese seaside theme park since 2004.

SPECIFICATIONS	
Type:	Soviet aircraft carrier
Displacement:	38,608 tonnes (38,000 tons)
Dimensions:	273m x 47.2m x 8.2m (895ft 8in x 154ft 10in x 27ft)
Machinery:	Quadruple screws, turbines
Top speed:	32 knots
Main armament:	Four 76.2mm (3in) guns, plus missiles
Aircraft:	36
Launched:	December 1972

1968    1972

SHIP TYPES 1950–1999

Giuseppe Garibaldi

Giuseppe Garibaldi has six decks with 13 watertight bulkheads. A 'ski-jump' launch ramp is mounted on the bows for vertical take-off and landing aircraft. This enables the aircraft to take off with a higher gross weight of fuel. It carries AV-8B Harrier jets or Agusta helicopters, or a combination of both, and has had several missile refits.

RADAR SYSTEMS
AN/SPS-52C early warning radar, SPS-702 CORA surface search, SPN-749 navigation, SPN-728 approach, RTN-30 and RTN-10X fire control radar.

AIRCRAFT
Up to 16 AV-8B Harrier II jump-jets, or 18 Augusta helicopters, or usually a combination of these.

GUNS
Three Selex NA 21 systems control three 40mm/70mm twin Oto Melara guns with an air target range of 4km (2.5 miles) and surface range of 12km (7.45 miles).

MACHINERY
COCAG drive with four Fiat-built General Electric LM2500 gas turbines and six diesel motors. Power output 60MW (81,000hp).

Giuseppe Garibaldi

SPECIFICATIONS	
Type:	Italian aircraft carrier
Displacement:	13,500 tonnes (13,370 tons)
Dimensions:	180m x 33.4m x 6.7m (590ft 6in x 109ft 6in x 22ft)
Machinery:	Quadruple screws, gas turbines
Top speed:	30 knots
Main armament:	Missile launchers, six torpedo tubes
Aircraft:	16 Harriers, or 18 helicopters
Complement:	550 plus 230 air wing
Launched:	1983

The WWII Peace Treaty banned Italy from having an aircraft carrier, which meant that at the time of launch *Giuseppe Garibaldi* did not receive its Harriers and was classed as an aircraft-carrying cruiser. The ban was eventually lifted and in 1989 the Italian Navy obtained fixed-wing aircraft to operate from the ship.

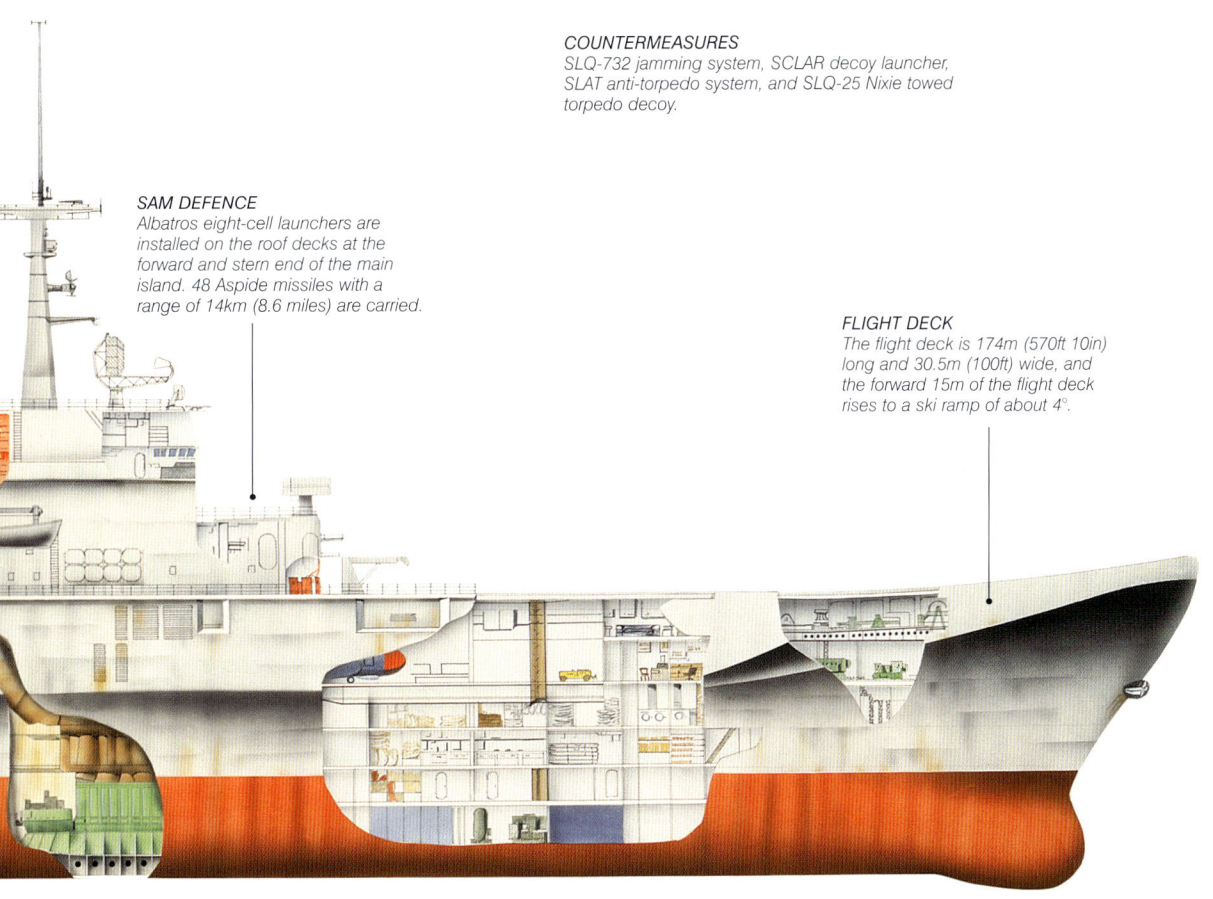

COUNTERMEASURES
SLQ-732 jamming system, SCLAR decoy launcher, SLAT anti-torpedo system, and SLQ-25 Nixie towed torpedo decoy.

SAM DEFENCE
Albatros eight-cell launchers are installed on the roof decks at the forward and stern end of the main island. 48 Aspide missiles with a range of 14km (8.6 miles) are carried.

FLIGHT DECK
The flight deck is 174m (570ft 10in) long and 30.5m (100ft) wide, and the forward 15m of the flight deck rises to a ski ramp of about 4°.

SHIP TYPES 1950–1999

Helicopter Carriers & Small Aircraft Carriers

The vastly increased importance of the helicopter as an element in anti-submarine action has made it, in effect, an extendable arm of the modern warship. In addition, the helicopter carrier can transport, service and fuel a larger number of helicopters to take part in a various situations, from military invasion to humanitarian aid.

Iwo Jima

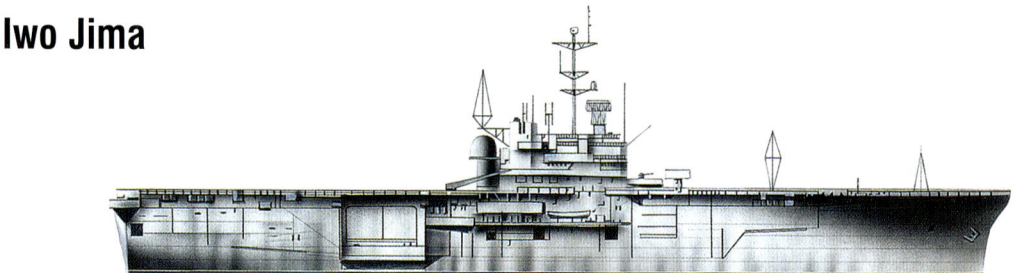

Iwo Jima was the first ship designed specifically to carry and operate helicopters, along with a Marine battalion of 2000 troops, plus artillery and support vehicles. In the 1970s, Sea Sparrow missile launchers were installed. A boiler explosion damaged the ship in 1990; it was stricken in 1993 and broken up in 1995.

SPECIFICATIONS	
Type:	US assault ship
Displacement:	18,330 tonnes (18,042 tons)
Dimensions:	183.6m x 25.7m x 8m (602ft 8in x 84ft x 26ft)
Machinery:	Single screw, turbines
Top speed:	23.5 knots
Main armament:	Four 76mm (3in) guns
Aircraft:	20 helicopters
Complement:	667, 2057 marines
Launched:	September 1960

Jeanne D'Arc

A multi-purpose cruiser, helicopter carrier and assault ship, *Jeanne D'Arc* could transport 700 men and eight large helicopters. In 1975, Exocet missiles were fitted, giving it a full anti-ship role. It also functioned as a training ship, providing facilities for up to 198 cadets at a time. It was struck from the list in 2009.

SPECIFICATIONS	
Type:	French helicopter carrier
Displacement:	13,208 tonnes (13,000 tons)
Dimensions:	180m x 25.9m x 6.2m (590ft 6in x 85ft x 20ft 4in)
Machinery:	Twin screws, turbines
Top speed:	26.5 knots
Main armament:	Four 100mm (3.9in) guns
Aircraft:	Eight
Complement:	627 including cadets
Launched:	September 1961

TIMELINE			
1960 	1961 	1964 	

HELICOPTER CARRIERS & SMALL AIRCRAFT CARRIERS

Moskva

SPECIFICATIONS	
Type:	Soviet helicopter carrier
Displacement:	14,800 tonnes (14,567 tons)
Dimensions:	191m x 34m x 7.6m (626ft 8in x 111ft 6in x 25ft)
Machinery:	Twin screws, turbines
Top speed:	30 knots
Main armament:	One twin SUW-N-1 launcher, two twin SA-N-3 missile launchers
Aircraft:	18 helicopters
Complement:	850, including air wing
Launched:	1964

Moskva was the first helicopter carrier built for the Russian Navy, completed in 1967 to counteract the threat from the US nuclear-powered missile submarines that began to enter service in 1960. A central block dominated the vessel and housed the major weapons systems. *Moskva* was scrapped in the mid-1990s.

Vittorio Veneto

SPECIFICATIONS	
Type:	Italian helicopter cruiser
Displacement:	8991 tonnes (8850 tons)
Dimensions:	179.5m x 19.4m x 6m (589ft 63ft 8in x 19ft 8in)
Machinery:	Twin screws, turbines
Top speed:	32 knots
Main armament:	Twelve 40mm (1.6in) guns, eight 76mm (3in) guns, four Teseo SAM launchers, one ASROC launcher
Aircraft:	Nine helicopters
Complement:	550
Launched:	February 1967

Vittorio Veneto was a purpose-built helicopter cruiser. A large central lift was set immediately aft of the superstructure, and two sets of fin stabilizers were fitted. Laid down in 1965, completed in 1969, the ship underwent a refit between 1981 and 1984. Withdrawn in 2003, it is intended to be a museum ship at Taranto.

Chakri Naruebet

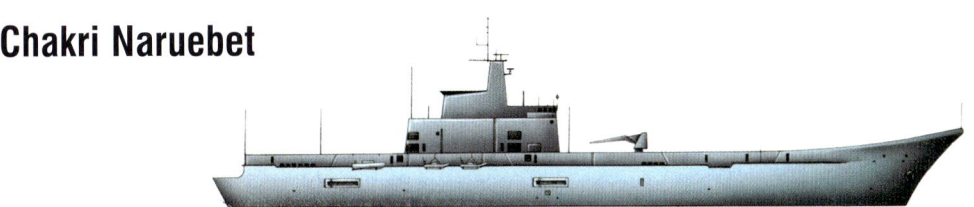

SPECIFICATIONS	
Type:	Thai light carrier
Displacement:	11,480 tonnes (11,300 tons)
Dimensions:	182.5m x 30.5m x 6.15m (599ft 1in x 110ft 1in x 20ft 4in)
Machinery:	Twin screw, turbines and diesels
Top speed:	26 knots
Main armament:	Two launchers for Mistral SAM
Aircraft:	10
Complement:	455 plus 162 aircrew
Launched:	1996

Spanish-built, modelled on Spain's *Principe de Asturias*, Thailand's only carrier is also the world's smallest. *Chakri Naruebet* carries Harrier AV-83 VSTOL jump-jets and helicopters, the Harriers also being bought from Spain. The ship was in service in 2010, but its operational status is unclear and it rarely goes to sea.

1967  1996

SHIP TYPES 1950–1999

Tarawa

Commissioned in 1976, equipped for air-land assault, *Tarawa* had a floodable well-deck for landing craft, and command and control facilities to undertake a flagship role. It was the first of a class of five, all built within the space of a few years in response to perceived threats during the Cold War.

Tarawa

USS *Tarawa* was the lead ship of the Navy's first class of amphibious assault ships able to incorporate the best design features and capabilities of several amphibious assault ships then in service.

SPECIFICATIONS	
Type:	US assault ship
Displacement:	39,388 tonnes (38,761 tons) full load
Dimensions:	249.9m x 38.4m x 7.8m (820ft x 126ft x 25ft 9in)
Machinery:	Twin screws, geared turbines
Top speed:	24 knots
Main armament:	Two RAM launchers, two 127mm (5in) guns, two 20mm (0.79in) Phalanx CIWS
Aircraft:	Up to 35 helicopters, 8 AV-8B Harrier II
Complement:	892 plus 1093 troops
Launched:	1973

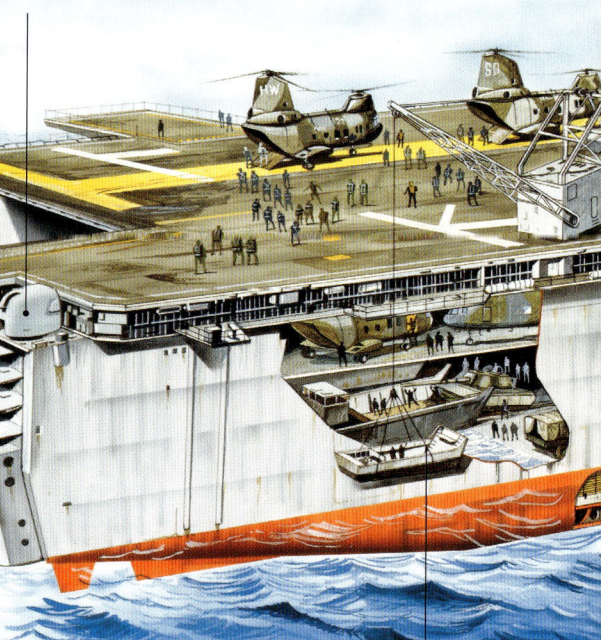

MEDICAL FACILITIES
Tarawa's facilities include 300-bed hospital, four operating rooms, and t dental operating rooms

ARMAMENT
Four Mk38 Mod 1 25mm (0.98in) Bushmaster cannon, five M2HB 12.7mm (0.5in) calibre machine guns, two Mk15 Phalanx CIWS, and two Mk49 RAM launchers.

WELL DECK
Internal roadways enabled vehicles to be driv from the garage space to the landing craft loading points.

TARAWA

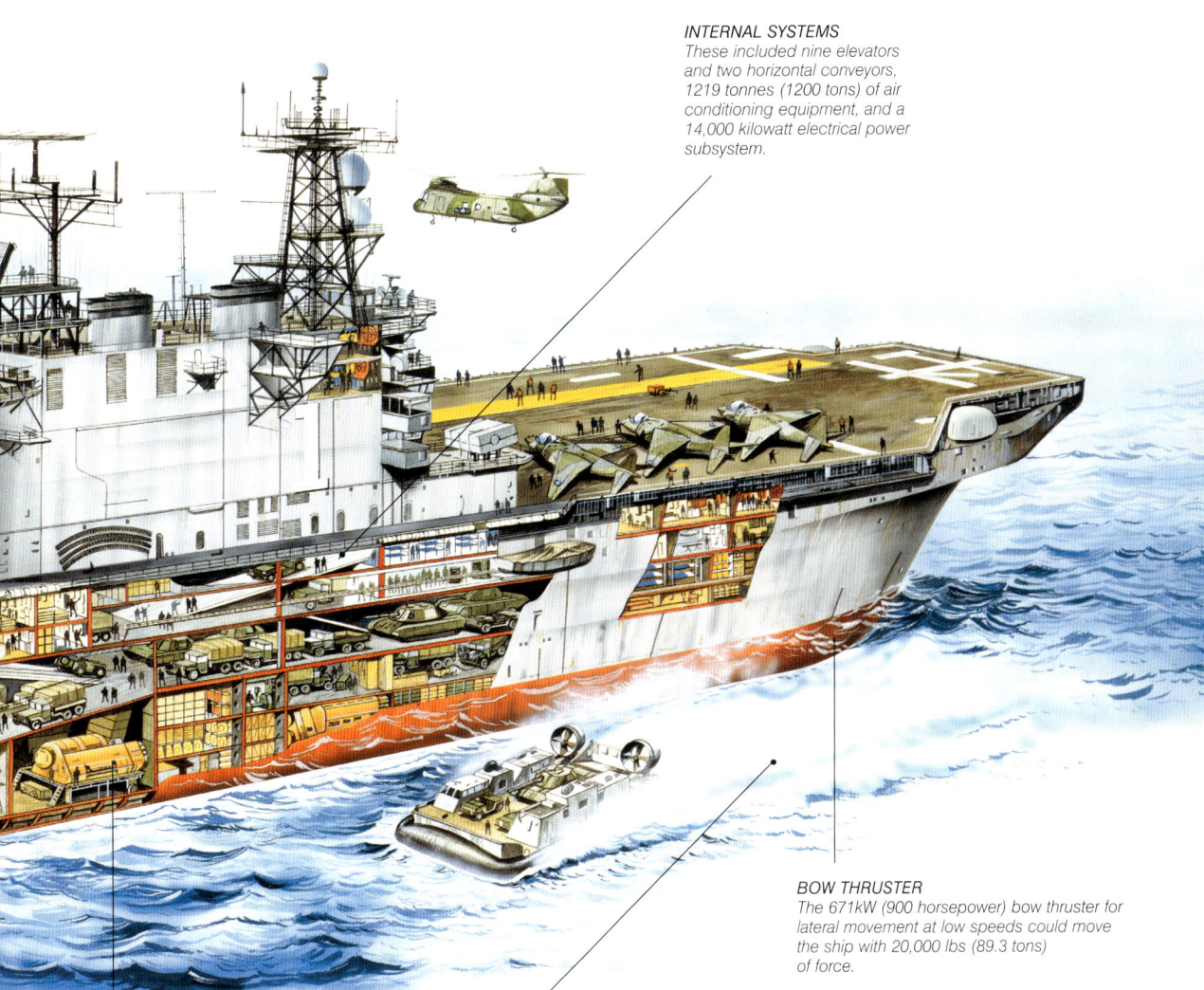

INTERNAL SYSTEMS
These included nine elevators and two horizontal conveyors, 1219 tonnes (1200 tons) of air conditioning equipment, and a 14,000 kilowatt electrical power subsystem.

BOW THRUSTER
The 671kW (900 horsepower) bow thruster for lateral movement at low speeds could move the ship with 20,000 lbs (89.3 tons) of force.

MACHINERY
The two boilers were the largest ever manufactured for the United States Navy, generating 406.4 tonnes (400 tons) of steam per hour, and developing 104,398kW (140,000hp).

BALLAST
Tarawa could ballast 12,192 tonnes (12,000 tons) of seawater for trimming the ship, while receiving and discharging landing craft from the well deck.

SHIP TYPES 1950–1999

Assault Ships

The needs of amphibious warfare, mobilizing specialist equipment and specialized vehicles, and with sophisticated communications, have been answered by a new generation of landing ships and command ships. These have systems more developed than the LSTs and converted merchant ships of the 1940s and '50s.

Intrepid

A 'landing platform dock', *Intrepid* could operate its own set of landing craft, and carry up to 700 troops. Above the landing dock were hangar and flight deck for six helicopters. In the Falklands War, the Argentinian surrender was signed on board *Intrepid*. Decommissioned in 1999, it was scrapped shortly after.

SPECIFICATIONS	
Type:	British assault ship (LPD)
Displacement:	12,313 tonnes (12,120 tons)
Dimensions:	158m x 24m x 6.2m (520ft x 80ft x 20ft 6in)
Machinery:	Twin screws, turbines
Top speed:	21 knots
Main armament:	Two 40mm (1.57in) guns, four Seacat anti-aircraft missile launchers
Complement:	566
Launched:	June 1964

Denver

The 11 ships of this class, enlarged versions of the *Raleigh* group, have greater capacity for carrying troops and support vehicles. Assault and landing craft are held in the comprehensive docking facility forming the rear section of the vessel. In recent years, *Denver* has brought post-tsunami aid to Taiwan and Sumatra.

SPECIFICATIONS	
Type:	US command ship
Displacement:	9477 tonnes (9328 tons)
Dimensions:	174m x 30.5m x 7m (570ft 3in x 100ft x 23ft)
Machinery:	Twin screws, turbines
Top speed:	21 knots
Main armament:	Eight 76mm (3in) guns
Complement:	447 plus 840 marines
Launched:	January 1965

TIMELINE

 1964 1965  1970

ASSAULT SHIPS

Mount Whitney

SPECIFICATIONS	
Type:	US command ship
Displacement:	19,598 tonnes (19,290 tons)
Dimensions:	189m x 25m x 8.2m (620ft 5in x 82ft x 27ft)
Machinery:	Single screw, turbines
Top speed:	23 knots
Main armament:	Four 76mm (3in) guns, two eight-tube Sea Sparrow missile launchers
Complement:	700
Launched:	January 1970

Modern warfare demands specialized command ships. *Mount Whitney*, flagship of the US Sixth Fleet from 2005, uses the same hull form and machinery as the Guam class, with flat open decks to allow maximum antenna placement. *Mount Whitney* has often been in 'hot-spot' situations, including the Black Sea in 2008.

Ivan Rogov

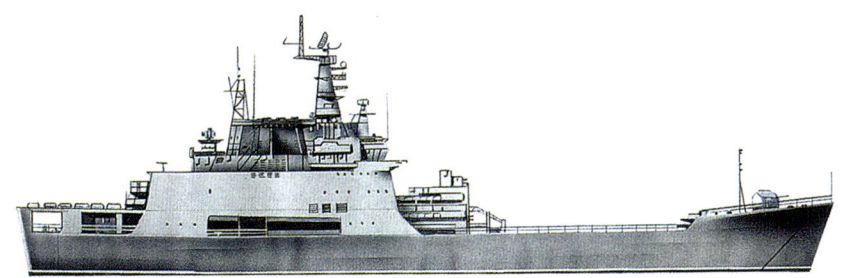

SPECIFICATIONS	
Type:	Soviet amphibious assault ship
Displacement:	13,208 tonnes (13,000 tons)
Dimensions:	158m x 24m x 8.2m (521ft 8in x 80ft 5in x 21ft 4in)
Machinery:	Twin screws, gas turbines
Top speed:	23 knots
Main armament:	Two 76mm (3in) guns, plus anti-aircraft missiles
Complement:	200
Launched:	1977

A long-range assault ship, carrying 550 troops, plus 40 tanks and other support vehicles, *Ivan Rogov* was fitted with a bow ramp, and a docking area 76m (250ft) long. The aft superstructure housed a helicopter. In 1979, it was transferred from the Black Sea to the Pacific Fleet, and stricken in 1996.

Whidbey Island

SPECIFICATIONS	
Type:	US dock landing ship
Displacement:	15,977 tonnes (15,726 tons)
Dimensions:	186m x 25.6m x 6.3m (609ft x 84ft x 20ft 8in)
Machinery:	Twin screws, diesel engines
Top speed:	20+ knots
Main armament:	Two 20mm (0.79in) Vulcan guns
Complement:	340
Launched:	June 1983

Whidbey Island's well deck accommodates four LCAC hovercraft or up to 21 smaller 61-tonne (60-ton) landing craft. The ship carries 450 troops, military vehicles and two assault and transport helicopters, and can fly Harrier jump jets. Assigned to Amphibious Group 2, it is currently deployed in the Persian Gulf.

SHIP TYPES 1950–1999

Corvettes/Patrol Ships: Part 1

Seaward extension of international boundaries and increasing levels of smuggling provide a role for the patrol ship. Lightweight but effective missile launchers and rapid-fire automatic guns endow small ships with heavy fire-power. Reconnaissance, surveillance and interception are their prime tasks.

Shanghai

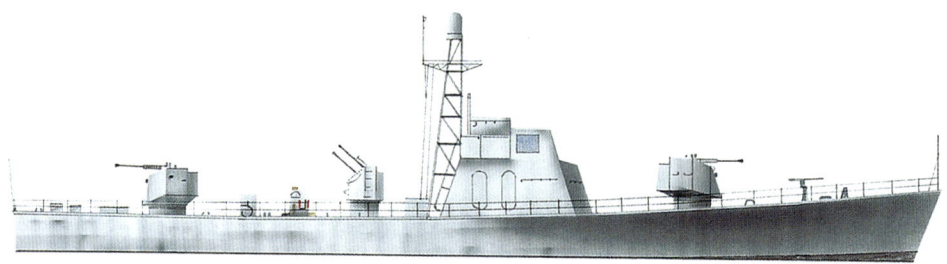

The Chinese Navy has many coastal patrol craft. The *Shanghai* vessels carry a relatively powerful armament of light weapons, plus depth charges and mines. Many have been exported to Asia, the Middle East and Africa, and others built under licence by European navies. Type 1 was in service until the early 1990s.

SPECIFICATIONS	
Type:	Chinese fast attack/patrol boat
Displacement:	137 tonnes (135 tons)
Dimensions:	38.8m x 5.4m x 1.7m (127ft 4in x 17ft 8in x 5ft 7in)
Machinery:	Quadruple screws, diesel engines
Top speed:	28.5 knots
Main armament:	Four 37mm (1.45in) guns, four 25.4mm (1in) cannon
Launched:	1962

Dardo

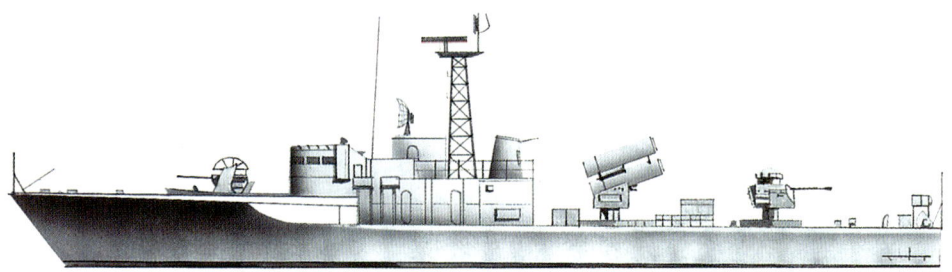

Dardo was one of four vessels whose functions could switch from minelayer (with an anti-aircraft gun and eight mines) to torpedo boat (with one 40mm/1.6in gun and 21 x 533mm/21in torpedoes). Conversion could be achieved in under 24 hours. Hybrid designs are not always successful, but these proved effective.

SPECIFICATIONS	
Type:	Italian motor gunboat
Displacement:	218 tonnes (215 tons)
Dimensions:	46m x 7m x 1.7m (150ft x 23ft 9in x 5ft 6in)
Machinery:	Twin screws, diesels and gas turbines
Top speed:	40+ knots
Main armament:	One 40mm (1.6in) gun, four 533mm (21in) torpedo tubes
Launched:	1964

TIMELINE

1962    1964    1966

CORVETTES/PATROL SHIPS: PART 1

Spica

Spica was the first of a group of fast attack craft designed for Baltic waters. Bases are built into the rocky coastline, and can withstand most weapons except nuclear. The gas turbines develop 12,720hp, for rapid acceleration. The design was adopted by several other navies. *Spica* is now a museum ship in Stockholm.

SPECIFICATIONS	
Type:	Swedish fast attack torpedo craft
Displacement:	218 tonnes (215 tons)
Dimensions:	42.7m x 7m x2.6m (140ft x 23ft 4in x 8ft 6in)
Machinery:	Triple screws, gas turbines
Main armament:	One 57mm (2.24in) gun, six 533mm (21in) torpedo tubes
Launched:	1966

Nanuchka I

This class of light but heavily armed missile craft was known as the *Nanuchka I*. Some variants carried two 57mm guns and all had fire control radar and hull-mounted sonar systems. *Nanuchka II* types were built for India and III for Algeria and Libya. All Russian class members were decommissioned by the end of the 1990s.

SPECIFICATIONS	
Type:	Russian corvette
Displacement:	670.5 tonnes (660 tons)
Dimensions:	59.3m x 12.6m x 2.5m (194ft 7in x 41ft 4in x 7ft 11in)
Machinery:	Twin screws, diesels
Top speed:	32knots
Main armament:	Six SS-N-9 SSM, one SA-N-4 SAM launcher, one 76mm (3in) gun
Launched:	1969

D'Estienne d'Orves

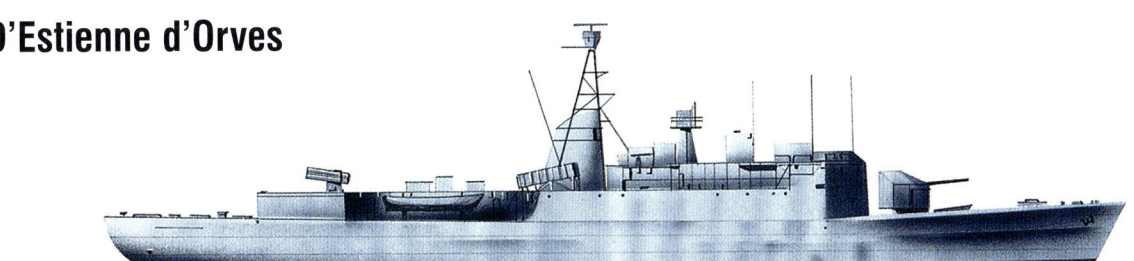

D'Estienne d'Orves was one of a group of 20 frigates, small by contemporary standards, that followed on from the *Commandant Rivière* group, a class of larger ships. Designed for anti-submarine work in coastal waters, they can also operate at long range. This ship became the Turkish Navy's *Beykoz* in 1999.

SPECIFICATIONS	
Type:	French light frigate
Displacement:	1351 tonnes (1330 tons)
Dimensions:	80m x 10m x 3m (262ft 6in x 33ft 10in x 9ft 10in)
Machinery:	Twin screws, diesel engines
Top speed:	23.3 knots
Main armament:	Four Exocet launchers, one 100mm (3.9in) dual-purpose gun
Launched:	June 1973

1969    1975

Corvettes/Patrol Ships: Part 2

Longer-range patrol work needs a larger vessel than even a large motor boat, and several navies have responded with a modern version of the corvette. Once a slow light escort ship, it is now more likely to be a fast missile-bearing patrol craft with a full array of radar search and possibly sonar detection equipment.

Beskytteren

Designed for patrols in North Atlantic and Arctic waters, *Beskytteren* also has a fishery protection role. It is a smaller, modified version of the Danish *Hvidbjørnen* class frigate. Navigational radar and sonar equipment are fitted, and hangar and flight deck for a Lynx helicopter are incorporated, in a compact vessel.

SPECIFICATIONS	
Type:	Danish patrol ship
Displacement:	2001.5 tonnes (1970 tons) full load
Dimensions:	74.4m x 12.5m x 4.5m (244ft x 41ft x 14ft 9in)
Machinery:	Single screw, three diesel motors
Top speed:	18 knots
Main armament:	One 76mm (3in) gun
Complement:	60
Launched:	1975

Fremantle

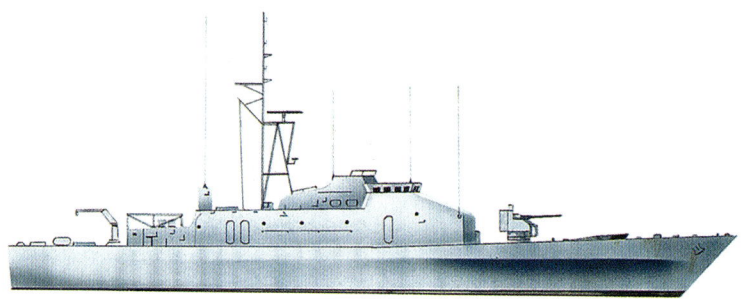

Lead ship of a class of 15, *Fremantle* was built in Lowestoft, England; the others were built at Cairns, Australia. They were faster than the *Attack*-class vessels that previously fulfilled the role of long-range coastal patrols to prevent smuggling and the landing of illegal immigrants. *Fremantle* served until 2006.

SPECIFICATIONS	
Type:	Australian fast patrol boat
Displacement:	214 tonnes (211 tons)
Dimensions:	41.8m x 7.1m x 1.8m (137ft 2in x 23ft 4in x 6ft)
Machinery:	Triple screws, diesel engines
Top speed:	30 knots
Main armament:	One 40mm (1.6in) gun
Launched:	1979

TIMELINE			
	1975	1979	1980

CORVETTES/PATROL SHIPS: PART 2

Badr

SPECIFICATIONS	
Type:	Egyptian fast patrol boat
Displacement:	355.6 tonnes (350 tons) full load
Dimensions:	52m x 7.6m x 2m (170ft 7in x 25ft x 6ft 7in)
Machinery:	Quadruple screws, four diesel engines
Top speed:	37 knots
Main armament:	Four SSM, one 76mm (3in) gun
Complement:	40
Launched:	1980

One of six boats packing a lot of hardware into a small hull, *Badr* has four OTO Melara/Matra Otomat Mk 1 anti-ship missiles, fired from box launchers mounted behind the deckhouse, and its weapons are directed by fire-control and target-tracking systems. The air-surface search radar dome is a conspicuous feature.

Kaszub

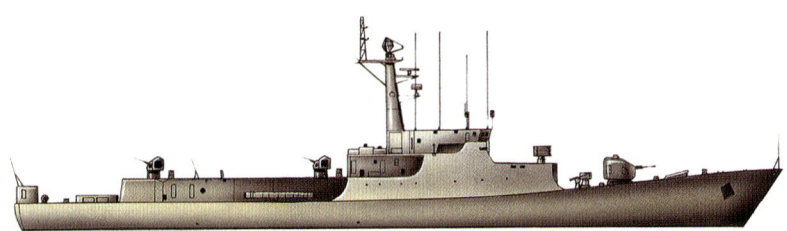

SPECIFICATIONS	
Type:	Polish corvette
Displacement:	1202 tonnes (1183 tons)
Dimensions:	82.3m x 10m x 2.8m (270ft 2in x 32ft 9in x 9ft 2in)
Machinery:	Quadruple screws, four diesel motors
Top speed:	28 knots
Main armament:	Two SA-N-5 SAM launchers, one 76mm (3in) gun, two 533mm (21in) torpedo tubes
Complement:	67
Launched:	1986

This Type 620 corvette, built in Poland, was to be the first of seven, but the collapse of the Warsaw Pact stopped development after *Kaszub*, which never received its intended Russian-made missile armament. Technical problems limit its usefulness, and it rarely puts to sea, though it is still on the active list in 2009.

Eilat

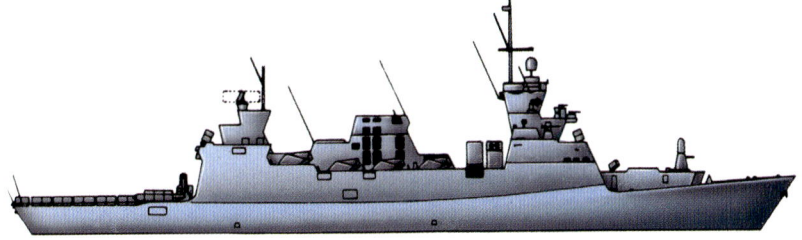

SPECIFICATIONS	
Type:	Israeli corvette
Displacement:	1295.4 tonnes (1275 tons) full load
Dimensions:	86.4m x 11.9m x 3.2m (283ft 6in x 39ft x 10ft 6in)
Machinery:	Twin screws, turbines plus turbo diesels
Top speed:	33 knots
Main armament:	Eight Harpoon SSM, eight Gabriel II SSM, one 76mm (3in) gun
Complement:	74
Launched:	1994

Designed on radar-dodging 'stealth' lines, *Eilat* is one of three well-armed small warships intended to lead Israel's large fleet of smaller attack craft. The forward gun position can be altered to mount different guns or a Phalanx CIWS system. A Dauphin helicopter is carried, and the vessel has sensor devices and radars.

1986  1994

SHIP TYPES 1950–1999

USS Long Beach

Completed in September 1961, *Long Beach* was the United States' largest non-carrier surface warship built since 1945. Off Vietnam in 1968, it shot down two MiG fighters in the first successful SAM naval action. In the 1980s, Harpoon missiles and Phalanx CIWS were installed. *Long Beach* was withdrawn from service in 1994.

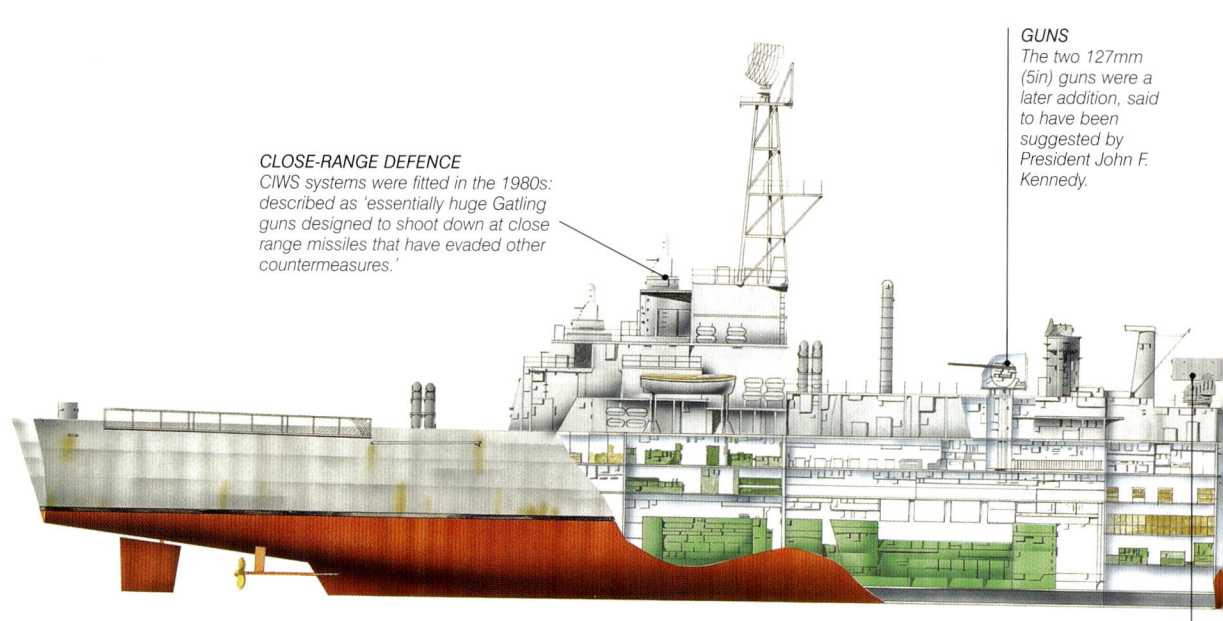

GUNS
The two 127mm (5in) guns were a later addition, said to have been suggested by President John F. Kennedy.

CLOSE-RANGE DEFENCE
CIWS systems were fitted in the 1980s: described as 'essentially huge Gatling guns designed to shoot down at close range missiles that have evaded other countermeasures.'

MACHINERY
Two CIW nuclear reactors powering two General Electric turbines. Total power output was 59,656kW (80,000shp). Range was effectively unlimited.

FINAL WEAPONS S
Harpoon and BGM-Tomahawk missiles replaced the origina and Talos systems. tube ASROC launch also fitted.

USS Long Beach

A deactivation ceremony took place on 2 July 1994 at Norfolk Naval Station. *Long Beach* was decommissioned on 1 May 1995, over 33 years after she had entered service. She is currently waiting to be recycled.

SPECIFICATIONS

Type:	US missile cruiser
Displacement:	16,624 tonnes (16,602 tons)
Dimensions:	219.8m x 22.3m x 7.2m (721ft 3in x 73ft 4in x 23ft 9in)
Machinery:	Twin screws, two nuclear reactors driving geared turbines
Top speed:	30+ knots
Main armament:	Eight Harpoon SSM, two Terrier SSM systems, two 127mm (5in) guns, two 20mm (0.79in) Phalanx CIWS, one ASROC launcher, six 2324mm (12.75in) torpedo tubes
Complement:	1107
Launched:	1959

SENSOR SYSTEMS
AN/SPS radar for surface search, bearing & range, target tracking, air search and fire control. AN/SQS-23 sonar.

MISSILES
A Talos missile fired by Long Beach in 1968 downed a Vietnamese jet 112.6km (70 miles) away: the first ship-to-air missile success in action.

HULL
Long Beach was the last US cruiser to be built with a traditional cruiser-type hull, long and relatively narrow.

SHIP TYPES 1950–1999

American Cruisers

While World War II marked the end of the battleship age, both the United States and Russia subsequently built many cruisers, though by the later 1950s the concept of the cruiser was obviously old-fashioned. New generation submarines, aircraft and missiles made them vulnerable. Smaller ships packed a more devastating punch.

Galveston

Galveston was one of six cruisers of World War II which were later refitted to carry Talos or Terrier missiles. The original guns were retained. The purpose was air defence and the ships were not expected to undertake deep sea missions. Galveston served until 1970, was stricken in 1973 and scrapped in 1975.

SPECIFICATIONS	
Type:	US cruiser
Displacement:	15,394 tonnes (15,152 tons)
Dimensions:	186m x 20m x 7.8m (610ft x 65ft 8in x 25ft 8in)
Machinery:	Quadruple screws, geared turbines
Top speed:	32 knots
Main armament:	Talos SAM system, six 152mm (6in) guns, six 127mm (5in) guns
Complement:	1382
Launched:	1945, converted 1958

Worden

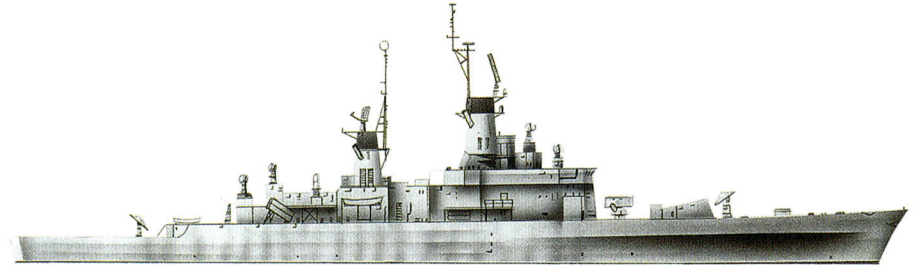

Worden was one of nine vessels replacing cruisers from World War II. The layout incorporated masts and gantries for a complex radar system. The class was refitted in the late 1960s and again in the late 1980s. In 1991, Worden became an anti-aircraft command vessel. Stricken in 1993, it was sunk as a target in 2000.

SPECIFICATIONS	
Type:	US cruiser
Displacement:	8334 tonnes (8203 tons)
Dimensions:	162.5m x 16.6m x 7.6m (533ft 2in x 54ft 6in x 25ft)
Machinery:	Twin screws, turbines
Top speed:	32.7 knots
Main armament:	Two 20mm (0.8in) Vulcan guns, two quad Harpoon launchers, two twin launchers for Standard SM-2 ER missiles
Launched:	June 1962

TIMELINE			
	1958	1962 	1976 

AMERICAN CRUISERS

Mississippi

SPECIFICATIONS	
Type:	US cruiser
Displacement:	11,176 tonnes (11,000 tons)
Dimensions:	178.5m x 19.2m x 9m (585ft 4in x 63ft x 29ft 6in)
Machinery:	Twin screws, nuclear-powered turbines
Main armament:	Two 127mm (5in) guns, two twin launchers for Tartar and Harpoon missiles, Asroc launcher
Launched:	July 1976

Mississippi was one of four ships with Mk 26 missile launchers and provision for a helicopter hangar and elevator in the stern. The hangars were replaced by three Tomahawk launchers in the 1980s. The 127mm (5in) Mk 45 guns fired 20 rounds per minute, with a range of over 14.6km (9.12 miles). It was broken up in 1997.

Ticonderoga

SPECIFICATIONS	
Type:	US guided missile cruiser
Displacement:	9052.5 tonnes (8910 tons)
Dimensions:	171.6m x 19.81m x 9.45m (563ft x 65ft x 31ft)
Machinery:	Twin screws, four gas turbines
Top speed:	30 knots
Main armament:	Eight Harpoon SSM, two Mk 26 launchers for SAM and ASROC torpedoes, two 127mm (5in) guns, six 324mm (12.75in) torpedo tubes
Complement:	343
Launched:	1981

Ticonderoga was lead ship of a class of 27, originally frigates but reclassified due to the scale of their armament. Later vessels in the class were enlarged to carry greater missile stocks. A full array of sensor equipment was carried, including the Aegis air defence system, and one helicopter. It was decommissioned in 2004.

Bunker Hill

SPECIFICATIONS	
Type:	US guided missile cruiser
Displacement:	9,754 tonnes (9600 tons)
Dimensions:	173m x 16.8m x 10.2m (567ft x 55ft x 34ft)
Machinery:	Twin reversible-pitch screws, four gas turbines
Top speed:	32.5 knots
Main armament:	Two 61-cell Mk 41 VLS systems, 122 RIM-156 SM-2ER Bock IV, RIM-162 ESSM, BGM-109 Tomahawk or RUM-139 VL Asroc; 8 RGM-84 Harpoon missiles
Complement:	400
Launched:	1985

First ship of the large *Ticonderoga* class to be equipped with the Mk 41 Vertical Launching System, *Bunker Hill* was first deployed in the Persian Gulf in 1987, and later participated in the Desert Shield and Desert Storm operations. Weapons systems were upgraded in 2006. In 2010 the ship assisted with disaster relief after the Haiti earthquake.

1981

1985

SHIP TYPES 1950–1999

Kirov

Kirov's superstructure supports radars and early-warning antennae. Most missile-launching systems are forward, below deck, leaving the aft section for the helicopter hangar and machinery. The two nuclear reactors are coupled with oil-fired turbine superheaters to intensify the heat of the steam, increasing power for more speed.

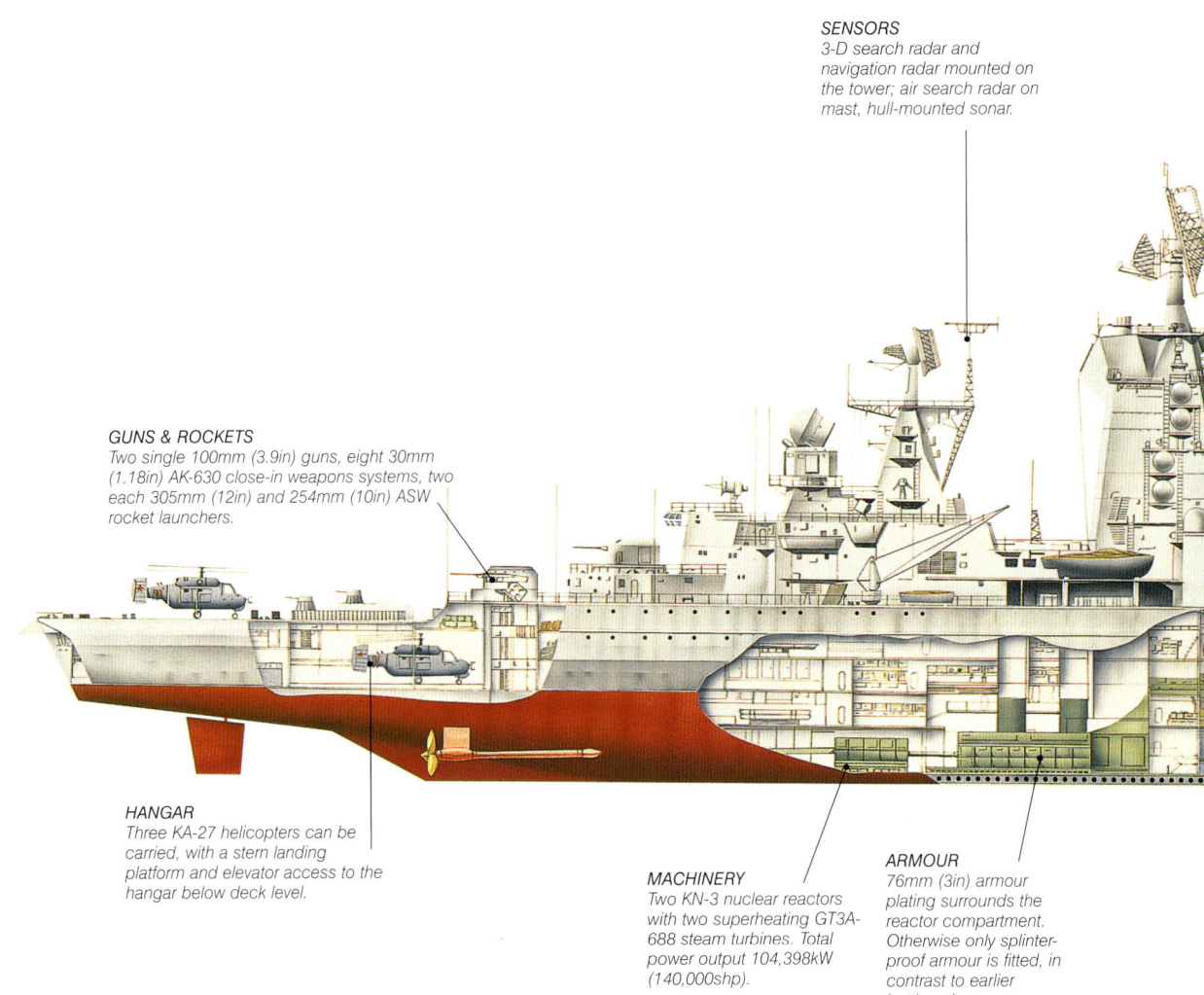

SENSORS
3-D search radar and navigation radar mounted on the tower; air search radar on mast, hull-mounted sonar.

GUNS & ROCKETS
Two single 100mm (3.9in) guns, eight 30mm (1.18in) AK-630 close-in weapons systems, two each 305mm (12in) and 254mm (10in) ASW rocket launchers.

HANGAR
Three KA-27 helicopters can be carried, with a stern landing platform and elevator access to the hangar below deck level.

MACHINERY
Two KN-3 nuclear reactors with two superheating GT3A-688 steam turbines. Total power output 104,398kW (140,000shp).

ARMOUR
76mm (3in) armour plating surrounds the reactor compartment. Otherwise only splinter-proof armour is fitted, in contrast to earlier battlecruisers.

Kirov

SPECIFICATIONS

Type:	Soviet guided-missile cruiser
Displacement:	28,448 tonnes (28,000 tons)
Dimensions:	248m x 28m x 8.8m (813ft 8in x 91ft 10in x 28ft 10in)
Machinery:	Twin screws, turbines, two pressurized water-type reactors
Top speed:	32 knots
Main armament:	Two 100mm (3.9in) guns, two twin SA-N-4 launchers, twelve SA-N-6 launchers plus 20 anti-ship missiles
Complement:	1600
Launch date:	December 1977

This ship had an impressive armament of missiles and guns as well as electronics. Its largest radar antenna was mounted on its foremast. *Kirov* suffered a reactor accident in 1990 while serving in the Mediterranean Sea. Repairs were never carried out, due to lack of funds and the changing political situation in the Soviet Union.

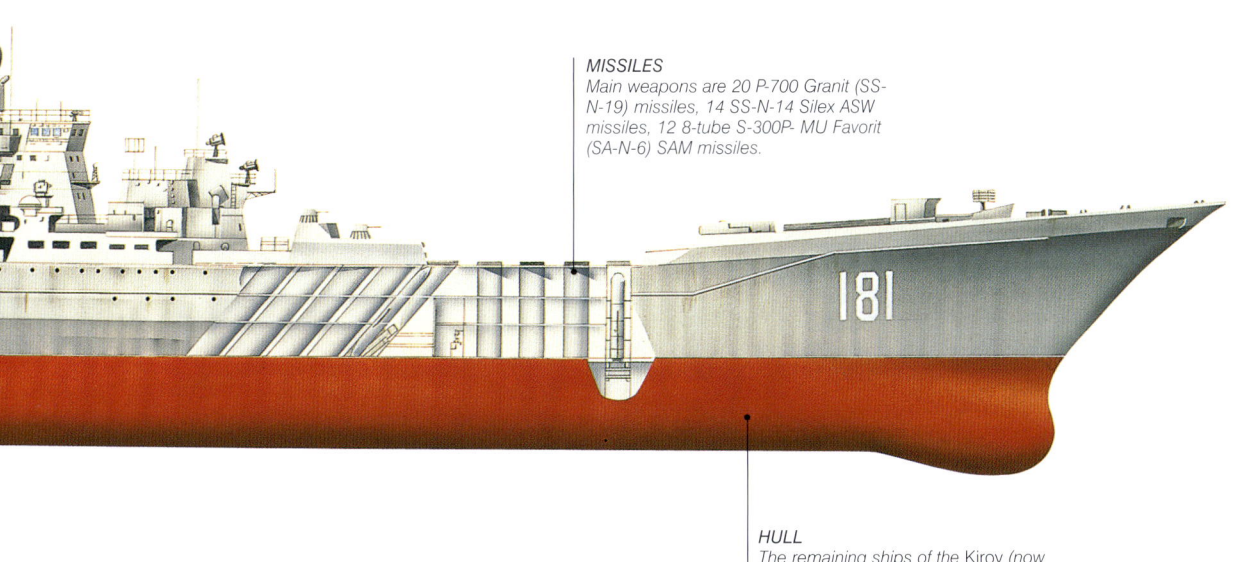

MISSILES
Main weapons are 20 P-700 Granit (SS-N-19) missiles, 14 SS-N-14 Silex ASW missiles, 12 8-tube S-300P- MU Favorit (SA-N-6) SAM missiles.

HULL
The remaining ships of the Kirov *(now renamed* Admiral Ushakov) *class are the world's largest non-carrier warships.*

Soviet Cruisers

The Soviet Union built up a substantial cruiser fleet in the 1950s, although building programmes were cut back from the original numbers. Despite efforts to modernize some of them, they were of diminishing strategic value. By later in the century, they were largely obsolescent and were retired or scrapped. Only a few remain active.

Admiral Senyavin

A *Sverdlov*-class heavy cruiser, this ship was extensively modified in 1971–72 to become a command ship in the event of nuclear war, and the rear guns were removed to install a helicopter deck and hangar. An SA-N-4 SAM launcher was fitted at the same time. It served with the Soviet fleet until stricken in 1991.

SPECIFICATIONS	
Type:	Soviet cruiser
Displacement:	16,723 tonnes (16,640 tons)
Dimensions:	210m x 22m x 6.9m (672ft 4in x 22ft 7in x 22ft)
Machinery:	Not known
Top speed:	32.5 knots
Main armament:	Twelve 152mm (6in) guns, ten 533mm (21in) torpedo tubes
Complement:	1250
Launched:	1952

Dmitry Pozharsky

Unlike *Admiral Senyavin*, this ship, sixth of the *Sverdlov* class to be built, retained its original (and increasingly out-of-date) armament. Sixteen ships of this class were built, out of a projected 30. Though obsolete, *Dmitry Pozharsky* remained on active service until 1987. Others were taken out of service 20 years earlier.

SPECIFICATIONS	
Type:	Soviet cruiser
Displacement:	16,906.3 tonnes (16,640 tons)
Dimensions:	210m x 22m x 6.9m (672ft 4in x 22ft 7in x 22ft
Machinery:	Not known
Top speed:	32.5 knots
Main armament:	Twelve 152mm (6in) guns, twelve 100mm (3.9in) guns, ten 533mm (21in) torpedo tubes
Complement:	1250
Launched:	1953

TIMELINE 1952 1953

Dmitri Donskoi

Of the 24 planned ships of this class, 17 were launched, but by the end of 1960 only 14 were operational. Nearly all were fitted for minelaying, mine stowage being on the main deck. The 152mm (6in) guns were mounted in triple turrets, two fore and two aft, each group having its own range-finders.

SPECIFICATIONS	
Type:	Soviet cruiser
Displacement:	19,507 tonnes (19,200 tons)
Dimensions:	210m x 21m x 7m (689ft x 70ft x 24ft 6in)
Machinery:	Twin screws, turbines
Main armament:	Twelve 152mm (6in) guns
Launched:	1953

Kerch

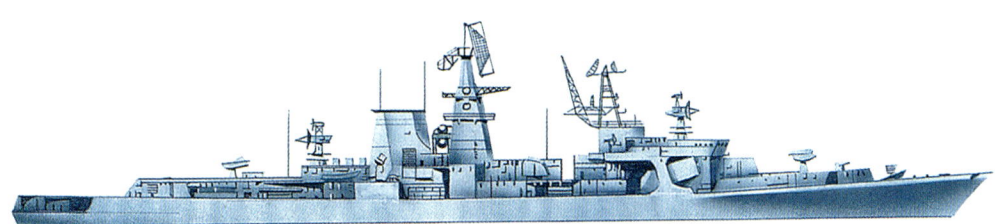

The largest vessels with all gas-turbine propulsion, the *Kerch* class developed 120,000hp, for a range of 5700km (3000 miles) at full speed, or 16,720km (8800 miles) at 15 knots. They had major AA and anti-submarine capabilities, a heavy gun armament, and a helicopter. *Kerch* remains in the Black Sea Fleet.

SPECIFICATIONS	
Type:	Soviet cruiser
Displacement:	9855 tonnes (9700 tons)
Dimensions:	173m x 18.6m x 6.7m (567ft 7in x 61ft x 22ft)
Machinery:	Twin screws, gas turbines
Main armament:	Four 76.2mm (3in) guns, two twin SA-N- 3 missile launchers
Complement:	525
Launched:	1973

Slava

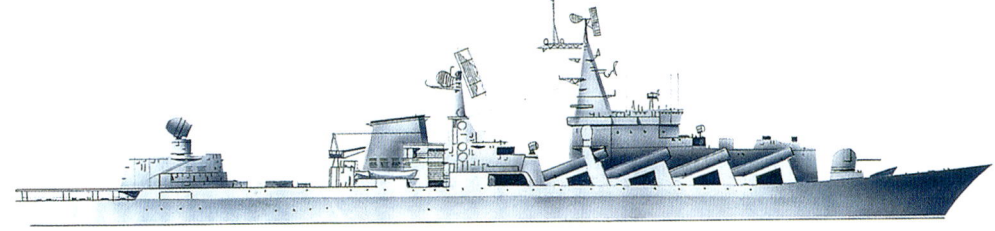

Slava is one of four ships, smaller versions of the *Kirov* class. The SS-N-12 missiles are in twin launchers along each side of the bridge. Complex radars are fitted on the massive foremast at the end of the bridge, with another mounted on top of the mainmast. *Slava* was in the South Ossetia war of 2008.

SPECIFICATIONS	
Type:	Soviet cruiser
Displacement:	11,700 tonnes (11,200 tons)
Dimensions:	186m x 20.8m x 7.6m (610ft 5in x 68ft 5in x 25ft)
Machinery:	Twin screws, turbines
Main armament:	Two 127mm (5in) guns, eight twin SS-N-12 launchers, eight launchers for SA-N-6 missiles plus two launchers for SAM missiles
Launched:	1979

1973    1979

SHIP TYPES 1950–1999

Cruisers of Other Navies

The traditional 'big' surface warship lingered on through the second half of the twentieth century, encouraged by a sense of national prestige and by the desire of admirals to have flagships. Attitudes changed, particularly perhaps after the sinking of the Argentinian *General Belgrano* by the British submarine *Conqueror* in 1982.

Babur

The British cruiser *Diadem* was acquired by Pakistan in 1956 and comprehensively refitted in 1956–57. In 1961 it became a naval training ship, and rarely went to sea, later becoming harbour-bound. In 1982 it was renamed *Jahangir* and a former British *Devonshire* class destroyer became *Babur*. It was broken up in 1985.

SPECIFICATIONS	
Type:	Pakistani cruiser
Displacement:	7638.3 tonnes (7518 tons)
Dimensions:	156m x 15m x 5.4m (512ft x 50ft 6in x 18ft)
Machinery:	Quadruple screws, geared tubines
Top speed:	32 knots
Main armament:	Eight 133mm (5.25in) guns
Armour:	76mm (3in) sides, 51–25mm (2–1in) deck
Complement:	530
Launched:	1942 (refitted 1956)

Coronel Bolognesi

One of two British *Fiji*-class cruisers sold to Peru, this was formerly HMS *Ceylon*. Modified before delivery, it received a new mast, increased anti-aircraft armament and improved bridge accommodation. Radar equipment was also updated, for long-range search, height-finding and fire-control. It remained active until 1982.

SPECIFICATIONS	
Type:	Peruvian cruiser
Displacement:	11,633 tonnes (11,450 tons)
Dimensions:	169.4m x 18.9m x 6.4m (555ft 6in x 62ft x 20ft 9in)
Machinery:	Quadruple screws, geared turbines
Top speed:	31.5 knots
Main armament:	Nine 152mm (6in) guns, eight 102mm (4in) guns
Complement:	920
Launched:	1942 (refitted 1960)

TIMELINE
1956  1960  1957

CRUISERS OF OTHER NAVIES

Prat

SPECIFICATIONS	
Type:	Chilean cruiser
Displacement:	12,405 tonnes (12,210 tons)
Dimensions:	185.4m x 18.8m x 6.95m (608ft 4in x 61ft 9in x 22ft 9in)
Machinery:	Quadruple screws, geared turbines
Top speed:	30 knots
Main armament:	Fifteen 152mm (6in) guns, eight 127mm (5in) guns
Armour:	127mm (5in) belt, 51mm (2in) deck
Complement:	868
Launched:	1936 (modernized 1957)

Formerly the US *Brooklyn* class cruiser *Nashville*, this World War II veteran was transferred to the Chilean Navy in 1951, as was *Brooklyn* itself, renamed *O'Higgins*. Both ships were refitted and modernized in the United States in 1957–58. *Prat* was decommissioned in 1984, while *O'Higgins* was stricken only in 1992.

Tiger

SPECIFICATIONS	
Type:	British cruiser
Displacement:	12,273 tonnes (12,080 tons)
Dimensions:	170m x 20m x 6.4m (555ft 6in x 64ft x 21ft 3in)
Machinery:	Quadruple screws, turbines
Top speed:	31.5 knots
Main armament:	Four 152mm (6in) guns, six 76mm (3in) guns
Launched:	October 1945/refitted 1959

Tiger was originally laid down in 1941, but work stopped in 1946 and it was finally completed to new plans in 1959, as one of the last cruisers to enter British service. However, it proved unsuitable for the conditions and requirements of the period, and after little use, was withdrawn in the 1960s and scrapped in 1986.

Caio Duilio

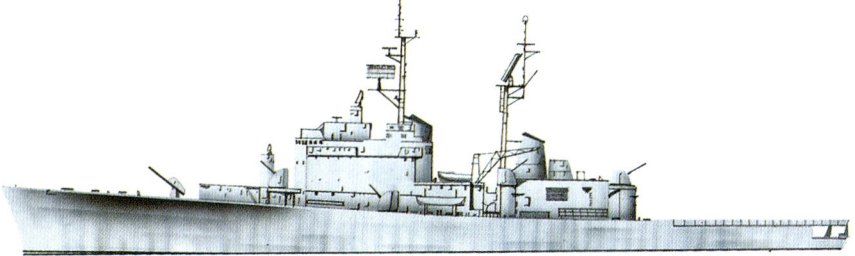

SPECIFICATIONS	
Type:	Italian cruiser
Displacement:	6604 tonnes (6506 tons)
Dimensions:	144m x 17m x 4.7m (472ft 4in x 55ft 7in x 15ft 4in)
Machinery:	Twin screws, geared turbines
Top speed:	31 knots
Main armament:	Eight 76mm (3in) guns, plus Terrier surface-to-air missiles
Complement:	485
Launched:	December 1962

Caio Duilio and its sister-ship *Andrea Doria* were helicopter cruisers for anti-submarine and air defence, designed to a new plan, having a wide beam in relation to their length. They carried three AB 212SW armed helicopters. In 1980, *Caio Duilio* became a training ship, and was decommissioned in 1991.

1959

1962

345

SHIP TYPES 1950–1999

Destroyers (guided missile): Part 1

The introduction of the guided missile and the new generation of long-range guided or homing torpedoes, as well as radar-directed, rapid-fire guns, made the medium-sized warship a more formidable fighting craft than ever before. Destroyer design, construction and ship-management entered a phase of rapid, significant change.

Farragut

SPECIFICATIONS	
Type:	US destroyer
Displacement:	5738.4 tonnes (5648 tons)
Dimensions:	156.3m x 15.9m x 5.3m (512ft 6in x 52ft 4in x 17ft 9in)
Machinery:	Twin screws, geared turbines
Top speed:	32 knots
Main armament:	One Terrier (later Standard) SAM missile system, one ASROC rocket-boosted ASW torpedo launcher, six 324mm (12.75in) torpedo tubes
Complement:	360
Launched:	1958

This class became the US Navy's first missile ships, and *Farragut* was among the first to carry the ASROC system, which fired rocket-boosted anti-submarine torpedoes. Later it was fitted with the Naval Tactical Data System for air defence command and control. Decommissioned in 1989, it was stricken in 1992.

Gremyaschiy

SPECIFICATIONS	
Type:	Soviet destroyer
Displacement:	4259 tonnes (4192 tons)
Dimensions:	138.9m x 14.84m x 4.2m (455ft 9in x 48ft 8in x 13ft 9in)
Machinery:	Twin screws, geared turbines
Top speed:	34.5 knots
Main armament:	Two SSN-N-1 SSM, two anti-submarine rocket launchers, six 533mm (21in) torpedo tubes
Complement:	310
Launched:	1959

The 'Krupny' class of nine destroyers were the first missile-armed ships in the Soviet fleet. The original SS-N-1 Scrubber missile system was soon removed and the class rearmed for anti-submarine warfare. With 16 57mm (2.24in) guns, the ship was lightly armed for self-defence, reducing its usefulness. It was stricken in 1995.

TIMELINE			
	1958 	1959 	1960 

DESTROYERS (GUIDED MISSILE): PART 1

Devonshire

SPECIFICATIONS	
Type:	British destroyer
Displacement:	6299 tonnes (6200 tons)
Dimensions:	158m x 16m x 6m (520ft 6in x 54ft x 20ft)
Machinery:	Twin screws, turbines plus four gas turbines
Top speed:	32.5 knots
Main armament:	Four 114mm (4.5in) guns, twin launcher for Seaslug missile
Complement:	471
Launched:	June 1960

Designed at the end of the 1950s, *Devonshire* and seven others were built to operate in the fall-out area of a nuclear explosion, with deck installations under cover. Later, Seacat missiles replaced the Seaslug and some of the class also carried the Exocet anti-ship missile. *Devonshire* was sunk as a target in 1984.

Boykiy

SPECIFICATIONS	
Type:	Soviet destroyer
Displacement:	4826 tonnes (4750 tons)
Dimensions:	140m x 15m x 5m (458ft 9in x 49ft 5in x 16ft 6in)
Machinery:	Twin screws, geared turbines
Top speed:	35 knots
Main armament:	Eight 57mm (2.24in) guns, plus missiles
Complement:	310
Launched:	1960

Boykiy was originally completed as a missile ship armed with SS-N-1 launchers. When these became obsolete in the mid-1960s, it was converted into an anti-submarine vessel. *Boykiy* served in the North Atlantic and the North Pacific. It was towed to Spain for breaking in 1988, grounding off Norway on the way.

Impavido

SPECIFICATIONS	
Type:	Italian destroyer
Displacement:	4054 tonnes (3990 tons)
Dimensions:	131.3m x 13.7m x 4.4m (430ft 9in x 45ft x 14ft 5in)
Machinery:	Twin screws, turbines
Top speed:	34 knots
Main armament:	Two 127mm (5in) guns, one Tartar missile launcher, six 533mm (21in) torpedo tubes
Complement:	340
Launched:	May 1962

Impavido was one of Italy's first two missile-armed destroyers. Derived from the *Impetuoso*-class destroyers, it had a US Mk 13 launcher for Tartar surface-to-air missiles. The after funnel was heightened to clear the fire control tracker on top of the aft structure. Modernized in 1976–77, *Impavido* was decommissioned in 1992.

1962

Destroyers (guided missile): Part 2

As usual with warship types, destroyers tended to get larger, offering a more substantial launch platform for various missiles. The proposed US *Zumwalt* class, to replace the *Arleigh Burkes* in the years after 2010, has an anticipated displacement of 12,000 tonnes (11,808 tons), equivalent to a heavy cruiser of 60 years ago.

Ognevoy

Project 61 from the 1960s produced 20 guided missile destroyers, known as the 'Kashin' class. The third completed, *Ognevoy*, was given cruise missiles and sonar and new air defence in the mid-1970s. Sensor equipment included air-search, navigation and fire-control radar. *Ognevoy* was broken up in 1990.

SPECIFICATIONS	
Type:	Soviet destroyer
Displacement:	4460.3 tonnes (4390 tons)
Dimensions:	144m x 15.8m x 4.6m (472ft 5in x 51ft 10in x 15ft 1in)
Machinery:	Twin screws, four gas turbines
Top speed:	18 knots
Main armament:	Two SA-N-1 SSM launchers, two RBU-6000 and two RBU-1000 anti-submarine rocket launchers, four 76mm (3in) guns, five 533mm (21in) torpedo tubes
Complement:	266
Launched:	1963

Duquesne

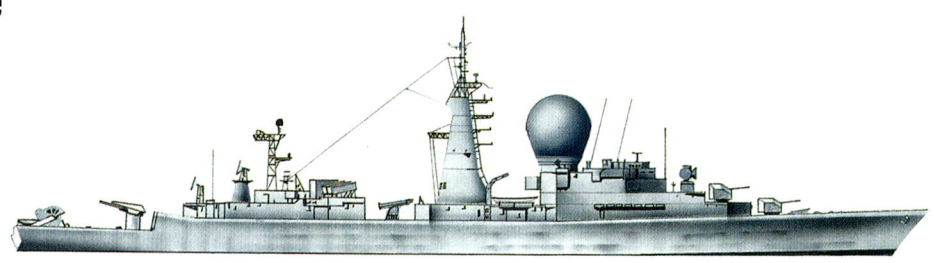

With its sister ship *Suffren*, *Duquesne* was the first French destroyer designed to carry surface-to-air missiles, serving as escort ships for the new generation of French aircraft carriers. *Duquesne* also received four Exocet missile launchers. Electronics were modernized in 1990–91, and it was decommissioned in 2007.

SPECIFICATIONS	
Type:	French destroyer
Displacement:	6187 tonnes (6090 tons)
Dimensions:	157.6m x 15.5m x 7m (517ft x 50ft 10in x 23ft 9in)
Machinery:	Twin screws, turbines
Top speed:	34 knots
Main armament:	Two 100mm (3.9in) guns, one Malafon anti-submarine missile launcher/four torpedo launchers
Launched:	February 1966

TIMELINE

1963  1966  1973

DESTROYERS (GUIDED MISSILE): PART 2

Duguay-Trouin

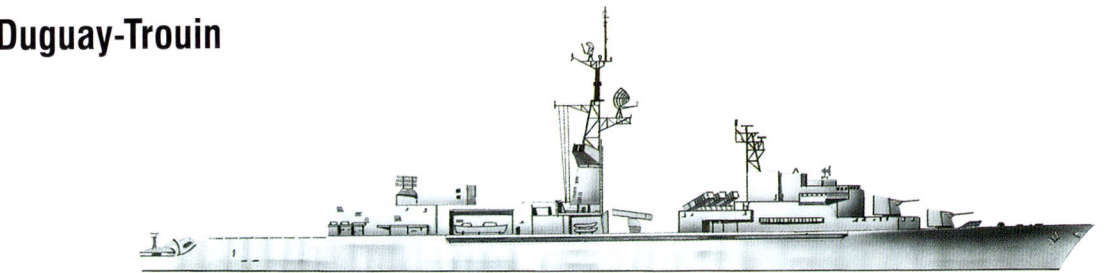

The three *Tourville*-class guided-missile destroyers were the first French warships of destroyer size purpose-built to operate two anti-submarine helicopters. In 1979, *Duguay-Trouin*'s Crotale missile launcher replaced a third gun turret, and new generation air-surveillance radar was fitted. It was decommissioned in 1999.

SPECIFICATIONS	
Type:	French destroyer
Displacement:	5892 tonnes (5800 tons)
Dimensions:	152.5m x 15.3m x 6.5m (500ft 4in x 50ft 2in x 21ft 4in)
Machinery:	Twin screws, turbines
Top speed:	32 knots
Main armament:	Two 100mm (3.9in) guns, one eight-cell Crotale launcher
Complement:	282
Launched:	June 1973

Spruance

Bigger than many former cruisers, the *Spruance* class was designed to offer a stable weapon-launcher, able to operate in difficult sea conditions. Its successful hull design was used, with modifications, on two other classes of US warship. After serving in the Atlantic fleet, *Spruance* was sunk as a target in 2006.

SPECIFICATIONS	
Type:	US destroyer
Displacement:	8168 tonnes (8040 tons)
Dimensions:	171.7m x 16.8m x 5.8m (563ft 4in x 55ft 2in x 19ft)
Machinery:	Twin screws, gas turbines
Top speed:	32.5 knots
Main armament:	Two 127mm (5in) guns, Tomahawk and Harpoon missiles
Complement:	296
Launched:	1973

Tachikaze

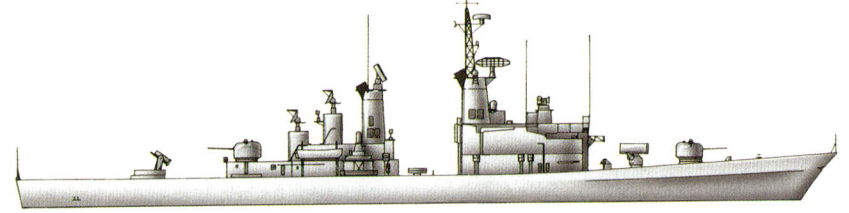

Like all Japanese post-war navy ships, *Tachikaze* was equipped with American weapons. Two 20mm (0.79in) Phalanx CIWS were added in 1983, when the Harpoon SSM were installed. It could also accommodate a SH-601 helicopter. From 1998 to decommissioning in January 2007, it was the Fleet Escort Force flagship.

SPECIFICATIONS	
Type:	Japanese destroyer
Displacement:	4877 tonnes (4800 tons)
Dimensions:	143m x 14.3m x 4.6m (469ft 2in x 46ft 10in x 15ft 1in)
Machinery:	Twin screws, geared turbines
Top speed:	32 knots
Main armament:	Eight Harpoon SSM, one Mk 13 Standard SAM launcher, one ASROC launcher, two 127mm (5in) guns
Complement:	277
Launched:	1974

 1974

Destroyers (guided missile): Part 3

Air and surface combat are usually seen as the prime role of the destroyer, though some navies have also fitted out destroyers for anti-submarine roles. CIWS (close-in weapons system) response systems are generally fitted, based on 20mm or 30mm (0.79in or 1.18in) guns, with a variety of missile and anti-missile systems, depending on the supplier.

Santisima Trinidad

Based on the Royal Navy's Type 42 destroyer, and carrying a Lynx helicopter, *Santisima Trinidad* was commissioned in 1981. In April 1982, it was the lead ship in Argentina's invasion of the Falkland Islands. In the late 1980s and 1990s, much of its equipment was cannibalized to keep its sister ship *Hercules* active.

SPECIFICATIONS

Type:	Argentinian destroyer
Displacement:	4419.6 tonnes (4350 tons)
Dimensions:	125m x 14m x 5.8m (410ft x 46ft x 19ft)
Machinery:	Twin screws, four gas turbines
Top speed:	30 knots
Main armament:	One GWS30 Sea Dart SAM missile launcher, one 114mm (4.5in) gun, six 324mm (12.5in) torpedo tubes
Complement:	312
Launched:	1974

Dupleix

Dupleix was one of eight ships built at Brest as anti-submarine vessels. A major innovation was the use of gas turbine engines, developing 52,000hp for a speed of 30 knots. All in the class had a double hangar aft for helicopters. The ships are well adapted for surface work, as well as the standard ASW role.

SPECIFICATIONS

Type:	French destroyer
Displacement:	4236 tonnes (4170 tons)
Dimensions:	139m x 14m x 5.7m (456ft x 46ft x 18ft 8in)
Machinery:	Twin screws, gas turbines, plus diesels
Top speed:	30knots
Main armament:	One 100mm (3.9in) gun, four MM38 Exocet SSM launchers, octuple Crote Navale SAM launcher, two fixed torpedo launchers
Complement:	216
Launched:	December 1978

TIMELINE

1974　　1978　　1982

DESTROYERS (GUIDED MISSILE): PART 3

Euro

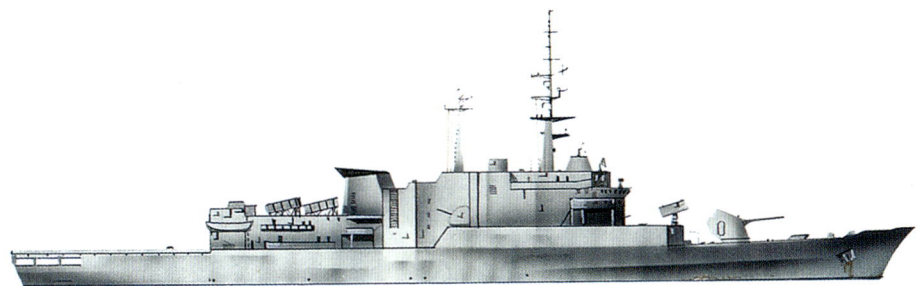

Euro entered service in 1983. The aft flight deck is 27m (88ft 6in) long and 12m (39ft 4in) wide, and a Variable Depth Sonar is streamed out on a 900m (984yd) long cable from a stern well. As the Italian Navy does not use the term 'destroyer', it is classed as a guided-missile frigate.

SPECIFICATIONS	
Type:	Italian destroyer
Displacement:	3088 tonnes (3040 tons)
Dimensions:	122.7m x 12.9m x 8.4m (402ft 6in x 42ft 4in x 27ft 6in)
Machinery:	Twin screws, diesels and gas turbines
Top speed:	29 knots (diesel), 32 knots (turbines)
Main armament:	One 127mm (5in) gun plus missiles
Launched:	December 1982

Mutenia

Built in Romania to Russian designs and using mostly Russian equipment, *Mutenia* was well equipped, having two Alouette III helicopters. It spent lengthy periods out of service, suffering from the problems of a one-off type as well as a lack of operating funds. In 1990–92, it was refitted with anti-submarine weapons.

SPECIFICATIONS	
Type:	Romanian destroyer
Displacement:	5882.6 tonnes (5790 tons)
Dimensions:	144.6m x 14.8m x 7m (474ft 4in x 48ft 6in x 23ft)
Machinery:	Twin screws, diesels
Top speed:	31 knots
Main armament:	Eight SSN-N-2C SSM, four 76mm (3in) guns, six 533mm (21in) torpedo tubes, two RBU-120 anti-submarine rocket launchers
Complement:	270
Launched:	1982

Hamayuki

Japan's Maritime Self Defence Force produced some versatile, well-armed ships in the 1980s. *Hamayuki* was fifth of 12 *Hatsuyuki* class ships and carried a Mitsubishi-built HSS 2B Sea King helicopter. Sensor equipment includes hull-mounted sonar, and air-search, sea-search and fire-control radar.

SPECIFICATIONS	
Type:	Japanese destroyer
Displacement:	3759.2 tonnes (3700 tons)
Dimensions:	131.7m x 13.7m x 4.3m (432ft 4in x 44ft 11in x 14ft 3in)
Machinery:	Twin screws, four gas turbines
Top speed:	30 knots
Main armament:	Eight Harpoon SSM, one Sea Sparrow SAM, one 76mm (3in) gun, two Mk15 Phalanx 20mm (0.79in) CIWS, one ASROC, six 324mm (12.7in) torpedo tubes
Complement:	190
Launched:	1983

Destroyers (guided missile): Part 4

Gas turbine propulsion, enabling rapid acceleration to maximum speed, is favoured for modern destroyers. The Soviet 'Kashin' class used gas turbines in the 1960s, as did the Canadian *Iroquois* class of the 1970s and the ships of the US *Spruance* class, launched between 1972 and 1980, and the *Arleigh Burke* class, still in service.

Edinburgh

SPECIFICATIONS	
Type:	British destroyer
Displacement:	4851 tonnes (4775 tons)
Dimensions:	141m x 14.9m x 5.8m (463ft x 48ft x 19ft)
Machinery:	Twin screws, gas turbines
Top speed:	30 knots
Main armament:	One 114mm (4.5in) gun, helicopter-launched Mk44 torpedoes, two triple mounts for Mk46 anti-submarine torpedoes, one Sea Dart launcher
Launched:	March 1983

Edinburgh was designed as an air-defence/ASW ship to work with a naval or amphibious task force. Its two helicopters carry air-to-surface weapons for use against lightly defended surface ships. Refitted in 1990, *Edinburgh* saw service off Iraq in the second Gulf War (2003) and had a further full refit in 2004–5.

Arleigh Burke

SPECIFICATIONS	
Type:	US guided missile destroyer
Displacement:	8534 tonnes (8400 tons)
Dimensions:	142.1m x 18.3m x 9.1m (266ft 3in x 60ft x 30ft)
Machinery:	Twin screws, gas turbines
Top speed:	30+ knots
Main armament:	Harpoon and Tomahawk missiles, 127mm (5in) gun
Launched:	1989

This class was designed to replace the *Adams* and *Coontz* class destroyers, which entered service in the early 1960s. *Arleigh Burke* was commissioned in 1991, to provide effective anti-aircraft cover, for which the SPY 1 D version of the Aegis system was fitted. It also has anti-surface and anti-submarine weapons.

TIMELINE

1983   1989   1991

Kongo

Kongo is based on the US *Arleigh Burke* class, its dimensions easily justifying cruiser designation. The flight deck has no hangar but can take a SH-60J Seahawk helicopter. Fitted with the Aegis air defence radar and missile system, the class has recently been modified to intercept North Korean ballistic missiles.

SPECIFICATIONS	
Type:	Japanese destroyer
Displacement:	9636.8 tonnes (9485 tons)
Dimensions:	160.9m x 20.9m x 6.2m (520ft 2in x 68ft 7in x 20ft 4in)
Machinery:	Twin screws, gas turbines
Top speed:	30 knots
Main armament:	Eight Harpoon SSM, two Mk41 VLS with Standard missiles and ASROC torpedoes, one 127mm (5in) gun, two 20mm (0.79in) Phalanx CIWS, six 324mm (12.75in) torpedo tubes
Complement:	300
Launched:	1991

Brandenburg

Brandenburg was lead ship of a class of four, identified as Type 123, and intended for air defence. They are equipped with air-search and air/surface search radar, two fire-control trackers and hull-mounted sonar. Two Lynx Mk88 helicopters are carried. Germany has built similar ships for Portugal and Turkey.

SPECIFICATIONS	
Type:	German destroyer
Displacement:	4343.4 tonnes (4275 tons)
Dimensions:	138.9m x 16.7m x 6.3m (455ft 8in x 57ft 1in x 20ft 8in)
Machinery:	Twin screws, gas turbines plus diesels
Top speed:	29 knots
Main armament:	Four MM38 Exocet SSM, one VLS for Sea Sparrow SAM, two 21-cell RAM launchers, one 76mm (3in) gun, six 324mm (12.75in) torpedo tubes
Complement:	219
Launched:	1992

Murasame

Commissioned in 1996, designed primarily for air defence but with anti-submarine potential, *Murasame* is a typically all-round member of the modern Japanese fleet. An SH-60J helicopter is carried, with hangar. The *Murasame* class has full radar search equipment, and both hull-mounted and towed sonar.

SPECIFICATIONS	
Type:	Japanese destroyer
Displacement:	5181.6 tonnes (5100 tons)
Dimensions:	151m x 16.9m x 5.2m (495ft 5in x 55ft 7in x 17ft 1in)
Machinery:	Twin screws, gas turbines
Top speed:	33 knots
Main armament:	Eight Harpoon SSM, two Mk41 VLS with Standard missiles and ASROC torpedoes, one 127mm (5in) gun, two 20mm (0.79in) Phalanx CIWS, six 324mm (12.75in) torpedo tubes
Complement:	170
Launched:	1994

SHIP TYPES 1950–1999

Destroyers (anti-submarine): Part 1

From its inception as a warship-type, torpedoes were the main armament of a destroyer, enabling it to be a threat to much larger ships. While many destroyers still carry torpedo tubes, these no longer define the destroyer as such. Some ships classed as destroyers have no torpedoes, relying on missiles and and ASW mortars.

St Laurent

SPECIFICATIONS	
Type:	Canadian destroyer
Displacement:	2641.6 tonnes (2600 tons)
Dimensions:	111.6m x 12.8m x 4m (366ft x 42ft x 13ft 2in)
Machinery:	Twin screws, turbines
Top speed:	28 knots
Main armament:	Four 76mm (3in) guns, two Limbo Mk10 anti-submarine mortars
Complement:	290
Launched:	1951

Seven ships formed the *St Laurent* class, the lead vessel being completed in 1955. In the early 1960s, the armament was updated and variable-depth sonar was mounted at the stern. A helicopter deck and hangar were built in. *St Laurent* was decommissioned in 1979 and sank under tow to the breakers in 1980.

Neustrashimyy

SPECIFICATIONS	
Type:	Soviet destroyer
Displacement:	3434 tonnes (3830 tons)
Dimensions:	133.8m x 13.6m x 4.4m (439ft 1in x 44ft 6in x 14ft 6in)
Machinery:	Twin screws, geared turbines
Top speed:	36 knots
Main armament:	Four 130mm (5in) guns, 10 533mm (21in) torpedo tubes
Complement:	305
Launched:	1951

Planned as lead ship of a large class, completed in 1955, *Neustrashimyy* ended up as a one-off. But it displayed many features to reflect the nuclear era, including air-conditioning and sealable crew accommodation. Its pressure-fired boiler design was used in many subsequent ships. It was broken up in 1975.

TIMELINE   1951   1952

DESTROYERS (ANTI-SUBMARINE): PART 1

Grom

Grom was the former Soviet *Smetlivy*, one of two destroyers transferred from the USSR Baltic Fleet to Poland in 1957. It was a member of a class comprising the first Russian destroyers built after World War II, and incorporating features from German destroyers. In service until 1973, *Grom* was scrapped in 1977.

SPECIFICATIONS	
Type:	Polish destroyer
Displacement:	3150 tonnes (3100 tons)
Dimensions:	120.5m x 11.8m x 4.6m (395ft 4in x 38ft 9in x 15ft)
Machinery:	Twin screws, turbines
Main armament:	Four 130mm (5.1in) guns, two 76mm (3in) anti-aircraft guns
Launched:	1952

Groningen

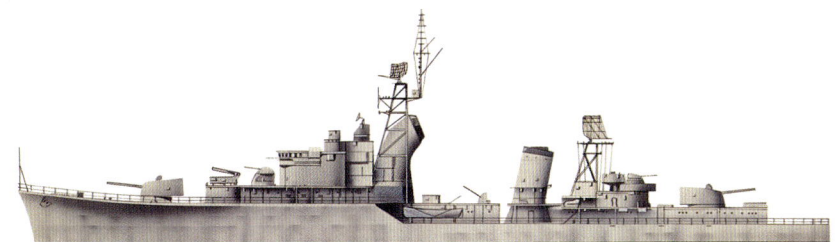

Groningen's class of eight had some side armour as well as deck protection. They were also some of the first destroyers to have no torpedo capability. Two short-range ASW rocket launchers were fitted. It was one of seven of the class sold to Peru in the 1980s. As *Galvez*, it was deleted in 1991.

SPECIFICATIONS	
Type:	Dutch destroyer
Displacement:	3119 tonnes (3070 tons)
Dimensions:	116m x 11.7m x 3.9m (380ft 3in x 38ft 6in x 13ft)
Machinery:	Twin screws, turbines
Top speed:	36 knots
Main armament:	Four 120mm (4.7in) guns
Launched:	January 1954

Almirante Riveros

This heavily-armed destroyer was one of a pair built in England. It returned to the UK for modernization work in 1975, when missile systems were fitted, replacing its secondary 40mm (1.57in) armament, and Squid anti-submarine mortars. It served for another 20 years. Decommissioned in 1998, it was sunk as a target in that year.

SPECIFICATIONS	
Type:	Chilean destroyer
Displacement:	3650 tonnes (3300 tons)
Dimensions:	122.5m x 13.1m x 4m (402ft x 43ft x 13ft 4in)
Machinery:	Twin screws, turbines
Top speed:	34.5 knots
Main armament:	Four 102mm (4in) guns, four MM38 Exocet SSM, one Seacat SAM system, six 324mm (12.75in) torpedo tubes
Complement:	266
Launched:	December 1958

1954

1958

Destroyers (anti-submarine): Part 2

Destroyer-borne ASW helicopters are fitted with sonobuoys, dipping sonar and magnetic anomaly detectors to identify potential submerged targets, and armed with torpedoes or depth charges. Helicopters have become of such combat value that some ships are identified as 'helicopter destroyers' or 'helicopter cruisers'.

Coronel Bolognesi

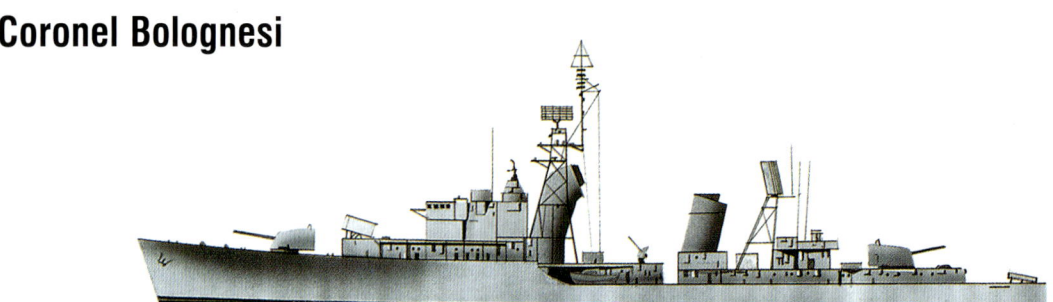

Coronel Bolognesi was formerly the Dutch *Overijssel*, of the *Friesland* class. Between 1980 and 1982, they were transferred to the Peruvian Navy, and fitted with Exocet missiles and other new weapons systems and sensors. *Coronel Bolognesi* arrived in Peru in July 1982 and was decommissioned in 1990.

SPECIFICATIONS	
Type:	Peruvian destroyer
Displacement:	3150 tonnes (3100 tons)
Dimensions:	116m x 12m x 5m (380ft 7in x 38ft 5in x 17ft)
Machinery:	Twin screws, turbines
Top speed:	36 knots
Main armament:	Four 120mm (4.7in) guns
Launched:	August 1955

Aragua

British-built, *Aragua* was one of the three *Nueva Esparta* class destroyers. Its two sister-ships were later given more up-to-date armament, including Seacat surface-to-air missiles, and their radar systems were also modernized. *Aragua* remained very much as delivered. It was withdrawn from service in 1975.

SPECIFICATIONS	
Type:	Venezuelan destroyer
Displacement:	3353 tonnes (3300 tons)
Dimensions:	122.5m x 13.1m x 3.9m (402ft x 43ft x 12ft 9in)
Machinery:	Twin screws, geared turbines
Top speed:	34.5 knots
Main armament:	Six 114mm (4.5in) guns, three 533mm (21in) torpedo tubes, two Squid anti-submarine mortars, two depth charge racks
Complement:	254
Launched:	1955

TIMELINE

1955   1966

DESTROYERS (ANTI-SUBMARINE): PART 2

Asagumo

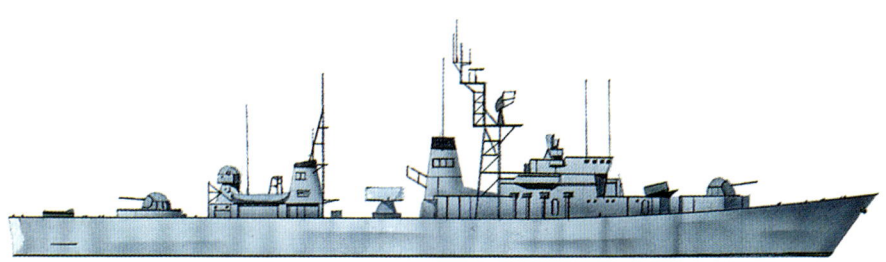

Asagumo and five sister-ships were typical of the mid period of Japanese destroyers after World War II. With 711 tonnes (700 tons) of oil fuel, *Asagumo* had a range of 11,400km (6000 miles) at 20 knots. The gunnery, radar and sensors were all supplied by the United States. It was decommissioned in 1998.

SPECIFICATIONS	
Type:	Japanese destroyer
Displacement:	2083 tonnes (2050 tons)
Dimensions:	114m x 11.8m x 4m (374ft x 38ft 9in x 13ft)
Machinery:	Twin screws, diesel engines
Main armament:	Four 76mm (3in) guns, six torpedo tubes
Launched:	1966

Audace

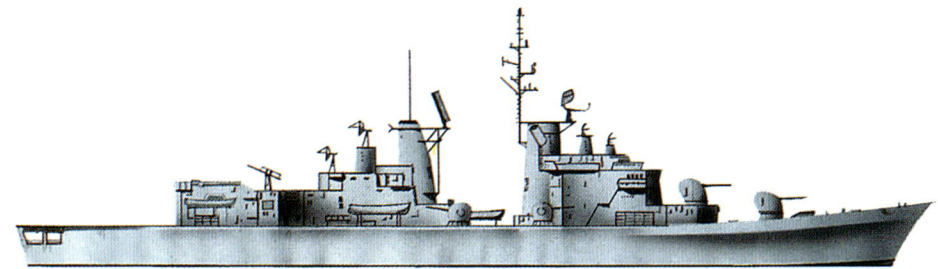

Audace was a multi-function fleet escort, its prime task being anti-submarine action. Two helicopters with weapons kit and sensors were carried. Some of its weapons had a poor arc of fire due to the height of the superstructure. Serving off Lebanon in 1982 and in the Gulf in 1990–91, it was decommissioned in 2006.

SPECIFICATIONS	
Type:	Italian destroyer
Displacement:	4470 tonnes (4400 tons)
Dimensions:	135.9 x 14.6m x 4.5m (446ft x 48ft x 15ft)
Machinery:	Twin screws, geared turbines
Top speed:	33 knots
Main armament:	Two 127mm (5in) guns, one SAM launcher
Launched:	1971

Haruna

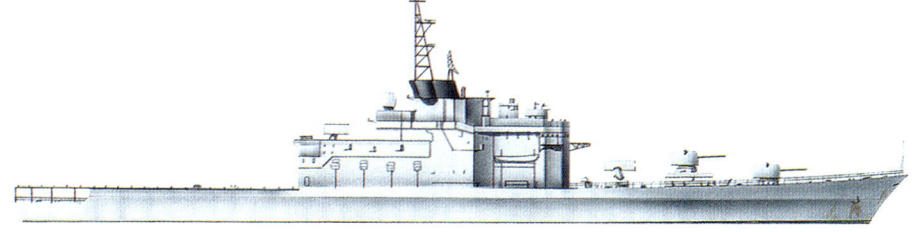

Haruna is a command ship for anti-submarine escort groups, its entire aft part devoted to facilities for three Sea King helicopters. The hangar occupies the full beam of the vessel. Automatic guns fire up to 40 rounds per minute. In 1986–87, *Haruna* underwent a major refit to improve its anti-aircraft defences.

SPECIFICATIONS	
Type:	Japanese destroyer
Displacement:	5029 tonnes (4950 tons)
Dimensions:	153m x 17.5m x 5.2m (502ft 5in x 57ft 5in x 17ft)
Machinery:	Twin screws, turbines
Main armament:	Two 127mm (5in) guns, Sea Sparrow missile launcher, six 324mm (12.75in) torpedo tubes
Launched:	February 1972

1971

1972

SHIP TYPES 1950–1999

Destroyers & Frigates (anti-submarine)

Around 200 crew are needed for a destroyer – not a large number in relation to the size of the ship and its firepower, and made possible by the use of technology. Post-2010 destroyers will include a 3-D phased array radar system in their equipment.

Gurkha

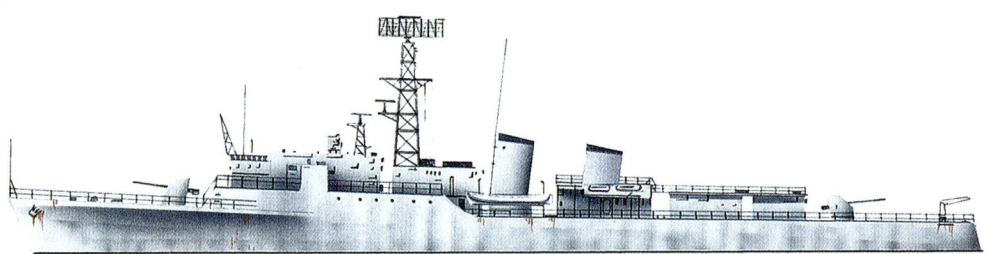

SPECIFICATIONS	
Type:	British frigate
Displacement:	2743 tonnes (2700 tons)
Dimensions:	109m x 12.9m x 5.3m (360ft x 42ft 4in x 17ft 6in)
Machinery:	Single screw, turbine and gas turbine
Top speed:	28 knots
Main armament:	Two 114mm (4.5in) guns, one Limbo three-barrelled anti-submarine mortar
Complement:	253
Launched:	July 1960

Gurkha was the third of seven all-purpose frigates of the 'Tribal' class, among the first British warships to be air-conditioned in all crew areas and most working spaces. Decommissioned in 1979, reactivated at the time of the Falklands conflict in 1982, *Gurkha* was sold to Indonesia in 1985, and laid up in 1999.

Georges Leygues

SPECIFICATIONS	
Type:	French destroyer
Displacement:	4236 tonnes (4170 tons)
Dimensions:	139m x 14m x 5.7m (456ft x 46ft x 18ft 8in)
Machinery:	Twin screws, gas turbines and diesel engines
Top speed:	30 knots
Main armament:	One 100mm (3.9in) gun, Exocet missiles
Launched:	December 1976

Georges Leygues and its seven sister destroyers are France's prime anti-submarine force. Gas turbine engines develop 52,000hp, while diesels develop 10,400hp; the cruising range at 18 knots on diesels is 18,050km (9500 miles). *Georges Leygues* carries two Lynx helicopters and has full hangar facilities.

TIMELINE 1960 1976 1978

DESTROYERS & FRIGATES (ANTI-SUBMARINE)

Glasgow

Glasgow was active in the Falklands War, and served at East Timor and in the South Atlantic patrol. It had air-search radar, and a fire control system, and carried one helicopter. Two triple 324mm (12.75in) anti-submarine torpedo tube sets were fitted. Decommissioned in 2005, it was broken up in Turkey in 2009.

SPECIFICATIONS	
Type:	British destroyer
Displacement:	4165 tonnes (4100 tons)
Dimensions:	125m x 14.3m x 5.8m (410ft x 47ft x 19ft)
Machinery:	Twin screws, gas turbines
Top speed:	30 knots
Main armament:	One 114mm (4.5in) gun, one twin Sea Dart mount
Launched:	April 1976

Cushing

Cushing was the last survivor of the *Spruance* class, sunk as a target in 2005. Anti-submarine ships, they carried two helicopters, plus the Phalanx CIWS air defence system, and Harpoon and Sparrow missiles. The first US Navy surface vessels fitted with gas turbines, they could run on a single engine at 19 knots.

SPECIFICATIONS	
Type:	US destroyer
Displacement:	7924 tonnes (7800 tons)
Dimensions:	161m x 17m x 9m (529ft 2in x 55ft 1in x 28ft 10in)
Machinery:	Twin screws, gas turbines
Top speed:	30 knots
Main armament:	Two 127mm (5in) guns, six 322mm (12.75in) torpedo tubes
Launched:	June 1978

Hatsuyuki

A radical departure from previous Japanese anti-submarine destroyer designs, *Hatsuyuki* resembles the French *Georges Leygues* class in its layout, although its weapons systems are of US origin. The propulsion machinery is British: two groups of gas turbines, one set developing 56,780hp, and the other 10,680hp.

SPECIFICATIONS	
Type:	Japanese destroyer
Displacement:	3760 tonnes (3700 tons)
Dimensions:	131.7m x 13.7m x 4.3m (432ft x 45ft x 14ft)
Machinery:	Twin screws, gas turbines
Top speed:	30 knots
Main armament:	One 76mm (3in) gun, one eight-cell Sea Sparrow launcher, two 20mm (0.79in) Phalanx CIWS
Complement:	190
Launched:	November 1980

1978    1980

SHIP TYPES 1950–1999

Tromp

Tromp and sister-ship *De Ruyter* acted as flagships to two long-range NATO task groups, for operating in the Eastern Atlantic. An octuple Sea Sparrow launcher with 60 reloads provided short-range anti-aircraft and anti-missile defence, and a later refit added a Goalkeeper point defence gun system. A single Lynx helicopter is carried.

Tromp

Replacing two cruisers in service with the Royal Netherlands navy, HNLMS *Tromp* and *De Ruyter* were among the largest and most capable of frigates afloat. Weapons fitted included Harpoon, Standard and Sea Sparrow missiles.

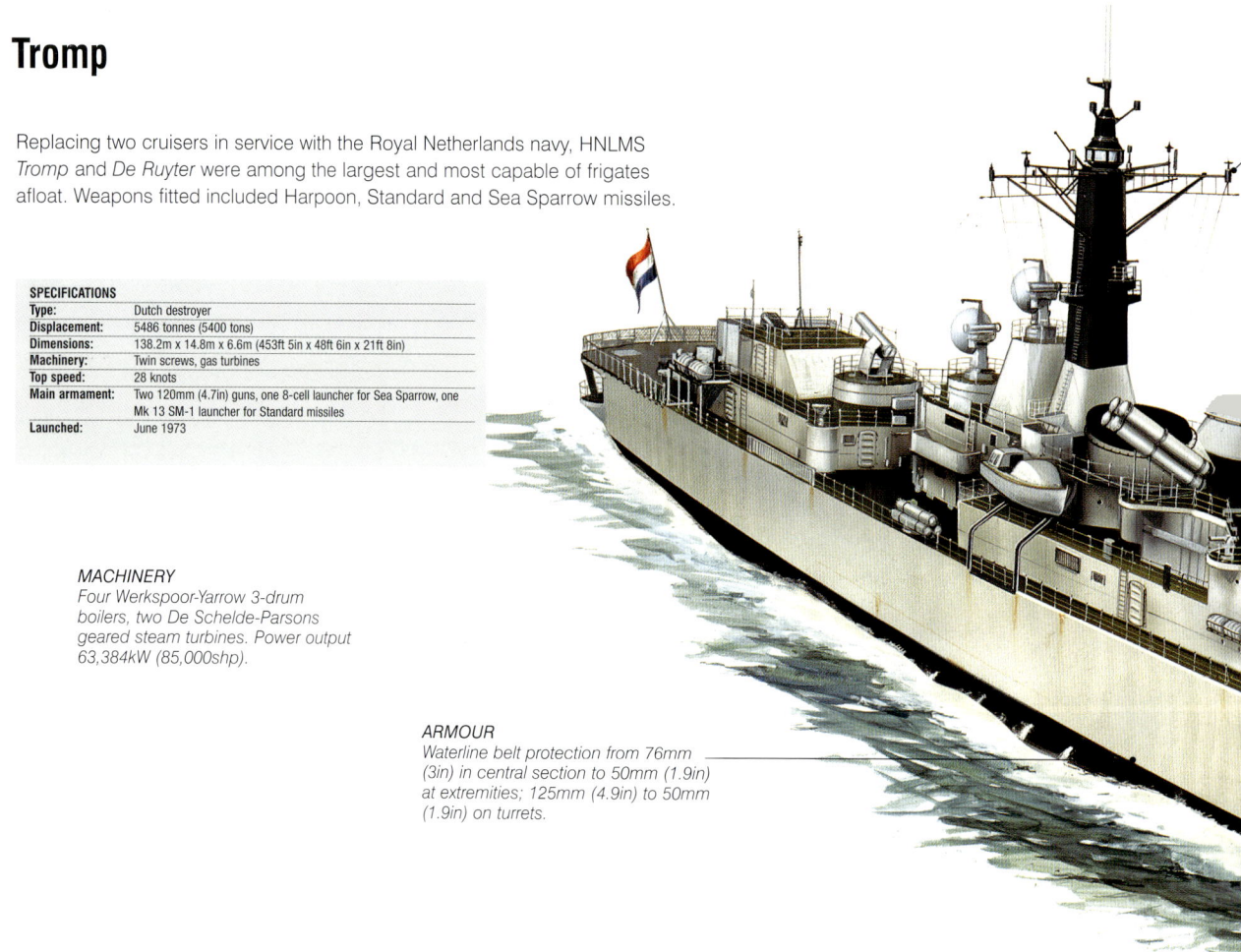

SPECIFICATIONS	
Type:	Dutch destroyer
Displacement:	5486 tonnes (5400 tons)
Dimensions:	138.2m x 14.8m x 6.6m (453ft 5in x 48ft 6in x 21ft 8in)
Machinery:	Twin screws, gas turbines
Top speed:	28 knots
Main armament:	Two 120mm (4.7in) guns, one 8-cell launcher for Sea Sparrow, one Mk 13 SM-1 launcher for Standard missiles
Launched:	June 1973

MACHINERY
Four Werkspoor-Yarrow 3-drum boilers, two De Schelde-Parsons geared steam turbines. Power output 63,384kW (85,000shp).

ARMOUR
Waterline belt protection from 76mm (3in) in central section to 50mm (1.9in) at extremities; 125mm (4.9in) to 50mm (1.9in) on turrets.

TROMP

MASTS
In original form the ship was unusual in having no separate masts, with extensions to the control tower and funnel serving instead.

UPGRADE
A major upgrade in 1985-88 brought new search and fire-control radar systems, decoy launchers and other countermeasures systems, and data links.

MISSILES
In 1993 eight Otomat Mk2 SSMs were installed and in 1996 the Bofors guns were replaced by Oto Melara twin 40L70 DARDO compact gun mountings.

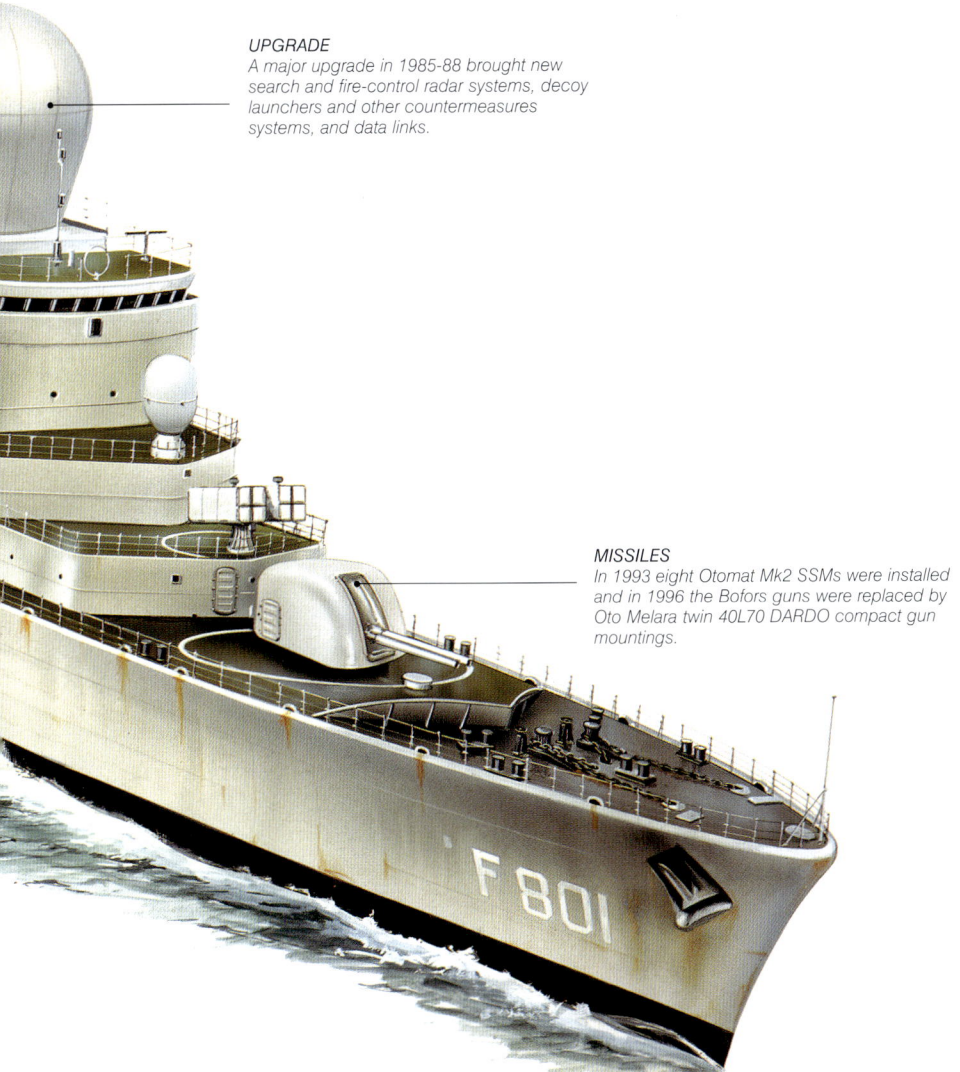

Frigates of the 1950s

It is not always easy to attach type-names to modern warships. 'Frigate' is a case in point. Earlier in the twentieth century, this described an escort ship, especially for merchant convoys. It was generally smaller and slower than a destroyer, and not armed with torpedoes. In the 1950s, this description was already ceasing to fit.

Grafton

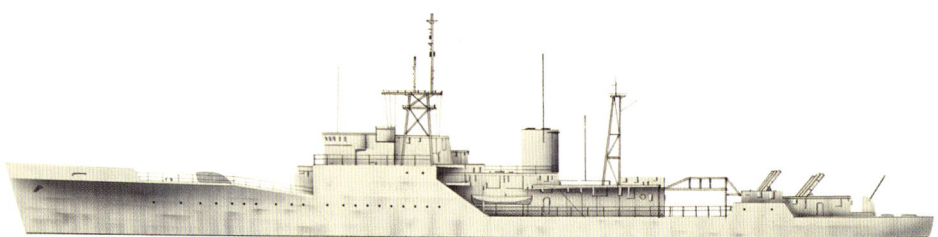

Largely prefabricated, the 12 frigates of *Grafton*'s class were too lightly gunned to be effective as escort ships. Their anti-submarine weapons consisted of two Limbo three-barrelled depth-charge launchers firing a pattern of large depth charges with great accuracy over a wide area. *Grafton* was broken up in 1971.

SPECIFICATIONS

Type:	British frigate
Displacement:	1480 tonnes (1456 tons)
Dimensions:	94.5m x 10m x 4.7m (310ft x 33ft x 15ft 6in)
Machinery:	Single screw, turbines
Top speed:	27.8 knots
Main armament:	Two 40mm (1.6in) guns
Launched:	September 1954

Centauro

Centauro was one of a class of four vessels built with US funds and equipped with automatic anti-submarine and medium anti-aircraft armament. The guns were mounted one above the other in the twin turrets, but this arrangement was later changed to conventional placing. *Centauro* was stricken in 1984.

SPECIFICATIONS

Type:	Italian frigate
Displacement:	2255 tonnes (2220 tons)
Dimensions:	104m x 11m x 4m (339ft x 38ft x 11ft 6in)
Machinery:	Twin screws, geared turbines
Main armament:	Four 76mm (3in) guns
Launched:	April 1954

TIMELINE

1954   1955

FRIGATES OF THE 1950S

Cigno

Of the same class as *Centauro* (see oppsite) but of greater displacement, *Cigno* shared the same features. The Italian-made 76mm (3in) guns were mounted in twin turrets and could fire 60 rounds per minute. In the 1960s, the turrets were replaced by three single 76mm (3in) mounts. *Cigno* was broken up in 1983.

SPECIFICATIONS	
Type:	Italian frigate
Displacement:	2455 tonnes (2220 tons)
Dimensions:	103m x 12m x 4m (339ft 3in x 38ft x 11ft 6in)
Machinery:	Twin screws, geared turbines
Main armament:	Four 76mm (3in) guns
Launched:	March 1955

Gatineau

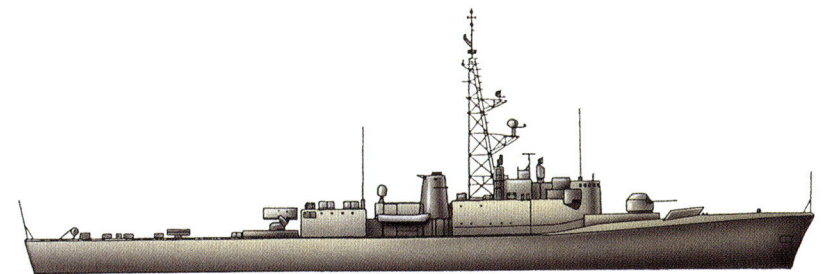

Developed from the *St Laurent* class, *Gatineau* was among four of its class to be modernized between 1966 and 1973, with variable-depth sonar and an ASROC launcher replacing an anti-submarine mortar and one 76mm (3in) gun. It served during the Gulf War. Decommissioned in 1996, *Gatineau* was broken up in 2009.

SPECIFICATIONS	
Type:	Canadian frigate
Displacement:	2641.6 tonnes (2600 tons)
Dimensions:	111.6m x 12.8m x 4.2m (366ft x 42ft x 13ft 2in)
Machinery:	Twin screws, geared turbines
Top speed:	28 knots
Main armament:	One Harpoon octuple SSM, two 76mm (3in) guns, one Mk15 Phalanx 20mm (0.79in) CIWS, six 324mm (12.75in) torpedo tubes
Complement:	290
Launched:	1957

Gemlik

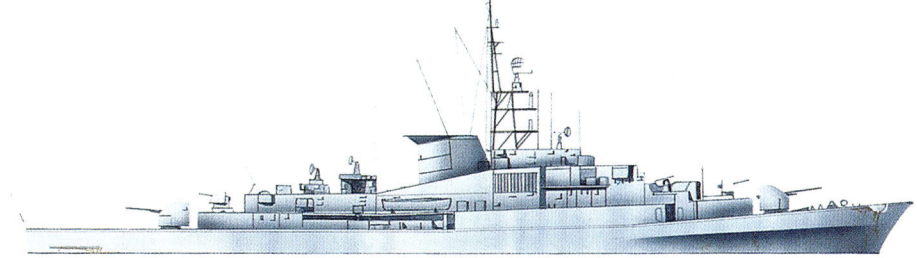

Emden, a *Köln*-class West German frigate, was transferred to the Turkish Navy in September 1983. It carried anti-submarine weapons, sensors and electronic counter-measures. Four launch tubes fired acoustic homing torpedoes. It could also lay up to 80 mines. After a fire, *Emden* was scrapped in 1994.

SPECIFICATIONS	
Type:	Turkish frigate
Displacement:	2743 tonnes (2700 tons)
Dimensions:	109.9m x 11m x 5.1m (360ft 7in x 36ft x 16ft 9in)
Machinery:	Twin screws, gas turbines/diesel engines
Top speed:	28 knots
Main armament:	Two 100mm (3.9in) guns, four 533mm (21in) torpedo tubes
Launched:	March 1959

1957  1959

Frigates of the 1960s & '70s: Pt1

Frigates, by the 1960s, were multi-task ships that fulfilled the role of the former light cruiser, able to provide a sufficiently powerful naval presence, whether helpful or punitive, in the event of some maritime incident or localized trouble-spot. Their missile armament equipped them for anti-aircraft or anti-submarine action, or both.

Carlo Bergamini

As well as fully automatic 76mm (3in) guns, this small but effective frigate carried a new type of single-barrelled mortar automatic depth charge discharger capable of firing 15 rounds per minute to a range of 920m (1000yd); two types of 304mm (12in) torpedo tube; and a helicopter. It was broken up in 1981.

SPECIFICATIONS	
Type:	Italian frigate
Displacement:	1676 tonnes (1650 tons)
Dimensions:	94m x 11m x 3m (308ft 3in x 37ft 3in x 10ft 6in)
Machinery:	Twin screws, diesel motors
Main armament:	Three 76mm (3in) guns
Launched:	June 1960

Dido

Third of the *Leander* class frigates, *Dido* was one of eight to receive the GWS 40 Ikara ASW missile system, from 1978. It also carried a Wasp (later replaced by a Lynx) light helicopter. In 1983, *Dido* was sold to New Zealand to become HMNZS *Southland*. It was stricken in 1995 and broken up in India.

SPECIFICATIONS	
Type:	British frigate
Displacement:	2844 tonnes (2800 tons)
Dimensions:	113m x 12m x 5.4m (372ft x 41ft x 18ft)
Machinery:	Twin screws, turbines
Top speed:	30 knots
Main armament:	Two 114mm (4.5in) guns, one quad launcher for Seacat missiles
Complement:	263
Launched:	December 1961

TIMELINE
1960
1961

FRIGATES OF THE 1960s & '70s – PT 1

Doudart de Lagrée

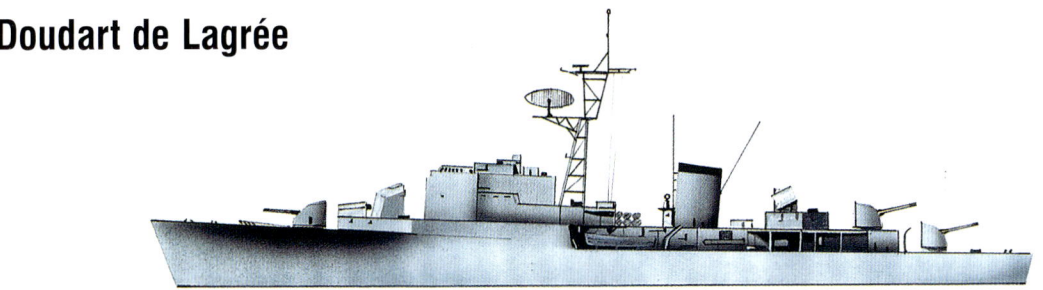

Doudart de Lagrée, intended for escort work and colonial patrol, could carry a force of 80 commandos. In the late 1970s, one gun turret was replaced by four Exocet missile launchers. Developments in building techniques and equipment design meant that the class was superseded, and the ship was stricken in 1991.

SPECIFICATIONS	
Type:	French frigate
Displacement:	2235 tonnes (2200 tons)
Dimensions:	102m x 11.5m x 3.8m (334ft x 37ft 6in x 12ft 6in)
Machinery:	Twin screws, diesels
Top speed:	25 knots
Main armament:	Three 100mm (3.9in) guns, twin anti-aircraft weapons
Complement:	210
Launched:	April 1961

Galatea

Galatea was an improvement of the Type 12 Rothesay class frigate. The missile system was housed on the extended superstructure forward of the bridge. The class was updated in the 1970s and 1980s. After serving in the Far East and Persian Gulf, Galatea was decommissioned in 1987 and sunk as a target in 1988.

SPECIFICATIONS	
Type:	British frigate
Displacement:	2906 tonnes (2860 tons)
Dimensions:	113.4m x 12.5m x 4.5m (372ft x 41ft x 14ft 9in)
Machinery:	Twin screws, turbines
Top speed:	28 knots
Main armament:	One anti-submarine Ikara missile launcher
Launched:	May 1963

Yubari

The Japanese Navy's *Ishikari* class was too small to carry the equipment, weapon stocks and electronic equipment vital for a late twentieth-century escort vessel, and the *Yubari* class is an enlarged version, with more fuel capacity and greater cruising range. A Phalanx CIWS was intended but not fitted.

SPECIFICATIONS	
Type:	Japanese frigate
Displacement:	1777 tonnes (1690 tons)
Dimensions:	91m x 10.8m x 3.5m (298ft 6in x 35ft 5in x 11ft 6in)
Machinery:	Twin screws, gas turbines and diesels
Top speed:	25 knots
Main armament:	Two quad Harpoon SSM launchers, one 76mm (3in) gun, one 375mm (14.75in) mortar, six 324mm (12.75in) torpedo tubes
Complement:	98
Launched:	1982

Frigates of the 1960s & '70s: Part 2

Distinctions between destroyers and frigates were increasingly blurred. Both types now routinely carried a helicopter, to aid in reconnoitring, anti-submarine attacks, and search-and-rescue missions. Many frigates were now equipped for anti-submarine warfare, with sonar detection and ASROC missile launchers.

Davidson

A *Garcia*-class destroyer escort, re-rated as a frigate from 1975, *Davidson* had gyro-driven stabilizers, enabling it to operate in heavy seas. A large box launcher held eight Asroc anti-submarine missiles. Twin torpedo tubes were later removed. Sold to Brazil in 1989 as *Paraibo,* it was decommissioned in 2002.

SPECIFICATIONS	
Type:	US frigate
Displacement:	3454 tonnes (3400 tons)
Dimensions:	126m x 13.5m x 7m (414ft 8in x 44ft 3in x 24ft)
Machinery:	Single screw, turbines
Top speed:	27 knots
Main armament:	Two 127mm (5in) dual-purpose guns
Complement:	270
Launched:	1964

Carabiniere

Supplementary gas turbines gave *Carabiniere* extra speed when needed. Mast and funnel were an integrated structure. Anti-submarine weapons were a single semi-automatic depth charge mortar and six torpedo tubes, and two helicopters. Anti-missile defence was provided by SCLAR rockets. It was withdrawn in 2008.

SPECIFICATIONS	
Type:	Italian frigate
Displacement:	2743 tonnes (2700 tons)
Dimensions:	113m x 13m x 4m (371ft x 43ft 6in x 12ft 7in)
Machinery:	Twin screws, diesels, gas turbines
Top speed:	20 knots (diesel), 28 knots (diesel and turbines)
Main armament:	Six 76mm (3in) guns
Launched:	September 1967

TIMELINE

1964　1967　1968

FRIGATES OF THE 1960s & '70s: PART 2

Alvand

SPECIFICATIONS	
Type:	Iranian frigate
Displacement:	1564.7 tonnes (1540 tons)
Dimensions:	94.5m x 10.5m x 3.5m (310ft x 34ft 5in x 11ft 6in)
Machinery:	Twin screws, gas turbines and diesels
Top speed:	40 knots
Main armament:	One SSM launcher, one Seacat SAM system, one 114mm (4.5in) gun, one Limbo Mk10 anti-submarine mortar
Complement:	135
Launched:	1968

Known as the *Saam* class until the lead ship's name changed to *Alvand* in 1985, these craft were a British Vosper Thornycroft design, in effect a scaled-down version of the Type 21 frigate. The Seacat launcher was later removed. One ship of this class was sunk by US aircraft in 1988, but *Alvand* remains in service.

Downes

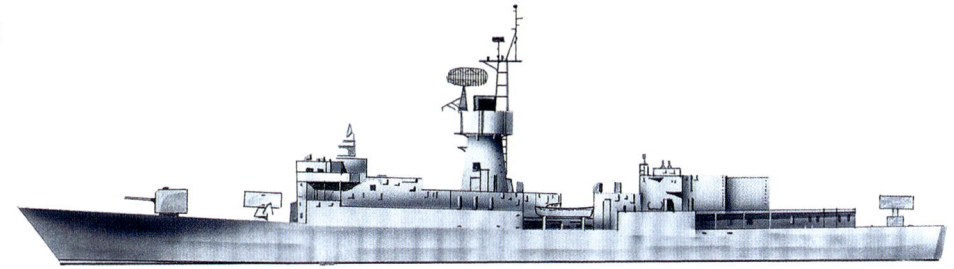

SPECIFICATIONS	
Type:	US frigate
Displacement:	4165 tonnes (4100 tons)
Dimensions:	126.6m x 14m x 7.5m (415ft 4in x 46ft 9in x 24ft 7in)
Machinery:	Single screw, turbines
Top speed:	28 + knots
Main armament:	One 127mm (5in) gun, one eight-tube Sea Sparrow missile launcher plus 20mm (0.79in) Phalanx CIWS
Launched:	December 1969

A large class (46 in total), these frigates were criticized for limited manoeuvrability and low anti-submarine capability. The midships tower structure was intended to carry an advanced electrical array, but this was not developed; *Downes* carried standard sea and air search radars instead. It was sunk as as a target in 2003.

Chikugo

SPECIFICATIONS	
Type:	Japanese frigate
Displacement:	1493 tonnes (1470 tons)
Dimensions:	93m x 11m x 4m (305ft 5in x 35ft 5in x 11ft 6in)
Machinery:	Twin screws, diesels
Main armament:	Two 76mm (3in) guns
Launched:	1970

Chikugo was one of 11 units laid down in 1968. These frigates were the smallest ships to carry the anti-submarine weapon ASROC. Light anti-aircraft armament was installed, as the class were intended for inshore patrolling, protected by land-based fighter aircraft and missiles. *Chikugo* was decommissioned in 1996.

1969

1970

SHIP TYPES 1950–1999

Frigates of the 1970s

While the functions of frigates and destroyers were tending to merge in deep-sea operations, a clear role for smaller versions of the frigate remained in coastal patrol work. Here there was a case for continued employment of the forward gun, in work that requires stop-and-search techniques and the interception of fast-moving craft.

Athabaskan

Athabaskan and three sister-ships were designed for anti-submarine warfare. Two hangars housed Sea King helicopters, giving the ships more flexibility than other anti-submarine vessels of the period. The armament now includes a SAM launcher, a Mk15 20mm (0.79in) Phalanx CIWS, and six 324mm (12.75in) torpedo tubes.

SPECIFICATIONS

Type:	Canadian frigate
Displacement:	4267 tonnes (4200 tons)
Dimensions:	129.8m x 15.5m x 4.5m (426ft x 51ft x 15ft)
Machinery:	Twin screws, gas turbines
Top speed:	30 knots
Main armament:	One 127mm (5in) gun, one triple mortar
Complement:	285
Launched:	1970

Izumrud

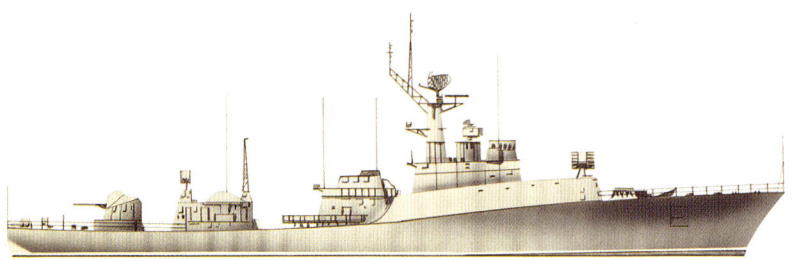

Used by the KGB Border Guard on inshore patrol, *Izumrud* carried twin 533mm (21in) torpedo tubes, SAM SA-N-4 missiles and rocket launchers. Turbines developed 24,000hp; the diesels produced 16,000hp. Range was 1805km (950 miles) at 27 knots, 8550km (4500 miles) at 10 knots. Disposal details are unknown.

SPECIFICATIONS

Type:	Soviet frigate
Displacement:	1219 tonnes (1200 tons)
Dimensions:	72m x 10m x 3.7m (236ft 3in x 32ft 10in x 12ft 2in)
Machinery:	Triple screws, one gas turbine, two diesel engines
Main armament:	Two 57mm (2.24in) guns, SAM missiles
Complement:	310
Launched:	1970

TIMELINE

1970  1972

FRIGATES OF THE 1970S

Najin

Equipped with Russian guns of World War II vintage and SS-N-2A missiles removed from redundant Soviet vessels, this was one of two similar ships built in North Korea in the early 1970s. Their later history is unclear. The names may have been changed and it is likely that both have been withdrawn from service.

SPECIFICATIONS	
Type:	North Korean frigate
Displacement:	1524 tonnes (1500 tons)
Dimensions:	100m x 9.9m x 2.7m (328ft x 32ft 6in x 8ft 10in)
Machinery:	Twin screws, diesels
Top speed:	33 knots
Main armament:	Two 100mm (3in) guns, three 533mm (21in) torpedo tubes
Complement:	180
Launched:	1972

Baptista de Andrade

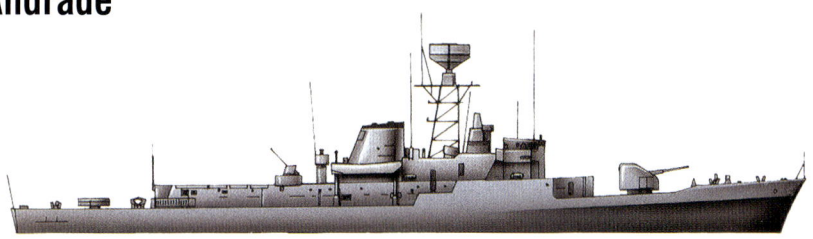

The four frigates of this class were ill-armed by contemporary standards, being deficient in anti-aircraft and anti-submarine defences. Portugal hoped to sell the quartet to Colombia in 1977, but the deal did not materialize. The *Andrades* are used only as coastal patrol vessels and are not deployed with NATO ships.

SPECIFICATIONS	
Type:	Portuguese frigate
Displacement:	1423.4 tonnes (1401 tons)
Dimensions:	84.6m x 10.3m x 3.3m (277ft 8in x 33ft 10in x 10ft 10in)
Machinery:	Twin screws, diesels
Top speed:	24.4 knots
Main armament:	One 100mm (3.9in) gun, six 324mm (12.75in) torpedo tubes
Complement:	113
Launched:	1973

Broadsword

Broadsword was the first general-purpose frigate designed to follow the *Leander* class. It was planned to build 26 units armed with missiles only, the main anti-submarine weapon being the Lynx helicopter. Later groups were fitted with extra weapons and sensors. *Broadsword* was sold to Brazil as *Greenhalgh* in 1995.

SPECIFICATIONS	
Type:	British frigate
Displacement:	4470 tonnes (4400 tons)
Dimensions:	131m x 15m x 4m (430ft 5in x 48ft 8in x 14ft)
Machinery:	Twin screws, gas turbines
Main armament:	Four M38 Exocet launchers, two 40mm (1.6in) guns
Complement:	407
Launched:	1975

Frigates of the 1970s & '80s

Most navies saw the frigate as the core-vessel of the surface fleet, capable of most tasks. Britain, for example, had 55 destroyers and 84 frigates in 1960. Twenty years later, it had 13 destroyers but still retained 53 frigates. The trend was very much towards fewer, but more versatile and comprehensively armed, warships.

Lupo

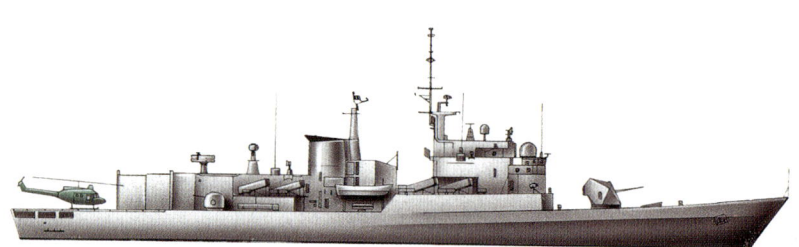

The *Lupo* class is an effective design, used by the Italian and other navies. Integral to the operating of *Lupo* was the SADOC automated combat control system, which enabled it to work with similarly fitted ships in an integrated group. Two helicopters are carried. *Lupo* was sold to Peru as *Palacios* in 2005.

SPECIFICATIONS	
Type:	Italian frigate
Displacement:	2540 tonnes (2500 tons)
Dimensions:	112.8m x 12m x 3.6m (370ft 2in x 39ft 4in x 12ft)
Machinery:	Twin screws, gas turbines plus diesels
Top speed:	35 knots
Main armament:	Eight Otomat SSM, one Sea Sparrow SAM launcher, one 127mm (5in) gun, six 324mm (12.75in) torpedo tubes
Complement:	185
Launched:	1976

Mourad Rais

Mourad Rais was Soviet-built and equipped, of the 'Koni' class of light frigate intended for export to nations allied with or friendly to Soviet Russia. Three were supplied to Algeria between 1978 and 1984, intended mainly for anti-submarine use. A Russian-managed modernization programme was under way in 2009–10.

SPECIFICATIONS	
Type:	Algerian frigate
Displacement:	1930.4 tonnes (1900 tons)
Dimensions:	95m x 12.8m x 4.2m (311ft 8in x 42ft x 13ft 9in)
Machinery:	Triple screws, diesels plus gas turbine
Top speed:	27 knots
Main armament:	One twin SA-N-4 SAM launcher, four 76mm (3in) guns, two RBU-6000 anti-submarine rocket launchers, two depth-charge racks
Complement:	110
Launched:	1978

TIMELINE   1976   1978   1980

FRIGATES OF THE 1970s & 80s

Godavari

SPECIFICATIONS	
Type:	Indian frigate
Displacement:	4064 tonnes (4000 tons)
Dimensions:	126.5m x 14.5m x 9m (415ft x 47ft 7in x 29ft 6in)
Machinery:	Twin screws, turbines
Top speed:	27 knots
Main armament:	Two 57mm (2.24in) guns, four SS-N-2C Styx missiles, SA-N-4 Gecko missiles
Complement:	313
Launched:	May 1980

Godavari is a modified British *Leander*-class frigate, but with Russian and Indian weapon systems as well. Two Sea King or Chetak helicopters can be housed in the hangar. The ship is an early example of the trend towards a smooth profile to minimize visibility on radar. Most of the armament is mounted on the foredeck.

Admiral Petre Barbuneanu

SPECIFICATIONS	
Type:	Romanian frigate
Displacement:	1463 tonnes (1440 tons)
Dimensions:	95.4m x 11.7m x 3m (303ft 1in x 38ft 4in x 9ft 8in)
Machinery:	Twin screws, diesels
Top speed:	24 knots
Main armament:	Four 76mm (3in) guns, two rocket launchers, four 533mm (21in) torpedo tubes
Complement:	95
Launched:	1981

Romania's navy operates in the Black Sea, and this vessel was intended for anti-submarine work and fitted with 16-tube RBU-2500 anti-submarine mortars. With three similar ships, it forms the 'Tetal' class. Sensor equipment included hull-mounted sonar, air/surface search radar and fire control radar.

Doyle

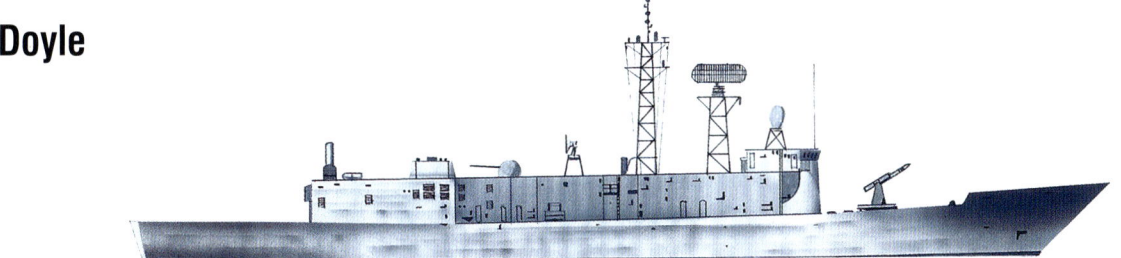

SPECIFICATIONS	
Type:	US frigate
Displacement:	3708 tonnes (3650 tons)
Dimensions:	135.6m x 14m x 7.5m (444ft 10in x 45ft x 24ft 7in)
Machinery:	Single screw, gas turbines
Top speed:	28 knots
Main armament:	One 76mm (3in) gun, Harpoon missile launcher
Launched:	May 1982

Doyle's profile is unlike that of previous frigates, an almost complete departure from earlier post-World War II designs. It reveals a warship reliant on missiles (not guns), built to have a minimal radar image, and with sophisticated radar and sonar detection systems. Its two helicopters carry anti-submarine weapons.

1981

1982

SHIP TYPES 1950–1999

Frigates of the 1980s

Advances in missile technology made ships of frigate type less dependent on the traditional 127mm (5in) guns, and in the 1980s they often carried only a single main gun. Some even dispensed with that, though guns are useful for firing salutes. CIWS systems, based on 20mm (0.79in) or 30mm (1.18in) gun combinations, were introduced.

Jacob van Heemskerck

The Chilean *Admiral Latorre* since 2005, this Dutch L-class missile frigate was completed in 1986 for air defence. Dispensing with the usual forward gun, it has only two 20mm guns. Surface-search, air/surface search and fire control radars are fitted, along with hull-mounted sonar. Its sister-ship was also sold to Chile.

SPECIFICATIONS	
Type:	Dutch frigate
Displacement:	3810 tonnes (3750 tons)
Dimensions:	130.2m x 14.4m x 6m (427ft x 47ft x 20ft)
Machinery:	Twin screws, gas turbines
Top speed:	30 knots
Main armament:	Eight Harpoon SSM, Standard SM-1MR SAM, Sea Sparrrow octuple launcher, Goalkeeper 30mm (1.18in) CIWS, four 324mm (12.75in) torpedo tubes
Complement:	197
Launched:	1983

Al Madina

Designed and built in France, *Al Madina* is one of four frigates supplied to Saudi Arabia in the mid-1980s and intended for general-purpose use, but chiefly ship-to-ship fighting. They can operate a SA 365F Dauphin helicopter, though it is not regularly carried. A full suite of radar equipment is fitted, and hull-mounted sonar.

SPECIFICATIONS	
Type:	Saudi Arabian frigate
Displacement:	2651.8 tonnes (2610 tons)
Dimensions:	115m x 12.5m x 4.9m (377ft 3in x 41ft x 16ft)
Machinery:	Twin screws, diesels
Top speed:	30 knots
Main armament:	Eight Otomat Mk 2 SSM, one Crotale SAM launcher, one 100mm (3.9in) gun, four 440mm (17.33in) torpedo tubes
Complement:	179
Launched:	1983

TIMELINE
1983   1984

FRIGATES OF THE 1980S

Kotor

SPECIFICATIONS	
Type:	Yugoslav frigate
Displacement:	1930.4 tonnes (1900 tons)
Dimensions:	96.7m x 12.8m x 4.2m (317ft 3in x 42ft x 13ft 9in)
Machinery:	Triple screws, diesels plus gas turbine
Top speed:	27 knots
Main armament:	Four SS-N-2C SSM, one twin SA-N-4 SAM launcher, two 76mm (3in) guns, six 324mm (12.75in) torpedo tubes, two RBU-6000 anti-submarine rocket launchers
Complement:	110
Launched:	1984

Built on the general plan of the Soviet 'Koni'-class frigates, *Kotor* and *Pula* were larger, with various structural variations. Armament and mechanical equipment were Russian and Western, reflecting the non-aligned staus of Yugoslavia (as it then was). *Kotor* is now part of Montenegro's navy, but not operational.

Jianghu III

SPECIFICATIONS	
Type:	Chinese frigate
Displacement:	1895 tonnes (1865 tons)
Dimensions:	103.2m x 10.83m x 3.1m (338ft 7in x 35ft 6in x 10ft 2in)
Machinery:	Twin screws, diesels
Top speed:	25.5 knots
Main armament:	Eight UJ-1 Eagle Strike SSM, four 100mm (3.9in) guns, two anti-submarine mortars, two depth-charge racks
Complement:	180
Launched:	1986

Following on from 'Jianghu I and II', this class incorporates more up-to-date anti-ship weaponry and a roomier superstructure. Low-powered, they are intended for coastal anti-submarine patrol work rather than deep-sea duty. Many boats have been sold to other navies, including Pakistan, Egypt and Thailand.

Inhaúma

SPECIFICATIONS	
Type:	Brazilian frigate
Displacement:	2001.5 tonnes (1970 tons)
Dimensions:	95.8m x 11.4m x 5.5m (314ft 3in x 37ft 5in x 18ft)
Machinery:	Twin screws, diesels and gas turbine
Top speed:	27 knots
Main armament:	Four MM40 Exocet SSM, one 114mm (4.5in) gun, six 324mm (12.75in) torpedo tubes
Complement:	162
Launched:	1986

Inhaúma was intended as the first of 16 light patrol ships, forming a major element in the Brazilian Navy. Designed in Germany, they carry a range of equipment, including a Swedish fire-control system, British combat data system, American engines, and French missile systems. The flight deck takes a Lynx helicopter.

1986

SHIP TYPES 1950–1999

Frigates of the 1980s & '90s

Stealth technology is standard in modern frigates. Superstructures and hulls are designed to offer a minimal radar cross section, with low profiles and large areas of smooth walling. This reduces air resistance, improving speed and manoeuvrability. At the same time, air and surface search radar has widened its detection capacity.

Halifax

Canada's 'City' class are big frigates with a large funnel offset to port. *Halifax* was completed in June 1992. The armament carried is chiefly for surface and aerial defence, but the helicopter that each ship carries is normally equipped for anti-submarine action. A comprehensive ship-by-ship class refit began in 2007.

SPECIFICATIONS	
Type:	Canadian frigate
Displacement:	4826 tonnes (4750 tons)
Dimensions:	134.1m x 16.4m x 4.9m (440ft x 53ft 9in x 16ft 2in)
Machinery:	Twin screws, gas turbine and diesel
Top speed:	28 knots
Main armament:	Eight Harpoon SSM, two VLS for Sea Sparrow SAM, one 57mm (2.24in) gun, one Mk 15 Phalanx 20mm (0.79in) CIWS, four 324mm (12.75in) torpedo tubes
Complement:	225
Launched:	1988

Neustrashimyy

Introduced to improve the Soviet Navy's anti-submarine capacities, this class has four ships. The flat-flared hull, divided superstructure and funnel shape reduce and disperse the ship's radar returns. Its own sensors include towed sonar. In 2008–09, *Neustrashimyy* was deployed to the Somali coast to help combat piracy.

SPECIFICATIONS	
Type:	Soviet frigate
Displacement:	3556 tonnes (3500 tons)
Dimensions:	130m x 15.5m x 5.6m (426ft 6in x 50ft 11in x 18ft 5in)
Machinery:	Twin screws, gas turbines
Top speed:	32 knots
Main armament:	One SS-N-25 SSM launcher, one SA-N-9 SAM launcher, two CADS-N-1 gun/missile CIWS, one RBU-12000 anti-submarine rocket launcher
Complement:	210
Launched:	1988

TIMELINE 1988 1989

FRIGATES OF THE 1980s & '90s

Thetis

SPECIFICATIONS	
Type:	Danish patrol ship
Displacement:	3556 tonnes (3500 tons)
Dimensions:	112.5m x 14.4m x 6m (369ft 1in x 47ft 3in x 19ft 8in)
Machinery:	Single screw, diesels
Top speed:	21.5 knots
Main armament:	One 76mm (3in) gun, depth-charge racks
Complement:	61
Launched:	1989

The *Thetis* class of four ships was intended to strengthen Denmark's fleet in the late twentieth and early twenty-first centuries. It was intended to mount Harpoon and Sea Sparrow missiles, but this plan was abandoned at the end of the Cold War and the class serve as lightly armed, outsize fishery protection ships.

Floréal

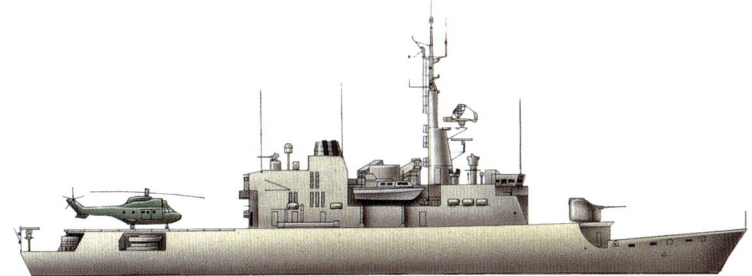

SPECIFICATIONS	
Type:	French frigate
Displacement:	2997 tonnes (2950 tons)
Dimensions:	93.5m x 14m x 4.3m (307ft x 46ft x 14ft)
Machinery:	Twin screws, diesels
Top speed:	20 knots
Main armament:	Two MM38 Exocet SSM, one 100mm (3.9in) gun
Complement:	80 plus 24 armed troops
Launched:	1990

Described as 'surveillance frigates' to protect France's 'exclusive economic zone', this class has been built using mercantile ship techniques and modular assembly, rather than the construction typical of warships. It can embark a helicopter up to Super Puma size. Two ships of the class were built for Morocco.

Nareusan

SPECIFICATIONS	
Type:	Thai frigate
Displacement:	3027.7 tonnes (2980 tons)
Dimensions:	120m x 13m x 3.81m (393ft 8in x 42ft 8in x 12ft 6in)
Machinery:	Twin screws, gas turbines and diesels
Top speed:	32 knots
Main armament:	Eight Harpoon SSM, one Mk 41 VLS for Sea Sparrow SAM, one 127mm (5in) gun, six 324mm (12.75in) torpedo tubes
Complement:	150
Launched:	1993

Built in China, to the design of the 'Jianghu' class, *Nareusan* was fitted out in Thailand, using Western machinery, weapons and electronic systems that make it more effective than the 'Jianghus'. Air/surface radar, navigation radar, fire-control radar and hull-mounted sonar are fitted, and it can embark a Lynx-type helicopter.

1990

1993

SHIP TYPES 1950–1999

Minehunters & Sweepers

In the second half of the twentieth century, mines became more varied in type and in the methods of laying. New generation 'smart' mines could be programmed in various ways to sense and counter the activity of minehunters. Several American ships were damaged by mines during operations in the Persian Gulf region.

Edera

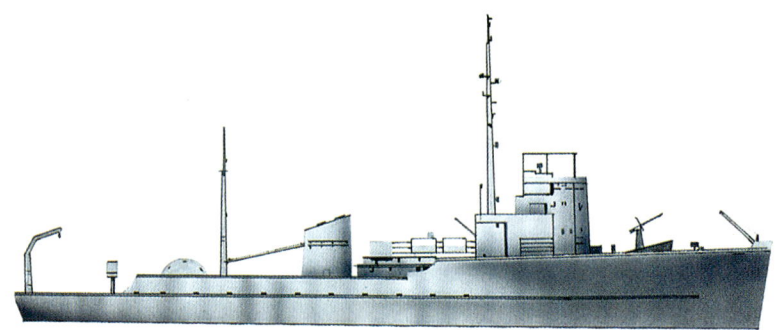

SPECIFICATIONS	
Type:	Italian minesweeper
Displacement:	411 tonnes (405 tons)
Dimensions:	44m x 8m x 2.6m (144ft x 26ft 6in x 8ft 6in)
Machinery:	Twin screws, diesel engine
Top speed:	14 knots
Main armament:	Two 20mm (0.8in) anti-aircraft guns
Complement:	38
Launched:	1955

Edera was one of the 19-strong *Agave* class of minesweepers, of non-magnetic wood and alloy composite construction, and designed for inshore minesweeping duties. During the 1960s, the class was part of Italy's countermining force. Fuel carried was 25 tonnes (25 tons), enough for 4750km (2500 miles) at 10 knots.

Bambú

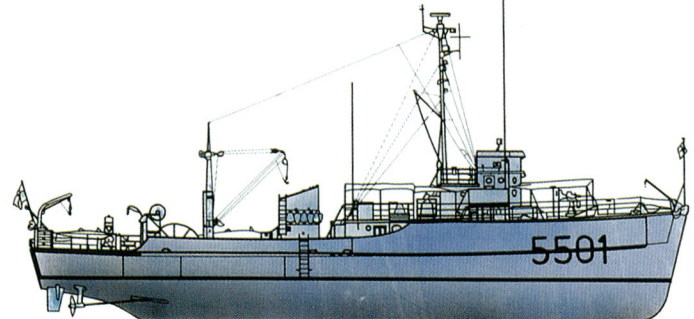

SPECIFICATIONS	
Type:	Italian coastal minesweeper
Displacement:	375 tonnes (370 tons)
Dimensions:	44.1m x 8.5m x 2.6m (144ft 5in x 28ft x 8ft 6in)
Machinery:	Twin screws, diesel engine
Top speed:	13 knots
Main armament:	Two 20mm (0.79in) anti-aircraft guns
Complement:	31
Launched:	1956

One of four converted American *Adjutant*-class minesweepers, *Bambú* entered service in 1956. Equipped with radar and sonar, it was wooden-hulled to defeat magnetic mines. Ships of this class were often assigned to United Nations' coastal patrol work in troubled regions. They were phased out in the 1990s.

TIMELINE

1955  1956  1957

MINEHUNTERS & SWEEPERS

Dromia

SPECIFICATIONS	
Type:	Italian minesweeper
Displacement:	132 tonnes (130 tons)
Dimensions:	32m x 6.4m x 1.8m (106ft x 21ft x 6ft)
Machinery:	Twin screws, diesel engine
Top speed:	14 knots
Main armament:	One 20mm (0.79in) gun
Launched:	1957

Dromia was one of 20 inshore minesweepers of the British 'Ham' class built in Italy between 1955 and 1957. They were designed to operate in shallow waters, rivers and estuaries, and when first built they were a new type of minesweeper, embodying many of the lessons learned during World War II and later hostilities.

Eridan

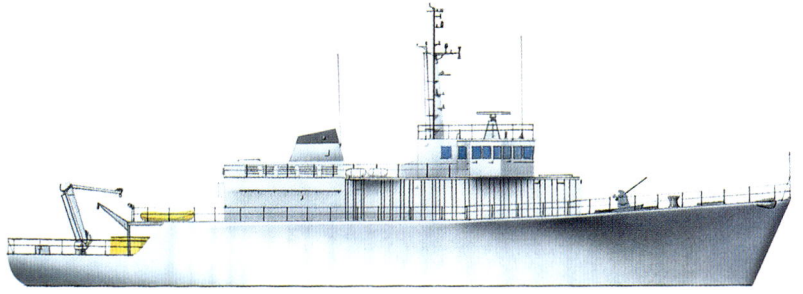

SPECIFICATIONS	
Type:	French minehunter
Displacement:	552 tonnes (544 tons)
Dimensions:	49m x 8.9m x 2.5m (161ft x 29ft 2in x 8ft 2in)
Machinery:	Single screw, diesel engine
Top speed:	15 knots
Main armament:	One 20mm (0.79in) gun
Launched:	February 1979

In the late 1970s, France, Belgium and the Netherlands combined to build 35 minehunters to a design that could be adapted by each nation. *Eridan* could be used for minehunting, minelaying, extended patrols, training, directing unmanned minesweeping craft, and as an HQ ship for diving operations.

Aster

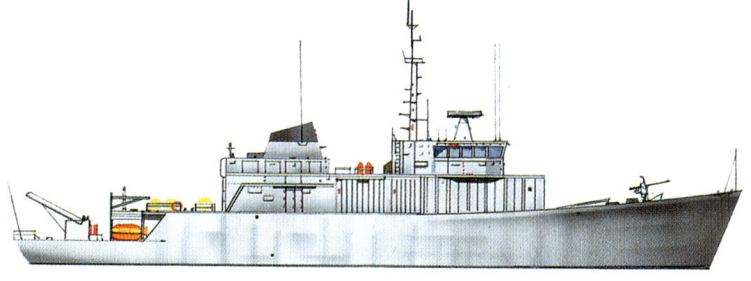

SPECIFICATIONS	
Type:	Belgian minehunter
Displacement:	605 tonnes (595 tons)
Dimensions:	51.5m x 8.9m x 2.5m (169ft x 29ft x 8ft)
Machinery:	Single screw, diesel engine, two manoeuvring propellers and one bowthruster
Top speed:	15 knots
Main armament:	One 20mm (0.79in) anti-aircraft gun
Launched:	1981

Aster is a Belgian example of the Tripartite minehunter design designed for NATO service. France, Belgium and the Netherlands each built its own hulls, which were fitted out in Belgium with French electronics and Dutch machinery. All vessels carry full nuclear, biological and chemical (NBC) protection and minesweeping equipment, and can be used as patrol and surveillance craft.

1979

1981

SHIP TYPES 1950–1999

Specialized Naval Ships

As in previous decades, fleet support required a variety of dedicated craft. The main difference was that the complexity of modern operating systems made it imperative to build ships for purpose rather than to adapt existing ones, though there were exceptions. Other specialisms included assault and landing ships.

Filicudi

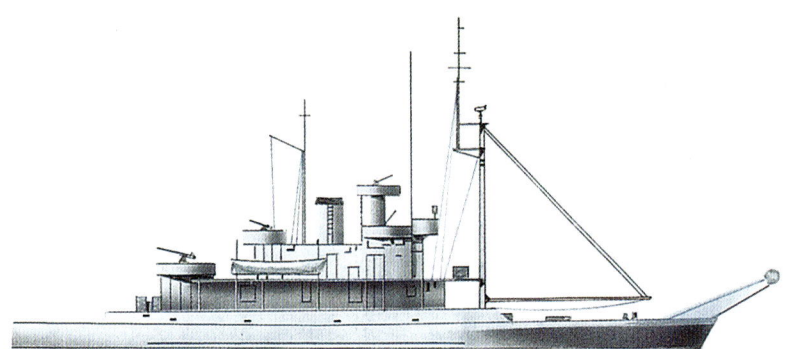

SPECIFICATIONS	
Type:	Italian net layer
Displacement:	847 tonnes (834 tons)
Dimensions:	50m x 10m x 3.2m (165ft 4in x 33ft 6in x 10ft 6in)
Machinery:	Twin screws, diesel-electric motors
Top speed:	12 knots
Main armament:	One 40mm (1.57in) gun
Launched:	September 1954

Filicudi and its sister *Alicudi* were based on a standard NATO design, and could lay nets of various depths across harbour entrances. A large, open deck for handling the nets is situated in the low bow section. A boom attached to the foremast controls the lifting and lowering of nets.

Caorle

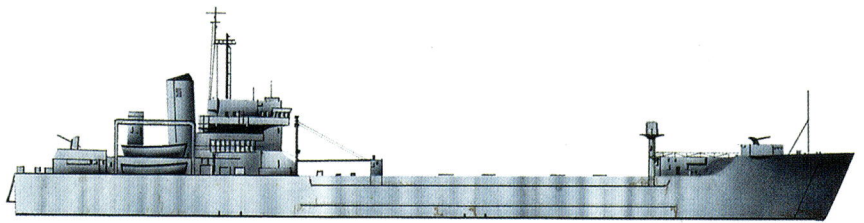

SPECIFICATIONS	
Type:	Italian landing ship
Displacement:	8128 tonnes (8000 tons)
Dimensions:	135m x 19m x 5m (444ft x 62ft x 16ft 6in)
Machinery:	Twin screws, diesel engines
Top speed:	17.5 knots
Main armament:	Six 76mm (3in) guns
Launched:	March 1957

In 1972, USS *York County* was sold to Italy, and renamed *Caorle*. It could carry up to 575 fully equipped assault troops, or a mixture of troops, tanks and other vehicles. A flat bottom and shallow draught allowed the bow to be grounded on a shallow beach for unloading. It was scrapped at Naples in 1999.

TIMELINE			
	1954	1957	1959

SPECIALIZED NAVAL SHIPS

Chazhma

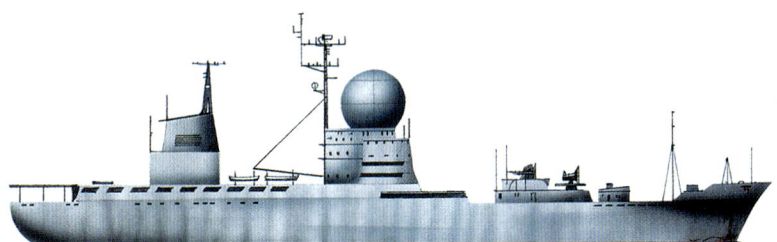

A 7381-tonne (7265-ton) bulk ore carrier of the *Dshankoy* class, *Chazhma* was converted into a missile range ship in 1963 to serve in the Pacific. A 'Ship Globe' radar was mounted in the dome above the bridge. A helicopter platform and hangar, built into the aft superstructure, let it operate one 'Hormone' helicopter.

SPECIFICATIONS	
Type:	Soviet missile range ship
Displacement:	13,716 tonnes (13,500 tons)
Dimensions:	140m x 18m x 8m (458ft x 59ft x 26ft)
Machinery:	Twin screws, diesel engines
Top speed:	15 knots
Launched:	1959

Deutschland

The first West German ship to exceed the post-war limit of 3048 tonnes (3000 tons), *Deutschland* carried a range of armaments for training purposes, including 100mm (3.9in) and 40mm (1.57in) guns, depth-charge launchers, mines and torpedoes. It was towed to India for scrapping in 1994.

SPECIFICATIONS	
Type:	German training ship
Displacement:	5588 tonnes (5500 tons)
Dimensions:	145m x 18m x 4.5m (475ft 9in x 59ft x 14ft 9in)
Machinery:	Triple screws, diesel motors, turbines
Top speed:	22 knots
Main armament:	Four 100mm (3.9in) guns
Complement:	500 including 267 cadets
Launched:	1960

Alligator class

The Project 1171 Nosorog large landing craft were designated 'Alligator' by NATO. Sixteen were built, with bow and stern ramps. All carried some weapons and at least one crane. Up to 30 armoured personnel carriers and their troops could be transported. Some were used in the South Ossetia War of 2008.

SPECIFICATIONS	
Type:	Soviet landing ship
Displacement:	4775 tonnes (4700 tons) full load
Dimensions:	112.8m x 15.3m x 4.4m (370ft 6in x 50ft 2in x 14ft 5in)
Machinery:	Twin screws, diesels
Top speed:	18 knots
Main armament:	Two/three SA-N-5 SAM launchers, one 122mm (4.8in) rocket launcher
Complement:	75 plus 300 combat troops
Launched:	1964

SHIP TYPES 1950–1999

Post-War Conventional Submarines: Part 1

The German and Japanese submarine fleets had been eliminated by the end of World War II, but the Russians, Americans and British still had substantial numbers. Post-war building programmes began only in the 1950s, stimulated by the Cold War.

Whiskey

About 240 of these attack submarines were built between 1951 and 1958. Four units were converted to early warning boats between 1959 and 1963, but from 1963 the long-range Bear aircraft reduced their strategic importance in some areas. By the 1980s, these submarines had disappeared from the effective list.

SPECIFICATIONS	
Type:	Soviet submarine
Displacement:	1066 tonnes (1050 tons) [surface], 1371 tonnes (1350 tons) [submerged]
Dimensions:	76m x 6.5m x 5m (249ft 4in x 21ft 4in x 16ft)
Machinery:	Twin screws, diesel engines [surface], electric motors [submerged]
Top speed:	18 knots [surface], 14 knots [submerged]
Main armament:	Two 406mm (16in), four 533mm (21in) torpedo tubes
Launched:	1956

Golf I

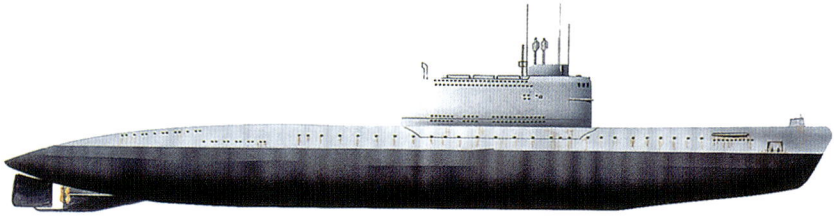

Twenty-three Golf I-class submarines were completed between 1958 and 1962, entering service at a rate of six to seven per year. The ballistic missiles were housed vertically in the rear section of the extended fin. Many boats in the class were modified after commissioning. All were withdrawn by 1990.

SPECIFICATIONS	
Type:	Russian missile submarine
Displacement:	2336 tonnes (2300 tons) [surface], 2743 tonnes (2700 tons) [submerged]
Dimensions:	100m x 8.5m x 6.6m (328ft x 27ft 11 in x 21ft 8in)
Machinery:	Triple screws, diesel engine (surface), electric motors [submerged]
Top speed:	17 knots (surface), 12 knots [submerged]
Main armament:	Three SS-N-4 ballistic missiles, ten 533mm (21in) torpedo tubes
Launched:	1957

TIMELINE

1956   1957

Grayback

SPECIFICATIONS	
Type:	US submarine
Displacement:	2712 tonnes (2670 tons) [surface], 3708 tonnes (3650 tons) [submerged]
Dimensions:	102m x 9m (335ft x 30ft)
Machinery:	Twin screws, diesel engines [surface], electric motors [submerged]
Main armament:	Four Regulus missiles, eight 533mm (21in) torpedo tubes
Launched:	1957

During construction, *Grayback* was altered to carry the first naval cruise missile, Regulus, and did so until 1964. Recommissioned in 1968 as an amphibious transport submarine for undercover missions, it carried 67 marines and their SEAL swimmer delivery vehicles. *Grayback* was sunk as a target in April 1986.

Daphné

SPECIFICATIONS	
Type:	French submarine
Displacement:	884 tonnes (870 tons) [surface], 1062 tonnes (1045 tons) [submerged]
Dimensions:	58m x 7m x 4.6m (189ft 8in x 22ft 4in x 15ft)
Machinery:	Twin screws, diesel [surface], electric drive [submerged]
Top speed:	13.5 knots [surface], 16 knots [submerged]
Main armament:	Twelve 552mm (21.7in) torpedo tubes
Launched:	June 1959

Eleven submarines of this class were launched between 1964 and 1970. The double hull had a deep keel to improve stability. They had good manoeuvrability, low noise, a small crew and were easy to maintain; several navies bought them. *Daphné* was decommissioned in 1989; the rest of the class followed by 1996.

Dolfijn

SPECIFICATIONS	
Type:	Dutch submarine
Displacement:	1518 tonnes (1494 tons) [surface], 1855 tonnes (1820 tons) [submerged]
Dimensions:	80m x 8m x 4.8m (260ft 10in x 25ft 9in x15ft 9in)
Machinery:	Twin screws, diesel [surface], electric motors [submerged]
Main armament:	Eight 533mm (21in) torpedo tubes
Launched:	May 1959

Dolfijn and three sister boats were built to a unique triple-hulled design – three cylinders arranged in a triangular shape. The upper cylinder housed the crew, navigational equipment and armament; the lower cylinders, the powerplant. Maximum diving depth was almost 304m (1000ft). *Dolfijn* was broken up in 1985.

Post-War Conventional Submarines: Part 2

In the 1960s, Japan, Italy and West Germany resumed the building of submarines, placing their forces within the NATO and US-Japanese defence agreements. Several non-aligned nations, notably Sweden, also produced effective submarine types.

Enrico Toti

The four vessels of this class were the first submarines to be built in Italy since World War II. The design was revised several times before the hunter/killer model, for use in shallow and confined waters, was finally approved. Withdrawn in 1992, *Enrico Toti* is now a museum vessel in Milan.

SPECIFICATIONS	
Type:	Italian submarine
Displacement:	532 tonnes (524 tons) [surface], 591 tonnes (582 tons) [submerged]
Dimensions:	46.2m x 4.7m x 4m (151ft 7in x 15ft 5in x 13ft)
Machinery:	Single screw, diesel engines [surface], electric motors [submerged]
Top speed:	14 knots surfaced, 15 knots submerged
Main armament:	Four 533mm (21in) torpedo tubes
Launched:	March 1967

Harushio

This was Japan's first post-World War II fleet submarine class, named for Oshio, though it had a different bow shape to its successors. The primary role, in Japan's Maritime Defence Force, was to act as targets in anti-submarine training exercises. *Harushio* was withdrawn and scrapped in 1984.

SPECIFICATIONS	
Type:	Japanese submarine
Displacement:	1676.4 tonnes (1650 tons) surfaced, 2184.4 tonnes (2150 tons) [submerged]
Dimensions:	88m x 8.2m x 4.9m (288ft 8in x 26ft 11in x 16ft)
Machinery:	Twin screws, diesel [surface], electric motors [submerged]
Top speed:	18 knots surfaced, 14 knots submerged
Main armament:	Eight 533mm (21in) torpedo tubes
Complement:	80
Launched:	1967

TIMELINE

1967   1968

POST-WAR CONVENTIONAL SUBMARINES: PART 2

U-12

SPECIFICATIONS	
Type:	German submarine
Displacement:	425 tonnes (419 tons) [surface], 457 tonnes (450 tons) [submerged]
Dimensions:	43.9m x 4.6m x 4.3m (144ft x 15ft x 14ft)
Machinery:	Single screw, diesel engine [surface], electric motors [submerged]
Top speed:	10 knots [surface], 17 knots [submerged]
Main armament:	Eight 533mm (21in) torpedo tubes
Launched:	1968

U-12 was one of the first class of German submarines built after World War II. They were a successful type, with over 40 boats serving in foreign navies. The hull was of a non-magnetic steel alloy. Diesel engines developed 2300hp, and the single electric motor developed 1500hp. *U-12* was decommissioned in 2005.

Näcken

SPECIFICATIONS	
Type:	Swedish submarine
Displacement:	995.7 tonnes (980 tons) [surface], 1169 tonnes (1150 tons) [submerged]
Dimensions:	49.5m x 5.7m x 5.5m (162ft 5in x 18ft 8in x 18ft)
Machinery:	Single screw, diesel engine [surface], electric motors [submerged]
Top speed:	20 knots [surface], 25 knots [submerged]
Main armament:	Six 533mm (21in), two 400mm (15.75in) torpedo tubes
Complement:	19
Launched:	1978

Näcken and its two sister craft were re-engined in 1987–88 with a closed-air independent propulsion system (AIP), which let them operate underwater for up to 14 days without surfacing. Withdrawn in the 1990s, they have been replaced by the Swedish-built *Vastergötland* class, which uses the same technology.

Kilo

SPECIFICATIONS	
Type:	Russian submarine
Displacement:	2336 tonnes (2300 tons) [surface], 2946 tonnes (2900 tons) [submerged]
Dimensions:	73m x 10m x 6.5m (239ft 6in x 32ft 10in x 21ft 4in)
Machinery:	Single screw, diesel engine [surface], electric motor [submerged]
Top speed:	12 knots [surface], 18 knots [submerged]
Main armament:	Six 533mm (21in) torpedo tubes
Launched:	1981

The 'Kilo' class were the first Soviet boats to use a modern teardrop hull form, which gives a good underwater speed-power ratio. Double-hulled, they are fast and highly manoeuvrable, well suited to operations in restricted waters. About 17 continue in service with Russia, and 33 in other fleets.

1978  1981

Post-War Conventional Submarines: Part 3

While by the 1980s the nuclear submarine had taken up the major strategic role, its deployment was confined to five navies. A significant tactical part was still played by conventionally powered boats, particularly for coastal patrol.

Galerna

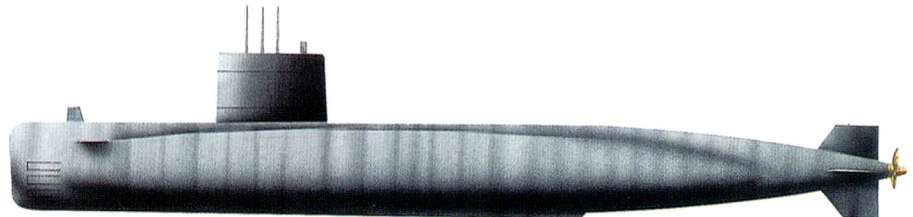

One of four medium-range submarines built in Spain to the design of the French *Agosta* class, *Galerna* marked a major step forward in Spanish submarine technology. The original weapon-stock was 16 reload torpedoes or nine torpedoes and 19 mines. State-of-the-art sonar kit is carried.

SPECIFICATIONS	
Type:	Spanish submarine
Displacement:	1473 tonnes (1450 tons) [surface], 1753 tonnes (1725 tons) [submerged]
Dimensions:	67.6m x 6.8m x 5.4m (221ft 9in x 22ft 4in x 17ft 9in)
Machinery:	Single screw, diesel engine [surface], electric motor [submerged]
Top speed:	12 knots surfaced, 20 knots submerged
Main armament:	Four 551mm (21.7in) torpedo tubes
Launched:	December 1981

Walrus

Walrus was not completed until 1991, due to a fire, and *Zeeleeuw*, commissioned in 1989, became class leader. The use of high-tensile steel gave a diving depth of 300m (985ft). New Gipsy fire control and electronic command systems reduced crew numbers to 49. A class refit in 2007 extended the service life of these boats.

SPECIFICATIONS	
Type:	Dutch submarine
Displacement:	2490 tonnes (2450 tons) [surface], 2845 tonnes (2800 tons) [submerged]
Dimensions:	67.5m x 8.4m x 6.6m (222ft 7in x 27ft 7in x 21ft 8in)
Machinery:	Single screw, diesel engines [surface], electric motors [submerged]
Top speed:	13 knots [surface], 20 knots [submerged]
Main armament:	Four 533mm (21in) torpedo tubes
Launched:	October 1985

TIMELINE

1981　　1985　　1986

Hai Lung

Hai Lung is a modified Dutch *Zwaardvis*-class, probably the most efficient design of the 1970s. They are quiet boats, with all machinery mounted on anti-vibration mountings. They carried up to 28 Tigerfish acoustic homing torpedoes, and in 2005 were upgraded to carry UGM-84 Harpoon anti-ship missiles.

SPECIFICATIONS	
Type:	Taiwanese submarine
Displacement:	2414 tonnes (2376 tons) [surface], 2702 tonnes (2660 tons) [submerged]
Dimensions:	66.9m x 8.4m x 6.7m (219ft 5in x 27ft 6in x 22ft)
Machinery:	Single screw, diesel engines [surface], electric motors [submerged]
Top speed:	11 knots [surface], 20 knots [submerged]
Main armament:	Six 533mm (21in) torpedo tubes
Complement:	67
Launched:	October 1986

Upholder

Designed as a new Royal Navy conventionally-powered patrol submarine, all four in the Upholder class were transferred to Canada in 1998. The teardrop-shaped hull is of high tensile steel, enabling dives to 200m (656ft). The class has had technical problems, and three were undergoing refits in 2009–10.

SPECIFICATIONS	
Type:	British submarine
Displacement:	2220 tonnes (2185 tons) [surface], 2494 tonnes (2455 tons) [submerged]
Dimensions:	70.3m x 7.6m x 5.5m (230ft 8in x 25ft x 18ft)
Machinery:	Single screw, diesel engine [surface], electric motors [submerged]
Top speed:	12 knots [surface], 20 knots [submerged]
Main armament:	Six 533mm (21in) torpedo tubes
Launched:	December 1986

Collins

Swedish-designed and Australian-built, this attack submarine was marred by mechanical and electronic problems when introduced in 1995 and the combat data management system was replaced. Three of the six boats in the *Collins* class are active, the others in reserve. Plans for replacement were put in hand in 2007.

SPECIFICATIONS	
Type:	Australian submarine
Displacement:	2220 tonnes (3051 tons) [surface], 2494 tonnes (3353 tons) [submerged]
Dimensions:	77.5m x 7.8m x 7m (254ft x 25ft 7in x 23ft)
Machinery:	Single screw, diesel-electric engines [surface], electric motor [submerged]
Top speed:	10 knots [surface], 20 knots [submerged]
Main armament:	Six 533mm (21in) torpedo tubes
Launched:	1993

 1993

SHIP TYPES 1950–1999

Nuclear Submarines: Part 1

Until 1954, the submarine was essentially a surface ship that could submerge. Experiments had been going on with power sources that would allow for indefinite submergence. A hydrogen peroxide motor was tried in the 1940s, but nuclear reaction offered the answer: in 1954 USS *Nautilus* became the first 'true' submarine.

Nautilus

The world's first nuclear-powered submarine, *Nautilus* was of conventional design. Early trials established many records, including nearly 2250km (1400 miles) submerged in 90 hours at 20 knots, and a passage beneath the ice over the North Pole. Stricken in 1980, *Nautilus* is preserved at Groton, Connecticut.

SPECIFICATIONS
Type:	US submarine
Displacement:	4157 tonnes (4091 tons) [surface], 4104 tonnes (4040) [submerged]
Dimensions:	98.7m x 8.4m x 6.6m (323ft 9in x 27ft 8in x 21ft 9in)
Machinery:	Twin screws, nuclear reactor, turbines
Top speed:	23 knots [submerged]
Main armament:	Six 533mm (21in) torpedo tubes
Complement:	105
Launched:	January 1954

Skipjack

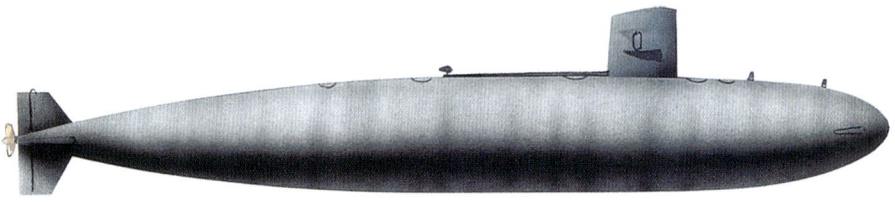

With a teardrop-form hull, and diving planes on the fin, *Skipjack* was fast and manoeuvrable. No stern tubes were fitted: the aft hull shape tapered sharply. It introduced the S5W fast-attack propulsion plant used in all subsequent attack and ballistic submarines until the *Los Angeles*. The class was withdrawn by the 1990s.

SPECIFICATIONS
Type:	US submarine
Displacement:	3124 tonnes (3075 tons) [surface], 3570 tonnes (3513 tons) [submerged]
Dimensions:	76.7m x 9.6m x 8.9m (251ft 8in x 31ft 6in x 29ft 2in)
Machinery:	Single screw, nuclear reactor, turbines
Top speed:	18 knots surfaced, 30 knots submerged
Main armament:	Six 533mm (21in) torpedo tubes
Complement:	93
Launched:	May 1958

TIMELINE

1954　　1958　　1959

NUCLEAR SUBMARINES: PART 1

USS Halibut

First deployed with cruise missiles, *Halibut* was used for secret intelligence work, often involving the retrieval of objects of military interest from the sea-bed. Midget submarines, carried in the former Regulus missile space, were used for this work. *Halibut* was decommissioned in 1976, and broken up in 1994.

SPECIFICATIONS	
Type:	US submarine
Displacement:	(3846 tons) surfaced, (4895 tons) submerged
Dimensions:	106.7m x 9m x 6.3m (350ft x 29ft 6in x 20ft 9in)
Machinery:	Twin screws, one nuclear reactor
Top speed:	15 knots [surfaced], 15.5 knots [submerged]
Main armament:	Five SSM-N-8 Regulus 1 or two SSM-N-9 Regulus II, six 533mm (21in) torpedo tubes
Complement:	111
Launched:	1959

George Washington

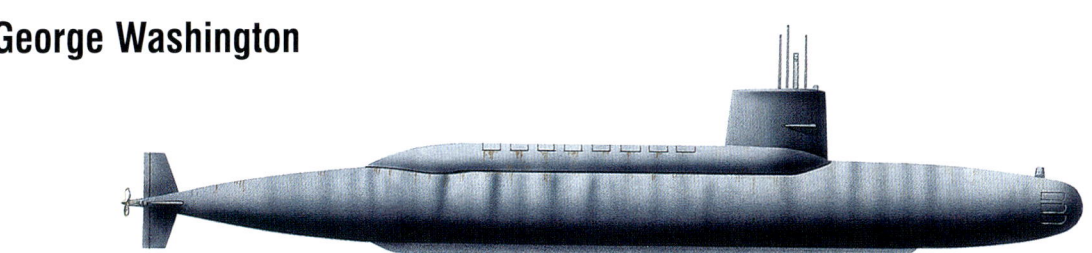

In 1955, the Soviet Union began modifying submarines to carry nuclear-tipped ballistic missiles. At the time, the United States was developing the Polaris A1 missile, and the submarine *Scorpion* was adapted to carry it. Renamed *George Washington*, it was 'de-missiled' in the 1980s, and decommissioned in 1986.

SPECIFICATIONS	
Type:	US ballistic missile submarine
Displacement:	6115 tonnes (6019 tons) [surface], 6998 tonnes (6888 tons) [submerged]
Dimensions:	116.3m x 10m x 8.8m (381ft 7in x 33ft x 28ft 10in)
Machinery:	Single screw, one pressurized water-cooled reactor, turbines
Top speed:	20 knots [surface], 30.5 knots [submerged]
Main armament:	Sixteen Polaris missiles, six 533mm (21in) torpedo tubes
Launched:	June 1959

Dreadnought

Britain's first nuclear-powered submarine, *Dreadnought* was a detect-and-destroy vessel. The form of the hull was based on the shape of a whale. Its power-plant was an American S5W reactor as fitted to the US *Skipjack* submarines. Laid up in 1982, *Dreadnought* was towed to Rosyth for disposal in the following year.

SPECIFICATIONS	
Type:	British submarine
Displacement:	3556 tonnes (3500 tons) [surface], 4064 tonnes (4000 tons) [submerged]
Dimensions:	81m x 9.8m x 8m (265ft 9in x 32ft 3in x 26ft)
Machinery:	Single screw, nuclear reactor, steam turbines
Top speed:	20 knots [surface], 30 knots [submerged]
Main armament:	Six 533mm (21in) torpedo tubes
Complement:	88
Launched:	October 1960

Resolution

Lead boat of a class of four, designed to carry Britain's nuclear deterrent armament of US Polaris missiles, *Resolution* went on its first patrol in 1968. It was intended that one of the four submarines would always be on active service. With the deployment of the *Vanguard* class with Trident missiles, *Resolution* was retired in 1994.

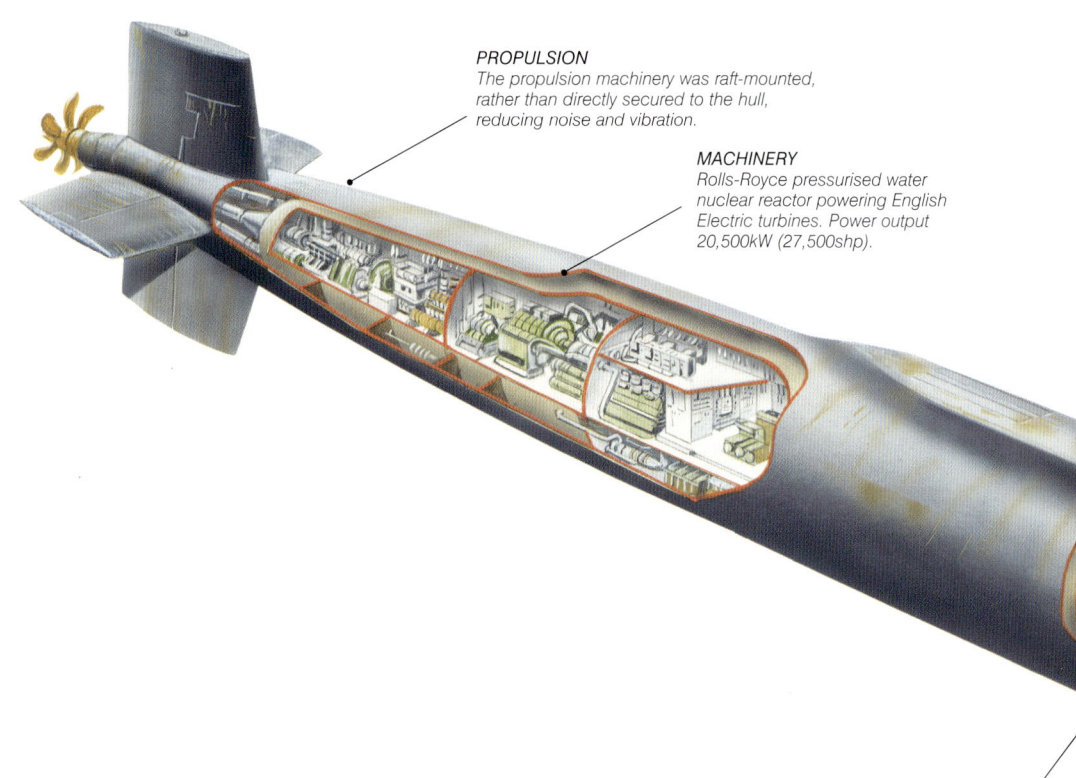

PROPULSION
The propulsion machinery was raft-mounted, rather than directly secured to the hull, reducing noise and vibration.

MACHINERY
Rolls-Royce pressurised water nuclear reactor powering English Electric turbines. Power output 20,500kW (27,500shp).

MISSILE COMPARTMENT
Vertically-mounted sixteen Polaris A3 missiles, in two rows of eight. These had a range of 4,631km (2,500 nautical miles) and multiple nuclear warheads.

Resolution

The *Resolution* class submarines were armed with the American Polaris SLBM and they took over the British deterrent role from the RAF in 1968. Their characteristics were very similar to the American *Lafayettes*.

SPECIFICATIONS

Type:	British submarine
Displacement:	7620 tonnes (7500 tons) [surface], 8636 tonnes (8500 tons) [submerged]
Dimensions:	129.5m x 10m x 9.1m (425ft x 33ft x 30ft)
Machinery:	Single screw, pressurized water reactor, geared steam turbines
Top speed:	20 knots [surfaced], 25 knots [submerged]
Main armament:	Sixteen UGM-27C Polaris A-3 SLBM, six 533mm (21in) torpedo tubes
Complement:	143
Launched:	September 1966

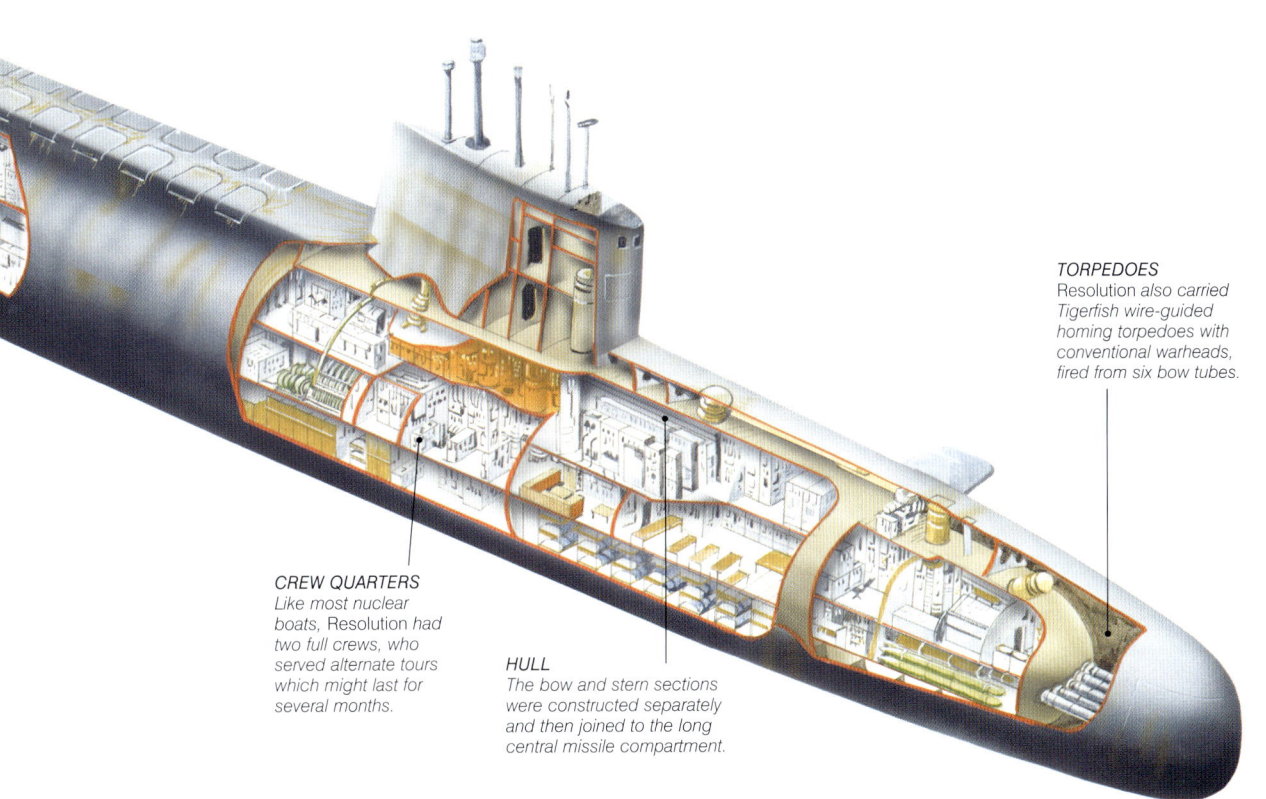

CONVERSION
The four Resolution class boats were adapted in the mid-1980s to carry new Polaris AT-K missiles with British Chevaline multiple re-entry warheads.

TORPEDOES
Resolution also carried Tigerfish wire-guided homing torpedoes with conventional warheads, fired from six bow tubes.

CREW QUARTERS
Like most nuclear boats, Resolution had two full crews, who served alternate tours which might last for several months.

HULL
The bow and stern sections were constructed separately and then joined to the long central missile compartment.

Nuclear Submarines: Part 2

Two US nuclear submarines, *Thresher* (1963) and *Scorpion* (1968), were lost in the 1960s. The loss of *Thresher* prompted the introduction of the Deep Sea Rescue Vessel (DSRV). Nuclear boats first carried conventional torpedoes but developments in rocket technology led to the introduction of the missile-firing submarine.

Daniel Boone

Daniel Boone was one of a sub-class of the *Lafayette* strategic missile nuclear submarines. Completed in April 1964, and fitted to carry UGM 73A Poseidon missiles, it was one of 12 boats adapted for the more reliable Trident type in 1980. With the advent of the *Ohio* class, *Daniel Boone* was retired in 1994.

SPECIFICATIONS	
Type:	US submarine
Displacement:	7366 tonnes (7250 tons) [surface], 8382 tonnes (8250 tons) [submerged]
Dimensions:	130m x 10m x 10m (425ft x 33ft x 33ft)
Machinery:	Single screw, single water-cooled nuclear reactor, turbines
Top speed:	20 knots [surface], 35 knots [submerged]
Main armament:	Sixteen Polaris missiles, four 533mm (21in) torpedo tubes
Launched:	June 1962

Warspite

Using old battleship names confirmed nuclear submarines as the new capital ships. One of five boats in Britain's first class of nuclear submarines, *Warspite* also had an emergency battery, diesel generator and electric motor. It was withdrawn in 1991, when hairline cracks were found in its primary coolant circuit.

SPECIFICATIONS	
Type:	British submarine
Displacement:	4368 tonnes (4300 tons) [surface], 4876 tonnes (4800 tons) [submerged]
Dimensions:	87m x 10m x 8.4m (285ft x 33ft 2in x 27ft 7in)
Machinery:	Single screw, pressurized water-cooled nuclear reactor, turbines
Top speed:	28 knots [submerged]
Main armament:	Six 533mm (21in) torpedo tubes
Launched:	1965

TIMELINE

1962   1965

NUCLEAR SUBMARINES: PART 2

George Washington Carver

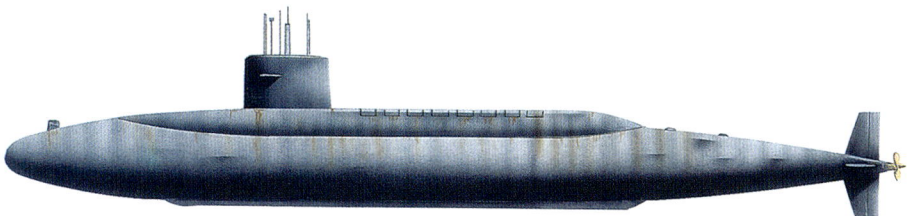

SPECIFICATIONS	
Type:	US submarine
Displacement:	7366 tonnes (7250 tons) [surface], 8382 tonnes (8250 tons) [submerged]
Dimensions:	129.5m x 10m x 9.6m (424ft 10in x 33ft 2in x 31ft 6in)
Machinery:	Single screw, one pressurised water-cooled nuclear reactor
Speed:	20 knots [surface], 30 knots [submerged]
Main armament:	Sixteen Trident C4 missiles, four 533mm (21in) torpedo tubes
Launched:	August 1965

One of 29 vessels in the *Lafayette* class, *George Washington Carver* could dive to depths of 300m (985ft), and the nuclear core provided enough energy to propel the boat for 760,000km (400,000 miles). Its missile tubes were deactivated in 1991 and it became an attack boat. It was stricken and sent for recycling in 1993.

Narwhal

SPECIFICATIONS	
Type:	US submarine
Displacement:	4374 tonnes (4246 tons) [surface], 4853.4 tonnes (4777 tons) [submerged]
Dimensions:	89.1m x 9.6m x 7.8m (292ft 3in x 31ft 8in x 25ft 6in)
Machinery:	Single screw, one pressurised water-cooled nuclear reactor
Speed:	26 knots [submerged]
Main armament:	Four 533mm (21in) torpedo tubes
Launched:	August 1965

The United States' 100th nuclear submarine, *Narwhal* was an attack boat, of the *Sturgeon* class. These were larger than the *Thresher* and *Permit* class, powered by an improved reactor. *Narwhal* was notably quiet and much of its activity was in reconnaissance, or eavesdropping. It was stricken in 1999.

Yankee

SPECIFICATIONS	
Type:	Soviet submarine
Displacement:	7823 tonnes (7700 tons) [surfaced], 9450 tonnes (9300 tons) [submerged]
Dimensions:	132m x 11.6m x 8m (433ft 10in x 38ft 1in x 26ft 4in)
Machinery:	Twin screws, nuclear reactors, turbines
Top speed:	13 knots [surface], 27 knots [submerged]
Main armament:	Sixteen SS-N-6 missile tubes, six 533mm (21in) torpedo tubes
Complement:	120
Launched:	1967

Project 667A, known to NATO as the 'Yankee' class, were more powerful than previous Russian nuclear submarines. Thirty-four boats were built, capable of firing missiles from underwater, and patrolled the US eastern seaboard. By the SALT arms limitation agreement, all strategic 'Yankees' were withdrawn by 1994.

1967

Nuclear Submarines: Part 3

France launched its first class of nuclear submarines armed with ballistic missiles with *Le Redoutable* in 1967, and China produced the 'Han' class in 1972. The invisibility of the nuclear submarine and the secrecy surrounding its cruising missions, together with its destructive power, added to the tensions of the Cold War.

Charlie II

Following from the 12 smaller 'Charlie I' (NATO code) as the Soviet Navy's Project 670M, the 'Charlie II' class carried SS-N-9 Siren anti-ship missiles, which could be fitted with nuclear warheads, and two sizes of torpedo. The class shadowed US carrier battle groups. Six were built, serving until the mid-1990s.

SPECIFICATIONS	
Type:	Soviet missile submarine
Displacement:	4368.8 tonnes (4300 tons) [surface], 5181.6 tonnes (5100 tons) [submerged]
Dimensions:	103.6m x 10m x 8m (340 x 32ft 10in x 28ft)
Machinery:	Single screw, nuclear reactor
Top speed:	24 knots surfaced
Main armament:	Eight SS-N-9 cruise missiles, four 533mm (21in) and four 406mm (16in) torpedo tubes
Complement:	98
Launched:	1967

Delta I

Between 1972 and 1977, Russia moved ahead in the Cold War with Project 667B – 18 large 'Delta'-class vessels, armed with new missiles that could out-range the US Poseidons. Initial tests showed the SS-N-48 missiles had a range of over 7600km (4000 miles). The class was scrapped between 1995 and 2004.

SPECIFICATIONS	
Type:	Russian submarine
Displacement:	11,176 tonnes (11,000 tons) submerged
Dimensions:	150m x 12m x 10.2m (492ft x 39ft 4in x 33ft 6in)
Machinery:	Twin screws, two nuclear reactors, turbines
Top speed:	19 knots [surface], 25 knots [submerged]
Main armament:	Twelve SS-N-48 missile tubes, six 457mm (18in) torpedo tubes
Launched:	1971

TIMELINE

NUCLEAR SUBMARINES: PART 3

Han

SPECIFICATIONS	
Type:	Chinese submarine
Displacement:	5080 tonnes (5000 tons) [submerged], surface displacement tonnage unknown
Dimensions:	90m x 8m x 8.2m (295ft 3in x 26ft 3in x 27ft)
Machinery:	Single screw, one pressurized-water nuclear reactor with turbine drive
Top speed:	25 knots [submerged]
Main armament:	Six 533mm (21in) torpedo tubes
Launched:	1972

The Chinese Navy went nuclear in the early 1970s with the 'Han'-class attack submarines. The highly streamlined hull shape, based upon the US vessel *Albacore*, is a departure from previous Chinese submarine designs. Five boats were completed, of which two or three were considered still operational in 2010.

Los Angeles

SPECIFICATIONS	
Type:	US submarine
Displacement:	6096 tonnes (6000 tons) [surface], 7010.4 tonnes (6900 tons) [submerged]
Dimensions:	109.7m x 10m x 9.8m (360ft x 33ft x 32ft 4in)
Machinery:	Single screw, pressurized-water nuclear reactor, turbines
Top speed:	31 knots [submerged]
Main armament:	Four 533mm (21in) torpedo tubes, up to eight Tomahawk cruise missiles
Complement:	127
Launched:	April 1976

Los Angeles was lead boat in the world's most numerous class of nuclear submarines, with 45 still serving in 2010. Later members of the class (built up to 1996) have been modified. Though intended as hunter-killer boats, they are capable of land attack with Tomahawk missiles, shown in Iraq and Afghanistan.

Ohio

SPECIFICATIONS	
Type:	US submarine
Displacement:	16,360 tonnes (16,764 tons) [surface], 19,050 tonnes (18,750 tons) [submerged]
Dimensions:	170.7m x 12.8m x 11m (560ft x 42ft x 36ft 5in)
Machinery:	Single screw, pressurized-water nuclear reactor, turbines
Top speed:	28 knots [surface], 30+ knots [submerged]
Main armament:	24 Trident missiles, four 533mm (21in) torpedo tubes
Launched:	April 1979

The *Ohio* class were the largest submarines built in the West, surpassed only by the Soviet 'Typhoon' class. The size was determined by the size of the reactor plant. *Ohio* was commissioned in 1981. Originally the class carried the Trident C-4 missile, but from the ninth boat they were built to carry the D-5 version.

1976  1979

Nuclear Submarines: Part 4

Improved reactors encouraged construction of large nuclear submarines. Boats of the United State's *Ohio* class were giants, but dwarfed by the Russian 'Typhoon' boats. Later types were smaller, on grounds of efficiency as well as cost (it was estimated that the United States had spent $700,000,000 on development by 1998).

Victor III

Russia's nuclear-powered hunter-killer submarines were codenamed 'Victor' by NATO. 'Victor III' could fire the SS-N-16 missile, which delivers a conventional homing torpedo to a greater range than otherwise possible. At least 43 'Victors' were launched, 26 of them being 'Victor IIIs', with some still operational in 2010.

SPECIFICATIONS
Type:	Soviet submarine
Displacement:	6400 tonnes (6300 tons) [submerged]
Dimensions:	104m x 10m x 7m (347ft 8in x 32ft 10in x 23ft)
Machinery:	Single screw, pressurized water-cooled nuclear reactor, turbines
Top speed:	30 knots
Main armament:	Six 533mm (21in) torpedo tubes
Launched:	1978

Typhoon

'Typhoon' is the largest submarine yet built, nearly half as big again as the US *Ohio* class. The missile tubes are situated in two rows in front of the fin. It can force a way up through ice up to 3m (9ft 10in) thick. *Dmitry Donskoi,* of this class, was test-firing new Bulava-M missiles in 2008–09.

SPECIFICATIONS
Type:	Russian submarine
Displacement:	25,400 tonnes (24,994 tons) [surface], 26,924 tonnes (26,500 tons) [submerged]
Dimensions:	170m x 24m x 12.5m (562ft 6in x 78ft 8in x 41ft)
Machinery:	Twin screws, pressurized water-cooled nuclear reactors, turbines
Top speed:	27 knots [submerged]
Main armament:	Twenty SS-N-20 nuclear ballistic missiles, two 533mm (21in) and four 650mm (25.6in) torpedo tubes
Launched:	1979

TIMELINE

1978   1979

NUCLEAR SUBMARINES: PART 4

San Francisco

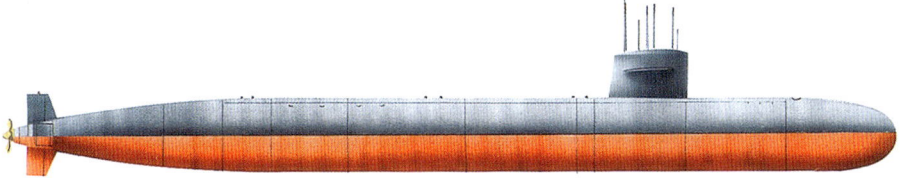

A *Los Angeles* class large attack submarine, *San Francisco* ran at full speed into an uncharted undersea mountain beneath the Pacific Ocean in January 2005, damaging the bows, but it managed to surface safely. Repaired with parts of withdrawn members of the class, it was restored to the fleet in 2008.

SPECIFICATIONS	
Type:	US submarine
Displacement:	6300 tonnes (6200 tons) [surface], 7010 tonnes (6900 tons) [submerged]
Dimensions:	110m x 10m x 9.8m (360ft x 33ft x 32ft 4in)
Machinery:	Single screw, nuclear powered pressurized-water reactor, turbines
Top speed:	30+ knots [submerged]
Main armament:	Four 533mm (21in) torpedo tubes. Harpoon and Tomahawk missiles
Launched:	October 1979

Oscar I

Project 949 was for a class of submarines combining the 'Typhoon' class's Arktika reactor with the 'Victor III' sonar systems, able to launch cruise missiles while submerged and to spend up to 50 days under water. The missiles were placed between the inner and outer pressure hulls, at an angle of 40° from the vertical.

SPECIFICATIONS	
Type:	Soviet submarine
Displacement:	tonnes (12,500 tons) [surface], 14,122 tonnes (13,900 tons) [submerged]
Dimensions:	143m x 18.21m x 8.99m (469ft 2in x 59ft 9in x 29ft 6in)
Machinery:	Twin screws, two pressurized water-cooled nuclear reactors
Top speed:	23 knots [submerged]
Main armament:	Four 533mm (21in) and four 650mm (25.6in) torpedo tubes launching SS-N-19, SS-N-15 and SS-N-16 Stallion missiles
Launched:	April 1981

Xia

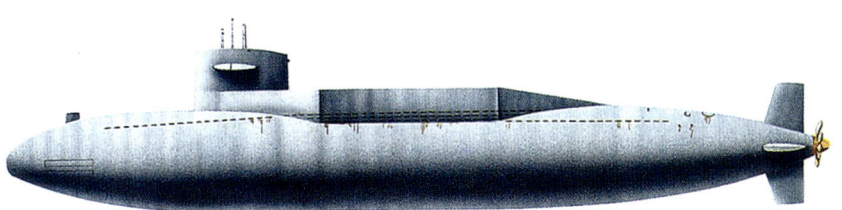

Type 092, 'Xia' was laid down in 1978. China's first ballistic missile submarine, it was an experimental craft. Two were built, of which one remains in service. The missiles were two-stage solid fuel rockets with inertial guidance for ballistic flight to 8000km (5000 miles), fitted with a nuclear warhead of two megatons.

SPECIFICATIONS	
Type:	Chinese submarine
Displacement:	8128 tonnes (8000 tons), submerged
Dimensions:	120m x 10m x 8m (393ft 8in x 32ft 10in x 26ft 3in)
Machinery:	Single screw, pressurized water-cooled nuclear reactor
Top speed:	22 knots [submerged]
Main armament:	Twelve tubes for CSS-N-3 missiles, six 533mm (21in) torpedo tubes
Launched:	April 1981

Ship Types 1950–1999

Nuclear Submarines: Part 5

In the Cold War, nuclear submarines shadowed enemy fleet groups, eavesdropping on naval exercises. Doubtless the practice continues, but operational boats fall into two categories: strategic missile submarines armed with long-range nuclear weapons, and 'hunter-killer' submarines to intercept and destroy enemy vessels.

Georgia

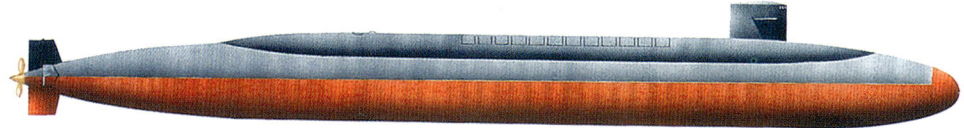

An *Ohio*-class boat, *Georgia* was redesignated SSGN (guided missile) when modified to carry cruise missiles in 2004. A major refit and overhaul followed in 2008. The fin is set far forward, ahead of the missile tubes. Its nuclear reactor is shielded from the engine, control centre and living quarters.

SPECIFICATIONS

Type:	US submarine
Displacement:	16,865 tonnes (16,600 tons) [surface], 19,000 tonnes (18,700 tons) [submerged]
Dimensions:	170.7m x 12.8m x 10.8m (560ft x 42ft x 35ft 5in)
Machinery:	Single screw, pressurized water-cooled nuclear reactor, turbines
Top speed:	28 knots [surface], 30+ knots [submerged]
Main armament:	Twenty-four Trident missiles (C4), four 533mm (21in) torpedo tubes
Launched:	November 1982

Sierra

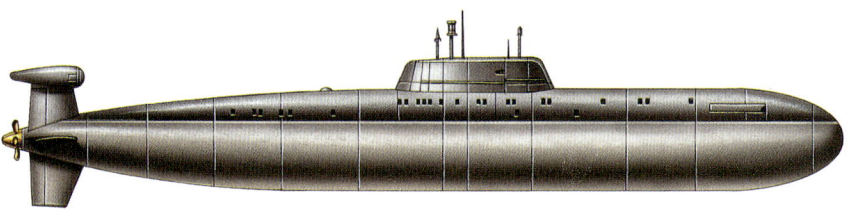

This was Project 945 and four boats were built before production switched to the 'Akula' boats of Project 971. Named 'Sierra' by NATO, the class used the Arktika reactor. Titanium-hulled, they had better safety provisions than previous Soviet nuclear submarines, including a crew escape pod. Three have been withdrawn.

SPECIFICATIONS

Type:	Russian submarine
Displacement:	7315 tonnes (7200 tons) [surface], 10,262 tonnes (10,100 tons) [submerged]
Dimensions:	107m x 12m x 8.8m (351ft 5in x 39ft 5in x 28ft 11in)
Machinery:	Single screw, pressurized water-cooled nuclear reactor, turbines
Top speed:	8 knots [surfaced], 36 knots [submerged]
Main armament:	Four 533mm (21in) and four 650mm (25.6in) torpedo tubes with provision for SS-N-22 and SS-N-16 missiles
Complement:	61
Launched:	1983

TIMELINE

1982   1983   1985

NUCLEAR SUBMARINES: PART 5

Torbay

SPECIFICATIONS	
Type:	British submarine
Displacement:	4877 tonnes (4800 tons) [surface], 5384 tonnes (5300 tons) [submerged]
Dimensions:	85.4m x 10m x 8.2m (280ft 2in x 33ft 2in x 27ft)
Machinery:	Pump jet, pressurized water-cooled reactor, turbines
Main armament:	Five 533mm (21in) tubes for Tigerfish torpedoes
Launched:	March 1985

Torbay was one of the *Trafalgar* class of fleet submarine ordered in 1977, with a longer-life nuclear reactor. The main propulsion and auxiliary machinery raft are suspended from transverse bulkheads to maximize sound insulation. Anechoic tiles also reduce the acoustic signature. Modernizing of the class is taking place.

Vanguard

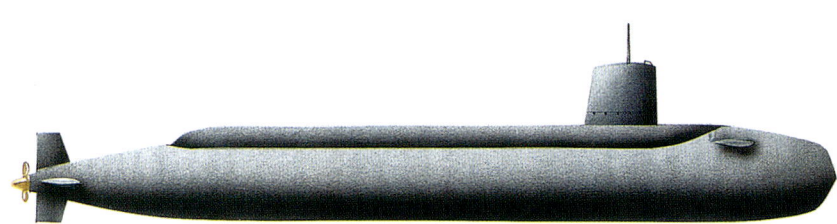

SPECIFICATIONS	
Type:	British submarine
Displacement:	15,240 tonnes (15,000 tons) [submerged]
Dimensions:	148m x 12.8m x 12m (486ft 6in x 42ft x 39ft 4in)
Machinery:	Single screw, pressurized water-cooled nuclear reactor
Top speed:	25+ knots [submerged]
Main armament:	Sixteen Trident D5 missiles, four 533mm (21in) torpedo tubes
Complement:	135
Launched:	1990

Vanguard carries 16 missiles in vertical launch tubes aft of the sail. Each can bear up to 14 warheads to targets more than 12,350km (6500 miles) distant. Like all submarines of this type, it operates independently, remaining submerged for months. The nuclear reactor is refitted and re-cored every eight years.

Le Triomphant

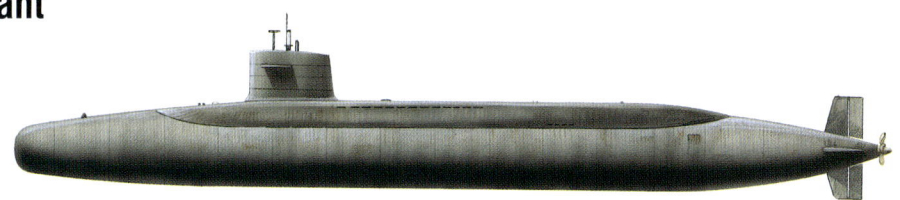

SPECIFICATIONS	
Type:	French submarine
Displacement:	12,842 tonnes (12,640 tons) [surface], 14,564.4 tonnes (14,335 tons) [submerged]
Dimensions:	138m x 17m x 12.5m (453ft x 55ft 8in x 41ft)
Machinery:	Single screw, nuclear reactor with pump jet propulsor
Top speed:	20 knots [surface] 25 knots [submerged]
Main armament:	M51 nuclear missiles from 2010
Launched:	1993

Le Triomphant is the first of France's 'new generation' missile submarines, commissioned in 1997 to replace the *Le Redoutable* class. It uses a new form of propeller. In February 2009, it and HMS *Vanguard* 'scraped' each other while on independent secret patrol beneath the Atlantic, but without consequences.

1990

1993

SHIP TYPES 1950–1999

Kursk

Kursk was an 'Oscar II' class nuclear submarine, an attack boat with nuclear missiles. In 1999, it was deployed in the Mediterranean. It sank after internal explosions while on exercises with the Northern Fleet in the Barents Sea, on 12 August 2000. All the crew perished. A complex salvage operation retrieved the wreck in October 2001.

Kursk

Kursk sank down to 354ft (108m). Russia, Britain and Norway launched a rescue operation, but ten days after the explosions, the remaining crew was declared dead. Twenty-three out of the crew of 118 survived the explosions, but they were trapped in a compartment and died when their air ran out.

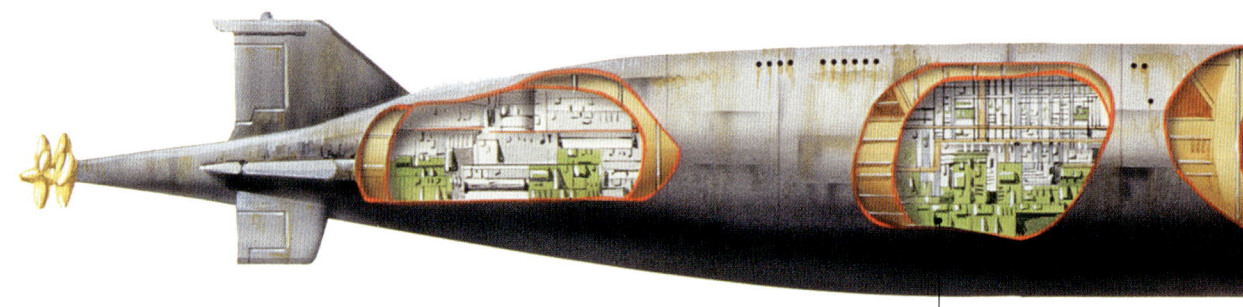

MACHINERY
Two pressurised water-cooled nuclear reactors powering two steam turbines. Power output 73,070kW (98,000shp).

FIFTH COMPARTMENT
This housed the nuclear reactors, and was protected by armoured steel walls 130mm (5.1in) thick, which withstood the blast.

KURSK

SPECIFICATIONS	
Type:	Russian submarine
Displacement:	14,834 tonnes (14,600 tons) [surface], 16,256 tonnes (16,000 tons) [submerged]
Dimensions:	154m x 18.21m x 8.99m (505ft 2in x 59ft 9in x 29ft 6in)
Machinery:	Twin screws, two pressurized water-cooled reactors powering steam turbines
Top speed:	16 knots [surface], 32 knots [submerged]
Main armament:	24 Granit cruise missiles, four 533mm (21in) and two 650mm (25.5in) torpedo tubes
Complement:	118
Launched:	1994

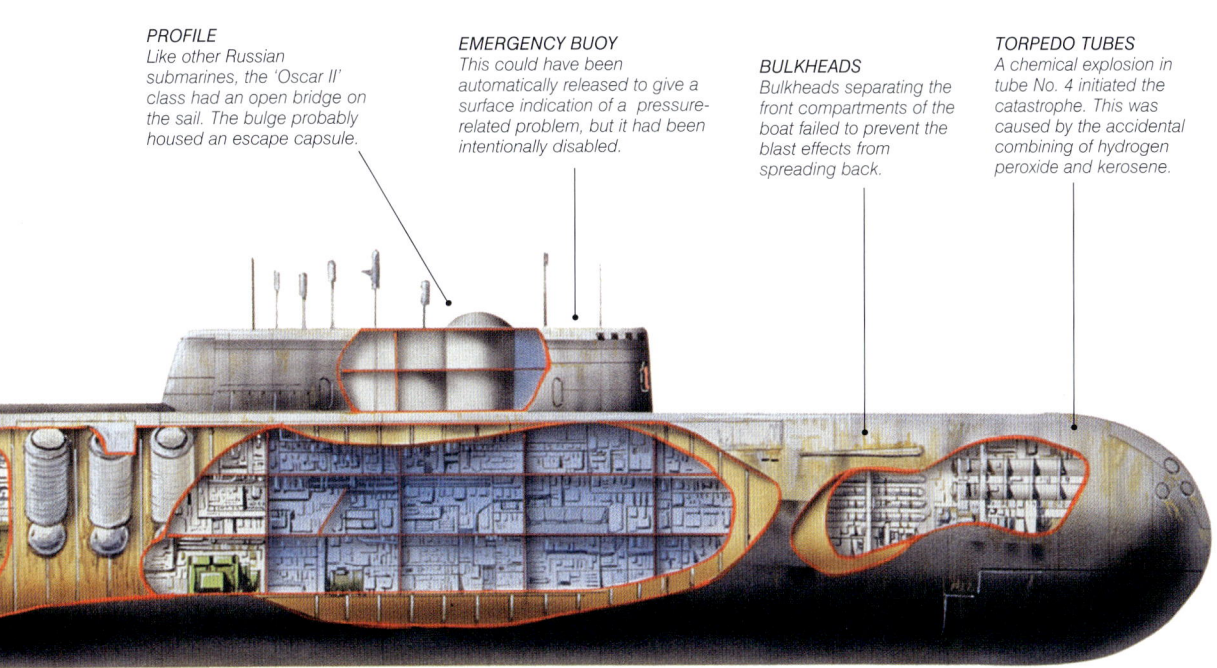

PROFILE
Like other Russian submarines, the 'Oscar II' class had an open bridge on the sail. The bulge probably housed an escape capsule.

EMERGENCY BUOY
This could have been automatically released to give a surface indication of a pressure-related problem, but it had been intentionally disabled.

BULKHEADS
Bulkheads separating the front compartments of the boat failed to prevent the blast effects from spreading back.

TORPEDO TUBES
A chemical explosion in tube No. 4 initiated the catastrophe. This was caused by the accidental combining of hydrogen peroxide and kerosene.

SECOND EXPLOSION
135 seconds after the first, a second larger explosion ripped open the third and fourth compartments.

SHIP TYPES 1950–1999

Support and Repair Ships

The concept of the rapid-deployment task force – able to move at short notice to remote destinations, for military reasons or to provide post-disaster aid – depends on support and repair ships, which can keep up with other vessels in the force and provide the essentials of an operating base, often with command functions as well.

Hunley

Hunley and its sister *Holland* were designed to provide repair and supply services to fleet ballistic missile submarines. With 52 workshops, *Hunley* could deal with the requirements of several submarines at once. It carried a helicopter for at-sea delivery. Decommissioned in 1994, it was broken up in 2007.

SPECIFICATIONS	
Type:	US submarine tender
Displacement:	19,304 tonnes (19,000 tons)
Dimensions:	182.6m x 25.3m x 8.2m (599ft x 83ft x 27ft)
Machinery:	Single screw, diesel-electric engines
Main armament:	Four 20mm (0.79in) guns
Complement:	2490
Launched:	September 1961

Engadine

Laid down in August 1965, the Fleet Auxiliary *Engadine* was designed to train helicopter crews in deep-water operations. The large hangar aft of the funnel held four Wessex and two WASP helicopters, or two of the larger Sea Kings. *Engadine* could also operate pilotless target aircraft. It was scrapped in 1996.

SPECIFICATIONS	
Type:	British helicopter support ship
Displacement:	9144 tonnes (9000 tons)
Dimensions:	129.3m x 17.8m x 6.7m (424ft 3in x 58ft 5in x 22ft)
Machinery:	Single screw, diesel engine
Top speed:	16 knots
Complement:	81 plus 113 training crew
Launched:	1966

TIMELINE

1961    1966    1970

SUPPORT AND REPAIR SHIPS

Basento

SPECIFICATIONS	
Type:	Italian naval water tanker
Displacement:	1944 tonnes (1914 tons)
Dimensions:	66m x 10m x 4m (216ft 6in x 33ft x 13ft)
Machinery:	Twin screws, diesels
Top speed:	12.5 knots
Armament:	Two light anti-aircraft guns
Launched:	1970

Basento was an auxiliary vessel supplying fresh water to the Italian fleet. Tank capacity is 1016 tonnes (1000 tons) and the ship's range is nearly 5700km (3000 miles) at 7 knots. The machinery space is placed aft. In 2009, Basento was given to Ecuador, to become a water supply ship for the arid Galapagos Islands.

Fort Grange

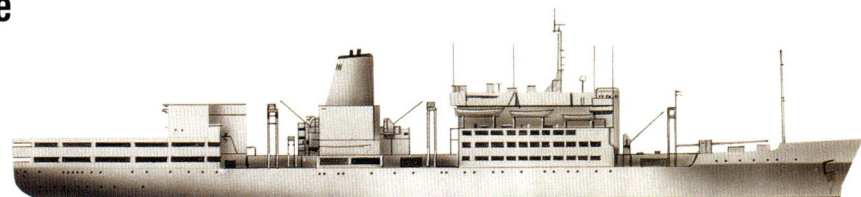

SPECIFICATIONS	
Type:	British fleet replenishment ship
Displacement:	23,165 tonnes (22,800 tons)
Dimensions:	183.9m x 24.1m x 8.6m (603ft x 79ft x 28ft 2in)
Machinery:	Single screw, diesels
Top speed:	22 knots
Main armament:	Two 20mm (0.79in) cannon
Complement:	140 plus 36 aircrew
Launched:	1976

Up to 3500 tonnes of stores can be carried on board, to refuel and restock ships at sea in operational conditions. In addition, it can fly up to four Sea King helicopters on combat missions. *Fort Grange* spent 1994–2000 in the Adriatic Sea. Renamed *Fort Rosalie* in 2000, it was refitted in 2008–09.

Frank Cable

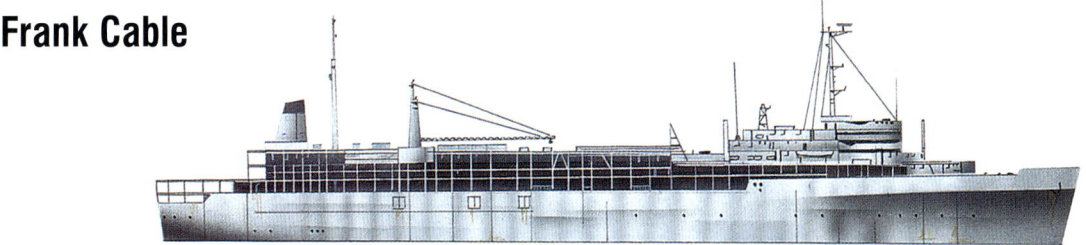

SPECIFICATIONS	
Type:	US submarine tender
Displacement:	23,368 tonnes (23,000 tons)
Dimensions:	196.9m x 25.9m x 7.6m (646ft x 85ft x 25ft)
Machinery:	Single screw, turbines
Top speed:	18 knots
Main armament:	Two 40mm (1.57in) guns
Launched:	1978

One of three improved versions of the *Spear* class, *Frank Cable* was equipped to support the *Los Angeles* class of submarine; up to four of this type can be handled simultaneously. These vessels are a far cry from World War II tenders, which were often old warships on their last role before scrapping.

SHIP TYPES 1950–1999

Bulk Carriers

Large bulk carriers have played an important part in international economic life. The transport of huge tonnages has reduced the cost of shipping heavyweight raw materials like coal and iron ore. Automation speeds up loading and unloading at each end of the ships' run, and the ships are managed by a handful of crew.

Yeoman Burn

Of typical bulk carrier design, with high superstructure and engines at the stern, *Yeoman Burn*'s most notable feature is the lattice booms of the self-loading and unloading machinery. This enables the ship to use ports that lack automated loading. The ship is now under German ownership as *Bernhard Olendorff*.

SPECIFICATIONS

Type:	Norwegian bulk carrier
Displacement:	78,740 tonnes (77,500 tons)
Dimensions:	245m x 32.2m x 14m (830ft 10in x 105ft 8in x 46ft)
Machinery:	Single screw, diesel engines
Top speed:	14.6 knots
Cargo:	iron ore, coal, limestone, salt, coke or grain in bulk
Routes:	International routes
Complement:	25
Launched:	October 1990

Jakob Maersk

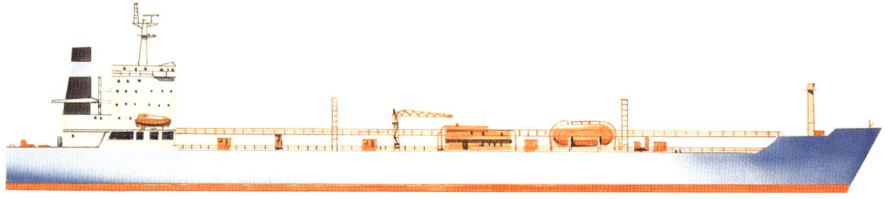

Small for a tanker, *Jakob Maersk* incorporated novel features, including bow and stern thrusters. Held in free-standing tanks in four holds, cargo is handled by eight multistage centrifugal pumps that can load or discharge two tanks at a time. The ship is now the LPG tanker *Maharshi Bhavatreya*.

SPECIFICATIONS

Type:	Danish tanker
Displacement:	42,523 tonnes (42,523 tons)
Dimensions:	185m x 27.4m x 12.5m (607ft x 90ft x 41ft)
Machinery:	Single screw, diesel engine
Top speed:	17.3 knots
Cargo:	Liquefied petroleum gas
Route:	Mediterranean Sea–Northern Europe
Complement:	23
Launched:	1991

TIMELINE

1990

1991

Front Driver

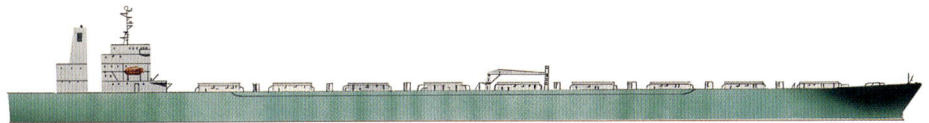

Front Driver is an OBO (oil/bulk ore) carrier. Nine holds with wing tanks can handle three types of oil cargo. The hull is made of 52 per cent high-tensile steel. The OBO concept was not widely followed, however. *Front Driver,* with 153,000 tonnes of coal, was the target of a Greenpeace demonstration in 2007.

SPECIFICATIONS	
Type:	Swedish cargo vessel
Displacement:	195,733 tonnes (192,651 tons)
Dimensions:	285m x 45m (935ft x 147ft 8in)
Machinery:	Single screw, diesel engine
Cargo:	iron ore, coal, limestone, salt, coke or grain in bulk
Routes:	International routes
Launched:	1991

Hakuryu Maru

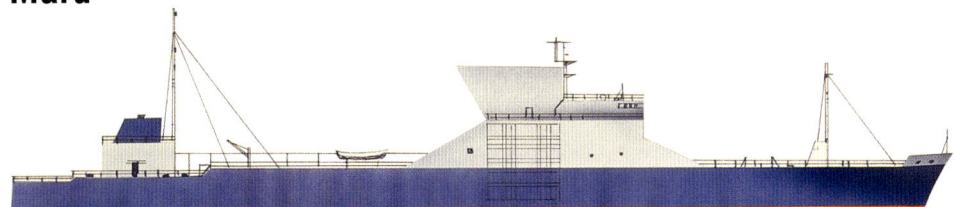

Hakuryu Maru was built specifically to handle and transport steel coils on pallet carriers. The hull has a double bottom with 1400 tonnes (1378 tons) of permanent iron and concrete ballast, to provide stable sea motion and, most importantly considering the loads involved, to limit heel to 3° while loading and unloading.

SPECIFICATIONS	
Type:	Japanese steel carrier
Displacement:	5278 tonnes (5195 tons)
Dimensions:	115m x 18m x 5m (377ft 4in x 59ft x 16ft 5in)
Machinery:	Single screw, diesel engine
Top speed:	15 knots
Route:	Fukuyama-other Japanese ports
Launched:	1991

Futura

Futura was one of the first bulkers built to improved safety standards, including a double hull, gas ventilating of tanks and the ability to ventilate tanks selectively as needed via ballast pipes. Pumping facilities within the double hull eliminate the need for separate spaces to house this equipment in the cargo area.

SPECIFICATIONS	
Type:	Dutch bulk carrier
Displacement:	76,127 tonnes (74,928 tons)
Dimensions:	228.6m x 32.2m x 14.5m (750ft x 105ft 6in x 47ft 6in)
Machinery:	Single screw, diesel engine
Top speed:	14.8 knots
Cargo:	iron ore, coal grain and other bulk cargoes
Routes:	International routes
Launched:	April 1992

Cargo Ships

SHIP TYPES 1950–1999

Modern cargo ships follow set routes, though international shipping agencies exist to find ships for specific cargoes, or vice versa. Many ships carry little or no cargo-handling equipment, and their increasing size confines them to deep-water ports with dockside cranes and conveyors. Machinery and ship-handling are automated.

Savannah

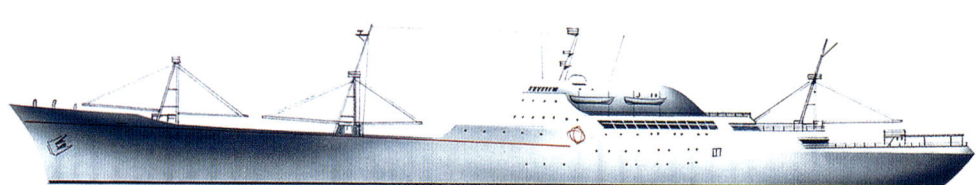

The first merchant ship powered by atomic propulsion, *Savannah* was meant to demonstrate the peaceful application of atomic energy. However, high operational costs made it commercially unviable and it was withdrawn from service in 1972. Its future as a museum ship was under debate in 2010.

SPECIFICATIONS	
Type:	US cargo ship
Displacement:	14,112 tonnes (13,890 tons)
Dimensions:	195m (639ft 9in) x 23.77m (78ft)
Machinery:	Twin screws, nuclear reactor, turbines
Top speed:	20.5 knots
Cargo:	Mixed freight
Complement:	124
Launched:	July 1959

Helena

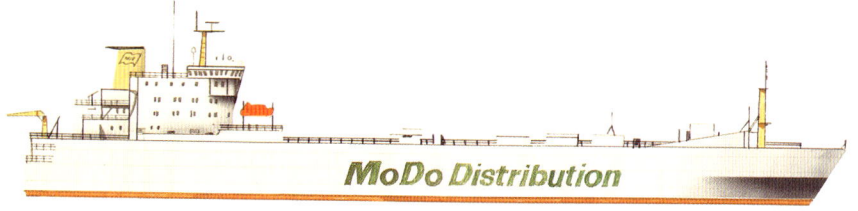

Helena is a roll-on, roll-off freighter with a full-length double bottom, and a double skin in the lower cargo areas and engine room. Traffic when loading is two-way, and all four decks are interconnected by ramps. Cargo-handling is monitored by closed-circuit display units in the wheelhouse and the engine room control centre.

SPECIFICATIONS	
Type:	Swedish cargo vessel
Displacement:	22,548 tonnes (22,193 tons)
Dimensions:	169m x 25.6m x 7m (554ft 6in x 84ft x 23ft)
Machinery:	Single screw, diesel engine
Top speed:	14.6 knots
Cargo:	Paper products, trailers, small cars and containers
Routes:	Swedish ports to Antwerp and other European ports
Launched:	1990

TIMELINE 1959 1990 1991

Hudson Rex

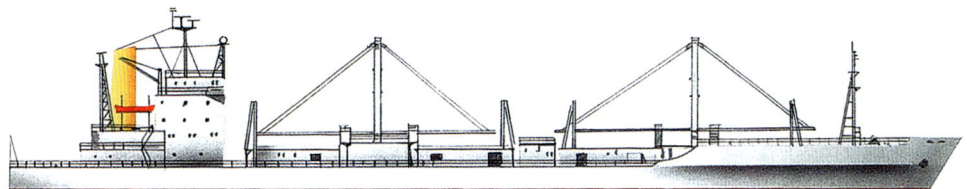

The design of *Hudson Rex* incorporates conventional derrick booms, operated by electro-hydraulic winches. Fans supply cold air to the refrigerated area, and there is a comprehensive insulation system. The refrigeration and temperature control system is installed in the engine room. The ship now sails as *Sun Maria*.

SPECIFICATIONS	
Type:	Panamanian cargo carrier
Displacement:	12,192 tonnes (12,000 tons)
Dimensions:	148.5m x 20.6m x 9.4m (487ft 3in x 67ft 7in x 31ft)
Machinery:	Single screw, diesel engine
Top speed:	19.2 knots
Cargo:	Refrigerated goods
Routes:	Netherlands–West Africa
Launched:	October 1991

Halla

The ship is a self-loader and unloader, using compressed air power to move its cargo through large-diameter tubes. The lattice tower supports discharge booms, and the machinery room is between the two holds. 1000 tonnes (984 tons) of cement can be loaded, and 500 tonnes (492 tons) unloaded, in 1 hour.

SPECIFICATIONS	
Type:	Korean cement carrier
Displacement:	10,427 tonnes (10,427 tons)
Dimensions:	111.8m x 17.8m x 7m (367ft 3in x 58ft 5in x 23ft)
Machinery:	Single screw, diesel engine
Top speed:	13 knots
Cargo:	bulk cement
Route:	South Korea–Japan
Complement:	27
Launched:	January 1991

Krasnograd

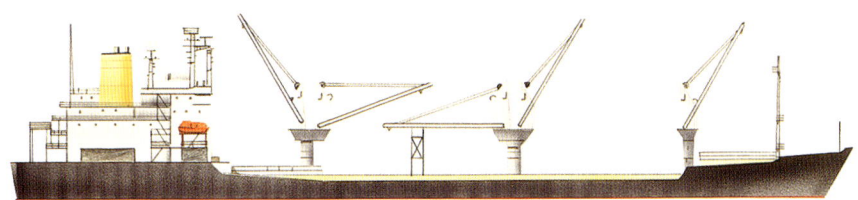

Krasnograd was one of the first foreign-built carriers to enter the Russian merchant fleet for years. The hull has two through-decks with four cargo holds. Containers of 6m (20ft) and 12m (40ft) offer a capacity of 728 TEU; 30 are refrigerated. The ship is now Greek-owned and Malta-registered as *Nordana Surveyor*.

SPECIFICATIONS	
Type:	Russian cargo ship
Displacement:	26,630 tonnes (26,630 tons)
Dimensions:	173.5m x 23m x 10m (569ft 3in x 75ft 6in x 32ft 10in)
Machinery:	Single screw, diesel engine
Cargo:	Containers
Routes:	International routes
Launched:	1992

SHIP TYPES 1950–1999

Jervis Bay

Jervis Bay moves between highly automated terminals, and unloading and reloading can be accomplished within 24 hours. The loading space is maximized by computer-assisted design, and on-board computers specify and record the location of every container carried on the ship. Carrying capacity is 4038 6m (20ft) units.

Jervis Bay

Despite its huge size, the *Jervis Bay* had a crew of just nine officers and 10 men. *Jervis Bay* and its sisters-ships were constructed to be employed mainly in the Europe–Far East service (accomplishing a round trip from Southampton to Yokohama and back in 63 days).

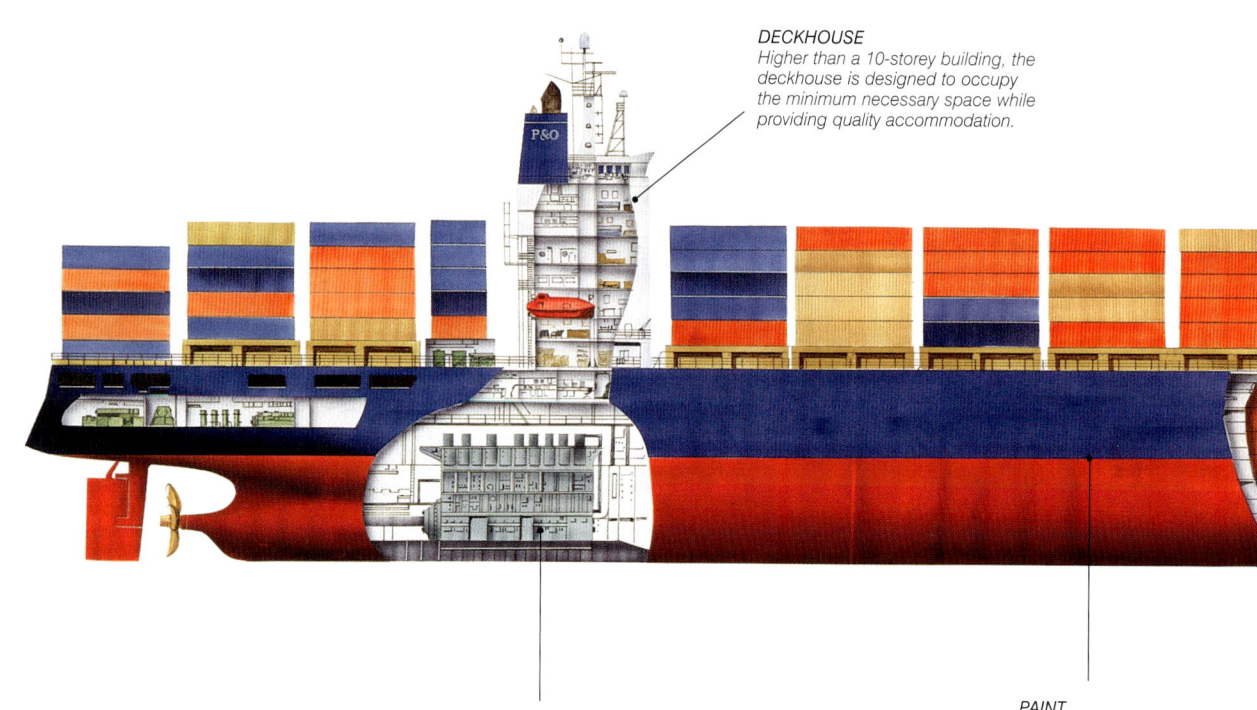

DECKHOUSE
Higher than a 10-storey building, the deckhouse is designed to occupy the minimum necessary space while providing quality accommodation.

MACHINERY
A Sulzer 9RTA 84C nine-cylinder diesel engine drives the massive propellor. Maximum power output is 34,412kW (47,000shp) at 100 rpm.

PAINT
Periodic dry-docking is needed to blast off growths and accretions and to repaint the hull with drag-reducing paint.

JERVIS BAY

SPECIFICATIONS	
Type:	British container ship
Displacement:	51,816 tonnes (51,000 tons)
Dimensions:	292.15m x 32.2m x 11.2m (985ft 6in x 105ft 6in x 36ft)
Machinery:	Single screw, diesel
Service speed:	23.5 knots
Cargo:	Containers
Routes:	Southampton–Japanese ports
Complement:	19
Launched:	1992

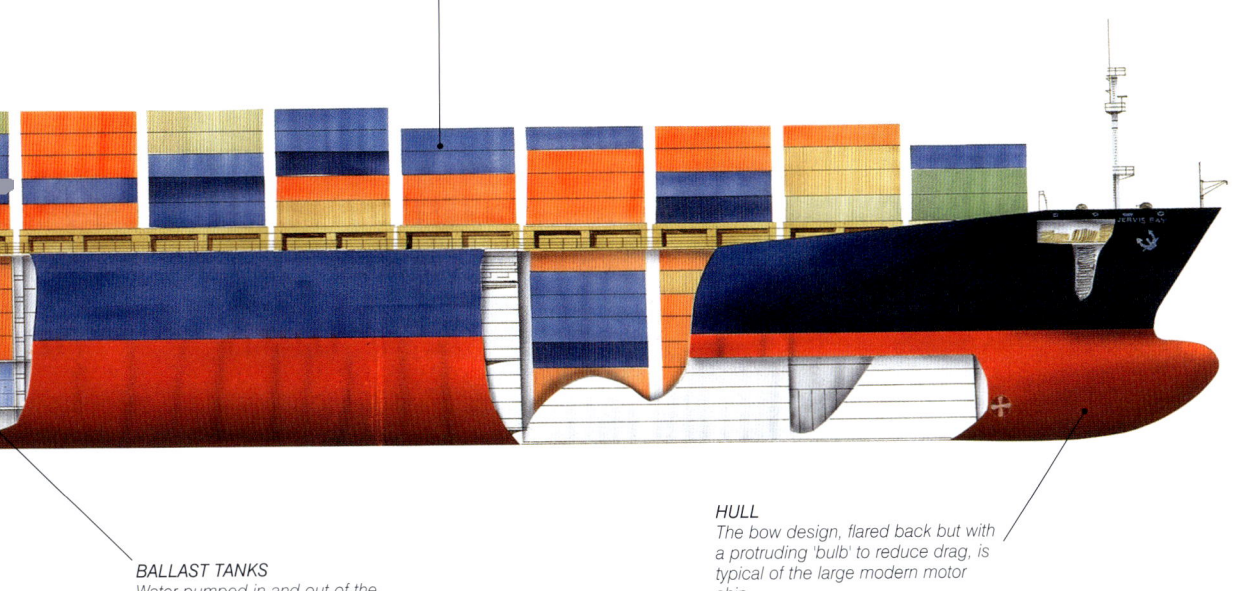

NAME
Passing into the ownership of A.P. Moller in 2006, and operated by Maersk Line, the ship was renamed MSC Almeria in 2008.

CONTAINERS
More than half the load is carried above deck level. 174 deck and 66 hold containers can be refrigerated.

HULL
The bow design, flared back but with a protruding 'bulb' to reduce drag, is typical of the large modern motor ship.

BALLAST TANKS
Water pumped in and out of the ballast tanks is a vital necessity to maintain stability during loading and unloading.

SHIP TYPES 1950–1999

Container Ships

The basic dimensions of all container ships are based on the standard international containers: 12m (40ft) and 6m (20ft) long. A ship designer's aim is to produce a hull that will hold the maximum number of loaded containers for the minimum usage of steel compatible with strength, safety and international marine regulations.

Ever Globe

Ever Globe was first owned by the Evergreen Marine Corporation, based in Taiwan and registered in Panama. It had three holds for containers, plus a massive deck area where more could be stacked. Sold and renamed twice, it was Scotland, then Hera. In January 2009, it was sold for scrapping in China.

SPECIFICATIONS	
Type:	Taiwanese container ship
Displacement:	43,978 tonnes (43,285 tons)
Dimensions:	231m x 32m (757ft 10in x 105ft)
Machinery:	Single screw, diesel engine
Routes:	Various
Launched:	1984

Hannover Express

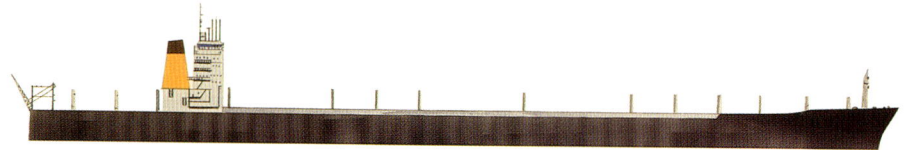

High-tensile steel construction allows 11 rows of containers to be stowed in the hull instead of 10. Additionally, rearranging the longitudinal beams allowed Hannover Express to carry heavy-lift cargoes, usually impossible with this type of vessel. The dimensions are 'Panamax', designed to fit the Panama Canal.

SPECIFICATIONS	
Type:	German container ship
Displacement:	76,330 tonnes (75,128 tons)
Dimensions:	294m x 32.2m x 13.5m (964ft 6in x 105ft 10in x 44ft 4in)
Machinery:	Single screw, diesel engine
Top speed:	23.8 knots
Routes:	International routes
Complement:	21
Launched:	October 1990

TIMELINE

1984   1990   1991

CONTAINER SHIPS

Kota Wijaya

Registered in Singapore, *Kota Wijaya* carries a combined load of 6m (20ft) and 12m (40ft) containers in six holds, with a capacity of 1186 TEU, plus 200 refrigerated containers on the upper deck. The hull is double-skinned over the midships section. Heeling tanks with water ballast provide stability while loading.

SPECIFICATIONS
Type:	Malayan container ship
Displacement:	22,695 tonnes (22,695 tons)
Dimensions:	184.5m x 27.6m x 9.5m (605ft 4in x 90ft 6in x 31ft 3in)
Machinery:	Single screw, diesel engines
Top speed:	19 knots
Routes:	Malaysia–Europe and Australia
Launched:	February 1991

Nedlloyd Europa

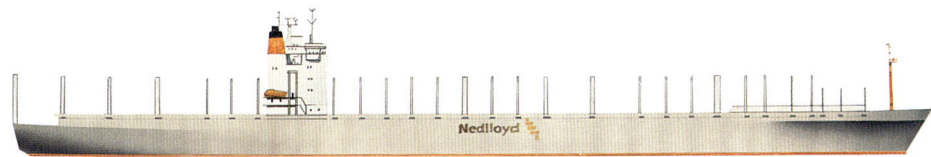

Nedlloyd Europa was the first ship to dispense with standard hatch covers, for a container guide-support system that extends from the holds up above the deck to secure deck-carried containers. Tests proved the safety of the design, which needs duplicate pumping and drainage systems. There are seven cargo holds.

SPECIFICATIONS
Type:	Dutch container ship
Displacement:	48,768 tonnes (48,000 tons)
Dimensions:	266m x 32.2m x 13m (872ft 9in x 105ft 9in x 42ft 8in)
Machinery:	Single screw, diesel engines
Top speed:	23 knots
Routes:	International routes
Launched:	September 1991

Hyundai Admiral

With the world's most powerful diesel engine (developing over 67,000bhp), *Hyundai Admiral* is highly automated: control centre monitors enable a single watch-keeping system to be used. The seven holds accommodate over 4400 containers. There is an area for dangerous cargo. The ship has a double hull.

SPECIFICATIONS
Type:	British container ship
Displacement:	62,131 tonnes (61,153 tons)
Dimensions:	275m x 37m x 13.6m (902ft 3in x 121ft 9in x 44ft 7in)
Machinery:	Single screw, diesel engines
Routes:	Britain–Far East
Launch date:	1992

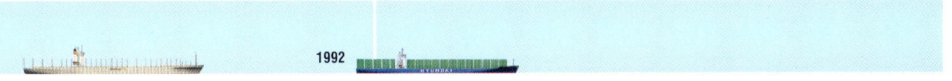

SHIP TYPES 1950–1999

Anastasis

In 1978, the Italian liner *Victoria* was converted by the US Mercy Ships charity into a hospital ship, visiting countries where medical aid was in short supply. Fitted out to provide surgical and dental treatment, *Anastasis* visited 275 ports, on 66 field assignments, in 23 nations. After 29 years of service, it was retired in 2007.

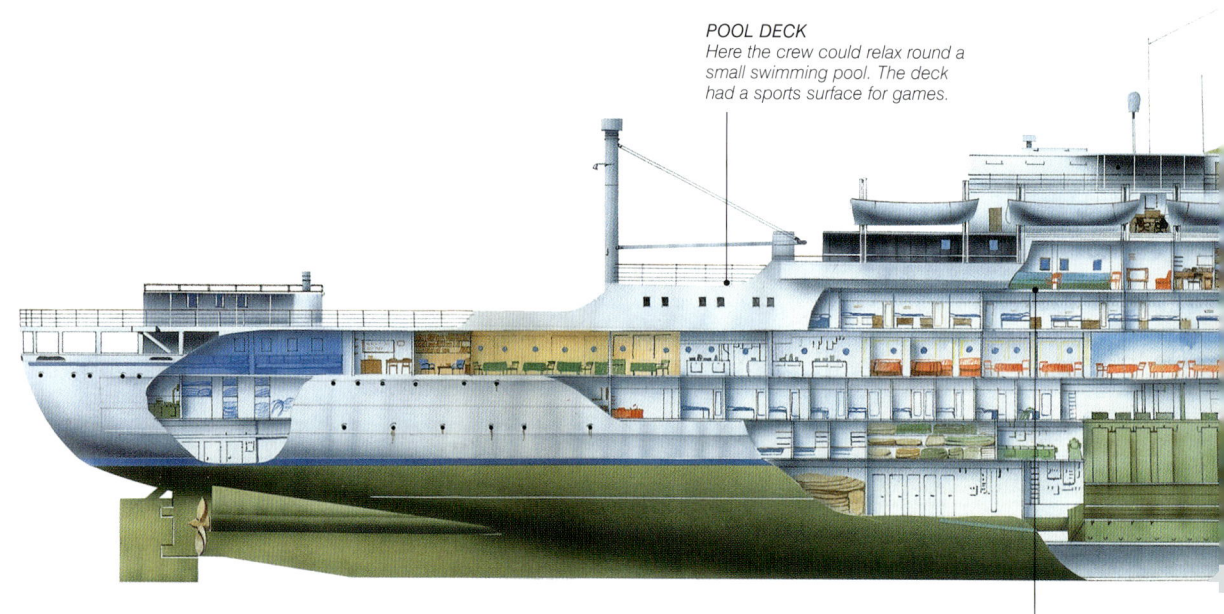

POOL DECK
Here the crew could relax round a small swimming pool. The deck had a sports surface for games.

CT SCANNER
A CT (computerised tomography) scanner was added to the ship's range of diagnostic and treatment facilities in 2002.

Anastasis

As a medical vessel *Anastasis* has delivered aid to some of the world's poorest countries. In the previous role as a passenger ship it sailed to Pakistan, India and the Far East.

SPECIFICATIONS	
Type:	Italian liner, later US private hospital ship
Displacement:	11,882 tonnes (11,695 tons)
Dimensions:	159m x 20.7m (521ft 6in x 67ft 10in)
Machinery:	Twin screws, diesels
Top speed:	19.5 knots
Complement:	420
Launched:	1953

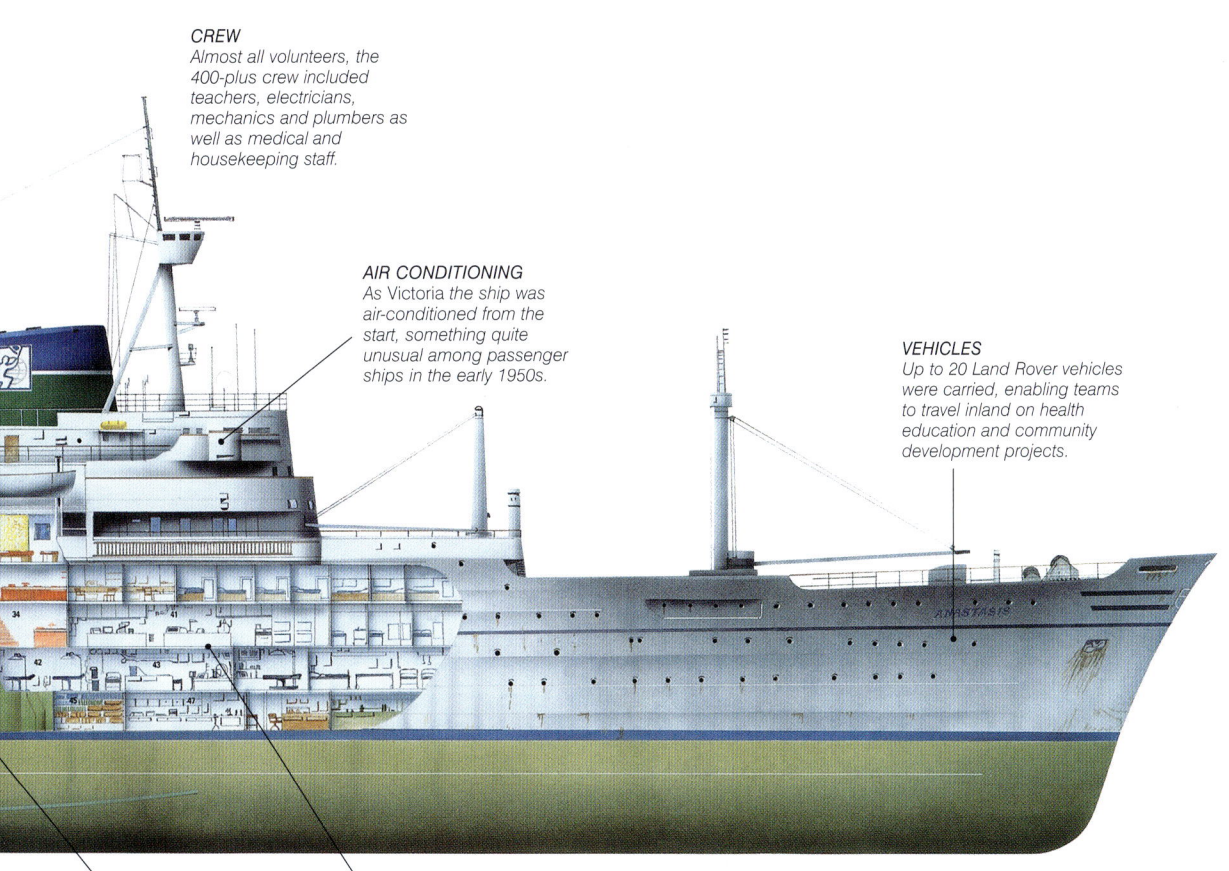

CREW
Almost all volunteers, the 400-plus crew included teachers, electricians, mechanics and plumbers as well as medical and housekeeping staff.

AIR CONDITIONING
As *Victoria* the ship was air-conditioned from the start, something quite unusual among passenger ships in the early 1950s.

VEHICLES
Up to 20 Land Rover vehicles were carried, enabling teams to travel inland on health education and community development projects.

MACHINERY
Two Fiat 7510 diesel engines each developing 5,995kW (8,040bhp). Much of the ship's secondary machinery had to be updated or replaced.

MEDICAL SUITES
Three operating theatres, a 40-bed ward for recuperation, and a two-bed intensive care unit were set up.

SHIP TYPES 1950–1999

Cruise Ships

Cruising as a holiday had been possible for more than a century, but took place on a limited scale. The availability of big ships, with adroit marketing and refits that included more entertainment and leisure facilities, combined to turn cruising into an all-year round marine industry. Soon custom-built cruise ships would be launched.

France

The third *France* was, by design, the longest passenger ship in the world when launched. In 1974, the government subsidy that had kept it in service was stopped, and it was withdrawn from service. In 1979 *France* was sold to the Norwegian Caribbean Line and refitted as a cruise ship, being renamed *Norway*.

SPECIFICATIONS	
Type:	French cruise ship
Displacement:	67,406 tonnes (66,344 tons)
Dimensions:	315.5m x 33.5m (1035ft x 110ft)
Machinery:	Four (later two) shafts, double-reduction turbines
Top speed:	30 (later 16) knots
Launched:	1961

Radisson Diamond

The big passenger ship found a new role as a cruise liner, but design changed radically. This ship is small compared to later examples, its catamaran design making it broad in relation to its length. Each hull has an engine, and boats can be launched from between them. Now *Asia Star*, it operates from Hong Kong.

SPECIFICATIONS	
Type:	US cruise ship
Displacement:	18,684 tonnes (18,400 tons)
Dimensions:	131m x 32m (423ft x 105ft)
Machinery:	Twin screws plus bow thrusters, diesels
Top speed:	12.5 knots
Launched:	1991

TIMELINE

1961

1991

CRUISE SHIPS

Society Adventurer

This expedition ship was renamed *Hanseatic* by new German owners in 1993. It can operate for up to eight weeks without taking on fuel or provisions. Range is 16,150km (8500 miles). For cruises to special-interest areas such as Antarctica, it has an observation lounge above the bridge, and carries 188 passengers.

SPECIFICATIONS	
Type:	Bahamian expedition ship
Displacement:	8,512 tonnes (8,378 tons)
Dimensions:	122.7m x 18m x 4.7m (402ft 8in x 59ft x 15ft 8in)
Machinery:	Twin screws, diesel engines
Launched:	January 1991

Majesty of the Seas

Built for Royal Caribbean Cruise Lines, *Majesty of the Seas* has promenade decks that are largely enclosed. It carries 2350 passengers on week-long cruises in the Caribbean Sea. Engines are low down and aft, maximizing passenger space and minimizing vibration and noise. It was partly refurbished in 2007.

SPECIFICATIONS	
Type:	Norwegian cruise ship
Displacement:	75,124 tonnes (73,941 tons)
Dimensions:	266.4m x 32.3m x 7.6m (874ft x 106ft x 25ft)
Machinery:	Single screw, diesels
Top speed:	21 knots
Launched:	1992

Europa

Rated 'best cruise ship' for nine successive years, *Europa* accommodates only 410 passengers. Novel aspects of the design include a propeller drive from externally mounted 'pods' that can be angled to increase manoeuvrability, and the propellers themselves are pullers rather than pushers. It was refitted in 2007.

SPECIFICATIONS	
Type:	German cruise ship
Displacement:	28,854.4 tonnes (28,400 tons)
Dimensions:	198.6m x 78ft x 39ft (644ft 6in x 78ft x 39ft)
Machinery:	Twin screws, diesel-electric
Top speed:	21 knots
Launched:	1999

1992  1999

SHIP TYPES 1950–1999

Canberra

Canberra served with P&O on the Pacific route in May 1961. Lavishly fitted, it could carry 2186 passengers. Requisitioned in 1982 as a troop ship for the Falklands campaign, it had several narrow escapes. It returned to the UK in July 1982 and, after a refit, returned to service. *Canberra* was scrapped in Pakistan in 1997–8.

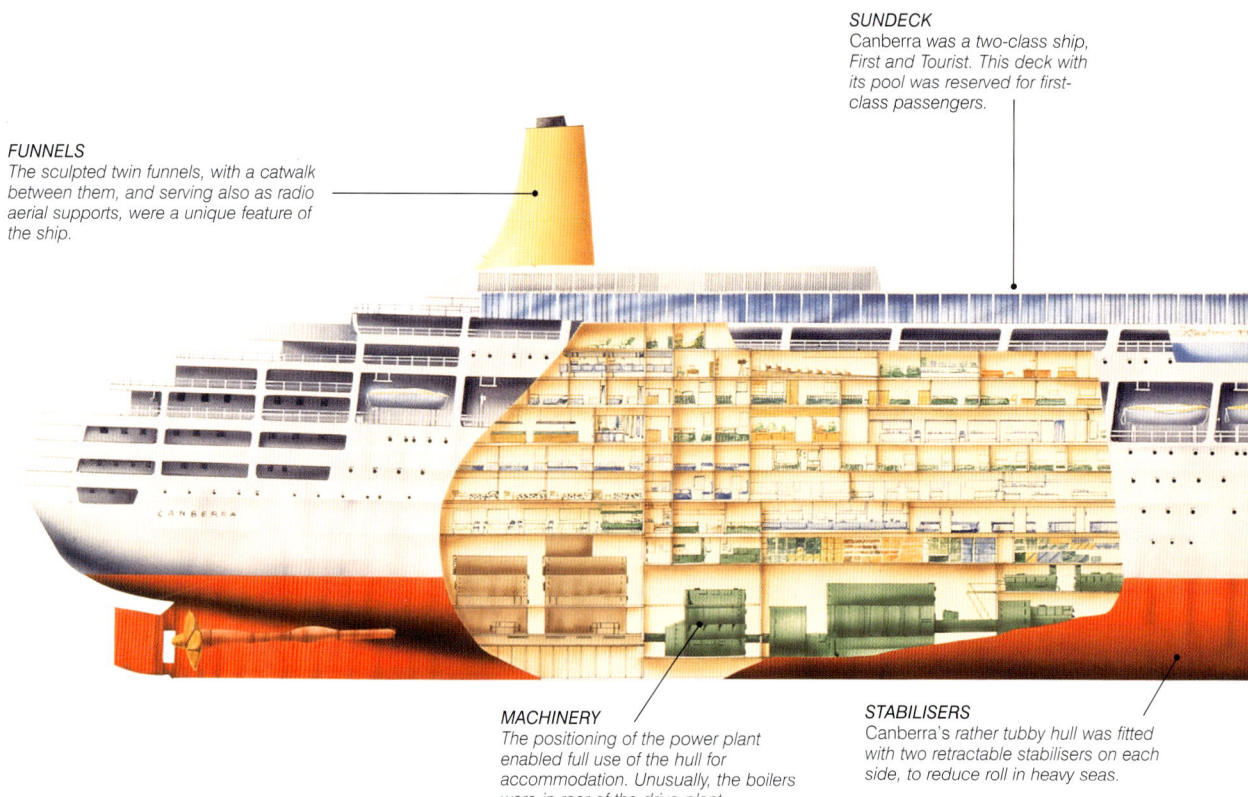

FUNNELS
The sculpted twin funnels, with a catwalk between them, and serving also as radio aerial supports, were a unique feature of the ship.

SUNDECK
Canberra was a two-class ship, First and Tourist. This deck with its pool was reserved for first-class passengers.

MACHINERY
The positioning of the power plant enabled full use of the hull for accommodation. Unusually, the boilers were in rear of the drive plant.

STABILISERS
Canberra's rather tubby hull was fitted with two retractable stabilisers on each side, to reduce roll in heavy seas.

Canberra

Canberra was built in Belfast, Northern Ireland in 1960 and entered service the following year. It was originally designed to serve as a passenger liner between Great Britian and Australia, but it was converted into a luxury cruise ship in 1974.

SPECIFICATIONS	
Type:	British liner
Displacement:	45,524 tonnes (44,807 tons)
Dimensions:	249m x 31m (817ft x 101ft 8in)
Machinery:	Twin screws, steam turbines, electric drive
Route:	Britain–Australia
Complement:	938
Launched:	March 1960

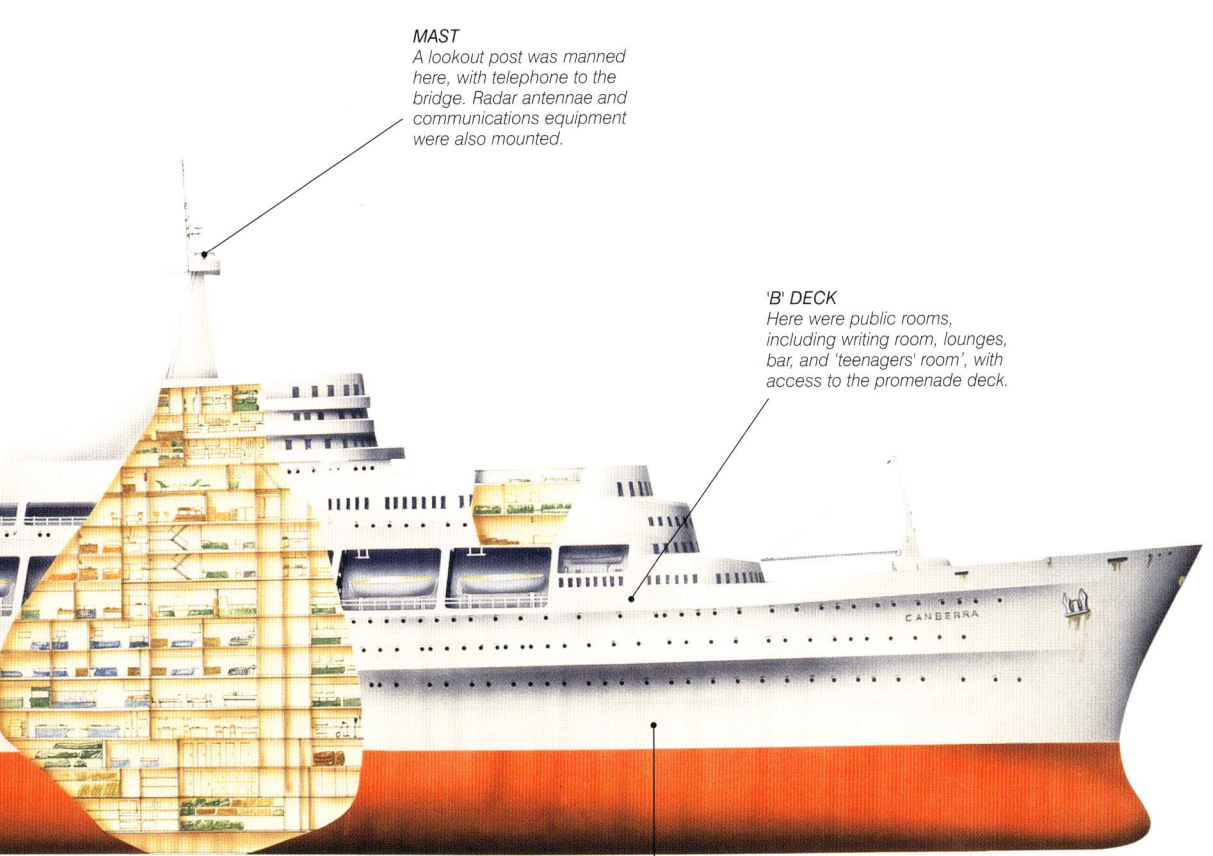

MAST
A lookout post was manned here, with telephone to the bridge. Radar antennae and communications equipment were also mounted.

'B' DECK
Here were public rooms, including writing room, lounges, bar, and 'teenagers' room', with access to the promenade deck.

CREW ACCOMMODATION
Crew cabins, some tourist class cabins, baggage rooms, store rooms and workshops were situated on 'G' deck at waterline level.

SHIP TYPES 1950–1999

Queen Elizabeth II

Queen Elizabeth II was the last of the transatlantic liners. Construction was beset by problems, and mechanical troubles delayed its maiden voyage. It was requisitioned as a troopship in the Falklands War of 1982. Re-engined, it later served successfully as a cruise ship. Withdrawn in 2008, it was bought to be a floating hotel at Dubai.

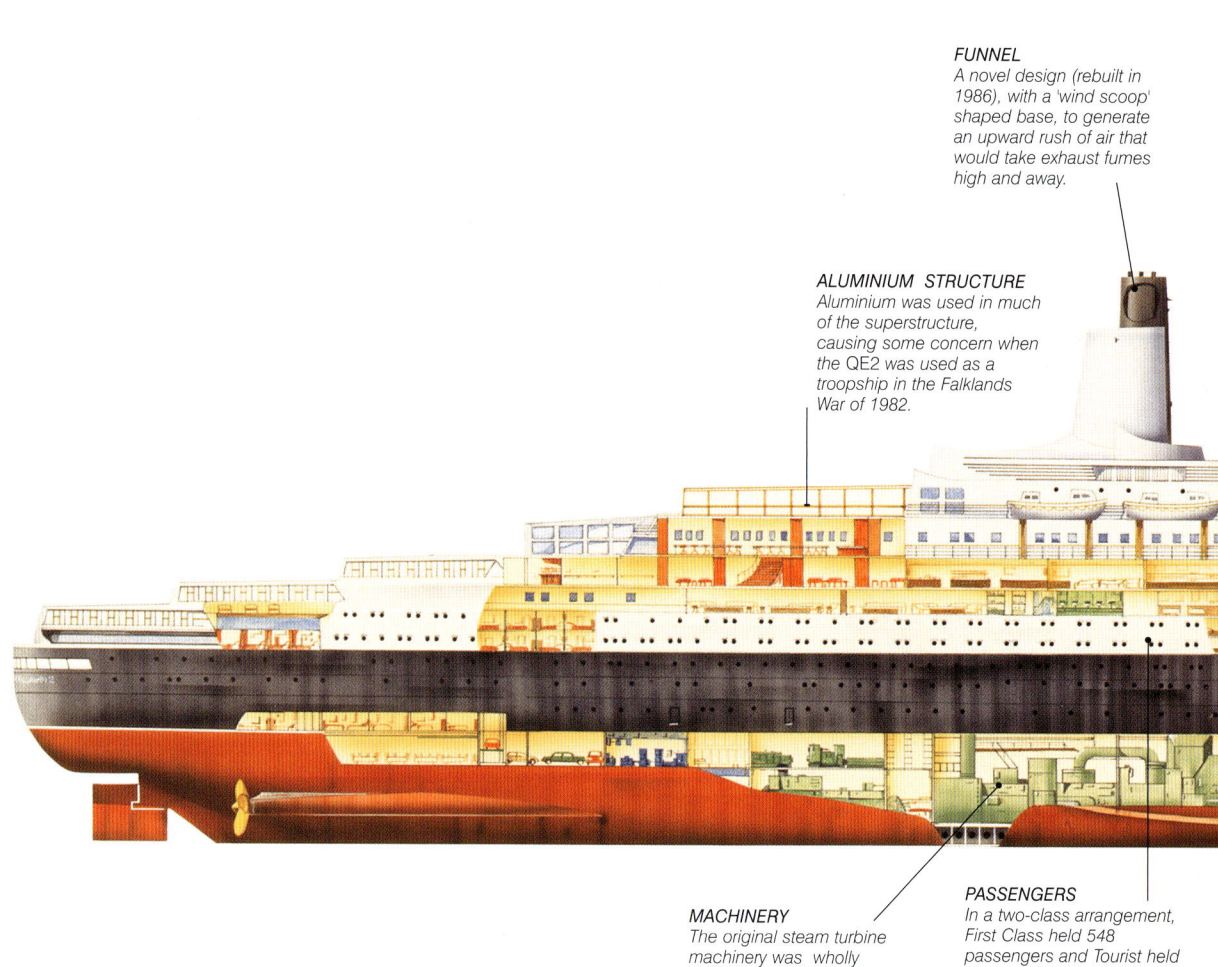

FUNNEL
A novel design (rebuilt in 1986), with a 'wind scoop' shaped base, to generate an upward rush of air that would take exhaust fumes high and away.

ALUMINIUM STRUCTURE
Aluminium was used in much of the superstructure, causing some concern when the QE2 was used as a troopship in the Falklands War of 1982.

MACHINERY
The original steam turbine machinery was wholly replaced in 1986-87 by nine MAN 9-cylinder diesels with electric drive.

PASSENGERS
In a two-class arrangement, First Class held 548 passengers and Tourist held 1690. Officers and crew numbered 795.

Queen Elizabeth II

In May 1982 the *QE2* took part in the Falklands War, carrying 3000 troops and 650 volunteer crew to the South Atlantic. It was refitted in Southampton in preparation for war service, this included the installation of three helicopter pads, the transformation of public lounges into dormitories and the covering of carpets with 2000 sheets of hardboard.

SPECIFICATIONS

Type:	British passenger liner
Displacement:	66,432 tonnes (65,836 tons)
Dimensions:	293.5m x 32.1m x 9.75m (963ft x 105ft x 32ft)
Machinery:	Twin screws, geared turbines (later diesel-electric)
Top speed:	29 knots
Routes:	North Atlantic; cruising
Launched:	1967

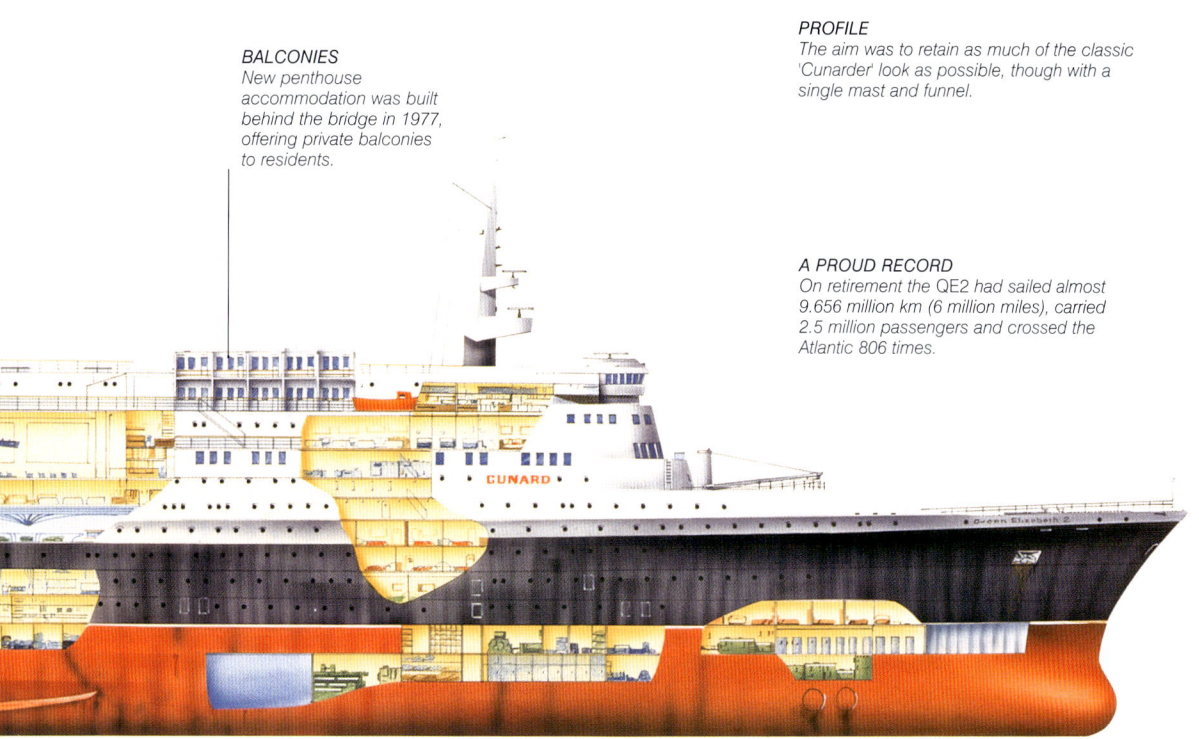

BALCONIES
New penthouse accommodation was built behind the bridge in 1977, offering private balconies to residents.

PROFILE
The aim was to retain as much of the classic 'Cunarder' look as possible, though with a single mast and funnel.

A PROUD RECORD
On retirement the QE2 had sailed almost 9.656 million km (6 million miles), carried 2.5 million passengers and crossed the Atlantic 806 times.

SHIP TYPES 1950–1999

Seagoing Ferries

Trends in travel and transport have encouraged the concept of the big, long-range car and truck ferry with comfortable accommodation and many amusements and attractions for passengers. The most notable examples ply the Baltic Sea and Japan–Asia routes and the tendency is for such vessels to get ever bigger.

Ishikari

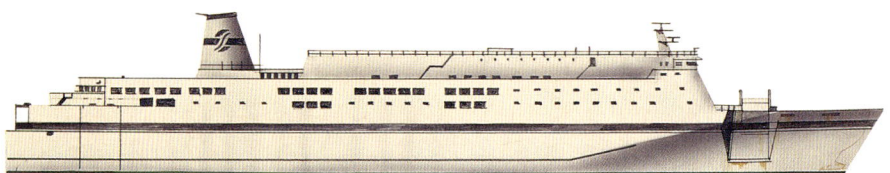

SPECIFICATIONS	
Type:	Japanese vehicle ferry
Displacement:	7050 tonnes (6938 tons)
Dimensions:	192.5m x 27m x 6.9m (631ft 6in x 88ft 7in x 22ft 8in)
Machinery:	Twin screws, diesel engines
Top speed:	21.5 knots
Route:	Between Japanese islands
Launched:	November 1990

Ishikari was one of Japan's first luxury, high-speed ferries, modelled on Baltic Sea ferries, and is able to carry 850 passengers, 151 cars and 165 trucks. The hull is designed for speed and economy, and it burns 76 tonnes (75 tons) of oil a day in regular service. The upper part houses nine separate decks.

Ferry Lavender

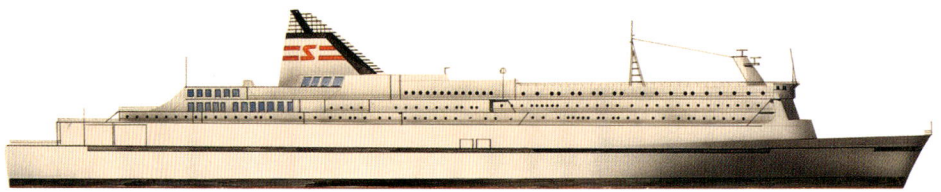

SPECIFICATIONS	
Type:	Japanese vehicle ferry
Displacement:	20,222 tonnes (19,904 tons)
Dimensions:	193m x 29.4m x 6.7m (632ft x 96ft 5in x 22ft 2in)
Machinery:	Twin screws, diesel engines
Top speed:	21.8 knots
Route:	Patras–Brindisi
Launched:	March 1991

A roll-on, roll-off passenger ferry, ordered by the Shin Nihonkai Ferry Company, *Ferry Lavender* was one of the biggest car ferries of its day. Able to carry 796 passengers, its two vehicle decks have access through bow and stern ramps. Greek-owned from 2004 as *Ionian King*, it now works between Greece and Italy.

TIMELINE

1990  1991

SEAGOING FERRIES

Tycho Brahe

The largest double-ended train ferry, *Tycho Brahe* works between Helsingør, Denmark, and Helsingborg, Sweden. It was designed to reach maximum speed after 1500m (1640yd), and to decelerate rapidly when 800m (875yd) from shore. It carries 260 lorries, 240 cars and nine railway coaches, and 1250 passengers.

SPECIFICATIONS	
Type:	Danish train ferry
Displacement:	10,871 tonnes (10,700 tons)
Dimensions:	111m x 28.2m x 5.7m (364ft 2in x 92ft 6in x 18ft 8in)
Machinery:	Quadruple thrusters, diesel engines
Top speed:	13.5 knots
Route:	Helsingør–Helsingborg
Launched:	1991

Frans Suell

From the keel of this Baltic Sea 'super-ferry' to the top of the wheelhouse, there are 12 decks, two of which are used to hold road vehicles. Accommodation is provided for 2300 passengers, with some cabins having balconies. Ownership passed to Silja as *Silja Scandinavia*, then to Viking Line as *Gabriella*.

SPECIFICATIONS	
Type:	Swedish ferry
Displacement:	35,850 tonnes (35,285 tons)
Dimensions:	169.4m x 27.6m x 6.25m (556ft 6in x 90ft 6in x 20ft 6in)
Machinery:	Twin screws, diesel engines
Route:	Stockholm–Helsinki
Launched:	January 1991

Condor Express

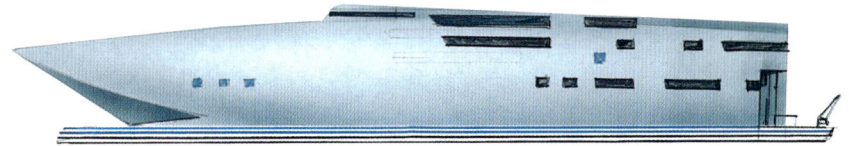

Built at the Condor yard in Hobart, Tasmania, this catamaran-hull ferry takes up to 200 cars and 776 passengers. Its four Ruston 20-cylinder diesel engines propel it at speeds in excess of 40 knots. With two sister craft, it provides a fast service between England's south coast, the Channel Islands and Brittany.

SPECIFICATIONS	
Type:	British car ferry
Displacement:	386 tonnes (380 tons)
Dimensions:	86.25m x 26m x 3.5m (282ft 10in x 85ft 3in x 11ft 6in)
Machinery:	Four water jets, diesels
Top speed:	40 knots
Route:	Poole–St Malo
Launched:	1997

SHIP TYPES 1950–1999

Multi-Product & Oil Tankers

Some disastrous groundings and oil spillages prompted a tighter international regime for construction and operation of VLCC (very large crude carrier) ships. Maximum permitted Panama Canal (Panamax) dimensions of 294.13m x 32.31m x 12.04m (965ft x 106ft x 39ft 6in) will be increased by 2014, enabling increases in ship sizes.

British Skill

British Skill was one of several ships built to replace ageing supertankers of previous decades. Like all big modern ships, controls are largely automated. It was an early user of Doppler radar for assisting with steering at low speed. In 2000, it was subject to a pirate attack in the South China Sea.

SPECIFICATIONS
Type:	British tanker
Displacement:	67,090 tonnes (66,034 tons) gross, 129,822 tonnes (127,778 tons) deadweight
Dimensions:	261m x 40m (856ft 5in x 131ft 5in)
Machinery:	Twin screws, diesel engines
Cargo:	Crude oil
Complement:	30–40
Launched:	1980

Mayon Spirit

Mayon Spirit has a double hull with a 2m (6ft 6in) space in the double bottom and more space in the wing tanks. There is a central cargo tank in a midship position and small side tanks. Carrying capacity is 120,043 cubic metres (4,239,285 cubic feet). Cargo is handled by three pumps monitored from the control room.

SPECIFICATIONS
Type:	Liberian tanker
Displacement:	100,000 tonnes (98,507 tons)
Dimensions:	244.8m x 41.2m x 14.4m (830ft 2in x 135ft 2in x 47ft 3in)
Machinery:	Single screw, diesel engine
Cargo:	crude oil
Complement:	38
Launched:	December 1981

TIMELINE

1980　　　1981　　　1990

MULTI-PRODUCT & OIL TANKERS

Helice

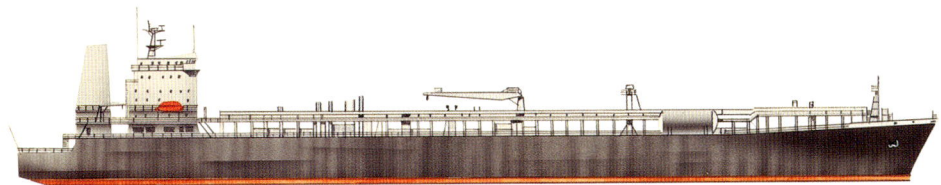

The four cargo holds have free-standing prismatic tanks built from carbo-manganese steel. Two control, or purge, tanks are situated on deck. The air can be changed up to eight times per hour in the largest hold if necessary. Now owned by Varun Line of India, it is renamed *Maharshi Vamadeva* and carries LPG.

SPECIFICATIONS	
Type:	Norwegian tank vessel
Displacement:	50,292 tonnes (49,500 tons)
Dimensions:	205m x 32.2m x 13m (672ft 7in x 105ft 8in x 42ft 8in)
Machinery:	Single screw, diesel engine
Top speed:	16 knots
Cargo:	liquefied petroleum gas
Launched:	September 1990

Landsort

Landsort was the first double-hulled oil tanker to comply with new regulations for this type. In 1997 Greek owners renamed it *Crudegulf*; in 2003 it became *Genmar Gulf*. Nine full-width tanks give capacity of 172,850 cubic metres (6,105,150 cubic ft). The space between the hulls is divided into 10 water ballast tanks.

SPECIFICATIONS	
Type:	Swedish tanker (VLCC)
Displacement:	165,646 tonnes (163,038 tons)
Dimensions:	274m x 48m x 17m (899ft 7in x 157ft 6in x 55ft 9in)
Machinery:	Single screw, diesel engine
Cargo:	crude oil and oil products of heavier specific gravity
Launched:	June 1991

Jo Alder

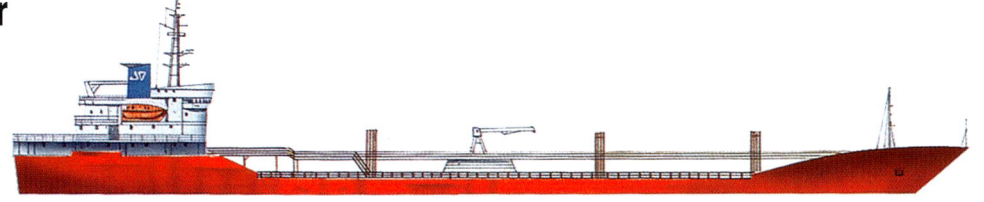

This specialized tanker for food products, non-contaminating chemicals and general petroleum products was renamed *Valdarno*, then *Monte Chiaro*. The hull is double-skinned and double-bottomed, with toughened longitudinal and transverse bulkheads. The engine room is designed for unmanned operation.

SPECIFICATIONS	
Type:	Italian tanker
Displacement:	12,801 tonnes (12,600 tons)
Dimensions:	139m x 21.2m x 8m (456ft 9in x 69ft 9in x 26ft 5in)
Machinery:	Single screw, diesel engine
Top speed:	14.5 knots
Cargo:	Liquids
Launched:	1991

1991

Specialized Vessels

SHIP TYPES 1950–1999

The spread of undersea oil drilling from shallow to deep water has extended the range of specialized surface ships needed to provide support vessels and to transport large structures. The spread of undersea fibre-optic and high-tension electricity cables has prompted a new generation of high-tech cable-laying ships.

Endurance

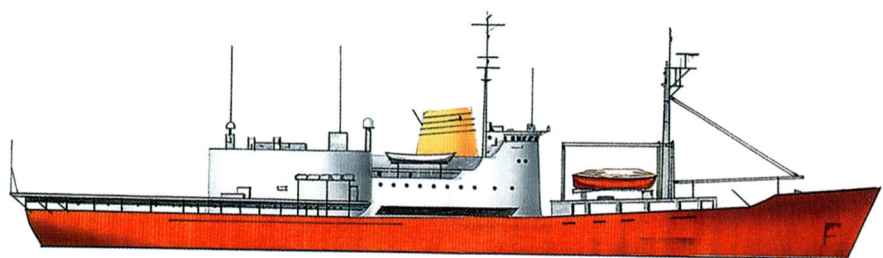

Anita Dan was built for the Lauritzen Line and renamed in 1967, when purchased by Britain for conversion to an ice patrol vessel. It entered service as support ship to the British South Atlantic Survey in 1968, and had a major refit in 1978. Weakened after hitting an iceberg in 1989, it was withdrawn in 1991.

SPECIFICATIONS	
Type:	British ice patrol ship
Displacement:	3657 tonnes (3600 tons)
Dimensions:	91.5m x 14m x 5.5m (300ft x 46ft x 18ft)
Machinery:	Single screw, diesel engine
Top speed:	14.5 knots
Main armament:	Two 20mm (0.79in) guns
Launched:	May 1956

Batcombe

A small tug-boat, *Batcombe* was equipped with foam and water tanks and high-pressure hose equipment to deal with fires on ships or in quayside installations. The hoses are mounted above the control room and the deckhouse has a rounded structure to give maximum field of access.

SPECIFICATIONS	
Type:	British fire-fighting tug
Dimensions:	18m x 5.4m (60ft x 18ft)
Machinery:	Single screw, diesel engines
Launched:	1970

TIMELINE

1956  1970   1982

SPECIALIZED VESSELS

AP.1-88

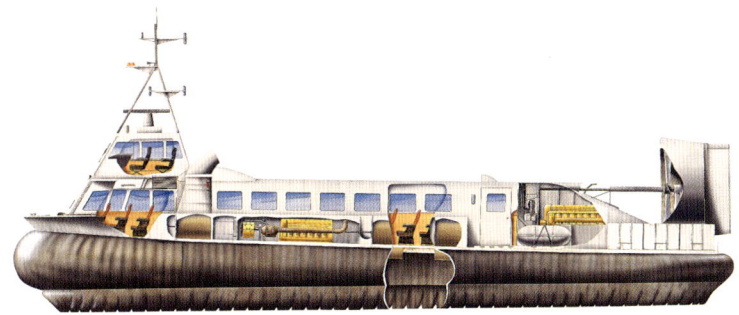

Advances in diesel engine design let hovercraft dispense with costly gas turbines, becoming commercially viable. This was the first commercial class, fitted as a passenger or cargo craft, able to carry 101 passengers or 12 tonnes of freight. A military version was produced, capable of mounting light cannon or missiles.

SPECIFICATIONS	
Type:	British air cushion vehicle
Maximum operating weight:	40.6 tonnes (40 tons)
Dimensions:	24.5m x 11m (80ft 4in x 36ft)
Machinery:	Four diesel engines driving air cushion fan
Top speed:	40 knots
Launched:	1982

KDD Ocean Link

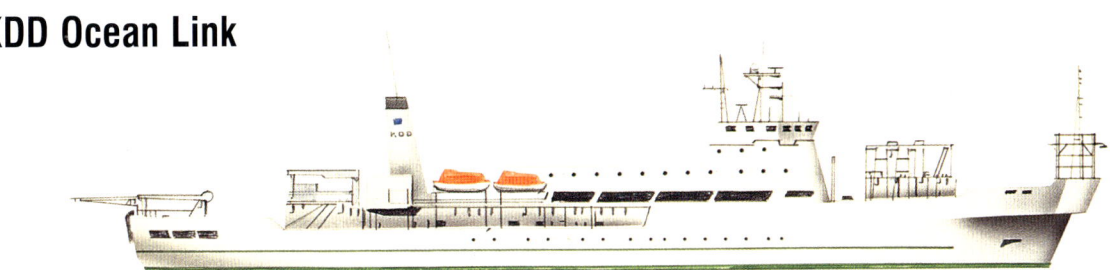

KDD Ocean Link can operate in the severe conditions of the North Pacific. Three large holds store the cables. High-speed Optical Fibre Cable is laid over the stern, while cable trenching is accomplished by a towed burial plough, fitted with TV camera and scanning sonar, and is monitored from the main control room.

SPECIFICATIONS	
Type:	Japanese cable layer
Displacement:	9662 tonnes (9510 tons)
Dimensions:	133m x 19.6m x 7.4m (437ft x 64ft 4in x 24ft 3in))
Machinery:	Twin screws, diesel engines
Launched:	August 1991

Sea Spider

Renamed *Team Oman*, it was built to lay the submarine cable between Sweden and Poland. It carries 5000 tonnes (4921 tons) of high-voltage cable on a 24m (78ft) diameter carousel, and 1600 tonnes (1574 tons) in a cable basket. Three cable engines with extending arms are mounted. A stern frame supports the trenching gear.

SPECIFICATIONS	
Type:	Dutch cable layer
Displacement:	4072 tonnes (4008 tons)
Dimensions:	86.1m x 24m x 4.5m (285ft x 78ft x 15ft)
Machinery:	Controllable pitch screw, diesel electric
Top speed:	9.5 knots
Launched:	1999

SHIP TYPES 1950–1999

James Clark Ross

Designed to carry out oceanographic research in the Antarctic region, with a strengthened bow and hull, *James Clark Ross* can pass through broken ice up to 1.5m (5ft) thick, or fragmented ice over 3m (10ft) thick. Capable of remaining at sea for up to 10 months at a time, the ship has fully equipped laboratory facilities.

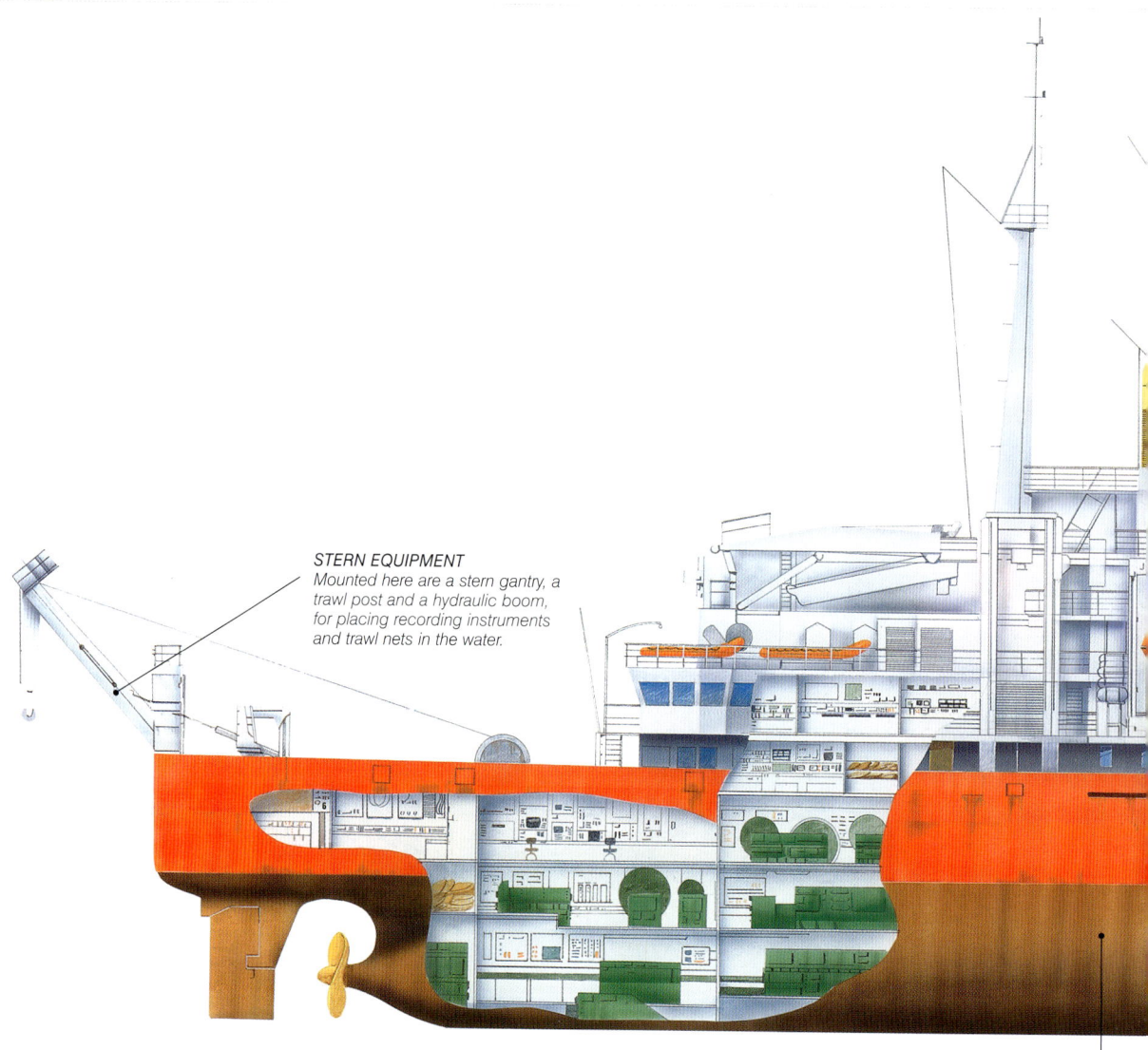

STERN EQUIPMENT
Mounted here are a stern gantry, a trawl post and a hydraulic boom, for placing recording instruments and trawl nets in the water.

HULL
A compressed air system enables the hull to roll from side to side, further breaking ice around the vessel.

James Clark Ross

This vessel is named after Admiral Sir James Clark Ross and is equipped for geophysical studies. It is designed with an extremely low noise signature to allow sensitive underwater acoustic equipment to operate effectively.

SPECIFICATIONS	
Type:	British research vessel
Displacement:	7439 tonnes (7322 tons)
Dimensions:	99m x 10.8m x 6.5m (325ft x 35ft 5in x 21ft 4in)
Machinery:	Single screw, diesel engines
Launched:	December 1990

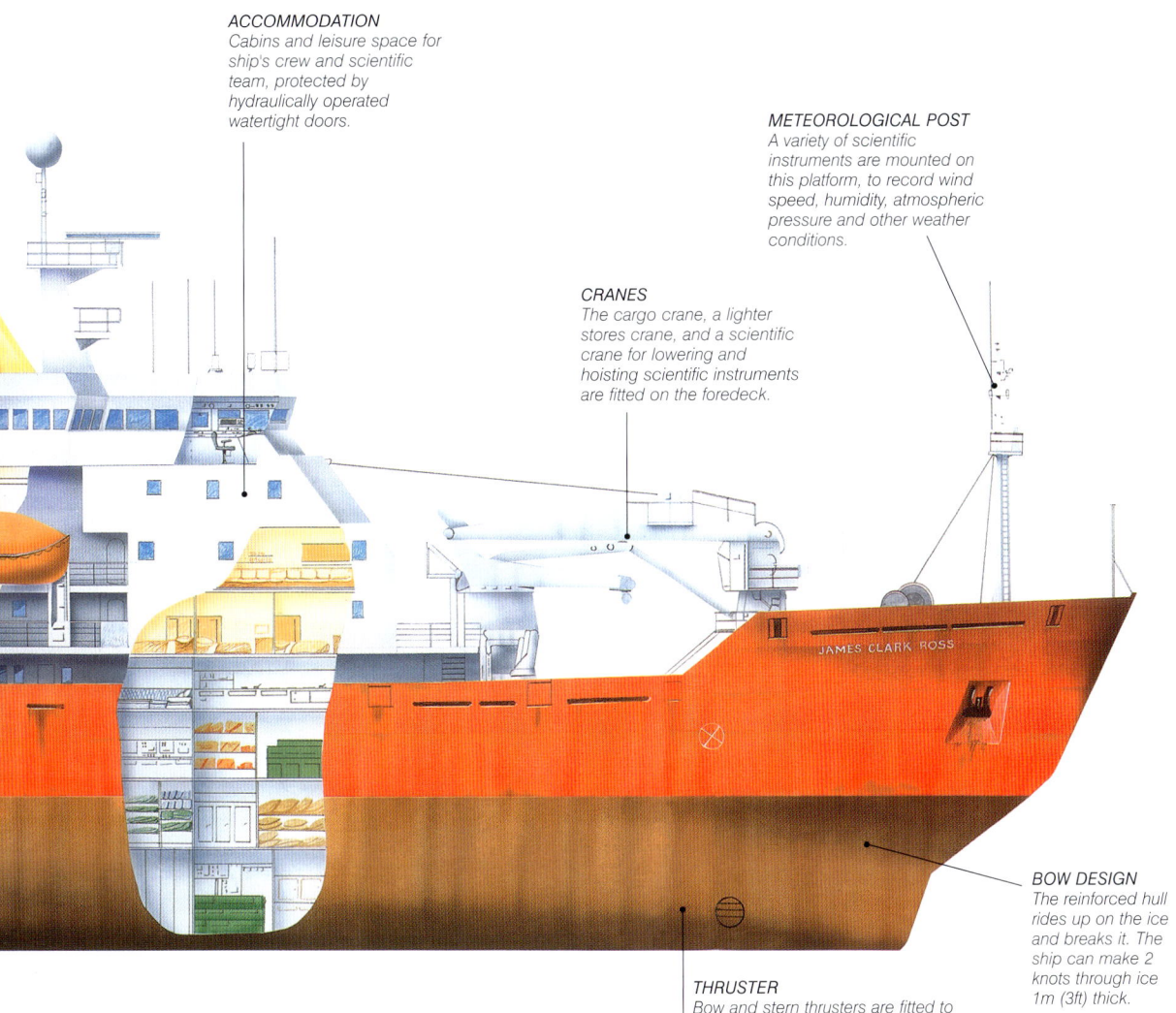

ACCOMMODATION
Cabins and leisure space for ship's crew and scientific team, protected by hydraulically operated watertight doors.

METEOROLOGICAL POST
A variety of scientific instruments are mounted on this platform, to record wind speed, humidity, atmospheric pressure and other weather conditions.

CRANES
The cargo crane, a lighter stores crane, and a scientific crane for lowering and hoisting scientific instruments are fitted on the foredeck.

BOW DESIGN
The reinforced hull rides up on the ice and breaks it. The ship can make 2 knots through ice 1m (3ft) thick.

THRUSTER
Bow and stern thrusters are fitted to help manouvrability and to hold the ship on station while working on geophysical projects.

SHIP TYPES 1950–1999

Twentieth-Century Unarmed Submersible Craft

A range of scientific, technical and military needs drove research into submarines that could go very deep or use long-term power sources. Sea-bed exploration and mapping is increasingly important. Remote-controlled craft are often used.

Trieste

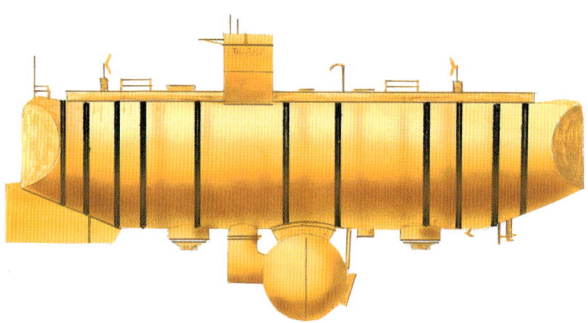

Designed by Auguste Piccard, *Trieste* was a large tank with a small crew sphere below. The tank held gasoline, lighter than water, enabling it to rise to the surface when water ballast was pumped out. In 1958, Piccard sold it to the US Navy, and in January 1960 it reached a record depth of 10,912m (35,800ft).

SPECIFICATIONS	
Type:	French bathyscaphe
Displacement:	50.8 tonnes (50 tons)
Dimensions:	18.1m x 3.5m (59ft 6in x 11ft 6in)
Machinery:	Twin screws, electric motor
Top speed:	1 knot
Launched:	1953

Aluminaut

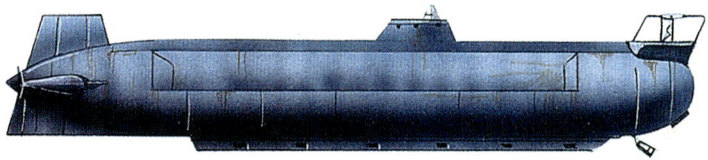

Constructed of aluminium 170mm (6.5in) thick, *Aluminaut* could attain depths of 4475m (14,682 ft). A side-scan sonar built up a map of the terrain on either side. *Aluminaut* was used in searching out the US H-bomb lost off Spain in 1966. Decommissioned in 1970, it is on exhibition at Richmond, Virginia.

SPECIFICATIONS	
Type:	US deep sea exploration vessel
Displacement:	Unknown
Weight:	81 tonnes (80 tons)
Length:	16m (51ft)
Top speed:	3 knots
Launched:	1965

TIMELINE

1953   1965

TWENTIETH-CENTURY UNARMED SUBMERSIBLE CRAFT

Deepstar 4000

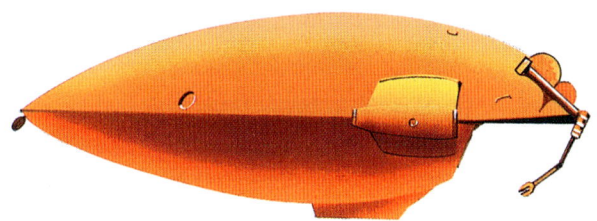

Deepstar 4000 was built between 1962 and 1964 by the Westinghouse Electric Corporation and the Jacques Cousteau group OFRS, as a scientific research and exploration submersible. The steel hull has 11 openings, and the two drive motors are attached externally. The craft carried a range of scientific equipment.

SPECIFICATIONS	
Type:	US submarine research craft
Displacement:	Unknown
Dimensions:	5.4m x 3.5m x 2m (17ft 9in x 11ft 6in x 6ft 6in)
Machinery:	Two fixed, reversible five hp AC motors
Top speed:	3 knots
Launched:	1965

Deep Quest

Deep Quest was built with fairing around a double sphere, one for the crew, the other for the propulsion unit. A deep search and recovery submarine, it could reach a depth of 2438 metres (8000ft). Vessels of this type remain vital when examining the seabed for sunken objects, pipelines and mineral deposits.

SPECIFICATIONS	
Type:	US submarine recovery craft
Displacement:	5 tonnes (5 tons)
Dimensions:	12m (39ft 4in) long
Machinery:	Twin reversible thrust electric motors
Service speed:	4.5 knots
Launched:	June 1967

India

Project 940 Lenok was designed for salvage and rescue operations, under sea or ice. Two DSRV (deep submergence rescue vessels) were carried in semi-recessed deck wells aft, and could link with the submerged parent boat. Two boats formed the class, both withdrawn in 1990 and scrapped in 1995.

SPECIFICATIONS	
Type:	Soviet rescue submarine
Displacement:	3251 tonnes (3200 tons) [surface], 4064 tonnes (4000 tons) [submerged]
Dimensions:	106m x 10m (347ft 9in x 32ft 10in)
Machinery:	Twin screws, diesel engines [surface], electric motors [submerged]
Top speed:	15 knots [surface], 11 knots [submerged]
Complement:	94
Launched:	1979

TWENTY-FIRST CENTURY SHIPS

Much attention is now given to reducing ships' environmental impact, both on the water and on the atmosphere. This applies both to construction and to daily operation.

Rising oil prices also push operators towards more efficient use of fuel. Overall ship dimensions are set to increase after widening of the Panama Canal and the deepening of the Suez Canal. The enormous cost of modern warships has led to a reduction in size of most navies, though a 'destroyer' of the 2010s has more destructive capacity than a battleship of the 1940s.

Left: The *Type 45* is the largest and most powerful destroyer ever built for Britain's Royal Navy, with a destructive power undreamt of when the first 'torpedo-boat destroyers' were built.

Twenty-First Century Warships:

The US Navy has focused its attention on two key types of surface ship. First is the large aircraft carrier, capable of providing a powerful platform for air strikes anywhere in the world's seas. Second is the amphibious assault ship, equipped to transport and land combat troops and their mechanized and armoured support vehicles.

Charles de Gaulle

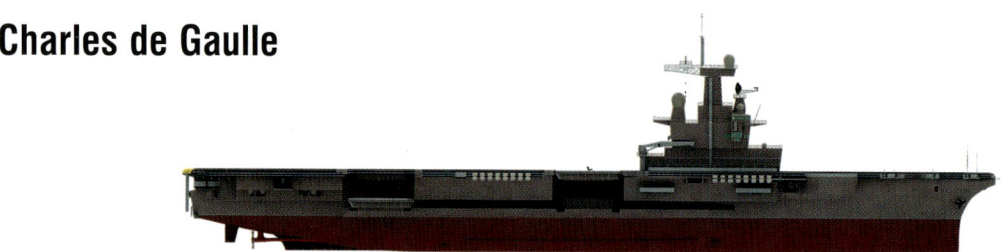

The only non-US nuclear-powered carrier, flying Super Etendard, Rafale, and E-2C Hawkeye aircraft. Propeller problems delayed commissioning until 2001 and reduced its operating speed. It saw active service in Operation Enduring Freedom in 2001-2, flying missions against al-Qaeda targets. It had a 15-month refit in 2007-8 including new propellers, but required further repairs in 2009.

SPECIFICATIONS	
Type:	French aircraft carrier
Displacement:	42,672 tonnes (42,000 tons)
Dimensions:	261.5m x 64.36m x 9.43m (858ft x 211ft 2in x 30ft 10in)
Machinery:	Twin screws, two pressurised water nuclear reactors, four diesel-electric motors
Top speed:	27 knots
Main armament:	Four SYLVER launchers, MBDA Aster SAM, Mistral short-range missiles
Aircraft:	40
Complement:	1350 plus 600 air wing
Launched:	1994

Ronald Reagan

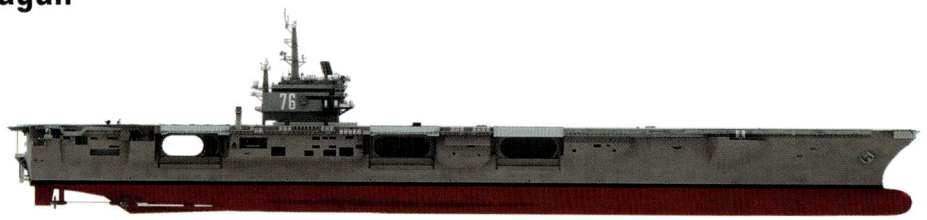

This ninth and penultimate ship in the *Nimitz* class has many new design features. Its island is placed further aft to give more open flight deck. Air traffic control and instrument landing guidance are included in a comprehensive range of systems. In 2008 *Reagan* launched over 1,140 sorties into Afghanistan. Its home port is San Diego, California.

SPECIFICATIONS	
Type:	US aircraft carrier
Displacement:	103,000 tonnes (101,000 tons)
Dimensions:	332.8m x 76.8m x 11.3m (1092ft x 252ft x 37ft)
Machinery:	Quadruple screws, two nuclear reactors, four turbines
Top speed:	30+ knots
Main armament:	Two Mk 29 ESSM launchers, two RIM-116 Rolling Airframe Missile launchers
Armour:	Classified
Aircraft:	90 aircraft
Complement:	3200 plus 2480 air wing
Launched:	March 2001

TIMELINE

1994　　　　2001　　　　2004

TWENTY-FIRST CENTURY WARSHIPS: 1

Mistral

Built partly in St Nazaire and partly in Brest, where it was completed, *Mistral* was commissioned in February 2006, and deployed off Lebanon later that year. For short-range missions, troop capacity can double to 900. Two landing barges and 70 vehicles are also carried. In 2010 it was announced that Russia was to buy a *Mistral*-type ship.

SPECIFICATIONS	
Type:	French amphibious assault ship
Displacement:	21,300 tonnes (20,959 tons) full load
Dimensions:	199m x 32m x 6.33m (652ft 9in x 105ft x 20ft 8in)
Machinery:	Twin screws, diesel-electric motors
Top speed:	18.8 knots
Main armament:	Two Simbad systems
Aircraft:	16 heavy or 35 light helicopters
Complement:	310 plus 450 troops
Launched:	Ooctober 2004

New York

Steel salvaged from the World Trade Centre was incorporated in the construction of this fifth ship in the *San Antonio* class, though it is actually named for NY state. It carries two air-cushion attack craft (LCAC) or one LCU (Landing Craft Utility). Delivered in August 2009, it has been troubled by main bearing failures in its engines.

SPECIFICATIONS	
Type:	US amphibious transport dock ship
Displacement:	25,298.4 tonnes (24,900 tons) full load
Dimensions:	208.5m x 31.9m x 7m (684ft x 105ft x 23ft)
Machinery:	Twin screws, turbo diesels
Top speed:	22 knots
Main armament:	Two Bushmaster II 30mm (0.18in) Close In guns, two RAM missile launchers
Aircraft:	Two CH-53E Super Stallion, two MV-22B Osprey tiltrotor aircraft, four CH-46 Sea Knight, four AH-1 Sea Cobra or UH-1 Iroquois helicopters.
Complement:	360 plus 700 marines
Launched:	December 2007

Zumwalt

New and still developing technologies are incorporated in this $1.1 billion-plus ship. Its hull, recalling the old ironclads, is claimed to have the radar print of a fishing boat. Automated systems in every department reduce crew numbers dramatically. Land attack as much as sea-based targets is envisaged as a potential mission. Three are currently under construction.

SPECIFICATIONS	
Type:	US multimission destroyer
Displacement:	14,797 tonnes (14,564 tons)
Dimensions:	182.9m x 24.6m x 8.4m (600ft x 80ft 8in x 27ft 7in)
Machinery:	Gas turbines, emergency diesels, powering advanced induction motors (AIM)
Top speed:	30.3 knots
Main armament:	20 Mk 57 VLS modules, Evolved Sea Sparrow and Tomahawk missiles, two 155mm (2.24in) advanced gun systems, two 57mm (6.1in) guns (CIWS)
Sensors:	AN/SPY multi-function radar, volume search radar, dual band sonar
Aircraft:	1 helicopter
Complement:	140
Launch date:	2015

Twenty-First Century Warships - 2

It takes great resources and a substantial industrial and naval infrastructure to sustain the design, building and operation of modern warships. Increasingly, navies and constructors of allied powers are joining forces to plan and fund the development of new warships: a trend particularly noticeable among the countries of the European Union.

Sachsen

The *Sachsen* class air-defence frigates are an enhanced version of the *Brandenburg* class and share features with the Spanish F100 class. Extensive countermeasures equipment include chaff and flare launchers, and detection systems include long-range air and surface surveillance and target indication radar. An STN Atlas Elektronik DSQS-24B bow sonar is fitted.

SPECIFICATIONS	
Type:	German frigate
Displacement:	5690 tonnes (5599 tons)
Dimensions:	143m x 17.4m x 5m (469ft x 57ft x 16ft 4in)
Machinery:	Twin controllable pitch screws, gas turbines and diesels (CODAG)
Top speed:	29 knots
Main armament:	Two Harpoon anti-ship missile systems, Sea Sparrow SAM system, two Mk32 double torpedo launchers, one 76mm (3in) Oto Melara gun
Aircraft:	Two NH90 helicopters
Complement:	230 plus 13 aircrew
Launched:	October 2000

Ma'anshan

This 'stealth' frigate carries formidable missile armament and a full range of radar systems, with many features developed from French originals. The sonar is however believed to be a Russian MGK-335 fixed sonar suite. Only two were built before the even more sophisticated *Type 054A* was introduced: an indication of the speed of Chinese naval development.

SPECIFICATIONS	
Type:	Chinese Type 054 frigate
Displacement:	4118 tonnes (4053 tons)
Dimensions:	134m x 16m (439ft 7in x 52ft)
Machinery:	Twin screw CODAD drive from four SEMT Pielstick diesel engines, most likely Type 16 PA6 STC
Top speed:	27-30 knots
Main armament:	Two quadruple launchers for YJ83 anti-ship cruise missiles, eight-cell Hong Qi7 short-range SAM system, four 6-barrel 30mm (1.18in) AK-630 CIWS, two Type 87 6-tube ASROC launchers, one 100mm (3.94in) gun
Aircraft:	One Kamov Ka 28 'Helix' or Harbin Z-9C helicopter
Launched:	September 2003

TIMELINE

2000      2003      2004   

TWENTY-FIRST CENTURY WARSHIPS - 2

Houbei class

SPECIFICATIONS	
Type:	Chinese missile boat
Displacement:	223.5 tonnes (220 tons) full load
Dimensions:	42.6m x 12.2m x 1.5m (139ft 7in x 40ft x 4ft 10in)
Machinery:	Twin water jet propulsors, diesels
Top speed:	36 knots
Main armament:	Eight C-801/802/803 anti-ship, or eight Hongniao long-range cruise missiles, twelve QW MANPAD surface-to-air missiles, one 30mm (1.18in) gun
Complement:	12
Launched:	April 2004

Navies are adopting missile-armed fast attack craft, more heavily armed than earlier patrol boats. This class, also known as Type 002, catamaran-hulled with stealth features, is in serial production in China. Detection equipment includes surface search and navigational radars and HEOS300 electro-optics. The two diesel engines generate 5,119 kW (6,865hp). Duties are coastal and inshore patrols.

Daring

SPECIFICATIONS	
Type:	British destroyer
Displacement:	8092 tonnes (7962.5 tons) full load
Dimensions:	152.4m x 21.2m x 7.4m (500ft x 69ft 6in x 24ft 4in)
Machinery:	Twin screws, integrated full electric propulsion, gas turbines
Top speed:	29+ knots
Main armament:	SYLVER missile launcher, MBDA Aster 15 and 30 missiles, 2 Phalanx 20mm (0.79in) CIWS
Aircraft:	One Lynx HMA 8 or Merlin HM 1 helicopter
Complement:	190
Launched:	February 2006

First of eight planned Type 45 destroyers, replacing Type 42, *Daring* was constructed in six 'blocks' in three different yards before final assembly. Its primary purpose is air defence and it has SAMPSON multi-function air tracking and S1850M three-dimensional air surveillance radars. But it is also fitted with MFS-7000 sonar and SSTDS underwater decoy systems.

Aquitaine

SPECIFICATIONS	
Type:	French FREMM-type frigate
Displacement:	6000 tonnes (5544 tons)
Dimensions:	142m x 20m x 5m (465ft 9in x 65ft 6in x 16ft 4in)
Machinery:	Twin screws, integrated full electric propulsion, gas turbines
Top speed:	27+ knots
Main armament:	MM-40 Exocet block 3, MU 90 torpedoes
Aircraft:	One NH90 helicopter
Complement:	108
Launched:	February 2012

Product of French-Italian co-operation, the FREMM multi-purpose frigate can be adapted to anti-air, anti-ship, and anti-submarine operation. *Aquitaine* and eight sister ships are due for launching from 2012; a further two will be deployed as anti-aircraft ships. Italy plans to build ten; six as general-purpose, four primarily for ASW action. Other NATO navies are likely to acquire them.

2006

2012

TWENTY-FIRST CENTURY SHIPS

Cruise Ships

The popularity of cruising continued into the 2000s and this was reflected by the construction of a new generation of 'super cruise ships', where the ship itself is the resort, fulfilling all needs and making few landfalls. The Gross Tonnage of such vessels, based on total enclosed volume, expressed in tons, reflects their huge enclosed space.

Queen Mary 2

If this is a liner, as owners Cunard claim, it is certainly the largest ever built. Its lines deliberately reflect the Cunarders of old. And it does make scheduled transatlantic runs in summer, with cruising at other times. Its height of 72m (236ft 2in) just gets it under New York's Verrazzano Narrows bridge. *QM2* accommodates 3506 passengers.

SPECIFICATIONS	
Type:	British cruise ship
Gross tonnage:	150,904 tonnes (148,528 tons)
Dimensions:	345m x 45m x 10.1m (1132ft x 147ft 6in x 33ft)
Machinery:	Four electric propulsion pods, powered by diesels and gas turbines
Top speed:	29.62 knots
Routes:	Transatlantic and worldwide
Complement:	1,253
Launched:	March 2003

Queen Victoria

Built by Fincantieri Marghera in Italy for the Cunard line, this ship made its maiden voyage in December 2007. It can take 2014 passengers on short or extended cruises to anywhere in the world, though it cannot traverse the Panama Canal. With 16 decks, of which 12 are for passengers, it has seven restaurants, a ballroom and a theatre.

SPECIFICATIONS	
Type:	British cruise ship
Gross tonnage:	91,440 tonnes (90,000 tons)
Dimensions:	294m x 36.6m x 8m (964ft 6in x 120ft x 26ft 2in)
Machinery:	Two azipod thrusters, diesel-electric
Service speed:	23.7 knots
Routes:	Worldwide
Complement:	2165
Launched:	January 2007

TIMELINE

2003   2007

CRUISE SHIPS

Poesia

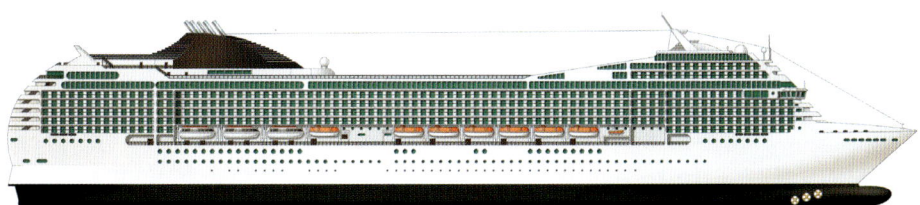

One of the Italian MSC cruise fleet, *Poesia* was built at St Nazaire, France, at a cost of $360 million. Passenger attractions include beauty salon, treatment rooms, gymnasium and jogging track, together with a range of restaurants, lounges and entertainments. Maximum accommodation is for 3605 persons, on 13 decks, with 13 elevators to ease movement.

SPECIFICATIONS	
Type:	Panama-registered cruise ship
Gross tonnage:	93,970 tonnes (92,490 tons)
Dimensions:	293.8m x 32.19m x 7.99m (963ft 10in x 105ft 6in x 26ft 2in)
Machinery:	Twin screws, diesels
Service speed:	23 knots
Routes:	Mediterranean
Complement:	987
Launched:	August 2007

Amacello

Said on its launch to inaugurate a new level of comfort in river cruising, *Amacello* holds 148 passengers on 4 decks. Its first cruise was in March 2008. Built for US-owned Amawaterways by Scheepswerf Grave in the Netherlands, it is one of a growing fleet plying not only in Europe, but on the Mekong in Vietnam.

SPECIFICATIONS	
Type:	Swiss river cruise-boat
Dimensions:	109.75m x 11.6m x 1m (360ft x 38ft x 3ft 3in)
Machinery:	twin screws, diesels
Routes:	Rivers Rhine, Danube
Complement:	41
Launched:	2007

Oasis of the Seas

The largest passenger vessel yet built, this ship can take 6296 passengers at maximum occupancy. With a height above the waterline of 72m (236ft 2in), its funnel has retractable flues to enable it to pass under certain bridges. It has no rudder, using its three thruster pods for steering. Based at Port Everglades, Florida, its maiden voyage was made in December 2009.

SPECIFICATIONS	
Type:	Bahamas-registered cruise ship
Gross tonnage:	225,282 tonnes (222,238 tons)
Dimensions:	360m x 60.5m x 9.3m (1181ft x 198ft x 31ft)
Machinery:	Three 20MW azimuth thrusters, powered by six diesel engines
Top speed:	22.6 knots
Routes:	Caribbean, Florida coast
Complement:	2165
Launched:	November 2008

2008

435

Twenty-First Century Cargo Ships

Every commercial ship burns oil, often high-sulphur content 'bunker oil'. Ships are estimated to contribute anything between 1.75 per cent and 4.5 per cent of atmospheric 'greenhouse gas' emissions, and much attention has been focused on ways in which this can be reduced. National and international regulations require ships to contain or process their own waste products.

Berge Bonde

Built by Imabari Shipbuilding, Japan, and owned by La Darien Navigacion, Berge Bond is an ore carrier, with nine holds. Fully loaded, it displaces 206,312 tonnes (203,011 tons) against a net tonnage (measurement of the space available for cargo, expressed in tonnage) of 66,443 tonnes (65,380 tons). In volume terms, its cargo capacity is 220,022m³ (7,766,776 cubic ft).

SPECIFICATIONS

Type:	Panama-registered bulk carrier
Gross tonnage:	104,727 tonnes (103,051 tons)
Dimensions:	299.94m x 50m x 18.1m (982ft x 164ft x 59ft 4in)
Machinery:	Single screw, diesels
Top speed:	15.1 knots
Cargo:	Mineral ore
Routes:	Worldwide
Launched:	2005

Emma Maersk

The world's biggest container ship when launched, *Emma Maersk*'s Wärtsila-Sulzer 14RT FLEX96-C diesel engine is also the world's biggest, weighing 2300 tons (2337 tonnes) and generating 109,000hp (82MW). Exhaust gases are used to generate electricity. The sub-waterline hull is painted with a silicone-based paint which reduces drag, deters barnacles and is not inimical to marine life.

SPECIFICATIONS

Type:	Danish container ship
Gross tonnage:	170,974 tonnes (168,239 tons)
Dimensions:	397m x 56m x 15.5m (1300ft x 180ft x 51ft)
Machinery:	Single screw, diesels
Service speed:	25.5 knots
Cargo:	Containers
Routes:	Chinese ports-Algeciras-Rotterdam-Bremerhaven
Complement:	13
Launched:	2006

TIMELINE 2005 2006 2008

TWENTY-FIRST CENTURY CARGO SHIPS

Grand Victory

While it is easy to feel all car carriers look the same, *Grand Victory* was designed with an innovatory, asymmetric stern fin and an unusual form of bulbous bow, aimed at greater manoeuvrability. Its engine was also designed to minimise emissions, noise and vibration. A ro-ro ship, with two boarding ramps, it carries cars on 12 decks.

SPECIFICATIONS	
Type:	Japanese car carrier
Gross tonnage:	60,164 tonnes (59,217 tons)
Dimensions:	199.99m x 35.8m x 9.62m (656ft x 117ft 5in x 31ft 8in)
Machinery:	Single screw, diesel
Top speed:	19.8 knots
Cargo:	6402 cars
Routes:	Japan-Asian and American ports
Launched:	June 2008

Auriga Leader

Hailed as 'ship of the year' by Lloyd's List in 2009, *Auriga Leader*'s deck is covered by 328 solar panels. The power they produce makes a very modest contribution to the ship's energy requirement, only 0.05 per cent of propelling power, but it is an experimental and unique vessel in this respect and further development is hoped for.

SPECIFICATIONS	
Type:	Japanese car carrier
Gross tonnage:	61,176 tonnes (60,213 tons)
Dimensions:	199.99m x 32.26m x 9.7m (656ft 1in x 105ft 9in x 31ft 10in)
Machinery:	Single screw, part solar-powered, diesels
Cargo:	6200 cars
Routes:	Japan-California
Launched:	2008

Cheikh el Mokrani

A member of the Mediterranean LNG Transport Corporation fleet, this ship shuttles across the Mediterranean Sea to maintain gas supplies in southern European countries. Total capacity is 75,500m³ (2,665,150 cubic ft) and the cargo tanks are finished and installed in line with the latest requirements of IMO and MARPOL. A bow thruster helps work the ship in harbours.

SPECIFICATIONS	
Type:	Bahamas-registered liquefied gas tanker
Gross tonnage:	52,855 tonnes (52,009 tons)
Dimensions:	219.95m x 22.55m x 9.75m (721ft 5in x 74ft x 32ft)
Machinery:	Single screw, steam turbines, bow thruster
Top speed:	17.5 knots
Cargo:	Liquefied natural gas
Routes:	Algerian ports to Spanish, French and Italian ports
Launched:	2008

TWENTY-FIRST CENTURY SHIPS

Specialized Vessels

Specialized ships have become even more specialised, sophisticated and capable in recent years. One of the key new technologies has been that of 'dynamic positioning', enabling a vessel to maintain a very precise station or line. In this field, even more than in general shipping, environmental impact is a major factor and is closely monitored.

Blue Marlin

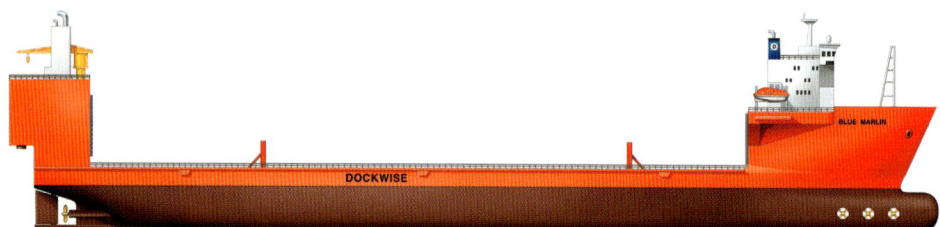

Specifications are of the reconstructed *Blue Marlin* (2004). Originally Norwegian-owned, the vessel was acquired by Dockwise Shipping of the Netherlands in 2001. It carries structures of up to 60,000 tonnes and can be submerged by 10m (33ft) for them to be floated on board. Major tasks have included carrying the 60,000 tonne oil platform 'Thunder Horse.'

SPECIFICATIONS

Type:	Dutch heavy lift ship
Displacement:	76,060 tonnes (74,843 tons) maximum load
Dimensions:	224.5m x 42m x 13.3m (712ft x 138ft x 44ft)
Machinery:	Single screw, diesels, two retractable peropulsors
Top speed:	14.5 knots
Complement:	60
Launched:	April 2000 (rebuilt 2004)

HAM 318

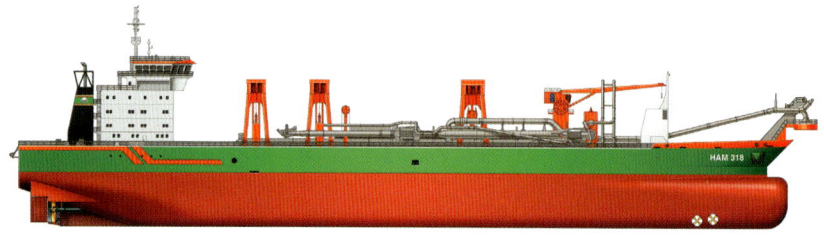

With two 12m (39ft 4in) diameter suction pipes, this hopper dredger can operate to a depth of 17m (55ft), discharging sludge through bottom doors or land-pipe. It can be used in clearing oil spillages and has storage for 2,800m^3 (98,840 cubic ft) of heavy oil. It is planned to increase its dredging depth to 110m (360ft).

SPECIFICATIONS

Type:	Dutch dredger
Displacement:	57,360 tonnes (56,442 tons)
Dimensions:	176.15m x 32m x 13m (577ft 9in x 105ft x 42ft 6in)
Machinery:	Twin controllable-pitch screws, diesels, two bow thrusters
Top speed:	17.3 knots
Complement:	45
Launched:	October 2001

TIMELINE 2000 2001

SPECIALIZED VESSELS

Tyco Reliance

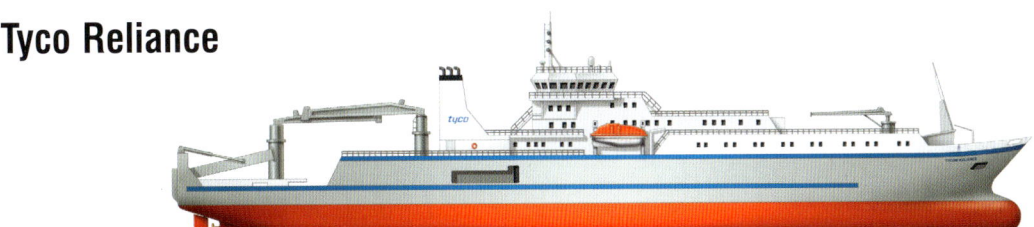

Built by Keppel Singmarine of Singapore, this deep sea cable layer is operated by Tyco Telecommunications. It is capable of carrying 5465 tonnes (5377.5 tons) of cable, and is equipped with Kongsberg Simrad SDP 21 dynamic positioning system. It carries a Perry Tritech ST200 remotely operated vehicle (ROV) for seabed work, and a trenching sea-plough.

SPECIFICATIONS	
Type:	Marshall Islands registered cable layer
Displacement:	12,184 tonnes (11,989 tons) full load
Dimensions:	140m x 21m x 8.4m (459ft 2in x 68ft 11in x 27ft 6in)
Machinery:	Two azimuth propulsors, bow and stern thrusters, diesel electric
Top speed:	13 knots
Complement:	80
Launched:	2001

Stena Drill MAX

Built in South Korea, capable of working in waters over 3,000m (10,000ft) deep and of drilling to a depth of 10,670m (35,000ft), in sub-Arctic conditions, this vessel uses dynamic positioning systems and multiple thrusters to remain on station. The deck can bear loads up to 15,000 tonnes (14,760 tons). A helicopter deck is fitted.

SPECIFICATIONS	
Type:	Swedish deep sea drilling ship
Displacement:	96,000 tonnes (94,464 tons)
Dimensions:	228m x 42m x 19m (748ft x 137ft 10in x 62ft 4in)
Machinery:	Six sets of azimuth thrusters, diesel electric
Top speed:	12 knots
Complement:	180
Launched:	2007

Crestway

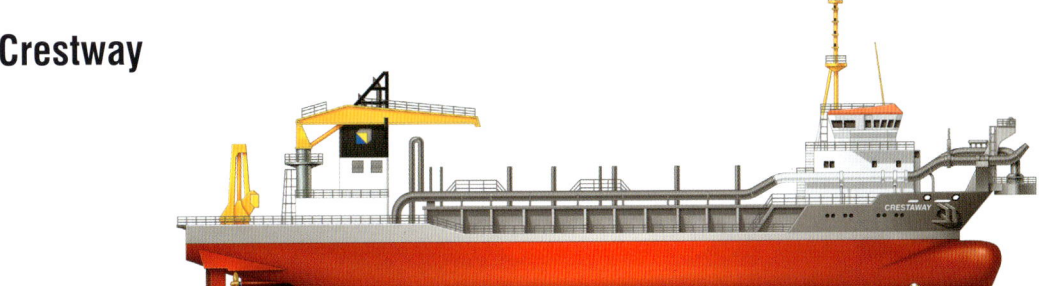

Operated by the Belgian dredging company Royal Boskalis, *Crestway* is a suction dredger able to work in depths of up to 33m (110ft) and with a hopper capacity of 5600m³. Ships like this are a major investment and can operate virtually anywhere, on channel deepening, foreshore restructuring, and similar large-scale tasks.

SPECIFICATIONS	
Type:	Cyprus-registered dredger
Gross tonnage:	5005 tonnes (4925 tons)
Dimensions:	97.5m x 21.6m x 7.6m (319ft 10in x 70ft 10in x 23ft 7in)
Machinery:	Two azimuth propulsors, bow and stern thrusters, diesel electric
Top speed:	13 knots
Complement:	14
Launched:	May 2008

2007

2008

Glossary

AA Anti-aircraft, as in 'anti-aircraft artillery' (AAA); air-to-air, as in 'air-to-air missile' (AAM).

Armour Plates of iron, later steel and alloys, later still more exotic metals such as titanium, added to the hull and essential components of a ship to protect its integrity, its vital parts and its crew from battle damage.

ASM Anti-submarine missile; anti-submarine mortar (also air-to-surface missile, air-to-ship/anti-ship missile).

ASW Anti-submarine warfare.

Axial fire Gunfire ahead or astern, along the major axis of the vessel.

Ballast The weight added to a ship or boat to bring her to the desired level of floatation and to increase stability.

Barge Most commonly, a flat-bottomed vessel of shallow draught used to carry cargo on inland waterways, both from port to port and to and from ocean-going ships.

Battlecruiser The made-up designation for a hybrid warship armed like a battleship but sacrificing passive protection in the form of armour plate for speed.

Battleship Originally the biggest and most powerful ships of the fleet, mounting guns of usually 10in (254mm) or larger calibre (the biggest were those of the Japanese Yamato class, which were 18.1in (460mm)), and heavily armoured.

Beam The width of a ship's hull.

Beam engine The original form of single-cylinder steam engine, the piston of which acted on a beam by way of a connecting-rod. The beam itself formed a simple Class I lever, its reciprocating action being translated into rotation by a link to a crank or eccentrically to a flywheel.

Bofors A Swedish armaments manufacturer, best known for its 40mm anti-aircraft gun.

Boiler A device for heating water to boiling point, to turn it into steam so that it could be employed to power machinery.

Bonaventure An extra mizzen sail; it fell out of use towards the end of the 17th century.

Boom A spar used to extend the foot of a sail; also a floating barrier, usually across the entrance to a harbour.

Bore The diameter of a cylinder or gun barrel.

Bowsprit A spar protruding over the bows of a sailing vessel, to serve as an outboard anchorage for the tack of a flying jib.

Break A change in the level of a deck, eg 'the break of the forecastle'.

Breech block The removable part of a gun's breech, through which projectile and charge could be loaded.

Breech-loading (BL) Guns loading from the breech, via a removable segment.

Broadside The side of the ship; the simultaneous firing of the guns located there.

Bulges/Blisters Chambers added to the outside of a warship's hull to provide protection against torpedoes; outer sections were generally water-filled, to absorb splinters, inner, air-filled, to diffuse blast.

Bulk Carrier A single-deck ship expressly designed to accommodate loose cargo such as grain or ore.

Bulkhead/Water-tight bulkhead A vertical partition employed to divide up a ship's internal space, both longitudinally and transversely. These partitions may be water-tight, in which case the openings in them to allow passage must be capable of being sealed, preferably by remote control.

Bunker/Bunkerage The part of a ship allocated to the storage of fuel; the fuel itself, and the quantity carried.

Calibre the diameter of the bore of a gun barrel; the number of times that diameter fits into the length of the barrel, expressed as 'L/(calibre)'; eg, a gun of 10in bore with a barrel 300in long would be described as '10in L/30', or just '10in/30'.

CAM ship Catapult-Armed Merchant ship A merchant ship equipped to fly off a fighter aircraft; a temporary expedient adopted during 1940.

Capital Ship A term coined around 1910 to describe the most important naval assets, and group together battleships and battlecruisers (chiefly to give extra credibility to the latter); it was later extended to include monitors.

Carrier battle group A force designation coined during World War II; it was made up of one or more fleet aircraft carriers together with associated defensive elements – destroyers and cruisers – but often included battleships, which had by then largely been relegated to the shore bombardment role.

Carronade A short-barrelled, lightweight muzzle-loading gun, produced by the Carron Ironworks in Scotland from the 1770s.

Casemate A fixed armoured box within which a gun was mounted. It allowed the weapon to be elevated and trained, and usually protruded from the hull or superstructure to increase its arc of fire.

Catamaran A boat (and later ship) with two hulls joined by a continuous deck or decks.

cb cabin class

Citadel/Central citadel A heavily-armoured redoubt within which the ship's main battery was housed.

Clipper An ultimately meaningless term used to describe any fast sailing ship, particularly one engaged in the grain, opium or tea trades, widely used in the mid-19th century.

Combined Carrier A cargo ship of the latter part of the 20th century, adapted to carry both bulk and containerised cargoes.

Composite construction A construction method employing iron or steel frames and wooden hull planking.

Compound engine A multi-cylinder steam engine in which the steam is employed at least twice, at decreasing pressures; theoretically, all multi-cylinder engines are compound engines, but those which employ the steam three times are known as triple-expansion, and those which employ it four times as quadruple-expansion engines.

Conbulker see Combined Carrier.

Corvette Originally a (French) sailing ship of war, too small to warrant a rate (and thus the equivalent of the British sloop); more recently, a warship smaller than a frigate or destroyer-escort.

Cruiser A warship, larger than a frigate or destroyer, much more heavily armed and often armoured to some degree, intended for independent action or to act as a scout for the battlefleet. Modern cruisers operate as defensive elements within carrier battle groups.

Cutter Originally a small, decked boat, lightly-armed, with a single mast and bowsprit, carrying a fore-and-aft (gaff) mainsail and a square topsail, with either two jibs or a jib and staysail, frequently used as an auxiliary to the fleet or on preventive duties.

CVA Attack aircraft carrier.

DDG Guided-missile destroyer.

DDH Helicopter destroyer.

Deadrise The angle to the vertical of the planking in the floor of a vessel's hull, and thus a measure of the 'sharpness' of her lines.

Deadweight see Tonnage.

Deck The continuous horizontal platforms, the equivalent of floors in a building, which separate a ship.

Derrick A form of lifting gear comprising a single spar attached at its heel low down to a mast or kingpost and pivoted there, equipped with stays, a topping lift and guy pendants, so that its attitude and position may be positively controlled, and with a block attached at its head, through which a runner may be rove and led, if necessary, to a winch.

Destroyer Originally torpedo-boat destroyer; a small warship of little more than 200 tons displacement, itself equipped to launch torpedoes, but also armed with light guns.

Destroyer-escort A small warship, bigger than a corvette of the period, designed and constructed to guard convoys of merchant ships, especially on the Atlantic routes, during World War II.

Diesel A form of internal-combustion engine which ignites its fuel/air mixture by compression alone, invented by Rudolf Diesel in 1892.

Diesel-electric A form of propulsion in which the compression-ignition internal-combustion engine drives a generator, which in turn drives an electric motor which turns the propeller shaft.

Displacement A measure of the actual total weight of a vessel and all she contains obtained by calculating the volume of water she displaces.

Draught (also Draft) The measure of the depth of water required to float a ship, or how much she 'draws'.

Dreadnought The generic name given to a battleship modelled after HMS Dreadnought, the first with all-big-gun armament; it fell into disuse once all capital ships were of this form.

Driver An additional sail hoisted on the mizzen; see Spanker.

ECM Electronic Countermeasures; measures taken to decoy or confuse an enemy force's sensors.

EEZ Economic Exclusion Zone; a coastal strip, 200nm wide measured from the mean low water mark, within which a nation is held to have the exclusive right to exploit natural resources; it supplements, but does not replace, the territorial limit (originally three miles, the effective range of coastal artillery, later extended to 12 miles).

Fast attack craft Gun, torpedo and/or guided-missile-armed warships, characterised by their small size and high speed. Such craft only ever had limited success.

Fire control A (centralised) system of directing the firing of a ship's guns, based on observation of the fall of shot relative to the target, taking into account movements of both the target and the firing platform.

Flag of Convenience see Registry.

Flare The outward (usually concave) curve of the hull of a ship towards the bow.

Floflo Float on/float off loading operations; see Lolo; Roro.

Flotilla In the Royal Navy up to World War II, an organised unit of (usually eight) smaller warships – destroyers and submarines in particular, but also minesweepers and fast attack craft; cruisers and capital ships were grouped into squadrons, and squadrons and flotillas made up fleets – derived from the diminutive of the Spanish flota, fleet.

Flush decked Commonly, a ship with no forecastle or poop.

Forced draught A means of increasing the efficiency of a ship's boilers by forcing air at higher than normal pressure through the furnace element.

Fore-and-aft Sails which, when at rest, lie along the longitudinal axis of a vessel; a vessel rigged with such sails.

Forecastle Originally the superstructure erected at the bows of a ship to serve as a fighting platform, later the (raised) forward portion and the space beneath it, customarily used as crews' living quarters. Pronounced fo'c'sle.

Frames The ribs of a vessel, upon which the hull planking is secured, set at right-angles to the keel.

Freeboard The distance between the surface of the water and the upper deck of a ship or the gunwale of a boat.

GLOSSARY

Frigate Originally, fifth- or sixth rate ships carrying their guns on a single deck, employed as scouts, and the counterpart of the later cruiser.

Gas turbine A rotary internal-combustion engine in which a fuel/air mixture is burned and the rapidly-expanding gas thus produced used to drive turbine blades arranged upon a shaft; a gas turbine bears the same relationship to a steam turbine that a reciprocating internal-combustion engine does to a reciprocating steam engine.

Gundeck The name given to the main deck in sailing warships of the Royal Navy.

Head The bows of a ship (and as in '(down) by the head'), and by extension in the plural, because they were traditionally located there, the latrines; also the top of a four-sided sail.

Headsail Those sails – jibs and staysails in the main, but also spinnakers – which are set before the (fore)mast.

Heel, to The act of temporarily tipping a vessel to one side, usually caused by the pressure of wind on sails.

Heeling tanks Ballast tanks set on a ship's sides to allow her to be deliberately heeled over.

Horsepower A measure of the power produced by an engine; one horsepower = 550 foot/pounds per second ('the power required to raise 550 pounds through one foot in one second') as defined by James Watt.

Ironclad The contemporary name for wooden warships clad with iron, and by extension, to the first iron warships; it continued in use up until the arrival of the dreadnought.

Jib A triangular sail (usually loose-footed) set on a forestay.
Jib-boom A continuation of the bowsprit.

Keel The main longitudinal timber of a ship or boat, effectively her spine and certainly her strongest member. In yachts, a downwards extension in the form of a wing (or wings) which balances the pressure of the wind upon the sails; also, the flat-bottom lighters used in ports in the northeast of England.

Ketch A two-masted sailing vessel; in modern terms, a yacht with a reduced mizzen stepped before the rudder post (see yawl).

Knot Internationally, the measure of a ship's speed – one nautical mile per hour.

Leeboard A primative form of drop-keel, hung over the side of a vessel from a forward pivot. Two were carried, one to port and one to starboard, though only the one on the lee side was employed.

Lifting screw A screw propeller designed to be lifted clear of the water, fitted to sailing ships with auxiliary machinery, the object of the exercise being to reduce drag when sailing.

Lighter A 'dumb' (ie, unpowered) barge, used as a transit vehicle to load and unload ships in port and also in places where proper port facilities are deficient.

Liner A ship carrying passengers to a fixed schedule, usually on trans-oceanic routes; the term became current from the mid-1800s. A cargo liner also operates on fixed schedules, with space for a limited number of passengers.

Magazine Secure storage for explosives.
Masts Spars, mounted vertically or close to it, normally stayed (guyed) at either side and fore and aft, employed to allow sails to be carried.
MGB/MTB Motor gun boat/motor torpedo boat; *see Fast attack craft*.
Minesweeper A small ship, roughly the size of a trawler (many were, in fact, converted fishing boats originally) adapted and equipped to locate and neutralise submarine mines. Later supplemented by specialist minehunters.
Mizzen The third mast, counting from the bows; since most ships had three masts, it was also the aftermost, and invariably carried a fore-and-aft steadying sail.

NATO North Atlantic Treaty Organisation.
Nautical mile Internationally, the measure of distance at sea which has become standardised at 6080ft (1852m).

OBO Ore/Bulk/Oil carrier.
Oerlikon A Swiss arms manufacturer whose 20mm cannon, widely acknowledged to be the best of its type, was adopted by both sides during World War II. Improved versions were still in production at the end of the 20th century.

Periscope An optical device allowing an observer to change his plane of vision. At sea they were commonly used to allow submerged submarines a view of the surface, and also in gun turrets.

Poop The short raised deck at the stern of a vessel, originally known as the aftercastle.
Propeller Properly speaking, the screw propeller; as essential to steam- and motor ships as their powerplant, the rotation of the screw propeller and the angle of its blades or vanes combine to generate thrust against the mass of water, which pushes the vessel through it.
Propulser Commonly, any propulsive device – a water jet, for example – which is not a propeller; the most effective is probably the Voith-Schneider.

Quarterdeck That part of the upper deck abaft the mainmast (or where the mainmast would logically be in a steam- or motor ship), traditionally the reserve of commissioned officers.
Quick-firing A designation applied to small- and medium-calibre guns to indicate that they used unitary ammunition (ie, with projectile and propellant cartridge combined).

Radar An acronym for Radio Direction and Range – a means of using electromagnetic radiation to locate an object.
Reserve Warships not in active commission are said to be in reserve; this may be a temporary measure, in which case maintenance work will be kept fully up to date, or a long-term measure, in which case the ship will be 'mothballed'.
Rudder A vertical board or fin hung on the centreline of the vessel at the stern post, originally (and still, in small boats) from simple hinges known as pintels, and connected either directly to the tiller or by ropes or chains to the steering wheel, which, when it is angled relative to the vessel's course, causes a change of direction.

SAM Surface-to-air missile.
Schooner-rigged A boat or ship with two or more masts of equal height (or with the foremast lower than the main and others), fore and aft rigged on all of them, with or without topsails.
Schnorkel/Snorkel A tube with a ball-valve at its upper extremity, which allows a submarine to take in air, and thus continue to operate its internal-combustion engines, while remaining below the surface.
Seabee A system of carrying loaded cargo barges aboard ocean-going ships to simplify on- and off-loading operations at terminal ports. Barges (more properly, lighters) were lifted on and off by means of an elevator at the stern of the ship; see LASH.
Sheer The upward curve of a ship's upper deck towards bow and stern.
Smooth-bore A gun with a smooth (ie, unrifled) barrel, used as naval ordnance until the second half of the 19th century.
Sonar An acronym for Sound Navigation and Ranging, a technique of using sound waves to detect objects underwater, and by extension, to the hardware employed; see also ASDIC.
Spanker Originally an additional sail hoisted on the mizzen mast to take advantage of a following wind, later taking the place of the mizzen course; see Driver.
Spar deck Strictly speaking, a temporary deck, but later used to describe the upper deck of a flush-decked ship.
Sponson A platform built outside the hull, at main- or upper deck level, usually to allow guns on the broadside to be sited so as to allow them to fire axially.
Squadron In the Royal Navy, originally an organised unit of (usually eight) major warships – cruisers and capital ships, but in the US Navy (and the practice became widespread), an organised unit of ships of any type, from minesweepers upwards, the term having taken over from flotilla.
Square-rigged A sailing vessel whose sails are set on yards, which when at rest are at right-angles to the longitudinal axis of the hull.
SSM Surface-to-surface missile.
SSN Nuclear-powered submarine.
Standing Rigging That portion of a ship's rigging – stays and shrouds, for example – which is employed to steady her masts; see also Running rigging.
Steam Turbine A rotary engine in which steam is used to drive turbine blades arranged upon a shaft.
Stem The foremost member of a ship's frame, fixed at its lower extremity to the keel.
Stern post The aftermost member of a ship's frame, fixed at its lower extremity to the keel.
Submarine A vessel capable of indefinite (or at least very prolonged) underwater operation.

Tack The lower forward corner of a fore-and-aft sail; a reach sailed (in a sailing vessel) with the wind kept on one side.
Tiller A wooden or metal bar attached rigidly to the rudder and used to control its movement.
Tonnage The load carrying capacity of a merchant ship or the displacement of a warship.
Topmast The second section of a mast, stepped above the lower mast, carrying the (upper and lower) topmast yard(s).
Topsail In a square-rigged vessel, the square sails set immediately above the course, from the topmast yard(s) (bigger ships carried paired topsails, upper and lower, for ease of working); in a fore-and-aft rigged vessel, the topsails may be either square or themselves fore-and-aft.
Torpedo A self-propelled explosive device, with or without some form of guidance, running on or below the surface of the sea.
Trawler A fishing boat (in fact, the largest are substantial ships) which drags behind it on two warps a roughly cone-shaped net. Modern trawlers have substantial refrigeration plant and freezers, and stay at sea for weeks at a time.
Triple-expansion A type of reciprocating compound engine, with a minimum of three cylinders of graduated sizes housing pistons connected to a common crankshaft; the steam, introduced at very high pressure into the smallest, is condensed, and passes to the second, slightly larger, cylinder, where it is condensed once more, and then passed to the largest cylinder).
Turbo-electric A form of propulsion in which the steam turbine drives a generator, which in turn drives an electric motor which turns the propeller shaft.
Turret Originally an armoured shell or covering for a gun, which rotated with the platform upon which the gun is mounted; later the armoured cover became an integral part of the rotating mounting, and itself supported the gun or guns.
Turret ship A design of cargo carrier developed in the 1890s, its upper deck being about half the full beam of the ship; slightly below this was the so-called 'harbour deck', which joined the main vertical plating in a wide-radius curve. It was basically a subterfuge, which came about as a result of the Suez Canal Company's policy of charging dues based on the ship's beam at the upper deck.

Yawl A two-masted sailing yacht with a reduced mizzen stepped abaft the rudder post (see ketch).

INDEX

Ships Index

A1, British submarine 163
Aboukir, British armoured cruiser 136
Acadia, Canadian hydrographic survey ship 213
Activity, British escort carrier 217
Admiral Graf Spee, German pocket battleship 234
Admiral Nakhimov, Russian cruiser 119
Admiral Petre Barbuneanu, Romanian frigate 371
Admiral Senyavin, Soviet cruiser 342
Adriatic, US liner 75
Affondatore, Italian turret battleship 57
Agano, Japanese cruiser 249
Agincourt, British battleship 56
Aigle, French destroyer 266
Akagi, Japanese aircraft carrier 99
Akitsuki, Japanese destroyer 277
Alabama, Confederate armed sloop 50–1
Alberto da Giussano, Italian fast destroyer 272
Alecto, British gunboat 52
Alligator class, Soviet landing ship 379
Al Madina, Saudi Arabian frigate 372
Almirante Cochrane, Chilean battleship 60
Almirante Latorre, British/Chilean battleship 121
Almirante Riveros, Chilean destroyer 355
Aluminaut, US deep sea exploration vessel 426
Alvand, Iranian frigate 367
Amacello, Swiss river cruise-boat 435
America, British liner/Italian royal yacht 39
America, US aircraft carrier 319
Amerigo Vespucci, Italian full rigged ship 188–9
Anastasia, Italian liner/US hospital ship 410–11
Aoba, Japanese cruiser 135
AP.1-88, British air cushion vehicle 423
Appalachian, US command ship 289
Aquila, Italian aircraft carrier 99
Aquitaine, French FREMM-type frigate 433
Arabia, UK passenger liner 74
Aradam, Italian submarine 298
Aragon, Spanish cruiser 61
Aragua, Venezuelan destroyer 356

Araguaya, Brazilian destroyer 281
Archibald Russell, British barque 186
Archimede, Italian submarine 302
Arctic, US passenger liner 73
Ardent, British destroyer 153, 262
Arethusa, British cruiser 284
Argonaut, US submarine (1897) 81
Argonaut, US submarine/minelayer (1927) 179
Ariadne, British cruiser/minelayer 291
Ariel, British sailing ship 41
Ariete, Italian destroyer 275
Ark Royal, British aircraft carrier 222
Arleigh Burke, US guided missile destroyer 352
Armide, French battleship 57
Artemis, US attack cargo ship 229
Artevelde, Belgian minelayer/royal yacht 291
Artigliere, Italian destroyer 273
Artiglio II, Italian salvage vessel 213
Asagumo, Japanese destroyer 357
Asashio, Japanese destroyer 274
Ashland, US landing ship 288
Askold, Russian cruiser 144
Assari Tewfik, Turkish battleship 57
Aster, Belgian minehunter 377
Astoria, US cruiser 246
Athabaskan, Canadian frigate 368
Atland, Swedish turret-hull cargo ship 190
Atlanta, Confederate ironclad 44
Atlanta, US cruiser 247
Atropo, Italian submarine 168
Attentive, British cruiser 138
Attilio Regolo, Italian cruiser 286
Attu, US escort carrier 221
Audace, Italian destroyer 357
Audacity, British escort carrier 216
Augusta Victoria, German liner 77
Augusto Riboty, Italian flotilla leader 155
Auriga Leader, Japanese car carrier 437
Aurora, Russian cruiser 118
Australia, Australian battlecruiser 109
Avon, British frigate 244

Avvoltoio, Italian torpedo boat 82

B1, British submarine 163
Babur, Pakistani cruiser 344
Badr, Egyptian fast patrol boat 335
Bahia, Brazilian cruiser 121
Baikal, Russian train ferry 210
Baleares, Spanish cruiser 257
Baleno, Italian destroyer 272
Balilla, Italian submarine 171
Ballarat, British cargo/passenger vessel 199
Balmoral Castle, British liner 200
Balny, French torpedo boat 83
Baltic, British merchant vessel 205
Baltic, Confederate ironclad 45
Baltimore, US heavy cruiser 231
Bambú, Italian minesweeper 376
Baptista de Andrade, Portuguese frigate 369
Barbara, German merchant vessel 193
Barbarigo, Italian submarine (1917) 172
Barbarigo, Italian submarine (1938) 302
Barham, British battleship 115
Basento, Italian naval water tanker 401
Batcombe, British fire-fighting ship 422
Bayan, Russian cruiser 126
Bayano, British escort vessel 183
Bayern, German battleship 115
Béarn, French aircraft carrier 97
Beaver, Canadian paddle steamer 37
Belfast, British cruiser 250
Bellona, British cruiser 251
Bengasi, Italian naval transport 160
Ben-My-Chree, British aircraft carrier 94
Benton, Union ironclad 45
Berge Bonde, Panama-registered carrier 436
Berlin, German cruiser 125
Berlin, light frigate 27
Beskytteren, Danish patrol ship 334
Birmingham, British cruiser 139
Bismarck, German battleship 214–15, 236–7
Black Prince, 123
Blenheim, British depot ship 161
Blitz, Austrian torpedo gunboat 87
Blücher, German liner 204
Blue Marlin, Dutch heavy lift ship 438

Bodryi, Soviet destroyer 260
Bombarda, Italian escort vessel/corvette 243
Bombardiere, Italian destroyer 275
Bombe, French torpedo gunboat 86
Bomb vessel (c.1780) 31
Borea, Italian destroyer 146
Bosna, Austrian river monitor 159
Boston, US cruiser 64
Bourrasque, French destroyer 153
Boykiy, Soviet destroyer 347
Brandenburg, German destroyer 353
Bremen, German liner 39
Breslau, German cruiser 141
Bretagne, French battleship 105
Brin, Italian submarine 300
Britannia, British paddle steamer 72
Britannic, British hospital ship 207
British Skill, British tanker 420
Broadsword, British frigate 369
Bronte, Italian naval fuel carrier 160
Bronzo, Italian submarine 303
Brooklyn, US cruiser 247
Bullfinch, British destroyer 89
Bunker Hill, US guided missile cruiser 339
Byedovi, Russian destroyer 147

C1, Japanese submarine 305
Cabotia, British cargo ship 191
Caio Duilio, Italian cruiser 345
Caio Mario, Italian cruiser 287
Cairo, US gunboat 45
Calatafimi, Italian destroyer 153
Caledonia, British liner 183
California, US paddle steamer 73
Calliope, British cruiser (1884) 65
Calliope, British cruiser (1914) 128
Canberra, British liner 414–15
Canis, Norwegian coasting cargo steamer 191
Canopus, British battleship 91
Caorle, Italian landing ship 378
Cap Trafalgar, German liner 183
Carabiniere, Italian frigate 366
Carelia, Finnish timber carrier 192
Carlo Bergamini, Italian frigate 364
Carmania, British liner 182
Caroline, British cruiser 139
Carpathia, British cargo liner 195

INDEX

Carthage, British liner 315
CB12, Italian midget submarine 305
C Class, British submarine 166
Centauro, Italian frigate 362
Chakri Naruebet, Thai light carrier 327
Chamäleon, Austrian minelayer 157
Chao Yung, Chinese cruiser 64
Chapayev, Soviet cruiser 285
Chaperon, US stern wheel steamer 75
Charles, French oared frigate 31
Charles de Gaulle, French aircraft carrier 430
Charleston, US cruiser 66
Charlie II, Soviet missile submarine 392
Charlotte Dundas, stern-wheeled steamboat 34
Chazhma, Soviet missile range ship 379
Chebeck, oar-assisted sailing warship 27
Cheikh el Mokrani, liquefied gas tanker 437
Chen Yuan, Chinese battleship 61
Chester, US cruiser 145
Chikugo, Japanese frigate 367
Chitose, Japanese seaplane carrier 226
Chiyoda, Japanese cruiser 67
Choctaw, Union ironclad 44
Christopher of the Tower, sailing warship 18
Cigno, Italian frigate 363
City of Rome, British liner 76
Clan Macalister, British cargo vessel 314
Clemenceau, French aircraft carrier 322
Clemenceau, French battleship 239
Clermont, sidewheel steamboat 35
Cleveland, British destroyer 263
Cockerill, Belgian cargo steamer 190
Collins, Australian submarine 385
Columbus, German liner 208
Comet, British destroyer 267
Comet, passenger steamship 35
Commandant de Rose, French steam schooner 187
Condé, French cruiser 124
Condor Express, British car ferry 419
Conqueror, British battleship 102
Constitution, sailing frigate 31
Conte di Cavour, Italian battleship 105
Conte di Savoia, Italian liner 311
Conte Verde, Italian liner 200
Corallo, Italian submarine 299
Cornwall, British cruiser 129

Coronel Bolognesi, Peruvian cruiser (1906) 120
Coronel Bolognesi, Peruvian cruiser(1942) 344
Coronel Bolognesi, Peruvian destroyer (1955) 356
Corrientes, Argentinian destroyer 88
Corsican, British liner 195
Cossack, British destroyer 264–5
Courageous, British aircraft carrier 95
Courbet, French battleship 90
Crescent, British destroyer 262
Crestway, dredger 439
Cunene, Portuguese cargo vessel 197
Curaçao, Dutch paddle steamer 36
Cushing, US destroyer 359
Cushing, US torpedo boat 85
Cutty Sark, British tea clipper 8–9, 42–3
Cyclop, German submarine salvage vessel 161
Czar, Russian liner 197

D1, British submarine 167
D 3 Type MTB, Soviet motor torpedo boat 283
Daffodil, British minesweeper/sloop 157
Daga, Italian escort ship 245
Dagabur, Italian submarine 299
Daino, Italian minesweeper 293
Dalmazia, Italian oiler 161
Danaide, Italian corvette 244
Dandolo, Italian submarine 300
Daniel Boone, US submarine 390
Danish warship (1390) 19
Danmark, Confederate steam warship 49
Dante Alighieri, Italian battleship 105
Daphné, French submarine 381
Dardo, Italian motor gunboat 332
Daring, British destroyer (1949) 267
Daring, British destroyer (2006) 433
Dar Pomorza, Polish sailing ship 187
Dauphin Royal, sailing warship 26
Davidson, US frigate 366
Decatur, US destroyer 146
Dédalo, Spanish aircraft carrier (1943) 217
Dédalo, Spanish seaplane carrier (1901) 94
Deep Quest, US submarine recovery craft 427
Deepstar 4000, US submarine research craft 427
Defence, British cruiser 123
De Grasse, French cruiser 257

Delfino, Italian submarine (1892) 81
Delfino, Italian submarine (1930) 296
Delhi, Indian cruiser 256
Delta I, Russian submarine 392
Denver, US command ship 330
Denver, US cruiser 126
Derbyshire, British liner 315
Derfflinger, German battlecruiser 110–11
De Ruyter, Dutch cruiser 258–9
Des Moines, US cruiser 249
D'Estienne d'Orves, French light frigate 333
Destructor, Spanish torpedo gunboat 86
Deutschland, German liner 204
Deutschland, German submarine 174–5
Deutschland, German training ship 379
Devonshire, British cruiser (1904) 123
Devonshire, British destroyer (1960) 347
De Zeven Provinzien, sailing warship 27
Diablo, US submarine 305
Diaspro, Italian submarine 298
Dido, British cruiser (1939) 251
Dido, British frigate (1961) 364
Discovery, British exploration ship 212
Dixmude, French aircraft carrier 217
Dmitri Donskoi, Soviet cruiser 343
Dmitry Pozharsky, Soviet cruiser 342
Dolfijn, Dutch submarine 381
Dolphin, US submarine 297
Domenico Millelire, Italian submarine 179
Doric, British liner 209
Doudart de Lagrée, French frigate 365
Downes, US frigate 367
Doyle, US destroyer (1942) 268
Doyle, US frigate (1982) 371
Dragone, Italian destroyer/escort 275
Dragonfly, British gunboat 282
Dreadnought, British battleship 100–1
Dreadnought, British submarine 387
Dromia, Italian minesweeper 377
Drum, US submarine 303
Duguay-Trouin, French cruiser (1923) 133
Duguay-Trouin, French destroyer (1973) 349
Duilio, Italian liner 208
Duncan, British destroyer 263
Duncan, US destroyer 269
Dunkerque, French battlecruiser 230
Dunkerque, French sailing cargo

ship 41
Dupleix, French cruiser (1930) 256
Dupleix, French destroyer (1978) 350
Dupuy de Lôme, French submarine 170
Duquesne, French destroyer 348
Durbo, Italian submarine 301
Dykkeren, Danish submarine 167

E20, British submarine 171
Eagle, British aircraft carrier (1918) 96
Eagle, British aircraft carrier (1946) 223
Edera, Italian minesweeper 376
Edgar Quinet, French cruiser 127
Edinburgh, British destroyer 352
Edsall, US destroyer escort 269
Effingham, British cruiser 129
Egypt, ancient
Cheops ship 10
Nile barge 11
reed boat 10
war galley 12
Eilat, Israeli corvette 335
Ekaterina II, Russian battleship 91
El Ictineo, Spanish submarine 78
Emanuele Filiberto Duca D'Aosta, Italian cruiser 254
Emden, German cruiser (1908) 140
Emden, German cruiser (1925) 135
Emerald, British cruiser 139
Emile Bertin, French cruiser 284
Emma Maersk, Danish container ship 436
Empire Windrush, British liner 314
Empress of Britain, Canadian liner (1905) 205
Empress of Britain, Canadian liner (1930) 310
Endurance, British ice patrol ship 422
Engadine, British helicopter support ship 400
Engadine, British seaplane carrier 95
English warship (c.1370) 19
Enrico Tazzoli, Italian submarine (1935) 297
Enrico Tazzoli, Italian submarine (1942) 304
Enrico Toti, Italian submarine (1928) 180
Enrico Toti, Italian submarine (1967) 382
Entemedor, US submarine 309
Enterprise, US aircraft carrier (1936) 218-19
Enterprise, US aircraft carrier

INDEX

(1960) 318
Erebus, British monitor 159
Eridan, French liner 209
Eridan, French minehunter 377
Erie, US gunboat 243
Erin, British battleship 103
Eritrea, Italian sloop 282
Ersh, Russian submarine 181
Espadon, French submarine (1901) 162
Espadon, French submarine (1926) 178
España, Spanish battleship 106
Espiègle, British minesweeper 292
Espora, Argentinian torpedo gunboat 87
Essex, US aircraft carrier 220
Etna, Italian cruiser (1885) 65
Etna, Italian cruiser (1942) 255
Etruria, British liner 76
Eugenio di Savoia, Italian cruiser 255
Euler, French submarine 168
Euridice, Italian cruiser 67
Euro, Italian destroyer 351
Europa, Danish liner 315
Europa, German cruise ship 413
Europa, German liner 209
Europa, Italian seaplane carrier 96
Eurydice, French submarine 179
Euterpe, Italian torpedo boat 83
Ever Globe, Taiwanese container ship 408
Exeter, British cruiser 130-1
Exmoor, British destroyer 267
Exmouth, British destroyer 263
Explorateur Grandidier, French liner 201
Extremadura, Spanish cruiser 144

F4, US submarine 169
Fairmile Type C, British motor gunboat 283
Falco, Italian flotilla leader 155
Farfadet, French submarine 162
Farragut, US destroyer (1898) 89
Farragut, US destroyer (1958) 346
Faulknor, British flotilla leader 155
Fenian Ram, Irish Republican submarine 79
Ferret, British destroyer 149
Ferry Lavender, Japanese vehicle ferry 418
Filicudi, Italian net layer 378
Fionda, Italian destroyer 277
Fiume, Italian cruiser 252
Fletcher, US destroyer 270-1
Floréal, French frigate 375
Florida, US cruiser 49
Flying Cloud, US sailing ship 40
Forban, French torpedo boat 85
Forbin, French cruiser 66
Foresight, British cruiser 122
Formby, British sailing ship 40
Formidable, British aircraft carrier 222
Forrestal, US aircraft carrier 318
Fort Grange, British fleet replenishment ship 401
Forth, British cruiser 65
Framée, French destroyer 89
France, French liner 206
Francesco Ferruccio, Italian cruiser 125
Franconia, British liner 206
Frank Cable, US submarine tender 401
Frans Suell, Swedish ferry 419
Fremantle, Australian fast patrol boat 334
Friant, French cruiser 68
Front Driver, Swedish cargo ship 403
Frunze, Russian destroyer 151
Fuad, Turkish despatch vessel 53
Fugas, Russian minesweeper 156
Fulmine, Italian destroyer 273
Fulton, sidewheel steamboat 35
Fulton, US submarine tender 295
Fu Lung, Chinese torpedo boat 83
Furious, British aircraft carrier 95
Furor, Spanish destroyer 88
Furutaka, Japanese cruiser 135
Fuso, Japanese battleship 117
Futura, Dutch carrier 403
Fuyutsuki, Japanese destroyer 277
Fylgia, Swedish cruiser 127

G1, British submarine 169
G5, Soviet torpedo gunboat 283
G40, German destroyer 151
G101, German destroyer 150
G132, German destroyer 147
Galatea, British cruiser (1914) 128
Galatea, British frigate (1963) 365
Galathée, French submarine 177
Galerna, Spanish submarine 384
Galileo Galilei, Italian liner/cruise ship 412
Galleass (1650s) 26
Galvani, Italian submarine 301
Galveston, US cruiser 338
Galway Castle, British liner 196
Gambia, British cruiser 251
Gambier Bay, US escort carrier 221
Gangut, Russian battleship 106
Garibaldino, Italian destroyer 148
Garland, British destroyer 149
Gatineau, Canadian frigate 363
Gatling, US destroyer 269
Gefion, German cruiser 68
Geiser, Danish cruiser 67
Gelderland, Dutch cruiser 69
Gemlik, Turkish frigate 363
General Garibaldi, Argentinian cruiser 69
Georges Leygues, French destroyer 358
Georges Philippar, French liner 310
George Washington, German liner 196
George Washington, US aircraft carrier 319
George Washington, US ballistic missile submarine 387
George Washington Carver, US submarine 391
Georgia, US submarine 396
Georgios Averroff, Greek cruiser 132
Gillis, US destroyer 152
Giovanni da Procida, Italian submarine 180
Giovanni delle Bande Nere, Italian cruiser 252
Giuseppe Garibaldi, Italian aircraft carrier 324-5
Giuseppe Miraglia, Italian seaplane carrier 98
Gladiator, British corvette 52
Glasgow, British cruiser (1909) 138
Glasgow, British cruiser (1936) 250
Glasgow, British destroyer (1976) 359
Glatton, British coast defence ship 158
Gloire, French battleship (1860) 54-5
Gloire, French cruiser (1900) 124
Gloire, French cruiser (1935) 257
Gneisenau, German battlecruiser (1936) 230
Gneisenau, German cruiser (1906) 125
Godavari, Indian frigate 371
Goeben, German battlecruiser 112
Golden Hind, English galleon 23
Golf I class, Russian missile submarine 380
Gorgon, British coast defence ship 62
Gorm, Danish coast defence ship 62
Göta Lejon, Swedish cruiser 287
Goteborg, Swedish destroyer 280
Gothland, Belgian liner 77
Gotland, Swedish cruiser 285
Goubet I, French submarine 80
Gouden Leeuw, Dutch minelayer 290
Graf Spee, German battlecruiser 113
Grafton, British frigate 362
Graf Zeppelin, German aircraft carrier 225
Grand Victory, Japanese car carrier 437
Grasshopper, British destroyer 148
Graudenz, German cruiser 141
Gravina, Spanish destroyer 280
Grayback, US submarine 381
Grayling, US submarine 167
Great Britain, British liner 38
Greece, ancient cargo ship 11 trireme 13
Gremyaschiy, Soviet destroyer 346
Grom, Polish destroyer 355
Gromki, Russian destroyer (1904) 147
Gromki, Russian destroyer (1913) 149
Gromki, Soviet destroyer (1936) 261
Gromoboi, Russian cruiser 69
Groningen, Dutch destroyer 355
Grosser Kurfürst, German battleship 107
Grouper, US submarine 304
Gryf, Polish minelayer 290
Guadiana, Portuguese destroyer 150
Guadiaro, Spanish minesweeper 293
Guam, US battlecruiser 231
Guglielmo Pepe, Italian destroyer 154
Guiseppe Garibaldi, Italian cruiser 253
Gurkha, British frigate 358
Gustav V, Swedish battleship 107
Gustave Zédé, French command ship (1934) 294
Gustave Zédé, French submarine (1893) 81
Gustave Zédé, French submarine (1913) 169
Gustavo Sampaio, Brazilian torpedo gunboat 87
Gwin, US destroyer 152
Gymnôte, French submarine 80

H4, US submarine 173
Haai, Dutch coast defence ship 63
Habaña, Spanish torpedo boat 84
Hachijo, Japanese escort 243
Hai Lung, Taiwanese submarine 385
Hajen, Swedish submarine 163
Hakuryu Maru, Japanese steel carrier 403
Halibut, US submarine 387
Halifax, Canadian frigate 374
Halla, Korean cement carrier 405
HAM 318, Dutch dredger 438
Hamakaze, Japanese destroyer 274
Hamayuki, Japanese destroyer 351

INDEX

Hampshire, British cruiser 122
Han, Chinese submarine 393
Hancock, US sailing frigate 30
Hannover Express, German container ship 408
Hanoverian, British liner 195
Hanseatic cog (1239) 15
Harald Haarfagre, Norwegian coast defence ship 63
Harriet Lane, US gunboat 53
Haruna, Japanese battlecruiser (1912) 113
Haruna, Japanese destroyer (1972) 357
Harushio, Japanese submarine 382
Hashidate, Japanese gunboat 242
Hatsuyuki, Japanese destroyer 359
Hatteras, US gunboat 53
Havock, British 'torpedo-boat destroyer' 85
Helena, Swedish cargo ship 404
Helgoland, German battleship 114
Helice, Norwegian tank vessel 421
Helle, Greek minelayer 156
Henri Poincaré, French submarine 181
Henry Grace à Dieu, Henry VIII's flagship 16–17
Hermes, British aircraft carrier (1919) 97
Hermes, British aircraft carrier (1953) 322
Herzogin Cecilie, German sail training ship 184–5
Highland Chieftain, British liner 201
Himalaya, British liner 39
H. L. Hunley, Confederate submarine 79
Hood, British battlecruiser 109
Hosho, Japanese aircraft carrier 97
Houbei class, Chinese missile boat 433
Housatonic, US cruiser 48
Howe, British battleship 238
Hudson Rex, Panamanian cargo carrier 405
Humber, British monitor 158
Humboldt, US liner 73
Hunley, US submarine tender 400
Hyundai Admiral, British container ship 409

I21, Japanese submarine 176
I201, Japanese submarine 308
I351, Japanese submarine 308
I400, Japanese submarine 309
Ibuki, Japanese battlecruiser 116
Impavido, Italian destroyer 347
Independence, US aircraft carrier 221
India, Soviet rescue submarine 427
Indiana, US battleship 239
Indianapolis, US cruiser 246
Indomitable, British aircraft carrier 223
Industry, Australian dredger/snag boat 212
Infanta Beatriz, Spanish passenger/cargo liner 201
Inflexible, British battlecruiser 108
Inhaúma, Brazilian frigate 373
Intelligent Whale, US submarine 79
Intrepid, British assault ship 330
Inverlago, Dutch–Venezuelan oil tanker 213
Invincible, British aircraft carrier 320–1
Iosco, US paddle gunboat 48
Iowa, US battleship 235
Iron Duke, British battleship 114
Isar, German cargo ship 193
Ise, Japanese battleship 117
Ishikari, Japanese vehicle ferry 418
Italia, Italian battleship 90
Italian cargo ship (c.1200) 15
Ivan Rogov, Soviet amphibious assault ship 331
Iwo Jima, US assault ship 326
Izumrud, Russian cruiser 127
Izumrud, Soviet frigate 368

J1, British submarine 170
Jacob van Heemskerck, Dutch cruiser (1939) 286
Jacob van Heemskerck, Dutch frigate (1983) 372
Jakob Maersk, Danish tanker 402
James Clark Ross, British research vessel 424–5
James Watt, British paddle steamer 36
Jason, US repair ship 295
Java, Dutch cruiser 134
Jeanne D'Arc, French helicopter carrier 326
Jervis Bay, British armed merchant cruiser 228
Jervis Bay, British container ship 406–7
Jianghu III, Chinese frigate 373
Jo Alder, Italian tanker 421
John Bowes, British coal carrier 38
John Fitch, experimental steamboat 34
John F. Kennedy, US aircraft carrier 319
Junyo, Japanese aircraft carrier 225

K26, British submarine 177
Kaga, Japanese aircraft carrier 98
Kaiser Franz Josef I, Austrian liner 207
Kaiser Friedrich III, German battleship 91
Karimoen, Dutch cargo ship 191
Karl Galster, German destroyer 278–9
Karlsruhe, German cruiser 141
Kasuga, Japanese cruiser 116
Kaszub, Polish corvette 335
KDD Ocean Link, Japanese cable layer 423
Kerch, Soviet cruiser 343
Kiautschou, German liner 194
Kiev, Soviet aircraft carrier 323
Kilo class, Russian submarine 383
Kirov, Soviet cruiser 255
Kirov, Soviet guided missile cruiser 340–1
Kniaz Souvarov, Russian battleship 119
Köln, German cruiser 142–3
Komet, German commerce raider 229
Kongo, Japanese destroyer 353
Königsberg, German light cruiser 140
Kormoran, German commerce raider 229
Kota Wijaya, Malayan container ship 409
Kotor, Yugoslav frigate 373
Krasnograd, Russian cargo ship 405
Krasnyi Kavkaz, Soviet cruiser 254
Kronprinz Wilhelm, German liner 182
Kruzenstern, Estonian full rigged cargo ship 187
Kursk, Russian submarine 398–9

L3, US submarine 171
L23, British submarine 176
La Champagne, French liner 77
La Dauphine, French caravel 23
Lady Hopetoun, Australian harbour inspection boat 210
Lake Champlain, British liner 194
Lancashire, British liner 198
Landsort, Swedish tanker 421
Lawhill, British sailing ship 41
LCI (L), US–British landing craft 288
Le Triomphant, French submarine 397
Lexington, US aircraft carrier 99
Liemba, East African lake steamer 211
Lightning, British torpedo boat 82
L'Indomptable, French destroyer 266
Lion, British battlecruiser 108
Littorio, Italian battleship 234
Long Beach, US missile cruiser 336–7
Los Angeles, US submarine 393
LSM (R), US landing craft/fire support ship 289
Luigi Cadorna, Italian cruiser 253
Lupo, Italian frigate 370
Lusitania, British liner 205

M1, British submarine 173
Ma'anshan, Chinese Type 054 frigate 432
Majesty of the Seas, Norwegian cruise ship 413
Marsala, Italian cruiser 132
Marshal Soult, British monitor 159
Matsonia, US cargo/passenger liner 207
Maya, Japanese cruiser 248
Mayon Spirit, Liberian tanker 420
Mediterranean cargo ship (c.800CE) 14
Memphis, US cruiser 134
Mendez Nuñez, Spanish cruiser 145
Michigan, US battleship 104
Mikura, Japanese escort ship 245
Minas Gerais, Brazilian battleship 120
Minnekahda, US liner 199
Minsk, Soviet destroyer 260
Mississippi, US cruiser 339
Mistral, French amphibious assault ship 431
Mizuho, seaplane/submarine support ship 226
Mogami, Japanese cruiser 248
Monadnock, US monitor 47
Monarch, British battleship 102
Monitor, US monitor 46
Montana, US armoured cruiser 137
Monterey, US monitor 47
Moreno, Argentinian battleship 121
Moskva, Soviet helicopter carrier 327
Mount Clinton, US passenger/cargo liner 199
Mount Whitney, US command ship 331
Mourad Rais, Algerian frigate 370
Murasame, Japanese destroyer 353
Mutenia, Romanian destroyer 351

N1, US submarine 172
Näcken, Swedish submarine 383
Nagara, Japanese cruiser 145
Nagato, Japanese battleship 117
Najin, North Korean frigate 369
Naldera, British liner 198
Nanuchka I, Russian corvette 333
Nareusan, Thai frigate 375

445

INDEX

Narwhal, US submarine 391
Nassau, German battleship 104
Natchez, US sidewheel steamer 70–1
Nautilus, US submarine (1930) 296
Nautilus, US submarine (1954) 316–17, 386
Nedlloyd Europa, Dutch container ship 409
Nerissa, British cargo/passenger liner 193
Neustrashimyy, Soviet destroyer (1951) 354
Neustrashimyy, Soviet frigate (1988) 374
Nevada, US battleship 107
New York, US amphibious dock ship 431
Nieuw Amsterdam, Dutch liner 311
Niña, Spanish sailing ship 22
North Carolina, US battleship 235
Norton Sound, US seaplane tender 295
Novgorod, Russian coast defence ship 63

Oasis of the Seas, Bahamas-registered cruise ship 435
Oberon, British submarine 178
Ognevoi, Soviet destroyer (1940) 261
Ognevoy, Soviet destroyer (1963) 348
Ohio, US submarine 393
Oscar I class, Soviet submarine 395
Oscar Huber, German river tug 211

Passaic, US monitor 46
Phoenicia
 bireme 12
 cargo ship 11
Pinguin, German commerce raider 228
Pisa, Italian cruiser 136
Pluton, French minelayer 157
Poesia, Panama-registered cruise ship 435
Pola, Italian cruiser 253
Powhatan, US cruiser 74
Prat, Chilean cruiser 345
Prinz Eugen, German heavy cruiser 231

Quaker City, US privateer 75
Queen Elizabeth, British battleship 103
Queen Elizabeth II, British liner 416–17
Queen Mary, British liner 312–13
Queen Mary 2, British cruise ship 434
Queen Victoria, British cruise ship 434

Radisson Diamond, US cruise ship 412
Resolution, British submarine 388–9
Retvisan, Russian battleship 118
Rex, Italian liner 311
Rome, ancient
 quinquereme 13
 trireme 13
Ronald Reagan, US aircraft carrier 7, 430
Royal Oak, British battleship 115
Royal William, British passenger–cargo steamship 37
Rurik, Russian cruiser 137
Ryujo, Japanese aircraft carrier 224

Sachsen, German frigate 432
St Laurent, Canadian destroyer 354
Salamander, Austrian battleship 56
San Francisco, US submarine 395
Sangamon, US escort carrier 216
San Giorgio, Italian cruiser 137
San Martin, Spanish galleon 20-1
Santisima Trinidad, Argentinian destroyer 350
Santissima Trinidad, Spanish ship of the line 32–3
São Gabriel, Portuguese sailing ship 22
Savannah, US cargo ship 404
Scandinavian longship (c.900CE) 14
Scharnhorst, German battlecruiser 232–3
Sea Spider, Dutch cable layer 423
Seraph, British submarine 303
Shanghai, Chinese fast attack/patrol boat 332
Shinano, Japanese aircraft carrier 227
Sierra, Soviet submarine 396
Silnyi, Soviet destroyer 261
Sims, US destroyer 268
Sirius, British paddle steamer 37
Skipjack, US submarine 386
Slava, Soviet cruiser 343
Society Adventurer, Bahamanian expedition ship 413
Sovereign of the Seas, English man of war 24–5
Spanish warship (não) (1450) 19
Spica, Swedish fast attack torpedo craft 333
Spruance, US destroyer 349
Stena Drill MAX, Swedish deep sea drilling ship 439
Stonewall, Confederate armoured ram ship 49
Surcouf, French submarine 181
Suwa Maru, Japanese cargo ship 197

Swedish cargo ship (c.1200) 15
Swift, British flotilla leader 154

T1, German light destroyer 276
T1, Japanese landing-ship 289
T 371, Soviet minesweeper 293
Tachikaze, Japanese destroyer 349
Taiho, Japanese aircraft carrier 227
Tarawa, US assault ship 328–9
Thetis, Danish patrol ship 375
Thistle, British submarine 301
Thomas W. Lawson, US sailing ship 186
Ticonderoga, US guided missile cruiser 339
Tiger, British battlecruiser (1913) 109
Tiger, British cruiser (1945) 345
Tintagel Castle, British corvette 245
Titanic, British liner 92–3, 202–3
Togo, German fighter direction ship 294
Tone, Japanese cruiser 249
Topaz, British coastal steamer 192
Torbay, British submarine 397
Trento, Italian cruiser 133
Trieste, French bathyscaphe 426
Trieste, Italian cruiser 133
Triumph, English galleon 23
Tromp, Dutch cruiser (1937) 285
Tromp, Dutch destroyer (1973) 360–1
Tsessarevitch, Russian battleship 119
Tsugaru, Japanese minelayer 291
Tsukuba, Japanese battlecruiser 112
Turtle, American submarine 78
Tycho Brahe, Danish train ferry 419
Tyco Reliance, cable layer 439
Tynwald, British anti-aircraft ship 242
Type 45, British destroyer 428–9
Typhoon, Soviet submarine 394

U-1, German submarine 166
U-2, German submarine 297
U-9, German submarine 164–5
U-12, German submarine 383
U-32, German submarine 299
U-47, German submarine 306–7
U-140, German submarine 173
U-2501, German submarine 309
Ulpio Traiano, Italian cruiser 287
Unebi, Japanese cruiser 61
Unicorn, British aircraft carrier 223
Unryu, Japanese aircraft carrier 227
Upholder, British submarine 385

Vanguard, British battleship (1870) 60
Vanguard, British battleship (1944) 239
Vanguard, British submarine 397
Vasilefs Georgios, Greek destroyer 281
Veinticinco de Mayo, Argentinian aircraft carrier 323
Venetian crusader ship (1268) 18
Viborg, Russian torpedo boat 84
Victor III, Soviet Submarine 394
Victoria, British battleship 58–9
Victory, British ship of the line 28–9
Vikrant, Indian aircraft carrier 323
Ville de Paris, French sailing warship 30
Vincenzo Gioberti, Italian destroyer 273
Vittorio Veneto, Italian battleship 235
Vittorio Veneto, Italian helicopter cruiser 327
Von der Tann, German battlecruiser 113

Walker, British destroyer 151
Walrus, Dutch submarine 384
Warrior, British battleship 55
Warspite, British battleship 103
Warspite, British submarine 390
Washington, French liner 72
Washington, US battleship 238
Wasp, US aircraft carrier 220
Whidbey Island, US dock landing ship 331
Whiskey class, Soviet submarine 380
Wichita, US cruiser 247
William G. Mather, US Great Lakes carrier 211
Winnebago, US monitor 47
Worden, US cruiser 338

X1, British submarine 177
Xia, Chinese submarine 395

Yamato, Japanese battleship 240–1
Yankee, Soviet submarine 391
Yeoman Burn, Norwegian carrier 402
YMS 100, US minesweeper 292
York, British cruiser 129
Yubari, Japanese frigate 365

Z30, German destroyer 276
Z51, German destroyer 281
Zuiho, Japanese aircraft carrier 224
Zuikaku, Japanese aircraft carrier 225
Zumwalt, US multimission destroyer 431

General Index

aircraft carriers
  up to 1929 94–9
  1930–49 216–27
  1950–99 318–25
  see also helicopter carriers
Algeria 370
American Civil War 44–51, 53, 74, 75
American War of Independence 30
Argentina
  19th century 69, 87, 88
  1900–29 121
  1950–99 323, 344, 350
assault ships, 1950–99 328–31
attack cargo ships, 1930–49 229
Australia
  1900–29 109, 210, 212
  1950–99 334, 385
Austria
  19th century 56, 87
  1900–29 157, 159, 207

Bahamas 413, 435, 437
battlecruisers
  1900–29 108–13
  1930–49 230–3
battleships
  1850s–90s 54–61, 90–1
  1900–29 114–21
  1930–49 234–41
  see also dreadnoughts
Belgium
  19th century 77
  1900–29 190
  1930–49 291
Brazil
  19th century 87
  1900–29 120–1
  1930–49 281
  1950–99 373
Britain
  18th century 28–9
  19th century 36–43, 52, 55–6, 58–60, 62, 65, 72, 74, 76, 82, 85, 89, 91
  1900–29 94–7, 100–3, 108–9, 114–15, 122–3, 128–31, 136, 138–9, 148–9, 151, 153–5, 157–9, 161, 163, 166–7, 169–71, 173, 176–8, 182–3, 186, 191–6, 198–203, 205–7, 209, 212, 364–5
  1930–49 216–17, 222–3, 228, 238–9, 242, 244–5, 250–1, 262–5, 267, 282–4, 288, 291–2, 301, 303, 312–15
  1950–99 320–2, 330, 345, 347, 352, 358–9, 362, 369, 385, 387–90, 397, 400–1, 406–7, 409, 414–17, 419–20, 422–5
  21st century 433–4
  see also England
bulk carriers, 1950–99 402–3

Canada
  19th century 37
  1900–29 205, 213
  1930–49 310
  1950–99 354, 363, 368, 374

Cape St Vincent, Battle of 28
cargo ships
  earliest 11
  early medieval 14–15
  19th century 40–3
  1900–29 190–3
  1950–99 404–5
  21st century 436–7
  see also bulk carriers; container ships; passenger–cargo ships
Chile
  19th century 60
  1900–29 121
  1950–99 345, 355
China
  19th century 61, 64, 83
  1950–99 332, 373, 393, 395
  21st century 432–3
Civil War ships 44–5, 48–51
coastal defence craft, 19th century 62–3
Cold War 328–9, 380, 392, 396
Columbus, Christopher 22
command ships, 1930–49 289
commerce raiders, 1930–49 228–9
container ships, 1950–99 406–9
Coral Sea, Battle of 246, 268
corvettes/patrol ships, 1950–99 332–5
Crimean War 39, 74
cruisers
  1860s 48–9
  1880s–90s 64–9
  1900s 122–7
  1910–29 128–35
  1930–49 246–59
  1950–99 336–45
  see also heavy cruisers; light cruisers
cruise ships
  1950–99 412–17
  21st century 434–5
Cyprus 439

Denmark
  19th century 62, 67
  1900–9 167
  1930–49 315
  1950–99 334, 375, 402, 419
  21st century 436
destroyers
  early 88–9
  up to 1929 146–53
  1930–49 260–81
  1950–99 (anti-submarine) 354–61
  1950–99 (guided missile) 346–53
Downs, Battle of 27
Drake, Sir Francis 23
dreadnoughts, 1900–29 100–7

early medieval ships 14–15, 18–19
early ships 10–11
East Africa 211
Egypt
  early ships 10–12
  1950–99 335
England
  16th century 16–17, 23

17th century 24–5
  see also Britain
escort vessels, 1930–49 242–5
Estonia 187
exploration craft
  15th/16th centuries 22–3
  1900–29 212

Falklands War
  Argentina 323, 344, 350
  Britain 320–1, 322, 330, 344, 358–9
Finland 192
fleet auxiliaries, 1900–29 160–1
flotilla leaders, 1900–29 154–5
France
  16th century 23
  18th century 30–1
  19th century 41, 54–5, 57, 66, 68, 72, 77, 80–1, 83, 85–6, 89–90
  1900–29 97, 105, 124, 127, 133, 153, 157, 162, 168–70, 177–9, 181, 187, 201, 206, 209
  1930–49 217, 230, 239, 256–7, 266, 284, 294, 310
  1950–99 322, 326, 333, 348–50, 358, 365, 375, 381, 397, 426
  21st century 430–1, 433
frigates
  17th century 27
  18th century 30–1
  1950s 362–3
  1960s & 70s 358, 364–7
  1970s 368–9
  1970s & 80s 370–1
  1980s 372–3
  1980s & 90s 374–5

galleons 20–1, 23
Gama, Vasco da 22
Germany
  19th century 39, 68, 77, 91
  1900–29 104, 107, 110–15, 125, 135, 140–3, 147, 150–1, 161, 164–5, 166, 173–5, 182–3, 184–5, 193–4, 196, 204, 208–9, 211
  1930–49 225, 228–33, 234, 236–7, 276, 278–9, 281, 294, 297, 299, 306–7, 309
  1950–99 353, 379, 383, 408, 413
  21st century 432
Gravelines, Battle of 20
Greece
  early ships 11, 13
  1900–29 132, 156
  1930–49 281
Gulf War (1991)
  France 322
  United States 319, 339
Gulf War (2003) 352
gunboats, 1930–49 282–3

heavy cruisers
  1900–29 136–7
  1930–49 231
helicopter carriers, 1950–99 326–7
Holland

17th century 26–7
  19th century 36, 63, 69
  1920–29 134, 191, 213
  1930–49 258–9, 285–6, 290, 311
  1950–99 355, 360–1, 372, 381, 384, 403, 409, 423
  21st century 438
hospital ships, 1950–99 410–11

India
  1930–49 256
  1950–99 323, 371
Indo-Pakistan War 323
Iran 367
Ireland 79
ironclads 44–5
iron steamships 38–9
Israel 335
Italy
  19th century 57, 65, 67, 81, 82–3, 90
  1900–29 96, 98–9, 105, 125, 132–3, 136–7, 146, 148, 153–5, 160–1, 168, 171–2, 179–80, 188–9, 200, 208, 213
  1930–49 234–5, 243–5, 252–5, 272–3, 275, 277, 282, 286–7, 293, 296–305, 311
  1950–99 324–5, 327, 332, 345, 347, 351, 357, 362–4, 366, 370, 378, 382, 401, 410–11, 412, 421

Japan
  19th century 61, 67
  1900–29 97–9, 112–13, 116–17, 135, 145, 176, 197
  1930–49 224–7, 240–3, 245, 248–9, 274, 277, 289, 291, 305, 308–9
  1950–99 349, 351, 353, 357, 359, 365, 367, 382, 403, 418, 423
  21st century 437
Java Sea, Battle of 130, 258
Jervis, Admiral Sir John 28
Jutland, Battle of
  Britain 103, 108–9, 114–15, 121, 123
  Germany 107, 110–11, 113–14

Korea 405
Korean War 270

lake steamers, 1900–29 210–11
landing craft, 1930–49 288–9
Leyte Gulf, Battle of 224–5, 241, 248, 277
Liberia 420
light cruisers
  1900–29 138–45
  1930–49 284–7
Lôme, Dupuy de 54

Malaya 409
Marshall Islands 439
Matapan, Battle of 235
Medina Sidonia, Duke of 20
men of war 24–5

447

INDEX

merchant ships, armed
  1900–29 182–3
  1930–49 228–9
Midway, Battle of
  Japan 98, 99, 241
  United States 218–19, 246
minehunters, 1950–99 377
minelayers
  1900–29 156–7
  1930–49 290–1
minesweepers
  1900–29 156–7
  1930–49 292–3
  1950–99 376–7
monitors
  19th century 46–7
  1900–29 158–9

Nelson, Horatio 28
North Korea 369
Norway
  19th century 63
  1900–29 191
  1950–99 402, 413, 421
nuclear submarines 386–99

paddle steamers, sidewheel
  early 1800s 35
  1820s–30s 36–7, 52
  1840s–60s 44–5, 48, 52–3, 70–5
paddle steamers, stern-wheel
  early 1800s 34
  1860s 45
  1880s 75
Pakistan 344
Panama 405, 435, 436
passenger–cargo ships
  1900–29 194–201
  1930–49 314–15
passenger liners
  19th century 38–9, 76–7
  1900–29 204–9
  1930–49 310–13
Pearl Harbor 98, 99, 224
Persian War 11
Peru
  1900–29 120
  1950–99 344, 356
Phoenicia 11, 12
Poland
  1900–29 187
  1930–49 290
  1950–99 335, 355
Portugal
  15th century 22
  1900–29 150, 197
  1950–99 369

repair/support ships
  1930–49 294–5
  1950–99 400–1
River Plate, Battle of 234
river vessels
  19th century 44–5, 70–1
  1900–29 210–11
Romania 351, 371
Rome 13
Russia, Imperial
  19th century 63, 69, 84, 91
  1900–17 106, 118–19, 126–7, 137, 144, 147, 149, 151, 156, 197, 210
Russian Federation 398–9, 405
Russo-Japanese War
  Russia 69, 116, 118, 126–7, 144, 147
  Japan 116
Ruyter, Admiral de 27

sailing ships
  early 10–13
  early medieval 14–15, 18–19
  15th century 22
  16th century 16–17, 20–1, 23
  17th century 24–7
  18th century 28–33
  19th century 40–3
  1900–29 184–9
Saudi Arabia 372
Saumarez, Admiral 28
seagoing ferries, 1950–99 418–19
Soviet Union
  1930–49 181, 254–5, 260–1, 283, 285, 293
  1950–99 323, 327, 331, 333, 340–3, 346–8, 354, 368, 374, 379–80, 383, 391–2, 394–6, 427
Spain
  15th century 22
  16th century 20–1
  18th century 32–3
  19th century 61, 78, 84, 86, 88
  1900–29 94, 106, 144–5, 201
  1930–49 217, 257, 280, 293
  1950–99 384
Spanish–American War 61, 88
Spanish Armada 20–1, 23
Spanish Civil War 201, 257, 297, 298, 299
specialized vessels
  1900–29 212–13
  1950–99 378–9, 422–5
  21st century 438–9
steamships
  early 34–5
  pioneering 36–9
submarines
  early 78–81
  1900–9 162–7
  post-1919 development 176–81
  1930s 296–301
  1950–99 380–5
  World War I 168–75
  World War II 302–9
  see also nuclear submarines

submersible craft 426–7
Sweden
  1900–29 107, 127, 163, 190
  1930–49 280, 285, 287
  1950–99 333, 383, 403–4, 419, 421
  21st century 439
Switzerland 435

Taiwan 385, 408
tankers, 1950–99 420–1
Terceiro, Battle of 20
Thailand 327, 375
torpedo boats
  19th century 82–7
  1930–49 283
torpedo gunboats 86–7
Trafalgar, Battle of 28, 32
Tsushima, Battle of 116, 118, 127, 147
Turkey
  19th century 53, 57
  1950–99 363

United States
  18th century 30–1, 78
  19th century 40, 44–51, 53, 64, 66, 70–1, 72–5, 79, 81, 85, 89
  1900–29 99, 104, 107, 126, 134, 137, 145–6, 152, 167, 169, 171–3, 179, 186, 199, 207, 211
  1930–49 216, 218–21, 229, 231, 235, 238–9, 243, 246–7, 249, 268–71, 288–9, 292, 295–7, 303–5, 309
  1950–99 318–19, 326, 328–31, 336–9, 346, 349, 352, 359, 366–7, 371, 381, 386–7, 390–1, 393, 395–6, 400–1, 404, 412, 426–7
  21st century 430–1

Venezuela 356
Vietnam War 231, 319, 336

war galleys 12–13
warships
  early 18–19
  16th century 16–17
  17th century 24–7
  18th century 28–33
  19th century (paddle-driven) 52–3
  19th century (screw-propelled) 54–61
  21st century 430–3
Whitehead, Robert 82
World War I
  Australia 109
  Austria 157, 159
  Britain 91, 94–5, 103, 108–9, 114–15, 122–3, 128–9, 130, 136, 138–9, 155, 157–8, 169–71, 173, 182–3
  Canada 205
  Chile 121
  France 105, 162, 168–70
  Germany 107, 110–15, 125, 140–1, 161, 164–5, 173–5, 182–3
  Greece 132
  Italy 105, 146, 168, 171–2
  Russia, Imperial 156
  United States 126, 137, 171–3
World War II
  Belgium 291
  Britain 95–7, 103, 130, 153, 161, 183, 216–17, 222–3, 228, 238, 242, 244–5, 250–1, 262–5, 267, 282–4, 288, 291–2, 301, 303
  Canada 310
  France 97, 133, 153, 230, 239, 256, 266, 284
  Germany 135, 228–33, 231, 234, 276, 278–9, 281, 294, 297, 299, 306–7, 309
  Greece 156, 281
  Holland 258–9, 285–6, 290
  India 256
  Italy 98–9, 133, 137, 153, 160, 235, 243–5, 252–5, 272–3, 275, 277, 282, 286–7, 293, 296–305
  Japan 98–9, 135, 224–7, 240–3, 245, 248–9, 274, 277, 289, 291, 305, 308–9
  Poland 290
  Soviet Union 181, 254–5, 260–1, 283, 293
  Spain 217, 293
  Sweden 280, 285, 287
  United States 99, 152, 216, 218–21, 229, 235, 238–9, 243, 246–7, 268–71, 289, 292, 295–7, 303–5, 309

Yugoslav Wars 320
Yugoslavia 373

Picture Credits

Art-Tech: 92/93 (MARS), 214/215 (Aerospace); BAE Systems: 428/429;
Getty Images: 8/9 (Robert Harding); U.S. Department of Defense: 5, 7, 316/317

All artworks © DeAgostini, Amber Books Ltd and Tony Gibbons except p430–433 © Military Visualisations Inc.